The Longman Handbook
of Modern British History
1714–1995

**Also by Chris Cook and John Stevenson**

British Historical Facts: 1760–1830
The Longman Handbook of Modern European History 1763–1991
British Historical Facts: 1688–1760
The Longman Companion to Britain since 1945
Britain in the Depression: Society and Politics, 1929–39, 2nd edn

**Other books by Chris Cook**

Post-war Britain: a Political History (*with Alan Sked*)
The Age of Alignment: Electoral Politics in Britain 1922–1929
A Short History of the Liberal Party 1900–1992
By-elections in British Politics (*ed. with John Ramsden*)
The Politics of Reappraisal 1918–1939 (*ed. with Gillian Peele*)
The Decade of Disillusion (*ed. with David McKie*)
Crisis and Controversy: Essays in Honour of A. J. P. Taylor (*ed. with Alan Sked*)
Trade Unions in British Politics (*ed. with Ben Pimlott*)
The Dictionary of Historical Terms
The Facts on File World Political Almanac
The Longman Guide to Sources in Contemporary British History
(*2 vols with David Waller* et al.)

**Other books by John Stevenson**

Popular Disturbances in England, 1700–1870, 2nd edn
British Society, 1914–1945
Order and Disorder in Early Modern England (*with A. J. Fletcher*)
The Working Class and Politics in Britain and America, 1929–1945
(*ed. with S. Salter*)
Third Party Politics since 1945

# The Longman Handbook of Modern British History 1714–1995

*Third Edition*

Chris Cook
John Stevenson

Longman
London and New York

Addison Wesley Longman Limited
Edinburgh Gate,
Harlow, Essex CM20 2JE, United Kingdom
*and Associated Companies throughout the world.*

*Published in the United States of America
by Addison Wesley Longman, New York.*

First published 1983
Second edition 1988
Fourth impression 1993
Third edition 1996

ISBN 0 582 29304 9 PPR

**British Library Cataloguing-in-Publication Data**

A catalogue record of this book is
available from the British Library

. **Library of Congress Cataloging-in-Publication Data**

Cook, Chris, 1945–
    The Longman handbook of modern British history, 1714–1995 / Chris
Cook, John Stevenson. – 3rd ed.
        p.   cm. – (The Longman handbooks to history)
    Includes bibliographical references and index.
    ISBN 0-582-29304-9 (pbk. : alk. paper)
        1. Great Britain–History–1714–1837–Handbooks, manuals, etc.
2. Great Britain–History–Victoria, 1837–1901–Handbooks, manuals,
etc. 3. Great Britain–History–20th century–Handbooks, manuals,
etc.   I. Stevenson, John, 1946–  . II. Title. III. Series.
DA470.C65   1996
941.07–dc20                                                      96-18356
                                                                          CIP

Set by 7 in 9.5/12 ITC New Baskerville
Produced through Longman Malaysia, VVP

# Contents

# Preface

This handbook has attempted to provide a convenient and accessible companion for both teachers and students of British history from 1714 to the present day. It is a much condensed work, bringing together a wealth of chronological, statistical and tabular information which is not to be found elsewhere within the confines of a single volume. The book covers not only political and diplomatic events but also the broader fields of social and economic history. It has been designed as a handbook for use by teachers as well as by sixth-formers and undergraduates. No book of this type can be entirely comprehensive. Rather, we have included those facts, figures and statistics that we believe are most needed for courses in later modern British history.

Chris Cook
John Stevenson
April 1996

# Acknowlegements

The publishers would like to thank the following for granting permission to reproduce copyright material: Routledge for the table *The population of England and Wales, 1695–1791* (p. 151) and the table *Comparative population growth* (p. 152); Macmillan Ltd and St Martin's Press Inc for the table *Commonwealth Immigrants in the United Kingdom, 1961–91* (p. 156); Faber and Faber Ltd for the table *Numbers transported to Australia from Great Britain and Ireland (males and females), 1788–1853* (p. 191); Oxford University Press for the table *Gregory King's estimate of the population and wealth of England and Wales, calculated for 1696* (p. 202); Methuen & Co. for the table *Patrick Colquhoun's estimate of the social structure of the United Kingdom, c. 1815* (pp. 203–4) and for the table *Religious affiliations in Irish provinces in 1861* (p. 327); Weidenfeld & Nicolson Ltd for the table *The 1851 Religious Census of England and Wales* (p. 241); Cambridge University Press, Dr B R Mitchell and Professor P M Deane for the following tables, *Principal components of British exports, 1760–1830* (p. 251), *Principal components of British imports, 1860–1939* (p. 251), *Principal components of British exports, 1830–1938* (p. 252), *Geographical distribution of British exports, 1701–98* (pp. 253–4), *The Schumpeter–Gilboy price index, 1714–1823* (p. 256), *The Rousseaux price index, 1800–1913* (p. 257), *Average price of wheat, 1771–1914* (pp. 258–9); ALCS and Professor D H Aldcroft for the table *Average money wages and real wages, 1913, 1920–38* (p. 262) © Derek H. Aldcroft. Reprinted by permission of ALCS on behalf of the copyright holder; Cambridge University Press for the following tables, *Money wages in Great Britian, 1790–1860* (p. 260), *Money wages and real wages in the United Kingdom, 1850–1906* (pp. 260–1), *Turnpike Acts by area, 1663–1839* (p. 271); Macmillan Ltd for the table *Shipping registered in English ports in the eighteenth century* (p. 273).

# List of abbreviations used in sources

| | |
|---|---|
| Mitchell and Deane, *Abstract* | B. R. Mitchell and P. Deane, *Abstract of British Historical Statistics* (Cambridge University Press, 1962) |
| Mitchell and Jones, *Second Abstract* | B. R. Mitchell and H. G. Jones, *Second Abstract of British Historical Statistics* (Cambridge University Press, 1971) |
| *Key Data, 1992/93* | Central Statistical Office, *Key Data, 1992/93* (London, HMSO, 1993) |
| *Annual Abstract* + date | *Annual Abstract of Statistics* (London, HMSO, date published) |
| Halsey (ed.), *Trends* | A. H. Halsey (ed.), *Trends in British Society since 1900* (London, Macmillan, 1972) |
| *Britain, 1994* | *Britain, 1994: An Official Handbook* (London, HMSO, 1994) |

# SECTION ONE

*Political history*

# Political chronology

Note: (i) In order to reflect the more personal character of politics and the less organized nature of parties in the eighteenth and the first half of the nineteenth centuries, governments up to 1868 are given the name of their principal minister or ministers. After 1868 governments are designated by their party label. (ii) In the eighteenth century leaders of administrations usually held the post of First Lord of the Treasury or one of the secretaryships of state, no formal office of Prime Minister existing. From the early nineteenth century this term came into more common usage and has been adopted from the 1820s for the description of leaders of administrations.

### 1714
**May** Schism Act passed. No person allowed to keep a school unless a member of the Anglican Church.

**July** Henry St John (Bolingbroke) secures dismissal of the Earl of Oxford and begins attempt to pack administration with Jacobite sympathizers. Severe illness of Queen Anne forces calling of Privy Council. Pro-Hanoverian Duke of Shrewsbury appointed Lord Treasurer in place of Oxford (30th).

**Aug.** Death of Queen Anne (1st); George I proclaimed King in London and leading cities. Bolingbroke dismissed from office.

**Sept.** George I arrives in England (18th). *Whig administration* formed under Lord Stanhope. Principal figures: Lord Stanhope (Secretary of State); Lord Halifax (First Lord of the Treasury); Lord Townshend (Secretary of State); Earl of Nottingham (Lord President of the Council); Lord Sunderland (Lord Lieutenant of Ireland).

### 1715
**Mar.** Meeting of first parliament of George I with large Whig majority.

**June** Bolingbroke, Ormonde and Oxford impeached. Flight of Bolingbroke and Ormonde; Oxford committed to the Tower. Widespread rioting followed by Riot Act strengthening power of magistrates by making many riots a capital offence.

**Sept.** Jacobite rising in Scotland under the Earl of Mar.
**Dec.** Pretender (James III) arrives in Scotland.

## 1716
**Feb.** Pretender flees Scotland after failure of England to rise in support. Impeachment of Jacobite leaders; execution of Derwentwater and Kenmure.
**May** Septennial Act extends maximum duration of parliaments to seven years.

## 1717
**Jan.** Triple Alliance formed between England, France and Holland to uphold the Treaty of Utrecht.
**Feb.** Convocation of the Church of England ceases to meet regularly.
**Apr.** Walpole and Townshend resign from administration.

## 1718
**Aug.** Quadruple Alliance formed between England, France, the Emperor and Holland.
**Dec.** War between England and Spain. Repeal of the Occasional Conformity Act and the Schism Act.

## 1719
**Dec.** Defeat of administration's Peerage Bill in House of Commons.

## 1720
**Jan.** Spain joins Quadruple Alliance, ending hostilities with England.
**Feb.** South Sea Company's scheme for taking over part of the National Debt in return for exclusive trade in the South Seas accepted by the House of Commons.
**June** South Sea stock reaches record level.
**Aug.** South Sea stock falls rapidly in value.
**Dec.** Walpole begins restoration of public credit. Secret Committee appointed to investigate affairs of South Sea Company. Directors of company expelled from the House of Commons; Chancellor of the Exchequer (Aislabie) sent to the Tower.

## 1721
**Feb.** Lord Townshend becomes Secretary of State in place of Stanhope.
**Apr.** *Walpole administration* formed. Principal figures: Robert Walpole (First Lord of the Treasury); Lord Townshend (Secretary of State); Carteret (Secretary of State).

**1722**

**Apr.** Death of Sunderland, Walpole's chief rival.

**May** Atterbury Plot by Jacobites discovered. Leading Jacobite sympathizers arrested.

**Oct.** Meeting of Parliament (9th). Habeas Corpus suspended; penal taxes levied on Catholics and non-jurors. Francis Atterbury (Bishop of Rochester) banished.

**1724**

**Apr.** Carteret becomes Lord Lieutenant of Ireland, Duke of Newcastle becomes Secretary of State and Henry Pelham Secretary at War.

**1725**

**Apr.** City Elections Act, regulating conduct of elections in London and increasing power of Court of Aldermen, passed by Walpole in spite of strong protests in the capital.

**Sept.** Treaty of Hanover between England, France and Prussia. Bolingbroke pardoned and returns to England where he helps to lead opposition to Walpole.

**1727**

**June** Death of George I (11th); accession of George II.

**1729**

**Nov.** Treaty of Seville with Spain; confirmation of *asiento* treaty allowing limited trade with Spanish colonies, Gibraltar ceded to England.

**1730**

**May** Lord Harrington replaces Townshend as Secretary of State.

**1731**

**Mar.** Treaty of Vienna; Austrian Emperor agrees to disband Ostend East India Company.

**1733**

**Mar.** Widespread opposition to Walpole's Excise Bill.

**Apr.** Walpole's majority in House of Commons reduced to 16 on Excise proposals; Walpole offers resignation to the King. Though remaining in office, Walpole postpones discussion of the Bill until June, effectively dropping the scheme.

**May** Walpole narrowly staves off defeat in the House of Lords over handling of South Sea Company affairs.

## 1734
**Mar.** Motion to repeal Septennial Act defeated. Bolingbroke gives up active opposition to Walpole and retires to France.

## 1735
**Jan.** Second parliament of George II's reign meets after general election of 1734, Walpole having lost 16 seats but still commanding a substantial majority.

## 1736
**Sept.** Porteous riots in Edinburgh.

## 1737
Frederick, Prince of Wales, quarrels with his father and sides openly with the opposition to Walpole.

## 1738
**Mar.** Spanish ill-treatment of British sailors taken up by the opposition to Walpole in the Commons and City of London.

## 1739
**Jan.** Convention of Pardo to settle differences with Spain submitted to Parliament and approved by only 28 votes.
**Oct.** Walpole forced to accede to demand for war with Spain. War of Jenkins' Ear.
**Nov.** Capture of Porto Bello by Admiral Vernon.

## 1741
**Feb.** Motion for Walpole's dismissal defeated by 184 votes.
**Apr.** Parliament dissolved. In subsequent general election Walpole's majority reduced to under 20 seats by defeats in Cornwall and Scotland.
**Dec.** Parliament reassembles and Walpole defeated in seven divisions.

## 1742
**Feb.** Walpole decides to resign after defeat over Chippenham election petition. *Carteret administration* formed. Principal figures: John Carteret (Secretary of State); Earl of Wilmington (First Lord of the Treasury).

## 1743
**Aug.** Henry Pelham becomes First Lord of the Treasury in place of the Earl of Wilmington.

## 1744

**Mar.** France declares war on Britain.

**Nov.** Carteret resigns after increasing disagreement in the Cabinet and Parliament about his foreign policy. *Pelham administration* formed. Principal figures: Henry Pelham (First Lord of the Treasury); Earl of Harrington (Secretary of State); Duke of Bedford (First Lord of the Admiralty).

## 1745

**May** Battle of Fontenoy. Marshal Saxe defeats Duke of Cumberland.

**July** Second Jacobite rebellion. The Young Pretender, Charles Edward Stuart, lands in Scotland (25th) and proclaims his father as James VIII of Scotland and James III of England. Highland clans rise in support.

**Sept.** The Pretender enters Edinburgh with 2,000 men (11th); Jacobite victory at Prestonpans (21st).

**Dec.** Pretender reaches Derby, but decides to retreat to Scotland because of lack of support in England (4th).

## 1746

**Feb.** Pelham, Newcastle, Hardwicke and Harrington resign after disagreements with the King over foreign policy. Bath and Granville attempt to form an administration. *Pelham administration* re-formed. Principal figures: H. Pelham (First Lord of the Treasury); Earl of Harrington (Secretary of State); Duke of Newcastle (Secretary of State); William Pitt the Elder (Vice-Treasurer of Ireland).

**Apr.** Defeat of Young Pretender and Jacobite forces at battle of Culloden (16th).

**May** Pitt becomes Paymaster-General of the Forces.

**Sept.** Flight of the Young Pretender to France.

## 1748

**Oct.** Treaty of Aix-la-Chapelle ends War of Austrian Succession.

## 1751

**May** Act passed for adoption of the reformed (Gregorian) calendar in England and the colonies. Year to begin from 1 January instead of 25 March; 11 days to be omitted from the calendar between 3 and 14 September 1752.

## 1753

**June** Jewish Naturalization Act passed, but repealed the following year because of popular opposition.

## 1754

**Mar.** Death of Pelham. *Newcastle administration* formed. Principal figures: Duke of Newcastle (First Lord of the Treasury); Earl of Holderness (Secretary of State); Henry Fox (Secretary at War); William Pitt (Paymaster).

## 1755

**May** Admiral Boscawen fails to prevent French reinforcements reaching North America. Subsidy treaties agreed with Hesse-Cassel and Russia to provide troops in the event of war.

## 1756

**May** War declared against France. Seven Years War begins.
**June** Loss of Minorca after failure of Admiral Byng to defeat French invasion fleet.
**Oct.** Henry Fox announces intention to resign after severe criticism of the conduct of the war in the House of Commons. Newcastle resigns; the King asks Fox to form an administration, but he refuses. Devonshire agrees to form an administration with Pitt (29th).
**Nov.** *Pitt–Devonshire administration* formed. Principal figures: Duke of Devonshire (First Lord of the Treasury); William Pitt (Secretary of State).

## 1757

**Apr.** The King demands Pitt's resignation after failures to achieve success in the war. George Grenville (Treasurer of the Navy) and Legge (Chancellor of the Exchequer) resign with Pitt. Widespread popular support shown for Pitt.
**July** After considerable negotiations *Pitt–Newcastle administration* formed. Principal figures: William Pitt (Secretary of State); Duke of Newcastle (First Lord of the Treasury); Henry Fox (Paymaster of the Forces).
**Oct.** Failure of Rochefort expedition; news of defeats in India and Canada leads to criticism of the conduct of the war in Europe.
**Nov.** Victory for Britain's ally, Frederick the Great, at Rossbach.
**Dec.** Victory of Frederick at Leuthen.

## 1758

**Apr.** At Second Treaty of Westminster, Prussia and Britain pledge themselves not to make a separate peace. Frederick granted an annual subsidy.
**July** Capture of Louisburg in North America (26th).
**Nov.** Occupation of Fort Duquesne by Colonel Forbes.

**1759**
**May** Capture of Guadeloupe.
**June** Capture of Fort Niagara in North America.
**July** Bombardment of Le Havre thwarts French plans for invasion of Britain.
**Aug.** Boscawen's defeat of French fleet at Lagos.
**Sept.** Wolfe's victory at battle of the Plains of Abraham (13th) and capture of Quebec (18th).
**Nov.** Defeat of French fleet by Admiral Hawke.

**1760**
**Sept.** Surrender of Montreal to the British; virtual loss of Canada by the French.
**Oct.** Death of George II (25th); accession of George III.

**1761**
**Oct.** Resignation of Pitt the Elder because of disagreements with colleagues about his war policy. *Bute–Newcastle administration* formed. Principal figures: Duke of Newcastle (First Lord of the Treasury); Earl of Bute (Secretary of State).

**1762**
**May** Duke of Newcastle resigns from government because of quarrel with Bute over foreign policy. *Bute administration* formed. Principal figures: Earl of Bute (First Lord of the Treasury); George Grenville (Secretary of State).
**June** John Wilkes starts *The North Briton* to attack the Bute administration.

**1763**
**Feb.** First Treaty of Paris signed, ending Seven Years War (for provisions, see p. 302).
**Mar.** Introduction of cider tax increases Bute's unpopularity.
**Apr.** Bute resigns in the face of increasing attacks in the press and Parliament. *Grenville administration* formed. Principal figures: George Grenville (First Lord of the Treasury and Chancellor of the Exchequer); Earl of Egremont (Secretary of State, later First Lord of the Admiralty); Earl of Halifax (Secretary of State). Wilkes arrested on a general warrant for an attack on the King in issue no. 45 of *The North Briton.*
**Dec.** Wilkes's arrest declared illegal by Chief Justice Pratt. Wilkes forced into exile after publication of *An Essay on Woman.*

## 1765

**Mar.** American Stamp Act passed to raise money for the defence of the American colonies by placing a charge on legal transactions. Six of the 13 colonies petitioned against the Act. (For American affairs, see also p. 281.)

**July** Grenville administration dismissed by the King. *First Rockingham administration* formed. Principal figures: Marquess of Rockingham (First Lord of the Treasury); Henry Seymour Conway (Secretary of State).

## 1766

**Jan.** Widespread petitioning movement against Stamp Act by English merchants.

**Mar.** Repeal of the Stamp Act with strong support of Pitt (now Earl of Chatham).

**July** *Chatham administration* formed. Principal figures: Earl of Chatham (Lord Privy Seal); Duke of Grafton (First Lord of the Treasury); Charles Townshend (Chancellor of the Exchequer).

## 1767

**June** Townshend's Revenue Act passed, imposing duties on tea and other articles imported into America to pay for defence and administration of the colonies.

## 1768

**Mar.** Wilkes elected MP for Middlesex.

**May** Industrial and pro-Wilkes riots in London; 11 people killed by soldiers at the 'massacre' of St George's Fields.

**Oct.** Resignation of Earl of Chatham. *Grafton administration* formed. Principal figures: Duke of Grafton (First Lord of the Treasury); Lord North (Chancellor of the Exchequer).

## 1769

**Feb.** House of Commons votes that Wilkes was guilty of a seditious libel for letter criticizing the government for the 'massacre' of St George's Fields; Wilkes expelled from the Commons; formation of the 'Supporters of the Bill of Rights' to support Wilkes and the cause of parliamentary reform.

**May** Cabinet decides to retain duties on tea in spite of strong opposition from the American colonists.

**June–July** Petitioning movement for reform of Parliament and reinstatement of Wilkes.

**1770**

**Jan.** Grafton resigns after securing a majority of 44 in the House of Commons after a motion on the administration's handling of the Middlesex election issue. *North administration* formed. Principal figure: Lord North (First Lord of the Treasury and Chancellor of the Exchequer).

**Mar.** Act repealing duties on paper, glass and paint, but retaining those on tea.

**Apr.** Edmund Burke publishes *Thoughts on the Causes of the Present Discontents*, accusing the King of dominating Parliament through 'influence' and calling for a revival of 'party'.

**1771**

**Mar.** Printers' Case. London printers reprimanded for publishing parliamentary debates and Lord Mayor and two aldermen of London imprisoned for a breach of the privileges of the House of Commons. But no serious attempts made to interfere with parliamentary reporting thereafter.

**1773**

**Oct.** Tea Act passed to aid finances of the East India Company by allowing direct export of tea to North America. American colonists resist imports and payment of duty.

**Dec.** Boston Tea Party. Protestors dump 340 chests of East India Company tea in Boston harbour.

**1774**

**Apr.** Motion in the House of Commons to repeal tea duty and pacify the colonists. Quebec Act passed granting toleration to Roman Catholics in Canada. Continental Congress meets at Philadelphia and agrees to defy coercive measures. Quebec Act passed for government of Canada.

**1775**

**Jan.** Chatham's motion proposing conciliation with the American colonies defeated.

**Mar.** Burke's conciliation proposals defeated.

**Apr.** British and American forces skirmish at Lexington (18th).

**May** Second Continental Congress meets at Philadelphia (10th).

**June** Battle of Bunker's Hill, Boston.

**Aug.** King's proclamation of rebellion in American colonies.

**1776**
**July** American Declaration of Independence.

**1777**
**Oct.** Surrender of British forces at Saratoga.

**1778**
**Feb.** Treaty of Amity and Commerce signed between France and the American colonists. Charles James Fox's motion for virtual abandonment of the war against America defeated in the Commons.
**Mar.–Apr.** Motions criticizing conduct of the war and urging reform of Parliament by reduction of Crown influence only narrowly defeated in Commons.

**1779**
**June** Spain declares war on Britain. Siege of Gibraltar begins.
**Dec.** First meeting of Yorkshire reformers under Christopher Wyvill to concert plans for reform of Parliament. Widespread agitation in Ireland for removal of trade and constitutional restrictions.

**1780**
**Feb.** Yorkshire petition for parliamentary reform presented. Beginning of widespread petitioning movement for 'economical reform'. Burke presents proposals for reform.
**Mar.** Convention of reformers in London.
**Apr.** Dunning's resolution 'that the influence of the Crown has increased, is increasing, and ought to be diminished' carried by 233 votes to 215. Further attempts to attack the Crown's influence defeated by the administration and its supporters.
**June** Protestant Association led by Lord George Gordon petitions Parliament for repeal of the Catholic Relief Act of 1778; followed by widespread rioting in London – the 'Gordon riots'.

**1781**
**Nov.** News of Cornwallis's surrender at Yorktown reaches England.

**1782**
**Feb.** Motion asserting the impracticability of the continued war with America passed in the House of Commons.
**Mar.** North only narrowly escapes defeat on two motions of no confidence. The King accepts North's resignation. *Second Rockingham*

*administration* formed. Principal figures: Marquess of Rockingham (First Lord of the Treasury); Charles James Fox (Foreign Secretary).

**May** Clerke's Act passed disqualifying government contractors from sitting in the Commons.

**June** Crewe's Act passed disfranchising revenue officers of the Crown.

**July** Burke's Civil Establishment Act passed controlling royal expenditure, pensions and offices. Paymaster's Office regulated. Death of Rockingham (1st) leads to formation of *Shelburne administration.* Principal figures: Earl of Shelburne (First Lord of the Treasury); William Pitt the Younger (Chancellor of the Exchequer); Thomas Townshend (Home Secretary).

**Nov.** Preliminaries of peace agreed with the American colonies.


## 1783

**Jan.** Preliminaries of peace signed with France and Spain.

**Feb.** Alliance of Fox and North and their supporters successfully challenges peace terms in the Commons; resignation of Shelburne.

**Apr.** *Fox–North administration* formed. Principal figures: Duke of Portland (First Lord of the Treasury); Lord North (Home Secretary); Charles James Fox (Foreign Secretary).

**Apr.** Pitt's proposals for parliamentary reform defeated in the Commons.

**Sept.** Treaty of Versailles signed between England, France and Spain (for details, see p. 302).

**Dec.** Fox's India Bill. Designed by Burke to transfer the authority of the East India Company to commissioners nominated by Parliament. Passes Commons but defeated in the Lords after pressure from the King. Ministers dismissed and *Pitt administration* formed. Principal figures: William Pitt (First Lord of the Treasury and Chancellor of the Exchequer); Lord Sydney (Home Secretary); H. Dundas (Treasurer of the Navy); Marquess of Carmarthen (Foreign Secretary); Duke of Rutland (Privy Seal).


## 1784

**Mar.** Parliament dissolved for general election. Pitt and his supporters gain a majority of over 100.

**June** Pitt introduces first Budget. Begins to reorganize government debts and finances. Duties reduced to deter smuggling, and window tax introduced. New loans raised and a large number of indirect taxes levied. 'Board for Taxes' set up to administer collection.

**July** Pitt's India Bill introduced, establishing a 'Board of Control' to administer the East India Company.

**1785**
**Apr.** Pitt's proposals for limited parliamentary reform defeated by 248 votes to 174. Pitt announces plans for a 'Sinking Fund' to liquidate the National Debt. Sets up five commissioners to investigate waste in government departments.

**1786**
**May** Pitt's 'Sinking Fund' established.
**Sept.** Commercial treaty signed between Britain and France. Duties lowered on trade in manufactured goods and wine between the two countries.

**1788**
**Nov.** King's illness starts 'Regency Crisis'. Fox and the Whigs demand unfettered powers for the Prince of Wales.

**1789**
**Feb.** Recovery of the King ends crisis.
**July** Storming of the Bastille in Paris (14th).
**Nov.** Meeting of the Revolution Society in London to celebrate the 'Glorious Revolution' of 1688–9; sermon preached by Dr Price welcoming the French Revolution.

**1790**
**Nov.** Burke publishes *Reflections on the Revolution in France*, bitterly attacking the revolution and its supporters.

**1791**
**Mar.** Publication of Thomas Paine's *Rights of Man* Pt I (Pt II published in February 1792).
**May** Burke and Fox quarrel publicly over the French Revolution.
**July** 'Church and King' riots in Birmingham against Dissenters.

**1792**
**Jan.** Formation of London Corresponding Society, first artisan-based political society.
**May** Proclamation against seditious publications.
**Nov.** Formation of loyalist associations against 'Republicans and Levellers' begins.

**Dec.** Pitt fortifies the Tower, calls out the militia and begins preparations for war. Further proclamation against seditious writings and trial of Paine (in his absence) for seditious libel.

### 1793

**Jan.** Execution of Louis XVI of France.
**Feb.** France declares war on Britain and Holland.
**May** Grey's motion for reform defeated by 282 votes to 41 in the Commons.
**Oct.** British Convention meets at Edinburgh.
**Nov.–Dec.** British Convention reassembles; dispersed by authorities and leaders tried and harshly sentenced (Jan.–Sept. 1794).

### 1794

**May** Arrest of leaders of English reform societies on charge of high treason. Secret committees appointed to investigate radical societies. Habeas Corpus suspended.
**July** Moderate Whigs under Portland join in the Pitt administration; Fox and his followers left in virtual isolation.
**Oct.–Nov.** Thomas Hardy and other radical leaders acquitted of high treason.

### 1795

**July** Widespread food rioting in England; demonstrations against the war in London.
**Oct.** Mass meeting organized by London Corresponding Society in London. Attack on the King's coach by anti-war protestors at opening of Parliament.
**Nov.–Dec.** Government introduces 'Two Acts', extending the law of treason and prohibiting mass meetings unless approved by the magistracy.

### 1796

**May** Failure of attempts to make peace with France.
**Dec.** Failure of French attempt to land at Bantry Bay, Ireland. Breakdown of further peace overtures to France.

### 1797

**Feb.** Bank crisis in Britain; temporary suspension of cash payments by the Bank of England. Defeat of Spanish fleet at Cape St Vincent. Failure of small French landing in Pembrokeshire.

**Apr.** Outbreak of naval mutiny at Spithead.

**May** Mutiny at Spithead settled; outbreak of mutiny at the Nore.

**June** Mutiny at the Nore suppressed and ringleaders hanged.

**Sept.** Negotiations for peace with France broken off.

**Oct.** Duncan defeats Dutch fleet at Camperdown.

**Nov.** Pitt's Finance Bill proposes new indirect taxes as well as an income tax.

## 1798

**Jan.** Pitt's Finance Bill approved by Parliament.

**Apr.** Remaining leaders of London Corresponding Society arrested.

**May** Outbreak of rebellion in Ireland.

**June** Defeat of Irish rebels at Vinegar Hill and suppression of rising in Ulster.

**Aug.** Landing of General Humbert and French troops in Ireland. Nelson defeats French fleet at the battle of the Nile.

**Sept.** Humbert's troops surrender.

**Oct.** Failure of French expedition to Lough Swilly and capture of Wolfe Tone.

## 1799

**Apr.** Pitt introduces income tax of 10 per cent.

**July** Combination Act passed, prohibiting combinations of workmen to raise wages. Act passed prohibiting certain named political societies, including the London Corresponding Society and the United Irishmen.

## 1800

**Jan.** Peace overtures from Napoleon rejected by Pitt.

**July** Second Combination Act passed, partly relaxing provisions of Act of 1799 (see p. 209).

**Aug.** Act of Union. Ireland merged with Great Britain and Irish parliament abolished.

## 1801

**Feb.** Resignation of Pitt because of the King's refusal to permit the introduction of Catholic Emancipation. *Addington administration* formed. Principal figures: Henry Addington (First Lord of the Treasury and Chancellor of the Exchequer); Duke of Portland (Home Secretary).

**Apr.** Danish fleet destroyed at Copenhagen.

**Oct.** Preliminary terms of peace agreed with France.

**1802**
**Mar.** Peace of Amiens signed with France (for details, see p. 303).

**1803**
**May** War resumed with France.

**1804**
**May** Resignation of Addington. *Second Pitt administration* formed. Principal figures: William Pitt (First Lord of the Treasury and Chancellor of the Exchequer); Lord Hawkesbury (Home Secretary).
**July** Napoleon's invasion army of 100,000 men and 2,000 transports assembled at Boulogne. Extensive anti-invasion preparations in England.

**1805**
**Aug.** Third Coalition formed with Britain, Austria and Russia. Napoleon begins movement of army of Boulogne to Central Europe.
**Oct.** Nelson defeats Franco-Spanish fleet at Trafalgar.

**1806**
**Jan.** Death of Pitt.
**Feb.** *Grenville administration* formed ('All the Talents'). Principal figures: Lord Grenville (First Lord of the Treasury); Charles James Fox (Foreign Secretary).
**Sept.** Death of Charles James Fox.
**Nov.** Napoleon's Berlin decrees close all European ports to British shipping.
**Jan.–Nov.** Orders in Council issued by Britain, in retaliation for Berlin decrees, ordering all neutral ships trading with Europe to proceed via Britain and pay duties.

**1807**
**Mar.** Resignation of 'All the Talents' ministry. *Portland administration* formed. Principal figures: Duke of Portland (First Lord of the Treasury); Spencer Perceval (Chancellor of the Exchequer).
**May** Act abolishing the slave trade.
**Sept.** Bombardment of Copenhagen.
**Nov.** Napoleon issues Milan decrees for confiscation of all neutral shipping calling at British ports.

**1808**
**Aug.** Convention of Cintra signed in Lisbon, allowing French to evacuate Portugal on easy terms. Widespread protests in England.

## 1809

**Jan.** Committee appointed to investigate the Duke of York's involvement in the sale of army commissions.

**June** Motion for parliamentary reform defeated in the Commons.

**Sept.–Oct.** Failure of Walcheren expedition. Resignation of Duke of Portland. *Perceval administration* formed. Principal figures: Spencer Perceval (First Lord of the Treasury and Chancellor of the Exchequer); Earl of Liverpool (Secretary for War and the Colonies).

## 1810

**Feb.** Government forced to appoint enquiry on the Walcheren expedition by vote in the House of Commons.

**Mar.** Government narrowly escapes defeat on motions of censure over Walcheren expedition.

**Apr.** Riots in London in support of radical MP Sir Francis Burdett.

**Oct.** George III suffers renewed bout of illness.

## 1811

**Feb.** Prince of Wales given virtually full powers as Prince Regent (confirmed 1812).

**Mar.** Beginning of Luddite disturbances in Midlands.

## 1812

**Jan.** Luddite disturbances spread to Yorkshire and Lancashire. Frame-breaking made capital offence.

**Mar.** Widespread petitions against Orders in Council.

**Apr.** Height of Luddite disturbances; attack on Rawfolds Mill; assassination of William Horsfall by Luddite sympathizers.

**May** Assassination of Spencer Perceval.

**June** *Liverpool administration* formed. Principal figures: Earl of Liverpool (First Lord of the Treasury); Viscount Sidmouth (Home Secretary); Viscount Castlereagh (Foreign Secretary); Sir Robert Peel (Home Secretary). Orders in Council revoked.

**July** Wellington defeats French at Salamanca.

## 1813

**June** Wellington's victory at Vittoria.

**Oct.** Defeat of Napoleon at battle of Leipzig.

## 1814

**Apr.** Abdication of Napoleon.

## 1815

**Mar.** Napoleon returns from Elba, beginning of the 'Hundred Days'. Widespread petitioning movement and riots in London against passing of the Corn Laws, imposing a high protective tariff against imports of grain.
**June** Defeat of Napoleon at Waterloo. Peace of Vienna signed (see p. 304).

## 1816

**Apr.** Income tax abolished after government defeat in the House of Commons. Beginning of widespread riots against distress in East Anglia and manufacturing districts.
**Oct.** First cheap edition of Cobbett's *Political Register* issued, the 'two-penny trash'.

## 1817

**Jan.** Attack on Prince Regent's coach leads to introduction of 'Gag Acts'; Habeas Corpus suspended, and restrictions placed on meetings.
**Mar.** March of the 'blanketeers' broken up by troops.
**June** Pentrich 'rising' in Derbyshire led by Jeremiah Brandreth.

## 1819

**Aug.** Reform meeting at St Peter's Fields, Manchester, broken up by troops ('Peterloo'); followed by 'Six Acts' restricting meetings and the press, and allowing magistrates to seize arms and prevent drilling.

## 1820

**Jan.** Death of George III; accession of George IV.
**Feb.** Cato Street conspiracy uncovered.
**June** George IV's estranged wife Caroline returns to claim her rights as Queen.
**Nov.** Government forced to abandon its attempt to deprive Queen Caroline of her title and dissolve her marriage to the King after widespread popular opposition.

## 1821

**Aug.** Riots in London at Queen Caroline's funeral.

## 1822

**Jan.** Peel becomes Home Secretary in place of Lord Sidmouth.
**Aug.** Castlereagh commits suicide; George Canning becomes Foreign Secretary.

**1823**

**Jan.** William Huskisson becomes President of the Board of Trade; Reciprocity of Duties Act passed (see p. 247).

**1824**

**Feb.** Act to repeal the laws relative to combinations (see pp. 210–11).

**1825**

**Nov.–Dec.** Financial crisis in England, widespread bankruptcies and commercial failures.

**Dec.** Second Act relating to combinations of workmen, amending Act of 1824 (see p. 211).

**1827**

**Feb.** Lord Liverpool paralysed by a stroke (17th).

**Apr.** *Canning administration* formed. Principal figures: Canning (First Lord of the Treasury and Chancellor of the Exchequer); Huskisson (President of the Board of Trade); Viscount Palmerston (Secretary at War).

**July** Treaty with France and Russia for pacification of Greece.

**Aug.** Death of Canning. *Goderich administration* formed. Principal figures: Viscount Goderich (First Lord of the Treasury); Huskisson (Secretary of State for War and the Colonies).

**1828**

**Jan.** Resignation of Goderich after internal Cabinet disputes with his colleagues. *Wellington administration* formed. Principal figures: Duke of Wellington (Prime Minister); Robert Peel (Home Secretary); Huskisson (Secretary of State for War and the Colonies).

**Feb.** Bill to repeal Test and Corporation Acts introduced by Lord John Russell and passed with minor amendments (May).

**May** Resignation of Huskisson and Canningites over failure of Parliament to approve the transfer of the franchises of Penryn and East Retford to Manchester and Birmingham. Catholic Emancipation Bill passes Commons but defeated in Lords.

**1829**

**Feb.** Wellington and Peel declare themselves in favour of Catholic Emancipation after election of Daniel O'Connell for County Clare. Widespread protests from 'Ultra' Tories.

**Apr.** Catholic Emancipation passed. Catholics admitted to Parliament and to almost all public offices. Irish freehold qualification raised from 40s. to £10.

**Sept.** Metropolitan Police Act comes into operation. London given force of 3,314 professional police.

## 1830

**June** Death of George IV; accession of William IV.

**July** Dissolution of Parliament for fresh elections.

**Sept.** Huskisson killed at inauguration of Liverpool & Manchester Railway.

**Nov.** Wellington declares against parliamentary reform (2nd); government defeated on a vote on the Civil List Accounts (15th); Wellington resigns (16th). *Grey administration* formed. Principal figures: Earl Grey (Prime Minister); Lord John Russell (Paymaster-General); Viscount Melbourne (Home Secretary); Viscount Palmerston (Foreign Secretary); H. Brougham (Lord Chancellor).

## 1831

**Mar.** First Reform Bill introduced into House of Commons by Lord John Russell. Passes second reading. (For fuller details of the reform movement see pp. 84–7).

**Apr.** Government defeated on Gascoyne's amendment objecting to the reduction in numbers of MPs for England and Wales. Parliament dissolved.

**June** Whigs returned after general election and second Reform Bill introduced into Parliament.

**July** Reform Bill receives second reading.

**Sept.** Reform Bill receives third reading.

**Oct.** Reform Bill rejected by House of Lords (8th). Riots in Nottingham and Derby (8–10th); riots in Bristol (29th–31st).

**Dec.** New Reform Bill introduced into Commons; passes second reading (18th).

## 1832

**Jan.** William IV agrees to creation of peers in order to obtain passage of reform.

**Mar.** Reform Bill passes third reading by 355 votes to 239 (22nd).

**Apr.** Reform Bill passes second reading in Lords.

**May** Government defeated on Lyndhurst's motion; resignation of ministers. 'May days' (9th–15th); Wellington asked to form an administration but unable to do so; the King forced to recall Grey and confirm assurances that peers will be created as necessary to ensure passage of Reform Bill.

**June** Reform Bill receives third reading in Lords and royal assent (4th and 7th). (For provisions of Reform Act, see p. 87).

**July** Scottish Reform Act passed.

**Aug.** Irish Reform Act passed.

## 1833

**Apr.** Irish Coercion Act passed.

**Aug.** Slavery abolished throughout British Empire; £20 million allocated as compensation to slave-owners.

## 1834

**July** Resignation of Earl Grey over question of extending Irish Coercion Act. Lord Melbourne becomes Prime Minister with leading ministers retaining places.

**Aug.** Poor Law Amendment Act passed, the 'New Poor Law'. Central board of commissioners appointed to administer system (for further details, see p. 151).

**Nov.** Ministry dismissed by the King and caretaker administration formed under Duke of Wellington. Principal figures: Duke of Wellington (Prime Minister and Secretary of State); Lord Lyndhurst (Lord Chancellor).

**Dec.** *Peel administration* formed. Principal figures: Sir Robert Peel (Prime Minister and Chancellor of the Exchequer); Lord Lyndhurst (Lord Chancellor); Duke of Wellington (Foreign Secretary). Parliament dissolved because majority in the Commons against the ministry. Peel issues 'Tamworth Manifesto' in an attempt to broaden base of support.

## 1835

**Feb.** New parliament meets.

**Apr.** Sir Robert Peel resigns after Whigs and Irish members combine in the 'Lichfield House Compact' to defeat Peel on the use of surplus revenues from the Irish Church. *Second Melbourne administration* formed. Principal figures: Lord Melbourne (Prime Minister); Viscount Palmerston (Foreign Secretary); Lord John Russell (Home Secretary).

**Sept.** Municipal Corporations Act. Members of town councils to be elected by ratepayers; town councils to publish accounts and budgets.

## 1836

**Aug.** Commutation of Tithes Act. Tithes to be paid in money and calculated on basis of average price of corn in previous seven years.

**1837**

**June** Death of William IV; accession of Queen Victoria.

**Nov.** First parliament of Queen Victoria's reign meets; Lord Melbourne continues as Prime Minister.

**1838**

**Aug.** National Charter drawn up (for fuller details of the development of Chartism, see pp. 224–5).

**Sept.** Anti-Corn Law League set up at Manchester under the leadership of John Bright and Richard Cobden.

**1840**

**Jan.** Penny postage introduced.

**Feb.** Marriage of Victoria and Prince Albert of Saxe-Coburg-Gotha.

**1841**

**Aug.** Following defeat of the government, *second Peel administration* formed. Principal figures: Sir Robert Peel (Prime Minister); Duke of Wellington (Minister without Portfolio); Sir James Graham (Home Secretary); William Ewart Gladstone (President of the Board of Trade from 1843).

**1842**

**June** New sliding scale of duties introduced to regulate the corn trade; duties on over 700 articles removed or reduced; income tax reimposed.

**1844**

**May** Bank Charter Act. Note-issuing and credit functions of Bank of England separated. Note circulation limited.

**1845**

**Oct.** First effects of Irish potato blight felt. Beginning of the Irish famine.

**Dec.** Peel resigns over desire to repeal Corn Laws (6th); resumes office (20th).

**1846**

**Jan.** Peel declares for a total repeal of the Corn Laws.

**June** Royal assent given to repeal of the Corn Laws; sliding scale abolished; duty retained until 1849; only a nominal duty of 1*s.* retained thereafter. Resignation of Peel after defeat of government on Irish Coercion Bill. *Russell administration* formed. Principal figures: Lord John

Russell (Prime Minister); Lord Palmerston (Foreign Secretary); Thomas B. Macaulay (Paymaster-General).

## 1848
**Apr.** Chartist demonstration at Kennington Common in support of third petition.

## 1849
**June** Repeal of the Navigation Laws.

## 1850
**Sept.** Re-establishment of Roman Catholic hierarchy in England.

## 1851
**Feb.** Russell announces intention of government to resign after defeat over Bill to reduce the county franchise to £10 (24th).
**Mar.** Russell announces that ministers to resume office after failure of attempts to form a new ministry.
**May** Opening of Great Exhibition in Hyde Park.
**Dec.** Dismissal of Palmerston for interference with internal affairs of France.

## 1852
**Feb.** *Earl of Derby's administration* formed. Principal figures: Earl of Derby (Prime Minister); Benjamin Disraeli (Chancellor of the Exchequer).
**Sept.** Death of Duke of Wellington.

## 1853
**Dec.** *Aberdeen administration* formed. Principal figures: Earl of Aberdeen (Prime Minister); Lord John Russell (Foreign Secretary); W. E. Gladstone (Chancellor of the Exchequer); Viscount Palmerston (Home Secretary).

## 1854
**Mar.** Alliance of Britain and France with Turkey. Declaration of war by England and France on Russia (28th), beginning of Crimean War (for details, see pp. 288–9).

## 1855
**Jan.** Resignation of Lord Aberdeen after criticism of the conduct of the Crimean War.

**Feb.** *Palmerston administration* formed. Principal figures: Lord Palmerston (Prime Minister); W. E. Gladstone (Chancellor of the Exchequer).

**1856**
**Mar.** Treaty of Paris concludes Crimean War (for details, see pp. 304–5).

**1857**
**Nov.** Commercial crisis in England. Bank Charter Act of 1844 suspended.

**1858**
**Feb.** Rejection of Palmerston's Conspiracy to Murder Bill leads to his resignation. *Second Derby administration* formed. Principal figures: Earl of Derby (Prime Minister); Disraeli (Chancellor of the Exchequer).
**June** Property qualification for Members of Parliament abolished.
**July** Jews admitted to Parliament. Act for the better government of India.

**1859**
**Mar.** Defeat of government on Reform Bill introduced by Disraeli.
**Apr.** Parliament dissolved.
**May** Government resigns after finding itself in a minority in new parliament.
**June** *Second Palmerston administration* formed. Principal figures: Lord Palmerston (Prime Minister); W. E. Gladstone (Chancellor of the Exchequer); Earl Russell (Foreign Secretary).

**1860**
**Jan.** Commercial treaty between Great Britain and France.

**1861**
**Nov.** 'Trent incident'. Two Confederate commissioners, Mason and Slidell, taken from the British steamer *Trent* by Federal (USA) warship.
**Dec.** Death of Prince Albert.

**1865**
**Oct.** Death of Lord Palmerston; Earl Russell assumes premiership.

**1866**
**Feb.** Gladstone introduces a Reform Bill.
**Mar.** The 'Cave of Adullam' formed (see Adullamites, p. 393).

**May** Financial crisis in England; widespread bank failures.

**June** Gladstone introduces Reform Bill to lower franchise qualifications in the boroughs and the counties. Defeat of the Bill by the revolt of the Adullamites leads to the resignation of the ministry. *Third Derby administration* formed. Principal figures: Earl of Derby (Prime Minister); Disraeli (Chancellor of the Exchequer).

**July** Demonstrations by Reform League in London; Hyde Park railings broken down by crowds (23rd).

### 1867

**Feb.** Disraeli introduces reform proposals. Fenians attempt to seize arsenal at Chester Castle and release prisoners at Clerkenwell prison. Rising in Ireland suppressed.

**May** Reform demonstration held in Hyde Park in defiance of government ban; resignation of Home Secretary, Spencer Walpole.

**Aug.** Second Reform Act passed (for details, see p. 88).

### 1868

**Feb.** Resignation of Lord Derby; Disraeli becomes Prime Minister.

**Dec.** Resignation of Disraeli and Conservatives following the general election. *Liberal government* formed. Principal figures: W. E. Gladstone (Prime Minister and Chancellor of the Exchequer); J. Bright (Board of Trade); E. Cardwell (War Office).

### 1869

**July** Disestablishment and disendowment of the Irish Church.

**Oct.** Opening of Suez Canal.

### 1870

**Jan.** Bankruptcy Act comes into force; imprisonment for debt ended.

**Aug.** Irish Land Act passed, providing for compensation for outgoing tenants, loans to be spent on improvements, restraint on evictions and establishment of courts of arbitration. Forster's Elementary Education Act. Establishment of School Boards made compulsory where educational provision deemed inadequate (for further details, see p. 158).

### 1871

**June** Abolition of religious tests at Oxford and Cambridge. Trade Union Act gives legal recognition to trade unions and protection of funds, though unions to remain liable to prosecution under provisions of 1825 Act.

**Aug.** Purchase of commissions in the army abolished.

## 1872
**July** Ballot Act passed.
**Aug.** Licensing Act restricting sale of intoxicating liquors.

## 1873
**Mar.** Gladstone defeated on Irish University Bill and resigns, but resumes office in the same month.
**June** Beginning of Ashanti War.

## 1874
**Feb.** Gladstone resigns following losses in general election. *Conservative government* formed. Principal figures: B. Disraeli (Prime Minister); Sir Stafford Northcote (Chancellor of the Exchequer); Earl of Derby (Foreign Secretary).
**July** New Licensing Act passed.

## 1875
**June** Artisans Dwellings Act.
**Aug.** Conspiracy and Protection to Property Act ends use of law of conspiracy in trade disputes and legalizes peaceful picketing. Employers and Workmen Act limits penalties for breach of contract.
**Dec.** British government purchases shares in the Suez Canal Company owned by the Khedive of Egypt for £4,000,000.

## 1877
**Jan.** Proclamation of Queen Victoria as Empress of India.

## 1878
**July** Treaty of Berlin (for details, see p. 305).

## 1879
**Jan.** Beginning of Zulu War in South Africa.

## 1880
**Feb.** Dissolution of Parliament for general election.
**Apr.** Resignation of ministers following general election. *Liberal government* formed. Principal figures: W. E. Gladstone (Prime Minister and Chancellor of the Exchequer); Sir William Harcourt (Home Secretary); Earl Granville (Foreign Secretary).

## 1881
**Mar.** Irish Coercion Act.
**Aug.** Irish Land Act (for details, see p. 315).

## 1882
**May** Murder of Lord Frederick Cavendish in Phoenix Park, Dublin (see p. 316).
**July** Bombardment of Alexandria. Resignation of John Bright as Chancellor of the Duchy of Lancaster. New Irish Coercion Act.

## 1883
**Aug.** Corrupt and Illegal Practices Act.

## 1884
**Mar.** Franchise Bill introduced.
**July** Franchise Bill blocked in the House of Lords.
**Nov.** Agreement reached between government and opposition on redistribution of seats. Third Reform Act passed (see pp. 88–9).

## 1885
**Mar.** Redistribution Act passed (see pp. 88–9).
**June** Resignation of Gladstone administration. *Conservative government* formed. Principal figures: Marquess of Salisbury (Prime Minister and Foreign Secretary); Lord Randolph Churchill (Secretary for India); J. Chamberlain (President of Local Government Board).
**Nov.** General election.
**Dec.** Results of general election leave Liberals as largest single party. 'Hawarden Kite'; Gladstone's support for Home Rule for Ireland widely reported.

## 1886
**Feb.** *Liberal government* formed. Principal figures: W. E. Gladstone (Prime Minister); Earl of Rosebery (Foreign Secretary); H. Campbell-Bannerman (Secretary for War). Gladstone announces intention to examine 'going nearer to the source and seat of the mischief' in Ireland. Lord Randolph Churchill in Belfast urges loyalists to resist attempts at repeal of the Union. Unemployed riots in London.
**Mar.** Resignation of Joseph Chamberlain and George Trevelyan from government.
**Apr.** Gladstone introduces Irish Home Rule Bill.
**June** Defeat of Home Rule Bill on second reading in Commons. Dissolution of Parliament and general election called.

**July** As a result of general election Gladstone resigns. *Conservative government* formed. Principal figures: Marquess of Salisbury (Prime Minister and Foreign Secretary); Lord Randolph Churchill (Chancellor of the Exchequer).

**Sept.** Parnell's Tenant Relief Bill defeated.

**Dec.** Resignation of Lord Randolph Churchill after disagreements over his Budget proposals. G. J. Goschen becomes Chancellor of Exchequer.

## 1887

**June** Celebration of Queen Victoria's Jubilee (21st).

**Aug.** Irish Tenants' Act and new Coercion Act passed.

**Nov.** 'Bloody Sunday'; meeting of Social Democratic Federation in Trafalgar Square broken up by police and troops.

## 1888

**Aug.** County Councils Act.

**Sept.** Commission formed to investigate complicity of Parnell and his colleagues in outrages in Ireland.

## 1889

**Aug.** Beginning of London dock strike led by Ben Tillett, Tom Mann and John Burns.

**Sept.** Dock companies concede 'docker's tanner', ending strike.

## 1890

**Feb.** Parnell cleared of involvement in Irish outrages.

**Nov.** Parnell cited as co-respondent in O'Shea divorce. Calls for Parnell to resign as leader of Irish Party.

**Dec.** Irish Nationalist Party split, majority seceding from Parnell's leadership.

## 1891

**Aug.** Abolition of fees for elementary education.

**Oct.** Gladstone outlines 'Newcastle Programme'. Death of Parnell.

**Nov.** J. Chamberlain renounces hope of Liberal Unionists rejoining Liberal Party.

## 1892

**July** General election returns small Liberal majority over Conservatives, but in a minority against all other parties.

**Aug.** Conservative administration defeated on vote of confidence.

*Liberal government* formed. Principal figures: W. E. Gladstone (Prime Minister); H. H. Asquith (Home Secretary); Earl of Rosebery (Foreign Secretary); H. Campbell-Bannerman (Secretary for War).

## 1893

**Jan.** Bradford Conference leads to formation of Independent Labour Party.
**Feb.** Gladstone introduces Second Irish Home Rule Bill.
**Sept.** Home Rule Bill passes third reading in the Commons by 34 votes (1st); defeated in the House of Lords by 419 votes to 41(8th).

## 1894

**Feb.** Employers' Liability Act defeated in the House of Lords.
**Mar.** Local Government Act passed, creating elected parish councils, urban district and rural district councils. Resignation of Gladstone. Queen summons Earl of Rosebery to take premiership. Death duties introduced in Harcourt's Budget.

## 1895

**June** Resignation of Liberal government after defeat on 'cordite' vote.
**July** General election returns Conservatives as largest single party. *Conservative government* formed. Principal figures: Marquess of Salisbury (Prime Minister and Foreign Secretary); A. J. Balfour (First Lord of the Treasury); Marquess of Lansdowne (Secretary for War); Joseph Chamberlain (Colonial Secretary).
**Dec.** Boundary dispute between British Guiana and Venezuela leads to crisis in relations between Britain and the United States (settled by Treaty of Washington, 1897). Jameson raid launched in South Africa.

## 1896

**Jan.** Chamberlain repudiates Jameson raid; 'Kruger telegram' of support from German Emperor to President Kruger on defeat of Jameson raid (3rd).
**Oct.** Lord Rosebery resigns Liberal leadership; Sir William Harcourt becomes effective party leader.

## 1897

**July** Committee of House of Commons reports on Jameson raid, censuring Rhodes but acquitting Chamberlain and the Colonial Office.
**Aug.** Workmen's Compensation Act passed; accidents at work to be paid for by employers.

## 1898

**June** Anglo-French Convention settles colonial boundaries in West Africa.

**Sept.** Defeat of dervishes at Omdurman and capture of Khartoum. Confrontation of French and British forces at Fashoda – the 'Fashoda Crisis'.

**Nov.** Marchand marches French forces away from Fashoda.

**Dec.** Campbell-Bannerman becomes leader of the Liberal Party, following departure of Harcourt and Morley from the leading circles of the party.

## 1899

**Mar.** Anglo-French Convention resolves spheres of influence dispute concerning Congo and Nile basins.

**Mar.–Apr.** Inconclusive talks with Germany about possibility of an alliance.

**May** Hague Conference to discuss disarmament and peace, leading to revision of laws of war and setting up of Court of Arbitration.

**May–June** Conference between Milner and Kruger to resolve differences between Boers and Uitlanders breaks down (31 May–5 June).

**Oct.** Outbreak of Boer War.

**Nov.** British overtures for an alliance with Germany rejected.

**Dec.** 'Black Week' (10th–15th); British defeats at Stormberg (10th), Magersfontein (11th) and Colenso (15th). Buller superseded by Lord Roberts with Lord Kitchener as Chief of Staff.

## 1900

**Feb.** Relief of Ladysmith (28th). Labour Representation Committee (LRC) formed after a meeting at Memorial Hall in London, with aim of electing Members of Parliament 'sympathetic with the needs and demands of the Labour movement'; political levy from unions agreed. Irish nationalists recombine under the leadership of John Redmond.

**May** Relief of Mafeking; widespread rejoicing in England (17th).

**Oct.** General election, known as the 'Khaki' election. Conservatives returned with reduced majority.

**Nov.** Salisbury gives up Foreign Office and replaced by Lansdowne.

## 1901

**Jan.** Death of Queen Victoria; accession of Edward VII (22nd).

**Feb.** Breakdown of peace negotiations between Kitchener and Botha at Middelburg.

## 1902

**Jan.** Alliance signed between Britain and Japan.
**Mar.** Boers sue for peace. Education Bill introduced.
**May** Peace with Boers signed at Vereeniging.
**July** Salisbury succeeded as premier by A. J. Balfour.
**Dec.** Education Act passed (see p. 159).

## 1903

**Mar.** Irish Land Purchase Act passed, sponsored by George Wyndham, Secretary for Ireland.
**May** Chamberlain announces his support for imperial preference at speech in Birmingham. Edward VII's visit to Paris opens way to more cordial relations with France.
**Sept.** Chamberlain and leading tariff reformers resign from cabinet to prosecute their campaign in the country at large. Cabinet reconstruction. Austen Chamberlain becomes Chancellor of the Exchequer; Alfred Lyttelton becomes Colonial Secretary.

## 1904

**Apr.** *Entente Cordiale* between Britain and France. Agreement over Morocco, followed by agreement over Siam, Egypt and Newfoundland.
**Oct.** Sir John ('Jacky') Fisher appointed First Sea Lord. Dogger Bank incident involving Russian fleet and British fishing vessels.

## 1905

**Apr.** Anglo-French military convention.
**Aug.** Anglo-Japanese Alliance. Unemployed Workmen Act passed. Unemployed registers formed under auspices of local government boards. Expenses to be defrayed by voluntary contribution.
**Nov.** Sinn Fein Party founded in Dublin.
**Dec.** Resignation of Balfour. *Liberal government* formed. Principal figures: Campbell-Bannerman (Prime Minister); Asquith (Chancellor of the Exchequer); Sir E. Grey (Foreign Secretary); Lord Haldane (Secretary for War); Lloyd George (President of Board of Trade).

## 1906

**Jan.** General election; Liberals returned with an overall majority of 84. Twenty-nine Labour MPs elected.
**Feb.** Parliament meets.
**Apr.** Education Bill introduced.
**July** Joseph Chamberlain paralysed by a stroke; effective end of his political career.

**Dec.** Trades Disputes Act passed, reversing Taff Vale decision. Government drop Education Bill after it has been mutilated by amendments in Lords.

### 1907

**Mar.** Third Imperial (Colonial) Conference in London.
**May** Introduction of the Territorial and Reserve Forces Bill to establish the Territorial Army.
**June** House of Commons approves Campbell-Bannerman's resolutions that if a Bill passed all its stages in the Commons three times it should become law, notwithstanding opposition by the Lords.
**Aug.** Anglo-Russian Agreement on Asia. Russia joins the *Entente.*

### 1908

**Apr.** Campbell-Bannerman resigns and Asquith becomes Prime Minister. Lloyd George becomes Chancellor of the Exchequer.
**July** Old Age Pensions Bill passed by Parliament.
**Oct.** Suffragette disturbances in Trafalgar Square.
**Nov.** Lords reject the Licensing Bill.

### 1909

**Mar.** Introduction of Navy Bill, a result of alarm at German shipbuilding. Four keels to be laid at once and four more if needed.
**Apr.** Lloyd George introduces his 'People's Budget'.
**July** Laying of the other four Dreadnought keels (provided for by Navy Act) is sanctioned by the government.
**Nov.** Lords reject the Budget. House of Lords upholds Osborne Judgment.
**Dec.** Parliament dissolved.

### 1910

**Jan.** General election. *Minority Liberal government* formed, dependent upon the support of the Irish Nationalist and Labour Parties.
**Apr.** Lloyd George Budget passed. Parliament Bill introduced with aim of reforming the House of Lords.
**May** Death of Edward VII. George V ascends the throne.
**June** Constitutional Conference between the leaders of the Liberal and Unionist Parties. A 'party truce' called while Conference tries to reach a compromise on the question of reform of the House of Lords.
**Oct.** Unionists reject Lloyd George's suggestion of a coalition.
**Nov.** Conference dissolves, having failed to reach agreement. Asquith

secures the King's pledge to create enough peers to pass the Parliament Bill if the Liberals win the election.

**Dec.** Liberals returned to power with very little change in the relative strengths of the parties.

## 1911

**May** National Insurance Bill introduced by Lloyd George.

**Aug.** Parliament Act passes House of Lords. The Lords lose their power of veto. House of Commons resolves to pay MPs £400 p.a. Dock strike. Two-day railway strike.

**Oct.** Churchill becomes First Lord of the Admiralty.

**Nov.** Balfour resigns leadership of the Unionist Party and is succeeded by Andrew Bonar Law. Suffragette riots, entailing extensive damage to property in London's West End.

**Dec.** National Insurance Bill receives royal assent.

## 1912

**Feb.** Miners' strike begins with the aim of securing a national minimum wage for miners.

**Mar.** A Bill to establish minimum district wages for miners is rushed through Parliament.

**Apr.** End of miners' strike. Introduction of third Irish Home Rule Bill.

**May** Strike of London dockers.

**Aug.** End of dockers' strike.

**Sept.** Two hundred thousand Ulstermen sign a 'Solemn Covenant' to oppose Home Rule. Anglo-French naval convention.

## 1913

**Jan.** Home Rule Bill rejected by House of Lords.

**July** Home Rule Bill again rejected by Lords.

**Oct.** Lloyd George begins his 'Land Campaign' for reform of rural social conditions.

## 1914

**Mar.** Suffragette riots in London. Curragh officers resign their commissions rather than act against Ulster resistance to Home Rule.

**May** Third reading of Home Rule Bill and Welsh Church (Disestablishment) Bill in Commons.

**June** Third reading of Plural Voting Bill. Assassination of Franz Ferdinand, Crown Prince of Austria, at Sarajevo.

**July** Buckingham Palace Conference attempts and fails to reach compromise on the exclusion of Ulster from the Home Rule Bill.

**Aug.** Britain declares war on Germany and Austria.

**Nov.** First battle of Ypres. Britain declares war on Turkey.

## 1915

**Apr.** Anglo-French landings at Gallipoli.

**May** Formation of *Coalition government*, which Conservatives join, under Asquith. Bonar Law becomes Colonial Secretary, Balfour replaces Churchill at the Admiralty, Curzon becomes Lord Privy Seal. Second battle of Ypres.

**Dec.** Robertson appointed Chief of Imperial General Staff. Haig succeeds French as British C. in C. on the Western Front.

## 1916

**Jan.** Allies evacuate Gallipoli peninsula. Introduction of conscription.

**Apr.** Easter Rising in Dublin suppressed.

**June** Naval battle at Jutland establishes British naval superiority.

**July–Nov.** Battle of the Somme.

**July** Lloyd George made Secretary for War.

**Dec.** Asquith resigns; Lloyd George forms new *Coalition government.* War Cabinet established with five members: Lloyd George (Prime Minister), Bonar Law (Chancellor of the Exchequer and Leader of the House), and Milner, Curzon and Arthur Henderson (Labour), who had no departmental responsibilities.

## 1917

**Feb.** Revolution in Russia led by Kerensky.

**Apr.** Battle of Vimy Ridge.

**June** Allenby takes command in Palestine.

**July** Hundred-day battle of Flanders begins.

**Oct.** Bolshevik Revolution in Russia.

**Nov.** British take Gaza. British take Passchendaele. Balfour Declaration that Britain favoured the establishment of a 'national home' for the Jewish people in Palestine.

**Dec.** Allenby enters Jerusalem.

## 1918

**Feb.** Representation of the People Act creates universal male and limited female suffrage.

**July** Second battle of the Marne.

**Sept.** General Allied offensive in West.

**Oct.** Turkey surrenders.

**Nov.** Allies grant armistice to Austria and then to Germany.

**Dec.** General election returns Lloyd George to power as head of a *Coalition government*, with 478 'Coalition' MPs returned, the vast majority being Conservatives. Lloyd George (Prime Minister), Bonar Law (Leader of the House), Austen Chamberlain (Chancellor of the Exchequer), Balfour (Foreign Secretary), Birkenhead (Lord Chancellor). Seventy Sinn Fein MPs refuse to take their seats.

## 1919

**Jan.** Paris Peace Conference begins. First Dáil Eireann elected. Irish Free State proclaimed.

**Jan.–Feb.** Engineers strike at Belfast and on the Clyde.

**Feb.** National Industrial Conference established. Sankey Commission on mining industry appointed in order to avoid miners' strike.

**Apr.** De Valera elected President of Sinn Fein Executive.

**Aug.** Sinn Fein declared an illegal organization.

**Sept.** Railway strike. Dáil Eireann proscribed; increase in acts of violence by Irish Republican Army.

**Oct.** End of railway strike. End of War Cabinet. Curzon replaces Balfour as Foreign Secretary.

**Dec.** Viscountess Astor becomes first woman MP to take her seat in Parliament.

## 1920

**Jan.** Versailles Treaty comes into force (for details, see p. 307).

**Apr.** Conscription abolished.

**June** Government begins recruiting 'Black and Tans', volunteers to suppress IRA.

**Oct.** Miners' strike.

**Nov.** Miners' strike ends.

**Dec.** Black and Tans set fire to the city of Cork. Government of Ireland Act passed, partitioning Ireland into six counties of Ulster, and the South. Each has a separate parliament.

## 1921

**Mar.** Anglo-Russian trade agreement signed. Coal Mines (Decontrol) Act returns mines to their owners after wartime government control.

**Apr.** Miners' strike. State of Emergency declared.

**May** Elections to Irish parliaments. Sinn Fein win overwhelming majority of seats in southern parliament, but do not recognize it.

**June** Miners' strike ends.

**Oct.** Conference to negotiate an Irish treaty in London.

**Dec.** 'Articles of Agreement for a Treaty' signed. When ratified, Southern Ireland will be the 'Irish Free State' with Dominion status within the Empire.

## 1922

**Sept.** 'Chanak crisis' caused by Turko-Greek war.

**Oct.** Carlton Club meeting of Conservative Party decides not to continue their coalition with Lloyd George. Lloyd George resigns. Formation of *Conservative government* under Bonar Law.

**Nov.** General election. Conservatives gain a comfortable majority (73 seats). Principal figures: Bonar Law (Prime Minister); Stanley Baldwin (Chancellor of the Exchequer); Curzon (Foreign Secretary).

**Dec.** Irish Free State comes into formal existence.

## 1923

**May** Bonar Law resigns because of ill-health and Baldwin becomes Prime Minister.

**Dec.** General election. No party is returned with an overall majority. Conservatives the largest party with 258 seats. Baldwin resumes office.

## 1924

**Jan.** Conservative government defeated on an amendment to the Address. Baldwin resigns. *First Labour government* takes office, dependent upon Liberal support in Parliament. Principal figures: James Ramsay MacDonald (Prime Minister and Foreign Secretary); Philip Snowden (Chancellor of the Exchequer); John Wheatley (Minister of Health).

**Feb.** Britain recognizes Soviet Russia.

**July** Beginning of London Conference on Reparations.

**Aug.** Conference accepts Dawes plan.

**Sept.** Hastings, the Attorney-General, withdraws a prosecution against J. R. Campbell for incitement to mutiny.

**Oct.** Labour government defeated on vote of censure over Campbell case. MacDonald resigns office. In general election, Conservatives win a large majority of seats.

**Nov.** Formation of *Conservative government.* Principal figures: Baldwin (Prime Minister); Churchill (Chancellor of the Exchequer); Austen Chamberlain (Foreign Secretary); Neville Chamberlain (Minister of Health); Birkenhead (Secretary for India).

## 1925

**Apr.** Britain returns to Gold Standard.

**July** 'Red Friday'; Triple Alliance of miners, railway, and transport unions threatens an embargo on transport of coal if miners' wages cut. Government averts strike by nine-month subsidy and setting up a Royal Commission into mining industry under Herbert Samuel.

**Dec.** Widows, Orphans and Old Age Pensions Act introduces contributory pensions; pensions to be given at 65 instead of 70. Treaty of Locarno signed in London. Irish Boundary Agreement.

## 1926

**Mar.** Samuel Commission reports: finds the government subsidy unsound, which signifies wage cuts.

**May** Miners refuse wage cuts and are 'locked out'. Nine-day General Strike.

**Oct.–Nov.** Imperial Conference in London. Britain and her Dominions are to be regarded as autonomous units of equal status.

**Nov.** Miners return to work.

## 1927

**May** Passage of Trade Disputes and Trade Unions Act: General Strikes made illegal and 'contracting-in' instituted as basis of trade union political levy to Labour Party.

**Aug.** Failure of conference on naval disarmament between Britain, USA and Japan. Unemployed Insurance Act reduces benefits.

## 1928

**Apr.** Voting age of women lowered from 30 to 21.

**May** Parliament rejects Revised Prayer Book.

## 1929

**Mar.** Passing of Local Government Act abolishes the guardians of the poor and transfers their responsibilities to county councils.

**May** General election. No party secures an overall majority. Labour has most seats (289).

**June** Formation of *Labour government*. Principal figures: MacDonald (Prime Minister); Arthur Henderson (Foreign Secretary); Snowden (Chancellor of Exchequer); J. H. Thomas (Lord Privy Seal); Margaret Bondfield (Minister of Labour).

**Oct.** 'Crash' of New York Stock Exchange. Anglo-Russian relations resumed. Irwin, Viceroy of India, makes a public promise of Dominion status for India.

**1930**

**Apr.** Naval Disarmament Conference in London. Naval treaty between Britain, France, Italy, Japan and USA.

**May** Sir Oswald Mosley resigns from government when Cabinet rejects his unemployment policy.

**Nov.** Round Table Conference on India in London.

**Dec.** Two and a half million unemployed.

**1931**

**Feb.** Mosley founds the 'New Party'. May Committee on economy established by government.

**July** Financial crisis in Europe. The May Committee recommends economies, including reduction of unemployment benefits.

**Aug.** Labour government breaks up on question of reducing unemployment benefits. Formation of *National Government* by MacDonald with four Labour, four Conservative and two Liberal Cabinet ministers. Principal figures: MacDonald (Prime Minister); Snowden (Chancellor of the Exchequer); Thomas, Sankey, Baldwin, Neville Chamberlain, Hoare, Cunliffe-Lister, Samuel (Home Secretary) and Reading (Foreign Secretary).

**Sept.** Britain goes off the Gold Standard. Second India Conference begins in London. Economy measures introduced.

**Oct.** General election. National Government win an overwhelming majority of seats (largely a Conservative majority). Labour badly beaten.

**Nov.** MacDonald forms second 'National' cabinet. Principal figures: MacDonald (Prime Minister); Baldwin (Lord President); Neville Chamberlain (Chancellor of the Exchequer); Snowden (Lord Privy Seal); Sir John Simon (Foreign Secretary).

**1932**

**Feb.** Beginning of two-year Disarmament Conference at Geneva.

**Mar.** Import Duties Act imposes 10 per cent general duty on imports.

**Apr.** Exchange Equalization Fund established to smooth variations in exchange rates. Import duty on manufactured goods raised to between 20 and 33⅓ per cent.

**July** Anglo-French Pact of friendship signed at Lausanne.

**July–Aug.** Ottawa Imperial Economic Conference.

**Sept.** Snowden, Samuel and Sinclair resign from government in protest at its protectionist policies.

**Oct.** Mosley launches British Union of Fascists.

**Nov.–Dec.** Third India Conference in London.

## 1933
**Jan.** Unemployment reaches almost 3 million. Hitler becomes Chancellor of Germany.
**Apr.** Anglo-German Trade Pact.
**Apr.–July** Embargo on Russian exports.
**June–July** World Monetary and Economic Conference in London.

## 1934
**Feb.** Anglo-Russian Trade Agreement.
**Oct.** Failure of Naval Disarmament Conference in London.

## 1935
**Apr.** Stresa Conference of Britain, France and Italy.
**June** MacDonald resigns. Baldwin becomes Prime Minister. Reconstruction of National Government: Simon (Home Secretary); Hoare (Foreign Secretary); Neville Chamberlain (Chancellor of the Exchequer); Cunliffe-Lister (Secretary for Air).
**Aug.** Government of India Bill passed.
**Nov.** General election returns *National Government* with a large majority, largely made up of Conservatives.
**Dec.** Hoare–Laval Pact between Britain and France over Abyssinia. Hoare resigns; Anthony Eden the new Foreign Secretary. Clement Attlee elected leader of the Labour Party.

## 1936
**Jan.** Death of George V. Edward VIII succeeds to the throne.
**Mar.** London Naval Convention signed by Britain, USA and France.
**July** Beginning of Spanish Civil War.
**Aug.** Anglo-Egyptian treaty terminates British military occupation.
**Sept.** 'Non-Intervention (in Spain) Committee' of all European powers meets in London.
**Oct.** Russia accedes to London Naval Convention.
**Dec.** Edward VIII abdicates. Accession of George VI. Irish Constitution (Amendment) and Executive Authority Acts abolish chief functions of governor-general and retains King for external relations only.

## 1937
**Jan.** Anglo-Italian Agreement signed.
**Apr.** Indian Constitution comes into force.
**May** Baldwin resigns. Neville Chamberlain becomes Prime Minister, with Simon (Chancellor of Exchequer), Eden (Foreign Secretary), Hoare (Home Secretary).

**June** Imperial Conference in London.

**July** Anglo-Russian and Anglo-German Naval Agreements signed.

## 1938

**Feb.** Eden resigns and is succeeded by Lord Halifax.

**Apr.** Agreement signed between Britain and Eire. Anglo-Italian Agreement on East Mediterranean and Red Sea.

**Sept.** Chamberlain meets Hitler at Berchtesgaden. British fleet mobilized. Munich Conference on Czechoslovakia, attended by Chamberlain, Daladier, Hitler and Mussolini.

**Oct.** Duff Cooper resigns as First Lord of the Admiralty.

**Nov.** Anglo-Italian Pact comes into force.

## 1939

**Mar.** British guarantee to Poland.

**Apr.** Russia proposes alliance with Britain and France against German aggression. Compulsory military service announced (operative from June).

**July** Ministry of Supply set up.

**Aug.** Emergency Powers Act.

**Sept.** Anglo-Polish Pact of mutual assistance. German–Soviet Non-aggression Pact. War declared on Germany (3rd).

## 1940

**Apr.** Germans invade Denmark and Norway.

**May** Invasion of France. Chamberlain resigns. Formation of *Coalition government* under Churchill. War Cabinet formed with Churchill as PM and Minister of Defence, Chamberlain (Lord President), Attlee (Lord Privy Seal), Halifax (Foreign Secretary), Arthur Greenwood (Minister without Portfolio). British troops evacuate Norway.

**June** British troops evacuate France at Dunkirk. Italy declares war on Britain.

**July** Germans occupy Channel Islands.

**July–Sept.** Battle of Britain.

**Sept.–Oct.** London 'Blitz'.

**Oct.** British troops land in Greece.

**Nov.** German air raids on Coventry.

## 1941

**Mar.** Roosevelt signs Lend-Lease Bill.

**May** Raid on London damages House of Commons. HMS *Hood* sunk. *Bismarck* sunk.

**June** Germans invade Russia.

**July** Anglo-Russian Alliance.

**Aug.** Roosevelt and Churchill issue Atlantic Charter.

**Dec.** Japanese attack US fleet at Pearl Harbor without warning. Germany and Italy declare war on USA.

### 1942

**Feb.** Fall of Singapore to Japanese.

**May** Anglo-Soviet treaty for 20 years. First 1,000-bomber raid on Cologne.

**Aug.** Raid on Dieppe. Alexander takes command of Middle East Army. Montgomery in command of 8th Army.

**Oct.–Nov.** Battle of El Alamein.

**Dec.** Publication of Beveridge Report on *Social Insurance and Allied Services.*

### 1943

**Jan.** Casablanca Conference: Allies demand unconditional surrender of Germany, Italy and Japan.

**Feb.** Ministry of Town and Country Planning set up.

**Sept.** Allies invade Italy.

**Oct.** Foreign secretaries of Britain, USA and USSR agree to found United Nations on the basis of their wartime alliance.

**Nov.–Dec.** Churchill, Roosevelt and Stalin meet at Tehran Conference.

### 1944

**June** Allies enter Rome. 'D-Day': Allied landing in Normandy.

**Aug.** Passage of Butler Education Act.

**Sept.** Battle of Arnhem.

**Oct.** Moscow Conference of Churchill and Stalin.

**Nov.** Address from the throne refers to a comprehensive health service and a uniform system of national insurance.

### 1945

**Feb.** Yalta Conference of Churchill, Stalin and Roosevelt.

**May** Germany surrenders. Labour Party leaves coalition and Churchill forms 'caretaker' government.

**July** General election gives Labour a huge majority. Formation of *first majority Labour government.* Principal figures: Attlee (Prime Minister); Herbert Morrison (Leader of the House); Aneurin Bevan (Minister of Health); Ernest Bevin (Foreign Secretary); Hugh Dalton (Chancellor of the Exchequer); Stafford Cripps (President of the Board of Trade).

**July–Aug.** Potsdam Conference.

**Aug.** British troops liberate Burma. Atom bombs dropped on Hiroshima and Nagasaki.

**Sept.** Japan surrenders.

**Dec.** Britain, USA and USSR agree in Moscow to provisional democratic government in Korea. Anglo-American Financial Agreement.

## 1946

**Mar.** Bank of England nationalized. Churchill's 'Iron Curtain' speech at Fulton, Missouri, USA.

**July** Coal Industry Nationalization Act passed. Irgun terrorists blow up British military HQ in King David Hotel, Jerusalem.

**Nov.** National Health Service Act passed (to take effect from July 1948).

**Dec.** Britain and USA arrange economic merger of their zones in Germany.

## 1947

**Jan.** Coal Industry Nationalization Act comes into effect.

**Feb.** Government announces that India will become independent by June 1948.

**Mar.** Anglo-French treaty of alliance.

**Apr.** School-leaving age raised to 15.

**June** US Secretary of State Marshall suggests US aid for Europe.

**Aug.** Act nationalizing electricity is passed. Inland Transport Act passed. India becomes independent.

**Nov.** Budget leak. Dalton resigns; Cripps becomes Chancellor of the Exchequer.

## 1948

**Jan.** Inland Transport Act becomes effective; railways are nationalized. Burma becomes independent.

**Apr.** US Economic Cooperation Act becomes effective, with $980 million of 'Marshall Aid' to be at Britain's disposal. Act nationalizing electricity becomes effective.

**May** Jews proclaim new state of Israel.

**July** 1947 Town and Country Planning Act becomes effective. Representation of the People Act passed. Berlin airlift by Britain and USA. End of bread rationing.

## 1949

**Mar.** End of clothes rationing.

**Apr.** North Atlantic Treaty Organization (NATO) established.

Conference of Commonwealth PMs redefines 'Commonwealth'. Independent republics who accept the Crown as a 'symbol of the free association of its independent member states' are to remain in Commonwealth. Ireland becomes a republic.
**May** Gas industry nationalized.
**Sept.** Sterling devalued from $4.03 to $2.80.
**Nov.** Royal assent given to Iron and Steel Nationalization Bill, but it is not to be effective until January 1951.

### 1950

**Jan.** Britain recognizes Communist government of China.
**Feb.** General election: Labour returned to office with a greatly reduced majority.
**May** Petrol rationing ends.
**June** North Korean troops enter South Korea. UN Security Council authorizes military aid to South Korea.
**Sept.** British troops in action in Korea.
**Oct.** Chinese troops enter Korean War. Cripps retires. Hugh Gaitskell becomes Chancellor of the Exchequer.

### 1951

**Jan.** New rearmament programme of £4,700 million announced.
**Feb.** Nationalization of iron and steel takes effect. Bevin resigns from Foreign Office and is replaced by Herbert Morrison.
**Apr.** Bevan resigns in protest at Cabinet decision to impose prescription charges (along with Harold Wilson and John Freeman).
**Oct.** General election. Establishment of *Conservative government* with majority of 16 seats. Principal figures: Churchill (Prime Minister); Eden (Foreign Secretary); R. A. Butler (Chancellor of the Exchequer); Maxwell Fyfe (Home Secretary).
**Dec.** London Foreign Exchange Market reopens after 12 years.

### 1952

**Jan.** Commonwealth Finance Ministers Conference in London to coordinate policy of the sterling area. Restrictions imposed on imports and hire-purchase.
**Feb.** Death of George VI. Queen Elizabeth II ascends throne.
**Mar.** Fifty-seven Labour MPs dissent from 'Party line' and vote against government defence motion.
**Oct.** Britain's first atom bomb exploded off Monte Bello Islands, Western Australia.

**1953**
**Feb.** Amnesty for wartime deserters declared.
**Mar.** Steel denationalized.
**Apr.** Road transport denationalized.
**June** Coronation of Elizabeth II. Britain gives *de facto* recognition to the Republic of Egypt.
**July** Korean armistice signed at Panmunjon.
**Sept.** End of sugar rationing after 14 years.

**1954**
**Mar.** London Gold Market reopens after 15 years.
**Apr.** Geneva Conference on Indo-China opens. Bevan resigns from Labour Party shadow cabinet over the party's Far Eastern policy.
**July** All food rationing ends. Anglo-Egyptian Agreement in Cairo to withdraw British troops from Suez Canal zone.
**Aug.** End of hire-purchase controls.
**Oct.** Anglo-Egyptian Suez Canal Agreement reached.

**1955**
**Feb.** Decision to proceed with manufacture of hydrogen bombs announced. Hire-purchase restrictions reintroduced.
**Apr.** Paris Agreement ratified: West Germany to join NATO and Britain to maintain four divisions and tactical air force on the Continent. USSR denounces 1942 treaty with Britain and France. Churchill resigns: Eden becomes Prime Minister, Harold Macmillan Foreign Secretary, Selwyn Lloyd Minister of Defence.
**May** General election gives Conservatives a majority of nearly 60.
**July** Summit Conference of Britain, France, USA and USSR at Geneva. Further hire-purchase restrictions.
**Dec.** Attlee retires. Gaitskell elected leader of the Labour Party. Cabinet reshuffle. Macmillan becomes Chancellor of the Exchequer, Selwyn Lloyd Foreign Secretary, Butler Lord Privy Seal and Leader of the House.

**1956**
**Feb.** House of Commons rejects motion to abolish the death penalty.
**June** British troops leave Suez.
**July** Nasser nationalizes Suez Canal.
**Aug.** Britain rejects request for independence by Central African Federation. Tripartite Declaration by Britain, France and USA against nationalization of Suez Canal.

**Oct.** Anglo-French invasion of Suez. British outline plan of a European Free Trade Area announced.

**Nov.** Cease-fire in Suez.

**Dec.** Anglo-French troops evacuate Suez. Britain draws £201 million from International Monetary Fund (IMF).

## 1957

**Jan.** Eden retires. Macmillan becomes Prime Minister and Peter Thorneycroft becomes Chancellor of the Exchequer.

**Mar.** Gold Coast given independence as Ghana.

**Apr.** Decision to discontinue 'call up' for National Service after 1960. Labour Party calls for an end to planned British hydrogen bomb tests.

**May** First British hydrogen bomb explosion in the Central Pacific.

**July** Electricity Bill enacted: Central Electricity Generating Board and Electricity Council replace Central Electricity Authority. Federation of Malaya Independence Act is given royal assent.

**Aug.** Council on Prices, Productivity and Incomes established.

**Sept.** Disarmament discussions in London end without agreement. Publication of Wolfenden report on prostitution.

## 1958

**Jan.** Treaties establishing European Economic Community (EEC) and Euratom come into force. Thorneycroft resigns in protest at failure of Cabinet to cut government expenditure. Heathcoat Amory becomes Chancellor of the Exchequer. Russia proposes 19-nation summit negotiations.

**Feb.** Britain and USA agree on the establishment of American missile bases in Britain. Campaign for Nuclear Disarmament (CND) set up with Earl (Bertrand) Russell as president.

**Apr.** First Aldermaston march organized by CND.

**June** British plan for Cyprus rejected by Greek government.

**July** Government decides to resume British nuclear tests. First life peers created.

**Oct.** Hire-purchase restrictions removed.

**Nov.** France formally rejects British proposal for a European Free Trade Area.

**Dec.** Partial convertibility between sterling and the American dollar announced.

## 1959

**Jan.** Britain recognizes Castro regime in Cuba.

**Feb.** London Agreement between Britain, Greece and Turkey on independence for Cyprus. Macmillan visits Moscow.

**Mar.** Air services agreement between Britain and USSR.

**Oct.** General election returns Conservatives with a majority of 100.

**Nov.** European Free Trade Association (EFTA) convention agreed.

**Dec.** Anglo-Russian Cultural Agreement reached.


## 1960

**Feb.** Macmillan addresses South African parliament on African nationalism – 'wind of change' speech. Britain agrees to the establishment of a US ballistic missile early warning system in Britain.

**Apr.** Blue Streak rocket abandoned as a military weapon. Hire-purchase restrictions reintroduced and credit squeeze begins. Togoland becomes independent.

**May** Opening and breakdown of Paris Summit Conference. EFTA treaty comes into effect.

**June** Somaliland given independence. Commons rejects Wolfenden Commission's recommendations on homosexuality.

**July** Selwyn Lloyd replaces Amory as Chancellor of the Exchequer.

**Aug.** Cyprus becomes independent.

**Oct.** Federation of Nigeria becomes independent. Labour Party Conference votes against existing party defence policy. Royal Navy's first nuclear submarine, *Dreadnought*, launched.

**Nov.** Gaitskell re-elected leader of the Labour Party. Britain announces that she will provide facilities for US Polaris submarines at Holy Loch.


## 1961

**Jan.** Hire-purchase controls relaxed.

**Feb.** Government announces an increase in National Health Service prescription charges.

**Mar.** First US nuclear submarine arrives at Holy Loch. Conference on discontinuance of nuclear weapons tests between Britain, USA and USSR begins at Geneva.

**July** British troops land in Kuwait following an appeal from Kuwaiti government. Macmillan announces government decision to apply for EEC membership. Anglo-American agreement to establish US Missile Defence Alarm Station in Britain. 'Pay pause' announced by Selwyn Lloyd; National Economic Development Council (NEDC) established.

**Aug.** IMF places £714 million at Britain's disposal. Failure of Geneva Conference. USSR to resume nuclear weapons tests.

**Oct.** Labour Party Conference votes against Polaris bases and German troops being stationed in Britain.

**Nov.** Official opening of negotiations for British entry into EEC at Brussels.

**Dec.** Tanganyika receives independence. Macmillan meets President Kennedy in Bermuda.

### 1962

**Mar.** Liberal wins Orpington by-election.

**Apr.** End of government's 'Pay pause'.

**July** Macmillan asks seven senior ministers for their resignations. Cabinet reconstructed: Butler (Deputy Prime Minister and First Secretary of State); Henry Brooke (Home Secretary); Reginald Maudling (Chancellor of the Exchequer). Government announces setting up of the National Incomes Commission.

**Aug.** Jamaica, Trinidad and Tobago become independent.

**Dec.** British troops quell uprising in Brunei. Macmillan meets Kennedy at Nassau. USA offers Polaris missiles for use on British submarines as part of a multilateral NATO force. British Railways Board replaces British Transport Commission under terms of the Transport Act. Beeching made chairman.

### 1963

**Jan.** Britain refused entry to the EEC. Death of Gaitskell.

**Feb.** Harold Wilson elected leader of the Labour Party.

**Mar.** Publication of Beeching Report on British Railways.

**Apr.** Polaris missile agreement signed by Britain and USA.

**June** House of Commons censures John Profumo, ex-Minister for War, for lying to House.

**July** Peerage Bill receives royal assent. Peers can now renounce titles.

**Aug.** Partial nuclear test ban treaty signed by Britain, USA and USSR.

**Oct.** Macmillan retires. Sir Alec Douglas-Home becomes Prime Minister. Iain Macleod and Enoch Powell refuse to serve under Home. Butler becomes Foreign Secretary, Lloyd Leader of the House, Anthony Barber Minister of Health, Edward Heath Secretary of State for Industry.

**Dec.** Zanzibar and Kenya become independent. Federation of Rhodesia and Nyasaland is dissolved.

### 1964

**Apr.** First GLC election won by Labour – majority of 27. Retail Price Maintenance abolished.

**Sept.** Malta gains independence. Northern Rhodesia becomes independent as Zambia.

**Oct.** General election. Formation of *Labour government*, with an overall majority of five. Principal figures: Harold Wilson (Prime Minister); James Callaghan (Chancellor of the Exchequer); George Brown (Deputy PM and Minister for Economic Affairs – a new department); Patrick Gordon Walker (Foreign Secretary). Fifteen per cent import surcharge announced.

**Nov.** Ban on sale of arms to South Africa.

**Dec.** IMF lends Britain $1,000 million. Statement of Intent on Productivity, Prices and Incomes signed by TUC and employers' organizations.

## 1965

**Jan.** National Health prescription charges abolished. Defeat of Patrick Gordon Walker in Leyton by-election. Succeeded as Foreign Secretary by Michael Stewart.

**Feb.** Establishment of National Board for Prices and Incomes. Gambia becomes independent.

**Apr.** Import surcharge cut to 10 per cent. TSR-2 fighter plane development cancelled.

**May** Britain draws $1,400 million from the IMF.

**June** Hire-purchase terms stiffened.

**July** Tightening of Exchange Controls. Home resigns leadership of Conservative Party. Edward Heath elected to replace him.

**Sept.** Five-Year National Plan aiming at a 25 per cent increase in GNP by 1970 announced.

**Oct.** Parliament passes Bill abolishing death penalty.

**Nov.** Rhodesia makes a Unilateral Declaration of Independence (UDI). Economic sanctions announced.

## 1966

**Jan.** White Paper announces proposed Industrial Reorganization Corporation. British government bans all trade with Rhodesia.

**Feb.** Hire-purchase terms stiffened.

**Mar.** General election. Labour win overall majority of 97.

**May** Official seamen's strike.

**July** End of seamen's strike. Minister of Technology, Frank Cousins, resigns in protest against government incomes policy. Prices and Incomes Bill introduced providing for an 'early warning' system on prices and incomes. Six-month wage freeze and stiff deflationary measures announced. George Brown resigns, but is persuaded to remain in office.

**Aug.** George Brown exchanges office with Foreign Secretary Michael Stewart. Sir Edward Compton named Britain's first parliamentary commissioner (Ombudsman).

**Nov.** End of import surcharge.

**Dec.** Wilson and Rhodesian leader Ian Smith hold negotiations on Rhodesia on board HMS *Tiger*. United Nations Security Council approves British resolution for mandatory sanctions against Rhodesia.

## 1967

**Jan.** Prime Minister and Foreign Secretary in Rome for EEC negotiations. Jeremy Thorpe elected leader of the Liberal Party following Jo Grimond's resignation.

**Feb.** Russian Prime Minister Kosygin in London; meets Queen at Buckingham Palace. Downing Street–Kremlin 'hot line' agreed upon.

**May** Wilson announces Britain's formal application to join the EEC.

**June** Arab–Israeli War. Arab oil embargo on Britain. Relaxation of hire-purchase restrictions.

**July** Defence cuts announced: withdrawal from East of Suez by mid-1970. Vesting date of British Steel Corporation.

**Aug.** Douglas Jay sacked in Cabinet reshuffle. Wilson takes over Department of Economic Affairs. Further relaxation of hire-purchase controls.

**Sept.** Arabs lift oil embargo. Dock strike begins in London and Liverpool.

**Oct.** Liverpool dockers return to work. HMS *Resolution*, Britain's first Polaris submarine, is commissioned.

**Nov.** Sterling devalued to $2.40 to the £. Aden becomes independent. Chancellor of the Exchequer, James Callaghan, exchanges offices with Roy Jenkins (Home Secretary).

**Dec.** France vetoes British application to join EEC.

## 1968

**Jan.** Public expenditure cuts announced.

**Mar.** Rush for gold in leading financial centres. Stock Exchange and banks closed in Britain. Resignation of Foreign Secretary George Brown. Summit meeting of Western Central Bankers agrees two-tier system for price of gold.

**Apr.** Cabinet reshuffle. Barbara Castle becomes Minister for Employment and Productivity. Birmingham immigration speech by Enoch Powell. Heath sacks him from shadow cabinet.

**June** National Health Service prescription charges re-introduced.
**Sept.** Basle arrangement for sterling area agreed. Swaziland becomes independent.
**Oct.** Failure of HMS *Fearless* talks on Rhodesia. Massive demonstration in London against the US involvement in Vietnam War.
**Nov.** Hire-purchase restrictions tightened. Credit squeeze imposed.

### 1969
**May** Voting age reduced to 18.
**June** Government drops its plans for legal restraints on unofficial strikes in return for a TUC pledge to deal with such disputes.
**Aug.** Three-day street battle in Londonderry following Apprentice Boys march. Army takes over security and police functions in Northern Ireland.
**Oct.** Department of Economic Affairs abolished.
**Dec.** EEC summit meeting at The Hague agrees to negotiations for British entry by June 1970. Parliament votes for permanent abolition of death penalty.

### 1970
**Jan.** Age of majority reduced to 18.
**June** General election. Formation of *Conservative government* with a majority of 30. Principal figures: Heath (Prime Minister); Macleod (Chancellor of the Exchequer); Home (Foreign Secretary); Maudling (Home Secretary).
**July** Death of Macleod. Barber becomes Chancellor of the Exchequer.
**Oct.** Government establishes new conglomerate ministries: Department of Trade and Industry; Department of the Environment.
**Dec.** Industrial Relations Bill introduced (became law in 1971).

### 1971
**Jan.** 'Angry Brigade' bomb attack on home of Robert Carr, Secretary for Employment.
**Feb.** Financial collapse of Rolls-Royce Limited. Aero-engine interests nationalized. First British soldier killed in Belfast.
**Mar.** One-day strike by 1.5 million engineers against Industrial Relations Bill. Chichester-Clark resigns Northern Ireland premiership and is succeeded by Brian Faulkner.
**June** EEC negotiations completed. Parliament endorses British entry.
**Aug.** Internment without trial introduced in Ulster.
**Sept.** TUC votes against registration under Industrial Relations Act.

**Oct.** Labour Party Conference overwhelmingly carries anti-EEC resolution.
**Nov.** Draft agreement signed between Britain and Rhodesia: Rhodesia to be independent if majority of population agree to negotiated terms.

## 1972

**Jan.** Miners' strike begins. Britain signs EEC treaty. 'Bloody Sunday' – 13 civilians killed by paratroopers in Londonderry.
**Feb.** State of Emergency declared in power crisis: large-scale power cuts begin, with 1.5 million workers laid off at the height of the crisis. Wilberforce enquiry's terms for settling miners' dispute published. Miners vote to return to work.
**Mar.** National Industrial Relations Court (NIRC) fines TGWU for contempt. 'Direct Rule' established for Northern Ireland: William Whitelaw Secretary of State.
**Apr.** 'Work-to-rule' on British Rail. NIRC orders 'cooling-off' period. NIRC imposes further fine for contempt on TGWU. Roy Jenkins, George Thompson and Harold Lever resign from Labour shadow cabinet over EEC.
**May** Pearce Commission concludes that the Rhodesian people are not generally in favour of the settlement plan: sanctions continue.
**June** Government decision to 'float' the pound.
**July** Robert Carr replaces Maudling as Home Secretary when Maudling resigns due to 'Poulson' corruption examination. Start of national dock strike following rejection of the Jones–Aldington proposals for modernization of the docks.
**Aug.** President Amin orders expulsion of 40,000 British Asians from Uganda. Intervention of official solicitor to release dockers imprisoned under Industrial Relations Act.
**Sept.** Thirty-two unions suspended by TUC for registering under Industrial Relations Act.
**Nov.** Government imposes immediate 90-day freeze on prices, pay, rent and dividend increases. Government defeat on new immigration rules.

## 1973

**Jan.** Britain becomes a member of EEC.
**Feb.** Start of foreign exchange crisis. Dollar devalued by 10 per cent.
**Mar.** Ulster referendum: overwhelming majority in favour of retaining links with Britain. White Paper proposes a Northern Ireland Assembly, elected by proportional representation.
**Apr.** Phase Two of counter-inflation policy comes into operation: £1 plus 4 per cent and a price code supervised by new Price Commission.

**June** New Northern Ireland Assembly elected.

**July** Assembly's first sitting ends in chaos.

**Oct.** Arab–Israeli War. Arabs cut oil supplies to West. Firemen begin series of unofficial strikes. Phase Three of counter-inflation policy launched: 7 per cent or £2.25 a week with threshold safeguards.

**Nov.** Electrical Power Engineers Association ban out-of-hours work. Miners ban overtime. Major rise in oil prices by the Organization of Petroleum Exporting Countries (OPEC). Eleven-man power-sharing executive proposed for Northern Ireland.

**Dec.** Rail drivers' union, the Amalgamated Society of Locomotive Engineers and Firemen (ASLEF), bans overtime. Emergency measures taken to conserve fuel: 50 mph speed limit, temperature control in offices, three-day working week announced from 31 December. Power engineers call off ban on out-of-hours working. Tripartite Conference (UK government, Northern Ireland executive-designate and Irish government) agree to establish a Council of Ireland – the Sunningdale Agreement.

## 1974

**Jan.** End of Direct Rule in Northern Ireland. New executive takes office. Lord Carrington made Secretary of new Energy Department. Parliament recalled for two-day debate on energy crisis. Loyalists expelled from Northern Ireland Assembly after angry scenes.

**Feb.** Eighty-one per cent majority favour strike action in ballot of miners. Heath calls general election and miners' strike begins. No party wins a clear majority in election and Heath enters abortive coalition negotiations with Liberals.

**Mar.** Wilson forms a minority *Labour government*. Principal figures: Callaghan (Foreign Secretary); Denis Healey (Chancellor of the Exchequer); Michael Foot (Secretary for Employment). End of three-day week and miners' strike. Food subsidies begin.

**Apr.** Britain demands renegotiation of EEC terms of entry.

**May** State of Emergency in Northern Ireland due to Protestant General Strike in protest at Sunningdale Agreement. Plan to establish a Council of Ireland postponed. General Strike called off. Northern Ireland Assembly suspended and Direct Rule from Westminster resumed.

**July** Industrial Relations Act 1971 repealed. Pay Board and statutory incomes policy abolished. NIRC abolished.

**Oct.** Guildford pub bombings by Provisional IRA; 5 killed and 70 injured. General election gives Labour an overall majority of three.

**Nov.** Birmingham pub bombings by Provisionals: 21 killed and 120 injured. Prevention of Terrorism Act passed, proscribing the IRA and giving police wider powers.

**Dec.** Government announces aid to British Leyland.

## 1975

**Jan.** Industry Bill introduced proposing National Enterprise Board and planning agreements. Referendum on EEC membership announced.

**Feb.** Heath withdraws as Conservative leader after defeat by Mrs Margaret Thatcher in first ballot of leadership election. Thatcher elected leader. Wilson–Brezhnev summit meeting in Moscow.

**Mar.** Meriden motor cycle cooperative set up. EEC summit meeting agreement on British renegotiation terms. British Cabinet accepts the terms.

**Apr.** Government accepts Ryder plan to invest £1,400 million in British Leyland over eight years.

**May** *Scottish Daily News* published by workers' cooperative. Elections for Northern Ireland Convention.

**June** Referendum gives two-to-one majority for remaining in EEC. In Cabinet reshuffle, Benn demoted from Employment to Energy.

**July** Government announces anti-inflation policy: £6 a week limit on pay increases until August 1976. TUC supports policy.

**Nov.** Chequers meeting of government, TUC, CBI and NEDC on strategy to regenerate British industry. Britain applies to IMF for £975 million loan.

**Dec.** End of internment without trial in Northern Ireland. Sex Discrimination and Equal Pay Acts come into force.

## 1976

**Mar.** Northern Ireland Convention dissolved: Direct Rule from Westminster continued. Wilson resigns as Prime Minister.

**Apr.** Callaghan defeats Foot in Parliamentary Labour Party ballot for leadership and becomes Prime Minister. Foot becomes Lord President of the Council, Crosland becomes Foreign Secretary.

**May** TUC endorses Stage 2 of government incomes policy (minimum £2.50, maximum £4 per week increases). Jeremy Thorpe resigns Liberal leadership; Grimond resumes leadership on a caretaker basis.

**June** Britain secures £3 billion standby credit from European and American Central Banks.

**July** David Steel elected Liberal leader.

**Sept.** Roy Jenkins resigns as Home Secretary to become President of the European Commission (succeeded by Merlyn Rees). Government seeks £2,300 million loan from IMF. Ian Smith accepts Anglo-American proposals for majority rule in Rhodesia in two years.

**Dec.** British Letter of Intent to IMF. Public spending cuts of £2,500 million, increased indirect taxation and BP share sale.

## 1977

**Jan.** Ian Smith rejects British proposals for transition to majority rule. Bullock Report on industrial democracy published: recommends worker-directors.

**Feb.** Death of Crosland; David Owen made Foreign Secretary. British Leyland toolroom workers' strike. Government defeated on guillotine motion on Devolution Bills for Scotland and Wales.

**Mar.** Lib–Lab Pact arranged, enabling government to defeat Conservative no-confidence motion.

**May** Eleven-day Loyalist general strike in Ulster called by United Ulster Action Council. Collapses through lack of support.

**July** Trade union demonstrations at Grunwick factory in support of claims for union recognition. Stage 3 of incomes policy announced: 10 per cent limit on earnings increases.

**Aug.** Violent clashes at National Front march, Lewisham, London.

**Sept.** Owen presents Ian Smith with Anglo-American proposals for Rhodesian settlement. National Front march in Manchester banned.

**Nov.** Firemen's strike for a 30 per cent pay increase.

## 1978

**Jan.** End of firemen's strike. Special Liberal Party Assembly votes to continue Lib–Lab Pact until July. Government suffers serious defeats in Commons on Scottish Devolution Bill. Amendments carried requiring minimum 'Yes' vote of 40 per cent of the whole electorate.

**Mar.** 'Internal settlement' agreed in Rhodesia between Ian Smith and three black nationalist leaders. Stricter controls on immigration proposed by House of Commons Select Committee.

**May** Ban on Zimbabwe African National Union (ZANU) and Zimbabwe African People's Union (ZAPU) lifted in Rhodesia. Labour government suffers several defeats on Budget – thresholds for higher tax rates raised to £8,000. Steel announces that Lib–Lab Pact will end in August.

**July** Government proposes 5 per cent pay guideline for 12 months beginning 1 August. Devolution Bills for Scotland and Wales receive royal assent.

**Oct.** Labour Party Conference at Blackpool rejects government's 5 per cent pay guidelines.

**Nov.** TUC General Council refuses to endorse government's 5 per cent pay limit.

**Dec.** Government wins vote of confidence following previous day's defeat on imposition of sanctions against private companies giving wage increases above 5 per cent.

## 1979

**Jan.** Secondary picketing in road haulage strike creates growing difficulties. About 150,000 laid off due to strike. White Rhodesians vote for limited form of majority rule. Labour government survives Commons vote on its handling of industrial relations.

**Feb.** Government–TUC 'concordat' with agreement on 5 per cent inflation within three years.

**Mar.** Devolution referendums. Wales votes 'no' overwhelmingly. Scotland has insufficient 'yes' vote (i.e. not 40 per cent of total electorate). Government is defeated in no-confidence vote, for first time since 1924. General election called.

**May** General election: formation of *Conservative government* with majority of 41. Principal figures: Thatcher (Prime Minister); Carrington (Foreign Secretary); Whitelaw (Home Secretary); Geoffrey Howe (Chancellor of the Exchequer).

**June** First direct elections to European Parliament. Conservatives win 60 of the 78 British seats.

**Aug.** Commonwealth Conference in Lusaka clears the ground for Lancaster House conference on Rhodesian settlement, which agrees to free elections.

**Dec.** Government introduces Employment Bill on picketing, secret ballot and closed shop. End of UDI in Rhodesia, Lord Soames arrives as governor to supervise elections.

## 1980

**Mar.** Robert Mugabe invited to form government in Rhodesia Zimbabwe after winning absolute majority in elections.

**Apr.** Rioting in St Paul's district of Bristol. End of steel strike. Zimbabwe gains full independence under Premier Mugabe.

**May** Iranian Embassy siege; SAS storm embassy and release hostages.

**June** British athletes decide to attend Moscow Olympic Games in spite of government displeasure.

**Aug.** Clegg pay commission abolished. Unemployment figures pass 2 million.

**Sept.** Large-scale cuts in local authority grants.

**Oct.** Labour Conference at Blackpool adopts new method of electing leader. James Callaghan announces retirement from leadership of Labour Party.

**Nov.** Government announces 6 per cent pay ceiling in public sector. Michael Foot elected leader of Labour Party.

### 1981

**Jan.** Special Wembley Conference of Labour Party votes for electoral college to select party leader. 'Gang of Four', Roy Jenkins, Shirley Williams, William Rodgers and David Owen, announce launching of a Council for Social Democracy.

**Feb.** National Coal Board announces pit closures (13th); plans withdrawn after strike threat (18th).

**Mar.** 12 MPs and 9 peers resign Labour whip and join the Social Democrats. Social Democratic Party launched at public meeting (26th).

**Apr.** Brixton riots; appointment of Lord Scarman to inquire into riots.

**May** IRA man Robert Sands dies after 66 days of hunger strike.

**July** Rioting by youths in Toxteth, Liverpool, Moss Side, Manchester, and several other towns and cities. Prince of Wales marries Lady Diana Spencer.

**Sept.** Formation of Liberal–SDP Alliance.

### 1982

**Jan.** Number of unemployed in United Kingdom passes 3 million. Opinion polls show Alliance 2 points ahead of Conservatives.

**Apr.** Argentine forces invade and take control of Falkland Islands (2nd) followed by South Georgia (for Falklands War, see pp. 295–6).

**June** Surrender of Argentinian forces in Falklands.

**July** IRA bombs in Hyde Park and Regent's Park kill 10 soldiers and injure 50 others.

**Dec.** Estimated 30,000 women demonstrate outside Greenham Common air base against siting of Cruise missiles.

### 1983

**Apr.** £1 coin introduced.

**May** Mrs Thatcher announces a general election in June.

**June** Conservative victory in general election with 144-seat majority

(9th). SDP–Liberal Alliance wins only 23 seats but 26 per cent of the vote (see p. 107). Formation of *Conservative government*; principal figures: Thatcher (Prime Minister); Lawson (Chancellor of the Exchequer); Howe (Foreign Secretary); Brittan (Home Secretary). Michael Foot announces he will stand down as Labour leader (12th); Roy Jenkins resigns as SDP leader, succeeded by David Owen (13th).

**July** Commons votes against restoration of capital punishment.

**Oct.** Neil Kinnock elected leader of Labour Party and Roy Hattersley deputy leader. Trade and Industry Secretary, Cecil Parkinson, resigns after disclosure of affair with former secretary.

**Nov.** First Cruise missiles arrive at Greenham Common.

**Dec.** Bomb in Harrods store kills six people and injures 91.

## 1984

**Jan.** Government bans trade unions at GCHQ communications centre in Cheltenham.

**Mar.** National Coal Board announces plans to close pits and shed 20,000 jobs (6th); National Union of Mineworkers (NUM) gives support for all-out strike. Civil servant Sarah Tisdall jailed for passing secret documents to *The Guardian*.

**Apr.** WPC Fletcher shot from Libyan embassy in St James's Square; police lay siege to embassy and eventually obtain removal of personnel.

**May** Serious disturbances outside Orgreave coking plant near Sheffield during mass picketing by striking miners. MP Tam Dalyell accuses Prime Minister of lying over the sinking of the Argentine ship *Belgrano*.

**July** Breakdown of talks between Britain and Argentina over future of Falklands.

**Aug.** TUC pledges support to miners' strike.

**Sept.** Leading 'wet', James Prior, leaves the government. At Labour Party Conference, Neil Kinnock supports the miners but condemns violence.

**Oct.** IRA bomb wrecks Grand Hotel, Brighton, where Mrs Thatcher and Conservative Party leadership are staying; five killed and senior figures Norman Tebbit and John Wakeham injured.

**Nov.** National Coal Board begins back-to-work drive in coal dispute. Government flotation of British Telecom successful, inaugurating process of 'privatizing' major public corporations.

**Dec.** NUM funds sequestered and receiver appointed to take control. Britain signs Sino–British declaration on future of Hong Kong, assuring its future as a capitalist centre for another 50 years after Britain's departure in 1997.

**1985**

**Jan.** Clive Ponting acquitted of breaching the Official Secrets Act over *Belgrano* affair.

**Feb.** Teachers begin series of selective pay strikes.

**Mar.** Miners vote to end strike.

**Apr.** Riot by Liverpool football fans in Heysel Stadium, Brussels, leaves 38 dead and 150 injured. English clubs banned from European competition.

**June** Social Services Secretary, Norman Fowler, announces major review of welfare, involving phasing out of SERPS (earnings-related pensions) and reorganization of other welfare benefits.

**Sept.** Major Cabinet reshuffle. Norman Tebbit becomes chairman of the Conservative Party. Serious riots in Handsworth area of Birmingham (9th). Riots in Brixton after accidental shooting of a woman by police officers.

**Oct.** Neil Kinnock attacks stand taken by militant members of Liverpool City Council in rate dispute with government, widely interpreted as attempt to reassert control over the party. Riots in Tottenham lead to death of PC Blakelock.

**Nov.** Anglo-Irish Agreement signed at Hillsborough by Mrs Thatcher and Dr Garret FitzGerald, giving Dublin government a say in Northern Irish affairs in return for recognition of the wishes of the majority population in Ulster.

**Dec.** Mass resignation by Ulster MPs in protest over Anglo-Irish Agreement, forcing 15 by-elections in Ulster.

**1986**

**Jan.** Westland affair leads to resignation of Defence Secretary Michael Heseltine and, a fortnight later, the Industry Secretary Leon Brittan. Beginning of Wapping print dispute after movement of printing of Murdoch newspapers to new plant at Wapping.

**Feb.** Government plans to sell off Austin Rover to Ford stopped by Commons revolt. Agreement signed to build Channel Tunnel.

**Mar.** High Court imposes surcharges on 81 members of Labour-controlled Lambeth and Liverpool councils. By end of month all 37 unions with political funds have voted to retain them.

**Apr.** Mrs Thatcher sanctions use of bases in Britain for American bombing of Libya (15th). Chernobyl nuclear accident spreads radioactive contamination across Britain, especially the North and West.

**June** Dissolution of Northern Ireland Assembly announced.

**July** Sir Geoffrey Howe makes journey to South Africa to explore possibilities of reform.

**Aug.** Mrs Thatcher stands out from other Commonwealth leaders on issue of economic sanctions against South Africa.

**Sept.** Liberal Assembly votes for non-nuclear amendment in defiance of party leadership, throwing Alliance defence policy into turmoil. Labour conference votes in favour of expulsion of American nuclear bases from Britain.

**Oct.** Jeffrey Archer forced to resign as Conservative Party deputy chairman following allegations in a Sunday newspaper. 'Big Bang' in City with deregulation of dealing.

**Nov.** Government announces increase in public spending in major reversal of earlier policy. Court in Australia begins hearing to prevent former MI5 officer Peter Wright publishing his memoirs. Government launches £20 million anti-AIDS campaign.

**Dec.** Investigations announced into Guinness takeover of Distillers group. Government decides to drop GEC Nimrod early-warning radar plane in favour of Boeing system.

**1987**

**Jan.** BBC Zircon programme banned and raid on Glasgow BBC offices by police. SDP–Liberal Alliance hold relaunch with compromise defence policy.

**Feb.** Wapping dispute ends. Greenwich by-election won by SDP's Rosie Barnes.

**Mar.** Russian leader Gorbachev announces new offer on intermediate missiles in Europe. Sizewell 'B' nuclear power station given go-ahead after marathon public enquiry. Government loses Wright case in Australia but seeks leave to appeal.

**May** Government announces June general election following relatively successful performance in local government elections and well-publicized visit by Mrs Thatcher to Moscow.

**June** Conservative victory in general election by 102 seats. New administration formed, principal figures: Thatcher (Prime Minister); Lawson (Chancellor of the Exchequer); Howe (Foreign Secretary). Government proceeds with plans for major reforms in education, further privatization and trade union reform. David Steel announces desire to press for a merger of SDP and Liberal parties. David Owen announces opposition.

**July** Injunctions granted to prevent publication of Wright's allegations and contents of his *Spycatcher* book. Jeffrey Archer awarded £500,000 damages for libel.

**Aug.** Ballot of SDP membership votes 57 to 43 per cent for opening merger talks with Liberals. David Owen resigns as leader, replaced by Robert Maclennan.

**Sept.** SDP conference supports opening merger talks with the Liberals. Labour leader, Kinnock, wins conference support for widespread policy review. Government loses appeal in Australia to prevent publication of Peter Wright's *Spycatcher.*

**Oct.** 'Black Monday' (19th) wipes £50 million off share values.

**Nov.** Government announces plans to replace rates with 'community charge' from April 1990.

**Dec.** Intermediate Nuclear Forces Treaty between USA and USSR promises large-scale cuts in medium and short-range nuclear missiles.


## 1988

**Jan.** Mrs Thatcher becomes the longest continuously serving prime minister in the 20th century. David Steel announces he will not stand for leadership of new merged party.

**Feb.** MPs vote to televise the House of Commons.

**Mar.** Liberals and SDP vote for the creation of a new merged party, the Social and Liberal Democrats (SLD). Gibraltar shootings: three IRA gunmen shot by SAS.

**Apr.** Government fails to stop TV documentary on the Gibraltar shootings, *Death on the Rock.*

**June** UK trade figures show £1.2 billion deficit, sparking fears of ending of economic growth.

**July** Government announces plans to privatize water companies. Government raises interest rates heralding end of 1980s' boom. Paddy Ashdown becomes new leader of the SLD. Education Act comes into force, introducing a national curriculum, regular testing, and possibility of schools opting out of local education authority control.

**Aug.** Further rise in interest rates following widening of trade deficit. Chancellor Lawson admits that the economy is in decline.

**Oct.** Government announces plans to privatize steel industry. Trade unionists at GCHQ are sacked.

**Nov.** Government proposes loan scheme for students.

**Dec.** Junior Health Minister, Edwina Currie, forced to resign after statement on presence of salmonella in eggs.


## 1989

**Feb.** Ayatollah Khomeini orders the death of Salman Rushdie for his book *The Satanic Verses;* anti-Rushdie demonstrations.

**May** Interest rates raised to 14 per cent. British government rejects EC Social Charter.

**June** Tiananmen Square massacre in Beijing. British government denies right of residency to Hong Kong holders of British passports. Labour secures significant gains in direct elections to European Parliament; Greens secure 15 per cent of vote and push Liberal Democrats into fourth place.

**July** Following disagreement with Mrs Thatcher over membership of the EMS and attitudes to Europe, Geoffrey Howe is replaced as Foreign Secretary by John Major; Howe becomes Leader of the Commons and Deputy Prime Minister.

**Aug.** Cruise missiles removed from Greenham Common following Intermediate Nuclear Forces Treaty.

**Sept.** Water companies privatized.

**Oct.** Interest rates rise to near record 15 per cent; share values show a major fall. 'Guildford Four' are released after 14 years in prison for IRA bombing. Nigel Lawson resigns as Chancellor, following public disagreement with Mrs Thatcher's private adviser, Alan Walters. John Major becomes Chancellor; Douglas Hurd Foreign Secretary.

**Nov.** East Germans allowed to pass freely into West Germany; Berlin Wall begins to be demolished. TV broadcasts of Parliament begin.

**Dec.** Mrs Thatcher defeats 'stalking horse' challenge by Sir Anthony Meyer for Conservative leadership. Czechs form non-communist government; Romanian revolution topples Ceauşescu.

## 1990

**Feb.** South African government removes bans on the Communist Party, the African National Congress (ANC), and other anti-apartheid groups; Nelson Mandela is released from prison after 27 years.

**Mar.** Riots follow anti-poll tax demonstration in Trafalgar Square.

**Apr.** Strangeways Prison riot and occupation (1st–25th). Parts of Iraqi 'Supergun' impounded by customs officers.

**June** David Owen's 'continuing SDP' is disbanded.

**July** London Declaration by NATO leaders formally ends the Cold War. Nicholas Ridley forced to resign over remarks about Germany. Assassination of Ian Gow MP by IRA.

**Aug.** Iraqi forces invade Kuwait; EEC, USA and Japan embargo Iraqi oil. Iraq seizes western hostages as a 'human shield'.

**Sept.** Iraq releases British men and women held hostage. Polly Peck chairman, Asil Nadir, questioned on fraud charges; shares in company suspended.

**Oct.** Britain joins the ERM; Germany reunited. Liberal Democrats take Eastbourne in by-election. Rome Summit of EEC agrees timetable for monetary union in spite of Thatcher's clear opposition.

**Nov.** Howe resigns (1st) from the government over Thatcher's comments on European monetary union in Commons debate of 30 Oct. Ireland elects Mary Robinson as its first woman president. Howe's resignation speech (13th) explicitly attacks Thatcher's policies and invites others 'to consider their own response'. The following day Michael Heseltine announces his challenge for the leadership. In the first ballot Thatcher fails to obtain the required majority by four votes (20th); she withdraws from the contest after consultation with her ministers, who reveal loss of support. John Major and Douglas Hurd enter the contest. In the second ballot (27th) Major secures two votes short of an overall majority, leading the other two candidates to withdraw, and becomes Prime Minister. Norman Lamont appointed Chancellor; Heseltine, Environment Secretary.

**Dec.** Heseltine promises far-reaching review of the poll tax. Iraq releases all western hostages.

## 1991

**Jan.** US and Allied air attack begins on Iraq (16th), Operation 'Desert Storm'.

**Feb.** IRA mortar attack on Downing Street. Allied land offensive begins in the Gulf War (24th); cease-fire called (28th).

**Mar.** Conservatives lose Ribble Valley by-election to the Liberal Democrats, forcing government to rethink its stand on the poll tax. Court of Appeal quashes convictions of the Birmingham Six.

**Apr.** Government announces that the poll tax will be replaced by a new tax.

**July** Bank of Credit and Commerce International (BCCI) collapses. John Major launches Citizen's Charter.

**Aug.** Attempted coup against President Gorbachev fails, heralding break-up of the Soviet Union.

**Nov.** Newspaper magnate Robert Maxwell, dies at sea; investigation of his companies reveals massive fraud.

**Dec.** Maastricht Treaty on political and economic union signed by EEC leaders. Britain secures opt-out from single currency and the Social Charter.

## 1992

**Jan.** First meeting of self-appointed Muslim Parliament of Great Britain, prompted by the Salman Rushdie affair. Britain and EC recognize Slovenian and Croatian Republics in former Yugoslavia.

**Feb.** Economic statistics show that the recession is the longest since 1945.

**Mar.** General election announced for 9 April. Ethnic fighting begins in Bosnia-Herzegovina.

**Apr.** Conservatives win 21-seat majority in general election in spite of poll predictions to the contrary. John Major forms a government. Principal figures: Major (Prime Minister); Norman Lamont (Chancellor of the Exchequer); Douglas Hurd (Foreign Secretary); Michael Heseltine (Trade and Industry Secretary). Neil Kinnock and Roy Hattersley resign their positions as leader and deputy leader of the Labour Party (13th). Chris Patten, defeated MP for Bath, becomes Governor of Hong Kong.

**May** Queen's Speech outlines further privatization and creation of a national lottery. Security service (MI5) to be placed on a statutory basis.

**June** Danish referendum rejects Maastricht, causing European Communities (Amendment) Bill to be suspended. Peerages for leading Thatcherites: Thatcher herself, Howe, Lawson, Parkinson and Tebbit.

**July** Details of British Rail privatization revealed (14th). John Smith elected leader of Labour Party (18th); Margaret Beckett becomes deputy leader.

**Aug.** Bank of England begins defence of sterling amid turbulence on foreign exchanges. Lord Owen succeeds Lord Carrington as EC peacemaker in former Yugoslavia.

**Sept.** Continuing pressure on pound. Débâcle of 'Black Wednesday' (16th): membership of ERM suspended when Lamont unable to halt the speculators. Resignation of Heritage Secretary, David Mellor.

**Oct.** Serious divisions over Europe at Conservative Party conference at Brighton. British Coal announces plans to close 31 pits, effectively decimating the industry and leaving 30,000 miners facing redundancy (13th); Conservative back-benchers revolt on the issue (21st).

**Nov.** Inquiry announced into Matrix-Churchill affair (10th). Queen to pay tax on her private income (26th).

## 1993

**Jan.** Single European Market comes into force. John Major issues writs for libel against *New Statesman* and *Scallywag* (over allegations of relationship with Clare Latimer).

**Mar.** Government defeated in Commons division on Maastricht Bill (8th). Reform of honours system announced, to give greater reward for merit (4th); Budget proposals for VAT on domestic fuel (initially at 8 per cent then 17.5 per cent from 1995) met with outcry (17th). IRA bombs Warrington, killing two children (20th). Heseltine announces £500 million pit rescue plan.

**Apr.** Britain and China agree to resume talks on Hong Kong, ending months of stalemate (13th). Huge IRA bomb blast in Bishopsgate, City of London (24th). Recession is officially declared to be at an end (28th).

**May** Conservatives lose Newbury on swing of 29 per cent to Liberal Democrats (6th). Sweeping Conservative county council losses the same day. Inflation falls to 1.3 per cent – lowest figure for 29 years (21st). Major's first high-level Cabinet reshuffle: Kenneth Clarke replaces Norman Lamont as Chancellor; Michael Howard becomes Home Secretary; other moves include John Gummer (to Environment), Gillian Shephard (to Agriculture), David Hunt (to Employment) and John Redwood (to Welsh Office).

**June** Gallup polls show John Major least popular prime minister since opinion polling began (4th); Norman Lamont's bitter Commons attack on Major (9th); Michael Heseltine suffers heart attack (21st); resignation of Michael Mates as Northern Ireland minister over links with fugitive Asil Nadir (24th).

**July** Additional defence cuts announced (beyond those proposed in the 1991 document *Options for Change*) (5th); House of Lords rejects referendum on Maastricht by 445 votes to 176, the largest turnout of the century (14th); Commons debate on Social Chapter opt-out ends in government defeat by 325 to 316 after tie in vote on Labour amendment (Speaker's casting vote given to government) (22nd). Government wins confidence vote, clearing way for ratification of Maastricht (23rd). Conservatives lose Christchurch by-election to Liberal Democrats on the largest swing against a Conservative government in modern times (29th).

**Aug.** Government ratifies Maastricht; the same day ERM totters on brink of complete collapse (2nd).

**Sept.** John Monks appointed new TUC general secretary (10th); government announces public sector pay freeze (14th); far-right British National Party (BNP) wins seat in Millwall ward of Tower Hamlets municipal by-election; government plans for Post Office privatization detailed. Labour Party conference passes John Smith's 'one member, one vote' (OMOV) motion (29th).

**Oct.** Major defence cuts announced, with privatization of Devonport and Rosyth dockyards (18th); Shankill bombing in Belfast, ten dead (23rd); Greysteel pub bombing (30th).

**Nov.** European Union (EU) established as Maastricht Treaty comes into force (1st). Queen's Speech outlines Sunday shopping reforms, coal privatization and reform of criminal justice (18th).

**Dec.** Home Secretary proposes 'Citizens' Army' to deter crime (4th). 'Downing Street declaration' by John Major and Irish Prime Minister Albert Reynolds on future of Northern Ireland opening way to all-party talks (15th).

## 1994

**Jan.** Resignation of Environment Minister Tim Yeo after scandal (5th); John Major reaffirms 'Back to Basics' policy (6th); Alan Duncan resigns over irregularities in council house purchase (8th); Earl of Caithness, Minister for Aviation and Shipping, resigns (9th); Westminster Council (a Conservative flagship) accused of 'gerry-mandering' (13th). Controversy continues over Pergau dam deal in Malaysia (25th).

**Feb.** Death of Conservative MP Stephen Milligan in bizarre circumstances (7th). Commons votes to lower homosexual age of consent to 18 (21st). Malaysia bans new UK trade deals in wake of Pergau affair (25th).

**Mar.** IRA mortar attack on Heathrow Airport (9th). Dispute over voting rights in enlarged European Union (15th); compromise later agreed (23rd).

**Apr.** VAT on fuel comes into force (at 8 per cent).

**May** Heavy Conservative losses to Labour and Liberal Democrats in local elections (5th). Death of John Smith from heart attack (12th).

**June** Fourth direct elections to Europe (9th): heavy Conservative losses to Labour; Liberal Democrats gain their first two MEPs. Conservatives also lose Eastleigh by-election to Liberal Democrats (third consecutive Liberal Democrat gain of a Conservative seat this parliament), finishing in third place. First in series of protracted strikes by signal workers on railways (15th). Loyalist gunmen murder six in bar in Loughinisland, County Down.

**July** Jacques Santer, Prime Minister of Luxembourg, chosen to succeed Delors as President of the European Commission (Britain having vetoed the Belgian Jean-Luc Dehaene) (15th). Cabinet reshuffle: casualties include John Patten, Peter Brooke, John MacGregor and Lord Wakeham. Jeremy Hanley appointed party chairman. Promotion for Jonathan Aitken, Stephen Dorrell and Brian Mawhinney (20th). Tony Blair elected leader of the Labour Party; John Prescott elected deputy leader (21st). Neil Kinnock appointed European Commissioner (29th).

**Aug.** Lord Archer admits 'grave error' when accused of irregular share dealing. IRA announce 'complete cessation' of military operations (31st). Cease-fire lasts until February 1996.

**Sept.** Broadcasting ban on Sinn Fein lifted. Liberal Democrat conference votes to decriminalize cannabis. John Major visits South Africa.

**Oct.** Tony Blair commits Labour to new social market economy and proposes reform of party constitution. Loyalist paramilitaries declare cease-fire. Conservative conference overshadowed by 'sleaze' allegations.

**Nov.** Nolan Committee established after 'cash for questions' revelations cause resignations of Tim Smith and Neil Hamilton.

**Dec.** Government defeat on planned VAT increase on fuel. Swing of 29 per cent to Labour as Dudley West by-election lost by Conservatives. Coal industry privatized.

## 1995

**Jan.** Austria, Sweden and Finland join European Union. Army ends daylight Belfast patrols. Widespread animal welfare demonstrations at Shoreham.

**Feb.** Joint Anglo-Irish document on future of Northern Ireland published. Barings Bank collapses (later rescued by Dutch ING group).

**Mar.** Norman Lamont votes with Labour against government's European policy.

**Apr.** Tony Blair wins victory in reform of Clause IV at special party conference.

**May** Worst postwar performance by Conservatives in local elections, losing over 2,000 seats. Report of Nolan Committee urges tough new measures to combat 'sleaze' in public life.

**June** Resignation of John Major as Conservative Party leader precipitates leadership contest. John Redwood resigns as Welsh Secretary to stand against him.

**July** Major wins comfortable victory over Redwood (218 votes to 89). However 111 MPs fail to support Major. Cabinet reshuffle: Heseltine Deputy Prime Minister, Rifkind to Foreign Office, Mawhinney Party Chairman, Virginia Bottomley moved from Health to National Heritage.

**Aug.** Resignation of James Molyneaux as leader of UUP after 16 years.

**Sept.** David Trimble elected UUP leader on third ballot (winning 466 out of 806 votes).

**Oct.** Metrication Day in Britain (pre-packed food etc. to be sold in metric units). Defection of Conservative MP Alan Howarth to Labour.

**Nov.** Nigeria suspended from membership of the Commonwealth following execution of Ken Soro-Wiwa and other human rights activists.
**Dec.** Defection of Conservative MP Emma Nicholson to Liberal Democrats (increasing their total to 25 MPs).

# British monarchs, 1702–1995

|  | Accession | Coronation |
|---|---|---|
| **House of Stuart** | | |
| Anne (1665–1714) | 8 Mar. 1702 | 23 Apr. 1702 |
| | | |
| **House of Hanover** | | |
| George I (1660–1727) | 1 Aug. 1714 | 20 Oct. 1714 |
| George II (1683–1760) | 14 June 1727 | 11 Oct. 1727 |
| George III (1738–1820) | 25 Oct. 1760 | 22 Sept. 1761 |
| George IV (1762–1830) | 29 Jan. 1820 (Prince Regent since 5 Feb. 1811) | 19 July 1821 |
| William IV (1765–1837) | 26 June 1830 | 8 Sept. 1831 |
| Victoria (1819–1901) | 20 June 1837 | 28 June 1838 |
| | | |
| **House of Saxe-Coburg-Gotha** (after 1917 House of Windsor) | | |
| Edward VII (1841–1910) | 22 Jan. 1901 | 9 Aug. 1902 |
| George V (1865–1936) | 6 May 1910 | 22 June 1914 |
| Edward VIII (1894–1972) | 20 Jan. 1936 | – (Abdicated, 11 Dec. 1936) |
| George VI (1895–1952) | 11 Dec. 1936 | 12 May 1937 |
| Elizabeth II (1926–) | 6 Feb. 1952 | 2 June 1953 |

# Genealogical charts

## The Stuart and Hanoverian lines

Unless otherwise stated, the dates are those of accession.

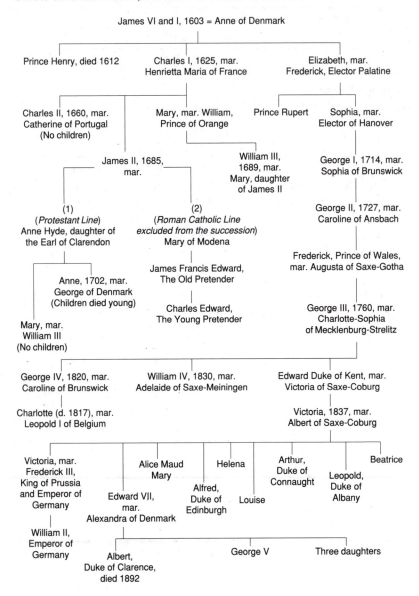

James VI and I, 1603 = Anne of Denmark

Prince Henry, died 1612

Charles I, 1625, mar.
Henrietta Maria of France

Elizabeth, mar.
Frederick, Elector Palatine

Charles II, 1660, mar.
Catherine of Portugal
(No children)

Mary, mar. William,
Prince of Orange

Prince Rupert

Sophia, mar.
Elector of Hanover

James II, 1685,
mar.

William III,
1689, mar.
Mary, daughter
of James II

George I, 1714, mar.
Sophia of Brunswick

(1)
(*Protestant Line*)
Anne Hyde, daughter of
the Earl of Clarendon

(2)
(*Roman Catholic Line
excluded from the succession*)
Mary of Modena

George II, 1727, mar.
Caroline of Ansbach

Anne, 1702, mar.
George of Denmark
(Children died young)

James Francis Edward,
The Old Pretender

Frederick, Prince of Wales,
mar. Augusta of Saxe-Gotha

Mary, mar.
William III
(No children)

Charles Edward,
The Young Pretender

George III, 1760, mar.
Charlotte-Sophia
of Mecklenburg-Strelitz

George IV, 1820, mar.
Caroline of Brunswick

William IV, 1830, mar.
Adelaide of Saxe-Meiningen

Edward Duke of Kent, mar.
Victoria of Saxe-Coburg

Charlotte (d. 1817), mar.
Leopold I of Belgium

Victoria, 1837, mar.
Albert of Saxe-Coburg

Victoria, mar.
Frederick III,
King of Prussia
and Emperor of
Germany

Alice Maud
Mary

Helena

Arthur,
Duke of
Connaught

Beatrice

Leopold,
Duke of
Albany

Edward VII,
mar.
Alexandra of Denmark

Alfred,
Duke of
Edinburgh

Louise

William II,
Emperor of
Germany

Albert,
Duke of Clarence,
died 1892

George V

Three daughters

# The family of Queen Victoria

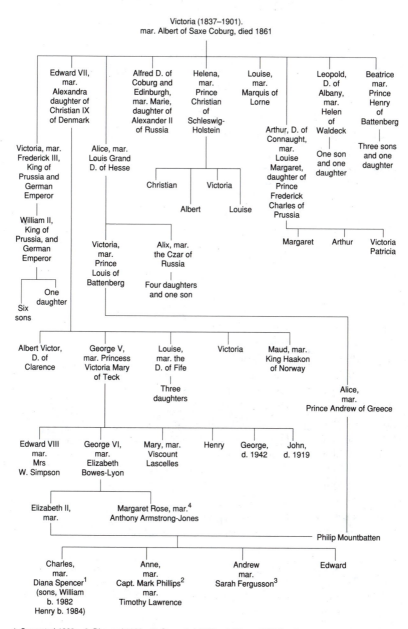

1 Separated 1992;  2 Divorced 1992;  3 Separated 1992;  4 Divorced 1978

# Lists of principal ministers

**Prime Ministers**

| | | |
|---|---|---|
| 1721 | 4 Apr. | Sir Robert Walpole (Earl of Orford) |
| 1741 | 16 Feb. | Earl of Wilmington |
| 1743 | 27 Aug. | Henry Pelham |
| 1754 | 16 Mar. | Duke of Newcastle |
| 1756 | 16 Nov. | Duke of Devonshire |
| 1757 | 2 July | Duke of Newcastle |
| 1760 | 25 Oct. | Duke of Newcastle (on the death of George II Newcastle resumed office the same day as First Lord of the Treasury under George III) |
| 1762 | 26 May | Earl of Bute |
| 1763 | 16 Apr. | George Grenville |
| 1765 | 13 July | Marquess of Rockingham |
| 1766 | 30 July | Earl of Chatham |
| 1768 | 14 Oct. | Duke of Grafton |
| 1770 | 28 Jan. | Lord North (Earl of Guildford) |
| 1782 | 27 Mar. | Marquess of Rockingham |
| 1782 | 4 July | Earl of Shelburne |
| 1783 | 2 Apr. | Duke of Portland |
| 1783 | 19 Dec. | William Pitt (the Younger) |
| 1801 | 17 Mar. | Henry Addington (1st Viscount Sidmouth) |
| 1804 | 10 May | William Pitt |
| 1806 | 11 Feb. | Lord William Wyndham Grenville |
| 1807 | 31 Mar. | Duke of Portland |
| 1809 | 4 Oct. | Spencer Perceval |
| 1812 | 8 June | Earl of Liverpool |
| 1820 | 29 Jan. | Earl of Liverpool (resumed office on accession of George IV) |
| 1827 | 10 Apr. | George Canning |
| 1827 | 31 Aug. | Viscount Goderich |
| 1828 | 22 Jan. | Duke of Wellington |
| 1830 | 22 Nov. | Earl Grey |
| 1834 | 16 July | Viscount Melbourne |

| 1834 | 17 Nov. | Duke of Wellington |
| 1834 | 10 Dec. | Sir Robert Peel |
| 1835 | 18 Apr. | Viscount Melbourne |
| 1837 | 20 June | Viscount Melbourne (resumed office on accession of Queen Victoria) |
| 1841 | 30 Aug. | Sir Robert Peel |
| 1846 | 30 June | Lord John Russell (Earl Russell) |
| 1852 | 23 Feb. | Earl of Derby |
| 1852 | 19 Dec. | Earl of Aberdeen |
| 1855 | 6 Feb. | Viscount Palmerston |
| 1858 | 20 Feb. | Earl of Derby |
| 1859 | 12 June | Viscount Palmerston |
| 1865 | 29 Oct. | Earl Russell |
| 1866 | 28 June | Earl of Derby |
| 1868 | 27 Feb. | Benjamin Disraeli (Earl of Beaconsfield) |
| 1868 | 3 Dec. | William Ewart Gladstone |
| 1874 | 20 Feb. | Benjamin Disraeli (Earl of Beaconsfield) |
| 1880 | 23 Apr. | William Ewart Gladstone |
| 1885 | 23 June | Marquess of Salisbury |
| 1886 | 1 Feb. | William Ewart Gladstone |
| 1886 | 25 July | Marquess of Salisbury |
| 1892 | 15 Aug. | William Ewart Gladstone |
| 1894 | 5 Mar. | Earl of Rosebery (Earl of Midlothian) |
| 1895 | 25 June | Marquess of Salisbury |
| 1901 | 23 Jan. | Marquess of Salisbury (resumed office on the accession of Edward VII) |
| 1902 | 12 July | Arthur James Balfour (Earl of Balfour) |
| 1905 | 5 Dec. | Sir Henry Campbell-Bannerman |
| 1908 | 7 Apr. | Herbert Henry Asquith (Earl of Oxford and Asquith) |
| 1910 | 8 May | Herbert Henry Asquith (Earl of Oxford and Asquith) (resumed office on accession of George V) |
| 1916 | 7 Dec. | David Lloyd George (Earl Lloyd-George of Dwyfor and Viscount Gwynedd) |
| 1922 | 23 Oct. | Andrew Bonar Law |
| 1923 | 22 May | Stanley Baldwin (Earl Baldwin of Bewdley) |
| 1924 | 22 Jan. | James Ramsay MacDonald |
| 1924 | 4 Nov. | Stanley Baldwin (Earl Baldwin of Bewdley) |
| 1929 | 5 June | James Ramsay MacDonald |
| 1935 | 7 June | Stanley Baldwin (Earl Baldwin of Bewdley) |
| 1936 | 21 Jan. | Stanley Baldwin (Earl Baldwin of Bewdley) (resumed office on accession of Edward VIII) |

| 1936 | 12 Dec. | Stanley Baldwin (Earl Baldwin of Bewdley) (resumed office on accession of George VI) |
| 1937 | 28 May | (Arthur) Neville Chamberlain |
| 1940 | 10 May | Winston Leonard Spencer Churchill (Sir) |
| 1945 | 26 July | Clement Richard Attlee (Earl Attlee) |
| 1951 | 26 Oct. | Winston Leonard Spencer Churchill (Sir) |
| 1952 | 7 Feb. | Winston Leonard Spencer Churchill (Sir) (resumed office on accession of Elizabeth II) |
| 1955 | 6 Apr. | Sir (Robert) Anthony Eden (Earl of Avon) |
| 1957 | 10 Jan. | Harold Macmillan (Lord Stockton) |
| 1963 | 19 Oct. | Sir Alec (Alexander Frederick) Douglas-Home (Lord Home of the Hirsel) |
| 1964 | 16 Oct. | (James) Harold Wilson (Sir) (Lord Wilson of Rievaulx) |
| 1970 | 19 June | Edward Heath (Sir) |
| 1974 | 4 Mar. | (James) Harold Wilson (Sir) (Lord Wilson of Rievaulx) |
| 1976 | 5 Apr. | (Leonard) James Callaghan (Lord Callaghan) |
| 1979 | 4 May | Margaret Hilda Thatcher (Baroness Thatcher of Kesteven) |
| 1983 | 10 June | Margaret Hilda Thatcher (Baroness Thatcher of Kesteven) |
| 1987 | 12 June | Margaret Hilda Thatcher (Baroness Thatcher of Kesteven) |
| 1990 | 28 Nov. | John Major |
| 1992 | 11 Apr. | John Major |

## Chancellors of the Exchequer

| 1714 | 13 Oct. | Sir Richard Onslow (Lord Onslow) |
| 1715 | 12 Oct. | Sir Robert Walpole (Earl of Orford) |
| 1715 | 15 Apr. | James Stanhope (Earl Stanhope) |
| 1718 | 20 Mar. | John Aislabie |
| 1721 | 21 Feb. | Sir John Pratt |
| 1721 | 3 Apr. | Sir Robert Walpole |
| 1742 | 12 Feb. | Samuel Sandys (Lord Sandys of Ombersley) |
| 1743 | 12 Dec. | Henry Pelham |
| 1754 | 8 Mar. | Sir William Lee |
| 1754 | 6 Apr. | Henry Bilson Legge |
| 1755 | 25 Nov. | Sir George Lyttelton (Lord Lyttelton) |
| 1756 | 16 Nov. | Henry Bilson Legge |
| 1757 | 13 Apr. | William Murray (Earl of Mansfield) |

| 1757 | 2 July | Henry Bilson Legge |
| 1761 | 19 Mar. | William Wildman Barrington-Shute (Viscount Barrington) |
| 1762 | 29 May | Sir Francis Dashwood (Lord le Despenser) |
| 1763 | 16 Apr. | George Grenville |
| 1765 | 16 July | William Dowdeswell |
| 1766 | 2 Aug. | Charles Townshend |
| 1767 | 11 Sept. | Lord Mansfield |
| 1767 | 6 Oct. | Frederick North, commonly called Lord North (Earl of Guildford) |
| 1782 | 1 Apr. | Lord John Cavendish |
| 1782 | 13 July | William Pitt |
| 1783 | 5 Apr. | Lord John Cavendish |
| 1783 | 27 Dec. | William Pitt |
| 1801 | 20 Mar. | Henry Addington (Viscount Sidmouth) |
| 1803 | 13 May | William Pitt |
| 1806 | 5 Feb. | Lord Henry Petty (Marquess of Lansdowne) |
| 1807 | 26 Mar. | Spencer Perceval |
| 1812 | 9 June | Nicholas Vansittart (Lord Bexley) |
| 1823 | 31 Jan. | Frederick John Robinson (Viscount Goderich) |
| 1827 | 20 Apr. | George Canning |
| 1827 | 3 Sept. | John Charles Herries |
| 1828 | 22 Jan. | Henry Goulburn |
| 1830 | 22 Nov. | John Charles Spencer, called Viscount Althorp (Earl Spencer) |
| 1834 | 10 Dec. | Sir Robert Peel |
| 1835 | 18 Apr. | Thomas Spring Rice (Lord Monteagle of Brandon) |
| 1839 | 26 Aug. | Sir Francis Thornhill Baring (Lord Northbrook) |
| 1841 | 3 Sept. | Henry Goulburn |
| 1846 | 6 July | Sir Charles Wood (Viscount Halifax) |
| 1852 | 27 Feb. | Benjamin Disraeli (Earl of Beaconsfield) |
| 1852 | 28 Dec. | William Ewart Gladstone |
| 1855 | 28 Feb. | Sir George Cornewall Lewis |
| 1858 | 26 Feb. | Benjamin Disraeli |
| 1859 | 18 June | William Ewart Gladstone |
| 1866 | 6 July | Benjamin Disraeli |
| 1868 | 29 Feb. | George Ward Hunt |
| 1868 | 9 Dec. | Robert Lowe (Viscount Sherbrooke) |
| 1873 | 30 Aug. | William Ewart Gladstone |
| 1874 | 21 Feb. | Sir Stafford Henry Northcote (Earl of Iddesleigh) |

| 1880 | 28 Apr. | William Ewart Gladstone |
| 1882 | 16 Dec. | Hugh Culling Eardley Childers |
| 1885 | 24 June | Sir Michael Edward Hicks Beach (Earl St Aldwyn) |
| 1886 | 6 Feb. | Sir William George Granville Venables Vernon Harcourt |
| 1886 | 3 Aug. | Lord Randolph Henry Spencer Churchill |
| 1887 | 14 Jan. | George Joachim Goschen (Viscount Goschen) |
| 1892 | 18 Aug. | Sir William Harcourt |
| 1895 | 29 June | Sir Michael Hicks Beach |
| 1902 | 12 July | Charles Thomson Ritchie (Lord Ritchie) |
| 1903 | 9 Oct. | Joseph Austen Chamberlain (Sir) |
| 1905 | 11 Dec. | Herbert Henry Asquith (Earl of Oxford and Asquith) |
| 1908 | 16 Apr. | David Lloyd George (Earl Lloyd-George of Dwyfor) |
| 1915 | 27 May | Reginald McKenna |
| 1916 | 11 Dec. | Andrew Bonar Law |
| 1919 | 14 Jan. | (Joseph) Austen Chamberlain (Sir) |
| 1921 | 5 Apr. | Sir Robert Stevenson Horne (Viscount Horne) |
| 1922 | 25 Oct. | Stanley Baldwin (Earl Baldwin) |
| 1923 | 11 Oct. | Arthur Neville Chamberlain |
| 1924 | 23 Jan. | Philip Snowden (Viscount Snowden) |
| 1924 | 7 Nov. | Winston Leonard Spencer Churchill (Sir) |
| 1929 | 8 June | Philip Snowden (Viscount Snowden) |
| 1931 | 9 Nov. | Arthur Neville Chamberlain |
| 1937 | 28 May | Sir John Allsebrook Simon (Viscount Simon) |
| 1940 | 13 May | Sir Howard Kingsley Wood |
| 1943 | 28 Sept. | Sir John Anderson (Viscount Waverley) |
| 1945 | 28 July | Hugh John Neale Dalton |
| 1947 | 17 Nov. | Sir Richard Stafford Cripps |
| 1950 | 25 Oct. | Hugh Todd Naylor Gaitskell |
| 1951 | 27 Oct. | Richard Austen Butler (Lord Butler of Saffron Walden) |
| 1955 | 22 Dec. | (Maurice) Harold Macmillan |
| 1957 | 14 Jan. | George Edward Peter Thorneycroft (Lord Thorneycroft) |
| 1958 | 7 Jan. | Derick Heathcoat Amory (Viscount Amory) |
| 1960 | 27 July | John Selwyn Brooke Lloyd (Lord Selwyn-Lloyd) |
| 1962 | 13 July | Reginald Maudling |
| 1964 | 16 Oct. | (Leonard) James Callaghan (Lord Callaghan) |
| 1967 | 30 Nov. | Roy Harris Jenkins (Lord Jenkins) |
| 1970 | 20 June | Iain Norman Macleod |
| 1970 | 25 July | Anthony Perrinott Lysberg Barber (Lord Barber) |

| 1974 | 5 Mar. | Denis Winston Healey (Lord Healey) |
| 1979 | 5 May | (Richard Edward) Geoffrey Howe (Sir) (Baron Howe) |
| 1983 | 9 June | Nigel Lawson (Baron Lawson of Blaby) |
| 1989 | 26 Oct. | John Major |
| 1990 | 28 Nov. | Norman Lamont |
| 1993 | 27 May | Kenneth Clarke |

## Secretaries of State for the Northern Department

Prior to 1782 there were two Secretaries of State: one for the Southern Department and one for the Northern Department, who shared domestic and foreign business. In 1782 the Southern Department became the Home Office and the Northern Department was converted into the Foreign Office.

| 1714 | 17 Sept. | Charles Townshend (Viscount Townshend) |
| 1716 | 12 Dec. | James Stanhope (Earl Stanhope) |
| 1717 | 15 Apr. | Earl of Sunderland |
| 1718 | 18–21 Mar. | Lord Stanhope |
| 1721 | 10 Feb. | Viscount Townshend |
| 1723 | 29 May | Sir Robert Walpole (Earl of Orford) (temp.) |
| 1730 | 19 June | William Stanhope (Earl of Harrington) |
| 1742 | 12 Feb. | Lord Carteret |
| 1744 | 24 Nov. | Earl of Harrington |
| 1746 | 10 Feb. | Earl Granville |
| 1746 | 14 Feb. | Earl of Harrington |
| 1746 | 29 Oct. | Earl of Chesterfield |
| 1748 | 6–12 Feb. | Duke of Newcastle |
| 1754 | 23 Mar. | Earl of Holderness |
| 1761 | 25 Mar. | Earl of Bute |
| 1762 | 27 May | George Grenville |
| 1762 | 14 Oct. | Earl of Halifax |
| 1763 | 9 Sept. | Earl of Sandwich |
| 1765 | 10–12 July | Duke of Grafton |
| 1766 | 23 May | Henry Seymour Conway |
| 1768 | 20 Jan. | Viscount Weymouth (Marquess of Bath) |
| 1768 | 21 Oct. | Earl of Rochford |
| 1770 | 19 Dec. | Earl of Sandwich |
| 1771 | 22 Jan. | Earl of Halifax |
| 1771 | 12 June | Earl of Suffolk |
| 1779 | 7 Mar. | Viscount Weymouth (Marquess of Bath) |
| 1779 | 27 Oct. | Viscount Stormont (Earl of Mansfield) |

## Secretaries of State for Foreign Affairs

| | | |
|---|---|---|
| 1782 | 27 Mar. | Charles James Fox |
| 1782 | 17 July | Lord Grantham |
| 1783 | 2 Apr. | Charles James Fox |
| 1783 | 19 Dec. | Earl Temple (Marquess of Buckingham) |
| 1783 | 23 Dec. | Marquess of Carmarthen (Duke of Leeds) |
| 1791 | 8 June | Lord Grenville |
| 1801 | 20 Feb. | Lord Hawkesbury (Earl of Liverpool) |
| 1804 | 14 May | Lord Harrowby (Earl of Harrowby) |
| 1805 | 11 Jan. | Lord Mulgrave (Earl of Mulgrave) |
| 1806 | 7 Feb. | Charles James Fox |
| 1806 | 24 Sept. | Viscount Howick (Earl Grey) |
| 1807 | 25 Mar. | George Canning |
| 1809 | 11 Oct. | Earl Bathurst |
| 1809 | 6 Dec. | Marquess Wellesley |
| 1812 | 4 Mar. | Viscount Castlereagh (Marquess of Londonderry) |
| 1822 | 16 Sept. | George Canning |
| 1827 | 30 April | Viscount Dudley and Ward (Earl of Dudley) |
| 1828 | 2 June | Earl of Aberdeen |
| 1830 | 22 Nov. | Viscount Palmerston |
| 1834 | 15 Nov. | Duke of Wellington |
| 1835 | 18 Apr. | Viscount Palmerston |
| 1841 | 2 Sept. | Earl of Aberdeen |
| 1846 | 6 July | Viscount Palmerston |
| 1851 | 26 Dec. | Earl Granville |
| 1852 | 27 Feb. | Earl of Malmesbury |
| 1852 | 28 Dec. | Lord John Russell (Earl Russell) |
| 1853 | 21 Feb. | Earl of Clarendon |
| 1858 | 26 Feb. | Earl of Malmesbury |
| 1859 | 18 June | Lord John Russell (Earl Russell) |
| 1865 | 3 Nov. | Earl of Clarendon |
| 1866 | 6 July | Lord Stanley (Earl of Derby) |
| 1868 | 9 Dec. | Earl of Clarendon |
| 1870 | 6 July | Earl Granville |
| 1874 | 21 Feb. | Earl of Derby |
| 1878 | 2 Apr. | Marquess of Salisbury |
| 1880 | 28 Apr. | Earl Granville |
| 1885 | 24 June | Marquess of Salisbury |
| 1886 | 6 Feb. | Lord Rosebery (Earl of Midlothian) |
| 1886 | 3 Aug. | Earl of Iddesleigh |
| 1887 | 14 Jan. | Marquess of Salisbury |

| 1892 | 18 Aug. | Lord Rosebery (Earl of Midlothian) |
| 1894 | 11 Mar. | Earl of Kimberley |
| 1895 | 29 June | Marquess of Salisbury |
| 1900 | 12 Nov. | Marquess of Lansdowne |
| 1905 | 11 Dec. | Sir Edward Grey (Viscount Grey of Falloden) |
| 1916 | 11 Dec. | Arthur James Balfour (Earl of Balfour) |
| 1919 | 24 Oct. | Earl Curzon (Marquess Curzon) |
| 1924 | 23 Jan. | James Ramsay MacDonald |
| 1925 | 7 Nov. | (Sir) (Joseph) Austen Chamberlain |
| 1929 | 8 June | Arthur Henderson |
| 1931 | 26 Aug. | Marquess of Reading |
| 1931 | 9 Nov. | Sir John Allesbrook Simon (Viscount Simon) |
| 1935 | 7 June | Sir Samuel John Gurney Hoare (Viscount Templewood) |
| 1935 | 22 Dec. | Sir (Robert) Anthony Eden (Earl of Avon) |
| 1938 | 1 Mar. | Viscount Halifax |
| 1940 | 22 Dec. | Sir (Robert) Anthony Eden (Earl of Avon) |
| 1945 | 27 July | Ernest Bevin |
| 1951 | 9 Mar. | Herbert Stanley Morrison (Baron Morrison of Lambeth) |
| 1951 | 28 Oct. | Sir (Robert) Anthony Eden (Earl of Avon) |
| 1955 | 20 Dec. | (John) Selwyn Brooke Lloyd (Baron Selwyn-Lloyd) |
| 1960 | 27 July | Earl of Home (Lord Home of the Hirsel) |
| 1963 | 20 Oct. | Richard Austen Butler (Baron Butler of Saffron Walden) |
| 1964 | 16 Oct. | Patrick Chrestien Gordon Walker (Baron Gordon-Walker) |
| 1965 | 22 Jan. | (Robert) Michael Maitland Stewart (Baron Stewart of Fulham) |
| 1966 | 11 Aug. | George Alfred Brown (Baron George-Brown) |

## Secretaries of State for Foreign and Commonwealth Affairs

| 1968 | 16 Mar. | (Robert) Michael Maitland Stewart (Baron Stewart of Fulham) |
| 1970 | 19 June | Sir Alec (Alexander Frederick) Douglas-Home (Lord Home of the Hirsel) |
| 1974 | 4 Mar. | (Leonard) James Callaghan (Lord Callaghan) |
| 1976 | 5 Apr. | (Charles) Anthony Raven Crosland |
| 1977 | 21 Feb. | David Anthony Llewellyn Owen (Lord Owen) |
| 1979 | 5 May | Lord Carrington |
| 1982 | 5 Apr. | Francis Pym (Lord Pym) |

| 1983 | 11 June | Sir Geoffrey Howe (Baron Howe) |
| 1989 | 24 July | John Major |
| 1989 | 26 Oct. | Douglas Hurd |
| 1995 | 5 July | Malcolm Rifkind |

**Secretaries of State for the Southern Department**

| 1714 | 27 Sept. | James Stanhope (Earl Stanhope) |
| 1716 | 22 June | Paul Methuen |
| 1717 | 16 April | Joseph Addison |
| 1718 | 16 Mar. | James Craggs |
| 1721 | 4 Mar. | Lord Carteret (Earl Granville) |
| 1724 | 6 Apr. | Duke of Newcastle upon Tyne |
| 1748 | 6–12 Feb. | Duke of Bedford |
| 1751 | 18 June | Earl of Holderness |
| 1754 | 23 Mar. | Sir Thomas Robinson (Lord Grantham) |
| 1755 | 14 Nov. | Henry Fox (Lord Holland) |
| 1756 | 4 Dec. | William Pitt (Earl of Chatham) |
| 1761 | 9 Oct. | Earl of Egremont |
| 1763 | 9 Sept. | Earl of Halifax |
| 1765 | 10 July | Henry Seymour Conway |
| 1766 | 23 May | Duke of Richmond |
| 1766 | 30 July | Lord Wycombe (Marquess of Lansdowne) |
| 1768 | 21 Oct. | Viscount Weymouth |
| 1770 | 19 Dec. | Earl of Rochford |
| 1775 | 9 Nov. | Viscount Weymouth |
| 1779 | 24 Nov. | Earl of Hillsborough (Marquess of Downshire) |

**Secretaries of State for Home Affairs**

| 1782 | 27 Mar. | Earl of Shelburne |
| 1782 | 10 July | Thomas Townshend (Viscount Sydney of St Leonards) |
| 1783 | 2 Apr. | Lord North (Earl of Guildford) |
| 1783 | 19 Dec. | Earl Temple (Marquess of Buckingham) |
| 1783 | 23 Dec. | Lord Sydney (Viscount Sydney of St Leonards) |
| 1789 | 5 June | Lord William Wyndham Grenville |
| 1791 | 8 June | Henry Dundas (Viscount Melville) |
| 1794 | 11 July | Duke of Portland |
| 1801 | 30 July | Thomas Pelham (Earl of Chichester) |
| 1803 | 17 Aug. | Charles Philip Yorke |
| 1804 | 12 May | Lord Hawkesbury (Earl of Liverpool) |
| 1806 | 5 Feb. | Earl Spencer |

| 1807 | 25 Mar. | Lord Hawkesbury (Earl of Liverpool) |
| 1809 | 1 Nov. | Richard Ryder |
| 1812 | 11 June | Viscount Sidmouth |
| 1822 | 17 Jan. | Sir Robert Peel |
| 1827 | 30 Apr. | William Sturges-Bourne |
| 1827 | 16 July | Marquess of Lansdowne |
| 1828 | 26 Jan. | Sir Robert Peel |
| 1830 | 22 Nov. | Viscount Melbourne |
| 1834 | 19 July | Lord Duncannon (Earl of Bessborough) |
| 1834 | 15 Dec. | Henry Goulburn |
| 1835 | 18 Apr. | Lord John Russell (Earl Russell) |
| 1839 | 30 Aug. | Marquess of Normanby |
| 1841 | 6 Sept. | Sir James Robert George Graham |
| 1846 | 6 July | Sir George Grey |
| 1852 | 27 Feb. | Spencer Horatio Walpole |
| 1852 | 28 Dec. | Viscount Palmerston |
| 1855 | 8 Feb. | Sir George Grey |
| 1858 | 26 Feb. | Spencer Horatio Walpole |
| 1859 | 3 Mar. | Thomas Henry Sutton Sotherton Estcourt |
| 1859 | 18 June | Sir George Cornewall Lewis |
| 1861 | 25 July | Sir George Grey |
| 1866 | 6 July | Spencer Horatio Walpole |
| 1867 | 17 May | Gathorne Hardy (Earl of Cranbrook) |
| 1868 | 9 Dec. | Lord Aberdare |
| 1873 | 9 Aug. | Robert Lowe (Viscount Sherbrooke) |
| 1874 | 21 Feb. | Sir Richard Assheton Cross (Viscount Cross) |
| 1880 | 28 Apr. | Sir William George Granville Venables Vernon Harcourt |
| 1885 | 24 June | Sir Richard Assheton Cross (Viscount Cross) |
| 1886 | 6 Feb. | Hugh Culling Eardley Childers |
| 1886 | 3 Aug. | Henry Matthews (Viscount Llandaff) |
| 1892 | 18 Aug. | Herbert Henry Asquith (Earl of Oxford and Asquith) |
| 1895 | 29 June | Sir Matthew White Ridley (Viscount Ridley) |
| 1900 | 12 Nov. | Charles Thompson Ritchie (Lord Ritchie) |
| 1902 | 12 July | Aretas Akers-Douglas (Viscount Chilston) |
| 1905 | 11 Dec. | Herbert John Gladstone (Viscount Gladstone) |
| 1910 | 19 Feb. | Winston Leonard Spencer Churchill (Sir) |
| 1911 | 24 Oct. | Reginald McKenna |
| 1915 | 27 May | Sir John Allesbrook Simon (Viscount Simon) |
| 1916 | 12 Jan. | Herbert Louis Samuel (Viscount Samuel) |

| 1916 | 11 Dec. | Sir George Cave (Viscount Cave) |
| 1919 | 14 Jan. | Edward Shortt |
| 1922 | 25 Oct. | William Clive Bridgeman (Viscount Bridgeman) |
| 1924 | 23 Jan. | Arthur Henderson |
| 1924 | 7 Nov. | Sir William Joynson-Hicks (Viscount Brentford) |
| 1929 | 8 June | John Robert Clynes |
| 1931 | 26 Aug. | Sir Herbert Louis Samuel (Viscount Samuel) |
| 1932 | 1 Oct. | Sir John Gilmour |
| 1935 | 7 June | Sir John Allesbrook Simon (Viscount Simon) |
| 1937 | 28 May | Sir Samuel John Gurney Hoare (Viscount Templewood) |
| 1939 | 3 Sept. | Sir John Anderson (Viscount Waverley) |
| 1940 | 3 Oct. | Herbert Stanley Morrison (Baron Morrison of Lambeth) |
| 1945 | 25 May | Sir Donald Bradley Somervell (Baron Somervell of Harrow) |
| 1945 | 3 Aug. | James Chuter Ede (Baron Chuter-Ede) |
| 1951 | 28 Oct. | Sir David Maxwell Fyfe (Earl of Kilmuir) |
| 1954 | 18 Oct. | Gwilym Lloyd-George (Viscount Tenby) |
| 1957 | 13 Jan. | Richard Austen Butler (Baron Butler of Saffron Walden) |
| 1962 | 13 July | Henry Brooke (Baron Brooke of Cumnor) |
| 1964 | 18 Oct. | Sir Frank Soskice (Baron Stow Hill) |
| 1965 | 23 Dec. | Roy Harris Jenkins (Lord Jenkins) |
| 1967 | 30 Nov. | (Leonard) James Callaghan (Lord Callaghan) |
| 1970 | 20 June | Reginald Maudling |
| 1972 | 19 July | (Leonard) Robert Carr (Baron Carr of Hadley) |
| 1974 | 5 Mar. | Roy Harris Jenkins (Lord Jenkins) |
| 1976 | 10 Sept. | Merlyn Rees (Lord Rees) |
| 1979 | 5 May | William Stephen Ian Whitelaw (Viscount Whitelaw) |
| 1983 | 10 June | Leon Brittan (Sir Leon Brittan) |
| 1985 | 2 Sept. | Douglas Hurd |
| 1989 | 26 Oct. | David Waddington (Lord Waddington) |
| 1990 | 28 Nov. | Kenneth Baker |
| 1992 | 11 Apr. | Kenneth Clarke |
| 1993 | 27 May | Michael Howard |

# Parliamentary reform

## The unreformed House of Commons

### The franchise (prior to 1832)

**England and Wales**: In the counties the voting qualification was the possession of freehold property valued for the land tax at 40 shillings per annum – the 40s. freeholder. In the boroughs various qualifications applied. The main types were:

(i) Scot and lot: right of voting vested in inhabitant householders paying poor rate.
(ii) Householder or 'potwalloper': right of voting vested in all inhabitant householders not receiving alms or poor relief.
(iii) Burgage: voting rights attached to property in the borough.
(iv) Corporation: right of voting confined to the corporation.
(v) Freeman: right of voting rested in the freemen of the borough.
(vi) Freeholder: right of voting lay with the freeholders.

**Scotland**: In the Scottish counties the franchise belonged to freeholders possessing land valued at 40s. 'of old extent' or to owners of land rated at £400 Scots (c. £35 sterling). In Sutherland the vote also extended to tenants of the Earl of Sutherland. The Scottish boroughs, or burghs, were combined in groups for the purpose of electing MPs by a process of indirect election. Voting was vested in the small burgh councils.

### The composition of the House of Commons in 1790

| Constituencies | MPs |
| --- | --- |
| *English boroughs* | |
| 196 boroughs each returning 2 members | 392 |
| 5 boroughs each returning 1 member | 5 |
| 2 boroughs (City of London and Weymouth) each returning 4 members | 8 |

*English counties*
40 counties each returning 2 members          80

*English universities*
2 universities each returning 2 members          4

*Welsh boroughs*
5 boroughs each returning 1 member          5
7 groups of boroughs each returning 1 member          7

*Welsh counties*
12 counties each returning 1 member          12

*Scottish burghs*
15 burghs each returning 1 member          15

*Scottish counties*
27 counties each returning 1 member          27
6 counties, grouped in pairs, 1 of each pair
alternately returning 1 member          3

*Total constituencies* 314          Total MPs   558

As a result of the Act of Union in 1800, 100 extra members representing Ireland were added to the existing members of the House of Commons.

### Size of electorates in English boroughs *c. 1790*

| Electors | Number of boroughs |
|---|---|
| Under 500 | 149 |
| 500–1 000 | 32 |
| Over 1 000 | 22 |

# The Reform Movement, 1714–1830

1716    Septennial Act extends duration of parliaments to seven years.
1729    Last Determinations Act fixes representation in disputed constituencies in perpetuity at the size 'last determined'.

1739    'Patriot' opposition begins to articulate programme for shorter parliaments and a reduction of patronage.

1768    Wilkes's expulsion from the House of Commons after election for Middlesex focuses attention on the subject of parliamentary reform.

1776    Major Cartwright's *Take Your Choice* outlines radical reform programme including universal suffrage and annual parliaments. Wilkes seeks leave to bring in a Bill for 'a just and equal Representation of the People of England in Parliament'.

1779    Yorkshire Association formed led by Christopher Wyvill to campaign for parliamentary reform.

1780    Convention of reformers in London, and petitions for reform sent in by several counties and towns. Dunning's motion passed condemning the increased power of the Crown over parliament. Society for Constitutional Information founded.

1782    'Economical reform' measures passed, limiting the number of government placeholders in the House of Commons.

1783    Pitt's proposals for a limited reform of parliament defeated in the House of Commons by 293 votes to 149.

1785    Pitt's proposals to redistribute 72 seats from 'decayed boroughs' to the counties and to slightly increase the electorate defeated in the House of Commons by 248 votes to 174.

1789    Meeting of London Revolution Society to celebrate the 'Glorious Revolution' of 1688 addressed by Dr Price welcoming the French Revolution for its stimulus to parliamentary reform and religious toleration.

1791    Publication of Thomas Paine's *Rights of Man* (Part I; Part II, 1792). Formation of reform societies in Sheffield and Manchester.

1792    London Corresponding Society founded by London artisans led by Thomas Hardy demands annual elections and 'an equal Representation of the Whole Body of the People'. Whig Society of the Friends of the People established.

1793    Charles Grey's motion for parliamentary reform defeated in the House of Commons by 282 votes to 41. British Convention of Reformers meets in Edinburgh.

1794    Leading reformers put on trial for high treason after plans for a new convention alarm government. Habeas Corpus suspended. Reformers acquitted.

1795    Mass meetings for reform in London and Sheffield. 'Two Acts' passed extending the law of treason to cover spoken words and banning most mass meetings.

1797    Last mass meeting of London Corresponding Society dispersed by police and troops. Rejection of Charles Grey's motion for parliamentary reform in the House of Commons by 256 votes to 91.

1798    Remaining leaders of London Corresponding Society arrested and imprisoned.

1799    London Corresponding Society and United Societies banned.

1800    Act of Union adds 100 extra members for Ireland to the House of Commons.

1806    William Cobbett lends support to cause of parliamentary reform.

1807    Sir Francis Burdett and Lord Cochrane elected as radical MPs for Westminster.

1809    Anti-bribery Act of J. C. Curwen passed. Burdett's motion for limiting duration of parliaments and extending franchise defeated.

1810    Thomas Brand's motion for limited parliamentary reform defeated.

1812    London Hampden Club founded to promote cause of parliamentary reform.

1816    Cobbett produces first cheap edition of the *Political Register*, disseminating reform ideas among the poorer classes. Spa Fields meetings in London addressed by Henry Hunt; petition for reform.

1817    Convention of reformers in London. Burdett's motion for reform defeated in the House of Commons.

1818    Sir Robert Heron's motion for triennial parliaments defeated in the House of Commons. Burdett's motions for annual parliaments, manhood suffrage, secret ballot and equal electoral districts defeated by 106 votes to nil.

1819    Reform meetings at Birmingham, Stockport and Manchester. Meeting at St Peter's Fields (Peterloo) broken up by magistrates and troops. Henry Hunt arrested. Widespread protests.

1821    Seats of Grampound transferred to Yorkshire. Lord Durham's Bill advocating triennial parliaments, equal electoral districts and ratepayer franchise defeated.

1822    Lord John Russell's motion to redistribute 100 members from the smallest boroughs defeated. County meetings organized by leading Whigs to promote cause of reform.

1826    Further reform proposals by Russell defeated in the House of Commons.

1827    Bill to redistribute seats of Penryn to Manchester and Birmingham defeated by the House of Lords.

1829    Formation of Birmingham Political Union.

1830    Wellington declares against need for parliamentary reform. Wellington's resignation leads to Grey and the Whigs taking office on a pledge to reform parliament.

Note: for events leading up to the first Reform Act, see Political chronology, p. 21.

## The Reform Act of 1832

**1. Disfranchisement clauses:**

(a) Fifty-six nomination or rotten boroughs returning 111 members of parliament lost representation.

(b) Thirty boroughs with less than 4,000 inhabitants lost 1 member of parliament each.

(c) Weymouth and Melcombe Regis gave up 2 of their 4 members. One hundred and forty-three seats made available for redistribution.

**2. Enfranchisement clauses:**

(a) Sixty-five seats awarded to the counties.

(b) Forty-four seats distributed to 22 large towns, including Birmingham, Manchester, Leeds, Sheffield and the new London metropolitan districts.

(c) Twenty-one smaller towns given 1 member each.

(d) Scotland awarded 8 extra seats.

(e) Ireland given 5 extra seats.

**3. Franchise qualifications:**

(a) Borough franchise regularized, right of voting vested in all householders paying a yearly rental of £10 and, subject to one-year residence qualification, £10 lodgers (if sharing a house and the landlord not in occupation).

(b) In the counties, franchise granted to 40s. freeholders; £10 copyholders; £50 tenants; £10 long leaseholders; £50 medium leaseholders. Borough freeholders could vote in counties if their freehold was between 40s. and £10, or if it was over £10 and occupied by a tenant.

# The Reform Act of 1867 (and Scotland, 1868)

## 1. Disfranchisement clauses:

  (a) Six boroughs returning 2 members and 5 boroughs returning 1 member totally disfranchised.

  (b) Thirty-five boroughs returning 2 members deprived of 1 member.

  (c) Peeblesshire and Selkirkshire to return 1 member conjointly instead of 1 each.

      Fifty-three seats made available for redistribution.

## 2. Enfranchisement clauses:

  (a) Nine new boroughs and London University to return 1 member each.

  (b) Five seats awarded to increase representation of Leeds, Liverpool, Birmingham, Manchester (from 2 seats to 3) and Salford (from 1 seat to 2).

  (c) Chelsea and Hackney each created 2-member seats.

  (d) Twenty-five seats awarded to the English counties.

  (e) One extra seat awarded to Wales (Merthyr Tydfil became 2-member seat).

  (f) Five additional seats awarded to Scottish burghs.

  (g) Three extra seats awarded to Scottish counties.

## 3. Franchise qualifications:

  (a) Borough franchise extended to all householders paying rates and to lodgers paying a rental of £10, subject to a one-year residence qualification.

  (b) County franchise extended to occupiers of property rated at £12 a year (£14 in Scotland) and to those with lands worth £5 a year.

# The Reform and Redistribution Acts of 1884–85

## 1. Disfranchisement clauses:

  (a) Thirteen boroughs returning 2 members and 66 boroughs returning 1 member in England and Wales merged in the counties.

  (b) Thirty-six boroughs returning 2 members in England and Wales deprived of 1 member.

(c) Two 2-member boroughs, Macclesfield and Sandwich, disfranchised.

(d) Two boroughs returning 1 member each in Scotland merged in the counties.

(e) Twenty-two boroughs returning 1 member each in Ireland merged in the counties.

(f) Three boroughs returning 2 members each in Ireland deprived of 1 member.

One hundred and thirty-eight seats made available for redistribution.

## 2. Enfranchisement clauses:

(a) London (including Croydon) to return 62 members instead of 22.

(b) Twenty-six seats added to provincial English boroughs.

(c) Six new provincial boroughs created in England and Wales returning 1 member each.

(d) Sixty-six additional members allocated to English and Welsh counties.

(e) Seven seats added to Scottish counties.

(f) Seven seats added to Aberdeen, Edinburgh and Glasgow.

(g) Twenty-one extra seats allocated to Irish counties.

(h) Four seats allocated to Belfast and Dublin.

## 3. Franchise qualifications:

The Representation of the People Act 1884 created a uniform franchise in both boroughs and counties of the United Kingdom on the basis of the 1867 borough franchise, to include:

(a) householders, subject to a one-year residential qualification and payment of rates;

(b) lodgers who occupied lodgings worth £10 a year, subject to a one-year residential qualification;

(c) an occupation franchise for those with lands or tenements worth £10 a year.

## The electorate

| | Electorate (000) | | Population (000) | |
|---|---|---|---|---|
| | England and Wales | UK | England and Wales | UK |
| 1831 | 435 | 516 | 14 000 | 24 000 |
| 1833 | 700 | 813 | 14 000 | 24 000 |
| 1866 | 1 000 | 1 310 | 22 000 | 31 000 |
| 1868 | 2 000 | 2 500 | 22 000 | 31 000 |
| 1883 | 2 600 | 3 100 | 26 000 | 35 000 |
| 1885 | 4 400 | 5 600 | 27 000 | 36 000 |

Percentage of all adults (male and female) entitled to vote (approx.)

| | (%) |
|---|---|
| 1831 | 5 |
| 1833 | 7 |
| 1867 | 16 |
| 1884 | 28½ |
| 1918 | 74 |
| 1928 | 97[*] |

* This figure is less than 100 per cent due to a six-month residence qualification before voters went onto the register.

## Adult males able to vote

| | England and Wales | Scotland | Ireland |
|---|---|---|---|
| 1833 | 1 in 5 | 1 in 8 | 1 in 20 |
| 1869 | 1 in 3 | 1 in 3 | 1 in 6 |
| 1885 | 2 in 3 | 3 in 5 | 1 in 2 |

# Legislation governing parliamentary representation and the conduct of elections, 1828–1995

1828    Polling limited in boroughs to eight days and providing for several polling places where necessary.

1832    First Reform Act (for detailed franchise and redistribution provisions, see p. 87). Time allowed for polling in each constituency reduced to two days (after 1853 reduced to one day in the boroughs); general elections still to take place over the course of a fortnight. Electoral register introduced.

1854    Corrupt Practices Prevention Act. Sponsored by Lord John Russell, the Act levied small fines for bribery, cheating and the use of undue influence and intimidation. Itemized accounts to be produced by candidates of their expenditure for examination by an election auditor.

1863    Office of election auditor replaced by that of returning officer.

1867    Representation of the People Act (for detailed franchise and redistribution provisions, see p. 88).

1868    Parliamentary Elections Act transferred jurisdiction over disputed elections from selected committees of the House of Commons to the judges in the high court. Penalties for bribery strengthened.

1872    Ballot Act introduced voting by secret ballot and increased the number of polling places.

1878    Registration system in English boroughs overhauled, regularizing electoral rolls.

1883    Corrupt and Illegal Practices Act. Maximum election expenses laid down for parliamentary elections. Severe penalties (including imprisonment) introduced for anyone found guilty of corrupt practices.

1884    Representation of the People Act (for detailed provisions, see pp. 88–9).

1885    Redistribution of Seats Act (for detailed provisions, see pp. 88–9).

1918    Representation of the People Act. Vote given to all men over 21 and to women over 30 if they were ratepayers or wives of ratepayers.

1928    Representation of the People (Equal Franchise) Act. Vote given to all women over 21.

1948    Representation of the People Act abolished plural voting – the practice of having one vote in the constituency in place of residence, *and* in the place of business or university where educated. Permanent Boundary Commissioners set up to report every three to seven years.

1958    Redistribution of Seats Act modifies rules governing Boundary Commissioners and requests reports every 10–15 years.

1969    Representation of the People Act reduces minimum age of voting from 21 to 18 years.

1973    Proportional Representation introduced into Northern Ireland for the Northern Irish Assembly.

1979    Euro-constituencies created for direct elections to European parliament.

1985    Representation of the People Act raises the deposit required of candidates from £150 (since it was first introduced in 1918) to £500, mainly to deter 'joke' candidates. The Act also introduced the concept of overseas voting by opening the franchise (for parliamentary and European elections) to British citizens who had lived abroad for up to five years and intended to return to the United Kingdom. That enfranchised an estimated 500,000 ex-patriates.

1989    Representation of the People Act facilitates the 'ex-patriate' vote by offering a proxy vote to any British citizen who has left in the last 20 years, to be cast in the constituency in which they were last registered.

# Elections and party politics

## General Elections, 1832–1992

Prior to 1832, the computation of election results is complicated by the vagueness of party lines, the number of uncontested elections and the presence of 'independent' candidates. All of these factors continued to operate to a greater or lesser degree after 1832, but the Reform Act of 1832 has generally been taken as the point from which an overall assessment of election results can be made in two-party terms. It should be noted, however, that the terms 'Conservative' (Tory) and 'Liberal' (Whig) represented for much of the nineteenth century only imprecise descriptions of political allegiance and cannot be regarded in the same way as the more definitive party labels of the twentieth century. For the complexity of political and party allegiance in the aftermath of the 1832 Reform Act, see N. Gash, *Reaction and Reconstruction in English Politics, 1832–52*, Oxford, Clarendon Press, 1965. The fullest reference source for election results in this period is F. W. S. Craig, *British Parliamentary Election Results, Volume 1 : 1832–1885*, London, Macmillan, 1977.

1832      The election followed the extension of the franchise by the 1832 Reform Act.

|                        | Seats |
| ---------------------- | ----- |
| Conservatives (*Tories*) | 175   |
| Liberals (*Whigs*)     | 483   |
| Total                  | 658   |

1835      Melbourne refused to serve as prime minister without Lord Althorp (who in Nov. 1834 was elevated to the House of Lords as 3rd Earl Spencer) to lead in the Commons. His only alternative suggestion to Althorp was Lord John Russell, whom the King would not accept. Consequently, Melbourne offered his resignation and William IV accepted it. Peel took office with a minority government. Eager to consolidate his party support and to show Conservative acceptance of the 1832 Reform Act, he decided to go to the country after three defeats in the House on the Irish Tithe Bill.

|  | Seats |
| --- | --- |
| Conservatives | 273 |
| Liberals | 385 |
| Total | 658 |

1837    By law Parliament had to dissolve within six months of the death of the monarch, in this case William IV.

|  | Seats |
| --- | --- |
| Conservatives | 313 |
| Liberals | 345 |
| Total | 658 |

1841    The Whig government, aware it was losing the confidence of the country, decided to go to the polls on what it hoped was a popular platform: vote by ballot and repeal of the Corn Laws.

|  | Seats |
| --- | --- |
| Conservatives | 367 |
| Liberals | 291 |
| Total | 658 |

1847    Peel resigned office following the defeat of an Irish 'coercion' Bill, though a more significant factor in his departure was the opposition of the Tory protectionists to his repeal of the Corn Laws in 1846.

|  | Seats |
| --- | --- |
| Conservatives (*Peelites and Protectionists*) | 324 |
| Liberals | 332 |
| Total | 656 |

1852    Derby's insistence that the Conservative Party adhere to Protection weakened the position of the government. Following a powerful attack by Gladstone on Disraeli's Budget the government was defeated and resigned. Dissolution followed.

|  | Seats |
| --- | --- |
| Conservatives (*including Peelites*) | 330 |
| Liberals | 324 |
| Total | 654 |

1857    Dissolution following the defeat of Palmerston's government on a motion of censure of its Chinese policy.

|  | Seats |
| --- | --- |
| Conservatives | 264 |
| Liberals (*including Peelites*) | 390 |
| Total | 654 |

1859    Palmerston's government, weakened by the appointment of the disreputable Lord Clanricarde to the Cabinet in 1857, was defeated on the Conspiracy to Murder Bill, introduced in consequence of the Orsini bomb attempt on the life of Napoleon III.

|  | Seats |
| --- | --- |
| Conservatives | 297 |
| Liberals | 357 |
| Total | 654 |

1865    Parliament was reaching the end of its seven-year life and many Liberals were anxious for an opportunity to state to the country their opinion on the question of franchise reform. In view of the unlikelihood of Palmerston, an opponent of reform, living the length of another parliament, yet sensing that Palmerston's personality might still prove an electoral asset, it was decided to dissolve.

|               | Seats |
| ------------- | ----- |
| Conservatives | 288   |
| Liberals      | 370   |
| Total         | 658   |

1868   Parliament dissolved following the considerable extension of the franchise by the 1867 Reform Act.

|               | Seats |
| ------------- | ----- |
| Conservatives | 271   |
| Liberals      | 387   |
| Total         | 658   |

1874   After six years of office Gladstone sensed the growing unpopularity of the government in the country, and its increasing weakness in Parliament. This, coupled with internal party difficulties which eventually prompted him secretly to resign the leadership, led him to dissolve on the question of finance, hoping to save the government's position by the popularity of a budget surplus.

|                    | Seats |
| ------------------ | ----- |
| Conservatives      | 342   |
| Liberals           | 251   |
| Irish Nationalists | 59    |
| Total              | 652   |

1880   The Cabinet faced the difficulty of carrying a highly unpopular Water Bill, or dropping it with loss of face. Suddenly by-election results appeared to indicate a movement of public opinion in the Conservatives' favour and Disraeli dissolved Parliament.

|                    | Seats |
| ------------------ | ----- |
| Conservatives      | 238   |
| Liberals           | 353   |
| Irish Nationalists | 61    |
| Total              | 652   |

1885    Despite the passage of the 1884 Reform Bill, the failures of the
        Liberal government at home and abroad, coupled with internal
        party divisions between Whigs, Moderates and Radicals, had
        weakened the administration. The Irish Nationalist MPs,
        annoyed at the attitude of the government towards Irish Home
        Rule, and tempted by the prospect of a Conservative
        government proving more sympathetic on the question, allied
        with the Conservatives to defeat the government on an
        increase in the beer and spirit duties. Gladstone resigned and
        the minority Conservative government which replaced him, as
        'caretaker' government, soon called the dissolution.

|                     | Seats |
| ------------------- | ----- |
| Conservatives       | 249   |
| Liberals            | 335   |
| Irish Nationalists  | 86    |
| Total               | 670   |

1886    The Liberal Party split on the question of Home Rule.
        Gladstone's Home Rule Bill was defeated by a combination of
        Conservatives and Liberal Unionists and a dissolution followed.

|                     | Seats |
| ------------------- | ----- |
| Conservatives       | 317   |
| Liberal Unionists   | 77    |
| Liberals            | 191   |
| Irish Nationalists  | 85    |
| Total               | 670   |

1892    Having fulfilled almost all his legislative commitments during a
        six-year parliament, Salisbury advised the Queen to dissolve
        Parliament. He probably hoped that the timing of the election
        would marginally favour the Unionist forces, and would return
        a Liberal government with only a small majority and a weak
        parliamentary position.

|                    | Seats |
| ------------------ | ----: |
| Conservatives      | 268   |
| Liberal Unionists  | 46    |
| Liberals           | 272   |
| Irish Nationalists | 80    |
| Others             | 4     |
| Total              | 670   |

1895   A weak Liberal government, which had failed to carry many of its major legislative proposals, was defeated, probably willingly, on the Army Estimates and resigned. Lord Salisbury became PM and dissolved in order to gain the parliamentary strength the new Cabinet required.

|                    | Seats |
| ------------------ | ----: |
| Conservatives      | 340   |
| Liberal Unionists  | 71    |
| Liberals           | 177   |
| Irish Nationalists | 82    |
| Total              | 670   |

1900   Knowing the Liberal Party to be divided on the question of the South African War, Salisbury dissolved when the war turned in Britain's favour, thus taking advantage of the extreme patriotism it had engendered.

|                    | Seats | Total vote | % share of total vote |
| ------------------ | ----: | ---------: | --------------------: |
| Conservatives      | 334   | 1 797 444  | 51.1                  |
| Liberal Unionists  | 68    |            |                       |
| Liberals           | 184   | 1 568 141  | 44.6                  |
| Irish Nationalists | 82    | 90 076     | 2.5                   |
| Labour             | 2     | 63 304     | 1.8                   |
| Others             | 0     | 544        | 0.0                   |
| Total              | 670   | 3 519 509  | 100.0                 |

1906    In 1905, with his party hopelessly divided on the tariff
        question, Balfour decided to resign. He hoped that the
        Liberals might split on the questions of Home Rule and the
        composition of a Liberal Cabinet, but Campbell-Bannerman
        succeeded in holding the party leadership and keeping his
        party together, and lost no time in going to the country to
        exploit the unpopularity and divisions of the Conservatives.

| | Seats | Total vote | % share of total vote |
|---|---|---|---|
| Conservatives (*Free Trade and Tariff Reform*) | 133 | 2 451 454 | 43.6 |
| Liberal Unionists (*Free Trade and Tariff Reform*) | 24 | | |
| Liberals | 400 | 2 757 883 | 49.0 |
| Irish Nationalists | 83 | 35 031 | 0.6 |
| Labour | 30 | 329 748 | 5.9 |
| Others | 0 | 52 387 | 0.9 |
| Total | 670 | 5 626 503 | 100.0 |

1910    Jan. The House of Lords having rejected Lloyd George's 1909
        'People's Budget', the government turned to the electorate for
        a mandate to force the Budget through the Lords.

| | Seats | Total vote | % share of total vote |
|---|---|---|---|
| Conservatives | 241 | 3 127 887 | 46.9 |
| Liberal Unionists | 32 | | |
| Liberals | 275 | 2 880 581 | 43.2 |
| Irish Nationalists | 82 | 124 586 | 1.9 |
| Labour | 40 | 505 657 | 7.6 |
| Others | 0 | 28 693 | 0.4 |
| Total | 670 | 6 667 404 | 100.0 |

1910    Dec. Having failed to reach a compromise with the Unionists on the question of reform of the House of Lords, and under pressure from his Irish Nationalist and Labour allies to carry out its reform, Asquith sought a clear mandate from the electorate for reform. Given such a mandate, he had the King's assurance that enough new peers would be created to pass a Reform Bill.

| | Seats | Total vote | % share of total vote |
|---|---|---|---|
| Conservatives | 237 ⎫ | 2 420 566 | 46.3 |
| Liberal Unionists | 35 ⎬ | | |
| Liberals | 272 | 2 295 888 | 43.9 |
| Irish Nationalists | 84 | 131 375 | 2.5 |
| Labour | 42 | 371 772 | 7.1 |
| Others | 0 | 8 768 | 0.2 |
| Total | 670 | 5 228 369 | 100.0 |

1918    Parliament had sat beyond its legal term due to the First World War. Lloyd George had made an electoral pact with the Conservative Party, and both wings of the wartime Coalition government were eager to exploit the popularity victory gave them.

| | Seats | Total vote | % share of total vote |
|---|---|---|---|
| Coalition Unionists | 335 | 3 504 198 | 32.6 |
| Coalition Liberals | 133 | 1 455 640 | 13.5 |
| Coalition Labour | 10 | 161 521 | 1.5 |
| (Coalition) | (478) | (5 121 359) | (47.6) |
| Conservatives | 23 | 370 375 | 3.4 |
| Irish Unionists | 25 | 292 722 | 2.7 |
| Liberals | 28 | 1 298 808 | 12.1 |
| Labour | 63 | 2 385 472 | 22.2 |
| Irish Nationalists | 7 | 238 477 | 2.2 |
| Sinn Fein | 73 | 486 867 | 4.5 |
| Independent and others | 10 | 572 503 | 5.3 |
| Total | 707 | 10 766 583 | 100.0 |

1922     The growing unpopularity of coalition with Lloyd George among the Conservative MPs and rank and file led to a split in the party, the majority of Conservatives refusing to continue the coalition for another election. Lloyd George therefore resigned office, and Bonar Law, the new PM and leader of the anti-coalition Conservatives, dissolved Parliament to consolidate a parliamentary base for his government.

|  | Seats | Total vote | % share of total vote |
|---|---|---|---|
| Conservatives | 345 | 5 500 382 | 38.2 |
| National Liberals | 62 | 1 673 240 | 11.6 |
| Liberals | 54 | 2 516 287 | 17.5 |
| Labour | 142 | 4 241 383 | 29.5 |
| Others | 12 | 462 340 | 3.2 |
| Total | 615 | 14 393 632 | 100.0 |

1923     Bonar Law had pledged that his government would not raise the issue of tariff reform during the life of the 1922 parliament. Possibly because he thought Lloyd George was about to take up a protectionist policy, Law's successor Baldwin spoke in favour of tariff reform in October. This indicated that an election was likely, but the reasons for calling it so quickly (Dec.) are not clear. Possibly it was to forestall a prolonged campaign by the opposition in favour of free trade.

|  | Seats | Total vote | % share of total vote |
|---|---|---|---|
| Conservatives | 258 | 5 538 824 | 38.1 |
| Liberals | 159 | 4 311 147 | 29.6 |
| Labour | 191 | 4 438 508 | 30.5 |
| Others | 7 | 260 042 | 1.8 |
| Total | 615 | 14 548 521 | 100.0 |

1924     The Liberals refused to support the minority Labour government over the Campbell case – an allegation that for political reasons a prosecution for incitement to mutiny had been withdrawn. After defeat in the House of Commons, MacDonald sought a dissolution.

|  | Seats | Total vote | % share of total vote |
|---|---|---|---|
| Conservatives | 419 | 8 039 598 | 48.3 |
| Liberals | 40 | 2 928 747 | 17.6 |
| Labour | 151 | 5 489 077 | 33.0 |
| Others | 5 | 181 857 | 1.1 |
| Total | 615 | 16 639 279 | 100.0 |

1929    Parliament was nearing the end of its (five-year) legal term. With by-elections going against the government Baldwin dissolved, seeking to save the position (before it deteriorated further) by fighting on the government's record and its 'safety first' approach.

|  | Seats | Total vote | % share of total vote |
|---|---|---|---|
| Conservatives | 260 | 8 656 473 | 38.2 |
| Liberals | 59 | 5 308 510 | 23.4 |
| Labour | 288 | 8 389 512 | 37.1 |
| Others | 8 | 293 880 | 1.3 |
| Total | 615 | 22 648 375 | 100.0 |

1931    The Labour Cabinet split on the question of reduction of unemployment benefits. Ramsay MacDonald formed a coalition or National Government of Conservatives, Liberals and those Labour ministers who would serve. The new government dissolved quickly, partly to gain a mandate to administer the country, partly to exploit the difficulties of the weakened Labour opposition.

|  | Seats | Total vote | % share of total vote |
|---|---|---|---|
| Conservatives | 473 | 11 978 745 | 55.2 |
| National Labour | 13 | 341 370 | 1.6 |
| Liberal Nationals | 35 | 809 302 | 3.7 |
| Liberals | 33 | 1 403 102 | 6.5 |
| (National Government) | (554) | (14 532 519) | (67.0) |
| Independent Liberals | 4 | 106 106 | 0.5 |

(cont.)

(*cont.*)

| | Seats | Total vote | % share of total vote |
|---|---|---|---|
| Labour | 52 | 6 649 630 | 30.6 |
| Others | 5 | 656 373 | 1.9 |
| Total | 615 | 21 944 628 | 100.0 |

**1935**    Following the resignation of MacDonald and the reorganization of the National Government in June, an election was predictable. Parliament was already four years old. The international tension between Italy and Abyssinia persuaded Baldwin that the time was opportune for dissolution and a campaign on the need for rearmament and collective security, thus 'stealing the clothes' of the Liberal and Labour parties.

| | Seats | Total vote | % share of total vote |
|---|---|---|---|
| Conservatives (*including National Labour and Liberal Nationals*) | 432 | 11 810 158 | 53.7 |
| Liberals | 21 | 1 422 116 | 6.4 |
| Labour | 154 | 8 325 491 | 37.9 |
| Others | 8 | 439 289 | 2.0 |
| Total | 615 | 21 997 054 | 100.0 |

**1945**    Parliament having been extended because of the war, Churchill wished to continue the coalition until the defeat of Japan. But with the defeat of Germany the Labour Party wished to dissolve the coalition and hold an election in the autumn. Churchill decided that the government could not function efficiently with the prospect of an election hanging over it. He ended the coalition and formed a 'caretaker' government which supervised the election.

| | Seats | Total vote | % share of total vote |
|---|---|---|---|
| Conservatives | 213 | 9 988 306 | 39.8 |
| Liberals | 12 | 2 248 226 | 9.0 |
| Labour | 393 | 11 995 152 | 47.8 |
| Others | 22 | 854 294 | 2.8 |
| Total | 640 | 25 085 978 | 100.0 |

1950    Their term of office coming to an end, and having carried much important legislation, Labour decided to go to the country.

|  | Seats | Total vote | % share of total vote |
|---|---|---|---|
| Conservatives | 298 | 12 502 567 | 43.5 |
| Liberals | 9 | 2 621 548 | 9.1 |
| Labour | 315 | 13 266 592 | 46.1 |
| Others | 3 | 381 964 | 1.3 |
| Total | 625 | 28 772 671 | 100.0 |

1951    With a narrow Commons majority constantly harassed by the opposition, and the government's impetus spent, Attlee decided that to postpone an election would only lead to further deterioration in the government's position.

|  | Seats | Total vote | % share of total vote |
|---|---|---|---|
| Conservatives | 321 | 13 717 538 | 48.0 |
| Liberals | 6 | 730 556 | 2.5 |
| Labour | 295 | 13 948 605 | 48.8 |
| Others | 3 | 198 969 | 0.7 |
| Total | 625 | 28 595 668 | 100.0 |

1955    Churchill's retirement from the premiership obviously meant a change of party leadership. Eden, the new PM, with the advantage of a rising standard of living and splits in the Labour Party, decided to dissolve after Butler's Budget had reduced income tax by 6d. in the pound.

|  | Seats | Total vote | % share of total vote |
|---|---|---|---|
| Conservatives | 344 | 13 286 569 | 49.7 |
| Liberals | 6 | 722 405 | 2.7 |
| Labour | 277 | 12 404 970 | 46.4 |
| Others | 3 | 346 554 | 1.2 |
| Total | 630 | 26 760 498 | 100.0 |

1959     Improvement in opinion polls and the economy, plus an easing of foreign problems and a recovery of party morale, persuaded Macmillan to take the opportunity to dissolve.

|  | Seats | Total vote | % share of total vote |
|---|---|---|---|
| Conservatives | 365 | 13 749 830 | 49.4 |
| Liberals | 6 | 1 638 571 | 5.9 |
| Labour | 258 | 12 215 538 | 43.8 |
| Others | 1 | 255 302 | 0.9 |
| Total | 630 | 27 859 241 | 100.0 |

1964     With Parliament nearing the end of its statutory life, Sir Alec Douglas-Home delayed dissolution for as long as possible in the hope of economic improvement and to let the party recover from the divisions resulting from a change of leadership.

|  | Seats | Total vote | % share of total vote |
|---|---|---|---|
| Conservatives | 304 | 12 001 396 | 43.4 |
| Liberals | 9 | 3 092 878 | 11.2 |
| Labour | 317 | 12 205 814 | 44.1 |
| Others | 0 | 348 914 | 1.3 |
| Total | 630 | 27 649 002 | 100.0 |

1966     Having only a precarious parliamentary majority, Wilson and his party decided to take the opportunity of an upswing in popularity, reflected in the Hull North by-election, to dissolve and improve their position.

|  | Seats | Total vote | % share of total vote |
|---|---|---|---|
| Conservatives | 253 | 11 418 433 | 41.9 |
| Liberals | 12 | 2 327 533 | 8.5 |
| Labour | 363 | 13 064 951 | 47.9 |
| Others | 2 | 452 689 | 1.7 |
| Total | 630 | 27 263 606 | 100.0 |

1970     From opinion polls and by-election trends Wilson believed he detected a ground swell of support for Labour and dissolved.

|  | Seats | Total vote | % share of total vote |
|---|---|---|---|
| Conservatives | 330 | 13 145 123 | 46.4 |
| Labour | 287 | 12 179 341 | 43.0 |
| Liberals | 6 | 2 117 035 | 7.5 |
| Others | 7 | 903 299 | 3.1 |
| Total | 630 | 28 344 798 | 100.0 |

1974     Feb. The confrontation between the miners and the Heath government, combined with the three-day week, led Heath to dissolve in order to seek a fresh mandate for his policy.

|  | Seats | Total vote | % share of total vote |
|---|---|---|---|
| Conservatives | 297 | 11 868 906 | 37.9 |
| Labour | 301 | 11 639 243 | 37.1 |
| Liberals | 14 | 6 063 470 | 19.3 |
| Others (Northern Ireland) | 12 | 717 986 | 2.3 |
| Scottish National Party | 7 | 632 032 | 2.0 |
| Plaid Cymru | 2 | 171 364 | 0.6 |
| Others | 2 | 260 665 | 0.8 |
| Total | 635 | 31 353 666 | 100.0 |

1974     Oct. Having made numerous policy statements during the summer, the Labour government decided that the opinion polls signified a Labour victory and dissolved the shortest parliament of the century. This, it was hoped, would gain a new mandate for the numerically weak government.

|  | Seats | Total vote | % share of total vote |
|---|---|---|---|
| Conservatives | 277 | 10 464 817 | 35.8 |
| Labour | 319 | 11 457 079 | 39.2 |
| ( cont.) | | | |

(*cont.*)

| | | | |
|---|---|---|---|
| Liberals | 13 | 5 346 754 | 18.3 |
| Others (Northern Ireland) | 12 | 702 094 | 2.4 |
| Scottish Nationalists | 11 | 839 617 | 2.9 |
| Plaid Cymru | 3 | 166 321 | 0.6 |
| Others | | 212 496 | 0.8 |
| Total | 635 | 29 189 178 | 100.0 |

1979    A minority Labour government, towards the end of its term of office, was defeated on a vote of confidence.

| | Seats | Total vote | % share of total vote |
|---|---|---|---|
| Conservatives | 339 | 13 697 690 | 43.9 |
| Labour | 269 | 11 532 148 | 36.9 |
| Liberals | 11 | 4 313 811 | 13.8 |
| Others (Northern Ireland) | 12 | 695 889 | 2.2 |
| Scottish Nationalists | 2 | 504 259 | 1.6 |
| Plaid Cymru | 2 | 132 544 | 0.4 |
| Others | 0 | 343 674 | 1.2 |
| Total | 635 | 31 220 015 | 100.0 |

1983    With a commanding lead in the opinion polls following the Falklands War of 1982, Mrs Thatcher waited for confirmation of the government's popularity in the municipal election results in May before calling a snap poll on 9 June.

| | Seats | Total vote | % share of total vote |
|---|---|---|---|
| Conservatives | 397 | 13 012 592 | 42.4 |
| Labour | 209 | 8 457 118 | 27.6 |
| Liberal/SDP | 23 | 7 780 589 | 25.4 |
| Plaid Cymru | 2 | 125 309 | 0.4 |
| Scottish Nationalists | 2 | 331 975 | 1.1 |
| Others (Northern Ireland) | 17 | 764 925 | 2.6 |
| Others | 0 | 198 387 | 0.5 |
| Total | 650 | 30 670 895 | 100.0 |

1987    Speculation about the date of the general election grew during the early months of 1987, the government benefiting from a number of favourable economic indicators which allowed it to introduce tax concessions in the Budget while remaining within its financial strategy. Favourable local election results led to the announcement of polling day as 11 June.

| | Seats | Total vote | % share of total vote |
|---|---|---|---|
| Conservatives | 375 | 13 763 747 | 42.2 |
| Labour | 229 | 10 029 270 | 30.8 |
| Liberal/SDP | 22 | 7 341 275 | 22.6 |
| Plaid Cymru | 3 | 123 589 | 0.3 |
| Scottish Nationalists | 3 | 416 873 | 1.4 |
| Others (Northern Ireland) | 17 | 730 152 | 2.3 |
| Others | 1* | 151 517 | 0.4 |
| Total | 650 | 32 556 423 | 100.0 |

*The Speaker

1992    John Major, who had succeeded Margaret Thatcher in Nov. 1990, delayed the election until 9 Apr. 1992. Opinion polls still pointed to the likelihood of a Conservative defeat but were proved mistaken by an apparent late swing to the Conservatives from Liberals cautious of 'letting in' a Labour government.

| | Seats | Total vote | % share of total vote |
|---|---|---|---|
| Conservatives | 336 | 14 092 891 | 41.9 |
| Labour | 271 | 11 559 735 | 34.4 |
| Liberal Democrat | 20 | 5 999 384 | 17.8 |
| Scottish Nationalists | 3 | 629 552 | 1.9 |
| Plaid Cymru | 4 | 154 439 | 0.5 |
| Others | 17 | 1 176 692 | 3.5 |
| Total | 651 | 33 612 693 | 100.0 |

# Famous by-elections, 1918–95

| Constituency | Date | Significance |
| --- | --- | --- |
| Newport | 18 Oct. 1922 | Conservative gain from Coalition Liberal; heralded downfall of Lloyd George coalition. |
| St George's Westminster | 19 Mar. 1931 | Conservative beats off Empire Crusade challenge. |
| East Fulham | 25 Oct. 1933 | Labour gain from Conservative; the 'pacifist' question. |
| Oxford | 27 Oct. 1938 | Conservative hold from Independent Progressive. An 'appeasement' by-election. |
| Bridgewater | 17 Nov. 1938 | Independent Progressive gains seat from Conservative. |
| Grantham | 25 Mar. 1942 | Independent defeats Conservative; first of series of wartime defeats of government candidates (e.g. Maldon, 25 June 1942, won by Tom Driberg). |
| Eddisbury | 7 Apr. 1943 | First victory by Common Wealth at by-election; further victories at Skipton and Chelmsford. |
| Motherwell | 12 Apr. 1945 | First ever by-election victory by Scottish Nationalists; seat gained from Labour. |
| Torrington | 27 Mar. 1958 | First Liberal victory at a by-election since 1929. |
| Orpington | 14 Mar. 1962 | The most sensational Liberal victory of the 1960s. The party swept to victory in a safe Tory seat. |
| Leyton | 21 Jan. 1965 | Defeat of Labour's Foreign Secretary Patrick Gordon Walker in a normally safe East London Labour stronghold. |
| Roxburgh, Selkirk and Peebles | 24 Mar. 1965 | David Steel won a safe Conservative seat to become the 'baby of the House' and eventual Liberal Party leader. |
| Carmarthen | 14 July 1966 | The first – and so far the only – Welsh Nationalist to win a seat in a by-election. |

## Famous by-elections 1918–95 (*cont*)

| Constituency | Date | Significance |
| --- | --- | --- |
| Hamilton | 2 Nov. 1967 | The first SNP by-election victory since the party won Motherwell in a wartime by-election in April 1945. Hamilton heralded the revival of the SNP. |
| Dudley | 28 Mar. 1968 | The by-election which saw the largest swing ever recorded to the Conservatives during the 1966–70 Wilson government. |
| Rochdale | 26 Oct. 1972 | First of the famous series of Liberal by-election victories of 1972–73. |
| Sutton and Cheam | 7 Dec. 1972 | A sensational Liberal victory in one of the safest Tory areas – the London suburbs. |
| Lincoln | 1 Mar. 1973 | Dick Taverne won a personal triumph as a Democratic Labour candidate having previously been the town's Labour MP. |
| Glasgow Govan | 8 Nov. 1973 | The first SNP by-election victory since Hamilton in 1967. |
| Walsall North | 4 Nov. 1976 | The safe Labour stronghold formerly held by John Stonehouse fell on a swing of 22.6 per cent to the Conservatives – the largest swing of the 1974–79 Parliament to a Conservative. |
| Liverpool Edge Hill | 29 Mar. 1979 | A sweeping Liberal victory by 8,133 votes in a hitherto safe Labour seat. The 32 per cent swing to the Liberals was the highest in postwar politics. |
| Warrington | 16 July 1981 | First major SDP by-election assault, led by Roy Jenkins, narrowly fails. |
| Crosby | 26 Nov. 1981 | Sensational SDP victory by Shirley Williams in normally safe Conservative seat. |
| Glasgow Hillhead | 25 Mar. 1982 | Roy Jenkins victorious for SDP. |

## Famous by-elections 1918–95 ( *cont* )

| Constituency | Date | Significance |
| --- | --- | --- |
| Ryedale | 8 May 1986 | Most spectacular Alliance gain from Conservatives of 1983–87 period. |
| Greenwich | 26 Feb. 1987 | Rosie Barnes secures first-ever SDP by-election gain from Labour. |
| Glasgow Govan | 19 Nov. 1988 | Swing of 33.2 per cent to SNP in sensational defeat for Labour. |
| Vale of Glamorgan | 4 May 1989 | Labour gain victory on a swing of 12.4 per cent, the largest swing in a seat *gained* by Labour since Liverpool West Toxteth in July 1935; seat gained from Conservatives. |
| Mid-Staffordshire | 22 Mar. 1990 | Labour increases its vote by 24.3 per cent, its best ever result in a postwar by-election; seat gained from Conservatives. |
| Eastbourne | 18 Oct. 1990 | First by-election victory for the newly formed Liberal Democrats on a swing of 20.1 per cent; seat gained from Conservatives. |
| Ribble Valley | 7 Mar. 1991 | The Liberal Democrats take an ultra-safe Conservative seat on a 24.8 per cent swing in what was seen as a verdict on the poll tax. |
| Newbury | 6 May 1993 | A sweeping Liberal Democrat victory, on a swing to them of 29 per cent from the Conservatives, in the first by-election since the 1992 general election. |
| Christchurch | 29 July 1993 | Following on from Newbury, the Liberal Democrats took this Conservative stronghold on the biggest swing in a by-election in the twentieth century (35.8 per cent). |
| Eastleigh | 9 June 1994 | The third successive Conservative seat to fall to the Liberal Democrats (on a swing of 21.4 per cent). Labour came second, the Conservatives third with 24.7 per cent of the vote. |

Famous by-elections 1918–95 (*cont*)

| Constituency | Date | Significance |
|---|---|---|
| Dudley West | 15 Dec. 1994 | Massive 29 per cent swing from Conservative to Labour as Labour sweep to victory. |
| Perth and Kinross | 25 May 1995 | SNP gains first-ever by-election victory from Conservatives, who finish third in a traditional stronghold. |

## European elections

The first direct elections to the 410-member European Parliament took place in June 1979. In Great Britain the result was as follows:

| Party | Votes | Votes (%) | Seats |
|---|---|---|---|
| Conservative | 6 504 481 | 50.6 | 60 |
| Labour | 4 253 210 | 33.0 | 17 |
| Liberal | 1 690 600 | 13.1 | – |
| Others | 421 553 | 3.3 | 1 (SNP) |
| Total | 12 869 844 | 100.0 | 78 |

In Northern Ireland, where proportional representation was used, three MEPs were elected.

The second direct elections to the European Parliament took place in June 1984. Although Labour improved considerably on its poor performance in 1979, the Liberal/SDP Alliance failed to secure any representation. The result was as follows:

| Party | Votes | Votes (%) | Seats |
|---|---|---|---|
| Conservative | 5 426 866 | 40.8 | 45 |
| Labour | 4 865 224 | 36.5 | 32 |
| Liberal/SDP Alliance | 2 591 659 | 19.5 | – |
| Others | 429 149 | 3.2 | 1 (SNP) |
| Total | 13 312 898 | 100.0 | 78 |

Northern Ireland again returned three MEPs by proportional representation.

The third direct elections to the European Parliament took place in June 1989. Labour achieved an impressive result, taking 45 seats, compared to the Conservatives on 32. The Liberal Democrats not only failed to win a seat, but also were humiliated by an upsurge in Green Party support. The Scottish Nationalists again returned a single MEP.

| Party | Votes | Votes (%) | Seats |
|---|---|---|---|
| Conservative | 5 331 077 | 34.6 | 32 |
| Labour | 6 153 640 | 40.0 | 45 |
| Liberal Democrats | 986 292 | 6.4 | – |
| SNP | 406 686 | 2.7 | 1 |
| Plaid Cymru | 115 062 | 0.8 | – |
| Others* | 2 409 886 | 15.5 | – |
| Total | 15 402 643 | 100.0 | 78 |

*Including 2 292 705 for the Green Party.

Northern Ireland again returned three MEPs by proportional representation.

The fourth direct elections to the enlarged European Parliament took place in June 1994. The Conservatives, at their lowest ebb in the opinion polls, suffered heavy losses to Labour, but the Liberal Democrats failed to sweep the south, taking only two seats in the south-west. The Scottish Nationalists polled well north of the border, finishing with two seats and 32.6 per cent of the total Scottish poll.

| Party | Votes | Votes (%) | Seats |
|---|---|---|---|
| Conservative | 4 268 531 | 27.9 | 18 |
| Labour | 6 753 863 | 44.2 | 62 |
| Liberal Democrat | 2 552 730 | 16.7 | 2 |
| SNP | 487 239 | 3.2 | 2 |
| Plaid Cymru | 162 478 | 1.1 | – |
| Others | 1 062 709 | 6.9 | – |
| Total | 15 287 550 | 100.0 | 84 |

Northern Ireland again returned three MEPs by proportional representation.

## Conservative Party

The origins of the Conservative Party have been variously traced to the seventeenth century, the era of party strife under Queen Anne, and the administration of Pitt the Younger. Other historians have preferred to date the decisive emergence of the Conservative Party from the resignation of Peel in 1846 or even from the Second Reform Act of 1867. Certainly the evolution of the Conservative Party represented no sharp break either in ideas or institutions with the older Tory Party. According to one authority the term 'Conservative Party' was first used in its modern political sense in an article in the *Quarterly Review* in Jan. 1830 (R. Blake, *The Conservative Party from Peel to Churchill*, Eyre and Spottiswoode, London, 1970, pp. 6–7) and the use of the term 'Conservative' by individuals has been recorded earlier. By 1832 the phrase 'Conservative Party' was in common use by politicians and journalists to describe the personalities, ideas and institutions previously referred to as Tory, though the latter remained in use.

1832    One hundred and seventy-five Conservative MPs returned at general election; Carlton Club founded.

1834    Peel forms Cabinet and is thus recognized as party leader. Publication of Peel's 'Tamworth Manifesto', identifying the Conservative Party as a party of moderate reform and attempting to extend the social composition of support for the party to the middle classes.

1834–5    Appearance of Conservative and Constitutional Associations.

1835    Peel's government leaves office after defeats on Irish Tithes Bill. Conservatives win 273 seats in general election.

1837    Conservatives win 313 seats and lose general election.

1839    Stanley and his Whig followers join Peel.

1841    Conservatives win general election with a majority of 78 (367 seats). Peel forms his second Cabinet.

1846    Party splits on Peel's repeal of the Corn Laws. Peel retains most of the Cabinet, the Chief Whip Sir J. Young and Bonham, the party's election manager. The 'Protectionists' are led by Lord George Bentinck, supported by Stanley and Disraeli.

1847    A divided Conservative Party wins 324 seats to the Liberals' 332. The party fund is used to support 'Peelite' candidates of whom 89 are elected. Stanley now leads the Protectionist Conservatives in the Lords; Bentinck leads in the Commons.

1848    Death of Bentinck. Leadership of party in the Commons put into commission under a committee of Granby, J. C. Herries and Disraeli, but Disraeli is the effective leader.

1850    Death of Peel.

1852    Lord Derby (Stanley) forms a Cabinet (Feb.). It falls on Disraeli's Budget. In the general election 330 Conservatives are returned, but the Peelites join a coalition government with the Liberals under Aberdeen (Dec.). Sir William Jolliffe made Chief Whip and Philip Rose, Disraeli's solicitor, made principal agent.

1855    Derby refuses to form a government when Aberdeen's ministry falls.

1857    Conservatives win 264 seats in general election.

1858    Derby forms the 'Who? Who?' ministry (Feb.).

1859    Derby resigns office and Palmerston forms a Whig government. M. Spofforth succeeds Rose as principal agent.

1865    Conservatives lose general election (288 seats).

1866    Liberal government defeated on Reform Bill by an alliance of Whigs and Conservatives. Derby forms a government (June).

1867    Disraeli introduces a Reform Bill which considerably extends the franchise. It is passed. Conference of Conservative Working Men's Associations in London (Apr.). Inaugural meeting of the National Union of Conservative and Constitutional Associations (Nov.).

1868    Derby retires and is succeeded by Disraeli who forms a government (Feb.). M. Spofforth forms a Central Board to organize for the election. Conservatives lose the Nov. election (276 seats).

1870    J. E. Gorst succeeds Spofforth as principal agent and sets up a Conservative Central Office.

1871    Gorst and Keith-Falconer become honorary secretaries of the National Union.

1872    Disraeli's Crystal Palace speech at London conference of the National Union links Conservative Party with the Empire and claims the working class should support both.

1874    Conservatives win 350 seats and Disraeli forms a Cabinet. Gorst's engagement as party agent ends.

1877    W. B. Skene becomes principal Conservative agent. Gorst ceases to be secretary of National Union.

1880    Conservatives lose general election, winning only 236 seats. Skene resigns. Central Committee set up under chairmanship of W. H. Smith to enquire into state of party organization. Gorst resumes position as principal agent (July). Rowland Winn becomes Chief Whip. Fourth Party ginger group of Lord

Randolph Churchill, J. E. Gorst, A. J. Balfour and H. Drummond-Wolff emerges.

1881    Lord Beaconsfield (Disraeli) dies. Party is now led by Lord Salisbury in the Lords and Sir H. Stafford-Northcote in the Commons – a dual leadership.

1882    E. Stanhope becomes chairman of the Central Committee – Gorst resigns as principal agent.

1883    G. C. T. Bartley becomes principal agent. Lord Randolph Churchill attacks party leaders at a National Union Conference. Primrose League founded by Churchill and Drummond-Wolff.

1884    Split in party organization. National Union threatened with eviction from Conservative Central Office premises. July quarrel between Churchill and leaders resolved. Hicks-Beach elected chairman of National Union Council. Central Committee abolished. Primrose League officially recognized.

1885    Lord Salisbury invited to form a Cabinet. Is thus recognized as party leader. Conservatives win 249 seats in general election (a defeat). Captain R. W. E. Middleton becomes Principal Agent (the first time the title is used officially) and Akers-Douglas becomes Chief Whip.

1886    Salisbury's minority government falls on Jesse Colling's 'three acres and a cow' amendment to the Address. Liberal Party splits on Home Rule. Conservatives and Liberal Unionists ally to defeat Home Rule Bill. Conservatives win election (317 seats). Salisbury PM, Churchill leader in Commons. In December Churchill resigns and a Liberal Unionist, Goschen, joins Cabinet as Chancellor of the Exchequer. W. H. Smith becomes Leader of the House.

1891    Smith dies, and A. J. Balfour becomes Leader of the House.

1892    Conservatives lose general election (268 seats).

1895    Conservatives win election (341 seats). Salisbury forms a government composed of Conservatives and Liberal Unionists.

1900    Conservatives win 'Khaki' election (334 seats). Salisbury forms another joint Conservative–Liberal Unionist government. Sir W. H. Walrond becomes Chief Whip.

1902    Salisbury retires and Balfour becomes PM. Liberal Unionist Duke of Devonshire leads in the Lords. A. Acland Hood is Chief Whip.

1903    Party splits on 'Tariff Reform' into Balfourites, Chamberlainites and Free Traders. Major Cabinet reconstruction. Lord

Lansdowne (a Liberal Unionist) leads the 'Unionists' in the Lords. Middleton retires as Principal Agent and is succeeded by L. Wells.

1905    Balfour resigns as Prime Minister.

1906    Conservatives defeated in general election, Unionist forces winning only 157 seats. Reorganization of party to give more strength to the regions is started. Percival Hughes succeeds A. Haig (appointed 1905) as Principal Agent.

1910    Party loses two general elections. Wins 273 seats in Jan., 272 in Dec.

1911    Party again reorganized. Acland-Hood resigns as Chief Whip and is replaced by Balcarres. New office of Chairman of the Party Organization is given to A. Steel-Maitland. Balfour resigns. Austen Chamberlain (a Liberal Unionist) and Walter Long enter leadership election, but withdraw in favour of Bonar Law. Lansdowne still leads in the Lords.

1912    Formal amalgamation of Conservative and Liberal Unionist parties. J. Boraston becomes Principal Agent.

1915    Conservatives enter wartime coalition Cabinet. Eight Conservatives given posts; Bonar Law becomes Colonial Secretary.

1916    Conservatives withdraw support for Asquith and Lloyd George succeeds him as PM. Bonar Law becomes Chancellor of the Exchequer.

1918    'Coupon election' in which Conservatives have an electoral pact with Lloyd George Liberals. Three hundred and thirty-five 'Coalition Unionists', and 23 other Conservatives are returned to support Lloyd George government.

1921    Law retires due to ill health. Austen Chamberlain elected leader at the Carlton Club.

1922    Party meeting at the Carlton declares against fighting another election alongside Lloyd George. Bonar Law returns and is given the title 'Leader of the Conservative and Unionist Party', the first time the Commons leader is officially recognized as leader of the whole party while in opposition. Party splits, Chamberlain, F. E. Smith and others adhering to Lloyd George. Conservatives win election (345 seats).

1923    Law retires and dies. Contest for premiership between Baldwin and Curzon. King appoints Baldwin. Baldwin calls an election on the tariff issue; Conservatives lose (258 seats).

1924    Conservatives win general election (419 seats). Party reunited and W. Churchill finally leaves Liberals to become Chancellor of the Exchequer.

1929    J. C. C. Davidson founds Research Department. Party loses general election (260 seats).

1931    Conservatives join the National Government. Four Conservative ministers serve in MacDonald's Cabinet, with Baldwin as the Lord President of the Council. Conservatives win 473 seats in general election and dominate the National Government. R. Topping becomes first General Director.

1935    Baldwin becomes PM when MacDonald resigns. Tacit electoral agreement with Simonite National Liberals. At general election 432 Conservatives are returned.

1937    Baldwin retires and the King invites Neville Chamberlain to form a government.

1938    Eden, the Foreign Secretary, resigns in protest against the government's policy of appeasement

1940    Neville Chamberlain resigns as Prime Minister due to dissatisfaction of Conservative back-benchers with his handling of the war, and Labour's refusal to serve under him in a coalition (May). Halifax renounces his claim to leadership and allows Churchill to become PM of coalition government; party leader from Oct. 1940.

1945    Victory in Europe leads to break-up of the coalition and a general election. Conservatives lose (213 seats). R. A. Butler becomes chairman of the Research Department. Formation of the Conservative Political Centre. Assheton, chairman of Party Organization, organizes Parliamentary Secretariat.

1946    Woolton becomes chairman of Party Organization.

1947    Woolton–Teviot agreement provides for union of Conservative and Liberal National parties at the constituency level, and the adoption of candidates who might be recommended by either headquarters.

1948    Maxwell Fyfe Committee Report is adopted by annual conference. Its proposals are aimed at democratizing the process of selection of candidates and securing more efficient party funding.

1950    Conservatives lose general election, but reduce Labour's majority (298 seats).

1951    Conservatives win general election (321 seats).

1955    Churchill retires as PM. Eden succeeds him. Conservatives win general election (344 seats).

1956    Suez crisis.

1957    Eden retires due to ill health. The Queen, following advice from senior Conservatives, chooses Harold Macmillan rather than R. A. Butler as his successor.

1958    Peter Thorneycroft resigns as Chancellor of the Exchequer and Enoch Powell as Financial Secretary to the Treasury: a 'little local difficulty'.

1959    Conservatives win general election (365 seats).

1963    Macmillan retires due to ill health. Sir Alec Douglas-Home emerges as leader, despite the challenge of R. A. Butler, Q. Hogg and R. Maudling. Macleod and Powell refuse to serve in government.

1964    Conservatives lose general election (304 seats).

1965    Under some pressure from the party, Home resigns. Edward Heath becomes the party's first elected leader, defeating Maudling and Powell in the ballot. *Putting Britain Right Ahead* is published and is basis of the Conservative election manifesto.

1966    Conservatives lose general election (257 seats).

1967    Conservatives win GLC elections.

1968    Powell raises the immigration issue in 'rivers of blood' speech and Heath dismisses him from the shadow cabinet.

1969    GLC Young Conservatives publish *Set the Party Free*, urging greater party democracy.

1970    Selsdon Park meeting of shadow cabinet. Manifesto published: *A Better Tomorrow*. Conservatives win general election (330 seats). Heath becomes PM.

1974    Three-day week. Conservatives win 296 seats in Feb. general election and Wilson forms government. Conservatives lose Oct. election (277 seats). Lord Home's Rules Committee rejects National Union Executive recommendation for an electoral college of area chairmen to select leader.

1975    Heath under pressure from the party stands for re-election. In ballot for party leadership Margaret Thatcher defeats Heath in first round, and H. Fraser, W. Whitelaw, J. Prior, G. Howe and J. Peyton in second.

1979    Conservatives win general election (339 seats). M. Thatcher becomes first woman prime minister.

1980    Conservatives win 60 of 78 British seats in first direct elections to the European Parliament.

1981    Major reconstruction of Thatcher Cabinet in response to growing criticism of economic policy, dismissing one of the most prominent 'wets', Sir Ian Gilmour, and switching another, James Prior, from the Department of Employment to the Northern Ireland office. Shirley Williams takes safe Conservative seat at Crosby (Nov.) for the SDP and opinion polls predict an Alliance victory in the next general election.

1982    Both Foreign Secretary, Lord Carrington, and Defence Secretary, John Nott, offer resignations following Argentine invasion of the Falkland Islands, but only the former resigns, although John Nott announces intention to resign at next election.

1983    Michael Heseltine appointed Secretary of State for Defence in January. Mrs Thatcher wins a resounding victory by 144 seats in the general election (June). Cecil Parkinson, party chairman, takes post as Minister for Trade and Industry but forced to resign after personal scandal (Sept.). John Selwyn Gummer becomes party chairman.

1984    James Prior announces his return to the back benches. Bomb at Grand Hotel, Brighton, during Conservative Party conference seriously injures Norman Tebbit and the Chief Whip, John Wakeham, and kills five others.

1985    Norman Tebbit replaces John Gummer as party chairman with Jeffrey Archer as his deputy.

1986    Westland affair leads to the resignation of Michael Heseltine, Defence Secretary, and Leon Brittan, Trade and Industry Secretary.

1987    Mrs Thatcher wins record third term of office in general election in June with 102-seat majority.

1989    Thatcher becomes longest-serving prime minister of the twentieth century.

1990    Fall of Margaret Thatcher. John Major becomes Prime Minister.

1991    Abandonment of poll tax. Government negotiates Maastricht Treaty.

1992    Conservatives win historic fourth successive election victory, overturning the opinion poll predictions (Apr.). John Major follows his victory with Cabinet reshuffle: new appointments include Kenneth Clarke (Home Secretary), Michael Heseltine (Trade and Industry), Malcolm Rifkind (Defence), Virginia Bottomley (Health), John Patten (Education), Michael Portillo (Chief Secretary to the Treasury) and David Mellor (Heritage). Norman Fowler becomes party chairman, following defeat of Chris Patten in general election. The October party conference at Brighton reveals serious divisions over European policy, the ERM and Maastricht. Opposition led by Norman Tebbit. Ground swell of opposition to Major leadership begins.

1993　Year of electoral disasters for Conservatives. Newbury by-election lost to Liberal Democrats on swing of 29 per cent (highest swing since 1972 Sutton and Cheam by-election) (May). Liberal Democrats and Labour make sweeping gains in county council elections, only Buckinghamshire left in Conservative control. In limited Cabinet reshuffle, following dismissal of Chancellor Norman Lamont, Major appoints Kenneth Clarke (Chancellor), Michael Howard (Home Secretary), John Gummer (Environment), David Hunt (Employment) and John Redwood (Welsh Secretary) (27 May).

1994　Heavy defeat for Conservatives in European elections. By-election defeats at Eastleigh (to Liberal Democrats) and Dudley West (to Labour).

1995　Sweeping Conservative losses in council elections (May). Major resigns party leadership (June) followed by victory over John Redwood (218–89) in July leadership contest. Sweeping Cabinet reshuffle: Heseltine Deputy Prime Minister, Rifkind Foreign Secretary, Mawhinney party chairman. Eurosceptics, although rebuffed, remain strong. Defection of Alan Howarth (to Labour) and Emma Nicholson (to Liberal Democrats).

## Liberal Party (since 1988, Liberal Democrats)

As with the term 'Conservative', 'Liberal' only emerged gradually in the nineteenth century to describe one of the major groupings in British politics. The parliamentary Liberal Party was only formed in the late 1850s through a fusion of Whigs, 'Peelites' and radicals, but the term was used earlier to describe the opponents of the Conservatives. Historians have used both the terms 'Liberal' and 'Whig' for the period 1832–67. Thereafter 'Whig' is normally applied to the landed, upper-class element in the Liberal Party.

1832　Liberals win 483 seats. Grey becomes PM.

1834　Grey resigns when Althorp, leader in the Commons, refuses to support the Irish Coercion Bill. Melbourne becomes PM, but resigns when Althorp is elevated to House of Lords.

1835　Liberals win 385 seats and Melbourne forms second Cabinet.

1836　Reform Club founded.

1837    Liberals win general election (345 seats).

1839    Melbourne resigns. Bedchamber crisis and Melbourne returns.

1841    Liberals lose general election (291 seats). Liberal government defeated in Commons and resigns.

1846    Conservative ministry breaks up. Lord John Russell forms a Liberal cabinet.

1847    Liberals win general election (332 seats). Lord John Russell PM.

1852    General election. Liberals win 324 seats. Whigs will no longer endure Russell's leadership and join a coalition with the Peelites under Aberdeen.

1855    Aberdeen government falls over conduct of Crimean War. Palmerston becomes PM when Russell fails to form a government.

1857    Liberals (including Peelites) win 390 seats. Palmerston defeated in a motion of censure on his Chinese policy.

1859    Palmerston's government defeated on Conspiracy to Murder Bill. Palmerston wins general election (357 seats). Willis' Rooms meeting where Whigs, radicals and Peelites agree to serve under Palmerston.

1860    Liberal Registration Association founded.

1865    Liberals win general election (370 seats). Palmerston dies. Russell becomes PM.

1868    Liberals win general election (387 seats). Gladstone becomes PM.

1874    Liberals lose election (251 seats). Gladstone resigns leadership. Liberal Registration Association recognized and becomes known as Liberal Central Association.

1875    Meeting of Liberal MPs elects Hartington leader in the Commons.

1877    Foundation of the National Liberal Federation; first president is Joseph Chamberlain.

1880    Liberals win general election (353 seats). Hartington refuses premiership and advises the Queen to make Gladstone PM, which she does.

1885    Government defeated on spirit duties and Gladstone resigns office. Liberals win general election (335 seats).

1886    Party splits on Home Rule Bill. Liberal Unionists led by Chamberlain and Hartington help Conservatives defeat the Bill. In general election Gladstonian Liberals badly beaten (191 seats). F. Schnadhorst becomes party agent (until 1892).

1887    National Liberal Club opened. Liberal Publication Department founded.

1891    'Newcastle Programme' adopted by conference, advocating extensive social reforms.

1892    Liberals win general election by a narrow majority (272 seats).

1894    Gladstone retires. Rosebery becomes PM. Harcourt leads the party in the Commons.

1895    Liberals lose the general election (177 seats). Rosebery privately refuses to work with Harcourt, and is titular leader only. Harcourt leads the party in the Commons, Kimberley in the Lords.

1896    Rosebery formally resigns leadership.

1898    Harcourt resigns leadership of Liberal MPs.

1899    Campbell-Bannerman elected leader of Liberals in the Commons. Herbert Gladstone becomes Chief Whip. Party divided on question of South African War.

1900    Three-way split in party on motion of censure on Joseph Chamberlain, Colonial Secretary. Liberals lose general election (184 seats). Liberal Imperialists found Liberal Imperialist Council under chairmanship of Sir Edward Grey.

1902    Foundation of Liberal League by the Liberal Imperialists, with Rosebery as president, Asquith, Fowler and Grey vice-presidents.

1903    Confidential electoral pact made with Labour Representation Committee, allowing a number of Labour candidates to stand unopposed by Liberals.

1905    Campbell-Bannerman becomes PM. Leading Liberal Imperialists join government.

1906    Liberals win general election (400 seats).

1908    Death of Campbell-Bannerman. Asquith becomes PM.

1909    Lloyd George's Budget rejected by Lords.

1910    Liberals win 275 seats in Jan. general election and Asquith forms minority government. They win 271 seats in Dec. and Asquith is again PM.

1914    Outbreak of war. Morley, Burns and C. P. Trevelyan resign from the government as Liberal pacifists.

1915    Coalition with Conservatives with Asquith remaining PM.

1916    Conservatives withdraw support from Asquith. He resigns and Lloyd George becomes PM. Party in Parliament therefore split, with two sets of whips – Lloyd George's government whips and Asquith's official Liberal whips.

1918    Lloyd George and the Coalition Liberals fight the general election in alliance with the Conservatives – the 'Coupon election'. One hundred and thirty-eight Coalition Liberals returned, 27 Asquithian Liberals. Asquith himself defeated, Lloyd George again PM.

1919     With Asquith out of Parliament, Maclean is elected sessional chairman of the parliamentary party. Thorne and Hogge appointed joint whips. Asquithian Liberals refuse the Lloyd George whip.

1920     Asquith wins Paisley by-election. Lloyd George floats the idea of Conservative–Liberal fusion. Liberal back-benchers oppose the idea. Coalition Liberals begin to form their own organization of constituency 'area advisory committees'.

1922     Carlton Club revolt of Conservative back-benchers against the coalition. Lloyd George resigns. Sixty-two Coalition Liberals and 54 Liberals returned in general election.

1923     Thorne resigns and Asquith makes V. Phillipps Chief Whip. Party agrees to reunion when Baldwin calls a general election on the question of 'Protection'. Joint manifesto by Asquith and Lloyd George and merger of organizations, but Lloyd George maintains his own headquarters and political fund. Liberals win 159 seats.

1924     Liberals help defeat Labour government over Campbell case. Forty Liberal MPs returned in general election.

1925     Asquith elevated to Lords as Lord Oxford and Asquith. Lloyd George elected chairman of the parliamentary party. Collins made Chief Whip. Seven MPs who voted against Lloyd George as chairman form the Radical Group, chaired by Runciman. Launching of the 'Liberal Million Fund'. Green Book, *The Land and the Nation*, published by the Liberal Land Committee. Lloyd George founds 'Land and Nation League'.

1926     Liberal Land Conference. Lloyd George and Asquith split over General Strike. Asquith resigns party leadership, succeeded by Lloyd George.

1927     Asquithians in party organization replaced by Lloyd George supporters. Hutchinson made Chief Whip. Asquithians form the Liberal Council. Samuel made chairman of the Organization Committee.

1928     Liberal Yellow Book, *Britain's Industrial Future*, published, the basis of *We Can Conquer Unemployment*, the Liberal election manifesto.

1929     Fifty-nine Liberals returned in general election. Liberals split on Labour government's Coal Bill.

1930     Hutchinson resigns demanding an anti-government policy. Sinclair made Chief Whip.

1931    Simon, Hutchinson and Brown resign Liberal whip in protest against the party's attitude to the Labour Budget. Formation of National Government. Several Liberals, led by Samuel, accept office in the coalition, and 21 MPs led by Simon establish a body to support the National Government. In general election, 35 Liberal National group (Simonites), 33 Liberals led by Samuel and four Independent Liberals (Lloyd Georgites) returned. Samuel and Simon, plus several of their followers, accept office in the National Government.

1933    Samuelites leave government in protest against its protectionist policies. Simonites remain.

1935    General election: 17 Samuelites and four Lloyd George Independents returned. Sinclair elected chairman of the parliamentary party.

1936    Foundation of Liberal Party Organization, incorporates all Liberal bodies except the Liberal Central Association. The National Liberal Federation is wound up.

1939    Liberals refuse to join a coalition under Chamberlain when Sinclair is not offered a post in the War Cabinet.

1940    Liberals join Churchill coalition, Sinclair becoming Secretary for Air.

1945    Liberals win 12 seats in general election. Sinclair loses seat and Clement Davies elected chairman of parliamentary party.

1946    Liberal Council wound up.

1947    Woolton–Teviot agreement for formal union of Conservatives and Liberal Nationals.

1950    Nine Liberal MPs returned in general election. Out of 475 Liberal candidates, 319 lose their deposits.

1951    Six Liberals returned at general election. Churchill offers Clement Davies the Ministry of Education. He declines the offer.

1952    H. F. P. Harris appointed to a new post of general director of the party.

1956    Davies resigns leadership. Jo Grimond elected chairman of the Liberal MPs.

1958    Mark Bonham-Carter wins Torrington by-election, first Liberal by-election victory since 1929.

1959    Liberals win six seats at general election.

1962    Eric Lubbock wins Orpington by-election.

1964    Liberals win nine seats in general election.

1965    David Steel wins Roxburgh, Selkirk and Peebles by-election.

1966    Liberals win 12 seats in general election.

1967    Grimond resigns. Jeremy Thorpe elected chairman of Liberal MPs.

1969    W. Lawler wins Birmingham Ladywood by-election for Liberals from Labour.

1970    Liberals win six seats in general election.

1972–3  Dramatic series of by-election victories in Rochdale, Sutton, Ely, Ripon and Berwick.

1974    Liberals win 14 seats in Feb. general election. Heath approaches Thorpe with offer of a coalition, but talks fail when Heath refuses to promise electoral reform. Liberals win 13 seats in Oct. general election.

1976    Thorpe resigns after party pressure due to his involvement with Norman Scott. An 'interregnum' leadership by Grimond until David Steel elected leader of the party.

1977    Liberals enter Lib–Lab Pact to sustain minority Callaghan government.

1978    End of Lib–Lab Pact.

1979    Liberals win by-election victory in Liverpool Edge Hill, and win 11 seats in general election.

1981    Formation of the Social Democratic Party. Liberals and Social Democrats agree at conferences to form an alliance to fight the next general election and to ally with each other in by-elections (Sept.). In July, Roy Jenkins almost overturns safe Labour majority at Warrington by-election. Bill Pitt wins Croydon NW for the Liberals (Sept.), and Shirley Williams wins safe Conservative seat of Crosby for the SDP (Nov.).

1982    Roy Jenkins wins Glasgow Hillhead for the SDP/Alliance (Mar.). After some dispute Liberals and SDP agree a 50:50 share of seats.

1983    Liberal Simon Hughes wins safe Labour seat of Bermondsey (Feb.), but Alliance fails to take Darlington. During general election campaign Alliance prime minister designate, Roy Jenkins, replaced by David Owen. Election results prove a disappointment for the Alliance with 26 per cent of the vote but only 23 seats. Following the general election David Owen was elected unopposed to replace Roy Jenkins as leader of the SDP.

1985    Alliance win Brecon and Radnor by-election (July).

1986    Joint commission of Liberals and SDP prepares proposals on defence policy representing a compromise position between the two parties. David Owen pre-empts publication of the report by announcing his commitment to maintaining the nuclear deterrent. Liberal Assembly (Sept.) rejects leadership's recommendations on replacement of Polaris; Alliance slumps in the polls after rift over defence policy.

1987    Relaunch of Alliance with compromise defence policy (Jan.). SDP win major by-election victory at Greenwich. Joint Alliance manifesto produced for the general election and David Owen and David Steel agree to campaign as joint Alliance leaders. In election, Alliance vote falls to 23 per cent and they gain only 22 seats. Immediately following the election David Steel calls for a formal merger of the two parties, but is opposed by David Owen and all but one SDP MP. SDP decide to hold a ballot on whether to hold merger talks with the Liberals; a majority of 57:43 per cent is announced in favour (Aug.). David Owen resigns as leader of the SDP.

1988    Liberal and SDP special conferences vote for merger of the two parties and formation of the Social and Liberal Democrats (Jan.). Launch of the new Social and Liberal Democrats. David Owen forms 'continuing SDP' (Mar.) with himself as leader; David Steel announces he will not stand in forthcoming leadership contest (June). Ashdown elected leader of Social and Liberal Democrats. Social and Liberal Democrats and 'continuing SDP' have separate conferences (Sept.). Tawney Society (SD think-tank) is disbanded (Nov.).

1989    Rival SLD and SDP candidates split the Alliance share of the vote at the Richmond (Yorks.) by-election allowing Conservative victory. Poll of SLD members agrees to adopt short title of Liberal Democrats (Feb.); Liberal Democrats pushed into fourth place (with 6.2 per cent of vote) in the direct elections to the European Parliament following surge in Green Party support (with 14.5 per cent) (June).

1990    SDP decides to cease campaigning as a political party (June). Liberal Democrats secure victory at the Eastbourne by-election in the wake of widespread opposition to the poll tax (Oct.). Replacement of Mrs Thatcher with John Major as Prime Minister and Conservative leader (Nov.).

1991    Liberal Democrats win Ribble Valley by-election, effectively ending Conservative attempts to retain the poll tax (Mar.); extensive Liberal Democrat gains in local elections (May). Liberal Democrat conference supports Ashdown in programme of extra spending on education, 'green' taxes on fuel and pro-federalism in Europe (Oct.).

1992    Ashdown survives revelation of former affair and his handling of the crisis boosts poll rating (Feb.). Liberal Democrats secure 20 MPs in general election on 18.3 per cent share of the vote, but fail to secure the balance of power in outright Conservative victory (Apr.). Speaking at Chard, Paddy Ashdown calls for cooperation on the centre left to prevent continuing Conservative hegemony. Labour response is unenthusiastic (May).

1993    Liberal Democrats win safe Conservative seat of Newbury in first by-election of the Parliament (May) on same day as sweeping gains in county council elections remove Conservative control from every council except Buckinghamshire; Liberal Democrats take Christchurch by-election (July) on largest anti-Conservative swing in modern times; accusations of racism over conduct of local party in Tower Hamlets (London) lead to three expulsions from the party (Dec.).

1994    Liberal Democrats win first seats in direct elections to Europe, capturing Cornwall and Plymouth West together with Somerset and Devon North (June). Liberal Democrats capture Eastleigh by-election on same day. Election of Tony Blair (July) to succeed John Smith as Labour Party leader causes Liberal Democrats to fall back in opinion poll ratings. Robert Maclennan elected president of SLD (Sept.).

1995    Liberal Democrats take Littleborough and Saddleworth by-election from Conservatives after bitter Labour campaign. Defection of Conservative MP Emma Nicholson to Liberal Democrats.

# Labour Party

1900    Labour Representation Committee (LRC) formed (27 Feb.). J. R. MacDonald secretary. Two MPs returned in 1900 election.

1902    Taff Vale decision undermines legal position of the trade unions.

1903    Electoral pact between MacDonald and Herbert Gladstone.

1906    Twenty-nine LRC MPs returned in general election. On their arrival in Parliament they assume the title 'Labour Party'. K. Hardie becomes chairman.

1910    Two general elections: 40 Labour MPs returned in the Jan. election, 42 in Dec.

1914    MacDonald resigns because the party will not oppose the War Estimates and Arthur Henderson becomes chairman of the parliamentary party.

1917    W. Adamson becomes chairman of the parliamentary party.

1918    Promulgation of new Labour Party Constitution prepared by Henderson and Sidney Webb. It allows individual membership of the party and formally commits it to a socialist programme. Sixty-three Labour MPs returned in general election. *Labour and the New Social Order* published and adopted by conference – it forms basis of policy for next 30 years.

1921    J. Clynes becomes chairman of the parliamentary party.

1922    MacDonald becomes chairman of parliamentary party. In the general election 142 Labour MPs are returned.

1923    General election returns 191 Labour MPs.

1924    January: MacDonald forms a minority Labour government. It is defeated over the Campbell case (Oct.), and the 'Red' or 'Zinoviev Letter' election follows, with 151 Labour MPs returned.

1926    General Strike (May).

1927    Electoral agreement with Co-operative Party.

1929    Labour wins 288 seats in the general election and forms a second minority government.

1931    Cabinet splits on question of reduction of unemployment benefits. MacDonald forms a National Government. Henderson becomes leader of the party. General election follows in which MacDonald and Snowden attack Labour Party. Labour win only 52 seats.

1932    George Lansbury elected party leader. Labour Party conference disaffiliates ILP.

1934    Publication of *For Socialism and Peace.*

1935    Labour win 154 seats in the general election. Clement Attlee elected leader by parliamentary party.

1937    Local constituency parties given more power by a change in party constitution.

1940    Labour leaders refuse to serve under Chamberlain, but enter Churchill's coalition government and accept wartime electoral truce.

1942    Publication of policy statement *The Old World and the New Society* which advocates retention of controls, planned production and public ownership.

1945    Labour withdraw from coalition which leads to dissolution of Parliament. A massive Labour victory (393 seats) allows Attlee to form the first majority Labour government. It begins a programme of nationalization and social reform, and establishes the National Health Service.

1950    Labour win election by a narrow majority. Total of Labour seats is 315.

1951    Resignations of Bevan, Wilson and Freeman from the government in protest at the imposition of prescription charges. General election sees Labour defeated with 295 seats, though they gain highest total vote.

1955    Division in party when Bevanites oppose manufacture and use of the hydrogen bomb. General election defeat for Labour, who win 277 seats. Attlee retires and Hugh Gaitskell elected leader.

1956    Publication of *The Future of Socialism* by Anthony Crosland.

1959    Labour defeated in general election, followed by Gaitskell's attempts to revise Clause IV of the party constitution.

1960    Death of Bevan. Leadership defeated over unilateral nuclear disarmament. Gaitskell makes 'fight and fight again' speech.

1961    *Signposts for the Sixties* adopted by annual conference. It plans for economic growth under Labour, upon which the social services and standard of living will depend. Unilateralists are defeated.

1963    Death of Hugh Gaitskell. Wilson defeats George Brown and James Callaghan in ballot to become leader.

1964    Labour win election with 317 seats; Wilson forms government with only a precarious majority.

1966    Wilson dissolves Parliament and Labour return to power with 363 seats.

1969    Struggle with the trade unions over the proposals for reform of trade union law embodied in *In Place of Strife*. Cabinet forced to drop its proposals.

1970    Labour defeated in general election, winning 287 seats.

1972    Formation of a TUC–Labour Party Liaison Committee.

1974    Wilson forms minority government with 301 seats after a stalemate election (Mar.). Enters a 'social contract' with the trade unions as an alternative to a statutory incomes policy. Labour win a second close election, taking 319 seats (Oct.).

1975    Labour ministers campaign for and against EEC in referendum campaign.

1976    Wilson resigns. Callaghan elected leader.

1977    The Labour government faces almost certain defeat in a 'no confidence' vote (Mar.). Callaghan and the Liberal leader, Steel, conclude the Lib–Lab Pact which secures the government's position.

1978    End of Lib–Lab Pact.

1979    Labour Government defeated on a vote of confidence and loses subsequent general election, gaining only 268 seats with a 5.2 per cent swing to the Conservatives. At the party conference (Oct.), sitting MPs required to submit to reselection during the life of each Parliament and final decisions on the content of the election manifesto given to the National Executive Committee. Committee of Inquiry set up to examine party organization.

1980    Committee of Inquiry begins work (Jan.). Party conference confirms decision on reselection but reverses decision on control of manifesto. Decision taken to take election of party leader out of sole hands of the Parliamentary Labour Party and replace them with an electoral college of MPs, constituency parties and trade unions. Special conference called for Jan. 1981 to decide on the precise composition of the electoral college. James Callaghan announces his retirement and Michael Foot elected leader under the old system over Denis Healey who becomes deputy leader (Nov.).

1981    Special Wembley conference votes for election of party leader by electoral college with 40 per cent votes for unions, 30 per cent Labour MPs and 30 per cent constituencies (Jan.). Following day, 'Gang of Four' announce launching of Council for Social Democracy. Social Democratic Party launched (Mar.) and 12 Labour MPs resign the party whip; Tony Benn announces his intention of standing against Denis Healey for deputy leadership (Apr.). At the Oct. conference Healey won by the narrowest of margins. Benn's candidature widely seen as symbolic of growing left-wing influence in the party. The NEC inaugurates enquiry into the Trotskyite group Militant Tendency.

1982    Report of NEC into Militant Tendency requires groups who operate within the party to register and meet specific conditions. NEC decides Militant fails to satisfy the conditions and begins action to expel leaders. Labour Party conference accepts unilateral nuclear disarmament as official policy.

1983    Labour Party loses Bermondsey by-election to the Liberals after bitter campaign against its left-wing candidate Peter Tatchell. Labour loses the general election with only 28 per cent of the vote, the lowest share since the 1920s. Michael Foot and Denis Healey announce intention of standing down as leader and deputy leader. Neil Kinnock elected leader and Roy Hattersley deputy leader, dubbed the 'Dream Ticket'.

1984    Miners' strike embarrasses Labour Party and TUC who seek to distance themselves from the more extreme statements of Arthur Scargill, the miners' leader, and picket-line violence. Tony Benn returns as MP for Chesterfield after losing his seat in 1983.

1985    At Labour conference Neil Kinnock vigorously attacks Arthur Scargill and the behaviour of left-wing councillors, especially in Liverpool. Widely seen as a major attempt to stem leftward drift of the party and restore confidence in moderate Labour supporters. NEC launches enquiry into running of the Liverpool District Party.

1986    NEC Report recommends expulsion of leading members of Liverpool District Party. In response, Liverpool and London councillors facing surcharges demand that Labour indemnify them on the party's return to power. After prolonged legal battle, leading Militant supporters in Liverpool expelled from the party.

1987    At general election, Labour loses heavily in spite of running a vigorous and highly professional campaign, and increasing its share of the vote to 32 per cent. Denis Healey announces resignation from shadow cabinet.

1988    Labour launches policy review. Kinnock comfortably defeats Tony Benn's leadership challenge; Hattersley in turn defeats John Prescott for deputy leadership (Oct.).

1989    Major electoral revival in European elections: Labour wins 45 seats, Conservatives win only 31 (June).

1990    Kinnock (having disowned poll tax 'outlaws' in the party in 1989) attacks 'toy town revolutionaries' after poll tax riots (Mar.).

1991    Kinnock denies pressure to stand down as leader (Sept.).

1992    Labour loses fourth successive general election (9 Apr.); Kinnock resigns (13 Apr.), Roy Hattersley to resign as deputy leader. John Smith elected leader with massive majority over Bryan Gould; Margaret Beckett is deputy leader (July). New shadow cabinet appointments include Jack Cunningham (foreign affairs), Gordon Brown (shadow chancellor), Tony Blair (home secretary) and Robin Cook (trade and industry). At party conference, Tony Blair and Gordon Brown elected to NEC (Sept.). Conference also reduces weight of unions' conference vote from 87 per cent to 70 per cent.

1993    John Smith proposes reduced role for unions in electing party leader and candidate selection (Feb.); the Plant Committee on the electoral system narrowly favours the supplementary vote method, abandoning first past the post (Mar.). Party conference passes John Smith's 'One Man One Vote' (OMOV) proposal (Sept.).

1994    Death of John Smith (12 May); Labour triumph in third direct elections to Europe, winning 62 seats to Conservatives' 18 (June). Tony Blair elected leader (July); John Prescott elected deputy leader. Labour win Dudley West by-election (Dec.).

1995    Labour's NEC endorses rewriting of Clause IV (Mar.). Special Party conference backs modernized Clause IV (April). Highly successful 'modernizing' conference at Brighton (Oct.).

# Other parties

## Alliance, The

An Alliance of the Liberal Party and the Social Democratic Party (SDP), formed in Sept. 1981 following the creation of the Social Democratic Party earlier in the year and the acceptance by both parties of the principle of an alliance at their conferences. The Alliance agreed to an equal share-out of seats for local and parliamentary elections and campaigned under a joint manifesto in both the 1983 and 1987 general elections. In addition, Alliance groups were formed on many local councils, following local election successes. At one point in 1981 the Alliance had an opinion poll rating of over 40 per cent, but obtained only 26 per cent and 24 per cent of the vote respectively in the two general elections of 1983 and 1987 in spite of an impressive string of by-election victories. Calls for a merger of the two parties immediately following the 1987 election and votes in favour of merger by the Liberals and the SDP at special conferences early in 1988 terminated the Alliance and created a new party, the Social and Liberal Democrats.

## Alliance Party of Northern Ireland

The Alliance Party was founded as a non-sectarian alternative to the existing Catholic and Protestant parties in 1970. Led by Oliver Napier until 1984 and then by John Cushnahan, the party has failed to obtain any MPs at Westminster. A moderate party, in favour of power-sharing and devolution, it follows the UK government line that the majority in Northern Ireland want to remain part of the UK: any changes must be made with the consent of the majority. It draws its support from all sides.

## British National Party

The British National Party had become by the 1990s the largest right-wing grouping in Britain. It was formed in 1982 following a split in the National Front. Led by John Tyndall and Richard Edmonds, it claims to have 1,300 members. Main areas of support are in the East Midlands, particularly Leicester, West Yorkshire and West Scotland, where it has strong links with loyalist groups. It won brief fame by winning a local by-election in the Isle of Dogs in 1993. The BNP has links with extreme right groups on the Continent. Their political hero is Jean-Marie Le Pen who has achieved the electoral success in France which the BNP has failed to achieve in Britain.

## British Union of Fascists

*See entry for New Party.*

## Common Wealth

The party was founded by Sir Richard Acland (Liberal MP for Barnstaple) in 1942. During the prevailing electoral truce (due to the war and the coalition government) its aim was to contest by-elections against 'reactionary' candidates, and it was not opposed by Labour or 'progressive' candidates. But in 1943 membership of the Common Wealth was proscribed by the Labour Party. Although it won three by-elections (Eddisbury 1943, Skipton 1944 and Chelmsford 1945) only one of the 23 candidates it ran in the 1945 general election was successful. This victory was at Chelmsford, where no Labour candidate ran, and the Common Wealth victor, E. Millington, subsequently joined the Labour Party. So too did Acland when the election results became known. Common Wealth contested no more elections, but survived for a time as an organization.

## Communist Party of Great Britain

The Communist Party (CP) was founded at a Unity Convention held in London in July–Aug. 1920. Most of the delegates at the conference were representatives of the British Socialist Party which had previously agreed to merge into the new party. Attempts in the early years to affiliate to the Labour Party were rebuffed. J. T. W. Newbold became the first Communist MP (for Motherwell) in 1922. In 1924 S. Saklatvala was elected for Battersea North (he had won the seat for Labour in 1923, even though he was a CP member). That same year the Labour Party declared that Communists could not become individual members of the Labour Party, and turned down Communist requests for affiliation in 1935, 1943 and 1946. Willie Gallagher was elected Communist MP for West Fife in 1935 and again in 1945, when he was joined by P. Piratin (Stepney, Mile End). Since the 1945 general election the CP has failed to return an MP, and there has been a steady decline in the total votes cast for it. In the Oct. 1974 general election all 29 Communist candidates lost their deposits. This may well explain the reappraisal of the party's position in 1977–78. The party was rent by internal division over the revision of its programme, *The British Road to Socialism*, and proposals to adopt a strategy based on building a 'Broad Democratic Alliance', laying emphasis on parliamentary methods and 'Euro-Communist' in tone. In 1979 the party's candidates polled 16,858 votes, but only 11,606 in 1983 with 35 candidates. Continuing splits with the Euro-Communist wing controlling the party machine and hard-liners in the *Morning Star* press were reflected in a split candidature in 1987 of 19 Communist candidates, 13 Red Front and 10 Workers' Revolutionary Party candidates. In Nov. 1991, delegates to the 43rd and final Congress of the Communist Party of Great Britain voted 135 to 72 to drop their name and the Leninist constitution, on which the party had been run for 71 years. A new name, Democratic Left, was chosen with a constitution embracing 'creative Marxism, feminism, anti-racism, ecology and other progressive traditions'.

## Democratic Left

*See above under Communist Party.*

## Democratic Unionist Party

Led by the Revd Ian Paisley, the DUP was formed in 1971 out of the earlier Protestant Unionist Party. It represents the more militant and populist wing of the loyalist community and has usually returned three MPs to Westminster. Initially a vehicle for Paisley's distinctive views, its deputy leader, Peter Robinson, has increasingly come to prominence, for example, leading a cross-border march in 1985 for which he was fined £15,000 by an Irish court. It strongly opposed the Anglo-Irish Agreement, boycotting Parliament for two years in 1985–87. It remains an essential element of any likely compromise political solution to the Northern Irish question, maintaining a powerful hold on popular Unionist opinion.

# Ecology Party

*See entry for Green Party.*

# Green Party

Founded in 1973 as the People's Party, becoming the Ecology Party in 1975, the party adopted its present name in Sept. 1985. The party campaigns to raise public consciousness about environmental and peace issues and promote an 'ecological' or 'green' perspective on economic matters. By 1987 the Green Party had an estimated 6,000 members and had almost 100 parish or community councillors, plus three district councillors. They fielded 133 candidates in the 1987 general election, compared with 53 in 1979, polling 89,854 votes, but losing their deposit in every seat. The Green Party's influence extends much wider than its parliamentary performance with the activities of the Greenpeace organization to alert public attention to environmental hazards. The party achieved a brief breakthrough in the 1989 European elections when it achieved its best ever results, with 14.9 per cent of the vote, and took second place in six Euro-constituencies, though obtaining no MEPs. The party benefited from growing environmental concerns aroused by Chernobyl, acid rain, the 'greenhouse effect' and pollution. Its membership also rose rapidly, making it an effective force in local politics. The party retains a loose structure and has no leader, only 'spokespersons'. It had consistently achieved over 4 per cent of support in national opinion polls since the summer of 1989 into 1990 but fell thereafter. In the 1992 election it polled only 170,000 votes. Membership is less than 8,000.

# Independent Labour Party

During the 1880s the idea of an independent party of labour proved slow to gain acceptance. Yet in 1892 J. K. Hardie, one of its main advocates, and three other candidates, were returned as independent labour members at the general election. These successes were followed by the foundation of a national organization, the Independent Labour Party (ILP), at Bradford in 1893.

In the 1895 election the ILP fielded 28 candidates but did not elect a single MP. Hardie lost his West Ham seat. In 1900 the ILP was one of the founding bodies of the Labour Representation Committee. Although affiliated to the Labour Party the ILP held its own conferences, sponsored its own candidates and maintained its own policies, even after the 1918 revision of the Labour Party Constitution. Throughout the 1920s differences with the Labour Party grew and the 37 ILP members among the 288 Labour MPs elected in 1929 were strong critics of MacDonald's government. Indeed the 1930 ILP conference decided to vote against the policy of the Labour government where it contradicted the ILP line. In 1932 the Labour Party conference disaffiliated the ILP. Accordingly, all 17 ILP candidates stood against Labour candidates in the 1935 election, and four were returned for various Glasgow divisions. In 1945 the ILP ran five candidates and three were successful, but after the death of the party's leader, James Maxton, in 1946, the ILP MPs joined the Labour Party.

In the 1950 and 1951 elections the ILP ran three candidates, in the 1955 and 1959 elections, two. All lost their deposits, a tale repeated in the cases of the three ILP candidates who stood at by-elections in the 1960s.

There have been no ILP candidates at general elections since 1964, except for a solitary candidate (Graham) in Halifax in 1970.

## Irish Nationalist Party

The Home Rule League was founded in Dublin in Nov. 1873, with the object of winning self-government for Ireland. In the 1874 general election 59 Home Rulers were returned for Irish constituencies, with all but two of these victories outside Ulster. The Home Rule MPs constituted themselves an independent and separate party at Westminster, with their own executive council, whips and secretaries. Their leader was Isaac Butt, but more active than he were C. S. Parnell and J. G. Biggar, who in 1875 devised the policy of parliamentary obstruction.

On Butt's death in 1879, W. Shaw was elected chairman. In the 1880 general election 61 Home Rulers were elected, and Parnell defeated Shaw in the election for chairman. The followers of Shaw refused to serve under Parnell, but did not form a separate party, and Parnell's party remained the one effective Home Rule organization in the House.

In 1885 the Parnellites won 86 seats (including one in England). This allowed Parnell to hold the balance between Conservatives and Liberals and helped persuade Gladstone to introduce his Home Rule Bill in 1886. In 1886 the Home Rulers won 85 seats but the party split in 1890 over Parnell's divorce case. Forty-five Nationalists demanded he resign his leadership, 26 continued to support him. He died in 1891, but the party remained divided, returning nine Parnellites and 71 anti-Parnellites in the 1892 election. John Redmond led the Parnellites following Parnell's death, J. McCarthy the anti-Parnellites. In 1895 12 Parnellites and 70 anti-Parnellites were returned. Only in 1900 did the Nationalists reunite under Redmond's leadership. Eighty-two National-ists were returned in 1900, 83 in 1906. In 1910 they found themselves again holding the balance between Liberals and Conservatives, having over 80 seats, and pressed Asquith to remove the House of Lords veto, thus opening the way for a Home Rule Bill to pass. But the First World War prevented implementation of the Act, and divisions over the war and the 1916 Easter Rebellion broke the hold of the party on the Irish electorate.

In 1918 only seven of its 58 candidates were elected, compared to Sinn Fein's 73, although T. P. O'Connor (the solitary Irish Nationalist MP for an English seat) was returned unopposed for Liverpool Scotland division until his death in 1929.

## Liberal National Party (National Liberal Party after 1948)

The Liberal National Group was formed in 1931 by 23 Liberal MPs who split from the official party to join the ranks of the National Government. In the 1931 general election they were opposed by Liberals, but not by Conservatives. They won 35 of the 41 seats they contested. In 1932 the 'Samuelite' Liberals left the National Government in protest at its protectionist policies, but the other Liberal Nationals, the 'Simonites', remained. In 1935, 33 of the 44 Liberal National candidates were returned. Between joining the National Government in 1931 and 1945 the Liberal Nationals were only opposed twice by Liberals (Denbigh 1935 and St Ives 1937). They were not opposed by a Conservative until 1946 (Scottish Universities). In 1940 E. Brown succeeded Sir J. Simon as leader. In the 1945 election Brown was defeated, and only 13 of the Liberal Nationals' 51 candidates were returned. The Woolton–Teviot agreement of May 1947 urged the constituency parties of the Conservatives and Liberal Nationals to combine, and in 1948 the party adopted the name National Liberal Party. In the 1966 Parliament only two MPs styled themselves Conservative and National Liberals, though two other members of the group were elected as Conservatives by Joint Associations. These four relinquished the room assigned to them in the House in 1966 and the group became fully integrated into the Conservative Party.

## Liberal Unionist Party

The Liberal Unionist Party was formed by those Liberals who left the party in opposition to Gladstone's 1886 Home Rule Bill. Ninety-three Liberals voted against the Bill, 46 of them radical Unionists who followed Joseph Chamberlain, the rest Whig and moderate Liberal Unionists who followed the Marquess of Hartington. Both groups set up organizations to fight the 1886 election: Hartington founded the Liberal Unionist Association, Chamberlain the National Radical Union. An electoral agreement with the Conservatives secured the return of 77 Liberal Unionists, mainly Hartingtonians. In 1889 Chamberlain restyled his organization the National Liberal Union and the two groups virtually amalgamated. In 1891 Hartington was elevated to the Lords as the Duke of Devonshire, and Chamberlain was elected leader of the Liberal Unionists in the Commons. In 1895 the Liberal Unionists took office in the Conservative government and the two parties became virtually fused. Separate organizations and funds were maintained until the two parties merged in 1912, but the merger was really a recognition of a *fait accompli.*

## National Front

The National Front (NF) was formed in early 1967 following the merger of the League of Empire Loyalists, the British National Party and members of the Racial Preservation Society. Shortly afterwards the Greater Britain Movement merged with the Front. The party's aims include an end to all coloured immigration, repatriation of immigrants living in Britain, withdrawal from the European Union, support for Ulster Unionists and stronger penalties for criminals.

In the 1970 municipal elections the NF won 10 per cent of the poll in some places, but in the general election all 10 NF candidates lost their deposits, despite an average NF vote of 3.6 per cent of the poll. That year Chesterton resigned from the NF after another internal struggle. O'Brien became chairman of the National Directorate. In 1972 John Tyndall replaced O'Brien. The NF polled 10,000 votes in the Leicester local elections of 1973, and won an average 6.8 per cent in the GLC elections it contested. At the West Bromwich by-election Martin Webster obtained 10 per cent of the votes cast, but at Hove the NF candidate won only 3 per cent of the votes.

The Front ran 36 candidates in the 1974 GLC elections and 54 in the Feb. general election. All 54 lost their deposits, but won an average of 3.3 per cent of the votes. At the Newham by-election the Front candidate beat the Conservative candidate into third place, though losing the election. Ninety candidates were run in Oct. of that year, all losing their deposits. In the same year Kingsley Read replaced John Tyndall.

In 1975 membership of the NF began to fall. Read, again voted head of the Directorate, expelled Tyndall who was reinstated by court action. A split occurred, with Read and others leaving to form the National Party.

At the 1979 general election, the Front ran 303 candidates. They polled 190,747 votes and shortly afterwards further internal rifts occurred. In 1982 a breakaway faction, led by John Tyndall, merged with other groups to form a new version of the British National Party. The party's vote fell back in 1983 to 0.1 per cent of the votes cast. It put up no candidates in 1987 and has been ineffectual in the 1990s.

## New Party

(*British Union of Fascists after 1932*)

Sir Oswald Mosley resigned from the Labour government in May 1930 when the Cabinet rejected his 'Memorandum' on unemployment. In Oct. 1930 a resolution at the Labour Party conference, calling upon the NEC to consider the Memorandum, was narrowly defeated. In December the main points of the Memorandum were published as the *Mosley Manifesto*. Seventeen Labour MPs signed the *Manifesto*, six of whom (Sir Oswald Mosley, Lady Cynthia Mosley, J. Strachey, O. Baldwin, W. J. Brown and R. Forgan) left the party to form the New Party in Feb. 1931. Baldwin and Brown resigned from the New Party almost immediately and Strachey left four months later. But a Conservative MP (Allen) and a Liberal (Dudgeon) joined the party. In the 1931 general election the New Party's 24 candidates were all defeated and only Mosley saved his deposit.

In 1932, after Mosley's visit to Italy, the New Party changed its name to the British Union of Fascists (BUF), adopting uniforms and mass rallies on the model of Continental fascist parties. The BUF urged a radical economic programme to solve the problem of unemployment and envisaged itself taking power in the event of a breakdown of conventional politics. By 1934 the BUF had obtained as many as 40,000 members and the backing of influential people, including Lord Rothermere, the proprietor of the *Daily Mail*. The violence of Mosley's supporters towards their opponents at the Olympia Meeting of June 1934, however, alienated public opinion, and improving economic circumstances limited the movement's appeal. The BUF did not contest the 1935 election and advised its members not to vote. In 1936 it changed its name to the British Union of Fascists and National Socialists (BUFNS) and adopted a distinctly anti-Semitic tone. A series of provocative marches through Jewish districts in London led to clashes between the police and anti-fascist demonstrators, notably at Cable Street in Oct. 1936, leading to the Public Order Act which banned the wearing of uniforms and provided for the prohibition of marches. The BUFNS gained some support in the London county council elections of 1937 in the East End of London, but failed to secure any seats. In May 1940 Mosley and other leading members were detained under the Emergency Powers Defence Regulations and in July the British Union was banned. In 1948 Mosley re-entered active politics by forming the Union Movement (see p. 148) which adopted a neo-fascist stance and called for a ban on immigration.

## Official Unionists

*See entry for Ulster Unionist Party.*

## Peelites

In 1846 112 Tories voted with Peel for repeal of the Corn Laws, but 242 voted with Bentinck for Protection. Many of those who went into the lobby with Peel did so not out of love of free trade, but because of their personal loyalty to Peel and the desire to maintain him as Prime Minister. Among the followers of Peel were all but three of the Cabinet ministers, the Chief Whip, Sir J. Young, and Bonham, the party's election manager. Peel thus had the support of the most important elements in the Conservative Party. Accordingly, the party fund was used to finance Peelite candidates in the 1847 general election, and 89 of them were returned.

The Peelites constituted not only the intellectual leadership, the administratively able and the middle class of the Tory party, but also formed a body of centre opinion which overlapped with moderate Liberalism, yet Peel failed to organize his followers in Parliament, up to his death in 1850. But in Dec. 1852 they were able to join the coalition formed by the Peelite PM Aberdeen on favourable terms, being given half the Cabinet offices.

## Plaid Cymru (Welsh Nationalist Party)

The party was founded in 1925 by John Saunders Lewis with the aim of obtaining independence for Wales. Since then it has run candidates at every general election and numerous by-elections, but without success until its president, Gwynfor Evans, won the 1966 Carmarthen by-election. In 1970 the Plaid ran 36 candidates and polled 175,000 votes, although none was elected. The party tended to attract a new influx of working-class support from South Wales to supplement the 'hard core' membership of the Welsh-speaking rural North Wales region. It also broadened its appeal by pursuing economic regeneration for the Welsh economy, encouragement for Welsh cultural activities, as well as full self-government for Wales. The adverse publicity attracted by the activities of the 'Free Wales Army' may have injured the party's prospects for a time, but in the Feb. 1974 election it won two seats (Caernarvon and Merioneth) and in Oct. 1974 Gwynfor Evans added a third, by again winning at Carmarthen. The lack of support for devolution in the Welsh referendum in early 1979 was taken as marking some decline in enthusiasm for Welsh nationalism. In the 1979 general election the party fielded 36 candidates, polling 132,000 votes and retaining two seats, with Evans again losing Carmarthen. Its vote in 1983 and 1987 fell back to *c.* 125,000 votes, but electing three MPs in the latter poll. Prior to the 1987 election, Plaid signed an agreement of cooperation with the Scottish Nationalist Party. In the 1992 general election, the party returned its largest number of seats so far (4), but its total poll was only 156,796.

## Scottish Crofters' Party

This party represented the protest of Highland smallholders against the Liberal Party's neglect of their grievances. The 1884 Reform Act opened the way for them to channel their protest into electoral activity of an effective nature. In the Highlands they possessed their own organization, and fought the 1885 election in alliance with the Highland Land League. Six candidates stood (three closely associated with the League) and five were returned, for Caithness-shire, Ross-shire, Argyllshire, Wick Burghs and Inverness Burghs. In 1886 victories followed at North-west Lanarkshire and Sutherlandshire. At the 1892 general election the Crofters' candidates threw in their lot with Gladstone, and stood as Gladstonian Liberals.

## Scottish National Party

The Scottish National Party (SNP) was formed in 1934 as a merger of two earlier groups: the National Party of Scotland founded in 1928 and the Scottish Party in 1930. From 1929 onwards the National Party contested elections, but it was not until 1945 that the SNP won its first seat. R. D. McIntyre won the Motherwell by-election, but was defeated at the general election three months later. In 1964 the party contested 15 seats, and in 1966 23 seats, but with no success. Then in 1967 Mrs W. Ewing won the Hamilton by-election. This encouraged the SNP to field 65 candidates in the 1970 general election, but of these only one, Stewart in the Western Isles, was elected, and 43 lost their deposits. It appeared that the SNP was again in decline, yet in 1973 Mrs Macdonald won the Glasgow Govan by-election. In 1974 the party won seven seats in the Feb. general election and in Oct. won 11 seats. Poor performances in the Hamilton by-election and the 1978 local elections signified a wane in Scottish nationalism. In 1979 the country voted only narrowly for devolution, thus relinquishing the possibility of devolution under the terms of the Act. In the 1979 general election the SNP won only two seats; the same number in 1983, but three in 1987. In 1987 its vote was 417,000 compared to 840,000 at its peak in Oct. 1974. Prior to the 1987 election the SNP signed an agreement to cooperate with Plaid Cymru in the next Parliament. More recently the party's fortunes have revived. The party won the Glasgow Govan by-election of Nov. 1988 on a swing of 33 per cent to overturn a 20,000 Labour majority. In the district elections the same year they forced the Conservatives into third place. In the 1992 general election the SNP polled 629,564 votes, still winning only three seats. In the 1994 direct elections to Europe the party captured two seats and in May 1995 it won the Perth and Kinross by-election from the Conservatives.

## Sinn Fein

Gaelic for 'ourselves alone'. Irish nationalist party founded in 1902 by Arthur Griffiths (1872–1922) and formed into the Sinn Fein League in 1907–8 when it absorbed other nationalist groups. The group rose to prominence in the 1913–14 Home Rule crisis when many Sinn Feiners joined the Irish Volunteers and many Dublin workers joined the organization. Sinn Fein members were involved in the Easter Rising in 1916 and one of the battalion commanders, Eamon de Valera (1882–1979), took over as leader in Oct. 1917. It successfully contested by-elections in 1917 and in 1918 won 73 out of 105 Irish seats, but its members refused to take their seats at Westminster, setting up an Irish parliament in Dublin. Banned by the British, Sinn Fein provided the main political organization in the campaign against British forces from 1919 to 1921. In 1922 it split over the treaty with Britain setting up the Irish Free State, de Valera leading the breakaway group who refused to accept the exclusion of Ulster. After the civil war between 'Free-Staters' and 'Republicans' in 1922–23, Sinn Fein continued to contest elections, but its elected representatives refused to take their seats in the Dail and take an oath of allegiance to the Crown. In 1926 de Valera formed a new party, Fianna Fail, abandoning the fundamentalist Sinn Feiners to a minority role, as a consequence of which they failed to return any seats in the general election of Sept. 1927. Sinn Fein continued in existence as the 'political wing' of the Irish Republican Army, winning four seats in the 1957 general election and operating as a fund-raising and propaganda body into the 1970s. In 1980 and 1981 Sinn Fein put up hunger strikers as candidates both for Westminster and the Dail. Bobby Sands was elected in a Westminster by-election in 1981 and two candidates for the Dail, though none took their seats. This success led to the joint politico-military strategy 'The Armalite in one hand, and the ballot in another', with Sinn Fein contesting the Northern Irish Assembly seats in 1982, gaining 10 per cent of the vote. Sinn Fein's leader, Gerry Adams, was elected to Westminster in 1983 for Belfast West, but as with other Sinn Fein candidates refused to take his seat. In 1986 Sinn Fein took the controversial decision to take any seats it won in the Irish Dail, ending its long-standing boycott of southern Irish politics. In 1983 it appeared that Sinn Fein was challenging the SDLP for the Catholic vote, taking 15 per cent as opposed to the SDLP's 18 per cent, but its support fell back in 1987. In 1992 Gerry Adams lost his seat.

## Social Democratic and Labour Party (Northern Ireland) (SDLP)

The SDLP, formed in 1970, grew out of the civil rights campaign of the late 1960s. Its first leader was Gerry Fitt who sat for Belfast West. He stood down in 1983 and was replaced by John Hume, who was elected for the Londonderry seat of Foyle. The SDLP is the major Catholic party of Ulster and has played an important part in all the attempts to create an acceptable political structure in Ulster, including the power-sharing executive of the early 1970s and the Anglo-Irish

(Hillsborough) Agreement of 1985. Since 1981 the SDLP's electoral position in the Catholic community has been under challenge from Sinn Fein, and in 1983 its vote was only 3 per cent ahead. Since 1983 the party has gained support at the expense of Sinn Fein. In 1987 it had two MPs and one MEP. In 1992 it returned four MPs. The party favours the unification of Ireland through peaceful means with the consent of the majority in the north. It strongly supports the Anglo-Irish Agreement.

## Social Democratic Party (SDP)

The SDP originated on 25 Jan. 1981 as the Council for Social Democracy, an organization led by four disillusioned Labour politicians (Shirley Williams, David Owen, William Rodgers and Roy Jenkins). The broad aims of the new party were set out in the Limehouse Declaration, followed on 26 Mar. 1981 by the setting up of the Social Democratic Party as a separate political party. Although its aims were to be decided by reference to its members, its leading members had expressed support for electoral reform through proportional representation, continued membership of the EU, multilateral disarmament and a reflationary economic strategy with an incomes policy and inflation tax. In Sept. 1981 the party joined an alliance with the Liberal Party to fight the next general election and to reach mutual agreement on the fighting of by-elections and local government elections. Party membership in Oct. 1981 stood at 66,000. The first SDP MP, Shirley Williams, was elected at the Crosby by-election in Nov. 1981. Roy Jenkins won Glasgow Hillhead in 1982 and was subsequently elected leader of the party. In the 1983 general election, the SDP campaigned in alliance with the Liberals, each fighting approximately half the seats, but returning only six MPs. In June 1983 David Owen succeeded Roy Jenkins as leader, unopposed. In 1986 serious rifts with the Liberal Party developed over defence policy, but the Alliance was relaunched early in 1987 and the SDP and Liberals campaigned under joint leadership in the subsequent general election. The party returned only five MPs, only David Owen of the 'Gang of Four' being returned to Parliament. Liberal calls for a merger in the wake of the election led to fierce controversy within the SDP and a ballot of SDP members about opening merger talks with the Liberals. A vote of 57 to 43 per cent in favour of merger talks led to David Owen's resignation as leader and a major split within the SDP appeared imminent. Owen was succeeded as leader by Robert Maclennan. In Jan. 1988 at Sheffield merger with the

Liberals was finally approved (by 273 votes to 28 with 49 abstentions). This merger was approved by a ballot of the SDP membership in Mar. and the Social and Liberal Democratic Party (now popularly known as the Liberal Democrats) launched on 3 Mar. 1988. Shortly afterwards Owen attempted to launch a rump SDP as an independent force but this rapidly became an ignominious failure.

## Social and Liberal Democratic Party

Formed in Mar. 1988 from a merger of the Liberal and Social Democratic parties under the temporary joint leadership of David Steel and Robert Maclennan. For events since 1988, see under main Liberal Party entry, pp. 122–8.

## Socialist Workers' Party (SWP)

The Socialist Workers' Party (formerly the International Socialist Group) was formed in 1976 as a Marxist party whose objective was to replace capitalism with socialism through revolution. It emphasized the need to establish universal socialist consciousness before such a revolution could occur. The SWP was uncompromising in its attitude to the Soviet Union. Unlike other Marxist organizations, International Socialists believed that the Soviet Union was not and never had been a socialist society but was a form of capitalist state where a class system operated. They adhered to the view that the October Revolution and subsequent development of the Soviet system failed because the Soviet interpretation of Marxist-Leninist theory was not international in character. The organization, which at its height secured approximately 3,000 members, was the largest of the far left political groups. Its members and supporters traversed a wider range of occupations and social backgrounds than many other left-wing organizations. Prominent members of the party included Paul Foot and Tony Cliff.

## Ulster Unionist Party

The Protestant Unionists dominated parliamentary and local representation in Ulster from 1921 until the 1970s, taking the Conservative Whip at Westminster, and representing Protestant interests in Ulster. The Unionist hegemony was broken in 1970–71 with the Sunningdale Agreement and the proposed Council of Ireland which bitterly divided the Unionist Party. The Ulster Unionists are the inheritors of the old Unionist organization and had 11 MPs in 1983, although it is now a less aristocratic and landed party. After a period of rivalry, the Ulster Unionists have increasingly made common cause with the breakaway Democratic Unionist Party led by the Rev. Ian Paisley in opposition to the Anglo-Irish Agreement of 1985. All Unionist MPs boycotted Westminster from 1985 until early in 1987. More recently the Unionists have reacted to the Downing Street Declaration (see p. 320) with a mixture of caution and anger. Their leader from 1979 to 1995 was James Molyneaux. In Sept. 1995 he was succeeded by David Trimble. The party returned 9 MPs in 1992.

## Union Movement

The successor, for a brief period in the postwar years, of Mosley's blackshirts (fascists). In 1948 Mosley, from his exile in France, formed the extreme-right Union Movement. Fascism gradually resurfaced in such old stamping-grounds as the East End. Mosley returned to fight North Kensington in the 1959 general election but lost his deposit. In 1966 he and three other Union Movement candidates stood again but gained an average 3.7 per cent of the vote. Most of his supporters found a home for their racist and anti-immigrant views in the National Front (see pp. 140–1).

## Welsh Nationalist Party

*See entry for Plaid Cymru.*

## Workers' Revolutionary Party (WRP)

Originally formed as the Socialist Labour League, the WRP became the most orthodox Trotskyist organization in Britain. Its members generally took the view that other Marxist groups were Stalinist and maintained that it was impossible to attain socialism by reforming capitalism. They prophesied the imminent downfall of capitalism with more regularity than socialists in other organizations. Between 1974 and 1983 the WRP fielded 101 candidates at parliamentary elections. All lost their deposit.

# SECTION TWO

*Social and religious history*

# Population

## The population of England and Wales, 1695–1791

|      | Population (millions) |           | Rate of growth (% per annum) |
|------|------------------------|-----------|------------------------------|
| 1695 | 5.2 | 1695–1701 | 1.2 |
| 1701 | 5.8 | 1701–11   | 0.3 |
| 1711 | 6.0 | 1711–21   | 0.1 |
| 1721 | 6.0 | 1721–31   | 0.1 |
| 1731 | 6.1 | 1731–41   | 0.2 |
| 1741 | 6.2 | 1741–51   | 0.4 |
| 1751 | 6.5 | 1751–61   | 0.4 |
| 1761 | 6.7 | 1761–71   | 0.6 |
| 1771 | 7.2 | 1771–81   | 0.5 |
| 1781 | 7.5 | 1781–91   | 1.0 |
| 1791 | 8.3 | 1791–1801 | 1.1 |

Source: N. Tranter, *Population since the Industrial Revolution: the case of England and Wales* (London, Croom Helm, 1973), p. 41. Census returns are only available from 1801; these figures are estimates based on data contained in the Parish Register Abstracts for baptisms, burials and marriages.

## Population, 1801–1991

|      | Population (millions) | | | Rate of growth |
|------|-----------------------|----------|---------|----------------|
|      | England and Wales | Scotland | Ireland | England and Wales annual average % increase |
| 1801 | 8.9  | 1.6 | 5.2 | 1.1  |
| 1811 | 10.2 | 1.8 | 6.0 | 1.43 |
| 1821 | 12.0 | 2.1 | 6.8 | 1.81 |
| 1831 | 13.9 | 2.4 | 7.8 | 1.58 |
| 1841 | 15.9 | 2.6 | 8.2 | 1.43 |
| 1851 | 17.9 | 2.9 | 6.5 | 1.27 |

(*cont.*)

## Population (*cont.*)

| | Population (millions) | | | Rate of growth |
|---|---|---|---|---|
| | England and Wales | Scotland | Ireland | England and Wales annual average % increase |
| 1861 | 20.1 | 3.1 | 5.8 | 1.19 |
| 1871 | 22.7 | 3.4 | 5.4 | 1.32 |
| 1881 | 26.0 | 3.7 | 5.2 | 1.44 |
| 1891 | 29.0 | 4.0 | 4.7 | 1.17 |
| 1901 | 32.5 | 4.5 | 4.5 | 1.22 |
| 1911 | 36.1 | 4.8 | 4.4 | 1.09 |
| 1921 | 37.9 | 4.9 | 4.3 (1926) | 0.49 |
| 1931 | 40.0 | 4.8 | 4.3 (1936) | 0.55 |
| 1951 | 43.8 | 5.1 | 4.3 | 0.48 |
| 1961 | 46.1 | 5.2 | 4.3 | 0.52 |
| 1971 | 48.7 | 5.2 | 4.5 | 0.26 |
| 1981 | 49.1 | 5.1 | 4.9 | 0.01 |
| 1991 | 51.1 | 5.1 | 5.1 | 0.02 |

Note: Figures for 1801 to 1991 based upon decennial census returns, with the exception of Irish figures based on census returns in 1926 and 1936. Figures for Ireland after 1911 represent the combined population totals for Northern Ireland and the Republic of Ireland.
Source: Mitchell and Deane, *Abstract*, pp. 6–7; *Britain, 1994*, p. 26.

## Comparative population growth (*annual average percentage increases*)

| | 1700–50 | 1750–1800 | 1800–50 | 1850–1910 | 1910–40 |
|---|---|---|---|---|---|
| England and Wales | 0.2 | 0.7 | 1.8 | 1.6 | 0.5 |
| Scotland | 0.6 | 0.5 | 1.6 | 0.9 | 0.4 |
| Ireland | 0.6 | 1.1 | 0.6 | 0.6 | 0.1 |
| France | 0.1 | 0.6 | 0.7 | 0.2 | 0.1 |
| Holland | 0.7 | 0.8 | 0.8 | 1.5 | 1.7 |
| Belgium | 0.8 | 0.7 | 0.9 | 1.2 | 0.4 |
| Norway | 0.4 | 1.0 | 1.3 | 1.0 | 0.8 |

Source: N. Tranter, *Population since the Industrial Revolution: the case of England and Wales* (London, Croom Helm, 1973), p. 43.

Birth and death rates in England and Wales, 1841–1990
(per 000 population)

|  | Births | Deaths |
|---|---|---|
| 1841–45 | 35.2 | 21.4 |
| 1846–50 | 34.8 | 23.3 |
| 1851–55 | 35.5 | 22.7 |
| 1856–60 | 35.5 | 21.8 |
| 1861–65 | 35.8 | 22.6 |
| 1866–70 | 35.7 | 22.4 |
| 1871–75 | 35.7 | 22.0 |
| 1876–80 | 35.4 | 20.8 |
| 1881–85 | 33.5 | 19.4 |
| 1886–90 | 31.4 | 18.9 |
| 1891–95 | 30.5 | 18.7 |
| 1895–1900 | 29.3 | 17.7 |
| 1901–5 | 28.2 | 16.1 |
| 1906–10 | 26.3 | 14.7 |
| 1911–15 | 23.6 | 14.3 |
| 1916–20 | 20.1 | 14.4 |
| 1921–25 | 19.9 | 12.1 |
| 1926–30 | 16.7 | 12.1 |
| 1931–35 | 15.0 | 12.0 |
| 1936–40 | 14.7 | 12.2 |
| 1941–45 | 15.9 | 12.8 |
| 1946–50 | 18.0 | 11.8 |
| 1951–55 | 15.3 | 11.7 |
| 1956–60 | 16.4 | 11.6 |
| 1961–65 | 18.1 | 11.8 |
| 1966–70 | 16.9 | 11.7 |
| 1971–75 | 13.4 | 11.7 |
| 1976–80 | 12.1 | 11.7 |
| 1981–85 | 12.7 | 11.7 |
| 1986–90 | 13.0 | 11.4 |

Sources: Mitchell and Deane, *Abstract*, pp. 8–10, 29–30, 34–5, 36–7;
Mitchell and Jones, *Second Abstract*, pp. 21–2; *Key Data, 1992/93*, pp. 10, 12.

## Birth and death rates in Scotland and Ireland, 1855–1990 (per 000 population)

|         | Scotland | | Ireland | |
|---------|--------|--------|--------|--------|
|         | Births | Deaths | Births | Deaths |
| 1855–59 | 33.8 | 20.4 | – | – |
| 1860–64 | 35.1 | 22.2 | – | – |
| 1865–69 | 35.1 | 21.8 | 26.4 | 17.0 |
| 1870–74 | 34.9 | 22.5 | 27.5 | 18.0 |
| 1875–79 | 35.1 | 21.2 | 25.8 | 18.9 |
| 1880–84 | 33.5 | 19.8 | 24.1 | 18.6 |
| 1885–89 | 31.9 | 18.7 | 23.1 | 18.1 |
| 1890–94 | 30.6 | 19.1 | 22.8 | 18.4 |
| 1895–99 | 30.1 | 18.1 | 23.4 | 17.9 |
| 1900–4  | 29.4 | 17.5 | 23.0 | 18.1 |
| 1905–9  | 28.1 | 16.3 | 23.4 | 17.2 |
| 1910–14 | 25.9 | 15.3 | 23.0 | 16.7 |
| 1915–19 | 21.7 | 15.6 | 20.5 | 17.2 |
| 1920–24 | 24.3 | 14.0 | 20.9 | 14.5 |
| 1925–29 | 20.3 | 13.7 | 21.4 | 15.1 |
| 1930–34 | 18.6 | 13.2 | 20.2 | 14.1 |
| 1935–39 | 17.7 | 13.2 | 19.8 | 14.3 |
| 1940–44 | 17.8 | 14.1 | 21.7 | 13.9 |
| 1945–49 | 19.6 | 12.8 | 21.9 | 12.0 |
| 1950–54 | 17.9 | 12.2 | 20.7 | 11.4 |
| 1955–59 | 18.9 | 12.1 | 21.4 | 10.9 |
| 1960–64 | 19.8 | 12.1 | 22.9 | 10.8 |
| 1965–69 | 18.4 | 12.1 | 22.3 | 10.6 |
| 1970–74 | 16.5 | 12.2 | 19.5 | 11.0 |
| 1975–79 | 13.8 | 12.3 | 18.2 | 10.7 |
| 1980–84 | 12.9 | 12.4 | 17.3 | 10.4 |
| 1985–90 | 13.6 | 11.7 | 17.6 | 10.4 |

Note: Figures before 1925 refer to the whole of Ireland, after 1925 to Northern Ireland only.

Sources: B. R. Mitchell, *European Historical Statistics, 1750–1970* (London, Macmillan, 1975), pp. 110, 113, 117, 120, 122, 124; *Annual Abstract* 1987, pp. 29–34; *Key Data, 1992/93*, pp. 10, 12.

## Selected urban populations, 1801–1991 (thousands)

|                    | 1801      | 1851  | 1901  | 1951  | 1991  |
|--------------------|-----------|-------|-------|-------|-------|
| Greater London*    | 1 117     | 2 685 | 6 586 | 8 348 | 6 889 |
| Birmingham         | 71        | 233   | 522   | 1 113 | 1 006 |
| Glasgow            | 77        | 357   | 762   | 1 090 | 688   |
| Leeds              | 53        | 172   | 429   | 505   | 717   |
| Sheffield          | 46        | 135   | 381   | 513   | 529   |
| Liverpool          | 82        | 376   | 685   | 789   | 480   |
| Manchester         | 75        | 303   | 645   | 703   | 438   |
| Bradford           | 13        | 104   | 280   | 292   | 475   |
| Edinburgh          | 83        | 202   | 394   | 467   | 440   |
| Bristol            | 61        | 137   | 339   | 443   | 397   |
| Belfast            | (1821) 37 | 103   | 349   | 444   | 287   |
| Coventry           | 16        | 36    | 70    | 258   | 306   |
| Cardiff            | 2         | 18    | 164   | 244   | 294   |

* Up to 1951 'Greater London' was defined as the Metropolitan Police District, an area reaching up to 15 miles from the centre of London. In 1951 it was redefined to refer to a slightly lesser area, but which still stretched beyond the boundaries of the London County Council to include built-up areas which formed part of the London conurbation. The 1991 figures relate to the most recent definition of 'Greater London' which was the area administered by the Greater London Council as established by the London Government Act of 1963.
Source: Mitchell and Deane, *Abstract*, pp. 24–7; *Britain, 1994*, p. 28.

## Migration to and from the United Kingdom, 1820–1989 (thousands)

|          | Outflow | Inflow |
|----------|---------|--------|
| 1820–29  | 216     | –      |
| 1830–39  | 668     | –      |
| 1840–49  | 1 495   | –      |
| 1850–59  | 2 440   | –      |
| 1860–69  | 1 841   | 300    |
| 1870–79  | 2 149   | 744    |
| 1880–89  | 3 570   | 1 089  |
| 1890–99  | 2 680   | 1 567  |
| (*cont.*) |        |        |

## Migration to and from the United Kingdom, 1820–1989 (*cont.*)

|         | Outflow | Inflow |
|---------|---------|--------|
| 1900–9  | 4 404   | 2 287  |
| 1910–19 | 3 526   | 2 224  |
| 1920–29 | 3 960   | 2 492  |
| 1930–39 | 2 273   | 2 361  |
| 1940–49 | 590     | 240    |
| 1950–59 | 1 327   | 676    |
| 1960–69 | 1 916   | 1 243  |
| 1970–79 | 2 554   | 1 900  |
| 1980–89 | 1 824   | 1 843  |

Note: Figures up to 1919 refer to all movements of citizen passengers to and from UK ports, including Ireland; figures from 1919 to 1963 are for UK and Commonwealth citizens migrating for permanent residence; figures from 1964 refer to all migration of UK and Commonwealth citizens, other than to and from Ireland.

Sources: Mitchell and Deane, *Abstract*, pp. 47–9; B. R. Mitchell, *European Historical Statistics, 1750–1970* (London, Macmillan, 1975), pp. 142, 146; D. Butler and A. Sloman, *British Political Facts, 1900–1979* (London, Macmillan, 1980), p. 298; *Population Trends 47*, London, HMSO, 1987, pp. 60–1; *Britain, 1994*, p. 28.

## Commonwealth immigrants in the United Kingdom, 1961–91 (Cumulative totals, defined by country of origin of head of household at census)

|      | W. Indian | Indian sub-continent | Australian | Others[1] | Total     |
|------|-----------|----------------------|------------|-----------|-----------|
| 1961 | 173 076   | 115 982              | 23 390[2]  | 285 962   | 596 755   |
| 1971 | 302 970   | 462 125              | 32 400     | 496 410   | 1 293 905 |
| 1981 | 295 179   | 628 589              | 61 916     | 280 466   | 1 666 120 |
| 1991 | 433 641   | 1 295 810            | n.a.       | n.a.      | 2 635 411 |

[1] Includes largely New Zealanders, Cypriots, Maltese, Canadians and South Africans.

[2] Persons born in Britain excluded from 1961 figure.

Source: D. Butler and G. Butler, *British Political Facts, 1900–1994* (London, Macmillan, 1994), p. 328.

# Education

## Education legislation and principal events

1780      Robert Raikes opens three Sunday schools in Gloucestershire and begins spread of the Sunday School Movement to other parts of the country.

1796      William Pitt as Prime Minister proposes extending the system of industrial schools for pauper children to all children working in industry, but the proposals are not implemented.

1798      Joseph Lancaster opens a school for 1,000 pupils in Borough Road, London, using the monitorial system in which the older children teach the younger.

1801      Royal Lancastrian Society founded and opens a number of voluntary schools using the monitorial system.

1811      The National Society for the Education of the Poor in accordance with the Principles of the Established Church is founded as an Anglican organization to rival the Nonconformist-based Royal Lancastrian Society. It also used the monitorial system, but only children who were regular churchgoers could attend National Schools.

1814      British and Foreign School Society formed out of the Royal Lancastrian Society. No religious barriers were imposed and with the National Society it provided the basis on which the state system was to develop.

1828      The Revd Thomas Arnold becomes headmaster of Rugby and begins the process of reform in the public schools by introducing the prefect system, the ideal of Christian duty and a more rigorous intellectual atmosphere. This influence spread to other schools through Vaughan at Harrow, Pears at Repton and Thring at Uppingham. Many public schools were founded from the 1830s on the new principles, providing education for the sons and daughters of the new middle classes.

1833      The Factory Act provides for the education of children working in textile factories. The first government grant, of £20,000, is made to education, shared between the British and Foreign Schools and the National Societies. A Committee of the Privy Council on Education set up in England and Wales, with the Lord President as head.

1839      The grant to the two educational societies is increased to £30,000 and government inspectors appointed to supervise schools receiving the grant. Thereafter the subsidy was regularly increased.

1840      The Grammar School Act gives the Court of Chancery the power to alter the original statutes of the schools, thereby adapting them to meet new needs.

1844      Lord Shaftesbury organizes 'Ragged Schools' for free education of the poorest children.

1858      The Newcastle Commission is appointed to survey the state of elementary education. One result of its recommendations was the establishment of the system of 'payment by results' in which the size of the government grant was dictated by the numbers of children in regular attendance and the number passing an annual examination in the three 'Rs' conducted by the school inspector.

1868      Public Schools Act. The Act regulated the administration of public schools and provided for the adaptation of their original charters to meet new circumstances.

1870      Education Act (Forster's). The first major Education Act. The existing 20,000 voluntary schools were given slightly increased grants. Where school places were insufficient, new school boards could be set up, or where the ratepayers demanded it, school boards could be rate-aided with powers to build schools and compel attendance. Board schools could provide religious instruction so long as it was not 'distinctive of any particular denomination'. School fees of a few pence each week were charged, but poorer parents could be excused payment. As a result of the Act voluntary schools and the new board schools constituted a dual system, each school's management committee dealing directly with Whitehall. Voluntary schools received no more rate aid and no more building grants.

1876      Education Act (Sandon's). The Act created school attendance committees for districts where there were no school boards and could compel attendance.

1880      Education Act. This made it compulsory for children to go to school between the ages of 5 and 10, when they could be exempted to work part-time in factories, if they had reached a certain educational standard.

1889    Education Act. County councils were empowered to levy a 1*d*. rate for technical education. The Board of Education was set up.

1891    Assisted Education Act. This made available a capitation grant of 10*s*. to all schools, enabling them to cease charging fees.

1891–95 From 1890 the system of payment by results was gradually dismantled and replaced by a system of block grants.

1893    Education (Blind and Deaf Children) Act. Made possible the establishment of special schools for the blind and deaf.

1902    Education Act (Balfour's). School boards were abolished and replaced by new local education authorities which were given the power to provide secondary education. In many cases new secondary schools were built and grants given to grammar schools.

1903    The Association to Promote the Higher Education of Working Men (from 1905 the Workers' Educational Association) founded by Albert Mansbridge. First branch opened in Reading in 1904.

1907    All secondary schools receiving grants from local education authorities to reserve 25 to 40 per cent of free places for children from elementary schools.

1918    Education Act (Fisher's), introduced by H. A. L. Fisher, President of the Board of Education. The Act raised the school-leaving age to 14 and abolished the remaining fees for elementary education in some schools. Provisions for the compulsory part-time education of children from 14 to 18 were not implemented because of government economies.

1926    Hadow Report published, recommending the division of schools into primary and secondary tiers, with transfer between tiers at the age of 11. The old 'elementary' schools would now become primary schools and different types of secondary education were envisaged with the school-leaving age raised to 15. The report was not implemented immediately because of government economies.

1936    Education Act. The Act raised the school-leaving age to 15, but was not enforced until 1944.

1944    Education Act (Butler's), introduced by R. A. Butler, Minister of Education. The Act raised the school-leaving age to 15 and provided free secondary education for all children, divided into three types – grammar schools, technical schools and secondary modern schools, selection for which was to be by an '11-plus' examination. Primary education was reorganized into infant and junior schools. Free school milk, subsidized meals and free medical and dental inspections to be provided in schools. Provisions were made for raising the school-leaving age to 16 (not implemented until 1973).

1951    General Certificate of Education (GCE) replaces School Certificate as principal examination leading to university entrance.

1959    McMeeking Committee reports in favour of improved technical training, including more apprenticeships and greater facilities for day-release schemes.

1960    Robbins Committee on higher education set up.

1963    Crowther Report recommends raising the school-leaving age to 16 and the provision of part-time education after 16. Conservative administration under Sir Alec Douglas-Home accepts the recommendation of the Robbins Committee for a doubling of university places over the next 10 years to 218,000, with an expansion in other areas of higher education to provide another 172,000 places. Colleges of technology to be developed as technological universities and postgraduate business schools to be established. Newsom Committee on secondary education recommends raising of school-leaving age and an alternative examination to GCE Ordinary Level.

1964    Labour Party elected to power with pledge to reorganize secondary education along comprehensive lines.

1965    Certificate of Secondary Education (CSE) introduced.

1969    Open University established, offering part-time degree studies to students of all ages via correspondence and broadcasting.

1973    School-leaving age raised to 16, having first been announced in 1964.

1976    Education Act requires local education authorities to submit proposals for comprehensive reorganization and limits the scope for taking up places in independent and direct-grant schools.

1980    Education Act by Conservative government strengthens position of parents on school governing bodies; relaxes obligations to provide milk and meals; and sets up scheme to finance able pupils to attend independent schools.

1981    Conservative government introduces major cuts in higher education.

1984    Confirmation of introduction of GCSE examination to replace 'O' Level and CSE examinations from 1987.

1987    AS Levels introduced to broaden A Level curriculum.

1988    Education Reform Act introduces national curriculum with attainment targets at 7, 11, 14 and 16. Control of school budgets passed to school governing bodies and schools allowed to 'opt out' of local education authority (LEA) control and apply for grant-maintained status. Polytechnics and larger colleges of higher education pass out of local authority control. University Funding Council replaces University Grants Committee. City Technology Colleges (CTCs) to be established outside LEA control, funded by local industry and private initiative (July). Higginson Report proposing five-subject A Level studies rejected by government. Government announces freezing of student grants at 1990 levels and a loan scheme. University teachers threaten exam boycott in pursuit of pay claim. Inner London Education Authority (ILEA) abolished.

1989    Education Minister Baker calls for doubling of numbers in higher education. University teachers call off exams boycott in return for a pay deal and system of appraisal (Apr.).

1990    Education (Student Loans) Act introduces loans to supplement higher education grants.

1992    Schools Act requires schools to submit annual reports on children's progress. Local authorities required to produce league tables of school performance. A new national schools inspectorate established on a contract basis with representatives from industry and commerce. Further and Higher Education Act moves 450 further education colleges and 113 sixth form colleges out of LEA control with separate Funding Councils. Polytechnics and large higher education colleges now allowed to call themselves universities. Council for National Academic Awards (CNAA) wound up.

1993    All six teaching unions call on Secretary of State John Patten to call off tests for 14 year olds; widespread boycott of tests occurs (June). Government accepts Dearing Committee recommendation (Aug.) to streamline classroom tests, scrap school league tables of results for 7 and 14 year olds, to slim down the core curriculum and concentrate on 'the three Rs', restrict tests for 7 and 11 year olds to English, maths and science, and freeze national tests for 14 year olds to the three core subjects until 1996. Education Act (July) sets up new funding agency for schools 'opting out' of LEA control; primary schools allowed to form 'clusters' to apply for grant-maintained status. Powers given to secretary of state to intervene in schools deemed as 'failing' and to close surplus school places; School Curriculum and Assessment Authority set up to replace National Curriculum Council.

1994    John Patten removed as Education Secretary (July) in Cabinet reshuffle following widespread criticism of his handling of opposition to educational changes.

1995    Education Secretary Gillian Shephard announces trial voucher scheme for nursery education.

## Expenditure on education in the United Kingdom, 1840–1990 (£ million)

| | |
|---|---|
| 1840 | 0.17 |
| 1850 | 0.37 |
| 1860 | 1.27 |
| 1870 | 1.62 |
| 1880 | 4.0 |
| 1890 | 5.8 |
| 1900 | 12.2 |
| 1910 | 17.9 |
| 1920 | 43.2 |
| 1930 | 50.1 |
| 1940 | 65.0 |
| 1950 | 272.0 |
| 1955 | 410.6 |
| 1960 | 917.3 |
| 1965 | 1 114.9 |
| 1970 | 2 592.0 |
| 1975 | 5 348.3 |
| 1980 | 13 049.0 |
| 1985 | 16 681.0 |
| 1990 | 23 956.0 |

Sources: Mitchell and Deane, *Abstract*, pp. 396–9; Halsey (ed.), *Trends*, p. 168: *Annual Abstract* 1987, p. 44; *Britain, 1994*, p. 119.

Percentage of children in different age groups attending
schools in England and Wales, 1901–90

|      | 2–4 years | 5–11 years | 12–14 years | 15–18 years |
|------|-----------|------------|-------------|-------------|
| 1901 | 2.8       | 89.3       | 41.5        | 0.3         |
| 1911 | –         | –          | 57.5        | 1.5         |
| 1921 | –         | –          | 65.8        | 3.2         |
| 1931 | 8.8       | 91.7       | 73.0        | 6.0         |
| 1938 | 10.0      | 92.4       | 74.5        | 6.6         |
|      | 2–4 years | 5–10 years | 11–14 years | 15–18 years |
| 1951 | 7.7       | 97.2       | 93.1        | 12.5        |
| 1961 | 10.8      | 99.9       | 99.1        | 19.6        |
| 1968 | 10.7      | 99.3       | 100.0       | 30.0        |
| 1976 | 23.7      | 100.0      | 100.0       | 36.0        |
| 1981 | 40.2      | 100.0      | 100.0       | 23.5[1]     |
| 1985 | 42.3      | 100.0      | 100.0       | 25.9[1]     |
| 1990 | 49.3      | 100.0      | 100.0       | 31.0        |

[1] Figures exclude pupils in further education and tertiary colleges.
Source: Halsey (ed.), *Trends*, p. 163; *Annual Abstract* 1987–.

# Social reform

## Factory and industrial legislation

1802    Health and Morals of Apprentices Act. The Act prohibited workhouse children apprenticed to textile factories from working more than 11 hours a day. They were also to have better accommodation and be provided with elementary education. The Overseer of the Poor and the local magistrates were to supervise the Act, but it failed to provide an efficient and independent inspectorate.

1819    Factory Act. Children under 9 years prohibited from working in cotton mills; those over 9 restricted to a 12-hour day.

1831    Truck Act. The Act prohibited payment in goods and tokens. All workers other than domestic servants to be paid entirely in coin. Factory Act: no young people under 18 to work more than 12 hours a day.

1833    Factory Act (also known as Althorp's Act). The Act applied only to textile factories and limited the hours of work for children and youths. Children aged from 9 to 12 to work a maximum of 9 hours a day and no more than 48 hours a week. Youths from 13 to 18 to work a maximum of 12 hours a day and no more than 69 hours a week. The employment of children under 9 was prohibited, except in silk factories, and night work by workers under 18 was banned, except in lace factories. Children from 9 to 11 (later raised to 13) were to have two hours' compulsory education every day. The first four factory inspectors were appointed.

1842    Mines Act. This followed on a Royal Commission into mining conditions. The Act prohibited women and girls and boys under 10 years of age from being employed underground. Inspectors of mines were appointed.

1842    Factory Act. The Act applied to textile factories and laid down that women and youths and young girls between 13 and 18 were not to work more than 12 hours a day. Hours of work for children under 13 were reduced from 9 to 6½ hours a day with three hours' education. The age at which children could start work was lowered from 9 to 8.

1847    Factory Act. The Act restricted working hours for women and young persons in textile factories to 10 a day.

1850    Factory Act. The Act specified the hours within which women and young persons could work. They were allowed to work only between 6 am and 6 pm with an hour's break for meals. They were not allowed to work after 2 pm on Saturdays. Although the Act effectively extended the permitted hours of work to 10½ per day, it was intended to imply limitations for men's hours by restricting the availability of assistance from women and young persons. This intention was circumvented by using child labour to do shift work alongside male workers.

1853    Factory Act. Intended to prevent the use of child labour for shift work, the Act laid down that children were to be employed only from 6 am to 6 pm with 1½ hours for meals.

1864    Factory Acts (Extension) Act. Special regulations for health and safety were made for six 'dangerous' industries including match-making, cartridge-making and pottery. Existing Factory Acts were made to apply to these industries, extending their provisions for the first time beyond textile mills and mines.

1867    Factory Acts (Extension) Act. The Act extended all existing Factory Acts to places employing more than 50 people.

1874    Factory Act. The Act raised the minimum working age to 9. Women and young people were to work no more than 10 hours a day in the textile industry. Children up to 14 only to work for half a day.

1878    Factory and Workshops Act. Regulations made governing conditions in workshops.

1891    Factory and Workshops (Consolidation) Act. Safety and sanitary regulations extended. Minimum working age in factories raised to 11.

1901    Factory and Workshops Act. Minimum working age raised to 12.

1909    Trade Boards Act. Boards were set up to fix minimum wages in a number of sweated industries, such as tailoring, paper box-making, chain and lace-making.

1918    Trade Boards Act. Trade boards extended to all low-paid trades and industries.

1937    Factory Act. Young persons under 16 not to work more than 44 hours in a week; those between 16 and 18, and women, no more than 48 hours a week. New regulations introduced governing lighting, ventilation and cleaning.

1946  National Insurance (Industrial Injuries) Act. In return for contributions collected under the National Insurance Act, benefits payable for injuries sustained at work or industrial diseases.

1961  Factories Act. Consolidated safety regulations in industrial premises, including all factories, warehouses, shipyards, docks and construction sites.

1963  Offices, Shops and Railway Premises Act. Consolidated safety regulations for commercial premises, including prevention of accidents and conditions of employment.

1965  Redundancy Payments Act provided graduated redundancy payments according to length of service of workers concerned. Nuclear Installations Act: regulations governing the granting of licences and safety in nuclear installations.

1974  Health and Safety at Work Act. Reorganized system under which safety and health at work was safeguarded and extended it to cover all those at work.

1975  Petroleum and Submarine Pipelines Act. Provided for the health and safety of all persons working in the offshore oil and gas industry.

1988  Control of Substances Hazardous to Health Regulations extends safeguards covering exposure to chemicals, fumes, dust and micro-organisms.

1993  Six new sets of health and safety regulations come into force, giving effect to EU directives concerning safety.

## Poor relief, health and social welfare

At the beginning of the eighteenth century the administration of poor relief was based upon the Poor Laws of 1597–98 and of 1601. By the former a poor rate was raised from the members of the parish for the support of the poor. Relief was given 'indoors', in the workhouse, and 'outdoors' to people in their own homes. The Act of 1597–98 empowered the overseers to erect a poorhouse out of the poor rates. Parish overseers were to provide work for paupers and were given the power to apprentice pauper children. Under the Act of 1601, the churchwardens of each parish and other substantial property owners were appointed overseers of the poor. Paupers were to be maintained out of poor rates with provisions for them to be set to work. Vagrants could be committed to Houses of Correction. By the 1662 Act of Settlement a stranger could be removed from the parish if he had no prospect of work within 40 days. Itinerant workmen had to carry a certificate from their own parish stating that they would be taken back. Settlement would otherwise be granted after 40 days' residence.

1691    Register of parishioners in receipt of poor relief to be kept.

1697    Settlement Act. Non-parishioners allowed into a parish if in possession of a Settlement Certificate from their own parish. Paupers and their families to carry a 'P' on their clothing to distinguish them.

1722    Knatchbull's Act. Parishes encouraged to build workhouses and permitted to contract out the care of paupers. 'Unions' could be formed between parishes too small to support a workhouse on their own. Illegitimate children were not to receive a Settlement Certificate and vagrant children could be apprenticed without their parents' consent.

1733    Bastardy Act. Obliged women with illegitimate children to name the father.

1782    Gilbert's Act. Parishes permitted to combine for more effective administration; able-bodied and infirm paupers to be separated and only the latter sent to the workhouse; work to be provided for able-bodied poor and wages supplemented from the poor rates if necessary. Orphan children to be boarded out and children under seven not to be separated from parents. Requirement to wear pauper's badge no longer necessary for paupers of good character. 'Guardians' to be appointed to administer relief.

1795    Speenhamland system. Resolution of the Berkshire magistrates at meeting at Speenhamland near Newbury in May to supplement wages from poor rates on a sliding scale dictated by the price of bread. Elements of the 'system' had been adopted informally as a result of Gilbert's Act, and the practice now became widespread in the agricultural counties of southern England. The system was later widely criticized because it encouraged farmers to pay low wages and demoralized the rural labourer.

1819    Poor Relief Act (also known as Sturges Bourne Act). This enabled parishes to appoint a representative Poor Law Committee with voting powers determined by their contribution to the poor rates. The Act was an attempt to ensure that substantial property owners had an influential say in the conduct of poor relief.

1834    Poor Law Amendment Act. The Act followed from the *Report of the Royal Commission on the Poor Laws, 1834* which expressed widespread dissatisfaction with the administration, effects and growing cost of poor relief. The Act attempted to abolish 'outdoor' relief for the able-bodied; relief was only to be granted to those who entered the workhouse after passing the 'workhouse test'. The workhouse regime was to be made as spartan as possible to discourage all but the truly needy from applying for relief. Parishes were to be united into Unions and Union workhouses substituted for parish workhouses, to be run by elected Boards of Guardians. The Act also established three central Poor Law Commissioners to supervise the implementation of the Act.

1836    Registration of births, marriages and deaths made compulsory.

1842    *Enquiry into the Sanitary Conditions of the Labouring Population of Great Britain*, written by Edwin Chadwick, secretary to the Poor Law Commissioners, revealed the totally inadequate drainage, sewerage and sanitation in the industrial areas.

1844    Poor Law Amendment Act. Owners and ratepayers were allowed votes for the election of guardians on a level with their assessment for poor rate. The Act also empowered mothers of illegitimate children to apply to the justices in petty sessions for a maintenance order against the father.

1845    Lunacy Act. Board of Commissioners set up to inspect asylums and other places where mentally ill were kept.

1847    Poor Law Commission abolished following the abuses revealed in the Andover Workhouse; replaced by a Poor Law Board responsible to a minister.

1848    Public Health Act allowed local boards of health to be set up and appoint medical officers of health.

1871    Local Government Board set up to supervise poor law and public health.

1872    Public Health Act. Appointment of medical officers of health made compulsory and sanitary authorities set up.

1875    Public Health Act. Local sanitary authorities given power to enforce sanitary regulations including drainage, sanitation and water supplies.

1906    Local authorities allowed to provide school meals.

1907    School medical examinations made compulsory and school medical services established.

1909    Old Age Pensions Act came into force, giving 5s. per week pension to people over 70 years old with incomes less than £31 10s. a year. Labour Exchanges set up to register vacant jobs and provide contact between employers and those requiring work.

1911    National Insurance Act. The Act provided insurance against sickness and unemployment to be paid for by contributions from the state, the employer and the employee. It covered those between 16 and 70 years of age, but was limited to industries where unemployment was recurrent. Maternity grants introduced.

1918    Ministry of Health established.

1919    Pensions raised to 10s. per week.

1925    Widows', Orphans' and Contributory Old Age Pensions Act provides for a contributory scheme for manual and lower paid non-manual workers for a pension of 10s. per week from age 65. The women's entitlement age to this pension reduced to 60 in 1940.

1929    Local Government Act. Boards of Guardians abolished and their functions transferred to county councils and county boroughs. Public assistance committees and public health committees set up by county and county borough councils.

1930    Poor Law Act. The Poor Law was renamed Public Assistance. Only the aged and the infirm now to apply for the workhouse, and outdoor relief could be granted. Mental Treatment Act made voluntary treatment possible for mental illness.

1931    Under the economy measures of the National Government a 'Means Test' was introduced for unemployment benefit.

1934    Local authorities allowed to provide subsidized or free milk at schools. Unemployment Assistance Board set up to administer unemployment benefit.

1942    Publication of Beveridge Report advocating a system of national insurance, comprehensive welfare and the deliberate maintenance of a high level of employment.

1944    Government White Papers *A National Health Service, Employment Policy*, and *Social Insurance* accept the major principles of a national health service, full employment and a comprehensive system of social welfare.

1946    National Insurance Act established a comprehensive 'welfare state' on the lines advocated by the Beveridge Report.

Compulsory insurance provided for unemployment, sickness and maternity benefits, old age and widows' pensions, and funeral grants. National Health Service Act provided a free medical service for everyone, including free hospital treatment, dental care and opticians' services. The Act came into force in 1948. Doctors and dentists now worked within the National Health Service though they continued to be able to treat private patients as well. Free milk for all schoolchildren introduced.

1948    National Assistance Act. The Act abolished all the Poor Law still in existence and provided cash payments for those in need and without any other source of income.

1961    Graduated pension scheme introduced in addition to flat-rate old age pension.

1966    System of earnings-related supplements for unemployment and sickness benefits introduced.

1967    Abortion Act provides for the legal termination of pregnancy if two registered doctors believe that continuation may injure the physical or mental health of the pregnant woman (or members of her family) or where there is substantial risk of mental or physical abnormalities. Family Planning Act allows local health authorities to provide a family planning service for all who seek it, either directly or through a voluntary body. Advice provided free with graduated charges for contraceptive devices according to the means of the patient.

1971    Abolition of free milk for schoolchildren. Introduction of Family Income Supplement to provide a cash benefit for poorer families with children.

1973    National Health Service Reorganization Act creates area health authorities to coordinate health services within the new local government boundaries set up in 1972.

1978    Health Services Act provides for the withdrawal of private medicine from National Health Service hospitals.

1985    Conservative White Paper *Reform of Social Security* proposes wide-ranging reform of the structure of social security.

1986    Social Security Act modifies state earnings-related pension scheme and encourages personal and occupational pension schemes. Income-related benefits introduced to replace Family Income Supplement, Supplementary Benefit and Housing Benefit. A Social Fund created to provide extra help for low-income families. Government launches £20 million anti-AIDS campaign.

1988    Social Security Act alters eligibility for Income Support and pattern of benefit contributions. Benefit withdrawn from school-leavers who do not join youth training scheme (YTS). Cold weather payments for elderly people to meet heating costs enacted.

1989    Children Act changes emergency protection orders for children. Children given stronger representation in care proceedings.

1990    National Health Service and Community Care Act provides for hospitals to opt out and become self-governing trusts; allows general practitioners to control own budgets; reorganizes system of local community care giving local authorities responsibility for care of elderly people in the community.

1991    Child Support Act sets up Child Support Agency (CSA) to reassess and enforce maintenance payments for children after divorce or separation and trace errant fathers. Mothers refusing 'unreasonably' to identify fathers face reductions in benefit. Act arouses widespread protest because of financial hardships caused to second families, highlighted by cases of suicide, and concern that the reform was aimed at saving the Treasury money rather than assisting single parents.

1994    Statutory Sick Pay Act implements changes to regulations for payment of sick pay by employers following Budget announcement of 1993. Social Security (Incapacity for Work) Act reforms benefit system for those too ill to work, replacing Sickness and Invalidity Benefits by new Incapacity Benefits.

# Housing

## Housing developments

1840    Select Committee on the Health of Towns exposes slum conditions in many industrial towns.

1851    Labouring Classes Lodging Houses Act permits local authorities to appoint commissioners to erect or purchase lodging houses for the working classes. Little used.

1868    Artisans' and Labourers' Dwellings Act (also known as Torrens' Act) gives local authorities powers to compel owners to demolish or repair insanitary houses.

1875    Artisans' and Labourers' Dwellings Improvement Act gives local authorities powers of compulsory purchase of areas 'unfit for human habitation'.

1885    Royal Commission on the Housing of the Working Classes reveals the poor state of housing in London and other major cities. The Commission recommended the appointment of additional sanitary inspectors, the rating of derelict land and government loans to build working-class housing.

1890    Housing of the Working Classes Act grants local councils further powers to close insanitary houses and to build council houses using money from the local rates.

1903    Ebenezer Howard founds a company to develop the first 'garden city' at Letchworth in Hertfordshire.

1915    Rent Restrictions Act introduces rent controls as a wartime measure.

1919    Housing and Town Planning Act or 'Addison' Act (after Dr C. Addison, Minister of Health) gives open-ended subsidies to local authorities to cover the cost of municipal housing schemes. Local authorities with populations over 20,000 were obliged to survey the housing needs of their district and draw up plans for housing development. A second Act provided a subsidy of £260 for houses built for sale or rent by private builders. Over 200,000 houses were built under the two Acts.

1920   Wartime rent controls continued and extended to higher-rated property. Welwyn 'garden city' started.

1922   Fresh grants under the Addison scheme cease as a result of economy measures.

1923   Housing Act offers a subsidy of £6 annually for 20 years for houses built by local authorities or private builders to agreed specifications. Almost 500,000 houses were built under its provisions before the subsidy was withdrawn in 1929, mainly by private builders for sale. Act regarded as a failure in terms of council-house building.

1924   Housing Act or 'Wheatley' Act (after C. I. Wheatley, Minister of Health) increases the state subsidy to £9 a year for 40 years on houses built for rent at controlled rents and makes provision for the expansion of the building trades. Over 500,000 council houses were built under the Act before it was suspended in 1932.

1930   Housing Act or 'Greenwood' Act (after A. Greenwood, Minister of Health) provides for slum clearance by local authorities with graduated subsidies according to the number of families rehoused and the cost of clearance. Local authorities obliged to produce five-year plans for slum clearance. Its operation was interrupted by the financial crisis of 1931 and the economy drive of 1931–33.

1933   Housing Act draws up fresh plans for slum clearance with subsidies under the Greenwood Act, aiming to clear 266,000 slum dwellings, build 285,000 houses and rehouse 1¼ million people.

1935   Housing Act or 'Hilton Young' Act (after E. Hilton Young, Minister of Health) provides for an Overcrowding Survey and obliges local authorities to make plans to end overcrowding.

1938   Rent Act removes rent control from houses worth more than £20 (£135 in London), but retains it on those below.

1946   New Towns Act sets up a number of development corporations entrusted with the building of new towns in various parts of the country.

1947   Town and Country Planning Act. County councils compelled to prepare plans for the development of their areas and given powers of compulsory purchase. Planning permission required for major alterations to buildings or changes in land use by owners.

1951   Conservative government pledges itself to build 300,000 houses per year. Housing subsidies for local authority housing raised from £22 to £35 per home. Local authorities empowered to license private contractors to build a greater number of council houses and encouragement given to private house-building.

1957    Rent Act of Conservative government abolishes rent control on 810,000 houses and allows rent increases for 4,300,000 houses still controlled.

1965    Rent Act of Labour government re-introduces rent control over the great majority of privately owned, unfurnished accommodation.

1968    Collapse of Ronan Point tower block in London, following a gas explosion, leads to widespread review of high-rise developments.

1972    Housing Finance Act forces local councils to charge 'fair rents' for subsidized council houses. Rent rebates and allowances to be given to those unable to afford the new rents.

1974    Housing Act increases aid to housing associations and introduces Housing Action Areas. Rent Act introduces protection for tenants in furnished accommodation; extends rent tribunal powers and tenants' rights.

1975    Community Land Act introduces a plan to bring development land within public control. Repealed 1979.

1976    Agricultural Rent Act. 'Tied' cottages abolished in rural areas.

1980    Housing Act gives council tenants right to buy their houses.

1985    Urban Housing Renewal Unit set up to assist local authorities improve run-down council estates.

1988    Housing Act. Introduces Housing Action Trusts to take over estate management where tenants vote for it.

1993    Government announces rent-to-mortgage scheme, allowing a million tenants to purchase their own homes.

1994    Government announces cut in value of mortgage interest tax relief to 15 per cent, effective from Apr. 1995.

Houses built in England and Wales, 1919–90

|          | Local authority | Private   | Total     |
|----------|-----------------|-----------|-----------|
| 1919–24  | 176 914         | 221 543   | 398 457   |
| 1925–29  | 326 353         | 673 344   | 999 697   |
| 1930–34  | 286 350         | 804 251   | 1 090 601 |
| 1935–39  | 346 840         | 1 269 912 | 1 616 752 |
| 1940–44  | –               | –         | 151 000   |
| 1945–49  | 432 098         | 126 317   | 588 415   |
| 1950–54  | 912 805         | 228 616   | 1 141 421 |
| 1955–59  | 688 585         | 623 024   | 1 311 609 |
| 1960–64  | 545 729         | 878 756   | 1 424 485 |
| 1965–69  | 761 224         | 994 361   | 1 755 585 |
| 1970–74  | 524 400         | 885 300   | 1 409 700 |
| 1975–79  | 542 292         | 746 506   | 1 288 798 |
| 1980–85  | 255 928         | 736 365   | 992 293   |
| 1986–90  | 155 500[1]      | 903 600   | 1 058 100 |

[1]Includes Housing Association construction.
Source: Halsey (ed.), *Trends*, p. 311; *Annual Abstract* 1987; 1994.

Types of housing tenure in England and Wales, 1914–90
(per cent)

|      | Owner-occupiers | Rented from local authority | Rented from private landlords | Others |
|------|-----------------|------------------------------|-------------------------------|--------|
| 1914 | 10.0            | 1.0                          | 80.0                          | 9.0    |
| 1939 | 31.0            | 14.0                         | 46.0                          | 9.0    |
| 1966 | 46.7            | 25.7                         | 22.5                          | 5.1    |
| 1970 | 50.0            | 30.0                         | 15.0                          | 5.0    |
| 1977 | 54.0            | 32.0                         | 9.0                           | 5.0    |
| 1985 | 61.9            | 27.3                         | 8.3                           | 2.5    |
| 1990 | 67.0            | 24.0                         | 7.0                           | 2.0    |

Source: Halsey (ed.), *Trends*, p. 308; *Annual Abstract* 1994.

# Environment

## Pollution and environmental control

1853–56 Smoke Abatement Acts for the metropolitan area.

1866    Sanitary Act empowers local authorities to act against smoke nuisances.

1875    Public Health Act includes smoke abatement section.

1881    Smoke Abatement Committee formed.

1891    Public Health (London) Act provides for limited control of smoke pollution.

1899    Coal Smoke Abatement Society formed.

1925    Council for the Preservation of Rural England set up.

1926    Public Health (Smoke Abatement) Act amends earlier legislation.

1929    Formation of the National Smoke Abatement Society. Publication of journal *Clean Air*.

1933    Report by Sir Raymond Unwin to the Greater London Regional Planning Committee proposes a 'green girdle' around London to provide recreational space.

1936    Public Health Act consolidates existing legislation on control of pollution.

1938    Green Belt Act protects 25,000 acres around the capital from future development.

1942    Scott Report recommends creation of National Parks.

1943    Ministry of Town and Country Planning set up.

1946    Simon Report on domestic fuel policy includes measures for preventing domestic smoke. First smokeless zone legislation introduced in the Manchester Corporation Act.

1947    Town and Country Planning Act provides statutory framework for planning procedures.

1949    National Parks and Access to the Countryside Act sets up National Parks with special protection for areas of outstanding beauty.

1951    First smokeless zone established in Coventry.

1952    Ridley Report on use of fuel and power resources recommends measures for smoke prevention. London smog disaster kills more than 4,000 people.

1955    London declared a smokeless zone.

1956    Clean Air Act passed.

1957    Major radioactive leak at Windscale nuclear plant.

1958    National Society for Clean Air established.

1960    Radioactive Substances Act passed.

1962    Further smog in London kills an estimated 750 people. Recognition of effect of Strontium 90.

1966    Aberfan disaster when sludge from coal tips kills 250 people.

1967    *Torrey Canyon* oil tanker disaster creates large-scale pollution on coasts of the south-west.

1968    Clean Air Act tightens control over air pollution.

1970    Department of the Environment established by combining several existing ministries. Royal Commission on Environmental Pollution established.

1972    UN Conference on the Human Environment held in Stockholm.

1974    Control of Pollution Act.

1975    Explosion at chemical plant at Flixborough draws attention to dangers of petrochemical plants near urban areas. Foundation of Ecology Party to campaign on behalf of environmental and conservation issues.

1976    Royal Commission on Environmental Pollution recommends inspectorate for all forms of pollution.

1979    Clean Air Council axed.

1980    First air quality standards established in the United Kingdom in line with EEC directives.

1981    Wildlife and Countryside Act establishes protection for animal and plant species.

1982    White Paper on radioactive waste management.

1983    Report of Royal Commission on Environmental Pollution recommending adoption of lead-free petrol accepted by the government. Royal Society agrees to investigate problem of acidification of surface waters in Norway and Sweden.

1984    Government announces plans for new powers controlling pesticides.

1986    Sellafield (Windscale) nuclear plant affected by radioactive leaks. Government announces four sites for possible dumping of low-level radioactive waste. Chernobyl nuclear accident in

USSR contaminates upland areas of northern and western Britain – bans imposed on the sale and slaughter of animals.

1987    Sizewell B power station given go-ahead after marathon public enquiry finds in its favour. Government announces abandonment of search for dumping sites for low-level nuclear waste. Ecology Party changes its name to the Green Party to contest general election, fielding 133 candidates.

1988    Commission of the European Community issues range of proposals including rules for protecting the ozone layer, for municipal waste incineration, for tighter control of hazardous waste, for protecting wild fauna and flora, and control of gases relevant to 'greenhouse effect'.

1989    Government publishes Environmental Protection Bill. EC directives controlling gases from car exhausts. Green Party obtains 15 per cent of the vote in the Euro-elections, pushing Liberal Democrats into fourth place.

1990    Government White Paper *The Common Inheritance* published committing government to reduce global warming, protect the ozone layer and reduce acid rain. Environmental Protection Act passes into law.

1992    'Earth Summit', UN Conference on Environment and Development, meets at Rio de Janeiro. UK Renewable Energy Advisory Group reports that renewable energy sources should 'make a significant contribution to future energy supply'.

1993    *Braer* oil tanker threatens major pollution of the Shetlands.

1994    Report of Royal Commission on Environmental Pollution urges major switch from private to public transport, from roads to railways.

1995    Following widespread protests by animal rights activists at British ports, government secures EU agreement restricting length of journeys for live animals.

# Women

## The status of women

1792    Mary Wollstonecraft's *Vindication of the Rights of Women* presents the first clear statement of the need for political and civil equality for women.

1839    Custody of Infants Act gives mothers of 'unblemished character' access to their children in the event of separation or divorce.

1848    Women admitted to London University.

1850    North London Collegiate Day School for girls established.

1854    Cheltenham Ladies' College founded.

1857    Matrimonial Causes Act sets up divorce courts. Women obtained limited access to divorce, though, unlike men, this could only be obtained on a specific cause other than adultery. Rights of access to children after divorce extended. Women given right to their property after a legal separation or a protection order given as a result of husband's desertion.

1867    John Stuart Mill publishes speech on *Admission of Women to Electoral Franchise*; followed by *The Subjection of Women* (1869).

1870    Married Women's Property Act allows women to retain £200 of their own earnings. Education Act provides elementary education for girls as well as boys.

1871    Newnham College, Cambridge, founded.

1872    London School of Medicine for Women opened. Hitchin College (later Girton College) moves to Cambridge.

1873    Custody of Infants Act extends access to children to all women in the event of separation or divorce.

1876    Medical schools opened to women.

1882    Married Women's Property Act allows women to own and administer their property.

1884    Married Women's Property Act makes a woman no longer a 'chattel' but an independent and separate person.

1886    Guardianship of Infants Act. Women could be made sole guardian of children if husband died.

1894    Local Government Act. Women eligible to vote for parochial councils.

1897    Foundation of National Union of Women's Suffrage Societies, a federation of existing women's suffrage groups under the presidency of Mrs Millicent Fawcett.

1903    Women's Social and Political Union formed by Mrs Emmeline Pankhurst and her daughters Christabel and Sylvia to campaign more militantly for female suffrage ('suffragettes').

1907    Qualification of Women (County and Borough Councils) Act. Women allowed to become councillors.

1910    Violent campaign for women's suffrage including demonstrations, arson attacks and picture slashing. Government only prepared to consider women's suffrage as part of a wider extension of the franchise. 'Hunger strikes' mounted in prisons.

1913    Emily Davidson kills herself by throwing herself in front of the King's horse at the Derby. 'Cat and Mouse' Act passed to permit release and reimprisonment of suffragettes on hunger strike.

1918    Representation of the People Act gives the vote to women over 30. Rights to vote given in local elections on similar terms. Women entitled to become MPs.

1919    Sex Disqualification Removal Act opens all professions to women except the Church. Lady Astor becomes first woman MP to take her seat.

1923    Women allowed to obtain divorce on grounds of adultery alone. Husband only allowed access to children if a desirable influence.

1925    Married Women's Property Act requires husband and wife to be treated as separate individuals in any property transaction.

1928    Representation of the People Act. Women over 21 given the vote in parliamentary and local elections.

1937    Divorce Act makes desertion and insanity grounds for divorce.

1945    Family Allowances Act grants allowances for children.

1948    National Health Service provides free health care for women.

1967    Abortion Act provides for legal termination of pregnancy (see p. 170). Family Planning Act allows local health authorities to provide a family planning service (see p. 170).

1969    Divorce Act liberalizes divorce laws by granting divorce on any grounds showing an 'irretrievable breakdown' in a marriage.

1970    Equal Pay Act designed to prevent discrimination in pay between men and women doing equal work; to come into operation by Dec. 1975.

1975    Sex Discrimination Act makes discrimination between men and women unlawful in employment, education, training and the provision of housing, goods, facilities and services. Discriminatory advertisements made illegal. Sex discrimination defined as treating a person less favourably than another on the grounds of his or her sex. Equal Opportunities Commission set up to assist enforcement of Equal Pay and Sex Discrimination Acts.

1984    Amendment to the Sex Discrimination Act entitles women to equal pay with men when doing work of the same, broadly similar, or of equal value.

1987    Sex Discrimination Bill prepared to bring 1975 Act into line with EEC directives, including one relating to the right of women to continue working until the same age as men.

1991    Child Support Act sets up Child Support Agency to secure maintenance from errant fathers. House of Lords decision declares that rape within marriage is an offence.

1992    Anglican Synod votes for ordination of women (Nov.). Representation of women in Commons reaches high of 58.

1994    The first 32 women priests are ordained in Bristol Cathedral.

# Press and broadcasting

## Major developments in the press

1702    First daily paper produced, the *Daily Courant*.

1712    Stamp Act introduced; newspapers subjected to tax and price increased.

1771    Printers' Case effectively frees the press to report parliamentary debates.

1785    *The Times* founded as the *Daily Universal Register*.

1797    Newspaper Act increases Stamp Duty on newspapers.

1814    Steam presses used to print *The Times*.

1821    *Manchester Guardian*, later *The Guardian*, founded.

1836    Reduction of Stamp Tax from 4*d.* to 1*d.*

1837    Invention of electric telegraph greatly facilitates collection of news.

1843    *News of the World* founded as Sunday newspaper.

1851    First news agency, Reuters, formed in London.

1855    Repeal of Stamp Duty on newspapers permits cheap press.

1870    Education Act provides basis of mass reading public.

1881    George Newnes produces *Tit-Bits* magazine for mass audience.

1896    *Daily Mail* founded by Alfred Harmsworth, later Lord Northcliffe (1865–1922); first mass circulation newspaper, priced at 1/2*d.*

1900    *Daily Express* started by Arthur Pearson (1866–1921).

1904    *Daily Mirror* refounded as 1/2*d.* illustrated newspaper, the first to make regular use of halftone photographs.

1908    Harmsworth acquires *The Times*.

1914    Press censorship introduced under Defence of the Realm Act of August 1914 and strengthened in subsequent amendments.

1922    Death of Lord Northcliffe. His newspaper empire passes to his brother, Lord Rothermere (1868–1940).

1926    *British Gazette* produced as official government organ during General Strike. TUC produced the *British Worker* as a response.

1932–33 Major circulation war between main newspapers. *Daily Herald* and *Daily Express* achieve circulations of over two million copies each per day.

1937    Total sale of all national dailies estimated at 10 million copies per day.

1939    Restrictions upon the press re-introduced during the Second World War under Defence Regulations.

1940    Newspapers limited in size, and circulations pegged at present rate due to shortage of newsprint. *Daily Worker* suppressed.

1949    First Royal Commission on the Press recommends setting up of Press Council to oversee all aspects of the press and handle complaints from the public.

1950    Total sale of all national daily newspapers reaches all-time peak of 17 million copies per day.

1953    Press Council set up according to recommendations of the Royal Commission of 1949.

1960    *News Chronicle* closed.

1962    Shawcross Commission on the Press reveals falling share of advertising revenue going to the press; expresses concern about growing concentration of the press; criticizes the growth of newspaper involvement with television; and advises admission of lay members and an independent chairman to the Press Council.

1973    Following the Report of the Committee on Privacy, further lay members appointed to the Press Council.

1976    *Evening Post* in Nottingham becomes first newspaper with direct input from journalists.

1977    McGregor Commission on the Press reveals increased concentration of ownership, growing economic difficulties, and greater division between 'quality' and 'popular' press.

1978    *Daily Star* launched from Manchester. Publication of *The Times* and *Sunday Times* suspended for 11 months.

1980    London *Evening News* closes; *Evening Standard* becomes *Standard*.

1981    *The Times* and *Sunday Times* bought by Murdoch's News International.

1982    *Mail on Sunday* becomes first photocomposed national newspaper.

1984    Robert Maxwell purchases Mirror Group Newspapers. Reuters News Agency floated as public company. Birmingham *Daily News* becomes first free daily.

1986    News International titles (*The Times, Sunday Times, Sun, News of the World*) move to Wapping. Eddy Shah launches *Today; Independent* launched; *Sunday Sport* launched.

1987    *Daily Telegraph, Sunday Telegraph, Observer* and *Evening Standard* move out of Fleet Street.

1989    *Financial Times* and Express Newspapers move from central London.

1990    *Independent on Sunday* and *European* launched.

1991    Press Complaints Commission replaces Press Council. Robert Maxwell dies leaving Mirror Group in disarray. Heritage Secretary, David Mellor, warns press they are 'drinking in the Last Chance Saloon' for invasions of privacy. Calcutt Commission set up to assess effectiveness of press self-regulation.

1993    Calcutt Report *Review of Press Self-Regulation* published and recommends introduction of a statutory complaints tribunal. Government announces intention of bringing forward proposals to deal with intrusion on private property and use of surveillance devices. Press Complaints Commission announces steps to strengthen voluntary regulation by increasing number of independent members, strengthening of code of practice and setting up a helpline service for members of public.


## Major developments in broadcasting

1901    First transatlantic radio message.

1922    Radio broadcasting begun by British Broadcasting Company.

1924    Baird transmits first successful television pictures.

1926    British Broadcasting Corporation (BBC) set up as a public corporation to take over radio broadcasting from the British Broadcasting Company.

1929    Experimental television broadcasts begun.

1936    First regular television broadcasts started from Alexandra Palace in North London.

1939    Television transmissions suspended for duration of the war.

1946    Television transmissions resumed.

1949    Report of the Broadcasting Committee rejects introduction of advertising and any breach in the BBC's monopoly.

1954    Television Act establishes commercial television under the overall control of the Independent Broadcasting Authority (IBA); programmes to be financed by advertising and transmitted by regionally based companies.

1955    First commercial television transmissions.

1962    Report of Pilkington Committee on Broadcasting criticizes 'trivial' nature of many television programmes, especially on the commercial channels. Recommendation that greater powers be given to the IBA over its programme companies rejected by the government.

1964    Partly as a response to the Pilkington Report, only the BBC permitted to go ahead with a second channel, BBC-2, which began transmission in April.

1966    Colour television introduced.

1972    Sound Broadcasting Act ends BBC monopoly of radio by allowing setting up of commercial radio stations.

1973    First commercial radio stations begin broadcasting.

1978    Government publishes proposals on future of broadcasting following report of Annan Committee. A fourth television channel to be established in which priority to be given to the minority and educational interests not catered for on existing channels, including a Welsh language service for Wales, to be financed by advertising and government grants.

1982    Channel 4 provides national television service under the control of the IBA.

1983    Cable Authority set up to supervise cable television networks.

1986    Peacock Committee rejects introduction of advertising to fund the BBC but recommends the development of wider choice for consumers in television output and an increase in sources of supply.

1987    Government forces BBC to halt programme on Zircon spy satellite.

1988    Government bans live broadcasting of IRA spokesmen. Government protests against Thames Television's *Death on the Rock* documentary about shootings of three IRA men in Gibraltar.

1989    Satellite TV transmissions begun by Rupert Murdoch's Sky TV.

1990    British Satellite Broadcasting (BSB) begins transmission in Apr. but merges (Nov.) to form BSkyB. Broadcasting Act creates Independent Television Commission to replace IBA and Cable Authority and license Channel 3, Channel 4, a new Channel 5, cable and satellite television. At least 25 per cent of all TV output to be bought from independent producers. Independent TV licences to be bought from highest bidders. New Radio Authority set up to allocate up to three national commercial stations, awarded by competitive tender, and supervise all independent radio. Broadcasting Standards Council put on a statutory basis.

1992    Government discussion paper, *The Future of the BBC*, published setting out framework for debate on the future of the BBC. BBC publishes own discussion document, *Extending Choice*.

1994    BBC announces plans for a 24-hour news and sports network to replace Radio 5. Heritage Secretary, Peter Brooke, announces that the BBC has passed vetting by independent consultants and would receive index-linked licence fees for the next three years. Government White Paper proposes a 10-year renewal of the BBC Charter in return for greater cost-effectiveness of BBC.

# Crime and police

## The development of the police

1792    Middlesex Justices Act provides for a force of professional magistrates and constables to operate in London.

1798    Thames Police Office set up to patrol the riverside districts of London.

1829    Metropolitan Police Act sets up a paid, uniformed police force for the metropolitan area excluding the City of London, under the authority of two Commissioners and the Home Secretary.

1833    Lighting and Watching Act permits any town with over 5,000 population to appoint paid watchmen.

1835    Municipal Corporations Act requires each of the 178 boroughs to appoint a watch committee and to set up a force of constables.

1839    County Police Act permits justices to set up a paid county police force. In 1840 it was authorized to amalgamate borough and county forces where desired.

1856    County and Borough Police Act compels all counties and boroughs to establish and maintain a police force. Three Inspectors of Constabulary appointed to assess their efficiency and report to Parliament; forces certified as efficient to qualify for an exchequer grant towards the cost of the force. Boroughs of under 5,000 people, maintaining their own forces, not to be eligible for a grant.

1877    Municipal Corporations (New Charters) Act prohibits newly incorporated boroughs of under 20,000 population from setting up police forces.

1888    Local Government Act abolishes police forces run by boroughs with less than 10,000 population. Control of the county police forces transferred to standing joint committees of county councillors and justices.

1919    Police Act, passed following strikes among metropolitan and provincial forces. It created the Police Federation and gave the Home Secretary powers to set nationwide pay and conditions of service.

1946    Police Act abolishes and amalgamates 45 of the smaller non-county police forces.

1964    Police Act encourages the setting up of joint crime and traffic squads. In 1966 amalgamation reduced the number of police forces in England and Wales from 117 to 49. Complaints against forces to be handled by an officer from an outside force.

1965    Metropolitan Police set up 'Special Patrol Group' (SPG) of 100 volunteers specially trained for riot control, gun use and intervention to support particular divisions at the command of Scotland Yard.

1969    Police National Computer Unit set up at Hendon to store information and provide direct links with the 800 police stations in England and Wales. Became operational in 1974.

1974    Diplomatic Protection Group of armed constables set up to provide protection for diplomatic premises in London.

1976    Police Act sets up a Police Complaints Board to deal with complaints from the public against the police.

1977    Members of Scotland Yard Obscene Publications Squad jailed for corruption. Sir Robert Mark, Commissioner of Metropolitan Police, reveals that almost 400 officers had left or been required to leave the Metropolitan Police since 1972 following investigations of corruption.

1981    Following inner-city riots (see p. 196), Scarman Report criticizes police community relations in urban areas, particularly in regard to ethnic minorities.

1984    Police and Criminal Evidence Act strengthens police powers of arrest for suspected offences. Home Office issues new codes of practice for the detention, treatment and questioning of arrested persons. Independent Police Complaints Authority set up.

1984–85 During the miners' strike the police set up a national system of allocating police resources and mount largest ever peace-time mobilization to police mining areas.

1985    Prosecution of Offences Act establishes independent Crown Prosecution Service for England and Wales.

1986    Public Order Act abolishes the common law offences of riot, rout and unlawful assembly and creates new public disorder offences of riot, violent disorder, affray and disorderly conduct; new regulations on processions and assemblies.

1987    Criminal Justice Act amends regulations relating to investigation and trial for fraud.

1988    Criminal Justice Act strengthens Attorney-General's right to extradite and challenge lenient sentences. Amends rules of evidence for criminal proceedings and allows courts to seize assets of convicted offenders.

1991    Criminal Justice Act aims to ensure greater consistency in sentencing; introduces range of 'community' penalties and new arrangements for early release of prisoners. War Crimes Act allows prosecution of UK residents who were suspected of war crimes during the Second World War.

1993    Criminal Justice Act to combat international fraud, drugs trade, money laundering.

1994    Police and Magistrates' Courts Act reconstitutes police authorities. Criminal Justice and Public Order Act extends sentencing of 10–13 year olds; greater range and duration of custodial sentences for young offenders; unconditional 'right to silence' ended; restrictions placed on bail; police given power to take DNA samples; measures to deal with trespass and limit New Age travellers, also to evict squatters; new anti-terrorist measures; also extends powers against obscenity and pornography.

## Committals for indictable offences in England and Wales, 1805–56

|      | Total  |      | Total  |      | Total  |      | Total  |
|------|--------|------|--------|------|--------|------|--------|
| 1805 | 4 605  | 1818 | 13 567 | 1831 | 19 647 | 1844 | 26 542 |
| 1806 | 4 346  | 1819 | 14 254 | 1832 | 20 829 | 1845 | 24 303 |
| 1807 | 4 446  | 1820 | 13 710 | 1833 | 20 072 | 1846 | 25 107 |
| 1808 | 4 735  | 1821 | 13 115 | 1834 | 20 168 | 1847 | 28 833 |
| 1809 | 5 330  | 1822 | 12 241 | 1835 | 20 731 | 1848 | 30 349 |
| 1810 | 5 146  | 1823 | 12 263 | 1836 | 20 984 | 1849 | 27 816 |
| 1811 | 5 337  | 1824 | 13 698 | 1837 | 23 612 | 1850 | 26 813 |
| 1812 | 6 576  | 1825 | 14 437 | 1838 | 23 094 | 1851 | 27 960 |
| 1813 | 7 164  | 1826 | 16 164 | 1839 | 24 443 | 1852 | 27 510 |
| 1814 | 6 390  | 1827 | 17 921 | 1840 | 27 187 | 1853 | 27 057 |
| 1815 | 7 818  | 1828 | 16 564 | 1841 | 27 760 | 1854 | 29 359 |
| 1816 | 9 091  | 1829 | 18 675 | 1842 | 31 309 | 1855 | 25 972 |
| 1817 | 13 932 | 1830 | 18 107 | 1843 | 29 591 | 1856 | 19 437 |

Note: The judicial statistics were altered and extended in 1857 to contain new categories of information.

Source: *British Parliamentary Papers*, 1836–1857.

## Crimes known to the police, 1857–1994

|      | England and Wales | Scotland |
|------|-------------------|----------|
| 1857 | 91 671            | –        |
| 1865 | 92 522            | –        |
| 1870 | 90 532            | 118 105  |
| 1875 | 82 316            | 123 169  |
| 1880 | 98 440            | 122 656  |
| 1885 | 86 905            | 114 865  |
| 1890 | 81 773            | 136 505  |
| 1895 | 81 323            | 134 357  |
| 1900 | 77 934            | 33 492   |
| 1905 | 94 654            | 39 804   |
| 1910 | 103 132           | 38 376   |
| 1915 | 77 972            | 33 915   |
| 1920 | 100 827           | 39 444   |
| 1925 | 113 986           | 33 070   |
| 1930 | 147 031           | 36 723   |
| 1935 | 234 372           | 59 753   |
| 1940 | 305 114           | 62 266   |
| 1945 | 478 394           | 86 075   |
| 1950 | 461 435           | 74 640   |
| 1955 | 438 085           | 74 773   |
| 1960 | 743 713           | 102 617  |
| 1965 | 1 133 882         | 140 141  |
| 1970 | 1 568 400         | 167 200  |
| 1975 | 2 105 600         | 232 482  |
| 1978 | 2 395 800         | 277 213  |
| 1980 | 2 688 200         | 364 600  |
| 1985 | 3 611 900         | 462 000  |
| 1990 | 4 543 600         | 959 100  |
| 1994 | 5 365 400         | n.a.     |

Note: Figures relate to indictable, generally more serious, offences, reported to or discovered by the police. Figures for Scotland up to 1895 also include minor, non-indictable, offences. The Theft Act, 1969, altered the categories of indictable offence, and the figures from 1970 are not strictly comparable to those before.

## Numbers transported to Australia from Great Britain and Ireland (males and females), 1788–1853

|      | Total |      | Total |      | Total |      | Total |
|------|-------|------|-------|------|-------|------|-------|
| 1788 | 759   | 1805 | –     | 1822 | 2 421 | 1839 | 3 711 |
| 1789 | –     | 1806 | 519   | 1823 | 2 735 | 1840 | 3 754 |
| 1790 | 1 246 | 1807 | 313   | 1824 | 1 887 | 1841 | 3 489 |
| 1791 | 2 035 | 1808 | 299   | 1825 | 2 750 | 1842 | 5 528 |
| 1792 | 780   | 1809 | 340   | 1826 | 2 178 | 1843 | 3 730 |
| 1793 | 322   | 1810 | 521   | 1827 | 3 693 | 1844 | 4 468 |
| 1794 | 84    | 1811 | 479   | 1828 | 3 925 | 1845 | 3 632 |
| 1795 | –     | 1812 | 526   | 1829 | 4 797 | 1846 | 2 106 |
| 1796 | 370   | 1813 | 602   | 1830 | 5 416 | 1847 | 1 705 |
| 1797 | 399   | 1814 | 1 262 | 1831 | 5 064 | 1848 | 1 634 |
| 1798 | 392   | 1815 | 1 093 | 1832 | 4 522 | 1849 | 3 416 |
| 1799 | 297   | 1816 | 1 288 | 1833 | 6 871 | 1850 | 3 204 |
| 1800 | 683   | 1817 | 2 013 | 1834 | 4 675 | 1851 | 2 111 |
| 1801 | 749   | 1818 | 3 350 | 1835 | 6 077 | 1852 | 2 578 |
| 1802 | 789   | 1819 | 2 706 | 1836 | 6 028 | 1853 | 1 569 |
| 1803 | 1 661 | 1820 | 3 989 | 1837 | 4 933 |      |       |
| 1804 | 340   | 1821 | 2 750 | 1838 | 5 178 |      |       |

Note: Transportation became increasingly common in the late eighteenth century as a substitute for capital punishment, but was gradually replaced by long-term imprisonment in the United Kingdom after 1840. As a result the numbers of those transported gradually declined, falling to almost negligible proportions after 1853, until it was finally ended in 1867.
Source: A. G. L. Shaw, *Convicts and the Colonies* (London, Faber, 1966), pp. 361–8.

## Prison population in England and Wales, 1880–1993 (daily average) (000)

| 1880 | 28.7 | 1930 | 11.3 | 1977 | 41.6 |
|------|------|------|------|------|------|
| 1890 | 18.3 | 1940 | 9.3  | 1985 | 46.3 |
| 1900 | 17.5 | 1950 | 20.0 | 1988 | 48.6 |
| 1910 | 22.0 | 1960 | 27.1 | 1993 | 45.6 |
| 1920 | 9.9  | 1970 | 39.0 |      |      |

Source: *Annual Reports* of the Prison Commissioners and Prison Department of the Home Office.

## Major popular disturbances and demonstrations

1715    Attacks upon dissenting meeting houses and chapels in the north-west and the Midlands by pro-Tory/Jacobite demonstrators. Most serious disturbances at Manchester, Birmingham and Oxford. Riot Act introduced to provide severer penalties against rioters.

1736    Porteus riots. Captain Porteus was the commander of a troop of soldiers in Edinburgh who opened fire on a crowd at the execution of a smuggler. Porteus was tried and condemned to death, but reprieved. A crowd attacked the prison he was held in and lynched Porteus (Sept.). The magistrates were reprimanded and the city fined £12,000. Attacks on Irish by English workmen in London. Attacks on informers.

1739–40    Food riots in East Anglia and West Country.

1740    Destruction of Newcastle Guildhall by pitmen and others after a man killed during a food riot.

1756–57    Widespread food riots in the Midlands and Forest of Dean; 'Shudehill fight' at Manchester.

1757    Militia Act riots against being balloted for the militia, mainly in Lincolnshire and Yorkshire.

1763–65    Machine-breaking by Spitalfields weavers and demonstrations against imports of foreign textiles.

1766    Widespread food riots. Major areas of disturbances in the West Country, Thames Valley, Midlands and East Anglia.

1768    Demonstrations in support of John Wilkes in London. 'Massacre' of St George's Fields: some of Wilkes's supporters killed by soldiers when demonstrating outside the King's Bench Prison (May).

1772–73    Renewed wave of food riots, mainly in East Anglia, the West Country, the Midlands and on Tayside.

1780    Gordon riots in London. Lord George Gordon led the Protestant Association in a campaign to repeal the Catholic Relief Act of 1778. A mass lobby of Parliament to present a petition on 2 June led to almost a week of rioting with attacks on the property of Catholics and prominent public buildings. Newgate prison burned and over 300 people killed or executed as a result of the riots.

1791    'Church and King' riots in Birmingham. House and property of Joseph Priestley and other dissenters destroyed by loyalists (July).

| 1794 | 'Crimp house' riots in London; attacks on recruiting houses for illegally obtaining recruits. |
|---|---|
| 1795–96 | Widespread food riots following poor harvests in 1794 and 1795. |
| 1795 | Attack on the King's coach at the opening of Parliament during huge anti-war demonstrations (29 Oct.). |
| 1796 | Riots against implementation of Supplementary Militia Act in Lincolnshire and Wales. |
| 1797 | Mutinies among fleets at Spithead and the Nore (May–June). |
| 1800–1 | Widespread food riots following harvest failures in 1799 and 1800. |
| 1809 | 'Old Price' riots at Drury Lane Theatre, London, against increased admission charges. |
| 1810 | Burdett riots. Demonstrations in London in support of radical MP Sir Francis Burdett. |
| 1811–12 | Luddite machine-breaking outbreaks (begin March 1811) in Midlands, Yorkshire, Lancashire and Cheshire. Renewed outbreaks occurred in 1814 and 1816. |
| 1816 | Widespread disturbances against high prices and unemployment on the conclusion of the Napoleonic Wars. Main centres in East Anglia and manufacturing districts. Spa Fields riot in London. Attack on gunshops and Tower of London by group of revolutionary followers of Thomas Spence. |
| 1817 | Attack on Prince Regent's coach at state opening of Parliament (Jan.). March of the 'blanketeers' from Manchester to present a petition for reform and against distress broken up by troops (Mar.). Failure of Pentrich 'rising' in Derbyshire led by Jeremiah Brandreth (June); Brandreth executed. |
| 1819 | Reform demonstration broken up at St Peter's Fields, Manchester. Eleven killed and nearly 200 wounded – the 'Peterloo Massacre'. |
| 1820 | Cato Street conspiracy to assassinate the Cabinet discovered. Arthur Thistlewood and fellow conspirators executed (Feb.). 'Battle of Bonnymuir' near Glasgow between weavers and troops. |
| 1821 | Two killed during riots at funeral of Queen Caroline (Aug.). |
| 1826 | Power-looms destroyed in Lancashire (Apr.–May). |
| 1830–33 | 'Captain Swing' disturbances among agricultural districts in southern England. Hundreds of demonstrations, riots, machine- |

breakings and arson attempts. Several hundred labourers transported. Reform disturbances in London (Nov. 1830).

1831    Riots in Bristol, Nottingham and Derby following Lords' rejection of the Reform Bill.

1833    Clerkenwell riot; reform demonstration broken up by police.

1839    'Bull Ring' riots in Birmingham. Pro-Chartist demonstrations (July). Newport 'rising' led by John Frost suppressed (Nov.).

1840    Chartist 'rising' in Dewsbury and Sheffield.

1842    'Plug-plot' riots and Chartist General Strike in the north and Potteries (July–Aug.).

1848    Chartist demonstration at Kennington Common (10 Apr.).

1852    Stockport riots between Catholics and Protestants; two Catholic churches sacked.

1855    'Sunday Trading' riots in Hyde Park, London, against Act prohibiting trading on Sundays.

1862    'Garibaldi' riots in Hyde Park, London, between Irish and Italians.

1866    Reform demonstration breaks down Hyde Park railings (July). Sheffield 'outrages': attacks upon non-union labour by Sheffield cutlers (Oct.).

1867    Reform League demonstration at Hyde Park in defiance of Home Secretary's ban (May). Fenian rescue of prisoners in Manchester (Sept.). Gunpowder attack by Fenians on Clerkenwell Prison (Dec.).

1868    'Murphy' riots in Ashton and Stalybridge; attacks on Irish Catholics provoked by anti-Catholic lecturer, William Murphy.

1886    'Black Monday': unemployed riots in West End of London, following meeting of Social Democratic Federation in Trafalgar Square (8 Feb.).

1887    'Bloody Sunday': meeting of Social Democratic Federation in Trafalgar Square broken up by police and troops (13 Nov.).

1893    Two people killed during clashes between troops and strikers at Acton Hall Colliery, near Featherstone.

1909    Serious sectarian riots in Liverpool.

1910    Disturbances during Cambrian Combine strike at Tonypandy in South Wales. Troops called out to disperse demonstrators.

1911    Clashes between police and strikers in Liverpool on 'Bloody Sunday' (13 Aug.) and two strikers shot by troops (15 Aug.). Two men shot at Llanelli (17 Aug.).

1919    Clashes between police and strikers during General Strike in

Glasgow, known as 'Bloody Friday' (31 June). Troops called to patrol city. Demobilization disturbances in London and at Rhyl, North Wales (Mar.). Police strike in Liverpool followed by rioting in central districts (Aug.).

1926    General Strike. Clashes between strikers and police in Glasgow, Hull, London and elsewhere. Four thousand strikers prosecuted for violence or incitement to violence; about 1,000 imprisoned.

1931    Widespread demonstrations against government economy measures. Clashes between National Unemployed Workers' Movement (NUWM) demonstrators and police in Bristol, Salford, Manchester, Dundee and other places (Oct.–Nov.).

1932    Clashes between unemployed demonstrators and police in Birkenhead and Liverpool (Sept.). NUWM 'hunger march' to London followed by clashes with police in Hyde Park and Central London (Oct.–Nov.). Serious riot in Dartmoor Prison.

1934    'Hunger march' to London mounted by the NUWM followed by mass lobby of Parliament (Feb.). Olympia meeting of British Union of Fascists (BUF) (June).

1934–35 Demonstrations mounted against new Unemployment Assistance Board regulations governing unemployment relief in South Wales, Scotland and Yorkshire. Some disturbances in South Wales (Oct.–Feb.).

1936    'Battle of Cable Street': fighting between police and anti-fascist demonstrators attempting to prevent BUF march through the Jewish districts of East London (4 Oct.). 'Jarrow March' of unemployed to London (Oct.). Further NUWM 'hunger march' to London protesting against unemployment (Nov.).

1937    Proposed march by BUF through East End prohibited under Public Order Act. March through Bermondsey leads to 113 arrests and 28 injured (July).

1938–39 Demonstrations in London by NUWM as part of campaign for 'winter relief' for the unemployed.

1958    Race riots in London (Notting Hill) and the Midlands.

1961    'Sit-down' demonstrations in London organized by Campaign for Nuclear Disarmament (CND).

1964–66 'Mods' versus 'Rockers' disturbances at seaside resorts, usually at Bank Holiday weekends.

1967    'Sit-in' at London School of Economics begins wave of similar demonstrations in several universities (Mar.). Anti-Vietnam War demonstration mounted by Vietnam Solidarity Campaign leads to disturbances outside American Embassy in Grosvenor Square (Oct.).

1968    Anti-Vietnam demonstrations in London lead to clashes with police in Grosvenor Square (Mar. and Oct.).

1973    Riot in Parkhurst Prison.

1974    Red Lion Square clashes between National Front and opponents, one man killed (June).

1976    Disturbances at West Indian carnival in London (Sept.). Hull Prison riot; an estimated £1 million worth of damage (Aug.–Sept.).

1977    Clashes between police and mass pickets at Grunwick strike (July–Sept.).

1979    Southall disturbances between police and anti-National Front demonstrators; one man killed (Apr.).

1980    Rioting in St Paul's area of Bristol by coloured youths (Apr.). Clashes in Lewisham between National Front and Anti-Nazi League (Apr.).

1981    Rioting in Brixton (Apr.), leads to setting up of Scarman Enquiry. Serious riots in Toxteth, Liverpool, and Moss Side, Manchester, followed by 'copycat' rioting by youths in many other towns and cities (July).

1983    Serious disturbances outside Warrington printing plant of *Stockport Messenger* as members of National Graphical Association attempt to enforce a closed shop (Nov.–Dec.).

1984–85    Series of disturbances during the miners' strike, principally between pickets and police forces protecting non-strikers. A Yorkshire miner is killed at Ollerton (Mar. 1984) and a taxi-driver carrying a working miner killed in South Wales (Dec. 1984). The largest confrontations took place outside the Orgreave Coke plant, near Sheffield (May–June 1984) when thousands of police and pickets struggled for control of access to the plant. In all, almost 12,000 miners were arrested during the course of the strike, many for public offences.

1985    Football supporter killed in riot by Leeds and Birmingham supporters (May). Thirty-eight people killed and 250 injured following the collapse of a wall during rioting between Liverpool and Juventus fans at the Heysel Stadium, Brussels (May). Riots in Handsworth area of Birmingham in which two Asian men die in a fire (Sept.). Rioting in Brixton following the police shooting and wounding of Mrs Cherry Groce (Sept.). Serious rioting at Broadwater Farm estate in Tottenham in which police constable killed (Oct.).

1986    Series of disturbances outside the Wapping printing works of Rupert Murdoch after the strike and dismissal of 5,500 print and other workers (May). Most serious night of violence in British gaols, affecting 19 institutions, during prison officers' dispute (May).

1987    Three hundred injured in demonstrations outside Wapping print works on anniversary of strike against Rupert Murdoch; widespread criticism of police behaviour (Jan.). Ninety-seven people arrested after disturbances at Notting Hill Carnival (Aug.).

1988    Serious riots and fires at Haverigg Prison, Cumbria, and Longriggend Remand Centre, Fife, the latter causing £1 million of damage (June).

1989    Following earlier disturbances, four-day riot at Risley Remand Centre leads to £2 million of damage.

1990    Series of anti-poll tax demonstrations across country (Mar.). Anti-poll tax rally in London attended by estimated 300,000 people, leads to rioting in Trafalgar Square (31 Mar.). Major riot at Strangeways Prison, Manchester (Apr.) leads to almost four-week siege of prison and estimated damage of several million pounds. Anti-poll tax demonstrators battle with police in Brixton (Oct.).

1991    Youths battle with police in series of disturbances in Leeds, Telford, Cardiff and Oxford (July–Aug.). Youths in Newcastle upon Tyne engage in three nights of arson, looting and affray.

1992    Five nights of disorder at estates in Coventry between youths and police (May). Riots in Hartcliffe area of Bristol with arson of shops and library (July). Attacks on police in Burnley and Huddersfield.

1993    Demonstrations against Twyford Down road scheme at Winchester. Beginning of series of protests against A12–M11 link road in London.

1994    Riots in Hyde Park against Criminal Justice and Public Order Bill (Feb.). Further protests over M11 route (Feb.). Protests in London by disabled people over failure to pass Disabled Persons Bill (Feb.). Further violence in Oct. at anti-Criminal Justice Bill demonstration.

1995    Widespread demonstrations at British ports over live animal exports (Jan.–Mar.). Riots in Manningham area of Bradford between Asian youths and police.

# Local government

## Local government and representation

1818    Vestries Act (also known as Sturges Bourne Act) establishes a system of voting according to land-ownership in electing parish officers.

1831    Vestries Act (also known as Hobhouse Act) provides for the election of members of parish vestries and a secret ballot if requested by five ratepayers. One-third of elected representatives to retire each year.

1835    Municipal Reform Act. All members of town councils to be elected by the ratepayers, and town councils to publish their accounts. Franchise in local elections extended to all males over 21 who had been owners or tenants of property for two and a half years and had paid rates. Towns with over 6,000 population were divided into wards for voting. Property qualifications introduced, restricting election of town councillors to property owners.

1855    Metropolis Management Act. The Act set up the Metropolitan Board of Works as the main authority for London.

1888    Local Government Act. Administration of counties, including levying of rates, maintenance of roads, bridges, lunatic asylums and poor relief transferred to county councils elected by ratepayers.

1889    Establishment of London County Council (LCC).

1894    Local Government Act creates rural and urban district councils. All county and parliamentary electors given the vote in local elections. Civil functions of parish vestries transferred to new parish councils and parish meetings.

1899    Local Government Act converts the London vestries into borough councils.

1918    Representation of the People Act establishes a common franchise for county councils, boroughs, rural and urban district councils. Men entitled to vote with six-month occupancy of premises or land within the area. Women over 30 entitled to vote under the same provisions or if married to a man entitled to vote.

1928    Representation of the People Act allows women over 21 to vote at local elections.

1929    Local Government Act gives county and county borough councils control over public assistance to the poor and sick.

1945    Representation of the People Act extends franchise in local government to all those registered for parliamentary elections.

1965    Two-tier system of local government established in London. Greater London Council (GLC) set up; responsible for general services and borough councils amalgamated to form larger units.

1972    Local government reorganization in England and Wales creates six metropolitan counties to run services in the major conurbations. Thirty-nine county councils with new boundaries established to run major services. A second tier of 375 district councils to provide local services and amenities. Abolition of 1,200 councils, including old county borough councils, but 7,000 smaller parish councils retained as a third tier of local government. Subsequent legislation introduced to reform local government along similar lines in Scotland.

1985    Local Government Act abolishes GLC and metropolitan county councils and transfers functions to London boroughs and to metropolitan district councils; some services are transferred to joint authorities, such as police, fire, and waste disposal.

1986    Restrictions placed upon local authority entitlement to block grants from central government with penalties for exceeding set limits. Government takes power to 'ratecap', i.e. fix a ceiling on rates set by selected authorities.

1987    Forty-five Liverpool councillors surcharged and barred from their council seats for setting an illegal rate in defiance of the government. The government confirms plans to replace domestic rates with a flat-rate community charge ('poll tax') in Scotland from 1989 and in England from 1991. Business rates to be set by central government rather than local authorities.

1988    Local Government Finance Act introduces poll tax or community charge.

1989    Poll tax comes into force in Scotland (1 Apr.). Local Government and Housing Act restrains political activity of local government and stops councils subsidizing rent and rates.

1990    Poll tax comes into force in England and Wales (1 Apr.) and meets widespread protests including riots in London and elsewhere.

1991    Michael Heseltine (Minister of Environment) announces introduction of new council tax to replace poll tax and a review of local government structure. As interim measure Chancellor Norman Lamont's Budget announces a £140-a-head cut in poll tax for 1991–92.

1992    Local Government Finance Act formally abolishes poll tax. Local Government Act sets up Local Government Commission for England (also Scotland and Wales) to recommend changes in structure, including more unitary authorities.

1994    Local Government Commission recommends abolition of Cleveland, Humberside and Avon counties and changes to structure of several English counties, including abolition of Berkshire.

1995    Elections take place for 14 English 'shadow' unitary authorities, though full shape of local government remains unclear. Proposals for Wales to take effect in April 1996 envisaged 22 all-purpose councils to replace the eight counties and 37 district councils. In Scotland, 29 single-tier authorities replaced two-tier structure from April 1996.

# Occupations and social structure

Gregory King's estimate of the population and wealth of England and Wales, calculated for 1696

| Rank | Number of families | Persons | Yearly income per family (£) | Yearly expenditure per family (£) | Total income of groups (£) |
|---|---|---|---|---|---|
| Temporal lords | 160 | 6 400 | 2 800 | 2 400 | 448 000 |
| Spiritual lords | 26 | 520 | 1 300 | 1 100 | 33 800 |
| Baronets | 800 | 12 800 | 880 | 816 | 70 400 |
| Knights | 600 | 7 800 | 650 | 498 | 39 000 |
| Esquires | 3 000 | 30 000 | 450 | 420 | 1 350 000 |
| Gentlemen | 12 000 | 96 000 | 280 | 268 | 3 360 000 |
| Clergy, superior | 2 000 | 12 000 | 60 | 54 | 120 000 |
| Clergy, inferior | 8 000 | 40 000 | 45 | 40 | 360 000 |
| Persons in the law | 10 000 | 70 000 | 140 | 119 | 1 400 000 |
| Sciences and liberal arts | 16 000 | 80 000 | 60 | 57.10s. | 960 000 |
| Persons in offices (higher) | 5 000 | 40 000 | 240 | 216 | 1 200 000 |
| Persons in offices (lower) | 5 000 | 30 000 | 120 | 108 | 600 000 |
| Naval officers | 5 000 | 20 000 | 80 | 72 | 400 000 |
| Military officers | 4 000 | 16 000 | 60 | 56 | 240 000 |
| Common soldiers | 35 000 | 70 000 | 14 | 15 | 490 000 |
| Freeholders (better sort) | 40 000 | 280 000 | 84 | 77 | 3 360 000 |
| Freeholders (lesser) | 140 000 | 700 000 | 50 | 45.10s. | 7 000 000 |
| Farmers | 150 000 | 750 000 | 44 | 42.15s. | 6 600 000 |

(*cont.*)

Gregory King's estimate of the population and wealth of
England and Wales, calculated for 1696 (*cont.*)

| Rank | Number of families | Persons | Yearly income per family (£) | Yearly expenditure per family (£) | Total income of groups (£) |
|---|---|---|---|---|---|
| Labouring people and servants | 364 000 | 1 275 000 | 15 | 15.5s. | 5 460 000 |
| Cottagers and paupers | 400 000 | 1 300 000 | 6.10s. | 7.6.3d. | 2 600 000 |
| Artisans, handicrafts | 60 000 | 240 000 | 40 | 38 | 2 400 000 |
| Merchants by sea | 2 000 | 16 000 | 400 | 320 | 800 000 |
| Merchants by land | 8 000 | 48 000 | 200 | 170 | 1 600 000 |
| Shopkeepers, tradesmen | 40 000 | 180 000 | 45 | 42.15s. | 1 800 000 |
| Common seamen | 50 000 | 150 000 | 20 | 21.10s. | 1 000 000 |
| Vagrants | | 30 000 | 2 | 3 | 60 000 |

Source: G. N. Clark, *The Wealth of England from 1496 to 1760* (Oxford,
1946), pp. 192–3.

Patrick Colquhoun's estimate of the social structure of the
United Kingdom, *c.* 1815 (000)

| | |
|---|---|
| Royalty and nobility | 3 |
| Baronets, knights and squires | 50 |
| Upper clergy, merchants and bankers | 40 |
| Upper civil servants and lawyers | 40 |
| Independent gentry | 150 |
| Upper doctors and other professionals | 20 |
| Army and navy officers | 70 |
| Lesser clergy | 75 |
| Upper freeholders | 300 |
| Shipowners, lesser merchants, shipbuilders, engineers and builders | 200 |
| Lesser professionals, civil servants and dissenting ministers | 250 |

(*cont.*)

Patrick Colquhoun's estimate of the social structure of the
United Kingdom, *c.* 1815 (000) (*cont.*)

| | |
|---|---:|
| Innkeepers | 375 |
| Shopkeepers and hawkers | 600 |
| Master craftsmen and manufacturers | 450 |
| Lesser freeholders | 900 |
| Farmers | 1 300 |
| Teachers, actors, clerks and shopmen | 320 |
| Artisans and other skilled workers | 4 500 |
| Agricultural labourers, miners, road and canal workers and seamen | 3 500 |
| Personal and household servants | 1 300 |
| Soldiers and sailors | 800 |
| Paupers, vagrants, prisoners and lunatics | 1 900 |

Source: G. D. H. Cole and R. Postgate, *The Common People, 1746–1946*,
6th edn (London, Methuen, 1963), p. 71.

Principal occupation groups in Britain in 1851 in order of size

| | Male | Female |
|---|---:|---:|
| Total population | 10 224 000 | 10 736 000 |
| Population of 10 years old and upwards | 7 616 000 | 8 155 000 |
| Agriculture: farmer, grazier, labourer, servant | 1 563 000 | 227 000 |
| Domestic service (excluding farm service) | 134 000 | 905 000 |
| Cotton worker, every kind, with printer, dyer | 255 000 | 272 000 |
| Building craftsman: carpenter, bricklayer, mason, plasterer, plumber, etc. | 442 000 | 1 000 |
| Labourer (unspecified) | 367 000 | 9 000 |
| Milliner, dressmaker, seamstress (seamster) | 494 | 340 000 |
| Wool-worker, every kind, with carpet-weaver | 171 000 | 113 000 |
| Shoemaker | 243 000 | 31 000 |
| Coal-miner | 216 000 | 3 000 |
| Tailor | 135 000 | 18 000 |
| Washerwoman | | 145 000 |
| Seaman (merchant), pilot | 144 000 | |
| Silk-worker | 53 000 | 80 000 |
| Blacksmith | 112 000 | 592 |
| Linen-, flax-worker | 47 000 | 56 000 |
| Carter, carmen, coachman, postboy, cabman, busman, etc. | 83 000 | 1 000 |

(*cont.*)

## Principal occupation groups in Britain in 1851 in order of size (*cont.*)

|  | Male | Female |
|---|---|---|
| Ironworker, founder, moulder (excluding iron-mining, nails, hardware, cutlery, files, tools, machines) | 79 000 | 590 |
| Railway driver, etc., porter, etc., labourer, platelayer | 65 000 | 54 |
| Hosiery worker | 35 000 | 30 000 |
| Lace-worker | 10 000 | 54 000 |
| Machine, boiler-maker | 63 000 | 647 |
| Baker | 56 000 | 7 000 |
| Copper-, tin-, lead-miner | 53 000 | 7 000 |
| Charwoman |  | 55 000 |
| Commercial clerk | 44 000 | 19 |
| Fisherman | 37 000 | 1 000 |
| Miller | 37 000 | 562 |
| Earthenware worker | 25 000 | 11 000 |
| Sawyer | 35 000 | 23 |
| Shipwright, boat-builder, block-, and mast-maker | 32 000 | 28 |
| Straw-plait worker | 4 000 | 28 000 |
| Wheelwright | 30 000 | 106 |
| Glover | 4 500 | 25 000 |
| Nailer | 19 000 | 10 000 |
| Iron-miner | 27 000 | 910 |
| Tanner, currier, fellmonger | 25 000 | 276 |
| Printer | 22 000 | 222 |

Source: Compiled from figures collected in 1851 census, *Parliamentary Papers* (1691), LXXXVIII, 1852–53.

## Occupational groups in Britain, 1911–81 (000)

|  | 1911 | 1921 | 1931 | 1951 | 1961 | 1971 | 1981 |
|---|---|---|---|---|---|---|---|
| Agriculture and fishing | 1 483 | 1 373 | 1 180 | 1 126 | 855 | 635 | 352 |
| Mining and quarrying | 1 308 | 1 469 | 1 040 | 841 | 722 | 391 | 336 |
| Manufacturing industries (*cont.*) | 6 147 | 6 723 | 5 981 | 7 902 | 8 383 | 8 136 | 5 974 |

## Occupational groups in Britain, 1911–81 (000) (*cont.*)

|  | 1911 | 1921 | 1931 | 1951 | 1961 | 1971 | 1981 |
|---|---|---|---|---|---|---|---|
| Building and contracting | 950 | 826 | 970 | 1 430 | 1 705 | 1 673 | 1 564 |
| Gas, electricity and water | 117 | 180 | 224 | 358 | 377 | 362 | 338 |
| Transport and communications | 1 260 | 1 359 | 1 430 | 1 705 | 1 673 | 1 564 | 1 422 |
| Distributive trades | n.a. | n.a. | 2 697 | 2 742 | 3 189 | 3 016 | 2 715 |
| Insurance, banking and finance | n.a. | 328 | 388 | 489 | 722 | 952 | 1 295 |
| Public administration: |  |  |  |  |  |  |  |
| national (inc. defence) | 452 | 480 | 368 | 1 036 | 798 | 812 | 589 |
| local | 555 | 457 | 541 | 602 | 629 | 760 | 931 |
| Professional scientific | n.a. | 868 | 1 018 | 1 536 | 2 120 | 2 901 | 3 649 |
| Miscellaneous services | n.a. | n.a. | 2 713 | 2 393 | 2 270 | 2 534 | 2 522 |
| Domestic service | n.a. | 1 390 | 1 509 | 499 | 362 | 239 | n.a. |

Source: Derived from Department of Employment *Gazette; Annual Abstract of Statistics.*

## Employment in Britain, 1980–93 (000) [1]

|  | 1980 | 1985 | 1990 | 1993 |
|---|---|---|---|---|
| Agriculture, forestry, fishing | 352 | 321 | 277 | 255 |
| Coal, oil, gas extraction | 355 | 273 | 157 | 103 |
| Gas, electricity, water supply | 361 | 309 | 284 | 247 |
| Metals, mechanical engineering | 3 867 | 2 840 | 2 646 | 2 156 |
| Chemicals and man-made fibres | 420 | 339 | 325 | 293 |
| Food, drink, tobacco | 705 | 575 | 524 | 459 |
| Textiles, leather, clothing | 716 | 550 | 477 | 401 |
| Timber, rubber, plastics, furniture | 554 | 473 | 540 | 438 |
| Paper, printing, publishing | 538 | 477 | 481 | 443 |
| Construction | 1 206 | 994 | 1 060 | 807 |
| Wholesale, retail, hotels, catering | 4 204 | 4 213 | 4 756 | 4 452 |
| Transport, post, telecommunications | 1 464 | 1 308 | 1 361 | 1 248 |
| Banking, insurance, finance | 1 669 | 2 039 | 2 701 | 2 577 |
| Public administration | 1 925 | 1 862 | 1 942 | 1 823 |
| Education | 1 586 | 1 557 | 1 735 | 1 806 |
| Health | 1 214 | 1 489 | 1 664 | 1 713 |

[1] In 1981 the industrial classification changed, making it impossible to compare later figures with earlier ones. Figures are for June each year.

# Labour

## Chronology of trade union history

1717    Reports of widespread combination of wool-workers in Devon and Somerset.

1718    Royal Proclamation against 'lawless clubs and societies'.

1719    Weavers' riots in Norwich and Colchester over the use of foreign calico; attacks on people wearing calico in London and campaign for an Act prohibiting their use mounted by the Weavers' Company. Keelmen's strike in the north-east.

1720    Weavers' riots in Tiverton over use of imported wool. Renewed rioting in London over delay in passing a Calico Act.

1723–26    Widespread stoppage and disturbances in the West Country woollen industry during a wage dispute. Acts passed in 1726 and 1728 to regulate wages.

1738–40    Renewed strikes and disturbances in the West Country over wage rates.

1740    Colliers' disturbances in the north-east to obtain wage rises.

1744    Keelmen's strike in the north-east against overloading of keels and a 'Contract' agreed with masters regulating wages and conditions.

1750    Disturbances in the West Country over the use of imported Irish wool. Strike of keelmen on the Tyne and Wear in defence of terms of 'Contract'. Strike broken by the use of troops.

1752    Strike of Norwich weavers to enforce regulation of the trade.

1755    Act obtained by Gloucestershire weavers to regulate wages ignored by clothiers; widespread disorder suppressed by the use of troops.

1758    London coal-heavers obtain an Act regulating the trade and placing them under the direction of the alderman for Billingsgate.

1762    Seamen's strike in Liverpool.

1765     Protracted colliers' strike in the north-east over the yearly 'bond'. Campaign of Spitalfields' weavers against imports of French silks achieves prohibitory Act.

1767–68  Widespread industrial disputes among the London trades including silk-weavers, coal-heavers, seamen, hatters, tailors, watermen, sawyers and coopers.

1768     Seamen's and keelmen's strikes in the north-east.

1773     Spitalfields Act obtained to regulate wages of London silk-weavers.

1775     Liverpool sailors' strike.

1778–79  Framework knitters' campaign for Act regulating wages defeated in Parliament. Disturbances in Nottingham following rejection of Bill. Machine-breaking in Lancashire directed at large spinning-jennies. Arkwright's factory at Birkacre, near Chorley, destroyed.

1792     Strikes of seamen along the east coast, of shipyard workers, Lancashire miners and several London trades. Power-loom factory of Messrs Grimshaw burnt down by Manchester weavers.

1793     Friendly Societies Act gives societies legal status and protection for their funds.

1797     Unlawful Oaths Act passed in wake of naval mutinies makes secret oath-taking illegal. Used subsequently to restrict trade union organization. Campaign of London watchmakers against taxes on their trade.

1799     Combination Act: passed as a result of petition of master millwrights of London for a Bill to outlaw combinations in the trade. Although combinations of workmen could already be prosecuted as conspiracies and for other offences in common law, the petition sought an Act similar to another 40 or so Acts passed during the eighteenth century to provide for summary prosecution (i.e. before a magistrate) of combinations in particular trades. On behalf of the government, Wilberforce suggested that the Act should apply to *all* combinations and this was supported by Pitt. The Act provided for summary prosecution before a single magistrate on the evidence of one or more witnesses. Workmen could be sentenced to three months in gaol or two months in a House of Correction with hard labour for: (a) combining to improve conditions or raise wages; (b) inducing others to leave work; (c) refusing to work with others; (d) attending meetings with the purpose of improving wages and conditions or persuading others to attend such a meeting or raise money for such a meeting; (e) contributing to the expenses of anyone tried under the Act; (f) holding money for a combination and refusing to answer questions about it.

1800     Objections to the 1799 Combination Act complained about the vagueness of its language; the use of summary jurisdiction; the possibility of employer-magistrates trying their own workmen; the compulsion to answer questions about money possibly held for a combination, thereby incriminating oneself or else face automatic sentence under the Act. Petitions for total repeal led by the Whig, Sheridan, were resisted by Pitt who claimed that provisions for summary prosecution of combinations were essential. The Combination Act of 1800, therefore, retained the principal features of the 1799 Act, but modified some of its features, notably: (a) two magistrates instead of one to try cases; (b) employer-magistrates prohibited from trying cases of men in their own trade; (c) an arbitration provision was introduced; (d) masters were prohibited from combining to reduce wages, increase hours or worsen conditions.

1801     Extensive strike of shipwrights in government dockyards led and organized by John Gast.

1802     Strike in civilian shipyards on Thames. Petition of clothiers in the south-west against gig-mills, followed by strikes and machine-breaking in the south-west and Yorkshire.

1803     First annual suspension of statutes regulating woollen industry. Strike of Tyne keelmen.

1805     Wool-workers petition for regulation of trade.

1807     Cotton-weavers petition for minimum wage bill.

1808     Manchester cotton-weavers' strike leads to widespread stoppage throughout the cotton district; 60,000 looms idle by June.

1809     Repeal of protective legislation in the woollen industry. Further strike of the Tyne keelmen.

1810     London printers of *The Times* prosecuted for conspiracy. Strike of Lancashire and Cheshire cotton-spinners, organized by 'General Union of Spinners'. Strike collapsed after four months.

1811     Beginning of Luddite campaign in Nottinghamshire directed at hosiers who refused to raise wages and end abuses in the trade. Frame-breaking spreads through hosiery districts of Nottinghamshire, Derbyshire and northern Leicestershire.

1812      Rejection of framework-knitters' Bill to regulate the trade leads to continued frame-breaking. Machine-breaking spreads to the Yorkshire croppers with attacks on mills around Huddersfield and Leeds and to Lancashire and Cheshire where attacks were made on power-looms. Frame-breaking made a capital offence. In Scotland, cotton-weavers mount a six-week strike covering the area from Aberdeen to Carlisle. Luddite attacks in Yorkshire reach climax in Apr. with unsuccessful attack on Rawfold's Mill of William Cartwright and in Lancashire with attacks on Westhoughton. Arrests of leaders and garrisoning of the north with over 10,000 troops gradually ends the main wave of machine-breaking.

1813      Clauses in Elizabethan Statute of Artificers empowering judges to fix wages repealed.

1814      Clauses in Elizabethan Statute of Artificers regulating apprenticeship abolished. Francis Place begins collecting evidence for campaign against the Combination Laws.

1815      Seamen's strike in north-eastern ports. Compromise settlement reached with shipowners.

1816      Strikes against lay-offs and wage reductions in iron-working districts. Renewed machine-breaking in textile districts.

1817      March of the 'blanketeers' (distressed Lancashire weavers) from Manchester for relief and parliamentary reform broken up by troops.

1818      Weavers' and spinners' strikes in Lancashire and attempts to form a 'General Union of the Trades'. Metropolitan Trades Committee sets up early general union, the 'Philanthropic Hercules'.

1819      Keelmen's strike on Tyneside.

1820      Scottish weavers' strike, and clashes with troops.

1821      Strikes and riots in Shropshire iron districts.

1824      Campaign for repeal of the Combination Laws managed by Francis Place and Joseph Hume MP. In February 1824 Hume moved resolutions in the House of Commons for committee to consider the laws on the emigration of artisans, the exportation of machinery and combinations of workmen. As a result Combination Act of 1824 was passed, virtually repealing all the provisions of the 1800 Act. Combination to alter wages or conditions now legal and freed from prosecution for conspiracy or other offences existing prior to the Combination Laws. Violence or threats in trade disputes made punishable by two months' hard labour on summary conviction before two magistrates not engaged in, or related to persons engaged in, the trade.

1825    The 1824 Act led to a rapid increase in trade union activity with extensive strikes, including some violence. This resulted in a new Act, the Combination Act of 1825, repealing the 1824 Act. It exempted from prosecution combinations which met to bargain over wages and conditions, but did not explicitly confer a right to strike. Violence, intimidation, molestation and obstruction (including picketing) in furtherance of a dispute made offenders liable to three months' imprisonment. The effect was to impose a narrow definition of legal activity for trade unions, confining them to peaceful collective bargaining over wages and hours only. Combinations to negotiate outside these limits could be prosecuted as criminal conspiracy 'in restraint of trade'. Also, many of the methods which unions might employ were liable to prosecution and were still ill-defined in law. *Trades Newspaper* founded by John Gast and others.

1829    General Union of Spinners formed by John Doherty in Manchester. Also launches Union of Trades.

1830    Union of Trades changes name to National Association for the Protection of Labour and forms branches in cotton districts, Midlands and Potteries. Strike of Northumberland and Durham Colliers' Union under leadership of Thomas Hepburn. Strike broken by eviction of colliers from their houses.

1831    Collapse of spinners' union after strikes early in the year; Doherty founds *Voice of the People* journal.

1832    Industrial unrest in South Wales. Merthyr occupied by miners. Exchange of goods made by cooperative production facilitated by National Equitable Labour Exchange. National Association for the Protection of Labour collapses. Operative Builders' Union formed as federation of building unions; executive was Grand Committee, appointed by Grand Lodge of 'Builders' Parliament' which met twice a year. Involved in a series of strikes and lock-outs to change contract system of labour. William Benbow's *Grand National Holiday and Congress of the Productive Classes* suggests idea of a general strike.

1833    Widespread 'turn-outs' of workmen lead to moves for general unions. Owenite Grand National Moral Union of the Productive Classes formed in Oct. at conference of delegates from Co-operative and Trade Societies 'to establish for the productive classes a complete dominion over the fruits of their own industry'. In Nov. Robert Owen and John Fielden establish the Society for Promoting National Regeneration with the intention of securing an eight-hour day by means of a limited general strike on 1 Mar. 1834.

1834    On 13 Feb. conference of trade union delegates in London decides to consolidate all trade unions in a single body with central committee and district lodges, the Grand National Consolidated Trades' Union (GNCTU) of Great Britain and Ireland. It had up to 16,000 fee-paying members, mainly in London and provincial skilled trades, but gained little support from several important groups, such as builders, potters, cotton-spinners and Yorkshire cloth-workers. Widespread strike movement by GNCTU defeated by lock-outs and internal divisions. Owen became Grand Master of reconstituted union known as British and Foreign Consolidated Association of Industry, Humanity and Knowledge, but most unions had seceded from the body and it was virtually defunct by the end of 1834. In Mar. 1834 six labourers (the 'Tolpuddle Martyrs') convicted and sentenced to transportation for seven years for administering illegal oaths in connection with the Agricultural Labourers' Friendly Society at Tolpuddle, Dorset. Widespread protests all over the country, including a peaceful demonstration of 40,000–50,000 in London. The men were eventually pardoned and allowed to return to England.

1837    Leader of the Cotton Spinners' Association deported after he had been charged with conspiracy over the murder of a 'blackleg' in Glasgow.

1842    Strikes of coal-miners and other workers merge into General Strike for the Charter. Widespread stoppage of work enforced over much of northern England by drawing plugs from engine boilers, hence called the 'Plug-plot' riots.

1844    Miners' Association strike in the north-east and Yorkshire. Strike defeated after four months in a spate of mass evictions and use of strike-breakers.

1851    Amalgamated Society of Engineers founded, the beginning of

'New Model Unionism'. Initial membership 12,000, rising to 33,000 in 1868 and 71,000 in 1891.

1853    Amalgamated Association of Operative Cotton Spinners formed.

1854    Imported Irish labour used to defeat Preston cotton-spinners' strike.

1855    Society benefit funds protected by Friendly Societies Act.

1858    Formation of National Miners' Association by Alexander MacDonald, and of Glasgow Trades Council. Nine-week strike in the Staffordshire collieries.

1859    Peaceful picketing allowed by Molestation of Workmen Act. Building workers' strike in London and intimidation in the Manchester building trade.

1860    London Trades Council and Amalgamated Society of Carpenters and Joiners formed. Coal Mines Regulation Act abolishes truck payment and regulates conditions of employment.

1864    First national conference of trade union delegates.

1865    Reform League formed to win enfranchisement for the working class.

1866    'Sheffield Outrages' (Oct.): attacks on non-union cutlery-workers by fellow workmen. As a result, Royal Commission on Trade Unions established. *Hornby* v. *Close* case, decision against trade union trying to recoup funds from a defaulting local treasurer raises doubts over the degree of protection for funds given by Friendly Societies Act of 1855. Short-lived United Kingdom Alliance of Organized Trades formed.

1867    Master and Servant Act amended to limit prosecution of strikers for breach of contract, but unions remain dissatisfied because criminal action still possible for 'aggravated cases'. The 'Junta' – Applegarth, Allan, Coulson, Odger and Guile – mastermind trade union case for Royal Commission, with Frederic Harrison as their nominee. Report of Royal Commission recommended legalization of trade unions.

1868    First Trades Union Congress (TUC) at Manchester; 34 delegates with no formal organization.

1869    Second TUC at Birmingham; 40 delegates representing 250,000 members.

1871    Trade Union Act and Criminal Law Amendment Act give unions legal recognition and right to protect their funds, although picketing was made illegal in any form. The TUC established its Parliamentary Committee and the Amalgamated Society of Railway Servants was formed. 'Nine Hours' strike by engineers in the north-east secures shorter hours.

1872    National Agricultural Union formed by Joseph Arch. Soon had 10,000 members and a weekly journal, *Labourers' Chronicle*, which reached a circulation of 30,000.

1874    Trade unionists Alexander MacDonald and Thomas Burt elected as MPs for Stafford and Morpeth respectively. Royal Commission on labour laws set up.

1875    Conspiracy and Protection of Property Act allows peaceful picketing and eliminated conspiracy from trades disputes unless they are illegal. Employers and Workmen Act limits penalty in breach of contract to civil damages. Henry Broadhurst becomes Secretary of the TUC.

1878    Nine-week strike of cotton-weavers in Lancashire; disturbances at Preston and Blackburn.

1880    Employers' Liability Act. Re-emergence of socialist influence in next few years.

1886    National Federation of Labour formed on Tyneside.

1887    Attack launched on Broadhurst at TUC, Keir Hardie accusing him of not serving the movement properly by collaborating with the employers.

1888    H. H. Champion's *Labour Elector* launched, advocating the establishment of an Independent Labour Party. Strike of the women match-makers of Bryant & May in London. The start of 'New Unionism'.

1889    In Mar., Will Thorn begins to organize gas workers, who successfully fought to reduce hours from 12 to eight per day. In Aug., the London dockers' strike saw the dockers winning 6*d.* per hour, and was followed by the establishment of the Dock, Wharf, Riverside and General Labourers Union under Ben Tillett. Miners Federation of Great Britain (MFGB) formed.

1890    Formation of Shipping Federation, the employers' response to New Unionism.

1892    Keir Hardie carries motion for a labour representation fund at TUC, although little progress is made.

1893    Independent Labour Party set up and National Free Labour Association established. Two people killed after clashes between strikers and soldiers at Ackton Hall Colliery, near Featherstone.

1894    Change in Standing Orders of TUC; representation now related to the number of members affiliated to TUC.

1896    *Lyons* v. *Wilkins* case; injunction against Amalgamated Trade Society of Fancy Leather Workers prevents them from picketing Lyons's premises. Employers' Federation of Engineering Associations formed.

1897–98 July 1897 to Jan. 1898, national lock-out in engineering industry ends in success for employers. Scottish TUC formed.

1898    Employers' Parliamentary Council formed to counter effects of TUC Parliamentary Committee.

1899    Formation of General Federation of Trade Unions to control a fund for mutual support in the event of strikes.

1900    Labour Representation Committee (LRC) formed, following Scottish Workers' Parliamentary Election Committee.

1901    Taff Vale case. A strike against the Taff Vale Railway Co., sanctioned by the Amalgamated Society of Railway Servants (ASRS), was opposed legally by Ammon Beasley, the company manager, on the strength of the *Lyons* v. *Wilkins* case. The legal case continued after the strike had ended, with the Law Lords under Lord Halsbury granting the injunction against the ASRS to stop picketing, and making the funds of the union liable for damages amounting to £23,000.

1905    'Caxton Hall Concordat' – mutual support by LRC and Parliamentary Committee of TUC for members standing for parliamentary election.

1906    Twenty-six Labour MPs elected in Jan. general election, following secret agreement between Ramsay MacDonald, secretary of the LRC, and Herbert Gladstone, Liberal Whip, aimed at securing trade union and working-class representation. Parliamentary Labour Party formed. Trades Disputes Act frees trade unions from liability for damages by strike, reversing Taff Vale judgement.

1907    ASRS threaten national railway strike, but government intervention secures agreement.

1908    Strike of Amalgamated Engineers in north-east ends in defeat after seven months.

1909    Miners' Federation formally affiliate to Labour Party. Trade Boards set up by Winston Churchill to fix wages in industries liable to cheap labour. Osborne judgement: judgement against ASRS prevents the trade unions from using their funds for political purposes.

1910    Ten months' strike by miners in South Wales, accompanied by rioting and the despatch of troops. Tom Mann publishes *Industrial Syndicalist* and then joins with Tillett and Havelock Wilson to form the National Transport Workers' Federation.

1911    Strikes of dockers and seamen joined in Aug. by railway unions, but settled after two days by Lloyd George's intervention. Two men killed by troops during clashes in Liverpool.

1912    Miners' national strike for minimum wage (Feb.), which continues until Apr. District minimum wages achieved. London dock strike collapses after use of blackleg labour to break the strike (May).

1913    Trade Union Act reverses the Osborne judgement, allowing the unions to use their funds for political purposes under certain circumstances. Eight-month strike of Irish Transport Union. National Union of Railwaymen formed by amalgamation of ASRS and other railway unions. ASLEF and Clerks' Union remain independent.

1914    Attempt to organize 'Triple Alliance' of miners, railwaymen and transport workers. Not able to organize properly before outbreak of First World War. Strike truce declared shortly after outbreak of the war by TUC.

1915    Beginning of Clydeside movement against 'dilution' of skilled trades by unskilled labour. 'Treasury agreement' negotiated between government and trade unions, relaxing trade practices and accepting compulsory arbitration. Later passed into law as Munitions of War Act. Arthur Henderson for Labour Party joins Cabinet (May). Miners' strike in South Wales in defiance of Treasury agreement; further unrest on Clydeside (July).

1916    Clyde Workers' Committee formed, leaders arrested and journals suppressed. Henderson enters War Cabinet, other Labour MPs join government (Dec.).

1917    Continuing strikes and unrest in munitions and other factories over dilution, conscription of skilled workers and rising prices, many led by unofficial committees of shop stewards. Government Commission of Enquiry into Industrial Unrest appointed. TUC decide to levy affiliate societies to increase efficiency of organization. Whitley Committee set up to report on 'Relations of Employers and Employees'. Recommends setting up of Whitley Councils, composed of employers and union leaders in each industry to discuss wages and conditions and more general problems. Not universally accepted, but Whitley Councils became established in sphere of government employment to bring sides together when in dispute.

1918    Widespread strikes against dilution and conscription, largest number of days lost for any year of the war. Police strikes in London and Merseyside.

1919    Forty Hours' strike in Glasgow called on 27 Jan., organized by Scottish TUC and Clyde Workers' Committee. Clashes with police on Friday 31 Jan. ('Bloody Friday') lead to arrest of strike leaders, calling in of troops and collapse of strike. Industrial Courts Act sets up permanent arbitration tribunal, known as the Industrial Court; can only advise. Sankey Commission looks into wages and nationalization in mining after threat of miners' strike; it accepts the principle of nationalization, but this repudiated by the government and mine-owners. National railway strike in opposition to 'Geddes Axe' (Sept.). Liverpool police strike leads to rioting. Police strikes in other cities fail; police forces purged of militants.

1920    Continuing widespread industrial unrest among miners and railwaymen, but most notably in transport, with the London dock strike. Performance before the Industrial Court earns Ernest Bevin the title of 'the dockers' KC'. 'Council of Action' formed to stop government interfering in Russian Revolution; loading of *Jolly George* with munitions blacked.

1921    Attempted action by revived Triple Alliance (Mar.–Apr.), but J.H. Thomas of railwaymen calls on miners to negotiate. On 'Black Friday' (15 Apr.) only the miners strike. TUC Coordinating Committee, led by Gosling and Bevin of transport workers, recommend a General Council with larger and wider powers than Parliamentary Committee.

1921–24 Number of amalgamations: Amalgamated Engineering Union (AEU), Transport and General Workers' Union (TGWU) and National Union of General and Municipal Workers established.

1925    Walter Citrine appointed TUC General Secretary.

1925–26 Miners' strike, leading to General Strike. In 1924 the mine-owners agreed to pay rises, but could not give them after the return to the Gold Standard and the fall of exports. Baldwin set up a Royal Commission under Herbert Samuel, but its report was unfavourable to the miners who, led by A. J. Cook, coined the slogan 'not a penny off the pay, not a second on the day'. A temporary government subsidy ran out on 1 May 1926, and all sides prepared for a lock-out. The TUC agreed to support the miners and when negotiations were broken off on 3 May because compositors stopped production of the *Daily Mail*, the General Strike began. The government, using the time gained by the Samuel Commission and the subsidy, was prepared, and troops, police and volunteers maintained essential services. Moderate union leaders became worried about the direction of the strike, and led by J. H. Thomas set up a Negotiating Committee to meet with Samuel and seek a solution. They accepted the Cabinet offer, though many saw this as a surrender, and work was resumed on 12 May. The miners continued their strike for almost six months, but were eventually forced to accept wage cuts and longer hours.

1927    Trades Disputes and Trade Union Act amends 1913 Act and imposes 'contracting in' for political levy, stopping some money going to Labour Party, and outlawing general strikes and sympathetic strikes.

1928    Amalgamation of TGWU with Workers' Union, third largest of general unions. The Mond–Turner talks initiate a new policy of union–business cooperation in industry. They went on through 1929 and were supported at the TUC despite left-wing protests.

1929    *Daily Herald* becomes official newspaper for trade union and Labour Party views.

1931    Fall of second Labour government; the General Council of the TUC refuses to accept spending cuts and Ramsay MacDonald forms National Government. The TUC, led by Bevin, maintains support for Labour Party as independent body.

1931–32    Reconstruction of National Joint Council, which became National Council of Labour, formalizing links between the TUC and the political side of the Labour movement. This gave the General Council more political influence.

1932    Cotton strike against wage cuts in textile industry.

1930–35    Economic depression reduces union membership. Miners badly hit, falling from 804,236 members in 1929 to 588,321 in

1939; surpassed in 1935 as largest union by TGWU. Some unions grew, like the AEU, the Electrical Trades Union and the General and Municipal Workers.

1938       Government officially approach TUC on mobilization for war effort.

1939–45    Wide legislation by government in industrial sphere. Bevin becomes Minister of Labour. Control of Employment Act gives government power to direct labour. Order 1305 legally restricts strikes and lock-outs and imposes compulsory arbitration. The Bridlington Agreement, 1939, between TUC affiliated unions restricts 'poaching' members from each other. Increase in memberships of most unions during war years.

1944       National Union of Mineworkers formed to replace MFGB with more centralized organization.

1946       Repeal of 1927 Trades Disputes and Trade Union Act.

1951       Order 1305 withdrawn after unsuccessful prosecution of dock strikers.

1956       Frank Cousins becomes General Secretary of TGWU. *Bonsor* v. *Musicians' Union* decides that a member was wrongfully expelled from trade union and was entitled to damages for breach of contract.

1958       National Arbitration Tribunal, remnant of Order 1305 and valued by unions, goes out of existence. London busmen's strike.

1956–62    Struggle in Electrical Trades Union over alleged malpractices of Communist leadership. Moderates led by Byrne, Cannon and Chapple defeat Communists, but only after litigation and expulsion of the union from the TUC and Labour Party.

1962       National Economic Development Council formed with TUC participation.

1964       Department of Economic Affairs set up under George Brown, Prices and Incomes Board under Aubrey Jones. *Rookes* v. *Barnard* case makes threat to strike to injure a third party illegal, even if in furtherance of a trade dispute; *Stratford* v. *Lindley* case determines that strike action not in furtherance of a trade dispute is not protected by 1906 Act.

1965       Trades Disputes Act reverses Rookes–Barnard judgement and gives trade unions further legal immunities.

1966       National seamen's strike defeated. Prices and Incomes Bill passed into law. Cousins resigns from Cabinet.

1968     One-day national stoppage by Amalgamated Union of Engineering and Foundry Workers against government's prices and incomes policy (15 May). Report of Donovan Commission on Industrial Relations (June); led by Woodcock, Clegg and Kahn-Freund, it argued against legal intervention and for improved voluntary agreements in industrial relations.

1969     Government White Paper *In Place of Strife* contemplates state intervention in industrial relations and legal sanctions against 'wildcat' strikes. Dropped after opposition from the TUC.

1970–71  Conservative government, committed to new legal framework for industrial relations, passes Industrial Relations Act in Aug. 1971, which gives the government wide-ranging and unique powers, and sets up a National Industrial Relations Court and system of registration for unions. Schemes provoke massive TUC opposition and most unions refuse to register or cooperate with it in any way.

1972     Miners' strike begins with widespread power cuts and industrial disruption (Jan.). State of Emergency declared as power crisis worsens and 1½ million workers laid off. Wilberforce Committee reports and grants many of miners' demands; strike called off (Feb.). *Heaton* v. *TGWU*: first test for the National Industrial Relations Court set up under the Industrial Relations Act (Mar.). It decided against the union in a blacking dispute, fining them £5,000 and a further £50,000 for contempt, the TGWU refusing to acknowledge the Court. Further fine in Apr. for contempt. Attempt by railway unions to start industrial action leads to government initiating its 'cooling-off' period and compulsory ballot allowed under the Act (Apr.). Ballot voted six to one in favour of action and not used by government again. Union action over decasualization of labour in docks (July) leads to the imprisonment of the 'Pentonville Five' for ignoring an order from the NIRC to stop blacking containers; led to national dock strike. *Goad* v. *AUEW*: James Goad excluded from union and appeals to NIRC. Union refuses to acknowledge the Court and fined £5,000, with £50,000 for contempt. Highest number of days lost in strikes since 1926.

1974     Miners' strike again (Jan.), following 81 per cent poll in favour of strike. Heath defeated in Feb. election called on the union issue. Labour government's Trade Union and Labour

Relations Act repeals most of the Industrial Relations Act, although the NlRC survived for a short while, sequestering £280,000 of the AEU's funds for non-payment of fines. Fines paid anonymously when AEU threatened a national stoppage. Court abolished in July. 'Social Contract' initiated between trade unions and government: attempt to achieve industrial peace by agreement and without legal intervention.

1975    TUC accepts flat-rate pay increase norm (July). Employment Protection Act gives statutory authority to the Advisory, Conciliation and Arbitration Service to arbitrate, if requested, in industrial disputes, and extends the rights of individual employees and trade unions (Nov.).

1976    Stage Two 4½ per cent pay limit agreed with TUC. Employment Protection Act comes into force.

1977    Stage Three sets earnings increase limit at 10 per cent. Firemen's strike; servicemen called in to deal with fires.

1978    Unions reject 5 per cent wage norm (Oct.); beginning of widespread industrial action during winter months by lorry drivers, water workers, hospital and municipal workers, the so-called 'winter of discontent'.

1979    Conservative government wins general election (May), pledged to reform various aspects of trade union law, including the 'closed shop', secondary picketing and use of secret ballot before strikes.

1980    First national steel strike since 1926 (Jan.–Apr.) gains 16 per cent wage increase but leaves way open to massive rationalization of the industry. 'Day of Action' (14 May), a one-day strike against government trade union legislation, receives only limited support. Employment Act restricts picketing to employees involved in a dispute and their place of work; expands exemptions from closed shop, and offers funds for secret ballots before strikes and for election of trade union officials.

1981    Three railwaymen dismissed for failing to join a union win compensation from British Rail following a decision by the European Court of Human Rights. The decision strengthens determination of the government to further reform of closed-shop legislation.

1982    Employment Act bans pre-entry closed shop and closed shops only permitted to exist where a ballot shows 85 per cent support. Retiring miners' president urges moderation on

NUM and miners vote by a small majority against a strike. Arthur Scargill succeeds Gormley as national president of the NUM. Special Wembley conference (Apr.) of the TUC plans campaign against Conservative Employment Acts.

1983   Conservative election manifesto promises further legislation to force trade unions to hold ballots on strikes and over payment of the political levy (June). National Graphical Association fined and has assets sequestered in *Stockport Messenger* dispute following its attempts to enforce a closed shop at Warrington printing plant (Nov.–Jan. 1984) and is forced to concede. Overtime ban imposed by NUM (Oct.), following NUM conference decision to oppose pit closures in July – 'rule 41'.

1984   Government bans trade unions at Government Communications Headquarters at Cheltenham. TUC calls 'Day of Action' (28 Feb.), but House of Lords rules in favour of the government's action. Chairman of Coal Board, Ian MacGregor, announces pit closures and loss of 20,000 jobs, without compulsory dismissals; NUM executive sanctions strikes in Yorkshire and Scotland and calls on other areas to support under 'rule 41' without recourse to a national ballot (Mar.). Flying pickets enforce national stoppage and beginning of a series of confrontations between police and pickets. NUM secures only patchy support from other unions and a national dock strike (July) breaks down. South Wales Mineworkers have funds sequestered for failure to pay fines over picketing (Sept.) and NUM has assets seized by order of High Court (Oct.). Coal Board begins pre-Christmas 'back to work' drive and 15,000 miners return to work. Violent incidents at Orgreave (May–June) lead to many arrests and in Dec. a taxi-driver is killed by miners when driving a working miner to work in South Wales.

1985   Following failure of negotiations a special delegate conference of the NUM decides on a return to work without agreement (Mar.). Union of Democratic Mineworkers set up, largely composed of Nottinghamshire miners who had opposed and worked through the coal strike (Aug.). The new *Today* newspaper breaks with tradition in Fleet Street by securing a one-union deal with the electricians and the use of new print technology.

1986    Wapping dispute between Rupert Murdoch and the print unions when following a strike he sacks 5,500 workers and transfers printing to a newly constructed plant at Wapping using members of the electricians' union. Picketing of the plant fails to stop the movement of papers and fines and sequestrations force the print unions to accept defeat. Widespread disruption in schools as a result of selective strikes by teachers in support of pay claim. Government imposition of a pay settlement and termination of existing negotiating machinery, the Burnham Committee, leads to further action. Trade unions complete ballots on retention of political funds. All 37 unions vote to retain them.

1987    Some teachers' unions call off industrial action, but others continue. Miners agree to industrial action against new Coal Board disciplinary procedures.

1988    Employment Act gives trade union members the right to ignore a union ballot on industrial action, outlaws industrial action to establish or preserve closed shops and introduces new restrictions on industrial action and election ballots.

1989    Employment Act limits cases going to full industrial tribunals; removes restrictions on employment of women and children; abolishes Training Commission.

1990    Employment Act constrains closed shop by making it unlawful not to employ non-union members; makes all secondary action other than picketing unlawful; forces unions to repudiate unofficial action.

1992    The Trade Union and Labour Relations (Consolidation) Acts bring together all collective employment rights, including trade union finances, elections, dismissal and time off.

1993    Government abolishes 26 wages councils. John Major refuses to reconsider ban on trade unions at GCHQ at Cheltenham. Michael Howard, Home Secretary, announces legislation to ban strikes by prison officers. Labour leader, John Smith, secures union backing for changes in Labour Party constitution.

1994    National Union of Rail, Maritime and Transport Workers calls series of one-day and two-day strikes against Railtrack. TUC invites two Conservative ministers to speak at TUC headquarters.

## Chartism: table of events

Note: For definition of Chartism see Glossary (p. 395).

1832    Reform Act.

1834    *Mar.* Tolpuddle Martyrs sentenced.
        *July* New Poor Law.

1835    Municipal Reform Act (including provision for reform of borough police).

1836    *Apr.* Foundation of Association of Working Men to procure a Cheap and Honest Press.
        *May* Newspaper duty reduced to 1*d.*
        *June* Foundation of London Working Men's Association (LWMA).

1837    *Jan.* Foundation of East London Democratic Association.
        *May* Birmingham Political Union revived; committee of LWMA and radical MPs prepare the Charter.
        *Nov. Northern Star* issued for first time (at 4½*d.*) at Leeds.

1838    *May* People's Charter published, London. National Petition published, Birmingham.
        *June* Foundation of Great Northern Union, Leeds, by Feargus O'Connor. Foundation of Northern Political Union, Newcastle.
        *Dec.* The first arrest: Revd J. R. Stephens for addressing open-air meeting in Hyde.

1839    *Feb.* General Convention of the Industrious Classes opens (4th) at British Hotel, Charing Cross.
        *Mar.* Major-General Sir C. Napier takes command of Northern District (until September 1841).
        *May* Convention moves to Birmingham; divisions appear between 'Physical' and 'Moral' Force Chartists. Several moderate delegates leave.

1839    *June* Chartist petition with 1,280,000 signatures presented to Parliament (14th); rejected (12 July) by 235 votes to 46.
        *July* Bull Ring riots, leading to the Birmingham, Bolton and Manchester Police Acts (repealed 1842).
        *Sept.* Convention dissolved (after failure of Sacred Month).
        *Nov.* Newport rising, to free Vincent. John Frost and other participants arrested, tried and transported.

1840    *Jan.* Abortive 'risings' in Dewsbury and Sheffield.
        *July* National Charter Association (NCA) founded (Manchester). Lovett released (imprisoned since July 1839).

1841    *Apr.* Foundation by Lovett of the National Association of the United Kingdom for Promoting the Political and Social Improvement of the People.
*Aug.* General election. O'Connor released (imprisoned since Mar. 1840).

1842    *Apr.* First Complete Suffrage Union Conference at Birmingham. NCA Convention (London) (12th).
*May* Second National Petition rejected by Parliament.
*Aug.* Plug riots. Trough of trade cycle, meaning wage cuts and unemployment.
*Dec.* Collapse of Second Complete Suffrage Union Conference (Birmingham).

1843    *Sept.* Chartist Convention at Birmingham accepts Land Plan.

1844    *Aug.* O'Connor–Cobden debate, Northampton.

1845    *Sept.* Agricultural Co-operative Society founded. Foundation of the Society of Fraternal Democrats.

1846    *June* Repeal of the Corn Laws.

1847    *May* Ten Hours Act. O'Connorville, first land settlement opened.

1848    *Feb.* French Revolution. Publication of *Communist Manifesto.*
*Apr.* Chartist Convention, London. Kennington Common meeting. O'Connor presents the National Petition (10th); it is rejected.
*May* National Assembly. Arrests of Chartist leaders in North.
*June* Clashes between police and Chartists in East End of London.
*Aug.* Abortive risings at Ashton, Dukinfield, Stalybridge and Oldham.

1849    *Dec.* Chartist Delegate Conference.

1850    *Jan.* Foundation of the National Reform League (Bronterre O'Brien).
*Mar.* National Charter League (O'Connorite).
*Aug.* Chartist Land Company dissolved by Act of Parliament.

1851    *Jan.* O'Connorite Convention (Manchester).
*Mar.* London Conference adopts wide programme.

1852    *Jan.* Harney buys *Northern Star,* which becomes the *Star of Freedom.* Ernest Jones and Harney quarrel: O'Connor insane.

1854    *Mar.* Labour parliament, Manchester (Jones).

1858    *Feb.* Last Chartist Convention.

## Trade union membership and trade disputes

| Year | Total number of trade unions | Total number of union members | Total number of trade union members affiliated to TUC | Number of stoppages beginning in year | Aggregate duration in working days of stoppages in progress in year |
|---|---|---|---|---|---|
| 1893 | 1 279 | 1 559 000 | 1 100 000 | 599 | 30 440 000 |
| 1894 | 1 314 | 1 530 000 | 1 000 000 | 903 | 9 510 000 |
| 1895 | 1 340 | 1 504 000 | 1 076 000 | 728 | 5 700 000 |
| 1896 | 1 358 | 1 608 000 | 1 093 191 | 906 | 3 560 000 |
| 1897 | 1 353 | 1 731 000 | 1 184 241 | 848 | 10 330 000 |
| 1898 | 1 326 | 1 752 000 | 1 200 000 | 695 | 15 260 000 |
| 1899 | 1 325 | 1 911 000 | 1 250 000 | 710 | 2 500 000 |
| 1900 | 1 323 | 2 022 000 | 1 200 000 | 633 | 3 090 000 |
| 1901 | 1 322 | 2 025 000 | 1 400 000 | 631 | 4 130 000 |
| 1902 | 1 297 | 2 013 000 | 1 500 000 | 432 | 3 440 000 |
| 1903 | 1 285 | 1 994 000 | 1 422 518 | 380 | 2 320 000 |
| 1904 | 1 256 | 1 967 000 | 1 541 000 | 346 | 1 460 000 |
| 1905 | 1 244 | 1 997 000 | 1 555 000 | 349 | 2 370 000 |
| 1906 | 1 282 | 2 210 000 | 1 700 000 | 479 | 3 020 000 |
| 1907 | 1 283 | 2 513 000 | 1 777 000 | 585 | 2 150 000 |
| 1908 | 1 268 | 2 485 000 | 1 705 000 | 389 | 10 790 000 |
| 1909 | 1 260 | 2 477 000 | 1 647 715 | 422 | 2 690 000 |
| 1910 | 1 269 | 2 565 000 | 1 662 133 | 521 | 9 870 000 |
| 1911 | 1 290 | 3 139 000 | 2 001 633 | 872 | 10 160 000 |
| 1912 | 1 252 | 3 416 000 | 2 232 446 | 834 | 40 890 000 |
| 1913 | 1 269 | 4 135 000 | – | 1 459 | 9 800 000 |
| 1914 | 1 260 | 4 145 000 | 2 682 357 | 972 | 9 880 000 |
| 1915 | 1 229 | 4 359 000 | 2 850 547 | 672 | 2 950 000 |
| 1916 | 1 225 | 4 644 000 | 3 082 352 | 532 | 2 450 000 |
| 1917 | 1 241 | 5 499 000 | 4 532 085 | 730 | 5 650 000 |
| 1918 | 1 264 | 6 533 000 | 5 283 676 | 1 165 | 5 880 000 |
| 1919 | 1 360 | 7 926 000 | 6 505 482 | 1 352 | 34 970 000 |
| 1920 | 1 384 | 8 348 000 | 6 417 910 | 1 607 | 26 570 000 |
| 1921 | 1 275 | 6 633 000 | 5 128 648 | 763 | 85 870 000 |
| 1922 | 1 232 | 5 625 000 | 4 369 268 | 576 | 19 850 000 |
| 1923 | 1 192 | 5 429 000 | 4 328 235 | 628 | 10 670 000 |
| 1924 | 1 194 | 5 544 000 | 4 350 982 | 710 | 8 420 000 |
| 1925 | 1 176 | 5 506 000 | 4 365 619 | 603 | 7 950 000 |
| 1926 | 1 164 | 5 219 000 | 4 163 994 | 323 | 162 233 000 |
| 1927 | 1 159 | 4 919 000 | 3 874 842 | 308 | 1 170 000 |
| 1928 | 1 142 | 4 806 000 | 3 673 144 | 302 | 1 390 000 |

*(cont.)*

## Trade union membership and trade disputes ( *cont.* )

| Year | Total number of trade unions | Total number of union members | Total number of trade union members affiliated to TUC | Number of stoppages beginning in year | Aggregate duration in working days of stoppages in progress in year |
|---|---|---|---|---|---|
| 1929 | 1 133 | 4 858 000 | 3 744 320 | 431 | 8 290 000 |
| 1930 | 1 121 | 4 842 000 | 3 719 401 | 422 | 4 400 000 |
| 1931 | 1 108 | 4 624 000 | 3 613 273 | 420 | 6 980 000 |
| 1932 | 1 081 | 4 444 000 | 3 367 911 | 389 | 6 490 000 |
| 1933 | 1 081 | 4 392 000 | 3 294 581 | 357 | 1 070 000 |
| 1934 | 1 063 | 4 590 000 | 3 388 810 | 471 | 960 000 |
| 1935 | 1 049 | 4 867 000 | 3 614 351 | 553 | 1 960 000 |
| 1936 | 1 036 | 5 295 000 | 4 008 647 | 818 | 1 830 000 |
| 1937 | 1 032 | 5 842 000 | 4 460 617 | 1 129 | 3 410 000 |
| 1938 | 1 024 | 6 053 000 | 4 669 186 | 875 | 1 330 000 |
| 1939 | 1 019 | 6 298 000 | 4 866 711 | 940 | 1 360 000 |
| 1940 | 1 004 | 6 613 000 | 5 079 094 | 922 | 940 000 |
| 1941 | 996 | 7 165 000 | 5 432 844 | 1 251 | 1 080 000 |
| 1942 | 991 | 7 867 000 | 6 024 411 | 1 303 | 1 527 000 |
| 1943 | 987 | 8 174 000 | 6 642 317 | 1 785 | 1 808 000 |
| 1944 | 963 | 8 087 000 | 6 575 654 | 2 194 | 3 714 000 |
| 1945 | 781 | 7 875 000 | 6 671 120 | 2 293 | 2 835 000 |
| 1946 | 757 | 8 803 000 | 7 540 397 | 2 205 | 2 158 000 |
| 1947 | 734 | 9 145 000 | 7 791 470 | 1 721 | 2 433 000 |
| 1948 | 735 | 9 319 000 | 7 937 091 | 1 759 | 1 944 000 |
| 1949 | 726 | 9 274 000 | 7 883 355 | 1 426 | 1 807 000 |
| 1950 | 732 | 9 289 000 | 7 827 945 | 1 339 | 1 389 000 |
| 1951 | 735 | 9 535 000 | 8 202 079 | 1 719 | 1 694 000 |
| 1952 | 719 | 9 583 000 | 8 088 450 | 1 714 | 1 792 000 |
| 1953 | 717 | 9 523 000 | 8 093 837 | 1 746 | 2 184 000 |
| 1954 | 703 | 9 556 000 | 8 106 958 | 1 989 | 2 457 000 |
| 1955 | 694 | 9 726 000 | 8 263 741 | 2 419 | 3 781 000 |
| 1956 | 674 | 9 762 000 | 8 304 709 | 2 648 | 2 083 000 |
| 1957 | 674 | 9 813 000 | 8 337 325 | 2 859 | 8 412 000 |
| 1958 | 665 | 9 626 000 | 8 176 252 | 2 629 | 3 462 000 |
| 1959 | 658 | 9 610 000 | 8 128 251 | 2 093 | 5 270 000 |
| 1960 | 654 | 9 821 000 | 8 299 393 | 2 849 | 3 024 000 |
| 1961 | 635 | 9 883 000 | 8 312 875 | 2 701 | 3 046 000 |
| 1962 | 626 | 9 887 000 | 8 315 332 | 2 449 | 5 798 000 |
| 1963 | 607 | 9 934 000 | 8 325 790 | 2 068 | 1 755 000 |
| 1964 | 641 | 10 218 000 | 8 771 012 | 2 524 | 2 277 000 |

( *cont.* )

## Trade union membership and trade disputes (*cont.*)

| Year | Total number of trade unions | Total number of union members | Total number of trade union members affiliated to TUC | Number of stoppages beginning in year | Aggregate duration in working days of stoppages in progress in year |
|------|------|------|------|------|------|
| 1965 | 629 | 10 325 000 | 8 867 522 | 2 354 | 2 925 000 |
| 1966 | 621 | 10 262 000 | 8 787 282 | 1 937 | 2 398 000 |
| 1967 | 602 | 10 190 000 | 8 725 604 | 2 116 | 2 787 000 |
| 1968 | 582 | 10 193 000 | 8 875 381 | 2 378 | 4 690 000 |
| 1969 | 561 | 10 472 000 | 9 402 170 | 3 116 | 6 846 000 |
| 1970 | 538 | 11 179 000 | 10 002 204 | 3 906 | 10 980 000 |
| 1971 | 520 | 11 127 000 | 9 894 881 | 2 228 | 13 551 000 |
| 1972 | 479 | 11 349 000 | 10 001 419 | 2 497 | 23 909 000 |
| 1973 | 519 | 11 456 000 | 10 022 224 | 2 873 | 7 197 000 |
| 1974 | 507 | 11 764 000 | 10 363 724 | 2 922 | 14 750 000 |
| 1975 | 501 | 12 193 000 | 11 036 326 | 2 282 | 6 012 000 |
| 1976 | 473 | 12 386 000 | 11 515 920 | 2 016 | 3 284 000 |
| 1977 | 481 | 12 846 000 | 11 865 390 | 2 703 | 10 142 000 |
| 1978 | 462 | 13 112 000 | 12 128 078 | 2 471 | 9 405 000 |
| 1979 | 454 | 13 498 000 | 12 172 508 | 2 080 | 29 474 000 |
| 1980 | 453 | 12 947 000 | 11 601 413 | 1 330 | 11 964 000 |
| 1981 | 438 | 12 106 000 | 11 005 984 | 1 328 | 4 266 000 |
| 1982 | 414 | 11 593 000 | 10 510 157 | 1 528 | 5 313 000 |
| 1983 | 408 | 11 337 000 | 10 087 144 | 1 352 | 3 754 000 |
| 1984 | 394 | 11 086 000 | 9 855 204 | 1 221 | 27 135 000 |
| 1985 | 375 | 10 994 000 | 9 580 502 | 887 | 6 402 000 |
| 1986 | 370 | 10 821 000 | 9 586 000 | 1 074 | 1 920 000 |
| 1987 | 335 | 10 539 000 | 9 243 000 | 1 016 | 3 546 000 |
| 1988 | 330 | 10 475 000 | 9 127 000 | 781 | 3 702 000 |
| 1989 | 315 | 10 376 000 | 8 652 000 | 701 | 4 128 000 |
| 1990 | 309 | 10 158 000 | 8 405 000 | 630 | 1 903 000 |
| 1991 | 287 | 9 947 000 | 8 193 000 | 369 | 761 000 |
| 1992 | 275 | 9 585 000 | 7 762 000 | 253 | 528 000 |

Sources: H. Pelling, *A History of British Trade Unionism*, 4th edn (Harmondsworth, Penguin, 1987), pp. 297–300; G. S. Bain and R. Price, *Profiles of Union Growth: A Comparative Statistical Portrait of Eight Countries* (Oxford, Blackwell, 1980), pp. 37–8; Department of Employment *Gazette* (London, HMSO).

# Religion

## Major events in British church history, 1714–1995

1714    Bolingbroke passes Schism Act by which teachers were required to declare their conformity to the Established Church; aimed at restricting the dissenting academies.

1716    Dr Williams founds the Williams Library. Non-jurors negotiate for reunion with the Greek Church, but fail.

1717    Convocation prorogued by government after it censures Bishop Hoadly's *The Nature of the Kingdom, or Church of Christ* which declares against tests of orthodoxy and argues that sincerity is the only requirement of Christian profession. Convocation does not meet for business again until 1852.

1719    Repeal of Occasional Conformity and Schism Acts. Presbyterians meet at Salter's Hall to protest against the subscription to a belief in the Trinity by the clergy.

1721    Toleration Act passed by Irish parliament.

1722    Francis Atterbury, Bishop of Rochester, arrested and banished for corresponding with the Pretender.

1723    Penal levy of £100,000 placed on Catholics.

1727    Walpole introduces first annual Bill of Indemnity allowing Dissenters to escape penalties of the Test and Corporation Acts by taking the sacrament after rather than before election to office. Independent, Baptist and Presbyterian congregations form General Body of Protestant Dissenting Ministers.

1728    Moravian mission established in England.

1729    John Wesley, Junior Fellow of Lincoln College, Oxford, and friends begin to meet at Oxford in a strict religious society, dubbed as 'Methodists'. Doddridge establishes a Presbyterian Academy at Market Harborough.

1730    Tindal's *Christianity as Old as the Creation* declares that Christ merely confirmed the law revealed by the light of nature.

1732    Organization of Protestant dissenting deputies to act as pressure group for Dissenters.

1736    Bishop Warburton's *Alliance of Church and State* argues for the Established Church and a Test Act. Attempt to relieve Quakers from tithes fails.

1738    John Wesley returns from America, falls under the influence of Peter Böhler, a Moravian, and is converted on 24 May. George Whitefield undertakes missionary work in America.

1739    Wesley follows Whitefield's example of preaching in the open air. Methodist Society meets in Old Foundry, Moorfields, London.

1740    Wesley severs his connection with the Moravians. Begins to employ lay preachers and build chapels. Controversy with Whitefield over Calvinist doctrine of predestination.

1742    Dodwell's *Christianity Not Founded on Argument* attacks both Deists and Christians for belief in the harmony of reason and revelation.

1743    Methodists produce rules for 'classes'. Welsh Calvinistic Methodist body founded by Whitefield.

1744    First Methodist Conference held at Foundry Chapel, London, consisting of John and Charles Wesley, four clergy and four lay preachers. Resolves that bishops are to be obeyed 'in all things indifferent', canons to be observed 'as far as can be done with a safe conscience' and 'societies to be formed wherever the preachers go'.

1746    Persecution of Scottish episcopal clergy for Jacobitism. Meetings of more than five banned and clergy forbidden to act as private chaplains.

1747    Methodist societies grouped into circuits.

1749    Calvinists under Whitefield desert Wesley; Whitefield becomes chaplain to Lady Huntingdon.

1756    Wesley's *Twelve Reasons Against a Separation from the Church* attempts to restrain breakaway tendencies among his followers.

1760    Wesley's lay preachers take out licences as dissenting teachers and administer the sacraments. Condemned by Charles Wesley. Board of Deputies of British Jews established.

1762    Warburton attacks Wesley and 'enthusiasm'.

1768    Lady Huntingdon founds a seminary at Trefecca.

1770    Wesley denounces Calvinism at conference; General Baptist New Communion established.

1771    Feathers Tavern petition against subscription to the Thirty-nine Articles; rejected by 217 to 17 in Parliament. Several clergy leave Established Church and become Unitarians.

1777    City Road Chapel, London, founded by Methodists.

1778    Sir George Savile obtains Catholic Relief Act. Roman Catholic worship permitted. New oath of allegiance. Protestant Association founded.

1779    Dissenting ministers and schoolmasters relieved from subscription to the Thirty-nine Articles.

1780    Gordon riots following campaign by Protestant Association against Catholic Relief Act of 1778. Mass petition of Parliament leads to riots in London with attacks on houses, chapels and embassies of Catholics. Raikes founds Sunday schools at Gloucester.

1781    Lady Huntingdon's Connexion separates from Church of England.

1782    Charles Simeon ordained curate of Trinity Church, Cambridge; introduces evangelical movement into the University.

1784    Wesley ordains Coke and Asbury as 'Superintendents' in America.

1787    Beaufoy's motion for repeal of the Test and Corporation Acts is defeated in the House of Commons. Beilby Porteus becomes Bishop of London and leads the Evangelical Revival within the Church of England, assisted by Hannah More, William Wilberforce and other members of what became known as the 'Clapham Sect'.

1789    Dr Richard Price, Unitarian preacher and theologian, preaches sermon at the annual dinner of the London Revolution Society (4 Nov.), welcoming the French Revolution for its stimulus to reform in civil and ecclesiastical affairs.

1790    Motions for repeal of Test and Corporation Acts withdrawn from Parliament without a division.

1791    Attacks on Dissenters at Birmingham, Priestley's house destroyed by mob. Death of Wesley.

1794    Paley's *Evidence of Christianity* assumes the existence of a personal God and infers the probability of revelation. Paine's *Age of Reason* attacks Christianity from a deistic standpoint. Stonyhurst College founded for Roman Catholic students.

1795    Separation of Methodist and Anglican Churches made final as a result of breakdown of plans for reconciliation. Maynooth College founded in Ireland to provide seminary for Catholic priests other than in France.

1797    Methodist New Connexion secedes from main Wesleyan body.

1799    Church Missionary Society agreed on in principle by evangelical group (fully established in 1801).

1801    Pitt's proposals for Catholic relief blocked by opposition of the King.

1804    British and Foreign Bible Society founded.

1807    William Wilberforce, Henry Thornton, Sir James Stephen, Lord Teignmouth, Granville Sharp and John Venn form the 'Clapham Sect' and campaign for various philanthropic causes, including the end of the slave trade.

1808    Expulsion of Hugh Bourne from Wesleyan Methodist Conference for open-air preaching.

1811    Welsh Calvinistic Methodists leave Church of England. Sidmouth's Bill to limit itinerant preaching defeated after protests from dissenting groups.

1812    Grattan's proposal for Catholic relief defeated. Unitarian Relief Act passed; Conventicle and Five-Mile Acts repealed. Primitive Methodist Connexion formed by Hugh Bourne and William Clowes.

1814    Wesleyan Missionary Society organized. Death of prophetess Joanna Southcott; followers, known as the New Israelites, found chapel in London.

1815    Bryanites or 'Bible Christians' separate from Methodists.

1816    Motion for Catholic relief defeated in the Lords.

1817    Military and Naval Officers' Oath Bill opens all ranks in the army and navy to Catholics.

1818    Church Building Society founded. At its instigation Parliament grants £1 million for church building and appoints a Commission to superintend its distribution.

1820    Revd Darby leaves Church of England and founds Plymouth Brethren, teaching a rigid Calvinism and the priesthood of all believers.

1826    Rose preaches at Cambridge on duties of the clergy and founds modern High Churchmanship.

1828    Repeal of Test and Corporation Acts, hence admitting Nonconformists to Parliament. Church Building Act passed.

1829    Catholic Emancipation passed; Catholics permitted to sit in Parliament.

1831    Formation of Congregational Union of England and Wales.

1832    Palmer's *Origines Liturgicae* prepares the way for the Oxford Movement and Rose founds *British Magazine* for defence of High Church principles. Church Inquiry: Commissioners appointed.

1833    Keble's Assize Sermon on 'National Apostasy' denounces suppression of 10 Irish bishoprics and is later declared by

Newman to have inaugurated the Oxford Movement. *Tracts for the Times* begin to appear. Nonconformists allowed to celebrate marriages in their chapels.

1834    Lords defeat admission of Nonconformists to university degrees. Wesleyan Methodist Association founded.

1835    Wiseman returns to England to lecture on the beliefs and system of Catholicism. Pusey joins the High Church movement.

1836    Tithes paid in kind commuted into a rent charge to vary with the price of corn. Ecclesiastical Commissioners incorporated. Newman's *Prophetical Office of the Church* defines the theory of the Oxford Movement. Church Pastoral Aid Society founded. Solemnization of Marriages Act permits licences to be issued for marriage in register offices and Nonconformist chapels.

1837    Additional Curates Society founded to provide extra clergy.

1838    Pluralities Act and Acts for building and enlarging churches passed. Froude's *Remains*, edited by Newman and Keble, condemns the Reformation.

1840    New Church Discipline Act. Jewish Reform Movement founded.

1841    Tait and three other Oxford tutors issue protest against Tract 90, in which Newman explained the Thirty-nine Articles in a Catholic sense. Newman censured and persuaded to end the Tracts. Miall founds *The Nonconformist.*

1843    Newman resigns as vicar of St Mary's. Pusey forbidden to preach for two years. New Parishes Act. 'Disruption' in Scotland and formation of Free Church of Scotland.

1844    Ward's *Ideal of a Christian Church* condemned by Oxford authorities. Nonconformists found Liberation Society.

1845    Ward joins the Roman Catholic Church; Newman follows. Pusey, Marriott and Mozley lead the Anglo-Catholic Party.

1846    The Evangelical Alliance formed to oppose Romanism, Puseyism and rationalism.

1847    United Presbyterian Church of Scotland formed.

1849    Wesleyan Methodist Reformers formed after 'Fly-sheets' controversy leads to expulsion from main body.

1850    Re-establishment of Catholic hierarchy to English sees. Manning (later Cardinal) joins Roman Catholic Church. Pusey censured for use of Catholic devotional literature. Beginning of 'papal aggression' scare in England.

1851    Census of church attendance reveals only half the population regularly attend Sunday worship (see p. 241).

1852    Convocation recommences.

1854    Act for extending licences of dissenting places of worship.

1859    Darwin publishes the *Origin of Species by Natural Selection*, starting controversy about the literal truth of the Bible.

1860    At meeting of British Association in Oxford, Bishop Wilberforce attacks and Huxley defends Darwin's theory of evolution. English Church Union founded to organize High Church movement. *Essays and Reviews* published and arouse considerable controversy over their 'broad church' views, attaching little importance to nicety of dogma but stressing Christian virtues. Act for opening grammar schools to Dissenters.

1861    Convocation condemns *Essays and Reviews.*

1862    *The Pentateuch*, by Dr Colenso, Bishop of Natal, asserts the Bible contains 'unhistorical parts'. Condemned by Convocation and excommunicated.

1863    Bishop of London's fund for remedying spiritual destitution founded.

1864    Newman publishes his spiritual autobiography, *Apologia pro Vita Sua.*

1865    'General' William Booth assumes leadership of a Christian Mission for the 'evangelization of the very lowest classes', later called the Salvation Army. Church Association formed to oppose ritualism. Manning appointed Catholic Archbishop of Westminster.

1866    Pope condemns efforts to promote Anglican and Catholic reunion. Act for removing religious oaths for public offices.

1868    Compulsory church rates abolished by Gladstone. Irish Church Disestablishment Bill introduced by Gladstone.

1869    Irish Church Disestablishment passed, effective from 1 Jan. 1871.

1870    Suffragan bishops appointed. Keble College, Oxford, founded. Declaration of Papal Infallibility by Vatican Council.

1871    Motion for disestablishment of English Church obtains 96 votes. Act for abolition of religious tests at the universities.

1874    Gladstone's pamphlets on Vaticanism declare papal decree of 1870 inconsistent with civil allegiance.

1876    Presbyterian Church of England formed.

1877    Methodist Conference admits laity.

1878    General William Booth formally constituted as superintendent of Salvation Army with control over funds, property and the power to nominate successor. Catholic hierarchy restored in Scotland.

1880    Burials Act allows Christian Dissenters to hold services in the churchyard of the parish.

1881    Revised version of the New Testament appears.

1882    General Booth sets forth his principles in the *Contemporary Review*, upholding the gospel, opposing sectarianism and requiring implicit obedience from his 'soldiers', aiming at the reformation of 'drunkards and other reprobates'.

1888    *Lux Mundi*, a collection of essays, defines the position of the new Oxford Movement.

1889    Mansfield Congregational College, Oxford, founded.

1890    General Booth publishes *In Darkest England, and the Way Out*, an exposé of destitution and poverty among the 'submerged tenth'. Bishop of Lincoln prosecuted in the Archbishop's Court for High Church practices. First Mosque opened at Woking, Surrey.

1891    Church's *History of the Oxford Movement* published.

1892    Conference held at Grindelwald discusses reunion of Established Church and Nonconformist bodies.

1894    Informal discussions begin about Catholic and Anglican reunion. Bill for disestablishment of Anglican Church in Wales fails to reach second reading in Parliament.

1895    Construction of Catholic Cathedral at Westminster begun.

1896    Pope condemns Anglican Orders and attempt at reconciliation comes to an end.

1898    Benefices Act forbids the public sale of advowsons and increases the power of bishops. Renewed attacks by Low Church Anglicans upon the ritualist party.

1899    Protestant agitation continues and archbishops pronounce against use of incense and processional lights. Balfour declares in favour of a Catholic university in Ireland.

1900    Free Church of Scotland and United Presbyterian Church of Scotland unite.

1901    Jewish Progressive Movement founded.

1904–5  Great Welsh revival. Large increases in membership of Nonconformist churches.

1906    Royal Commission appointed to consider Welsh Disestablishment.

1907    United Methodist Church formed from several of existing separate Methodist churches.

1910    World Missionary Conference at Edinburgh sees beginning of modern ecumenical movement.

1914    Disestablishment of the Anglican Church in Wales (effective 1920).

1921    Church of Scotland Act confirms its complete independence in all spiritual matters.

1924    Inter-denominational conference at Birmingham urges church-men to pay greater attention to social questions.

1927–8  Revised Prayer Book controversy. House of Commons rejects attempt by Church of England to modernize the Prayer Book.

1932    Following a conference at the Albert Hall in London, the Wesleyan Methodists, the Primitive Methodists and the United Methodists join to become the Methodist Church.

1942    William Temple becomes Archbishop of Canterbury.

1958    Death of Pius XII; Pope John XXIII elected.

1959    Second Vatican Council convened, the first since 1870; begins reappraisal of Roman Catholic liturgy and policy.

1960    Lord Fisher becomes first Archbishop of Canterbury to visit the Pope since the Reformation.

1962    Consecration of new Coventry Cathedral. First Hindu temple opened in Britain (London).

1963    Controversy aroused by the radical theology of the Bishop of Woolwich's (John Robinson) *Honest to God.* Sales reach 300,000 copies.

1964    Dr Coggan, Archbishop of York, advocates 'marriage' between Anglican and Methodist churches.

1965    Dr Heenan, Roman Catholic Archbishop of Westminster, created cardinal.

1969    The Sharing of Church Buildings Act enables agreements to be made by two or more churches for the sharing of church buildings.

1970    Translation of the New English Bible completed.

1972    United Reformed Church formed from the merger of the Congregational Church of England and Wales and the English Presbyterian Church. General Synod of the Church of England fails to approve a scheme for Anglican–Methodist unity, already approved by Methodists.

1979    Revised Prayer Book introduced for Anglican services.

1981    Further merger of Free Churches as Reformed Association of the Churches of Christ.

1982    Pope John Paul II visits Britain.

1985    Church of England report 'Faith in the City' criticized by the government for depiction of inner-city problems.

1986    Church of England passes measure allowing women to become deacons.

1988    First Jain temple opened in Britain at Leicester.

1992    Decision taken at General Synod of Church of England to allow ordination of women to the priesthood, subject to approval in Parliament.

1994    First women ordained as priests of the Anglican Church; several prominent defections from the Anglican Church to Roman Catholicism. Church of England reveals heavy losses in property dealing and urgent need for economy.

1995    Turnbull Commission report recommends sweeping changes in administrative structure of Church of England. Opening of Hindu temple in Neasden, north London – the largest centre for Hindu worship outside India itself.

## The Church of England: clergy and Easter Day communicants, 1801–1993

|      | Clergy | Easter Day communicants (000s) |      | Clergy | Easter Day communicants (000s) |
|------|--------|-------------------------------|------|--------|-------------------------------|
| 1801 | –      | 535   | 1901 | 23 670 | 1 945 |
| 1811 | 14 531 | 550   | 1911 | 23 193 | 2 293 |
| 1821 | –      | 570   | 1921 | 22 579 | 2 236 |
| 1831 | 14 933 | 605   | 1931 | 21 309 | 2 311 |
| 1841 | 15 730 | 755   | 1941 | n.a.   | 2 018 |
| 1851 | 16 194 | 875   | 1951 | 18 196 | 1 867 |
| 1861 | 17 966 | 995   | 1961 | 18 749 | 2 159 |
| 1871 | 19 411 | 1 110 | 1966 | 20 008 | 1 899 |
| 1881 | 20 341 | 1 225 | 1993 | 10 250 | 1 100 |
| 1891 | 22 753 | 1 490 |      |        |       |

Sources: A. D. Gilbert, *Religion and Society in Industrial England: Church, Chapel and Social Change, 1740–1914* (London, Longman, 1976), p. 28; Halsey (ed.), *Trends*, p. 424; *Britain, 1994*, p. 425.

## Nonconformist church membership in England, 1750–1900 (000)

|      | Congregationalists | Baptists | Presbyterians |
|------|--------------------|----------|---------------|
| 1750 | 15                 | 10       | –             |
| 1790 | 26                 | 20       | –             |
| 1838 | 127                | 100      | 10            |
| 1850 | 165                | 140      | 15            |
| 1880 | 190                | 200      | 56            |
| 1900 | 257                | 239      | 78            |

Source: A. D. Gilbert, *Religion and Society in Industrial England: Church, Chapel and Social Change, 1740–1914* (London, Longman, 1976), p. 37.

## Nonconformist church membership in Wales, 1815–1900 (000)

|      | Congregationalist | Baptist | Presbyterians |
|------|-------------------|---------|---------------|
| 1815 | 23                | –       | –             |
| 1838 | 43                | 25      | 110           |
| 1851 | 60                | 35      | –             |
| 1870 | –                 | 60      | 245           |
| 1880 | 116               | 80      | 275           |
| 1890 | 130               | 91      | 288           |
| 1900 | 150               | 107     | 324           |

Source: C. Cook and B. Keith, *British Historical Facts, 1830–1900* (London, Macmillan, 1975), pp. 226–9.

## Church membership in Scotland, 1831–1901 (000)

|        | Episcopal Church | Presbyterian Church of Scotland | Free Church | United Presbyterian Church | Wesleyan Methodist | Baptist |
|--------|------------------|---------------------------------|-------------|----------------------------|--------------------|---------|
| 1831   | –                | –                               | –           | –                          | 4                  | –       |
| 1841   | –                | –                               | –           | –                          | 4                  | –       |
| 1851   | 14               | –                               | 199         | –                          | 4                  | –       |
| 1861   | –                | –                               | 243         | 154                        | 4                  | –       |
| (*cont.*) |               |                                 |             |                            |                    |         |

Church membership in Scotland, 1831–1901 (000) (*cont.*)

|      | Episcopal Church | Presbyterian Church of Scotland | Free Church | United Presbyterian Church | Wesleyan Methodist | Baptist |
|------|----------|---------|------|--------------|----------|---------|
| 1871 | –  | 436 | –   | 163 | 5 | 9  |
| 1881 | –  | 528 | 312 | 175 | 5 | 10 |
| 1891 | 36 | 600 | 337 | 185 | 7 | 12 |
| 1901 | 47 | 662 | 288 | 194 | 8 | 17 |

Source: C. Cook and B. Keith, *British Historical Facts, 1830–1900* (London, Macmillan, 1975), pp. 222–30.

Nonconformist church membership in the United Kingdom, 1900–90 (000)

|      | Baptist Union | Congregational Union | United Reformed | Presbyterian Church of England | Presbyterian Church of Scotland |
|------|-------|-------|-----|----|-------|
| 1900 | 366 | 436 | –   | 76 | 1 164 |
| 1910 | 419 | 494 | –   | 87 | 1 220 |
| 1920 | 405 | –   | –   | 84 | 1 278 |
| 1930 | 406 | 390 | –   | 84 | 1 281 |
| 1940 | 382 | 459 | –   | 82 | 1 269 |
| 1950 | 338 | 387 | –   | 82 | 1 273 |
| 1960 | 318 | 212 | –   | 71 | 1 293 |
| 1970 | 293 | 165 | –   | 57 | 1 134 |
| 1975 | 256 | –   | –   | –  | –     |
| 1977 | –   | –   | 175 | –  | 1 003 |
| 1987 | –   | –   | 136 | –  | 870   |
| 1990 | 232 | –   | 120 | –  | 787   |

Note: Figures for the Baptist Union relate to the whole of the British Isles. In 1972 the Congregational Union and the Presbyterian Church in England merged to form the United Reformed Church.
Source: D. Butler and A. Sloman, *British Political Facts, 1900–1979*, 5th edn (London, Macmillan, 1980), pp. 470–2; *Britain, 1994*, pp. 426–7.

## Methodist membership in England and Wales, 1767–1914, and Great Britain, 1921–90

| | | | | | | | |
|---|---|---|---|---|---|---|---|
| 1767 | 22 410 | 1821 | 215 466 | 1881 | 630 575 | 1941 | 778 712 |
| 1771 | 26 119 | 1826 | 267 652 | 1886 | 676 542 | 1946 | 746 757 |
| 1776 | 30 875 | 1831 | 288 182 | 1891 | 690 022 | 1951 | 741 596 |
| 1781 | 37 131 | 1836 | 364 641 | 1896 | 702 411 | 1956 | 742 444 |
| 1786 | 46 559 | 1841 | 435 591 | 1901 | 732 668 | 1961 | 723 529 |
| 1791 | 56 605 | 1846 | 452 238 | 1906 | 800 234 | 1966 | 678 776 |
| 1796 | 77 402 | 1851 | 490 000 | 1911 | 783 723 | 1976 | 567 400 |
| 1801 | 91 825 | 1856 | 443 493 | 1914 | 777 886 | 1987 | 527 400 |
| 1806 | 109 135 | 1861 | 513 628 | 1921 | 801 861 | 1990 | 468 000 |
| 1811 | 143 311 | 1866 | 547 613 | 1926 | 839 797 | | |
| 1816 | 189 777 | 1871 | 570 936 | 1932 | 838 019 | | |
| 1819 | 194 670 | 1876 | 610 846 | 1936 | 818 480 | | |

Sources: A. D. Gilbert, *Religion and Society in Industrial England: Church, Chapel and Social Change, 1740–1914* (London, Longman, 1976), p. 31; Halsey (ed.), *Trends*, p. 433; *Britain, 1994*, p. 426.

## The Roman Catholic Church, 1720–1990

| | Estimated Catholic population | Churches and chapels | Actual Mass attendants |
|---|---|---|---|
| 1720 | 115 000 | – | 61 600 |
| 1780 | 69 376 | – | 37 200 |
| 1840 | 700 000 | 469 | 371 500 |
| 1851 | 900 000 | 597 | 482 000 |
| 1891 | 1 357 000 | 1 387 | 726 000 |
| 1911 | 1 710 000 | 1 773 | 915 000 |
| 1921 | 1 915 475 | 1 932 | – |
| 1941 | 2 414 002 | 2 580 | – |
| 1961 | 3 553 500 | 4 222 | 2 018 000 |
| 1969 | 4 143 854 | 4 770 | – |
| 1976 | 5 004 000 | – | – |
| 1987 | 5 700 000 | – | – |
| 1990 | 5 624 000 | 4 297 | – |

Sources: A. D. Gilbert, *Religion and Society in Industrial England: Church, Chapel and Social Change, 1740–1914* (London, Longman, 1976), p. 46; Halsey (ed.), *Trends*, p. 421; *Britain, 1994*, p. 427.

## The 1851 Religious Census of England and Wales

|  | Persons present at church on census Sunday | % of total population | % of those 'at church' on census Sunday |
|---|---|---|---|
| Church of England | 2 971 268 | 17 | 47 |
| Nonconformist | 3 110 782 | 17 | 49 |
| Roman Catholic | 249 389 | 1 | 4 |
| Other | 24 793 | 0.1 | 0.4 |
| Total | 6 356 222 | 35 | 100 |

Note: The government's Census of Religious Worship was a unique attempt to enumerate religious attendance in the nineteenth century. It was based on a return of all those attending places of worship for morning, afternoon or evening services on a given Sunday in 1851. For further details see K. S. Inglis, 'Patterns of religious worship in 1851', *Journal of Ecclesiastical History*, ii, No. 1 (1960).
Source: G. Best, *Mid-Victorian Britain, 1851–75* (London, Weidenfeld and Nicolson, 1971), p. 179.

## Buddhists, Hindus, Muslims and Sikhs in Britain, 1970–93 (000)

|  | 1970 | 1975 | 1993 |
|---|---|---|---|
| Buddhists | 6 | 21 | 25 |
| Hindus | 50 | 100 | 320 |
| Muslims | 250 | 400 | 1 000[1] |
| Sikhs | 75 | 115 | 300 |
| Jews | 450 | 450 | 300[1] |

[1]estimated
Source: Derived from HMSO, *Social Trends* No. 8 (1977); *Britain, 1994*, pp. 428–9.

# SECTION THREE

*Economic history*

# Agriculture

Percentage area of each county enclosed by Act of
Parliament in the eighteenth and nineteenth centuries

| | | | | | |
|---|---|---|---|---|---|
| Northampton | 51.5 | Warwick | 25.0 | Hereford | 3.6 |
| Huntingdon | 46.5 | Wiltshire | 24.1 | Somerset | 3.5 |
| Rutland | 46.5 | Gloucester | 22.5 | Stafford | 2.8 |
| Bedford | 46.0 | Middlesex | 19.7 | Essex | 2.2 |
| Oxford | 45.6 | Worcester | 16.5 | Sussex | 1.9 |
| Yorkshire, East Riding | 40.1 | Derby | 15.9 | Northumberland | 1.7 |
| Leicester | 38.2 | Hertford | 13.1 | Cumberland | 1.1 |
| Cambridge | 36.3 | Yorkshire, North Riding | 11.6 | Durham | 0.7 |
| Buckingham | 34.2 | Dorset | 8.7 | Westmorland | 0.6 |
| Nottingham | 32.5 | Suffolk | 7.5 | Cheshire | 0.5 |
| Norfolk | 32.3 | Hampshire | 6.4 | Monmouth | 0.4 |
| Lincoln | 29.3 | Surrey | 6.4 | Shropshire | 0.3 |
| Berkshire | 26.0 | Yorkshire, West Riding | 6.3 | Lancashire, Kent, Devon, Cornwall | 0.0 |

Source: G. Slater, *The English Peasantry and the Enclosure of Common Fields*
(London, Constable, 1907), pp. 140–7.

## Number of parliamentary Enclosure Acts per decade

| | | | | | |
|---|---|---|---|---|---|
| 1720–29 | 25 | 1760–69 | 385 | 1800–9 | 847 |
| 1730–39 | 39 | 1770–79 | 660 | 1810–19 | 853 |
| 1740–49 | 36 | 1780–89 | 246 | 1820–29 | 205 |
| 1750–59 | 137 | 1790–99 | 469 | | |

Source: G. R. Porter, *The Progress of the Nation*, Vol. I (London, C.
Knight, 1836), pp. 155–6.

The pace of enclosure by Act of Parliament accelerated during the
eighteenth century, reaching a peak during the Napoleonic Wars.

Although enclosure continued after 1830 it was on a smaller scale than in the preceding decades.

## The corn trade: imports and exports of wheat and flour by Great Britain (annual average per decade)

|         | Imports | Exports |
|---------|---------|---------|
|         | (000s of quarters) | |
| 1700–9  | n       | 104.8   |
| 1710–19 | n       | 108.8   |
| 1720–29 | 11.5    | 116.0   |
| 1730–39 | n       | 296.9   |
| 1740–49 | 1.3     | 290.7   |
| 1750–59 | 16.2    | 329.0   |
| 1760–69 | 97.0    | 235.0   |
| 1770–79 | 130.0   | 87.0    |
| 1780–89 | 153.0   | 129.0   |
| 1790–99 | 405.0   | 83.0    |

|         | Imports | Exports |
|---------|---------|---------|
|         | (000s of hundredweights) | |
| 1800–9  | 1 989.0 | n       |
| 1810–19 | 2 617.0 | n       |
| 1820–29 | 1 631.0 | n       |
| 1830–39 | 3 743   | n       |
| 1840–49 | 10 676  | n       |
| 1850–59 | 19 326  | n       |
| 1860–69 | 33 692  | n       |
| 1870–79 | 50 406  | n       |
| 1880–89 | 70 282  | n       |
| 1890–99 | 85 890  | n       |
| 1900–9  | 102 551 | n       |
| 1910–19 | 104 502 | n       |
| 1920–29 | 108 699 | n       |
| 1930–39 | 110 422 | n       |
| 1940–49 | 94 775  | n       |
| 1950–59 | 82 625  | n       |

n = negligible

Source: Mitchell and Deane, *Abstract,* pp. 94–5, 97–9; Mitchell and Jones, *Second Abstract,* p. 61.

# Trade

## Major trade and tariff agreements, 1760–1995

1786      Commercial treaty signed with France. France reduced duties on British exports of manufactured goods in return for preferential treatment for French wines and luxury goods.

1807–12  Orders in Council issued by Britain in retaliation for Napoleon's 'Continental System'. All neutral ships trading with Europe compelled to proceed via British ports and pay duties.

1812      Orders in Council revoked after widespread protests by commercial community and unrest in the manufacturing districts.

1815      Corn Law passed prohibiting import of wheat into Britain until price of wheat on the domestic market reached 80s. per quarter. Passed in order to protect the interests of British farmers who had invested heavily in agricultural production during the Napoleonic Wars, the Act aroused considerable opposition from commercial interests led by the Anti-Corn Law League.

1822–25  Revision of mercantilist Navigation Acts begun by Thomas Wallace, Vice-president of the Board of Trade, and continued by William Huskisson as Secretary to the Board of Trade. Obsolete penalties on Dutch shipping were removed; restrictions on shipping of other European nations considerably eased; but imperial trade was still reserved to British or colonial shipping.

1823      Huskisson obtains Reciprocity of Duties Act in order to permit reduction of duties with individual countries on a reciprocal basis. By 1830 such treaties concluded with most European states.

1824–25  Huskisson reduces tariffs on imports and exports to an average of 20 per cent (maximum of 30 per cent). Over 1,000 Customs Acts repealed and remaining tariffs codified.

1826      Consolidated tariff brought into operation for the whole of the United Kingdom.

| | |
|---|---|
| 1828 | 'Sliding scale' introduced to modify operation of Corn Law of 1815. High duties on imports now only payable when domestic price of corn low, and progressively reduced as price rose. Though a step towards free trade in line with the other commercial legislation of the 1820s, it failed to satisfy manufacturers and consumers. |
| 1842–45 | Sir Robert Peel reduces or abolishes duties on a wide range of raw materials, food and manufactured goods. |
| 1846 | Repeal of the Corn Laws. Free trade in corn established apart from minor registration dues (removed in 1869). |
| 1853 | Gladstone halves duties on fruit and dairy produce, cotton yarn. |
| 1860 | Gladstone abolishes all duties on fruit, dairy produce, and on all manufactured goods. Free Trade treaty signed with France. |
| 1914–18 | Temporary duties imposed on a wide range of luxury goods to restrict home consumption and economize on the use of merchant shipping in wartime. |
| 1921 | Safeguarding of Industries Act places duties on goods from countries with depreciated currencies. Preference given to products from the Empire. |
| 1925 | Duties imposed on imports of motor vehicles, musical instruments and films. Imperial preferences (reduced duties) for trade with British colonies and Dominions. |
| 1932 | Import Duties Act passed in wake of financial crisis of 1931. General duties of 10 per cent placed on most manufactured goods, and committee appointed to revise duties as necessary. Ottawa Agreement signed with Dominions for limited scheme of imperial preference. Wheat Act imposes levy on foreign wheat and guarantees domestic price to help agriculture. |
| 1944 | Britain signs Bretton Woods Agreement setting up International Monetary Fund (IMF). Member states bound themselves not to devalue currencies except under certain conditions, not to discriminate against other member states by tariffs and not to restrict international payments. The agreement came into force in 1947. |
| 1947 | Britain signatory to General Agreement on Tariffs and Trade (GATT), lowering tariff and trade restrictions. |
| 1959 | Britain organizes European Free Trade Association (EFTA) as a customs union. |
| 1973 | Britain becomes a member of the European Economic Community (EEC) and accepts programme of gradual adjustment of tariffs and customs to bring her into line with |

| 1975 | Referendum confirms Britain's membership of EEC and acceptance of conditions of entry into European market, including reduction of trading links with Commonwealth countries. |
| 1979 | Britain enters European Monetary System (EMS) but not Exchange Rate Mechanism (ERM), leaving her currency free to fluctuate in value. Exchange controls scrapped. |
| 1986 | Britain signs Single European Act permitting free movement of goods and services by 1993 within the European Community. Uruguay Round of GATT talks commences. |
| 1990 | Britain enters ERM (Oct.). |
| 1991 | Britain negotiates a potential opt-out from a single European Bank and currency at Maastricht. |
| 1992 | Britain forced out of Exchange Rate Mechanism. |
| 1993 | Single European Market comes into effect. |
| 1994 | Uruguay Round of GATT comes to successful conclusion. |

existing members and curtail imperial preferences.

## Imports and exports, 1700–1850 (annual averages per decade in £ million)

|         | Imports | Exports | Re-exports |
|---------|---------|---------|------------|
| 1700–9  | 4.8     | 4.4     | 1.7        |
| 1710–19 | 5.6     | 4.8     | 2.2        |
| 1720–29 | 6.8     | 4.9     | 2.8        |
| 1730–39 | 7.8     | 5.9     | 3.2        |
| 1740–49 | 7.3     | 6.6     | 3.6        |
| 1750–59 | 8.3     | 8.8     | 3.5        |
| 1760–69 | 10.7    | 10.0    | 4.8        |
| 1770–79 | 12.1    | 9.3     | 5.1        |
| 1780–89 | 13.8    | 10.2    | 4.3        |
| 1790–99 | 21.8    | 17.5    | 9.4        |
| 1800–9  | 28.7    | 25.4    | 12.2       |
| 1810–19 | 31.6    | 35.0    | 11.7       |
| 1820–29 | 38.3    | 46.1    | 10.0       |
| 1830–39 | 52.0    | 76.0    | 11.6       |
| 1840–49 | 79.4    | 124.5   | 17.0       |

Note: Figures for England and Wales to 1790; for Great Britain 1790–1850. Official values throughout. Figures rounded up to nearest £100,000.
Source: Mitchell and Deane, *Abstract,* pp. 279–83.

## Imports and exports, 1860–1989 (annual averages per decade in £ million)

|         | Imports  | Exports  |
|---------|----------|----------|
| 1860–69 | 260.9    | 159.7    |
| 1870–79 | 360.6    | 218.1    |
| 1880–89 | 393.6    | 230.3    |
| 1890–99 | 435.8    | 237.1    |
| 1900–9  | 570.4    | 333.3    |
| 1910–19 | 937.5    | 504.6    |
| 1920–29 | 1 259.2  | 791.4    |
| 1930–39 | 841.0    | 438.9    |
| 1940–49 | 1 672.1  | 768.5    |
| 1950–59 | 3 615.8  | 2 835.2  |
| 1960–69 | 5 433.4  | 4 817.7  |
| 1970–79 | 23 408.2 | 21 058.2 |
| 1980–89 | 79 648.7 | 69 174.7 |

Note: Figures for imports based on computed values 1860–69; declared values 1871–1939; current values 1940–89. Exports at current prices. Figures 1940–45 include munitions.
Source: Mitchell and Deane, *Abstract*, pp. 283–4; *Annual Abstract* 1970–.

## Exports of manufactures (England), 1700–1800 (% of total exports)

|      | Woollens | Linen | Cotton | Iron |
|------|----------|-------|--------|------|
| 1700 | 57.3     | –     | 0.5    | 1.6  |
| 1750 | 45.9     | 2.1   | –      | 4.4  |
| 1772 | 42.2     | 7.3   | 2.3    | 8.0  |
| 1790 | 34.8     | 4.2   | 10.0   | 6.3  |
| 1800 | 28.5     | 3.3   | 24.2   | 6.1  |

Source: Mitchell and Deane, *Abstract*, pp. 293–5.

Principal components of British imports, 1760–1830 (% of total value)

| | Corn | Other foods | Textile raw materials | Other raw materials | Other |
|---|---|---|---|---|---|
| 1760–69 | 2 | 36 | 16 | 6 | 40 |
| 1770–79 | 3 | 32 | 16 | 6 | 43 |
| 1780–89 | 3 | 31 | 18 | 5 | 43 |
| 1790–99 | 5 | 35 | 15 | 4 | 41 |
| 1800–9 | 5 | 42 | 19 | 6 | 28 |
| 1810–19 | 5 | 41 | 26 | 8 | 20 |
| 1820–29 | 3 | 35 | 33 | 10 | 19 |

Source: Mitchell and Deane, *Abstract*, pp. 285–9.

Principal components of British exports, 1760–1830 (% of total value)

| | Cotton | Woollen goods | Iron and steel | Other materials | Other |
|---|---|---|---|---|---|
| 1760–69 | 2 | 44 | 6 | 6 | 42 |
| 1770–79 | 3 | 43 | 7 | 7 | 40 |
| 1780–89 | 7 | 35 | 6 | 7 | 45 |
| 1790–99 | 15 | 30 | 7 | 7 | 41 |
| 1800–9 | 39 | 24 | 5 | 4 | 28 |
| 1810–19 | 53 | 16 | 4 | 3 | 24 |
| 1820–29 | 62 | 12 | 4 | 2 | 20 |

Source: Mitchell and Deane, *Abstract*, pp. 293–5.

Principal components of British imports, 1860–1939 (% of total value)

| | Foodstuffs | Textile raw materials | Other raw materials | Manufactured goods | Other |
|---|---|---|---|---|---|
| 1860–69 | 30 | 30 | 16 | 2 | 22 |
| 1870–79 | 30 | 35 | 12 | 2 | 21 |
| 1880–89 | 35 | 27 | 12 | 3 | 23 |
| (*cont.*) | | | | | |

Principal components of British imports, 1860–1939 (% of total value) (*cont.*)

|  | Foodstuffs | Textile raw materials | Other raw materials | Manufactured goods | Other |
|---|---|---|---|---|---|
| 1890–99 | 35 | 21 | 12 | 4 | 28 |
| 1900–9 | 32 | 19 | 14 | 6 | 29 |
| 1910–19 | 31 | 19 | 16 | 6 | 28 |
| 1920–29 | 30 | 17 | 16 | 5 | 32 |
| 1930–39 | 29 | 11 | 18 | 7 | 35 |

Source: Mitchell and Deane, *Abstract*, pp. 298–301.

Principal components of British exports, 1830–1938 (% of total value)

|  | Cottons | Other textiles | Iron and steel | Machinery | Coal | Vehicles |
|---|---|---|---|---|---|---|
| 1830–39 | 48 | 24 | 11 | 1 | 1 | – |
| 1840–49 | 45 | 25 | 15 | 1 | 2 | – |
| 1850–59 | 36 | 24 | 18 | 2 | 2 | – |
| 1860–69 | 36 | 26 | 15 | 3 | 3 | – |
| 1870–79 | 33 | 22 | 16 | 4 | 4 | – |
| 1880–89 | 32 | 17 | 15 | 5 | 5 | – |
| 1890–99 | 28 | 16 | 14 | 7 | 7 | – |
| 1900–9 | 26 | 12 | 14 | 7 | 10 | 3 |
| 1910–19 | 25 | 15 | 12 | 5 | 10 | 2 |
| 1920–29 | 24 | 12 | 12 | 7 | 8 | 4 |
| 1930–38 | 14 | 10 | 12 | 10 | 9 | 5 |

Source: Mitchell and Deane, *Abstract*, pp. 302–6.

## Principal components of British imports, 1954–92 (% of total value)

|      | Food, drink and tobacco | Basic raw materials | Fuels and lubricants | Semi-manufactures | Finished manufactures |
|------|------|------|------|------|------|
| 1954 | 39 | 30 | 10 | 15 | 5 |
| 1964 | 32 | 20 | 11 | 21 | 15 |
| 1976 | 16 | 10 | 18 | 26 | 28 |
| 1985 | 11 | 6 | 12 | 69 | |
| 1992 | 11 | 4 | 6 | 78 | |

Sources: *Pears Cyclopaedia, 1980* (London, Pelham Books, 1980); *Annual Abstract* 1987, pp. 229–30.

## Principal components of British exports, 1954–92 (% of total value)

|      | Food, drink and tobacco | Basic raw materials | Fuels and lubricants | Metals | Engineering products | Textiles | Other manufactured goods |
|------|------|------|------|------|------|------|------|
| 1954 | 6 | 4 | 6 | 13 | 38 | 12 | 18 |
| 1964 | 7 | 4 | 3 | 12 | 45 | 6 | 20 |
| 1976 | 7 | 3 | 5 | 9 | 39 | 4 | 31 |
| 1985 | 6 | 3 | 21 | 6 | 31 | 2 | 24 |
| 1992 | 8 | 2 | 6 | 4 | 34 | 2 | 22 |

Sources: *Pears Cyclopaedia, 1980* (London, Pelham Books, 1980); *Annual Abstract* 1987–.

## Geographical distribution of British exports, 1701–98 (official values, £ million)

|      | Europe | North America | West Indies |
|------|------|------|------|
| 1701 | 3.7 | 0.3 | 0.2 |
| 1731 | 3.9 | 0.4 | 0.4 |
| 1751 | 6.3 | 1.0 | 0.4 |
| 1773 | 3.8 | 2.5 | 1.2 |
| (*cont.*) | | | |

Geographical distribution of British exports, 1701–98 (official values, £ million) (*cont.*)

|  | Europe | North America | West Indies |
|---|---|---|---|
| 1781 | 3.3 | 1.4 | 1.3 |
| 1790 | 5.3 | 3.3 | 1.7 |
| 1798 | 3.8 | 5.7 | 4.6 |

Source: Mitchell and Deane, *Abstract*, p. 312.

Geographical distribution of British trade, 1760–1992 (% of total)

|  | 1760 | 1800 | 1850 | 1900 | 1938 | 1970 | 1985 | 1992 |
|---|---|---|---|---|---|---|---|---|
| South America | 15 | 18 | 16 | 8 | 10 | 5 | 2 | 2 |
| Africa | 1½ | 15 | 3 | 3 | 7 | 10 | 6 | 4 |
| North America | 15 | 1½ | 15 | 25 | 17 | 20 | 16 | 13 |
| Asia | 12 | 12 | 12 | 12 | 12 | 12 | 10 | 10 |
| Europe | 43 | 35 | 33 | 44 | 32 | 25 | 63 | 64 |
| Others | 13½ | 18½ | 21 | 8 | 22 | 28 | 3 | 7 |

Sources: Mitchell and Deane, *Abstract*, pp. 312–26; *Facts in Focus* (Harmondsworth, Penguin, 1972), p. 150; *Annual Abstract* 1987–.

The balance of payments of the United Kingdom, 1816–1990 (annual averages in £ million, all figures rounded)

|  | Balance of visible trade | Balance of invisible trade | Net balance |
|---|---|---|---|
| 1816–20 | −11 | +18 | +7 |
| 1821–25 | −8 | +18 | +10 |
| 1826–30 | −15 | +17 | +3 |
| 1831–35 | −13 | +19 | +6 |
| 1836–40 | −23 | +26 | +3 |
| 1841–45 | −19 | +25 | +6 |
| 1846–50 | −26 | +30 | +5 |
| 1851–55 | −33 | +41 | +8 |
| 1856–60 | −34 | +60 | +26 |
| 1861–65 | −59 | +81 | +22 |
| (*cont.*) | | | |

The balance of payments of the United Kingdom, 1816–1990 (annual averages in £ million, all figures rounded) (*cont.*)

| | Balance of visible trade | Balance of invisible trade | Net balance |
|---|---|---|---|
| 1866–70 | –65 | +106 | +41 |
| 1871–75 | –64 | +139 | +75 |
| 1876–80 | –124 | +149 | +25 |
| 1881–85 | –99 | +161 | +61 |
| 1886–90 | –89 | +177 | +88 |
| 1891–95 | –134 | +186 | +52 |
| 1896–1900 | –159 | +199 | +40 |
| 1901–5 | –177 | +226 | +49 |
| 1906–10 | –144 | +290 | +146 |
| 1911–13 | –140 | +346 | +206 |
| 1920–24 | –258 | +419 | +161 |
| 1925–29 | –398 | +481 | +83 |
| 1930–34 | –328 | +301 | –27 |
| 1935–38 | –356 | +332 | –24 |
| 1946–50 | –160 | +104 | –56 |
| 1951–55 | –345 | +326 | –19 |
| 1956–60 | –94 | +226 | +132 |
| 1961–65 | –218 | +176 | –42 |
| 1966–70 | –297 | +441 | +144 |
| 1971–75 | –2 263 | +1 219 | –1 044 |
| 1976–80 | –1 969 | +2 393 | +424 |
| 1981–85 | –2 397 | +3 937 | +3 608 |
| 1986–90 | –17 222 | +5 352 | –11 870 |

Sources: P. Deane and W. A. Cole, *British Economic Growth, 1688–1959*, 2nd edn (Cambridge University Press, 1967), p. 36; Mitchell and Jones, *Second Abstract*, p. 142; Central Statistical Office, *United Kingdom Balance of Payments 1967–78* (London, HMSO, 1978); *Key Data, 1992/3*, p. 29.

# Prices and wages

The Schumpeter–Gilboy price index, 1714–1823 (index of consumer goods including cereals; 1701 = 100)

| | | | | | | | | | |
|------|-----|------|-----|------|-----|------|-----|------|-----|
| 1714 | 103 | 1736 | 87 | 1758 | 106 | 1780 | 110 | 1802 | 174 |
| 1715 | 104 | 1737 | 93 | 1759 | 100 | 1781 | 115 | 1803 | 156 |
| 1716 | 99 | 1738 | 91 | 1760 | 98 | 1782 | 116 | 1804 | 161 |
| 1717 | 95 | 1739 | 89 | 1761 | 94 | 1783 | 129 | 1805 | 187 |
| 1718 | 93 | 1740 | 100 | 1762 | 94 | 1784 | 126 | 1806 | 184 |
| 1719 | 97 | 1741 | 108 | 1763 | 100 | 1785 | 120 | 1807 | 186 |
| 1720 | 102 | 1742 | 99 | 1764 | 102 | 1786 | 119 | 1808 | 204 |
| 1721 | 100 | 1743 | 94 | 1765 | 106 | 1787 | 117 | 1809 | 212 |
| 1722 | 92 | 1744 | 84 | 1766 | 107 | 1788 | 121 | 1810 | 207 |
| 1723 | 89 | 1745 | 85 | 1767 | 109 | 1789 | 117 | 1811 | 206 |
| 1724 | 94 | 1746 | 93 | 1768 | 108 | 1790 | 124 | 1812 | 237 |
| 1725 | 97 | 1747 | 90 | 1769 | 99 | 1791 | 121 | 1813 | 243 |
| 1726 | 102 | 1748 | 94 | 1770 | 100 | 1792 | 122 | 1814 | 209 |
| 1727 | 96 | 1749 | 96 | 1771 | 107 | 1793 | 129 | 1815 | 191 |
| 1728 | 99 | 1750 | 95 | 1772 | 117 | 1794 | 136 | 1816 | 172 |
| 1729 | 104 | 1751 | 90 | 1773 | 119 | 1795 | 147 | 1817 | 189 |
| 1730 | 95 | 1752 | 93 | 1774 | 116 | 1796 | 154 | 1818 | 194 |
| 1731 | 88 | 1753 | 90 | 1775 | 113 | 1797 | 148 | 1819 | 192 |
| 1732 | 89 | 1754 | 90 | 1776 | 114 | 1798 | 148 | 1820 | 162 |
| 1733 | 85 | 1755 | 92 | 1777 | 108 | 1799 | 160 | 1821 | 139 |
| 1734 | 88 | 1756 | 92 | 1778 | 117 | 1800 | 212 | 1822 | 125 |
| 1735 | 89 | 1757 | 109 | 1779 | 111 | 1801 | 228 | 1823 | 128 |

Source: Mitchell and Deane, *Abstract*, pp. 468–9.

The Rousseaux price index, 1800–1913 (index of total agricultural and principal industrial products; average of 1865 and 1885 = 100)

| | | | | | | | | | |
|---|---|---|---|---|---|---|---|---|---|
| 1800 | 175 | 1823 | 120 | 1846 | 109 | 1869 | 107 | 1892 | 82 |
| 1801 | 188 | 1824 | 122 | 1847 | 115 | 1870 | 110 | 1893 | 82 |
| 1802 | 152 | 1825 | 133 | 1848 | 100 | 1871 | 115 | 1894 | 74 |
| 1803 | 161 | 1826 | 117 | 1849 | 95 | 1872 | 128 | 1895 | 72 |
| 1804 | 159 | 1827 | 117 | 1850 | 95 | 1873 | 127 | 1896 | 73 |
| 1805 | 170 | 1828 | 112 | 1851 | 91 | 1874 | 121 | 1897 | 74 |
| 1806 | 166 | 1829 | 110 | 1852 | 94 | 1875 | 117 | 1898 | 78 |
| 1807 | 161 | 1830 | 109 | 1853 | 112 | 1876 | 115 | 1899 | 84 |
| 1808 | 189 | 1831 | 112 | 1854 | 125 | 1877 | 110 | 1900 | 91 |
| 1809 | 206 | 1832 | 109 | 1855 | 125 | 1878 | 101 | 1901 | 86 |
| 1810 | 193 | 1833 | 107 | 1856 | 124 | 1879 | 98 | 1902 | 86 |
| 1811 | 178 | 1834 | 112 | 1857 | 127 | 1880 | 102 | 1903 | 86 |
| 1812 | 196 | 1835 | 112 | 1858 | 111 | 1881 | 99 | 1904 | 83 |
| 1813 | 203 | 1836 | 123 | 1859 | 115 | 1882 | 101 | 1905 | 86 |
| 1814 | 202 | 1837 | 118 | 1860 | 120 | 1883 | 101 | 1906 | 93 |
| 1815 | 164 | 1838 | 119 | 1861 | 115 | 1884 | 95 | 1907 | 97 |
| 1816 | 144 | 1839 | 130 | 1862 | 120 | 1885 | 88 | 1908 | 87 |
| 1817 | 161 | 1840 | 128 | 1863 | 121 | 1886 | 83 | 1909 | 91 |
| 1818 | 160 | 1841 | 121 | 1864 | 119 | 1887 | 81 | 1910 | 97 |
| 1819 | 147 | 1842 | 111 | 1865 | 117 | 1888 | 84 | 1911 | 102 |
| 1820 | 132 | 1843 | 105 | 1866 | 120 | 1889 | 84 | 1912 | 104 |
| 1821 | 121 | 1844 | 108 | 1867 | 118 | 1890 | 87 | 1913 | 106 |
| 1822 | 116 | 1845 | 110 | 1868 | 115 | 1891 | 86 | | |

Source: Mitchell and Deane, *Abstract*, pp. 471–3.

The Sauerbeck–*Statist* price index, 1900–65 (overall index of consumer goods, raw materials and food; average of 1866–77 = 100)

| | | | | | | | | | |
|---|---|---|---|---|---|---|---|---|---|
| 1900 | 75 | 1907 | 80 | 1914 | 85 | 1921 | 155 | 1928 | 120 |
| 1901 | 70 | 1908 | 73 | 1915 | 108 | 1922 | 131 | 1929 | 115 |
| 1902 | 69 | 1909 | 74 | 1916 | 136 | 1923 | 129 | 1930 | 97 |
| 1903 | 69 | 1910 | 78 | 1917 | 179 | 1924 | 139 | 1931 | 83 |
| 1904 | 70 | 1911 | 80 | 1918 | 192 | 1925 | 136 | 1932 | 80 |
| 1905 | 72 | 1912 | 85 | 1919 | 206 | 1926 | 126 | 1933 | 79 |
| 1906 | 77 | 1913 | 85 | 1920 | 251 | 1927 | 122 | 1934 | 82 |

(*cont.*)

The Sauerbeck–*Statist* price index, 1900–65 (overall index of consumer goods, raw materials and food; average of 1866–77 = 100) (*cont.*)

| | | | | | | | | | |
|---|---|---|---|---|---|---|---|---|---|
| 1935 | 84 | 1942 | 151 | 1949 | 274 | 1956 | 384 | 1963 | 374 |
| 1936 | 89 | 1943 | 155 | 1950 | 324 | 1957 | 376 | 1964 | 401 |
| 1937 | 102 | 1944 | 160 | 1951 | 401 | 1958 | 355 | 1965 | 404 |
| 1938 | 91 | 1945 | 164 | 1952 | 380 | 1959 | 356 | | |
| 1939 | 94 | 1946 | 186 | 1953 | 366 | 1960 | 359 | | |
| 1940 | 128 | 1947 | 230 | 1954 | 361 | 1961 | 354 | | |
| 1941 | 142 | 1948 | 260 | 1955 | 370 | 1962 | 360 | | |

Sources: Mitchell and Deane, *Abstract*, pp. 474–5; Mitchell and Jones, *Second Abstract*, p. 187.

Average price of wheat, 1771–1914 (by calendar year; per imperial quarter)

| | *s.* | *d.* | | *s.* | *d.* | | *s.* | *d.* |
|---|---|---|---|---|---|---|---|---|
| 1771 | 48 | 7 | 1793 | 49 | 3 | 1815 | 65 | 7 |
| 1772 | 52 | 3 | 1794 | 52 | 3 | 1816 | 78 | 6 |
| 1773 | 52 | 7 | 1795 | 75 | 2 | 1817 | 96 | 11 |
| 1774 | 54 | 3 | 1796 | 78 | 7 | 1818 | 86 | 3 |
| 1775 | 49 | 10 | 1797 | 53 | 9 | 1819 | 74 | 6 |
| 1776 | 39 | 4 | 1798 | 51 | 10 | 1820 | 67 | 10 |
| 1777 | 46 | 11 | 1799 | 69 | 0 | 1821 | 56 | 1 |
| 1778 | 43 | 3 | 1800 | 113 | 10 | 1822 | 44 | 7 |
| 1779 | 34 | 8 | 1801 | 119 | 6 | 1823 | 53 | 4 |
| 1780 | 36 | 9 | 1802 | 69 | 10 | 1824 | 63 | 11 |
| 1781 | 46 | 0 | 1803 | 58 | 10 | 1825 | 68 | 6 |
| 1782 | 49 | 3 | 1804 | 62 | 3 | 1826 | 58 | 8 |
| 1783 | 54 | 3 | 1805 | 89 | 9 | 1827 | 58 | 6 |
| 1784 | 50 | 4 | 1806 | 79 | 1 | 1828 | 60 | 5 |
| 1785 | 43 | 1 | 1807 | 75 | 4 | 1829 | 66 | 3 |
| 1786 | 40 | 0 | 1808 | 81 | 4 | 1830 | 64 | 3 |
| 1787 | 42 | 5 | 1809 | 97 | 4 | 1831 | 66 | 4 |
| 1788 | 46 | 4 | 1810 | 106 | 5 | 1832 | 58 | 8 |
| 1789 | 52 | 9 | 1811 | 95 | 3 | 1833 | 52 | 11 |
| 1790 | 54 | 9 | 1812 | 126 | 6 | 1834 | 46 | 2 |
| 1791 | 48 | 7 | 1813 | 109 | 9 | 1835 | 39 | 4 |
| 1792 | 43 | 0 | 1814 | 74 | 4 | 1836 | 48 | 6 |

(*cont.*)

Average price of wheat, 1771–1914 (by calendar year; per
imperial quarter) (*cont.*)

| | *s.* | *d.* | | *s.* | *d.* | | *s.* | *d.* |
|---|---|---|---|---|---|---|---|---|
| 1837 | 55 | 10 | 1863 | 44 | 9 | 1889 | 29 | 9 |
| 1838 | 64 | 7 | 1864 | 40 | 2 | 1890 | 31 | 11 |
| 1839 | 70 | 8 | 1865 | 41 | 10 | 1891 | 37 | 0 |
| 1840 | 66 | 4 | 1866 | 49 | 11 | 1892 | 30 | 3 |
| 1841 | 64 | 4 | 1867 | 64 | 5 | 1893 | 26 | 4 |
| 1842 | 57 | 3 | 1868 | 63 | 9 | 1894 | 22 | 10 |
| 1843 | 50 | 1 | 1869 | 48 | 2 | 1895 | 23 | 1 |
| 1844 | 51 | 3 | 1870 | 46 | 11 | 1896 | 26 | 2 |
| 1845 | 50 | 10 | 1871 | 56 | 8 | 1897 | 30 | 2 |
| 1846 | 54 | 8 | 1872 | 57 | 0 | 1898 | 34 | 0 |
| 1847 | 69 | 9 | 1873 | 58 | 8 | 1899 | 25 | 8 |
| 1848 | 50 | 6 | 1874 | 55 | 9 | 1900 | 26 | 11 |
| 1849 | 44 | 3 | 1875 | 45 | 2 | 1901 | 26 | 9 |
| 1850 | 40 | 3 | 1876 | 46 | 2 | 1902 | 28 | 1 |
| 1851 | 38 | 6 | 1877 | 56 | 9 | 1903 | 26 | 9 |
| 1852 | 40 | 9 | 1878 | 46 | 5 | 1904 | 28 | 4 |
| 1853 | 53 | 3 | 1879 | 43 | 10 | 1905 | 29 | 8 |
| 1854 | 72 | 5 | 1880 | 44 | 4 | 1906 | 28 | 3 |
| 1855 | 74 | 8 | 1881 | 45 | 4 | 1907 | 30 | 7 |
| 1856 | 69 | 2 | 1882 | 45 | 1 | 1908 | 32 | 0 |
| 1857 | 56 | 4 | 1883 | 41 | 7 | 1909 | 36 | 11 |
| 1858 | 44 | 2 | 1884 | 35 | 8 | 1910 | 31 | 8 |
| 1859 | 43 | 9 | 1885 | 32 | 10 | 1911 | 31 | 8 |
| 1860 | 53 | 3 | 1886 | 31 | 0 | 1912 | 34 | 9 |
| 1861 | 55 | 4 | 1887 | 32 | 6 | 1913 | 31 | 8 |
| 1862 | 55 | 5 | 1888 | 31 | 10 | 1914 | 34 | 11 |

Source: Mitchell and Deane, *Abstract*, pp. 488–9.

Real wages in London and Lancashire, 1700–96 (1700 = 100)

| | London wages | Lancashire wages |
|---|---|---|
| 1700 | 100 | 100 |
| 1710 | 74 | 71 |
| 1720 | 108 | 130 |
| 1730 | 122 | 149 |

(*cont.*)

## Real wages in London and Lancashire, 1700–96 (1700 = 100) (*cont.*)

|        | London wages | Lancashire wages |
|--------|-------------|------------------|
| 1740   | 97          | 112              |
| 1750   | 129         | 143              |
| 1760   | 122         | 127              |
| 1770   | 103         | 169              |
| 1780   | 98          | 160              |
| 1790   | n.a.        | 175              |
| 1796   | n.a.        | 152              |

(n.a. = not available)
Note: Wages relate to wages of men in full employment.
Source: E. W. Gilboy, 'The cost of living and real wages in eighteenth-century England', *Review of Economic Statistics* Vol. 18 (1936).

## Money wages in Great Britain, 1790–1860 (1840 = 100)

| 1790 | 70  | 1816 | 117 | 1845 | 98  |
|------|-----|------|-----|------|-----|
| 1795 | 82  | 1820 | 110 | 1850 | 100 |
| 1800 | 95  | 1824 | 105 | 1855 | 117 |
| 1805 | 109 | 1831 | 101 | 1860 | 115 |
| 1810 | 124 | 1840 | 100 |      |     |

Source: P. Deane and W. A. Cole, *British Economic Growth, 1688–1959* (Cambridge University Press, 1969), p. 23.

## Money wages and real wages in the United Kingdom, 1850–1906 (1850 = 100)

|        | Money wages | Real wages |
|--------|-------------|------------|
| 1850   | 100         | 100        |
| 1855   | 116         | 94         |
| 1860   | 114         | 105        |
| 1866   | 132         | 117        |
| 1871   | 137         | 125        |
| 1874   | 155         | 136        |
| 1877   | 152         | 132        |
| 1880   | 147         | 132        |
| (*cont.*) |          |            |

## Money wages and real wages in the United Kingdom, 1850–1906 (1850 = 100) (*cont.*)

|      | Money wages | Real wages |
|------|-------------|------------|
| 1883 | 150         | 142        |
| 1886 | 148         | 142        |
| 1891 | 162         | 166        |
| 1896 | 162         | 177        |
| 1900 | 179         | 184        |
| 1906 | 181         | 194        |

Source: P. Deane and W. A. Cole, *British Economic Growth, 1688–1959* (Cambridge University Press, 1969), p. 25.

## Money wages, the cost of living and real wages, 1880–1914 (1914 = 100)

|      | Money wages | Cost of living | Real wages |      | Money wages | Cost of living | Real wages |
|------|-------------|----------------|------------|------|-------------|----------------|------------|
| 1880 | 72 | 105 | 69  | 1898 | 87  | 88  | 99  |
| 1881 | 72 | 103 | 71  | 1899 | 89  | 86  | 104 |
| 1882 | 75 | 102 | 73  | 1900 | 94  | 91  | 103 |
| 1883 | 75 | 102 | 73  | 1901 | 93  | 90  | 102 |
| 1884 | 75 | 97  | 77  | 1902 | 91  | 90  | 102 |
| 1885 | 73 | 91  | 81  | 1903 | 91  | 91  | 99  |
| 1886 | 72 | 89  | 81  | 1904 | 89  | 92  | 97  |
| 1887 | 73 | 88  | 84  | 1905 | 89  | 92  | 97  |
| 1888 | 75 | 88  | 86  | 1906 | 91  | 93  | 98  |
| 1889 | 80 | 89  | 90  | 1907 | 96  | 95  | 101 |
| 1890 | 83 | 89  | 93  | 1908 | 94  | 93  | 101 |
| 1891 | 83 | 89  | 92  | 1909 | 94  | 94  | 100 |
| 1892 | 83 | 89  | 94  | 1910 | 94  | 96  | 98  |
| 1893 | 83 | 90  | 92  | 1911 | 95  | 97  | 97  |
| 1894 | 83 | 85  | 98  | 1912 | 98  | 100 | 97  |
| 1895 | 83 | 83  | 100 | 1913 | 99  | 102 | 97  |
| 1896 | 83 | 83  | 100 | 1914 | 100 | 100 | 100 |
| 1897 | 84 | 85  | 98  |      |     |     |     |

Source: E. C. Ramsbottom, 'The course of wage rates in the United Kingdom', *Journal of the Royal Statistical Society* Vol. 98 (1935).

Average money wages and real wages, 1913, 1920–38 (1930 = 100)

|  | Annual money wages | Annual real wages |  | Annual money wages | Annual real wages |
|---|---|---|---|---|---|
| 1913 | 52.4 | 82.8 | 1929 | 100.4 | 96.7 |
| 1920 | 143.7 | 91.2 | 1930 | 100.0 | 100.0 |
| 1921 | 134.6 | 94.1 | 1931 | 98.2 | 105.1 |
| 1922 | 107.9 | 93.2 | 1932 | 96.3 | 105.7 |
| 1923 | 100.0 | 90.8 | 1933 | 95.3 | 107.6 |
| 1924 | 101.5 | 91.6 | 1934 | 96.4 | 108.1 |
| 1925 | 102.2 | 91.7 | 1935 | 98.0 | 108.3 |
| 1926 | 99.3 | 91.2 | 1936 | 100.2 | 107.7 |
| 1927 | 101.5 | 95.8 | 1937 | 102.8 | 105.4 |
| 1928 | 100.1 | 95.2 | 1938 | 106.3 | 107.7 |

Note: Figures cover most manufacturing and service industries, but exclude salary-earners.
Source: D. H. Aldcroft, *The Inter-war Economy: Britain, 1919–1939*, 2nd edn (Batsford, 1973), pp. 352, 364.

Prices and wages, 1950–79 (1955 = 100)

|  | Retail price index | Weekly wage rates | Weekly earnings | Real wage rates | Real earnings |
|---|---|---|---|---|---|
| 1950 | 77 | 73 | 68 | 96 | 91 |
| 1955 | 100 | 100 | 100 | 100 | 100 |
| 1960 | 114 | 124 | 130 | 109 | 114 |
| 1965 | 136 | 151 | 175 | 112 | 129 |
| 1970 | 170 | 202 | 250 | 119 | 147 |
| 1977 | 407 | 579 | 661 | 142 | 162 |
| 1979 | 499 | 759 | 844 | 152 | 169 |

Prices, wages and disposable incomes, 1971–92 (1971 = 100)

|      | Retail prices | Average earnings | Real average earnings | Real disposable incomes |
|------|--------------|-----------------|----------------------|------------------------|
| 1971 | 100.0 | 100.0 | 100.0 | 100.0 |
| 1972 | 107.5 | 111.7 | 103.9 | 108.4 |
| 1973 | 117.3 | 127.2 | 108.4 | 115.4 |
| 1974 | 136.0 | 150.0 | 110.3 | 114.4 |
| 1975 | 168.7 | 189.7 | 112.4 | 114.9 |
| 1976 | 196.7 | 220.5 | 112.1 | 114.5 |
| 1977 | 228.0 | 240.3 | 105.4 | 112.0 |
| 1978 | 246.7 | 271.2 | 109.9 | 120.6 |
| 1979 | 279.9 | 313.1 | 111.9 | 127.6 |
| 1980 | 330.4 | 378.2 | 114.5 | 129.6 |
| 1981 | 369.6 | 426.5 | 115.4 | 128.7 |
| 1982 | 401.4 | 466.7 | 116.3 | 128.0 |
| 1983 | 419.6 | 506.2 | 120.6 | 131.4 |
| 1984 | 440.7 | 536.5 | 121.7 | 134.8 |
| 1985 | 467.3 | 581.9 | 124.5 | 138.5 |
| 1986 | 483.2 | 627.9 | 129.9 | 144.9 |
| 1987 | 503.3 | 676.7 | 134.5 | 150.0 |
| 1988 | 528.0 | 735.5 | 139.3 | 158.6 |
| 1989 | 569.2 | 802.4 | 141.0 | 167.2 |
| 1990 | 622.9 | 880.4 | 141.3 | 172.0 |
| 1991 | 659.5 | 951.4 | 144.2 | 171.9 |
| 1992 | 684.2 | 1 009.2 | 147.5 | 175.2 |

# Production

## Coal output, 1800–1993

| | Total UK output (million tons) | % exported | | Total UK output (million tons) | % exported |
|------|------|------|------|------|------|
| 1800 | 11.0 | 2.0 | 1900 | 225.2 | 25.9 |
| 1816 | 15.9 | 2.5 | 1905 | 236.1 | 20.1 |
| 1820 | 17.4 | 1.4 | 1910 | 264.4 | 23.5 |
| 1825 | 21.9 | 1.4 | 1915 | 253.2 | 17.2 |
| 1830 | 22.4 | 2.2 | 1920 | 229.5 | 10.8 |
| 1835 | 27.7 | 2.7 | 1925 | 243.2 | 20.9 |
| 1840 | 33.7 | 4.8 | 1930 | 243.9 | 22.5 |
| 1845 | 45.9 | 5.5 | 1935 | 222.3 | 17.4 |
| 1850 | 49.4 | 6.8 | 1940 | 224.3 | 8.8 |
| 1855 | 61.5 | 8.1 | 1945 | 182.2 | 1.8 |
| 1860 | 80.0 | 9.2 | 1950 | 216.3 | 6.2 |
| 1865 | 98.2 | 9.3 | 1955 | 221.6 | 5.5 |
| 1870 | 110.4 | 13.4 | 1960 | 193.6 | 2.6 |
| 1875 | 131.9 | 13.5 | 1965 | 187.5 | 2.0 |
| 1880 | 146.8 | 16.3 | 1970 | 133.4 | 1.0 |
| 1885 | 159.4 | 19.3 | 1978 | 122.0 | 1.4 |
| 1890 | 181.6 | 21.3 | 1988 | 103.8 | 1.1 |
| 1895 | 189.7 | 22.6 | 1993 | 80.8 | 0.7 |

Sources: Mitchell and Deane, *Abstract*, pp. 115–19, 120–1; Mitchell and Jones, *Second Abstract*, pp. 66, 68; *CSO: Key Data, 86* (HMSO, 1986); *Britain, 1994*, pp. 217–18.

## Coal production, employment and collieries, 1954–93

|         | Output (million tonnes) | Labour force (000) | Number of collieries |
|---------|-------------------------|--------------------|----------------------|
| 1954/55 | 221.6                   | 695.0              | 850                  |
| 1967/68 | 170.9                   | 391.9              | 376                  |
| 1977/78 | 119.0                   | 240.5              | 231                  |
| 1985/86 | 104.5                   | 154.6              | 133                  |
| 1988/89 | 103.8                   | 87.0               | 86                   |
| 1992/93 | 80.8                    | 44.0               | 50[*]                |

Note: *In 1992 closure plans for 31 collieries were announced by British Coal, though 21 were examined in a review in 1993.
Source: *Britain, 1987* (London, HMSO, 1987), p. 281; *Britain, 1994*, p. 217.

## Steel production, 1870–1992 (000 tons)

| 1870 | 300    | 1930 | 7 000  | 1985 | 15 700 |
|------|--------|------|--------|------|--------|
| 1880 | 1 250  | 1940 | 12 000 | 1990 | 16 700 |
| 1890 | 3 500  | 1950 | 16 000 | 1992 | 14 900 |
| 1900 | 5 000  | 1960 | 24 000 |      |        |
| 1910 | 6 500  | 1970 | 28 000 |      |        |
| 1920 | 9 000  | 1980 | 11 300 |      |        |

Sources: Mitchell and Deane, *Abstract*, pp. 136–7; *Annual Abstract* 1987, p. 157; *Britain, 1994*, p. 158.

## Cotton production and exports, 1750–1977 (annual average per decade)

|         | Raw cotton (retained imports, 000lb) | Exports of piece goods (million yd) |
|---------|--------------------------------------|-------------------------------------|
| 1750–59 | 2 820                                | –                                   |
| 1760–69 | 3 531                                | –                                   |
| 1770–79 | 4 797                                | –                                   |
| 1780–89 | 14 824                               | –                                   |
| 1790–99 | 28 645                               | –                                   |
| (*cont.*) |                                    |                                     |

Cotton production and exports, 1750–1977 (annual average per decade) (*cont.*)

| | Raw cotton (retained imports, 000lb) | Exports of piece goods (million yd) |
|---|---|---|
| 1800–9 | 59 554 | – |
| 1810–19 | 96 339 | 227 |
| 1820–29 | 173 000 | 320 |
| 1830–39 | 302 000 | 553 |
| 1840–49 | 550 000 | 978 |
| 1850–59 | 795 000 | 1 855 |
| 1860–69 | 803 000 | 2 375 |
| 1870–79 | 1 244 000 | 3 573 |
| 1880–89 | 1 473 000 | 4 575 |
| 1890–99 | 1 556 000 | 5 057 |
| 1900–9 | 1 723 000 | 5 649 |
| 1910–19 | 1 864 000 | 5 460 |
| 1920–29 | 1 498 000 | 4 239 |
| 1930–39 | 1 360 000 | 1 970 |
| 1940–49 | 1 074 000 | 621 |
| 1950–59 | 928 000 | 596 |
| 1960–69 | 469 000 | – |
| 1970–77 | 311 000 | – |

Sources: Mitchell and Deane, *Abstract*, pp. 177–81; Mitchell and Jones, *Second Abstract*, pp. 90–1; *Economic Trends* (London, HMSO, 1972–8).

Ships built and registered in the United Kingdom, 1790–1913 (000 tons)

| | | | | | |
|---|---|---|---|---|---|
| 1790 | 68.7 | 1840 | 211.3 | 1890 | 652.0 |
| 1800 | 134.2 | 1850 | 133.7 | 1900 | 739.0 |
| 1810 | 84.9 | 1860 | 212.0 | 1910 | 601.0 |
| 1820 | 66.7 | 1870 | 342.7 | 1913 | 975.2 |
| 1830 | 75.5 | 1880 | 403.8 | | |

Source: Mitchell and Deane, *Abstract*, pp. 221–2.

## Total shipping completed in the United Kingdom, 1900–85 (000 tons)

| | | | | | | | |
|---|---|---|---|---|---|---|---|
| 1900 | 1 440 | 1925 | 800 | 1950 | 1 400 | 1975 | 1 203 |
| 1905 | 1 625 | 1930 | 950 | 1955 | 1 350 | 1980 | 431 |
| 1910 | 1 150 | 1935 | 680 | 1960 | 1 303 | 1985 | 225 |
| 1913 | 1 950 | 1939 | 1 000 | 1965 | 1 204 | | |
| 1920 | 2 400 | 1945 | 1 250 | 1970 | 1 297 | | |

Sources: Mitchell and Deane, *Abstract*, pp. 221–2; *Facts in Focus* (Harmondsworth, Penguin Books, 1972), p. 114; *Annual Abstract* 1987, p. 172.

## Motor vehicles produced, 1908–94 (000)

| | | | | | | | |
|---|---|---|---|---|---|---|---|
| 1908 | 10 | 1933 | 286 | 1965 | 1 722 | 1985 | 1 311 |
| 1913 | 34 | 1938 | 445 | 1970 | 1 641 | 1994 | 1 621 |
| 1923 | 95 | 1948 | 500 | 1975 | 1 648 | | |
| 1928 | 212 | 1960 | 1 353 | 1979 | 1 479 | | |

Sources: *The Motor Industry of Great Britain*, annual reports; *Annual Abstract* 1987, p. 173; *Britain, 1994*, p. 166.

# Finance

## Major legislation concerning finance and banking

1694    Bank of England founded (Bank of Scotland, 1695).

1716    'Sinking Fund' established to redeem National Debt.

1720    South Sea Bubble. A spate of speculation in the shares of the South Sea Company, promoted by members of the government, is followed by a collapse, causing financial and political crisis. Walpole eventually restores public credit.

1733    Walpole introduces excise scheme to discourage smuggling and reduce land tax. Widespread opposition forces him to withdraw.

1773    Stock Exchange founded.

1799    Income tax introduced to pay for the war with France. Abolished 1802, reimposed 1803.

1816    Income tax abolished.

1826    Legalization of joint-stock banks outside a 65-mile radius of London.

1831    Land tax ceases to be collected.

1833    Bank Act, making Bank of England notes the legal tender.

1842    Income tax reimposed at 7*d.* in the £.

1844    Bank Charter Act. Note issue and central banking functions of the Bank of England regularized.

1855    Limited Liability Act limits responsibility of investors in the event of bankruptcy of the company.

1890    Bank of England becomes responsible for foreign exchange and gold reserves.

1894    Estate, or 'death', duties introduced.

1909    Supertax or 'surtax' on incomes over £2,000 per year introduced.

1914    Britain goes off Gold Standard as a result of First World War.

1925    Britain goes back on to Gold Standard.

1931    Financial crisis; Britain leaves Gold Standard.

1940    Purchase tax introduced to reduce spending on luxury goods; essential items exempt. Tax added to the price paid by the customer.

1946    Bank of England nationalized.
1949    Devaluation of the pound by 30.5 per cent.
1965    Capital gains tax and corporation tax introduced.
1966    Selective employment tax (SET) introduced.
1967    Devaluation of the pound by 14.3 per cent.
1972    Pound allowed to 'float'.
1973    Purchase tax and selective employment tax abolished; value added tax (VAT) introduced, levied on all goods and services, bringing British taxation into line with the European Economic Community.
1975    Capital transfer tax introduced to replace estate duty.
1980    Controls on international movement of currency and property abolished.
1986    'Big Bang' in the City of London with changes in rules governing share-dealing in the Stock Exchange and introduction of automated share quotation.
1990    Britain enters European Exchange Rate Mechanism (ERM).
1991    Britain obtains an opt-out clause in Maastricht Treaty against automatic entry in a Single European Currency or European Central Bank.
1992    Britain leaves the ERM system, allowing the pound to float and effectively devaluing its currency.

## National income, 1855–1992 (at factor cost)

|      | Total (£ million) |      | Total (£ million) |      | Total (£million) |
|------|-------------------|------|-------------------|------|------------------|
| 1855 | 636               | 1905 | 1 776             | 1960 | 20 809           |
| 1860 | 694               | 1910 | 1 984             | 1965 | 28 807           |
| 1865 | 822               | 1915 | 2 591             | 1970 | 39 567           |
| 1870 | 936               | 1920 | 3 664             | 1975 | 82 179           |
| 1875 | 1 113             | 1925 | 3 980             | 1980 | 171 204          |
| 1880 | 1 076             | 1930 | 3 957             | 1985 | 264 019          |
| 1885 | 1 115             | 1935 | 4 109             | 1992 | 456 387          |
| 1890 | 1 385             | 1938 | 4 671             |      |                  |
| 1895 | 1 447             | 1950 | 10 784            |      |                  |
| 1900 | 1 750             | 1955 | 15 511            |      |                  |

Sources: Mitchell and Deane, *Abstract,* pp. 367–8; *Annual Abstract* 1987, p. 283; *Britain, 1994,* p. 109.

# Unemployment

Total numbers registered unemployed, Great Britain, 1922–94 (000s; average for 12 months)

| | | | | | | | |
|------|-------|------|-----|------|-------|------|-------------------|
| 1922 | 1 543 | 1941 | 350 | 1960 | 360   | 1979 | 1 382             |
| 1923 | 1 275 | 1942 | 123 | 1961 | 341   | 1980 | 1 590             |
| 1924 | 1 130 | 1943 | 82  | 1962 | 463   | 1981 | 2 422             |
| 1925 | 1 226 | 1944 | 75  | 1963 | 573   | 1982 | 2 809[1]          |
| 1926 | 1 385 | 1945 | 137 | 1964 | 380   | 1983 | 2 988[1]          |
| 1927 | 1 088 | 1946 | 374 | 1965 | 329   | 1984 | 3 038[1]          |
| 1928 | 1 217 | 1947 | 480 | 1966 | 353   | 1985 | 3 149[1]          |
| 1929 | 1 216 | 1948 | 310 | 1967 | 556   | 1986 | 2 984[1]          |
| 1930 | 1 917 | 1949 | 308 | 1968 | 554   | 1987 | 2 700[1]          |
| 1931 | 2 630 | 1950 | 314 | 1969 | 534   | 1988 | 2 370[1]          |
| 1932 | 2 745 | 1951 | 253 | 1970 | 579   | 1989 | 1 798[1]          |
| 1933 | 2 521 | 1952 | 414 | 1971 | 724   | 1990 | 1 664[1]          |
| 1934 | 2 159 | 1953 | 342 | 1972 | 899   | 1991 | 2 291[1]          |
| 1935 | 2 036 | 1954 | 285 | 1973 | 575   | 1992 | 2 607[1]          |
| 1936 | 1 755 | 1955 | 232 | 1974 | 542   | 1993 | 2 992[1]          |
| 1937 | 1 484 | 1956 | 257 | 1975 | 866   | 1994 | 2 790[1]          |
| 1938 | 1 791 | 1957 | 312 | 1976 | 1 332 |      |                   |
| 1939 | 1 514 | 1958 | 457 | 1977 | 1 450 |      |                   |
| 1940 | 963   | 1959 | 475 | 1978 | 1 381 |      |                   |

[1]Changes introduced in the method of recording unemployment statistics have removed significant numbers of people from unemployment totals.

Sources: Mitchell and Deane, *Abstract*, p. 66; Mitchell and Jones, *Second Abstract*, p. 43; *Britain, 1979* (London, HMS0, 1979), p. 310; *Annual Abstract* 1987, p. 116; *Key Data, 1993/4*, p. 17.

# Transport

## Turnpike Acts by period, 1663–1839 (England)

|  | Number of Acts passed |  | Number of Acts passed |
|---|---|---|---|
| 1663–1719 | 37 | 1761–72 | 205 |
| 1720–29 | 46 | 1773–91 | 65 |
| 1730–39 | 24 | 1792–1815 | 173 |
| 1740–50 | 39 | 1816–39 | 139 |
| 1751–60 | 184 |  |  |

## Turnpike Acts by area, 1663–1839

|  | Number of Acts passed |
|---|---|
| Home Counties | 73 |
| Southern | 134 |
| East Anglia | 61 |
| Western | 102 |
| Far West | 68 |
| Northants, Cambs, Hunts. and Beds | 45 |
| South Midlands | 58 |
| North Midlands | 84 |
| East Midlands | 75 |
| Yorkshire and Lancashire | 148 |
| Far North | 64 |

Source: W. Albert, *The Turnpike Road System of England, 1663–1844* (Cambridge University Press, 1972).

# Major canal developments

1757    Sankey Canal completed from St Helens to the Mersey.

1761    Bridgewater Canal completed from Worsley to Manchester.

1769    Birmingham Canal completed from Wednesbury to Birmingham.

1772    Bridgewater Canal extended to the Mersey at Runcorn. Staffordshire & Worcestershire Canal completed.

1774    Bradford Canal completed.

1776    Chesterfield Canal completed.

1777    Trent & Mersey Canal completed.

1778    Oxford Canal opened from Banbury to Coventry.

1779    Stroudwater Canal opened.

1789    Thames & Severn Canal completed.

1790    Forth & Clyde Canal completed. Oxford Canal reaches Oxford.

1792    Shropshire Canal completed.

1794    Glamorgan Canal opened from Merthyr Tydfil to Cardiff.

1796    Lune aqueduct completed.

1797    Ashton and Shrewsbury Canals completed.

1798    Huddersfield, Ashton to Stalybridge, and Hereford to Gloucester Canals completed.

1799    Barnsley Canal completed.

1800    Peak Forest Canal completed.

1801    Grand Junction (London–Buckingham) Canal completed.

1802    Nottingham Canal completed.

1804    Rochdale Canal completed.

1810    Kennet & Avon trunk canal completed.

1813    Aylesbury branch of Grand Junction Canal completed.

1814    Grand Western Canal (Loudwell–Tiverton) completed.

1815    Grand Junction (Northampton branch) completed.

1816    Leeds & Liverpool Canal completed.

1819    North Wiltshire and Sheffield Canals completed.

1822    Caledonian Canal completed; Edinburgh & Glasgow Union Canal completed.

1824    Thames & Medway Canal completed.

1826    Lancaster Canal completed.

1827    Harecastle New Tunnel completed and Gloucester & Berkeley Canal completed.

1830    Hereford Union Canal completed.

1831    Liskeard & Looe, Portsmouth & Arundel, and Macclesfield Canals completed.

1833    Glastonbury Canal completed.
1835    Birmingham & Liverpool Canal completed.
1839    Manchester & Salford Canal completed.
1842    Chard Canal completed.
1847    Par Canal opened.
1853    Droitwich Junction Canal completed.
1894    Manchester Ship Canal completed.

## Shipping registered in English ports in the eighteenth century (000 tons)

|              | 1702  | 1788  |
|--------------|-------|-------|
| London       | 140.0 | 315.3 |
| Newcastle    | 11.0  | 106.1 |
| Liverpool    | 8.6   | 76.1  |
| Sunderland   | 3.9   | 53.6  |
| Whitehaven   | 7.2   | 52.3  |
| Hull         | 7.6   | 52.1  |
| Whitby       | 8.3   | 47.9  |
| Bristol      | 17.3  | 37.8  |
| Yarmouth     | 9.9   | 36.3  |

Source: R. Davis, *The Rise of the English Shipping Industry* (London, Macmillan, 1962), p. 35.

## Shipping registered in the United Kingdom, 1790–1993 (000 tons)

| 1790 | 1 383 | 1870 | 5 691  | 1950 | 18 219 |
|------|-------|------|--------|------|--------|
| 1800 | 1 699 | 1880 | 6 575  | 1960 | 21 131 |
| 1810 | 2 211 | 1890 | 7 979  | 1970 | 25 825 |
| 1820 | 2 439 | 1900 | 11 514 | 1975 | 33 700 |
| 1830 | 2 202 | 1910 | 16 768 | 1985 | 14 300 |
| 1840 | 2 768 | 1920 | 18 111 | 1993 | 13 600 |
| 1850 | 3 565 | 1930 | 20 322 |      |        |
| 1860 | 4 659 | 1940 | 17 891 |      |        |

Sources: Mitchell and Deane, *Abstract*, pp. 217–19; *Britain, 1994*, p. 257.

## Tonnage cleared by major ports, 1880, 1937, 1992 (000 tons)

| 1880 | | 1937 | | 1992[1] | |
|---|---|---|---|---|---|
| London | 12 900 | London | 62 600 | London | 48 900 |
| Liverpool | 10 300 | Liverpool | 35 000 | Tees ports | 43 800 |
| Cardiff | 8 000 | Southampton | 27 500 | Sullom Voe | 41 400 |
| Newcastle | 5 200 | Tyne ports | 18 300 | Grimsby | 40 800 |
| Hull | 3 400 | Cowes | 16 100 | Milford Haven | 35 600 |
| Glasgow | 2 500 | Cardiff | 15 400 | Southampton | 29 600 |
| Newport | 2 400 | Belfast | 15 200 | Liverpool | 27 800 |
| South Shields | 1 900 | Glasgow | 13 000 | Forth ports | 23 300 |
| Southampton | 1 700 | Hull | 12 300 | Felixstowe | 17 000 |
| Sunderland | 1 600 | Plymouth | 12 200 | Medway | 14 300 |
| Middlesbrough | 1 200 | Dover | 8 200 | Dover | 13 100 |
| Grimsby | 1 200 | Manchester | 7 700 | | |

[1]Figures for 1992 are in metric tonnes.
Sources: C. Cook and J. Stevenson, *Longman Atlas of Modern British History* (London, Longman, 1978), p. 54; *Britain 1987: An Official Handbook* (HMSO, 1987), *Britain, 1994*, p. 259.

## Railway mileage and passengers carried in the United Kingdom, 1845–1993

| | Miles open | Passengers carried (million) | | Miles open | Passengers carried (million) |
|---|---|---|---|---|---|
| 1845 | 2 441 | 30.4 | 1905 | 19 535 | 1 170.0 |
| 1850 | 6 084 | 67.4 | 1910 | 19 986 | 1 276.0 |
| 1855 | 7 293 | 111.4 | 1915 | – | – |
| 1860 | 9 069 | 153.5 | 1920 | 20 312 | 1 579.0 |
| 1865 | 11 451 | 238.7 | 1925 | 20 400 | 1 232.6 |
| 1870 | 13 562 | 322.2 | 1930 | 20 265 | 844.3 |
| 1875 | 14 510 | 490.1 | 1935 | 20 152 | 856.2 |
| 1880 | 15 563 | 596.6 | 1940 | 19 931 | 691.1 |
| 1885 | 16 594 | 678.1 | 1945 | 19 863 | 1 055.7 |
| 1890 | 17 281 | 796.3 | 1950 | 19 471 | 704.0 |
| 1895 | 18 001 | 903.5 | 1955 | 19 061 | 730.2 |
| 1900 | 18 680 | 1 114.6 | 1960 | 18 369 | 721.3 |

(*cont.*)

Railway mileage and passengers carried in the United Kingdom, 1845–1993 (*cont.*)

|      | Miles open | Passengers carried (million) |      | Miles open | Passengers carried (million) |
|------|-----------|------------------------------|------|-----------|------------------------------|
| 1965 | 14 920    | 580.5                        | 1985 | 10 410    | 697.4                        |
| 1970 | 11 799    | 823.9                        | 1993 | 10 300    | 745.0                        |
| 1977 | 11 169    | 702.0                        |      |           |                              |

Sources: Mitchell and Deane, *Abstract*, pp. 225–7; Mitchell and Jones, *Second Abstract*, p. 104; *Annual Abstract* 1987, p. 200; *Britain, 1994*, p. 253.

Motor vehicles in use, 1905–92 (000)

|      | Private cars | Goods vehicles | All vehicles* |
|------|-------------|----------------|---------------|
| 1905 | 16          | 9              | –             |
| 1910 | 53          | 30             | 144           |
| 1915 | 139         | 85             | 407           |
| 1920 | 187         | 101            | 650           |
| 1925 | 580         | 224            | 1 510         |
| 1930 | 1 056       | 348            | 2 274         |
| 1935 | 1 477       | 435            | 2 570         |
| 1939 | 2 034       | 488            | 3 149         |
| 1945 | 1 487       | 473            | 2 553         |
| 1950 | 2 258       | 895            | 4 409         |
| 1955 | 3 526       | 1 109          | 6 465         |
| 1960 | 5 526       | 1 397          | 9 439         |
| 1965 | 8 917       | 1 602          | 12 940        |
| 1970 | 11 515      | 1 622          | 14 950        |
| 1978 | 14 069      | 2 216          | 17 654        |
| 1985 | 16 453      | 2 704          | 21 166        |
| 1992 | 20 700      | 2 637          | 24 800        |

*'All vehicles' includes buses, trams, taxis and motor cycles, as well as cars and goods vehicles.

Sources: Mitchell and Deane, *Abstract*, p. 230; Mitchell and Jones, *Second Abstract*, p. 106; *Annual Abstract* 1987, p. 193; *Britain, 1994*, p. 246.

## Air transport: passengers carried, 1938–92 (000)

| | |
|------|------------|
| 1938 | 220[1] |
| 1950 | 1 157[1] |
| 1958 | 3 985[1] |
| 1965 | 10 868[1] |
| 1977 | 34 600 |
| 1988 | 71 400 |
| 1992 | 83 000 |

[1]UK airlines only.

Sources: Mitchell and Jones, *Second Abstract*, p. 108; *Key Data, 1992/3*, p. 55.

# SECTION FOUR

*Foreign affairs and defence*

# Military and naval

## British wars and campaigns

### Jacobite rebellions 1715 and 1745

**The '15**

The Earl of Mar raised the Stuart standard at Braemar on 6 Sept. 1715. The rebellion faltered when Mar failed to dislodge the royal army under Argyll from Sheriffmuir, north of Stirling, on 13 Nov., and on the same day a Jacobite army surrendered at Preston. The Pretender landed in Scotland on 22 Dec., but as Argyll advanced the Jacobite army dispersed, and James sailed again for France on 5 Feb. 1716.

**The '45**

Prince Charles Edward, the Young Pretender, raised his standard at Glenfinnan on 19 Aug. 1745. He occupied Edinburgh on 17 Sept. and defeated a royalist army under Sir John Cope at Prestonpans on 20 Sept. On 31 Oct. Charles led an army of 5,000 men south into England. The Jacobites reached Derby on 4 Dec., but their hopes of an English uprising were disappointed, and the decision to retreat was taken the following day. The rebellion had its last success with a victory at Falkirk on 17 Jan. 1746, but on 16 Apr. the Duke of Cumberland decisively defeated the Jacobites at Culloden, near Inverness. After several months as a fugitive, Charles Edward escaped to France in Sept. 1746.

### War of the Quadruple Alliance 1718–20

Following the Spanish occupation of Sardinia in Nov. 1717 and Sicily in July 1718, the Quadruple Alliance was formed by France, Austria, England and Holland on 2 Aug. 1718 to oppose Philip of Spain's designs on Italy and France. On 11 Aug. 1718 Admiral Byng destroyed the Spanish fleet off Cape Passaro. The English fleet then supported Austrian operations in Sicily and carried out raids on the Galician coast in Oct. 1719. The war was ended by the Treaty of The Hague on 17 Feb. 1720, by which Philip gave up his claims. Fighting took place briefly between Spain and France and England in 1727 over the implementation of the terms of the Treaty of The Hague. The dispute over Philip's son's succession to the Italian duchies was resolved by the Treaty of Seville in Nov. 1729.

## War of the Austrian Succession 1740–48

Colonial conflicts, and particularly the incident in which Captain Jenkins claimed to have had his ear cut off by a Spanish official, led Britain to declare war on Spain on 19 Oct. 1739. This war became part of a wider European conflict when Frederick the Great of Prussia launched his campaign to seize Silesia from Maria Theresa of Austria on 16 Dec. 1740. King George II, commanding in person an army of British, Hanoverian and Dutch troops in support of Maria Theresa, defeated the French at Dettingen on 27 June 1743. In May 1745 the French began an advance into the Austrian Netherlands, defeated the Duke of Cumberland at Fontenoy on 10 May and completed their conquest of Flanders. In 1747 the French invaded Holland and defeated the allies at Lauffeld on 2 July. At sea, Admiral Anson, who had carried out a circumnavigation and raided Spanish possessions, 1740–44, defeated the French at the first battle of Finisterre on 3 May 1747. Admiral Hawke achieved a similar victory over a convoy escort in a second battle in Oct. In North America, Louisburg was captured from the French in June 1745, but in India, Madras was lost in Sept. 1746. They were exchanged by the Treaty of Aix-la-Chapelle signed on 18 Oct. 1748, which brought the war in Europe to a close.

## Seven Years War 1756–63

Britain and France declared war on 17 May 1756, but the war in Europe began when Frederick the Great invaded Saxony in Aug. In 1757 a French army invaded Hanover and defeated the allies at Hastenbeck on 26 July. The Duke of Cumberland signed the Convention of Kloster-Seven on 8 Sept., disbanding his army, but this was repudiated after Frederick the Great's victory at Rossbach on 5 Nov. 1757. Ferdinand of Brunswick took command of the allied army and Pitt began the payment of subsidies to Frederick the Great. On 1 Aug. 1759 Ferdinand routed the French at Minden, and on 31 July 1760 saved Hanover by a victory at Warburg. While Prussia bore the brunt of the fighting in Europe, in North America Britain mounted a fourfold attack on the French in 1758. This culminated in Wolfe's victory before Quebec on 13 Sept. 1759 and the capture of the city. On 8 Sept. 1760 the Marquis de Vaudreuil surrendered Montreal and with it French Canada. French plans to invade England were disrupted by Admiral Boscawen's victory at Lagos Bay on 18 Aug. 1759 and Hawke's victory at Quiberon Bay on 20 Nov. A French expedition to Ireland surrendered at Kinsale in Feb. 1760. Following the outbreak of war with Spain in Jan. 1762, Britain seized Havana and Manila. The death of Empress Elizabeth of Russia on 5 Jan. 1762 led to a peace treaty between Prussia and Russia on 5 May 1762. Britain, France, Spain and Portugal signed the Treaty of Paris on 10 Feb. 1763, and Prussia, Austria and Saxony concluded the Treaty of Hubertusburg on 15 Feb.

## War of American Independence 1775–83

The first shots of the war were fired on 19 Apr. 1775 when British troops sent from Boston to destroy stores of the Massachusetts Militia at Concord were opposed at Lexington. George Washington was appointed commander-in-chief of the rebels' Continental Army on 15 June 1775. An American attack on Canada failed, but in Mar. 1776 the British were forced to evacuate Boston. The Americans issued their Declaration of Independence on 4 July 1776. In Sept. 1776 the British occupied New York, and Washington retreated across the Delaware river into Pennsylvania. However, on 26 Dec. 1776 he recrossed the river and defeated an army of Hessian auxiliaries at Trenton. In 1777 a British plan to divide the rebels by a threefold attack, with Burgoyne advancing from Canada, in cooperation with St Leger from Lake Ontario and Howe from New York, was a complete failure and resulted in Burgoyne's surrender at Saratoga on 17 Oct. 1777. In 1778 the scope of the conflict widened as France declared war on Britain on 17 June. Spain declared war on 21 June 1779, and Britain declared war on Holland on 20 Dec. 1780. British command of the seas was further challenged by the Armed Neutrality of the North formed by Russia, Sweden and Denmark in 1780. In 1781 General Cornwallis was besieged at Yorktown by Washington and Rochambeau on land and by the French fleet under de Grasse, and forced to surrender on 19 Oct. This ended any chance of a British suppression of the rebellion, but command of the seas was restored by Admiral Rodney's victory over de Grasse at the battle of the Saints in the West Indies on 12 Apr. 1782. Peace was concluded and the independence of the United States recognized by the Treaty of Versailles signed on 3 Sept. 1783.

## Expeditions and naval operations 1793–1814

1793     France, already at war with Austria, Prussia and Piedmont, declared war on Britain and Holland on 1 Feb., and on Spain on 7 Mar. In Aug. Admiral Hood occupied Toulon after a royalist uprising, but French successes on land forced him to evacuate on 19 Dec. In Dec. a British expedition arrived too late to aid royalist rebels in La Vendée.

1793–95   Campaign in the Low Countries: the Duke of York was sent to the Low Countries at the head of a force of British, Dutch, Hanoverians and Hessians. He was defeated at Hondschoote in Sept. 1793 and Tourcoing in May 1794. In July 1794 the French reoccupied Brussels and the Austrians retreated towards the Rhine, while the British fell back into Holland. The British forces were evacuated from Bremen in Apr. 1795.

1793–98   Campaign in the West Indies: in Nov. 1793, 7,000 men under Grey sailed with a squadron under Jervis to the West Indies. By 1796 military action, particularly involving slave revolts, and disease, had resulted in 40,000 dead and 40,000 incapacitated. The campaign was brought to a close by the evacuation of San Domingo in Oct. 1798.

1794     Howe defeated the French fleet off Ushant (1 June), but a vital French food convoy was able to reach Brest safely. British forces occupied Corsica (Aug.).

1795     In June *emigrés* landed from British ships at Quiberon Bay. They were defeated by Hoche, 16–20 July, and a small British force was evacuated, 20–21 July. In Nov. an expedition of 2,500 men sailed to La Vendée but did not disembark.

1797     Jervis defeated Spanish fleet at Cape St Vincent (14 Feb.). Duncan defeated Dutch fleet at Camperdown (11 Oct.).

1798     In June rebels in Ireland were defeated at Vinegar Hill. A force of 1,200 French under General Humbert landed in Killala Bay on 22 Aug., but Cornwallis forced their surrender on 8 Sept. Nelson destroyed the French fleet at the battle of the Nile (1 Aug.). In Nov. the British captured Minorca.

1798–1800   British forces supported uprising by Maltese against the French who surrendered on 5 Sept. 1800.

1799     Expedition to Holland: on 27 Aug. British troops under Abercromby landed at the Helder; the Dutch navy in the Texel surrendered. Russo-British forces, now under the Duke of York, planned to advance on Amsterdam, but were checked in the battle of Bergen-op-Zoom on 19 Sept. Further attacks on 2 and 6 Oct. made little progress. By the Convention of Alkmaar on 18 Oct. the allies agreed to evacuate Holland.

1801    Campaign against the French in Egypt: on 8 Mar. British troops under Abercromby landed at Aboukir Bay. An attack on Alexandria failed on 13 Mar., but a French counter-attack was beaten off on 21 Mar., though Abercromby was fatally wounded. His successor, General Hutchinson, advanced on Cairo, which the French agreed to evacuate in June. The French forces remaining in Alexandria surrendered on 31 Aug. Nelson, second-in-command to Sir Hyde Parker, defeated the Danes in the battle of Copenhagen, 2 Apr.

1805    Nelson defeated Franco-Spanish fleet in the battle of Trafalgar (21 Oct.), but was himself fatally wounded.

1806    In June an expedition of 6,000 men under General Sir David Baird captured the Cape of Good Hope from the Dutch.

1806–7  Expeditions to South America: in June 1806, Home Popham, who had escorted Baird to Cape Town, took 1,500 men under Beresford to Buenos Aires. Beresford was forced to surrender by a local uprising in Aug. 1806. In 1807 General Whitelocke led a second expedition to South America. He occupied Montevideo, but his attack on Buenos Aires failed and he was forced to evacuate the country.

1807    Danish fleet captured in the second battle of Copenhagen (2–7 Sept.).

1809    Walcheren expedition: in July 40,000 men under Chatham sailed for the Scheldt estuary to take Antwerp. They were delayed by the resistance of Flushing and suffered heavy losses when fever broke out. Half the force returned to England in Sept.; the rest remained to garrison Walcheren, but were evacuated in Dec.

1810    Mauritius and Réunion captured.

1811    Java captured.

1813    Graham sent to Holland with 6,000 men to support an Orangeist revolt. But the Prussians failed to take part in an intended attack on Antwerp, and after an unsuccessful attack on Bergen-op-Zoom, Graham's force remained largely inactive until the end of the war.

## Peninsular War 1808–14

The French conquest of Portugal in 1807 was followed by the invasion of Spain in Mar. 1808 and the imposition of Napoleon's brother, Joseph, as King of Spain. To encourage resistance to the French, a British army under Sir Arthur Wellesley reached Lisbon on 1 Aug. 1808. The French were defeated at Roliça (17 Aug.) and Vimeiro (21 Aug.), but were allowed to evacuate Portugal by the Convention of Cintra (30 Aug.). Sir John Moore took command in Portugal and advanced into Spain. He was forced to retreat before Napoleon and was killed evacuating his army from Corunna on 16 Jan. 1809. In Apr. 1809 Wellesley landed with a British army at Lisbon and defeated the French at Talavera on 28 July, for which he was created Viscount Wellington. When the French invaded Portugal in 1810, Wellington took shelter behind the fortified lines of the Torres Vedras, and in 1811 Masséna was forced to retreat. In 1812 Wellington defeated the French at Salamanca (22 July) and entered Madrid. In 1813 he won another victory at Victoria (21 June) and invaded southern France. Before hostilities were suspended in 1814, Wellington defeated Soult at Orthez (27 Feb.) and Toulouse (10 Apr.).

## War of 1812

Grievances, arising from British conduct of the maritime war against the French, led the United States to declare war on Britain on 19 June 1812. An American plan for a threefold attack on Canada failed, and a British force under General Brock forced the surrender of Detroit on 16 Aug. 1812. In Apr. 1813 the Americans captured and burnt Toronto, and in Sept. defeated the British in the battle of Lake Erie and recaptured Detroit. In Aug. 1814 a force of 4,000 British veterans landed in Chesapeake Bay, defeated the Americans at Bladensburg and burnt parts of Washington. A peace treaty was signed at Ghent in Belgium on 24 Dec. 1812, largely restoring the pre-war situation. Before news of the peace reached America, General Pakenham was killed on 8 Jan. 1815 leading an unsuccessful British attack on New Orleans.

## Waterloo Campaign 1815

Following Wellington's advance from Spain, and allied attacks on Paris, the capital fell on 30 Mar. 1814 and Napoleon went into exile. Napoleon returned to France from Elba on 1 Mar. 1815 and resumed power. Faced by the renewal of the victorious coalition against him, he planned to take the allied armies in Belgium by surprise. On 16 June

Napoleon attacked Blücher's Prussians at Ligny, while engaging the Anglo-Dutch Army at Quatre Bras. Both allied armies were able to conduct orderly retreats. On 17 June Napoleon sent Grouchy to prevent Blücher joining Wellington, but Blücher had retreated towards Wavre and not Liège as he imagined. Thus, Grouchy was absent when the battle of Waterloo was fought on 18 June. French attacks failed to drive Wellington from his defensive positions, and the arrival of Blücher in the late afternoon ensured the total defeat of the French. Napoleon abdicated on 22 June.

## Chronology of conflicts in India 1744–1818

### First Carnatic War
25 July 1746: Count de la Bourdonnais defeated British fleet at Negapatam, and with Dupleix, the French governor-general, captured Madras in Sept.
1746–48: unsuccessful attempts by the French to capture Fort St George and Pondicherry from the British. 18 Oct. 1748: Treaty of Aix-la-Chapelle: Madras returned to Britain in exchange for Louisburg.

### 1749–54 Second Carnatic War
Conflict between British and French East India Companies supporting rival native forces. In 1751 Robert Clive captured Arcot, capital of the pro-French Nawab of the Carnatic, Chanda Sahib, who was besieging the English garrison at Trichinopoly. Clive successfully withstood a siege of over 50 days.

1754    Dupleix recalled to France.

1756    Surajah Dowlah, Nawab of Bengal, captured Calcutta (20 June) imprisoning 146 Europeans in the 'Black Hole' where 123 died.

1757    Robert Clive and Admiral Watson recaptured Calcutta (2 Jan.). Clive routed Surajah Dowlah at Plassey (23 June).

1758    French force under Comte de Lally-Tollendal reached Pondicherry, and captured Fort St David in June.

1758    Lally unsuccessfully besieged Madras (Dec. 1758–Feb. 1759).

1760    Eyre Coote defeated Lally at Wandewash (22 Jan.).

1761    Lally's surrender at Pondicherry (15 Jan.) marked the end of the French bid for power in India.

1764    Mutiny in Bengal army (23 Oct.) crushed by Major Munro at Buxar.

### 1766–69 First Mysore War
Ended when Hyder Ali concluded a defensive alliance with East India Company.

## 1779–82 First Maratha War

Gwalior stormed by Captain Popham in 1780. Peace by the Treaty of Salbai.

## 1780–84 Second Mysore War

1780    Hyder Ali invaded the Carnatic, but was defeated by Coote at Porto Novo (June), Pollilur (Aug.) and Sholingarh (Sept.).

1782    French under Admiral de Suffren captured Trincomalee (Aug.), and sent aid to Hyder Ali.

1784    Ali's son, Tippoo Sahib, made peace by the Treaty of Mangaloore.

## 1789–92 Third Mysore War

Tippoo Sahib attacked the ruler of Travancore, an ally of Britain. Cornwallis invaded Mysore, stormed the capital Bangalore and besieged Tippoo in Seringapatam. Tippoo made peace in Mar. 1792.

1795–96 Ceylon captured from the Dutch.

## 1799 Fourth Mysore War

After a small French force had landed in Mysore, Wellesley declared war, and Tippoo Sahib was killed when Seringapatam was stormed in May 1799.

## 1803–5 Second Maratha War

In 1803 Arthur Wellesley defeated Sindhia of Gwalior at Assaye (23 Sept.) and Argaum (29 Nov.). General Lake stormed Aligarh (4 Sept.) and defeated the Marathas at Delhi (16 Sept.) and Laswari (1 Nov.). Sindhia submitted 20 Dec. Further uprisings by Marathas suppressed, 1804–5.

1814    Britain invaded Nepal (Nov.). The Gurkhas were forced to make peace in 1816.

## 1817 Third Maratha War

Attacks by Marathas and bands of marauding robbers called Pindaris. On 21 Dec. 1817 Sir Thomas Hyslop crushed the army of Maratha leader, Holkar, at Mahidput. In 1818, Lord Rawdon-Hastings hunted down the Pindaris; the ruler of the Marathas, the Peshwa, surrendered on 2 June.

## *Wars with Burma 1824–26, 1852–53, 1885–92*

The threat of a Burmese invasion of India led to a British declaration of war on 5 Mar. 1824. An expedition under Sir Archibald Campbell imposed the Treaty of Yandabo on 24 Feb. 1826. An appeal for protection by British merchants at Rangoon in 1852 resulted in a further expedition which captured Rangoon. South Burma was annexed in Dec. 1852. In 1885, as a result of King Thibaw's confiscation of the property of the Bombay-Burma Company, a British amphibious force invaded Burma and on 1 Jan. 1886 it was annexed as a province of the Indian Empire. Guerrilla warfare continued until 1892.

## Battle of Navarino 1827

By the Treaty of London signed on 6 July 1827 France, Russia and England threatened action in support of the Greeks who were fighting for their independence from the Ottoman Empire, unless the Turks agreed to an armistice. On 8 Sept. 1827 the Egyptian fleet landed fresh troops at Navarino to suppress the Greek rebellion. On 20 Oct. the Egyptian–Turkish fleet was destroyed by the action of British, French and Russian squadrons. Russia subsequently declared war on Turkey on 26 Apr. 1828, and Greek independence was recognized by the Treaty of London of 7 May 1832.

## Wars with China 1839–42, 1856–60

The 'Opium War' of 1839–42 originated in drastic action taken by the Chinese against British merchants in an attempt to curb the opium trade. An expedition under Sir Hugh Gough captured Canton on 24 May 1841. Shanghai was captured on 19 June 1842, and peace was concluded by the Treaty of Nanking on 29 Aug. 1842. Chinese seizure of the British ship, the *Arrow*, at Canton in Oct. 1856 led to renewed fighting. Canton was taken and the Taku forts near Tientsin were silenced. The Treaty of Tientsin was signed on 26 June 1858. However, in 1859 a naval force under Admiral James Hope was repulsed at the Taku forts on the way to obtain ratification of the treaty. A British and French expedition led by Sir Hope Grant captured the Taku forts and occupied Peking on 9 Oct. 1860. The Treaty of Peking, ending the war, was signed on 24 Oct. 1860.

## Afghan wars 1839–42, 1878–81

Fears regarding the threat to India posed by Russian activity in Afghanistan led to a British invasion which captured Kabul on 7 Aug. 1839. Following an uprising, General Elphinstone's force was massacred at Gardamak on 13 Jan. 1842, while attempting to withdraw. Parts of Kabul were destroyed by a punitive expedition in Sept. 1842, but the country was then evacuated. A further British invasion was mounted in 1878. A British force was defeated at Maiwand on 27 July 1880, but Sir Frederick Roberts relieved Kandahar on 1 Sept. A pro-British government was established and the evacuation of Afghanistan completed by Apr. 1881.

### Conquest of Sind (India), 1843

Following friction between the rulers of Sind and the British, the British Residency in the capital, Hyderabad, was attacked. Sir Charles Napier marched to its relief, defeated the enemy at Miari on 17 Feb. 1843 and proceeded to conquer the territory. He summed up his campaign in a one-word message to the governor-general: 'Peccavi' ('I have sinned').

### Maori wars 1843–48, 1860–70

The Maoris' resentment of encroachment by British settlers in New Zealand led to periods of guerrilla warfare. The uprisings were suppressed by a combination of the local militia, helped by troops from Britain and Australia, and diplomacy.

### Sikh wars 1845–46, 1848–49

On 11 Dec. 1845 a Sikh army crossed the Sutlej into British Indian territory. Sir Hugh Gough beat off an attack at Mudki on 18 Dec., and then defeated the Sikhs at the battle of Ferozeshah on 21–22 Dec. Further defeats were inflicted by the British at Aliwal (29 Jan. 1846) and Sobraon (10 Feb. 1846), and by the Treaty of Lahore, signed on 11 Mar. 1846, the Punjab became a British protectorate. A mutiny at Multan on 20 Apr. 1848 sparked off a Sikh uprising. Gough invaded the Punjab and fought inconclusive battles at Ramnagar (22 Nov. 1848) and Chilianwala (13 Jan. 1849), before finally defeating the Sikhs at Gujerat on 21 Feb. 1849. The Punjab was subsequently annexed.

### Crimean War 1854–55

Turkey declared war on Russia on 23 Sept. 1853. The Turkish fleet was destroyed at Sinope on 30 Nov. 1853, and a Franco-British fleet entered the Black Sea to protect the Turkish coast. France and Britain declared war on Russia on 28 Mar. 1854. In Sept. 1854 an allied force landed on the Crimean Peninsula and besieged Sebastopol. Major battles fought were Alma (20 Sept.), Balaclava (25 Oct.) and Inkerman (5 Nov.). The French capture of the Malakoff strongpoint on 8 Sept. 1855 led to the Russian evacuation of Sebastopol. The Russians accepted a preliminary peace on 1 Feb. 1856 and the Treaty of Paris was signed in Mar. 1856. British losses were 4,600 killed and 13,000 wounded; a further 17,500 died of disease.

## Persian War 1856–57

On 1 Nov. 1856 Britain declared war on Persia, which had occupied Herat in Afghanistan. Sir James Outram led an invasion of Persia, and by a peace treaty signed in Mar. 1857 the Shah agreed to evacuate Afghanistan.

## Indian Mutiny 1857–58

The mutiny broke out at Meerut on 10 May 1857. From there the mutineers marched on Delhi and seized the city. The mutiny spread rapidly and the British were besieged at Cawnpore and Lucknow. At Cawnpore they surrendered on 26 June to Nana Sahib, who then massacred his prisoners. In Sept. 1857 the British recaptured Delhi. Sir Henry Havelock reached Lucknow, but was himself besieged there until relieved in Nov. by Sir Colin Campbell, who evacuated the defenders. Lucknow was finally recaptured in Mar. 1858. In Central India Sir Hugh Rose defeated Tantia Topi at Gwalior on 19 June 1858. Peace was proclaimed on 8 July 1858.

## Abyssinian War 1867–68

An expedition of British and Indian troops led by Sir Robert Napier was sent to rescue diplomats and Europeans held by King Theodore of Abyssinia in his capital, Magdala. Theodore's army was defeated at Arogee and he committed suicide on 10 Apr. 1868. Magdala was stormed and the hostages rescued on 13 Apr.

## Ashanti campaign 1873–74

After initial fighting, Sir Garnet Wolseley, the administrator and commander-in-chief on the Gold Coast, mounted an expedition against Kumasi, the capital of the Ashanti, who were threatening British settlements. Kumasi fell in Feb. 1874 and peace was imposed. Further expeditions took place against the Ashanti in 1896 and 1900, the latter leading to the annexation of the territory.

## Zulu War 1878–79

The Zulus under Chief Cetewayo ignored a British demand on 11 Dec. 1878 for the establishment of a British protectorate over Zululand. Lord Chelmsford invaded Zululand on 11 Jan. 1879, but part of his army was annihilated at Isandhlwana on 22 Jan. The defence of Rorke's Drift during the following night saved Natal from being overrun. After the arrival of reinforcements, Chelmsford defeated Cetewayo in the battle of Ulundi on 4 July 1879.

## First South African War 1880–81

Great Britain annexed the Transvaal Boer Republic in 1877. In Dec. 1880 the Boers proclaimed their independence. General Sir George Colley, leading British troops from Natal, was defeated and killed at Majuba Hill on 27 Feb. 1881. The British government decided on withdrawal. An armistice was signed on 6 Mar. 1881, and peace made by the Convention of Pretoria on 5 Apr. 1881. The Boers were granted their independence under British suzerainty.

## Egyptian War 1882

A nationalist uprising led by Colonel Arabi against the growth of European influence in Egypt resulted in June 1882 in the deaths of many Europeans in riots in Alexandria. As a result British forces bombarded and occupied Alexandria and Colonel Arabi's revolt was crushed at the battle of Tel-el-Kebir on 13 Sept. 1882.

## The Sudan 1884–85, 1896–99

In Oct. 1883 an Egyptian army led by Colonel Hicks was defeated at El Obeid by the Sudanese forces of the Mahdi. In Jan. 1884 General Gordon was sent to Khartoum to bring back the Egyptian garrison, but he remained and was cut off. A relief expedition under Sir Garnet Wolseley arrived on 28 Jan. 1885, two days after Khartoum had fallen and Gordon been killed. The British government undertook the reconquest of the Sudan in 1896. The Sudanese were defeated on 2 Sept. 1898 at the battle of Omdurman, and on 19 Jan. 1899 an Anglo-Egyptian condominium was established over the Sudan.

## Second South African War 1899–1902

The war began in Oct. 1899 following the rejection of a Boer ultimatum to the British government to disband military preparations. In the first phase of the war British troops were defeated and forced on the defensive; Mafeking, Kimberley and Ladysmith were besieged. In Feb. 1900 the British counter-offensive relieved Kimberley and Ladysmith. After further fighting, Mafeking was relieved in May and the Boer capital, Pretoria, was captured on 5 June 1900. Eighteen months of guerrilla warfare then followed before peace was brought about by the Treaty of Vereeniging, signed on 31 May 1902. British casualties were 5,774 killed and 22,829 wounded; the Boers lost an estimated 4,000 killed.

## Expedition to Tibet 1903–4

A British expedition led by Colonel Younghusband invaded Tibet to force the Dalai Lama to enter into negotiations about the frontier with India. After fierce fighting, Younghusband reached Lhasa on 3 Aug. 1904, and a treaty was signed on 7 Sept.

## First World War 1914–18

Britain declared war on Germany on 4 Aug. 1914 after the German invasion of Belgium. Pre-war military planning had committed the British Expeditionary Force to fighting alongside the French. The Germans, advancing according to the Schlieffen Plan, were halted at the battle of the Marne in Sept. 1914. The defensive power of modern weapons led to the development of trench warfare on the Western Front. Despite the use of poison gas and tanks, the major British attacks on the Somme (1916) and at Ypres (1917) failed to achieve a breakthrough. The German offensive in Mar. 1918 was initially successful, but the Allies were able to counter-attack as German morale weakened. The Armistice was signed on 11 Nov. 1918. The Western Front was the crucial theatre in the First World War, and British campaigns against the Turks at Gallipoli in 1915 and in the Middle East were very much sideshows. At sea the greatest naval battle of the war was fought at Jutland (31 May to 1 June 1916) between the British and German fleets. More important as regards the final outcome of the war was the defeat of the German U-boats (which had brought Britain close to starvation in 1917) by the adoption of the convoy system. Casualties suffered by the British Empire in the conflict were 908,000 killed and 2,090,000 wounded.

## Anglo-Irish conflict 1916–21

Rebellion broke out in Dublin on Easter Monday, 24 Apr. 1916. The rebellion was suppressed by 1 May, and Sir Roger Casement and leaders of the risings were tried and executed. Open warfare began again in 1919, and atrocities by the Irish Republican Army were matched by those committed by a special force brought in by the British, the Black and Tans. Peace was formally established by a treaty recognizing the dominion status of the Irish Free State signed on 6 Dec. 1921.

### British intervention in Russia 1918–19

In 1918 small expeditions composed of British, French and American troops seized Murmansk and occupied Archangel, in order to aid the White Russian forces against the Bolsheviks. Sporadic operations were conducted for over a year until the final evacuation of allied troops in Sept. 1919.

### Amritsar 'massacre' 1919

Fears of a revolt in the Punjab led Brigadier-General Dyer, commander of the garrison at Amritsar, to order his men to open fire on an unarmed mob which had refused to disperse. Some 379 Indians were killed and 1,208 wounded. A commission of enquiry heavily censured Dyer and the shootings embittered Anglo-Indian relations.

### Third Afghan War 1919

In May 1919 Amir Amanullah declared a holy war (Jihad) against Britain, crossed the border and occupied Bagh. While Jalalabad and Kabul were bombarded by the RAF, a British expedition drove the Afghans out of Bagh and forced the Khyber Pass into Afghanistan. An armistice was agreed on 31 May and the Treaty of Rawalpindi was signed on 8 Aug.

### Second World War 1939–45

German forces invaded Poland on 1 Sept. 1939, which led to declarations of war by Britain and France on 3 Sept. The Germans invaded the Low Countries on 10 May 1940, and France was compelled to sign an armistice on 22 June. The British army was evacuated from Dunkirk, while in the 'Battle of Britain' the German Luftwaffe failed to defeat the RAF and establish air superiority which would have made an attempted invasion of Britain possible. Italy declared war on 10 June 1940, and Britain attacked Italian forces in North Africa. Allied forces eventually drove the Germans and Italians out of North Africa, captured Sicily and invaded the Italian mainland, forcing the Italians to make a separate peace on 3 Sept. 1943. The British and American air forces conducted a costly strategic bombing offensive against Germany in 1942 and 1943, but it was mainly German losses in Russia which paved the way for the success of the Allied invasion of Europe, launched on D-Day, 6 June 1944. The Allies linked up with the Russians on the Elbe on 28 Apr. 1945 and the Germans accepted unconditional surrender terms on 7 May. In the Far East Japan attacked the American base at Pearl Harbor on 7 Dec. 1941, and within six months the Japanese were masters of South-East Asia and Burma. The Allied counter-offensive culminated in the dropping of the first atomic bombs on Hiroshima and Nagasaki in Aug. 1945. The Japanese surrendered on 14 Aug. 1945. Casualties suffered by the British Empire in the conflict were 486,000 killed and 590,000 wounded.

## Palestine 1945–48

A period of guerrilla warfare was waged by Jewish Zionists against British mandate forces and the Arab population, to achieve an independent Jewish nation. On 22 July 1946 the King David Hotel in Jerusalem, housing the British headquarters, was blown up, with the loss of 91 lives. With the proclamation of the independence of Israel on 14 May 1948, Britain surrendered her League of Nations mandate over Palestine and withdrew her armed forces.

## Malayan emergency 1948–60

The Federation of Malaya was proclaimed on 1 Feb. 1948. Communist guerrilla activity began, and on 16 June a state of emergency was declared. In Apr. 1950 General Sir Harold Briggs was appointed to coordinate anti-Communist operations by Commonwealth forces. He inaugurated the Briggs Plan for resettling Chinese squatters in new villages to cut them off from the guerrillas. After the murder of the British high commissioner, Sir Henry Gurney, on 6 Oct. 1951, General Sir Gerald Templer was appointed high commissioner and director of military operations on 15 Jan. 1952, and on 7 Feb. a new offensive was launched. On 8 Feb. 1954 British authorities announced that the Communist Party's high command in Malaya had withdrawn to Sumatra. The emergency was officially ended on 31 July 1960.

## Korean War 1950–53

The invasion of South Korea by North Korea on 25 June 1950 led to intervention by United Nations forces, following an emergency session of the Security Council. The advance of United Nations forces into North Korea on 1 Oct. 1950 led to the entry of the Chinese into the war on 25 Nov. on the side of the North. An armistice was signed at Panmunjon on 27 July 1953. Casualties suffered by the British contribution to the United Nations force were 686 killed, 2,498 wounded and 1,102 missing.

## Cyprus emergency 1952–59

Agitation for union with Greece ('enosis') by the Greek population of Cyprus led to terrorism and guerrilla warfare against British forces and the Turkish minority by EOKA, the militant wing of the enosis movement. It was led by Colonel Grivas, and supported by Archbishop Makarios, who was deported to the Seychelles in Mar. 1956. A cease-fire came into effect on 13 Mar. 1959, prior to the establishment of the independent republic of Cyprus on 16 Aug. 1960.

## Mau Mau revolt 1952–60

Violence by the Mau Mau, an African secret society in Kenya, led to a British declaration of a state of emergency on 20 Oct. 1952. Leading Kikuyu nationalists were arrested and Jomo Kenyatta was given a seven-year prison sentence in Oct. 1953. A separate East African command consisting of Kenya, Uganda and Tanganyika was set up under General Sir George Erskine. In campaigns in the first half of 1955 some 4,000 terrorists in the Mount Kenya and Aberdare regions were dispersed. Britain began to reduce her forces in Sept. 1955; the state of emergency in Kenya ended on 12 Jan. 1960.

## Suez 1956

Following Egyptian nationalization of the Suez Canal on 26 July 1956, Israel invaded Sinai on 29 Oct. When Egypt rejected a cease-fire ultimatum by France and Britain, their air forces began to attack Egyptian air bases on 31 Oct. On 5 Nov. Franco-British forces invaded the Canal Zone, capturing Port Said. Hostilities ended at midnight on 6–7 Nov., following a cease-fire call by the United Nations. Allied losses were 33 killed and 129 wounded.

## 'Confrontation' between Indonesia and Malaysia 1963–66

When the Federation of Malaysia was established on 16 Sept. 1963, President Sukarno of Indonesia announced a policy of 'confrontation', on the grounds that it was 'neo-colonialist'. There followed a campaign of propaganda, sabotage and guerrilla raids into Sarawak and Sabah. An agreement ending 'confrontation' was signed in Bangkok on 1 June 1966 (ratified 11 Aug.). In the conflict Commonwealth forces lost 114 killed and 181 wounded, the Indonesians 590 killed, and 222 wounded.

## Aden 1964–67

On 18 Jan. 1963 Aden acceded to the South Arabian Federation. British troops were involved in frontier fighting with the Yemen, and in suppressing internal disorders in Aden. A large-scale security operation was launched in Jan. 1964 in the Radfan region, north of Aden. On 26 Nov. 1967 the People's Republic of South Yemen was proclaimed, and the British military withdrawal from Aden was completed on 29 Nov. In the period 1964–67 British security forces lost 57 killed and 651 wounded in Aden.

## Northern Ireland 1969–

As a result of a request by the government of Northern Ireland, facing severe rioting, British troops moved into Londonderry on 14 Aug. 1969 and into Belfast on 15 Aug. The first British soldier was killed by a sniper in Belfast on 6 Feb. 1971. Internment without trial was introduced on 9 Aug. 1971; it was ended on 7 Dec. 1975. Direct rule from London was imposed from 30 Mar. 1972. At the peak in Aug. 1972 there were 21,500 British soldiers in Northern Ireland. Thereafter, a policy of 'normalization' led to a reduction of the number of regular troops to under 10,000 by the mid-1980s, with increasing security work carried out by police and the part-time Ulster Defence Regiment. Over 3,160 persons had died in the conflict by the end of Aug. 1994 when the IRA called a 'complete cessation' of military operations. The cease-fire was ended early in 1996.

## Falkland Islands 1982

Argentina has sustained a long-standing claim to the sovereignty of the Falkland Islands and on 2 Apr. 1982 the Argentine dictatorship under General Galtieri launched a successful invasion of the Islands, forcing its garrison of 18 Royal Marines to surrender. Argentine forces also seized the island of South Georgia. On 5 Apr. a British Task Force set sail to recapture the islands and on 7 Apr. an exclusion zone of 200 miles was declared around the island. On 25 Apr. South Georgia was recaptured and on 1 May air attacks began on the Argentine garrison on the Falklands. The next day the Argentine cruiser *Belgrano* was sunk by a British submarine and on 4 May HMS *Sheffield* was hit by an Exocet missile. On 21 May British troops went ashore at San Carlos. Two British frigates, the *Ardent* and *Antelope*, were sunk and others damaged by air attack, but British troops took Darwin and Goose Green by the end of May and on 11–14 June an attack on Port Stanley led to the surrender of the Argentine forces. During the conflict 255 British and 720 Argentine troops were killed. A large permanent garrison and modern airstrip were placed on the island for their future security.

### Gulf War 1990

On 2 Aug. 1990, Iraq invaded Kuwait. UN Resolution 660, condemning the invasion and calling for immediate and unconditional withdrawal, was passed the same day. The United States ordered naval forces to the Gulf on 3 Aug., and sent troops to Saudi Arabia on 7 Aug. (Operation 'Desert Shield'). UN Resolution 661, imposing economic sanctions on Iraq, was passed on 6 Aug. On 8 Aug. Iraq announced the annexation of Kuwait. On 29 Nov. UN Resolution 678 sanctioned the use of force if Iraq had not withdrawn by 15 Jan. 1991. Britain joined the Allied forces (led by the United States), contributing land, sea and air forces. The Allied offensive against Iraq (Operation 'Desert Storm') began shortly before midnight GMT on 16 Jan. The Allied ground offensive began on 24 Feb. Kuwait City was entered by the Allies on 26 Feb. With Kuwait liberated and the Iraqi army defeated, President Bush ordered a cease-fire, which came into effect on 28 Feb. During the conflict, Allied forces lost 166 killed, 207 wounded and 106 missing or captured. Iraqi losses were estimated by some to be 200,000.

## Major military legislation and administrative reforms

1757    Militia Act creates county-based force raised by ballot for use in emergencies under the command of lord-lieutenants and responsible to the home secretary.

1792    Barrack-building programme begun to provide accommodation for troops in ports and major manufacturing areas.

1794    First secretary of state for war appointed. Volunteer regiments formed to resist a French invasion.

1797    In aftermath of the naval mutinies, Mutiny Act makes it treasonable to incite disaffection among the armed forces. Pay rises awarded to both army and navy.

1832    All naval business consolidated under the Board of Admiralty.

1847     Life service in the army abolished; replaced by a minimum term of 10 years.

1852     Militia Act reorganizes militia and places it under the control of the secretary at war.

1853     Continuous Service Act reorganizes naval service with fixed terms of enlistment.

1854–55 Secretary of state for war takes overall control of the armed forces, though discipline and command of the army reserved to the commander-in-chief at the Horse Guards. Board of Ordnance abolished and duties of secretary at war combined with secretary of state for war.

1856     Staff college set up at Sandhurst.

1858     Creation of the Indian Army. Army of the East India Company transferred to the control of the Crown.

1859     Volunteer force created to protect against threat of French invasion.

1862     Fixed terms of enlistment made compulsory in the navy.

1867     Army of Reserve Act plans formation of a trained reserve of 80,000 men.

1868     Edward Cardwell becomes secretary for war and begins period of reform.

1870     War Office Act reorganizes War Office, incorporating the Horse Guards. Army Enlistment Act fixes terms of enlistment at 12 years, part on active service, part with the reserve.

1871     Purchase of commissions abolished. Flogging suspended in the navy in peacetime.

1872     Cardwell reorganizes regimental structure on basis of linked battalions, one to serve abroad, one to remain at home. Regiments to have local attachment for recruiting.

1879     Flogging in navy suspended in wartime.

1881     Flogging abolished in the army. Regular and militia battalions of the army amalgamated into territorial regiments with local designation and depot.

1902     Committee of Imperial Defence created.

1904     Office of commander-in-chief abolished; Army Council established and General Staff created.

1906     Richard Haldane becomes secretary for war and begins series of 'Haldane reforms'.

1907     British Expeditionary Force created for commitment to the Continent in the event of European war. Territorial Reserve Forces Act abolishes militia and volunteers and replaces them with Territorial regiments organized by county associations.

1914–15  Kitchener's 'New Army' raised from volunteers.

1916  Conscription introduced by Military Service Acts.

1918  Royal Air Force formed from British Royal Flying Corps. Air Board, later Air Ministry, established.

1923  Royal Tank Corps formed.

1931  Pay cuts in the armed forces provoke mutiny among naval units at Invergordon.

1939  Territorial Army doubled from 13 to 26 divisions. Compulsory Training Act calls reservists up for six months' training. Conscription introduced some months before Second World War (May).

1940  'Local Defence Volunteers' or 'Home Guard' formed for defence against invasion.

1946  Ministry of Defence created.

1947  National Service Act provides for continuation of compulsory military service; at first for 12 months; extended to two years in 1950.

1948  Britain signs Brussels treaty with France and Benelux countries, committing herself to military assistance in the event of an attack on Europe; confirmed in NATO treaty of 1949. British Army of the Rhine (BAOR) henceforth to be part of the NATO forces in Germany.

1957  Defence White Paper envisages reduction in conventional armed forces and greater reliance upon nuclear deterrence and a strategic reserve stationed in the United Kingdom.

1958–61  Large-scale amalgamation of existing regiments.

1960  National Service abolished.

1963  War Office, Admiralty and Air Ministry brought under the control of the Ministry of Defence. Defence Council set up under the secretary of state to exercise the powers previously wielded by each service.

1966  Territorial Army greatly reduced and replaced by smaller Territorial and Army Volunteer Reserve (TAVR).

1967  Further amalgamations of regiments and brigades.

1968  Announcement of withdrawal of British forces from East of Suez by 1971.

1976  Britain withdraws its forces from Singapore, except for a small contribution to the integrated air defence system; New Zealand troops remain, along with Australian air forces in Malaysia (Mar.).

1982    Argentine invasion of Falkland Islands/Malvinas (Mar.).
        Dispatch of British task force to reconquer islands (Apr.).
        Reconquest completed June (see pp. 295–6). Conservative
        govern- ment decides to replace Polaris submarines with new
        fleet of Trident II submarines (Mar.).
1983    First Cruise missiles arrive at Greenham Common (Nov.).
1985    Home Service Force established, linked with Territorial Army,
        of 5,000 to protect domestic civilian and military installations.
1989    Cruise missiles removed from Greenham Common (Aug.).
1990    Invasion of Kuwait by Iraq (Aug.). British forces join Allies to
        eject Iraqi invaders (see. p. 296).
1991    'Options for Change' programme of reducing and restruct-
        uring armed forces (modified in 1993).
1993    British troops sent to Bosnia as part of peacekeeping force in
        former Yugoslavia. First Trident submarine, HMS *Vanguard*,
        launched.
1994    BAOR renamed United Kingdom Support Command – a 25,000-
        strong force to serve as a multinational rapid reaction force.
1995    Biggest reorganization of the British army since 1945 brings
        nearly 140,000 regular and part-time soldiers under a single
        Land Command based at Erskine barracks, Witton, Salisbury.
        Its commander is General Sir John Wilsey.

## Strengths of army, navy and air force 1714–1990

|        | Army    | Navy    | Air force |
|--------|---------|---------|-----------|
| 1714   | 16 347  | 10 000  | –         |
| 1745   | 74 187  | n.a.    | –         |
| 1756   | 49 749  | 50 000  | –         |
| 1761   | 67 776  | 88 355  | –         |
| 1762   | 17 536  | 89 061  | –         |
| 1777   | 90 734  | 45 000  | –         |
| 1783   | 54 678  | 110 000 | –         |
| 1793   | 17 013  | 45 000  | –         |
| 1802   | 84 445  | 94 461  | –         |
| 1815   | 204 386 | 85 384  | –         |
| 1820   | 92 586  | 23 000  | –         |
| 1830   | 88 848  | 29 000  | –         |
| 1850   | 99 128  | 39 000  | –         |
| (*cont.*) |      |         |           |

## Strengths of army, navy and air force 1714–1990 (*cont.*)

|        | Army       | Navy     | Air force  |
|--------|-----------|----------|-----------|
| 1855   | 223 224   | 70 000   | –         |
| 1870   | 113 221   | 61 000   | –         |
| 1880   | 131 859   | 58 800   | –         |
| 1890   | 153 483   | 68 800   | –         |
| 1900   | 430 000   | 114 880  | –         |
| 1914*  | 733 514   | 147 667  | –         |
| 1918†  | 3 759 500 | n.a.     | 290 743   |
| 1920   | 435 000   | 133 000  | 28 000    |
| 1930   | 333 000   | 97 000   | 33 000    |
| 1939   | 1 128 000 | 214 000  | 215 000   |
| 1945   | 3 007 300 | 852 600  | 1 124 400 |
| 1950   | 377 600   | 140 000  | 202 000   |
| 1960   | 264 300   | 97 800   | 163 500   |
| 1970   | 173 000   | 87 000   | 113 000   |
| 1979   | 163 681   | 72 900   | 86 310    |
| 1986   | 162 100   | 68 200   | 93 100    |
| 1990   | 153 000   | 63 000   | 90 000    |

*Jan.  †Nov.

Source: C. Cook and B. Keith, *British Historical Facts 1830–1900* (London, Macmillan, 1975), p.185; *Parliamentary Papers*, 1868–69, XXXV, pp. 639–51; *Britain, 1994*, pp. 315–16.

# Treaties

## Key British defence treaties and alliances

1717    Triple Alliance between Britain, France and The Netherlands signed at The Hague to oppose Philip V's ambitions in France and Italy, 4 Jan. This became the Quadruple Alliance after the accession of Austria on 2 Aug. 1718.

1720    Treaty of The Hague ended the War of the Quadruple Alliance, 17 Feb.

1725    Treaty of Hanover, 3 Sept., created defensive league between Britain, France and Prussia to counterbalance alliance between Austria and Spain signed earlier in the year.

1727    Treaty of Paris, 31 May, between Austria and Britain, France and Prussia ended brief conflict. A peace treaty with Spain was signed at the Pardo on 6 Mar. 1728.

1729    Treaty of Seville for peace and friendship between Britain, France and Spain was concluded on 9 Nov.

1731    Treaty of Vienna between Britain, Spain, The Netherlands and Austria, 22 July. Britain and The Netherlands guaranteed the Pragmatic Sanction in return for which the Emperor suspended the Ostend East India Company.

1741    Treaty of Hanover, 24 June: Britain offered Maria Theresa support against Prussia and France. George II concluded treaty with France for the neutrality of Hanover, 7 Sept.

1745    Quadruple Alliance against Prussia signed at Warsaw by Austria, England, The Netherlands and Saxony, 8 Jan. Convention of Hanover between Britain and Prussia, 26 Aug.

1748    Treaty of Aix-la-Chapelle ending War of the Austrian Succession signed on 18 Oct. by Britain, France and The Netherlands (also accepted by Spain, Austria, Madeira, Genoa and Sardinia by Dec.). Maria Theresa recognized, but Silesia ceded to Prussia. Succession of House of Hanover in its German states and Great Britain confirmed.

1750    Treaty of alliance with Austria and Bavaria signed at Hanover,

22 Aug. Treaty of alliance with Austria and Russia signed at St Petersburg, 30 Oct.

1755    Treaty with Russia for defence of Hanover, 30 Sept.

1756    Treaty of London with Prussia to oppose attacks in Germany, 16 Jan.

1758    Subsidy treaty with Prussia, 11 Apr.

1762    Preliminary articles of peace signed by Britain, France and Spain, 3 Nov.

1763    Peace of Paris, 10 Feb. between France, Spain and Britain ended Seven Years War. France ceded to England Canada, Cape Breton Island, Granada and Senegal; the Mississippi recognized as the frontier between Louisiana and the British colonies. England restored to France Goree in Africa, and all conquests in India. Spain ceded Florida to England, but received back all conquests in Cuba.

1782    Provisional articles of peace signed by Britain and the United States at Paris, 30 Nov.

1783    Preliminaries of peace signed with France and Spain, 20 Jan. Treaty of Versailles signed by Britain, France, Spain and the United States, 3 Sept. Recognition of the independence of the United States and establishment of its boundaries. United States' fishing rights established on Grand Bank, Newfoundland coast, and in the Gulf of St Lawrence. Navigation of the Mississippi to be open to both Great Britain and the United States. Great Britain ceded Tobago and Senegal to France and Florida to Spain.

1784    Treaty of peace and friendship with The Netherlands signed in Paris, 20 May.

1786    Treaty of commerce and navigation with France, 26 Sept.

1788    Defensive alliance with The Netherlands to maintain the peace of Europe, 15 Apr. Defensive alliance with Prussia to maintain the peace of Europe, 13 Aug.

1790    Alliance with Prussia and The Netherlands, 9 Jan. Convention with The Netherlands, the Holy Roman Empire and Prussia concerning the Austrian Netherlands, 10 Dec.

1793    Convention with Russia for concerted action against France, 25 Mar. Treaty of alliance with Sardinia against France, 25 Apr. Convention with Spain against France, 25 May. Convention with Sicily against France, 12 July. Convention with Prussia against France, 14 July. Convention with the Emperor against France, 30 Aug. Treaty with Portugal against France, 26 Sept.

1794    Agreement with Spain against France, 11 Jan. Subsidy treaty between Britain, The Netherlands, and Prussia, 19 Apr.

1795    Defensive alliance with Russia, 18 Feb. Loan convention with the Emperor, 4 May. Defensive alliance with the Emperor, 20 May.

1796    Loan convention with the Emperor, 16 May.

1798    Treaty of alliance against France with the King of the Two Sicilies, 1 Dec. Provisional treaty with Russia to act against France, 29 Dec.

1799    Treaty of alliance with Turkey against France, 5 Jan. Convention with Russia against France, 22 June.

1800    Subsidy treaty with Bavaria, 16 Mar. Convention with the Emperor, 20 June. Preliminary convention with Denmark, 29 Aug.

1801    Convention with Russia, 17 June (accessions: Denmark, 23 Oct. 1801, Sweden, 30 Mar. 1802); grants British right to search vessels. Preliminary articles of peace with France, 1 Oct.

1802    Treaty of Amiens, 27 Mar.: peace with France, Spain and the Bavarian Republic. Surrender of all conquests made by England to France and her allies except Ceylon and Trinidad. Malta restored to the Knights of St John and Minorca to Spain. France recognized Ionian Republic and evacuated the Sicilies, the Papal States, Portugal and Egypt.

1805    Treaty with Russia, 11 Apr., for the purpose of restoring the balance of power in Europe (accessions: Austria, 9 Aug.; Sweden, 3 Oct.).

1807    Convention of friendship and amity with Portugal, 22 Oct.

1808    Convention of Cintra permits evacuation of defeated French army from Portugal on British ships, 30 Aug.

1809    Treaty of alliance with Austria against France, 24 Apr.

1812    Treaties of peace, union and friendship with Russia and Sweden, 18 July.

1813    Treaty of subsidy and concert with Sweden against France, 3 Mar. Convention with Prussia signed at Reichenbach, 14 June, to provide subsidies for war with France. Convention with Russia signed at Reichenbach, 27 June, to provide subsidies for war with France. Preliminary treaty of alliance with Austria signed at Toplitz, 3 Oct.

1814    Treaties of union, concert and subsidy signed with Austria, Prussia and Russia at Chaumont, 1 Mar. Convention for suspension of hostilities with France, 23 Apr. Treaty of peace with France signed at Paris, 30 May. France restricted to her boundaries in 1792 and forced to recognize the independence of The Netherlands, the German and Italian states and Switzerland. England restored all French colonies except Tobago, St Lucia and the Ile de France (Mauritius), and also retained Malta, Heligoland and the Cape of Good Hope. Treaty of peace with United States signed at Ghent, 24 Dec.

1815    Treaty of alliance with Austria, Prussia and Russia against Napoleon signed at Vienna, 25 Mar., each power engaging to furnish 180,000 men. Act of the Congress of Vienna signed by Britain, Austria, France, Portugal, Prussia, Russia and Sweden, 9 June. Treaty of peace with France signed at Paris, 20 Nov.

1827    Treaty with France and Russia for pacification of Greece signed at London, 6 July.

1830    Protocol signed with France and Russia concerning Greek independence, 3 Feb.

1831    Protocol of conference regarding the separation of Belgium and The Netherlands signed by Britain, Austria, France, Prussia and Russia, 20 Jan.

1832    Convention regarding the sovereignty of Greece signed by Britain, France, Russia and Bavaria, 7 May.

1834    Treaty of Quadruple Alliance with France, Spain and Portugal for the pacification of the Iberian Peninsula, 22 Apr. Agreement with Russia to respect the integrity and independence of Persia, 5 Sept.

1839    Treaty between Britain, Austria, France, Prussia, Russia and Belgium regarding Belgium and The Netherlands, 19 Apr.

1840    Convention between Britain, Austria, Prussia, Russia and Turkey for the pacification of the Levant, 15 July.

1841    Convention between Austria, France, Prussia, Russia and Turkey regarding the Dardanelles, 13 July.

1842    Treaty of Nanking between Britain and China ending the Opium War, 29 Aug.; Hong Kong was ceded to Britain and the five treaty ports were opened to foreign trade.

1846    Treaty with the United States settling the Oregon boundary with Canada, 15 June.

1854    Treaty of alliance with Austria and France, 2 Dec.

1855    Treaty with France and Sweden and Norway regarding the integrity of the United Kingdoms of Sweden and Norway, 21 Nov.

1856    Peace of Paris ending the Crimean War signed by Britain,

Austria, France, Prussia, Russia, Sardinia and Turkey, 30 Mar. Treaty between Britain, Austria and France guaranteeing the independence and integrity of the Ottoman Empire, 15 Apr.

1864   Geneva Convention regarding the amelioration of the condition of the wounded in armies in the field, 22 Aug.

1871   Treaty concerning the navigation of the Black Sea and the Danube between Britain, Austria, France, Germany, Italy, Russia and Turkey, 13 Mar. Treaty between Britain and the United States regarding the amicable settlement of disputes, 8 May.

1878   Treaty arising out of the Congress of Berlin signed by Britain, Austria-Hungary, France, Germany, Italy, Russia and Turkey for the settlement of Balkan problems, 13 July. Agreement between Britain and Turkey regarding British government of Cyprus, 14 Aug.

1881   Final Act for the settlement of the frontier between Greece and Turkey agreed between Britain, Austria-Hungary, France, Germany, Italy and Russia, 18 Sept.

1885   General Act of the 15-nation conference at Berlin regarding affairs of Central Africa, 26 Feb. Declaration regarding Egyptian finances and the free navigation of the Suez Canal by Britain, Austria-Hungary, France, Germany, Italy and Russia, 17 Mar. Agreement between Britain and Germany regarding spheres of action in Africa, 29 Apr. Protocol between Britain and Russia regarding the Afghan frontier, 10 Sept.

1888   Convention respecting the free navigation of the Suez Canal, 29 Oct.

1889   Final Act of the conference on the affairs of Samoa, 14 June.

1890   Convention with China relating to Sikkim and Tibet, 17 Mar. Agreement with Zanzibar placing Zanzibar under the protection of Britain, 14 June. Agreement between Britain and Germany regarding Zanzibar, Heligoland and spheres of influence in Africa, 1 July. Declarations exchanged with France respecting territories in Africa, 5 Aug.

1891   Agreement with France regarding spheres of influence in Africa, 26 June.

1893   Protocol with Germany respecting the delimitation of the Anglo-German boundary in East Equatorial Africa, 8 July. Arrangements with France fixing boundary between British and French possessions on the Gold Coast, 12 July. Protocol with France respecting territories in the region of the Upper

Mekong, 31 July. Agreement with Afghanistan respecting frontier between India and Afghanistan, 12 Nov. Agreement with Germany respecting boundaries in Africa, 15 Nov.

1894     Protocol between Britain and Italy regarding spheres of influence in eastern Africa, 5 May.

1897     Convention with France concerning Tunis, 18 Sept.

1898     Convention with France concerning spheres of influence east and west of the Niger, 14 June. Convention with Germany regarding Portuguese Africa and Timor, 30 Aug.

1899     International conventions for the pacific settlement of international disputes; for adapting to maritime warfare the principles of the Geneva Convention; and with respect to the laws and customs of war by land, 29 July. Conventions with Germany and the United States relating to Samoa, 7 Nov.–2 Dec. Exchange of notes with the United States accepting the commercial policy of the 'open door' in China, Sept.–Dec.

1900     Agreement with Germany regarding China, 16 Oct. Both parties agree to restrain foreign territorial aggression in China and maintain the 'open door' for trade.

1902     Anglo-Japanese Alliance signed, 30 Jan. Concluded initially for five years, both powers recognized the special interests of each other in China, and Japan's interests in Korea. Agreement to remain neutral in the event of war with a third power, or provide assistance in the event of war with two other powers. Renewed in Aug. 1905 and modified to provide for mutual support in the event of attack by another power.

1904     Anglo-French *Entente (Entente Cordiale)* signed, 8 Apr. Although no formal military alliance was arranged, there was an unwritten understanding of mutual assistance if required. Agreed that Egypt and Morocco to be under British and French influence respectively. Disputes over Newfoundland, Madagascar and Siam settled.

1907     Anglo-Russian *Entente* signed, 31 Aug. Settled outstanding differences over Afghanistan, Tibet and Persia, paving the way for Russia to side with Britain and France against Germany in 1914.

1914     Triple *Entente* signed between Britain, France and Russia, 3 Sept., agreeing not to make a separate peace with Germany.

1915     Secret Anglo-Russian treaty signed, 12 Mar. Agreed that Constantinople and the Straits to go to Russia after the conclusion of the war. Britain obtained concessions in Persia and Asiatic Turkey in return. Secret Treaty of London signed, 25 Apr. Italy agreed to declare war on the central powers in return for territorial concessions from the Austro-Hungarian Empire, including the Tyrol, Istria and North Dalmatia.

1916    Sykes–Picot agreement between Britain and France reached in Jan. to partition Turkish Empire in Asia. Syria allotted to France and Mesopotamia to Britain, with British outlet to the Mediterranean at Haifa. The agreement was subject to Russian consent, obtained in May 1916 when Turkish Armenia was allotted to Russia.

1919    Peace treaty signed between Germany and the Allied powers at Versailles, 28 June. Germany surrendered Alsace-Lorraine to France; the Rhineland was declared a demilitarized zone to be occupied by the Allies for 15 years; territory was ceded to Belgium, Denmark, Poland and Czechoslovakia; the German army was limited to 100,000 men and denied tanks or aircraft; and Germany was stripped of all overseas colonies which were placed under League of Nations control or 'mandate'. The treaty declared German responsibility for the war and made her liable for the payment of reparations. The treaty also contained the Covenant of the League of Nations. Peace treaty of St Germain with Austria signed, 10 Sept. Austrian territory ceded to Italy, Yugoslavia, Poland, Czechoslovakia and Romania. Hungary became a separate state; union of Austria and Germany forbidden; Austrian army reduced to 30,000 men and the state made liable for reparations. Peace treaty of Neuilly with Bulgaria signed, 27 Nov. Territory ceded to Greece and Yugoslavia and army reduced to 20,000 men.

1920    Peace treaty between Hungary and the Allied powers, 4 June. Hungary reduced to two-thirds pre-war size and army limited to 35,000 men. Treaty of Sèvres with Turkey, 10 Aug.; never ratified by the Turks.

1921    Articles of agreement for a treaty between Great Britain and Ireland signed, 6 Dec. Irish Free State created with Dominion status; six counties of Ulster excluded. Washington Four Power treaty signed, 13 Dec.: Britain, Japan, France and United States agree not to strengthen their island possessions in the Pacific.

1922    Washington Nine Power treaty signed, 6 Feb.: naval limits agreed; Britain, America and Japan to have battleships in ratio 5 : 5 : 3; no battleships over 35,000 tons to be constructed and no battleships or cruisers built for 10 years.

1923    Treaty of Lausanne with Turkey signed, 23 Aug. Treaty made necessary by Turkey's refusal to accept the Treaty of Sèvres. Turkey surrendered parts of the Ottoman Empire occupied by non-Turks, but retained Constantinople and eastern Thrace in Europe. Smyrna ceded by Greece, but all other Aegean Islands except Imbros and Tenedos ceded by Turkey. Turkey recognized annexation of Cyprus by Britain and Dodecanese by Italy. Bosporus and Dardanelles demilitarized.

1925    Locarno treaties, 15 Oct.: France, Germany and Belgium agreed to the inviolability of the Franco-German and Belgo-German frontiers and the existence of the demilitarized zone of the Rhineland; this was guaranteed by Britain and Italy. Franco-Polish and Franco-Czech treaties of mutual guarantee were also signed.

1928    Kellogg–Briand Pact signed by Britain, France, Germany, Italy, Japan and the United States renouncing aggressive war, 27 Aug.

1930    London Naval treaty signed by Britain, France, Italy, Japan and the United States limiting naval armaments, 22 Apr. Building of capital ships suspended for six years and existing numbers reduced.

1935    Anglo-German Naval Agreement, 18 June, limiting the German navy to 35 per cent of the British, with submarines at 45 per cent or equality in the event of danger from Russia.

1936    London Naval treaty, 25 Mar. Warships limited to 14-inch guns and size of aircraft carriers reduced. Not implemented by Japan, Italy or France. Montreux Convention by which Turkey was permitted to refortify the Straits (July). Non-intervention Agreement with regard to Spanish Civil War signed by major powers, 7 Aug. Abrogated by Germany and Italy.

1937    Anglo-Italian 'Gentleman's Agreement' to maintain the *status quo* in the Mediterranean, 2 Jan.

1938    Munich Agreement: agreement reached by Britain, France, Italy and Germany, by which territorial concessions were made to Germany, Poland and Hungary at the expense of Czechoslovakia, 29 Sept. The rump of Czechoslovakia was to be guaranteed against unprovoked aggression, but German control was extended to the rest of Czechoslovakia in Mar. 1939.

1939    Franco-British guarantee to Poland, 31 Mar. Agreed to lend support if independence threatened. British guarantee to

Romania and Greece, 13 Apr. Offered support in the event of external threat.

1941 Atlantic Charter published by Britain and United States pledging preservation of world freedom, 14 Aug.

1942 'United Nations' (principally United States, Great Britain, Soviet Union, China) declare will not make separate peace, 1 Jan. Anglo-American Mutual Aid Agreement, 23 Feb., confirmed 'lend-lease' arrangements between Britain and United States and pledged reduction of trade barriers after the war. Anglo-Soviet treaty, 26 May.

1945 Yalta Agreement between leaders of Britain, Russia and the United States, 11 Feb. Agreement to split Germany into zones of occupation after the war, try war criminals and set up United Nations. United Nations Charter signed, 26 June. Potsdam Agreement, 2 Aug.: leaders of Russia and United States arrange regular meetings to settle problems; trials of war criminals arranged; reparations to be taken from war zones by occupiers.

1947 Peace treaties with Italy, Bulgaria, Finland, Hungary and Romania, 10 Feb. Treaty of Dunkirk: 50-year alliance with France, 4 Mar. Defence agreement with Burma, 29 Aug.; ended by Burma, 3 Jan. 1953. Defence agreement with Ceylon, 11 Nov.

1948 Twenty-year mutual defence treaty with Jordan, 15 Mar.; ended 14 Mar. 1957. Treaty of Brussels, 17 Mar. signed by Britain, Belgium, France, Luxembourg and The Netherlands for collective military aid and economic and social cooperation; amended and expanded by Paris agreements of 23 Oct. 1954, when the Brussels Treaty Organization was renamed Western European Union.

1949 North Atlantic Treaty signed in Washington by Britain, Belgium, Canada, Denmark, France, Iceland, Italy, Luxembourg, The Netherlands, Norway, Portugal and the United States; joined later by Greece, Turkey and the German Federal Republic.

1951 Peace treaty with Japan, 8 Sept.

1953 Treaty of friendship and alliance with Libya, 29 July: in 1967 Libya requested the withdrawal of all British forces and liquidation of bases.

1954 Geneva Conventions on Indo-China, 20 July. Laos and Cambodia become independent; Vietnam divided at 17th parallel. South-East Asia collective defence treaty signed in Manila, 8 Sept., by Britain, Australia, France, New Zealand, Pakistan, the Philippines, Thailand and the United States. Pakistan left the South-East Asia Treaty Organization (SEATO) on 7 Nov. 1973. On 24 Sept. 1975 the SEATO Council agreed to disband the organization, but not to abrogate the treaty.

1955    Britain joined Turkey and Iraq in the Baghdad Pact, 4 Apr.; later joined by Pakistan and Iran. The name was changed to the Central Treaty Organization (CENTO) on 21 Aug. 1959. Austrian State treaty signed by Britain, France, Soviet Union, United States and Austria re-establishing Austria as a sovereign, independent and neutral state, 15 May. Simonstown naval cooperation agreement with South Africa, 4 July; revised Jan. 1967; ended 16 June 1975.

1957    Treaty of defence and mutual assistance with Malaysia, 12 Oct.

1959    Britain joins European Free Trade Association (EFTA), 20 Nov. Britain signs treaty for the demilitarization of Antarctica, 1 Dec.

1960    Defence agreement with Nigeria, Nov.; abrogated by joint decision, 21 Jan. 1962.

1963    Britain signs the Partial Test Ban treaty prohibiting nuclear tests in the atmosphere, in outer space and under water, 5 Aug.

1967    Britain signs the Outer Space treaty banning the development of weapons of mass destruction in outer space, 27 Jan.

1968    Britain signs Non-Proliferation treaty intended to prevent the spread of nuclear weapons, 1 July.

1971    Britain signs Sea-Bed treaty banning the installation of weapons of mass destruction on the ocean floor, 11 Feb.

1972    Treaty of Accession to European Economic Community and European Atomic Energy Community, 22 Jan. Effective from 1 Jan. 1973. Britain signs the Chemical and Bacteriological Convention, prohibiting the development, production and stockpiling of bacteriological and toxic weapons, 10 Apr.

1975    Helsinki Agreement on Security and Cooperation in Europe, 1 Aug.

1976    International (UN) Convention on Economic and Social Rights and on Civil and Political Rights, 20 May.

1979    Britain signs International Agreement on trans-national air pollution.

1984    Sino-British Declaration on the future of Hong Kong, assuring its future as a capitalist entity for 50 years after Britain's departure in 1997.

1985    Anglo-Irish Agreement signed at Hillsborough by British and Irish Premiers, giving the Irish government a consultative role in Northern Irish affairs while guaranteeing the wishes of the majority population in the North.

1986    Single European Act signed by member states and ratified by their parliaments. European flag adopted (Feb.).

1988    Delors' reforms of the European budget agreed, putting controls on farm spending and expanding structural funds. Committee set up under Delors to prepare plans for European Monetary Union (EMU) (Feb.). Mrs Thatcher makes Bruges speech attacking attempts to create a European 'superstate' (Sept.).

1989    Third direct elections to European Parliament. Madrid Summit receives Delors Plan for three-stage plan for European Monetary Union (Jan.). Agreement reached that first stage of EMU would start on 1 July 1990 with all 12 members beginning to adhere to the EMS. Austria applies to join EEC (Apr.).

1990    Britain joins EMS (Oct.). Inter-government conference on EMU plans further development of EMU (Dec.).

1991    Luxembourg plan for inter-government conference at Maastricht turned down (Oct.). Maastricht Summit gives Britain opt-out clauses over monetary union and social charter.

1992    Several currencies (including sterling) forced to suspend membership of EMS following speculation.

1993    British parliament eventually passes Maastricht Bill (receives Royal Assent, July).

1994    European Union comes into force (Jan.).

# Ireland

## Major events in Irish history, 1714–1995

1720  Act of 6 Geo 1: formal assertion of British parliament's right to legislate for Ireland.

1722  William Wood, an Englishman, granted a patent to coin money for Ireland.

1724  Swift publishes his *Drapier's Letters*.

1756  Money Bill defeated in Irish parliament because preamble states surplus revenue belongs to the Crown not to the nation.

1778  Widespread volunteer movement to repel French invasion and assert Irish rights. Gardiner's Relief Act permitted Catholics to lease land if they took oath of allegiance.

1779  Demonstration of armed volunteers in Dublin (4 Nov.).

1780  Grattan's 'declaration of independence' by Irish parliament adjourned as inexpedient; Irish magistrates refuse to operate the Mutiny Act. Perpetual Mutiny Act passed by British parliament.

1782  Ulster Volunteers meet at Dungannon and pass a patriot programme (15 Feb.). Grattan's motion, postponed for a second time in February, passed unanimously (16 Apr.). 'The Constitution of 1782' repeals the legislative authority of the British parliament and alters Poyning's Law, to end the power of the chief governor, and Council of Ireland to originate or alter Bills; only Bills enacted by the Irish parliament were to be transmitted to the King. Perpetual Mutiny Act replaced by a Biennial Act. Irish judges granted same security of tenure as their English counterparts.

1783  Renunciation Act confirms the legislative and judicial independence of Ireland.

1791  Society of United Irishmen founded by Theobald Wolfe Tone and others in Belfast for religious equality and radical reform. Similar societies set up elsewhere.

1792  Catholic Relief Act removes restrictions on Roman Catholics in education, marriage and the professions they could follow. Provisions for granting political rights defeated. Catholic Convention in Dublin (Dec.); petitions for further concessions.

1793      Catholic Relief Act admits Roman Catholics to municipal and parliamentary franchise on the same terms as Protestants with the right to bear arms and hold most civil and military offices except in Parliament.

1794–95      Earl Fitzwilliam becomes Viceroy of Ireland and commits the government to Catholic relief. Grattan's Bill to admit Roman Catholics to Parliament rejected (May). First 'Orange Society' founded in response to sectarian fighting.

1796–97      Insurrection Act passed giving government repressive powers to deal with the disturbances. United Irishmen take up arms and are suppressed by the military.

1798      Outbreak of rebellion, 23 May; initially successful in Wexford, but eventually suppressed. General Humbert lands at Killala Bay, 22 Aug. Forced to surrender at Ballinamuch, and the rising in Connaught ended within a month with the recapture of Killala. Hardy's expedition to Lough Swilly fails (Oct.); Wolfe Tone is captured.

1799      Act establishes virtual martial law in Ireland.

1800      Act of Union receives Royal Assent (1 Aug.). It establishes 'The United Kingdom of Great Britain and Ireland'; succession of the Crown to be governed by the same provisions as the union with Scotland; Irish parliament abolished; 32 Irish peers (28 temporal, 4 spiritual) to sit in the House of Lords and 100 members (64 county, 35 borough and 1 university) in the House of Commons. The churches were united, but the financial systems remained distinct. Ireland was to provide two-seventeenths of United Kingdom expenditure.

1803      Emmett's 'rising' suppressed. He and 21 others executed.

1816–17      Partial failure of potato crop produces famine conditions in several areas; relief committees set up.

1822      Further failure of potato crop; major public works programme started to provide employment.

1823      Catholic Association founded by O'Connell to campaign for political and other rights.

1828      Election of O'Connell for Co. Clare forces consideration of granting Catholics right to sit in Parliament.

1829      Catholic Emancipation Act. Roman Catholics made eligible for all offices of state except regent, lord lieutenant and lord chancellor. No oath of supremacy required to sit in either House of Parliament.

1832    Irish Reform Act receives Royal Assent, 7 Aug.

1833    Irish Church Temporalities Act suppresses 10 sees and reduces the revenues of the rest. Surplus revenues to be administered for purely ecclesiastical purposes.

1836    Potato famine.

1838    Tithe Act removes a popular source of grievances.

1840    Irish Municipal Corporations Act enfranchises £10 householder, abolishes 58 corporations, establishes 10 new ones, and overhauls municipal administration. 'Young Ireland' Party formed.

1842    *The Nation* magazine founded by group of 'Young Ireland' journalists to promote nationalism.

1843    O'Connell begins programme of mass meetings to promote repeal of the union at Trim (16 Mar.), but forced to cancel monster meeting at Clontarf (Oct.) when government declared it illegal. O'Connell arrested, tried for sedition and conspiracy and sentenced to a year's imprisonment and a fine, but judgement reversed in the House of Lords.

1845    Grant to Irish Catholic college at Maynooth increased in spite of bitter opposition in Parliament. Irish National Education Board formed.

1845–50 Great famine due to successive failures of potato crop as a result of blight. Irish population fell from 8,178,124 in 1841 to 6,552,386 in 1851 as a result of deaths and emigration.

1847    'Young Ireland' set up the Irish Confederation under William Smith O'Brien. O'Connell's death at Genoa, 15 May. Thirty-nine repealers returned in the general election. John Mitchell begins publication of *United Irishman* newspaper, promoting radical agrarian reform.

1848    Arrest of Mitchell, 13 May; 'Young Ireland' rising in Tipperary easily suppressed and leaders transported (July). Encumbered Estates Act passed.

1849    Serious affray between Catholics and Protestants at Dolly's Brae.

1850    Establishment of Queen's University, Belfast. Irish Franchise Act increased voters from 61,000 to 165,000.

1851    First meeting of Catholic Defence Association.

1852    Warrenstown Tenant Right demonstration.

1853    Income tax extended to Ireland.

| 1858 | Fenian Brotherhood started by John O'Mahoney and James Stephens, directed at achieving nationhood 'soon or never'. |
|------|------|
| 1862 | Catholic University College founded in Dublin. |
| 1867 | Failure of Fenian insurrection. |
| 1868 | Election of Gladstone as Prime Minister. |
| 1869 | Disestablishment and Disendowment of the Irish Church. From Jan. 1871 the Church of Ireland was disestablished; all property except churches in use was vested in a body of commissioners for Irish Church temporalities. Compensation set at £16 million, half of the capital of confiscated property, the remainder to be used for public benefit. |
| 1870 | Land Act designed to protect the tenant. The Ulster custom was established by law where it already existed; elsewhere greater compensation was to be given for improvements and for disturbance. Agrarian disorder continued. Home Government Association formed by Irish Protestant Conservative lawyer, Isaac Butt. In 1873 re-formed as Home Rule League. |
| 1872 | Six Home Rulers in Parliament commit themselves to land reform and denominational education. |
| 1873 | Home Rule League founded in Dublin. |
| 1874 | Home Rule League led by Isaac Butt wins 59 seats in general election and initiates policy of 'obstruction'. |
| 1879 | Death of Isaac Butt; Land League formed by Michael Davitt (Parnell as president), for fair rents to be fixed by arbitration, fixity of tenure while rent was paid and freedom of tenant to sell his right of occupancy. |
| 1880 | Parnell becomes the new leader of the 61 Home Rulers returned in the general election. 'Boycotts' organized against those who offended against the Land League's code. Troops used to harvest crops on Lord Erne's land managed by Captain C. C. Boycott, who gave his name to the tactic used against him. |
| 1881 | New Coercion Act passed in Mar. But in Apr. Gladstone introduced a new Land Act conceding many of the basic demands of the Land League. Its reception was hostile and in Oct. Parnell was imprisoned in Kilmainham Gaol, and was not released until Apr. 1882. A 'No Rent' movement was launched in protest at the imprisonment. |
| 1882 | By the so-called 'Kilmainham treaty' Parnell promised to use his influence to end crime and disorder, while the government promised a new policy of conciliation. Spencer |

became new Viceroy and Lord Frederick Cavendish, Chief Secretary. On 6 May, Cavendish and T. H. Burke, the Under-Secretary, were murdered in Phoenix Park by 'the Invincibles'; New Crimes Bill introduced. National League founded by Parnell, closely linked to Irish parliamentary party.

1884    Franchise Act gave the counties (outside Ulster) to the Home Rulers.

1885    Redistribution Act. Number of Irish MPs unchanged despite the fall in population. Ashburne's Act: provided the advance to the tenant of the whole sum needed to buy his land, to be repaid over 49 years at 4 per cent. In three years the £5 million grant was exhausted. Eighty-five Home Rulers returned for Irish seats in the general election. They held the balance in the House of Commons and chose to support Gladstone because of a press rumour that he was in favour of Home Rule. Home Rule Bill defeated in Commons, 343–313 (93 Liberals voted against).

1886    General election: 85 Home Rulers returned, but in England Home Rule was heavily rejected. National League organizes a plan of campaign by tenants against landlords.

1887    Parnell accused of complicity in agrarian outrages in letter in *The Times*; cleared by committee of enquiry, who discovered the forgery.

1890    Parnell cited in Mrs O'Shea's divorce, which made continued alliance with the Liberals impossible. The Home Rulers split, 26 supporting Parnell, the majority disavowing him.

1891    Death of Parnell (Oct.). Chief Secretary Balfour encourages land purchase; £30 million made available. Congested Districts Board set up to assist poorest areas.

1892    Duke of Abercorn declares in Belfast, 'We will not have Home Rule' (June).

1893    Second Home Rule Bill; this would continue Irish representation at Westminster. Defeated in House of Lords. Edward Saunderson, MP for North Armagh, helps establish the Ulster Defence Union. Gaelic League founded.

1898    William O'Brien puts new life into the Home Rule movement with the United Ireland League, begun in Connaught with a policy of agrarian reform. Doctrine of 'Sinn Fein' ('ourselves alone') preached by *United Irishman*, a weekly paper published in Dublin by A. Griffith. James Connolly founds the Irish Socialist Republican Party.

| 1900 | Irish Nationalists reunited under Redmond; 82 returned in general election. |
|------|-----------------------------------------------------------------------------|
| 1902 | Sinn Fein founded by Arthur Griffith. |
| 1903 | 'Wyndham's Act' goes a long way to making sale of estates universal; £100 million made available for land purchase by tenants. |
| 1904 | Negotiations for a scheme for devolution between government and Irish Nationalists. |
| 1905 | Ulster Unionist Council established; a large representative body with a permanent executive committee. |
| 1906 | Eighty-three Irish Nationalists returned at the general election. Bill to introduce devolution rejected by Redmond, but no alternative offered by government. |
| 1907 | Augustine Birrell becomes Chief Secretary. Sinn Fein League organized for 'the re-establishment of the independence of Ireland'. |
| 1908 | Sinn Fein contests North Leitrim election; violence, but Redmond wins. Universities' Act founds Queen's University, Belfast, and National University of Ireland. |
| 1909 | Birrell Act to encourage land purchase eases financial clauses of Wyndham's Act. |
| 1910 | At the Jan. general election, 70 followers of Redmond and 11 independent Irish Nationalists returned. Sir Edward Carson leads the Ulster Unionists in opposition to plans for Home Rule. |
| 1911 | Carson declares in Belfast: 'We will yet defeat the most nefarious conspiracy that has ever been hatched against a free people.' Unionist Council prepares plans to take over civil administration in Ulster in event of Home Rule. |
| 1912 | Bonar Law, the Conservative leader, espouses Unionist cause 'as the cause of the Empire'. At Blenheim supports plans for Ulster resistance. Liberal government introduces a Home Rule Bill for the whole of Ireland. Ulster Volunteers formed as a military force to resist Home Rule. Ulster's 'Solemn League and Covenant' signed by over 200,000 Protestants. |
| 1913 | Home Rule Bill defeated in the House of Lords, but awaits automatic implementation under provisions of Parliament Act; idea of excluding Ulster from its provisions raised by Liberal government. Citizen Army, later known as the 'Irish Volunteers', formed in the South. |
| 1914 | Asquith persuades Redmond to accept exclusion of Ulster from operation of Home Rule for six years, but Carson rejects |

compromise. 'Mutiny' at the Curragh (headquarters of the British army in Ireland) following rumours of unwillingness of army officers to coerce the Ulster Protestants. Gun-running into Ulster and Dublin arms the two 'volunteer' forces. Conference at Buckingham Palace in July fails to reach agreement on Ulster's exclusion from Home Rule. Outbreak of First World War defers implementation of Home Rule.

1916    Easter Rising in Dublin by members of the Irish Republican Brotherhood crushed by British troops. Execution of leaders sparks off bitter anti-British feeling.

1917    'Irish Convention' organized by Lloyd George to discuss future government of Ireland. Two Sinn Fein candidates elected in by-elections at Roscommon and Longford. De Valera assumes leadership of Sinn Fein.

1918    Attempt to extend conscription to Ireland provokes widespread protest. Sinn Fein and Irish Volunteers declared illegal and leaders detained, but in December general election 73 Sinn Fein candidates elected.

1919    Sinn Fein members refuse to sit at Westminster and set up provisional government; unofficial parliament of the Irish Republic, Dail Eireann, meets in Dublin in Jan. De Valera escapes from Lincoln gaol and is elected president. Sinn Fein and Dail declared illegal. Clashes between Republican 'flying columns' and British forces. Irish Volunteers reconstituted as Irish Republican Army (IRA).

1920    Virtual guerrilla war between IRA and British forces. Black-and-Tans and auxiliaries recruited to assist Royal Irish Constabulary carry out reprisals. Government of Ireland Act passed in Dec. dividing Ireland into two: 'Northern Ireland', based on the six Ulster counties, and 'Southern Ireland', consisting of the remaining 26. Each part to have its own parliament, but accept the supremacy of Westminster where both to retain representatives. A Council of Ireland to be set up to coordinate matters relating to the whole of Ireland. Ulster politicians accept the Act, but Republicans refuse to agree to it and continue attacks on British forces.

1921    Southern elections return 124 Sinn Fein candidates out of 128, but members refuse to sit and parliament adjourned. Treaty signed with southern Irish, giving Southern Ireland dominion status as Irish Free State.

1922    Dail approves treaty with Britain by 64 votes to 57. De Valera leads anti-treaty 'Republican' faction and resigns as president. General election confirms majority support for pro-treaty group. Split in IRA, and anti-treaty group begins raids against Ulster and arms raids in South. Four Courts in Dublin occupied by anti-treaty forces; besieged by Free State forces and Republicans forced to surrender. Michael Collins assassinated in Republican ambush at Cork and widespread fighting between Free State and Republican forces. Executions of Republican leaders.

1923    Cease-fire accepted by de Valera and Republican group. Free Staters set up political party, Cumann na nGaedheal.

1925    Tripartite agreement signed in London confirming existing boundary between Northern Ireland and Irish Free State relieving Irish Free State of responsibilities for any share of British national debt and transferring powers of Council of Ireland relating to Northern Ireland to Northern Irish government.

1927    De Valera splits from Sinn Fein and founds Fianna Fail Party.

1932    Republican electoral victory in the South followed by hostility to Great Britain and tariff war. New constitution; name of Southern Ireland now 'Eire'.

1933    Cumann na nGaedheal changes name to Fine Gael.

1939    Irish proclaim neutrality in Second World War.

1949    The Republic of Ireland proclaimed in April, the British government formally accepting the complete independence of Southern Ireland, which leaves the Commonwealth.

1952    Revival of IRA activity; attacks on customs posts and police barracks on Ulster border.

1957    Southern Irish government acts against IRA in conjunction with Ulster government.

1962    'Terrorist' campaign against Ulster officially abandoned by IRA.

1972    Ireland signs treaty of accession to the European Economic Community.

1979    Visit of Pope John Paul II to Ireland.

1980    Meeting of Irish Premier, Charles Haughey, and Mrs Thatcher in London, followed by visit of Mrs Thatcher and Lord Carrington to Dublin to discuss Northern Ireland.

1983    New Ireland Forum discusses future settlement of the North.

1985    Anglo-Irish Agreement signed at Hillsborough.

1992    Meeting of Irish government with representatives of Northern

Ireland (June). Irish Foreign Minister, Dick Spring, indicates that articles 2–3 of the Irish Constitution are no longer sacrosanct.

1993    'Downing Street Declaration' by John Major and the Taoiseach, Albert Reynolds, opening way to all-party talks (Dec.).

1995    British and Irish governments publish 'Framework Document on future of Northern Ireland'.

## Major events in Northern Ireland, 1920–95

1920    Government of Ireland Act sets up Northern Ireland parliament with a Senate and House of Commons elected by proportional representation. Special constabulary created to assist in peacekeeping.

1921    Northern Ireland parliament opened and elections held, producing a large Unionist majority. Continuing guerrilla war by IRA against Ulster and British forces.

1922    Civil Authorities Act gives extensive powers to the Northern Irish Home Secretary to preserve public order in face of IRA attacks from the South.

1925    Tripartite agreement with Irish Free State and British government confirms existing boundary between Northern Ireland and the Irish Free State; Northern Ireland released from its share of the British national debt; powers of the Council of Ireland relating to Northern Ireland under the Government of Ireland Act of 1920 transferred to the Northern Ireland government. Full-time special constabulary dissolved but part-time 'B specials' retained for use in emergencies.

1926    Unemployment insurance agreement provides for payments to be made by British Treasury to assist social expenditure in Northern Ireland.

1929    Proportional representation in parliamentary elections withdrawn in favour of single-member constituencies.

1932    Two people killed after unemployed workers' demonstration in Belfast leads to rioting.

1933    De Valera elected MP for constituency of South Down, but refuses to take seat.

| 1935 | Serious sectarian rioting in Belfast; 11 killed and 600 injured. |
| 1937 | New Southern Irish constitution lays claim to 'the whole island of Ireland'. Beginning of renewed IRA campaign against Ulster. |
| 1938 | British government agrees to fund deficits in Northern Ireland budget, provided that the levels of social expenditure and taxation remain comparable with Britain. |
| 1941 | Major air raids on Belfast; 700 people killed and 1,500 wounded. |
| 1946 | Agreement that future Northern Irish budgets will be arranged in consultation with British government and that parity in services and taxation will be maintained with Britain. |
| 1949 | Social Services Agreement arranges for Britain to pay four-fifths of the excess cost of Northern Irish social services. |
| 1951 | National Insurance funds of Britain and Ulster merged and agreement reached for transfer of funds in case of need. |
| 1956 | Beginning of renewed IRA campaign against Ulster. |
| 1962 | Campaign against Ulster called off by IRA. |
| 1963 | Prime Minister Terence O'Neill begins attempt to develop amicable relations with the South. |
| 1965 | Exchange of visits between Prime Minister Terence O'Neill and Irish Premier, Sean Lemass. |
| 1966 | Revd Ian Paisley imprisoned for militant anti-Catholic activities. Secret Protestant Ulster Volunteer Force declared illegal after spate of attacks on Catholics. |
| 1967 | Northern Ireland Civil Rights Association set up. |
| 1968 | Civil Rights march in Dungannon. Rioting in Londonderry following Civil Rights march (Oct.). Cameron Commission set up to investigate disturbances. |
| 1969 | People's Democracy march from Belfast to Londonderry broken up (Jan.). General election weakens O'Neill's position at Stormont. Further rioting leads to call-up of 'B specials'. O'Neill resigns and replaced by Chichester-Clark (Apr.). British army sent into Belfast and Londonderry following sectarian fighting. IRA splits into 'Official' and 'Provisional' wings. Following report of Hunt Advisory Committee, Royal Ulster Constabulary disarmed and 'B specials' disbanded, the latter replaced by non-sectarian Ulster Defence Regiment. Housing allocation transferred from local government to Stormont. |
| 1970 | Growing violence leads to ban on parades. Army uses rubber bullets and CS gas to combat rioters. |

1971    First British soldier killed in Northern Ireland (Feb.).
        Chichester-Clark resigns as Northern Ireland premier and
        replaced by Brian Faulkner (Mar.). IRA bombing campaign
        intensifies, followed by introduction of internment without
        trial.

1972    'Bloody Sunday' (30 Jan.): holding of banned Civil Rights
        march in Londonderry leads to 13 people being shot by
        British soldiers. Stormont suspended and direct rule
        introduced (Mar.).

1973    Northern Ireland Assembly elected on proportional
        representation set up to replace Stormont. 'Bloody Friday' (21
        July): bomb explosions in Belfast. Operation 'Motorman':
        troops occupy Catholic 'no-go' areas in Belfast and
        Londonderry. Consultative document on 'power-sharing' in
        Northern Ireland agreed. Sunningdale talks between London
        and Dublin agree to setting up of a Council of Ireland and to
        preserve status of Northern Ireland as part of the United
        Kingdom (Dec.).

1974    Direct rule ended and beginning of 'power-sharing'
        experiment (Jan.). General Strike called by Protestant Ulster
        Workers' Council leads to resignation of Brian Faulkner and
        Northern Ireland executive (May). Direct rule reimposed. IRA
        extend bombing campaign to Great Britain.

1975    Elections held for a Constitutional Convention on Northern
        Ireland result in landslide victory for United Ulster Unionist
        Council. Majority report of Constitutional Convention
        recommends end of direct rule and re-establishment of a
        Northern Irish Assembly.

1976    Breakdown of talks between British government and Ulster
        representatives (Mar.). Direct rule continued. British
        ambassador in Dublin, Christopher Ewart-Biggs, assassinated
        by IRA. European Commission for Human Rights finds Britain
        guilty of torture in Northern Ireland. Peace Movement
        launched by Betty Williams and Mairead Corrigan.

1977    Ten-day strike (May) by Ulster Unionist Action Council in
        support of tougher action against the IRA and the
        implementation of the Constitutional Convention's Report
        ends in failure.

1978    European Court of Human Rights clears Britain of torture in
        Northern Ireland, but convicts it of 'inhuman and degrading
        treatment'.

1979    Airey Neave assassinated at the House of Commons by Irish National Liberation Army (Mar.). Earl Mountbatten assassinated by IRA in Irish Republic (Aug.). Devolution Conference of Northern Ireland political parties fails to reach agreement.

1980    Summit meetings held in May and Dec. between Irish Premier Charles Haughey and Mrs Thatcher. A communiqué after the May meeting affirms wish of the Irish government to secure the unity of Ireland 'by agreement and in peace' but only 'with the consent of a majority of the people in Northern Ireland'. Dec. meeting followed by joint studies on new institutional structures, citizenship rights, security, and economic and cultural cooperation. Republican prisoners mount 'dirty protest' for special status and begin hunger strikes in Oct. (called off in Dec.).

1981    Resumption of hunger strikes for special status leads to deaths of Bobby Sands and Francis Hughes (May). Rioting over hunger strikes leads to more than 50 deaths. Dr Garret FitzGerald becomes Irish Premier (June) and announces intention to make the Irish constitution less offensive to the North. Summit meeting with Mrs Thatcher (Nov.) leads to establishment of Anglo-Irish Intergovernmental Council to hold regular meetings at ministerial and official levels to discuss matters of common concern.

1982    Secretary of State for Northern Ireland, James Prior, introduces a Bill for Northern Ireland Assembly to resume legislative and executive powers by a process of gradual devolution. Elections for the Assembly result in 59 per cent of votes for Unionist candidates and 32 per cent to Nationalists (SDLP, 19 per cent; Sinn Fein, 10 per cent). Both the SDLP and Sinn Fein, however, boycott the Assembly.

1983    New Ireland Forum set up in Dublin on the initiative of John Hume, leader of the SDLP (May), and begins to prepare report on the way in which unity could be achieved with the North by consent. Participants include representatives of southern Irish parties and SDLP from the North.

1984    Report of New Ireland Forum (May) condemns terrorist activity in the North but calls for a unitary state, achieved by agreement and consent, embracing the whole of Ireland and providing guarantees for the protection and preservation of 'both the Unionist and the Nationalist identities'. Northern

Ireland Assembly begins work in June on proposals to strengthen the Assembly and move towards devolution. In July James Prior welcomes the Forum Report and Official Unionist report 'The Way Forward' and looks forward to further discussions between the parties in Northern Ireland and between the Irish and British governments. James Prior succeeded by Douglas Hurd as Northern Ireland Secretary (Sept.). IRA bomb explodes at Grand Hotel, Brighton, killing five people and narrowly missing Mrs Thatcher and the Conservative leadership (Oct.). Unofficial Kilbrandon Report in Nov. recommends a number of safeguards for the Catholic community in the North, including a Bill of Rights, allowance of flags and emblems, and joint police and judicial procedures. Dr FitzGerald and Mrs Thatcher meet (Nov.) for second summit of the Anglo-Irish Intergovernmental Council and issue communiqué outlining support for structures which will guarantee the rights of both communities in the North, opposition to violence, and cooperation in security matters. Mrs Thatcher, however, rejects co-federation or joint sovereignty as a solution.

1985    Alliance report *What Future for Northern Ireland?* proposes a joint British-Irish Parliamentary Council and Security Commission. In Nov., meeting of Mrs Thatcher and Dr FitzGerald at Hillsborough Castle, near Belfast, produces Anglo-Irish Agreement setting up a new Intergovernmental Conference concerned with Northern Ireland and with relations between the two parts of Ireland. Joint communiqué states aim of Anglo-Irish Agreement is to promote peace and stability in the North and to reconcile the two major traditions in Ireland, Unionist and Nationalist. Unionists denounce the agreement as a 'sell-out', calling for a referendum in the province. At a massive Loyalist demonstration in Belfast (23 Nov.), attended by upwards of 20,000 people, Unionist MPs pledge to resign their seats and force province-wide by-elections. First meeting of Anglo-Irish conference at Stormont (11 Dec.).

1986    Vote in Ulster by-elections in Jan. endorses Unionist opposition to Hillsborough Agreement, although Unionists lose a seat to the SDLP. Ulster Clubs emerge to coordinate grass-roots Protestant opposition to the Anglo-Irish Agreement. Unionist leaders meet Mrs Thatcher in Feb. but fail to obtain scrapping of Anglo-Irish Agreement and 24-hour general strike called for 3 Mar. Strike accompanied by widespread violence and intimidation, including attacks on the police. Campaign of intimidation mounted by Loyalists on police homes. United States grants $250 million of aid to Ulster. Because of Unionist boycott, Cabinet decides not to hold further elections to the Northern Ireland Assembly (June). Unionist MPs effectively boycott Westminster. Unionist MP Peter Robinson arrested for leading a mob across the Irish border (Aug.).

1987     Peter Robinson fined £15,000 for cross-border march (Jan.). Ulster Unionist MPs give up boycott of Westminster. Remembrance Day bombing at Enniskillen kills 11 people (Nov.).

1988     Three unarmed IRA members shot in Gibraltar by SAS while on bombing mission, leading to further accusations of 'shoot to kill' policy.

1990     Ian Paisley and James Molyneaux agree to take part in round-table talks, but fail to reach agreement.

1991     Peter Brooke, Northern Ireland Secretary, suspends Anglo-Irish Agreement to allow constitutional talks.

1992     IRA bomb in City of London causes widespread damage (Apr.). Intergovernmental Conference meets in London and announces suspension of meetings to allow talks to take place. Meeting of representatives of Northern Ireland and of Irish government (June); further discussions in London and Dublin (June–Sept.). Death toll in Northern Ireland from the Troubles passes 3,000 (Aug.). Irish Foreign Minister, Dick Spring, indicates that articles 2 to 3 of the Irish constitution are no longer sacrosanct. Mayhew announces to the Commons that the constitutional talks have been suspended without agreement (Nov.).

1993     Bomb planted by IRA in Warrington kills two children, causing widespread expressions of concern for a Northern Ireland settlement (Mar.). Bomb in City of London causes huge damage (Apr.). Bombings in Northern Ireland at Belfast, Portadown and Magherafelt cause an estimated £28 million damage (May). Exploratory talks between John Hume of the SDLP and Gerry Adams of Sinn Fein. Ulster Unionists save the government from defeat on the Maastricht Bill, leading to allegations of a 'deal' with John Major. Significant 'progress' reported in SDLP–Sinn Fein talks (Sept.). Shankhill Road bombing by IRA (Oct.) leads to considerable pressure for a peace initiative; Irish government offers six-point statement for peace which receives welcome from London. British government admits to several months of clandestine talks with IRA. Downing Street Declaration by John Major and Taoiseach, Albert Reynolds, opening way to all-party talks (Dec.). Sinn Fein demands release of IRA prisoners as a gesture; refused.

1994    IRA mortar attacks on Heathrow Airport (Mar.). IRA demands 'clarification' of British position. British insist on cessation of violence. Sinn Fein refuses to make definitive move towards peace at annual conference (July). IRA declare cease-fire, effective from midnight 31 Aug. Followed by Protestant militaries' own cease-fire. (IRA end cease-fire early in 1996.)

1995    British army ends daylight patrols in Belfast (Jan.). British and Irish governments publish 'Framework Document on future of Northern Ireland'. First official meeting for 23 years between British government minister and IRA representative (May). Release of private Lee Clegg provokes widespread disorder. Resignation of James Molyneaux as leader of Official Unionists: David Trimble elected to succeed him (Sept.). Continuing deadlock over 'decommissioning' of IRA arms.

## Religious affiliations in nineteenth-century Ireland

|  | 1834 | | 1881 | |
| --- | --- | --- | --- | --- |
|  | 000 | % | 000 | % |
| Roman Catholic | 6 436 | 81 | 3 952 | 77 |
| Anglican Church | 853 | 11 | 636 | 12 |
| Presbyterians | 643 | 7 | 486 | 9 |
| Others | 40 | 1 | 86 | 2 |

Source: figures compiled from R. Dudley Edwards, *An Atlas of Irish History* (London, Methuen, 1973), p. 127, and G. Best, *Mid-Victorian Britain, 1851–75* (London, Weidenfeld & Nicolson, 1971), p. 193.

Religious affiliations in Irish provinces in 1861 (%)

|           | Roman Catholics | All Protestants |
|-----------|-----------------|-----------------|
| Ulster    | 50.5            | 49.47           |
| Leinster  | 85.9            | 14.01           |
| Munster   | 93.8            | 6.07            |
| Connaught | 94.84           | 5.13            |

Source: R. Dudley Edwards, *An Atlas of Irish History* (London, Methuen, 1973), p. 129.

Religious affiliations in Ulster, 1911 and 1961

|               | 1911 | | | | 1961 | | | |
|---------------|---------|------|---------|------|---------|------|---------|------|
|               | Protestant | | Catholic | | Protestant | | Catholic | |
|               | No.     | %    | No.     | %    | No.     | %    | No.     | %    |
| Belfast       | 293 704 | 75.9 | 93 243  | 24.1 | 301 520 | 72.5 | 114 336 | 27.5 |
| Co. Antrim    | 154 113 | 79.5 | 39 751  | 20.5 | 206 976 | 75.6 | 66 929  | 24.4 |
| Co. Armagh    | 65 765  | 54.7 | 54 526  | 45.3 | 61 977  | 52.7 | 55 617  | 47.3 |
| Derry City    | 17 857  | 43.8 | 22 923  | 56.2 | 17 689  | 32.9 | 36 073  | 67.1 |
| Derry County  | 58 367  | 58.5 | 41 478  | 41.5 | 64 027  | 57.4 | 47 509  | 42.6 |
| Co. Down      | 139 818 | 68.4 | 64 485  | 31.6 | 190 676 | 71.4 | 76 263  | 28.6 |
| Co. Fermanagh | 27 096  | 43.8 | 34 740  | 56.2 | 24 109  | 46.8 | 27 422  | 53.2 |
| Co. Tyrone    | 63 650  | 44.6 | 79 015  | 55.4 | 60 521  | 45.2 | 73 398  | 54.8 |

Sources: *Census of Ireland*, 1911, Vol. 3, *Ulster*, Cd. 6051–1 (London, HMSO, 1912), and General Register Office, Northern Ireland, *Census of Population 1961*, County volumes, Tables XVI (Belfast, HMSO, 1964).

# Imperial

## Empire chronology, 1713–1995

1713    Treaty of Utrecht: Britain gains Gibraltar, Minorca, Hudson Bay, Nova Scotia and Newfoundland.

1729    Dispute over government of Carolina resolved and divided into North and South Carolina by Act of Parliament.

1733    Settlement of Georgia, the last of the 13 colonies, under the auspices of James Oglethorpe and associates.

1740    Unsuccessful expedition of Oglethorpe and colonists against Florida.

1744    French attack on Nova Scotia heralds beginning of Anglo-French struggle over colonies.

1745    Siege and capture of Louisburg in Canada by British colonial forces.

1748    Treaty of Aix-la-Chapelle between England, France and Spain. In reciprocal surrender of conquests, Cape Breton restored to the French. Formation of Ohio Company under Crown charter.

1750    Settlement begins on the Gold Coast.

1754    Benjamin Franklin proposes a union of all the American colonies under a president appointed by the Crown. Proposal rejected by Connecticut and later by the colonies and the Crown.

1755    War between England and France. Defeat of General Braddock at battle of Fort Duquesne in Canada.

1756    Capture of Forts Oswego and George by Marquis of Montcalm, commander of French armies in Canada, leads to temporary abandonment of British attacks on French positions in North America. Imprisonment of 146 British persons in 'Black Hole of Calcutta' by the Nabob of Bengal.

1757    Battle of Plessey; Clive is victorious in Bengal.

1759    General Wolfe captures Quebec after battle of the Plains of Abraham.

| | |
|---|---|
| 1760 | Battle of Wandewash breaks French power in India. |
| 1763 | Treaty of Paris: all French possessions in North America east of the Mississippi ceded to Great Britain; also Grenada, St Vincent, Tobago and the Windward Islands; Florida gained from Spain. |
| 1765 | Clive becomes governor of Bengal. Treaty of Allahabad restores the Nabobs. The East India Company's privileges are confirmed by the Mogul and extended to revenue collection. |
| 1766 | First Mysore War. |
| 1768 | Separate secretary of state for the colonies established. |
| 1769 | Cook's first Pacific voyage. |
| 1773 | Lord North's Regulating Act: British rule in India to be carried on in the name of the Crown. |
| 1774 | Warren Hastings becomes governor-general of Bengal. Quebec Act: Canada becomes a Crown colony. |
| 1776 | American colonies declare independence. |
| 1777 | General Burgoyne surrenders at Saratoga (see also p. 281). France enters the war against Britain. |
| 1779 | First Maratha War (see p. 286). |
| 1780 | Second Mysore War (see p. 286). |
| 1783 | Treaty of Versailles recognizes American independence. France recovered her trading stations in India, Senegal, St Lucia and Tobago; Britain retained Gibraltar. |
| 1784 | Pitt's India Act separates the commercial and political functions of the East India Company; the latter to be supervised by a Board of Control in London. |
| 1787 | Freetown, Sierra Leone, established as settlement for freed slaves. |
| 1788 | First convict settlement at Port Jackson (Sydney). Norfolk Island settled. Impeachment of Warren Hastings. |
| 1789 | Third Mysore War (see p. 286). |
| 1791 | Canada Act: Canada was divided into two provinces (Upper and Lower Canada), each with its own government subject to a joint governor-general. |
| 1794 | Seychelles captured. |
| 1800 | Malta captured. |
| 1802 | Ceylon ceded. |
| 1803 | Second Maratha War (see p. 286). |
| 1807 | Slave trade abolished by Britain. |
| 1808 | Crown takes over Sierra Leone. |
| 1813 | East India Company loses its monopoly of Indian trade. |

1814    St Lucia, Malta, Mauritius, British Guiana, Windward Islands and Cape of Good Hope ceded to Great Britain as colonies, after the defeat of Napoleon.

1817–18 Third Maratha War destroys Maratha power (see p. 286).

1821    North West Company and the Hudson's Bay Company amalgamate. Royal African Company abolished and forts taken over by the Crown as part of its West African settlements.

1823    New South Wales becomes a Crown colony.

1824    Burmese War (see pp. 286–7). Singapore ceded to Britain.

1827    Western Australia explored by Captain Stirling.

1830    Edward Gibbon Wakefield forms the Colonization Society.

1833    East India Company ceases to trade; governor-general of Bengal becomes governor-general of India. Indian Legislative Council established. Slavery abolished in the British Empire. Falkland Islands annexed.

1834    South Australia Act authorizes the establishment of a colony.

1835    Great Trek of Boer colonists from the Cape.

1837    Aborigines Protection Society founded. New Zealand Association begun by Wakefield. Rebellion of Papineau and Mackenzie in Canada.

1838    Earl of Durham becomes governor-general of Canada. Apprenticeship system in West Indies abolished.

1839    Aden annexed. First Afghan War (see pp. 287–8). First China 'Opium' War (see p. 287). Republic of Natal founded. Durham Report published. It suggests process of granting greater autonomy to colonies.

1840    Canada Act reunites Upper and Lower Canada in a single administration and legislature. New Zealand annexed: Treaty of Waitangi aims to protect Maoris by forbidding private sale and purchase of land. Transportation to New South Wales discontinued.

1841    Retreat from Kabul.

1842    Treaty of Nanking ends the war with China (see p. 287). Hong Kong is ceded to Britain, and five treaty ports (Amoy, Canton, Foochow, Ningpo and Shanghai) opened to British trade. Ashburton treaty settles the Maine boundary. Representative government established in New South Wales. Conquest of Burma and Assam begins.

1843    Maori Wars begin. Sind conquered. Natal annexed.

1845    First Sikh War (see p. 288).

| | |
|---|---|
| 1846 | Oregon treaty fixes the boundary of Canada at the 49th Parallel. Earl Grey's Act establishes two provinces in New Zealand, each with executive and legislative councils under the governor. |
| 1847 | Elgin becomes governor-general of a united Canada. Governor of Cape Colony becomes high commissioner for South Africa. |
| 1848 | Orange Free State becomes a Crown colony. Second Sikh War: Punjab annexed. Nova Scotia becomes the first colony with a responsible ministry. |
| 1849 | Navigation Acts repealed. |
| 1851 | Australian gold rush. Victoria becomes a separate colony. |
| 1852 | Rangoon annexed in Second Burmese War (see p. 287). By the Sand River Convention, Britain abandons attempts to control the Boer trekkers. Responsible government attained in New Zealand. |
| 1853 | Cape Colony gains representative government. |
| 1854 | Bloemfontein Convention: Orange Free State gains self-rule. Separate Colonial Office established. |
| 1855 | New South Wales, Victoria and Newfoundland granted responsible government. |
| 1856 | Oudh annexed. War with China renewed. South Australia and Tasmania gain responsible government. |
| 1857 | Indian Mutiny begins in Meerut in May, quickly spreading across northern India (see p. 289). When the revolt was quelled the Crown assumed direct control of India. A secretary of state for India was established with a Council of India to advise him. The East India Company's rule was abolished. |
| 1858 | Treaty of Tientsin secured, when Anglo-French forces defeated the Chinese. China repudiated the treaty in 1859. British Columbia becomes a Crown colony. |
| 1859 | Queensland becomes a separate colony with responsible government. Sir George Grey, Governor of Cape Colony, proposes a plan for South African federation. |
| 1860 | Britain attains full Free Trade. Maori Wars recur when the New Zealand Company breaks the Treaty of Waitangi (see p. 288). |
| 1861 | Lagos annexed. India Councils Act. Parliamentary committee agrees territories enjoying responsible government should make a greater contribution to their own defence. |

1864    Quebec Conference lays the foundation for the Dominion of Canada.

1865    Colonial Laws Validity Act: colonial legislatures could pass laws contrary to the common law of England, but not contrary to Acts of the imperial Parliament applying to the colony. Governor Eyre suppresses Morant rising in Jamaica.

1867    British North America Act creates the Dominion of Canada as a self-governing federation of four provinces. Straits Settlements becomes a Crown colony.

1869    Suez Canal opened. Hudson's Bay Company cedes its territorial rights to the Dominion of Canada. Rebellion led by Louis Riel in Canada.

1870    Manitoba admitted to Dominion of Canada.

1871    British Columbia joins the Dominion of Canada. Griqualand West annexed (diamond fields discovered there). Protectorate proclaimed in Basutoland. Dutch cede Gold Coast forts to Britain.

1872    Responsible government implemented in Cape Colony.

1873    Ashanti War (see p. 289). Prince Edward Island joins the Dominion of Canada.

1874    Fiji Islands annexed. Treaties with chiefs of Perak and Selangor by which British residents to give advice to the Malay rulers.

1875    Suez Canal shares purchased giving United Kingdom a majority holding. Lord Carnarvon launches plan for South African Confederation.

1876    Victoria created Empress of India. Lord Lytton becomes viceroy.

1877    Transvaal annexed.

1878    Cyprus occupied under the Treaty of Berlin. Dual control established in Egypt (Britain and France). Walvis Bay, South Africa, annexed. Second Afghan War begins.

1879    British Resident at Kabul murdered. Peace restored when Afghanistan independence recognized, 1880. Zulu War; British defeated at Isandhlwana, victorious at Ulundi (see p. 290).

1880    First Boer War begins (see p. 290).

1881    British defeated at Majuba Hill. Convention of Pretoria recognizes the Transvaal as an independent republic subject to the suzerainty of the Queen. Revolt of the Mahdi in the Sudan (see p. 290).

1882    British North Borneo Company chartered. Four territories organized from the Canadian prairies, Alberta, Athabasca, Assiniboine and Saskatchewan. Revolt of Arabi Pasha, defeated at Tel-el-Kebir (see p. 290). Britain occupies Egypt and assumes control of Egyptian finances.

1883    British force under Hicks Pasha defeated in the Sudan. Sir Evelyn Baring (Lord Cromer) appointed British agent and consul-general in Egypt. Sir J. R. Seeley's *Expansion of England* published.

1884    Imperial Federation League founded. Transvaal recognized as the South African Republic, when Britain abandoned her suzerainty. Berlin Conference opens. It established ground rules for partition of Africa. Britain takes possession of remainder of New Guinea after German annexations.

1885    Death of General Gordon at Khartoum. Crisis in Penjdeh, the disputed boundary area between Afghanistan and Russian Turkestan. Indian National Congress founded. Upper Burma invaded (see p. 287). Protectorate established in Bechuanaland. Federation of the Windward Islands.

1886    Royal Niger Company chartered for trade and government. Anglo-German treaties partition East Africa and the Pacific. Gold discovered in the Transvaal; Johannesburg founded. Annexation of Burma.

1887    First Colonial Conference. Protectorate proclaimed in British Somaliland.

1888    Imperial British East Africa Company chartered. Zululand annexed. Protectorates in Matabeleland, British North Borneo and Sarawak.

1889    British South Africa Company chartered; begins colonization in what became Rhodesia. Federation of Australia proposed by Sir Henry Parkes at Tenterfield.

1890    Anglo-German treaties concerning East Africa. Rhodes becomes prime minister of Cape Colony. Responsible government in Western Australia.

1891    Anglo-Portuguese colonial treaty recognizes British Protectorate in Nyasaland.

1892    India Councils Act introduces first Indian members to the Viceroy's legislative council. Gold discovered in Western Australia.

1893    Responsible government in Natal. Durand Line fixes the frontier between Afghanistan and British India.

1894    L. S. Jameson appointed administrator of Southern Rhodesia. Protectorate established in Uganda.

1895    Joseph Chamberlain appointed colonial secretary. British East Africa protectorate established. Jameson leads an unsuccessful raid into the Transvaal.

1896    Kitchener advances into the Sudan. Second Ashanti War: the monarchy was abolished and a protectorate established.

1897    Milner becomes high commissioner of the Cape. Second Colonial Conference on Queen's Diamond Jubilee. Royal Commission on the West Indies. Convention at Adelaide to prepare terms for Australian Federation.

1898    Niger convention with France. Wei-hai-wei leased. Confrontation with France at Fashoda on Upper Nile. Anglo-Egyptian condominium proclaimed over the Sudan after the defeat of the Mahdi at Omdurman. Curzon appointed viceroy of India.

1899    Anglo-French agreement concerning the Nile Valley. Royal Niger Company loses its powers to the Crown. Second Boer War begins: Britain defeated at Magersfontein, Stormberg and Colenso.

1900    Ladysmith, Kimberley and Mafeking relieved. Boxer Rising in China. First Pan-African Congress in London. Cook Islands annexed. Protectorate established in Tobago.

1901    Commonwealth of Australia established. North West Frontier Province created.

1902    Peace of Vereeniging: Transvaal and Orange Free State annexed. Colonial Conference decides to meet again every four years.

1904    Anglo-French *Entente*: acceptance of mutual spheres of influence in Africa.

1905    Partition of Bengal alienates Hindu nationalists. Alberta and Saskatchewan created as provinces of Canada.

1906    Transvaal gains responsible government. All India Muslim League formed: British promise Muslims separate electorates.

1907    Australia and New Zealand gain Dominion status. Imperial Conference: Dominions division established in the Colonial Office. Orange Free State gains responsible government. Gorst becomes British agent in Egypt and increases the powers of provincial councils.

1909    Morley–Minto constitutional reforms in India. India Councils Act.

1910     Union of South Africa formed.

1911     Coronation Durbar: Indian capital transferred from Calcutta to Delhi; division of Bengal abandoned.

1914     Protectorate proclaimed in Egypt. Cyprus annexed. Northern and Southern Nigeria protectorates joined together. France and Britain conquer German colonies except German East Africa.

1917     Balfour declaration promises the Jews a national home in Palestine. Montagu declaration states the eventual aim of full responsible government in India. Imperial War Conference includes India.

1918     Rhodesian Native National Congress formed.

1919     Nationalist revolt in Egypt. Massacre at Amritsar. Government of India Act enacts the Montagu–Chelmsford reforms. Dyarchy introduced – responsible government in certain departments.

1920     Gandhi wins control of Congress, and leads the non-cooperation movement in India. East African Protectorate becomes colony of Kenya.

1921     Southern Ireland granted Dominion status as the Irish Free State. Responsible government introduced in Malta. League of Nations mandate for Iraq accepted. National Congress in British West Africa formed.

1922     Palestine and Transjordan administered by Britain under League of Nations. Egyptian independence recognized with reservations. Increasing violence leads Gandhi to call off non-cooperation.

1923     Southern Rhodesia becomes a self-governing colony.

1924     Protectorate of Northern Rhodesia established. Irish Free State is the first Dominion to establish a separate diplomatic representative abroad.

1925     Cyprus becomes a colony.

1926     Imperial Conference declares Great Britain and the Dominions autonomous and equal though 'freely associated as members of the British Commonwealth of Nations'.

1927     Simon Commission sent to investigate the Montagu–Chelmsford system.

1929     Separate secretary of state for the Dominions established.

1930     Nehru proclaims independence of India. Gandhi begins second civil disobedience campaign. Round Table Conference begins.

1931     Statute of Westminster embodies the decisions of the 1926 Imperial Conference.

1932    Imperial Economic Conference at Ottawa establishes limited preferential duties.

1935    Government of India Act; establishes responsible government in the provinces.

1942    Cripps mission to India offers Dominion status after the war; rejected by Indian nationalists. Japanese capture Singapore – a major blow to Britain's imperial prestige in Asia.

1946    North Borneo becomes a colony. Sarawak ceded. Full independence granted to Transjordan.

1947    Independence granted to India and Pakistan (the latter in Muslim majority areas).

1948    Ceylon and Burma become independent. State of Israel formed. Beginning of a conflict with Communist guerrillas in Malaya.

1949    Ireland withdraws from the Commonwealth.

1950    India becomes the first republic to belong to the Commonwealth.

1952    Beginning of Mau Mau rebellion in Kenya (see p. 294).

1953    Southern Rhodesia, Nyasaland and Northern Rhodesia united in the Federation of Rhodesia and Nyasaland.

1956    Suez expedition. Mau Mau rebellion in Kenya suppressed.

1957    Ghana and the Malay states gain independence.

1958    West Indies Federation formed.

1960    Harold Macmillan's 'wind of change' speech presages African decolonization. Cyprus, Nigeria and British Somaliland gain independence.

1961    South Africa withdraws from the Commonwealth. Tanganyika, Sierra Leone and British Cameroons gain independence.

1962    West Indies Federation breaks up when Jamaica and Trinidad and Tobago become independent. Western Samoa and Uganda gain independence.

1963    Zanzibar and Kenya gain independence.

1964    Commonwealth Secretariat established. Malta gains independence. The Federation of Rhodesia and Nyasaland is dissolved; Nyasaland becomes the independent state of Malawi; Northern Rhodesia becomes Zambia.

1965    Southern Rhodesia unilaterally proclaims independence. Gambia becomes independent.

1966    Basutoland (Lesotho), Bechuanaland (Botswana), British Guiana (Guyana) and Barbados become independent.

1967    Aden gains independence.

1968    Mauritius and Swaziland gain independence.

1970    Fiji and Tonga gain independence.

1972    East Pakistan gains independence from Pakistan as Bangladesh.

1973    Bahamas gain independence.

1974    Grenada becomes independent.

1975    Papua New Guinea gains independence.

1976    Seychelles become independent.

1978    Dominica becomes independent.

1979    Rhodesian settlement reached; Britain and Patriotic Front conclude a cease-fire agreement; Kiribati (formerly known as the Gilbert Islands) becomes independent.

1980    Elections in Rhodesia, under supervision of monitoring force. Zimbabwe independent (Apr.). New Hebrides becomes independent state of Vanuatu (July).

1981    Belize becomes an independent republic.

1982    Argentine troops invade Falkland Islands and South Georgia (Apr.). British task force sent to recapture the islands (May–June) forces Argentine surrender. Maldive Islands gain independence.

1984    Brunei becomes independent. Sino-British agreement signed on the future of Hong Kong, guaranteeing its future as a capitalist system after its reversion to Chinese rule in 1997.

1985    Britain isolated amongst Commonwealth leaders over further sanctions against South Africa.

1987    Fiji leaves Commonwealth as a result of military coup.

1990    Independence of Namibia (formerly South-West Africa) recognized. Namibia becomes 50th member of the Commonwealth.

1994    After historic multi-racial elections, South Africa rejoins Commonwealth.

1995    Bermuda votes to remain a British colony. Cameroon becomes 52nd member of the Commonwealth (Nov.). Nigeria suspended from membership of Commonwealth.

# SECTION FIVE

*Biographies*

**Aberdeen** 4th Earl of, George Hamilton-Gordon (1784–1860): Hamilton-Gordon became Earl of Aberdeen in 1801. From 1806 to 1814 he was a Scottish representative peer, and served as ambassador extraordinary at Vienna in 1813. In 1814 he represented Britain in the negotiation of the Treaty of Paris. Later that year he was created a peer of the United Kingdom. He held office as Chancellor of the Duchy of Lancaster Jan.–June 1828, as Foreign Secretary 1828–30, as Secretary for War and the Colonies 1834–35 and as Foreign Secretary again from 1841 to 1846. After 1846 he was leader of the Peelite faction in the House of Lords. Between 1852 and 1855 he presided as Prime Minister over a coalition of Whigs and Peelites. In 1855 he resigned when Roebuck's motion for a committee of enquiry into the conduct of the Crimean War was carried.

**Adams** Gerry (1949– ): Republican activist and President of Sinn Fein. Provisional Sinn Fein MP for West Belfast, 1983–92 (though he refused to take his seat). Participated in unsuccessful secret talks with Home Secretary Whitelaw in June 1972. Principal spokesman for the strategy of the 'ballot paper in one hand and Armalite rifle in the other', but following talks with John Hume (*q.v.*) announced cease-fire on 31 Aug. 1994.

**Addington** Henry. *See* Sidmouth.

**Applegarth** Robert (1833–1925): Secretary of Amalgamated Society of Carpenters and Joiners (1862), and dominating figure in London Trades Council which advocated industrial conciliation and arbitration of disputes; he and four other union leaders assumed title 'Conference of Amalgamated Trades' in attempt to influence 1867 Royal Commission into unionism; cautious attitude of 'Junta' leaders helped disarm criticism of unionism.

**Arch** Joseph (1826–1919): Liberal MP 1885–86, 1892–1902; pioneer of agricultural trade unionism, forming first agricultural labourers' union, 1872; puritan and Primitive Methodist lay preacher.

**Ashdown** 'Paddy' (1941– ): Liberal politician and leader of the Social and Liberal Democrats since 1988. MP for Yeovil since 1983. Ex-soldier, followed by career in business and two periods of unemployment. Defeated Alan Beith for the leadership of the new merged party which emerged from the Alliance. Has energetically rebuilt the Liberal

Democrats into a significant force in local politics and through a series of by-election victories before and after the 1992 general election. Has moved the party towards a more defined position on defence, economic policy, and Europe. An enthusiastic modernizer of party organization and publicity.

**Asquith** Herbert Henry, 1st Earl of Oxford and Asquith (1852–1928): Asquith was Liberal MP for East Fife from 1886 to 1918 and for Paisley from 1920 to 1924. In 1925 he was created Earl of Oxford and Asquith. He was Home Secretary 1892–95, Chancellor of the Exchequer 1905–8 and Prime Minister 1908–16. During 1914 he was also Secretary for War. He resigned the premiership in 1916 and became leader of the opposition. In 1926 he resigned the leadership of the Liberal Party when it failed to endorse his censuring of Lloyd George for refusing to attend a shadow cabinet. Asquith's term as PM was a troubled one, embracing the Budget, House of Lords and Ulster crises, suffragette militancy and the outbreak of the First World War. His replacement by Lloyd George and their subsequent feuds did great harm to the Liberal Party.

**Attlee** Clement Richard, 1st Earl Attlee (1883–1967): Attlee was Labour MP for Limehouse Stepney 1922–50, and for West Walthamstow 1950–55. He served as Parliamentary Private Secretary to Ramsay MacDonald 1922–24 and as Under-Secretary for War in 1924. He was Chancellor of the Duchy of Lancaster 1930–31 and Postmaster-General in 1931. He was elected leader of the Labour Party in 1935. In the wartime Coalition government he took office as Lord Privy Seal 1940–42, Secretary for the Dominions 1942–43 and as Lord President of the Council 1943–45. He was Deputy Prime Minister 1942–45 and Prime Minister 1945–51. During 1945–46 he was also Minister of Defence. He was Leader of the Opposition 1951–55 and was created an earl in 1955. Attlee's rise to the leadership of the Labour Party was facilitated by the disruption of the party in 1931. As Labour Prime Minister he presided over an active and able Cabinet which introduced the National Health Service, comprehensive social welfare and nationalized many basic industries.

**Attwood** Thomas (1783–1856): MP for Birmingham from 1832. Founder of the Birmingham Political Union which conducted a vigorous campaign for parliamentary reform in the early 1830s; fanatical believer in currency reform; became closely associated with

Chartists and in July 1839 presented Chartist 'monster petition' to House of Commons.

**Baldwin** Stanley, 1st Earl Baldwin of Bewdley (1867–1947): Baldwin was Conservative MP for his father's old constituency of Bewdley, Worcs., 1908–37. In 1917 he became Joint Financial Secretary to the Treasury and held that post until 1921. He was President of the Board of Trade 1921–22 and Chancellor of the Exchequer 1922–23. He served as Prime Minister 1923–24 and 1924–29. From 1931 to 1935 he sat in the National government as Lord President of the Council, and in 1932–33 was also Lord Privy Seal. His final term as Prime Minister ran from 1935 to 1937, when he resigned. In 1937 he was created an earl. In many ways Baldwin's achievements as PM were considerable. He succeeded in uniting a divided party and in pursuing a conciliatory course through the difficult inter-war years. However, his handling of the questions of rearmament and mass unemployment has tended to obscure his more successful endeavours.

**Balfour** Arthur James, 1st Earl of Balfour (1848–1930): Balfour was Conservative MP for Hertford 1874–85, for Manchester East 1885–1906, and for the City of London 1906–22. He was created an earl in 1922. Balfour served as Parliamentary Private Secretary to his uncle, Lord Salisbury, 1878–80. In 1885 he was President of the Local Government Board and in 1886 was Secretary for Scotland. He was Chief Secretary for Ireland between 1887 and 1891, and Leader of the Commons and First Lord of the Treasury 1891–92 and 1895–1902. He became Prime Minister in 1902, resigning in 1905. He resigned the leadership of the Conservative Party in 1911. In 1914 he was made a member of the Committee of Imperial Defence and attended meetings of the War Cabinet, 1914–15. He served as First Lord of the Admiralty 1915–16 and as Foreign Secretary 1916–19. He was Lord President of the Council 1919–22 and 1925–29. A well-connected Conservative, Balfour proved a highly intelligent and able administrator in most offices, but as PM and party leader he gave an impression of indecision and indifference on the question of Tariff Reform which split the party. After the Liberal government's reform of the House of Lords, accusations of ineffectuality and nepotism helped persuade Balfour to resign the leadership.

**Bath** 1st Earl, William Pulteney (1684–1764): MP 1705–42; Secretary of War, 1714–17; Whig politician prominent in opposition to Walpole; joined with Bolingbroke (*q.v.*) in attempt to form united party of opposition, and encouraged alliance between Whig and Tory factions opposed to Walpole; declined two invitations from George II to form ministry after Walpole's fall, 1742; failed to organize government with Granville (*q.v.*) in 1746.

**Beaconsfield** 1st Earl of. *See* Disraeli.

**Bentham** Jeremy (1748–1832): Jurist and utilitarian philosopher who expounded doctrine of 'the greatest happiness of the greatest number'; publications included *A Fragment on Government* (1776) attacking form of law in England, and *Introduction to Principles of Morals and Legislation* (1789); advocated reform and codification of criminal law and more logical poor law; formative influence on Edwin Chadwick, Francis Place, Henry Brougham and Robert Peel (*qq.v.*).

**Bevan** Aneurin (1897–1960): Labour MP for Ebbw Vale 1929–60; Minister of Health 1945–51; Minister of Labour 1951; deputy leader of Labour Party 1959–60; emerged from Welsh coal-mining background to become spokesman for South Wales miners in General Strike of 1926; pioneered National Health Service, resigning in protest at Gaitskell's (*q.v.*) proposals to introduce Health Service charges to meet defence expenditure. Led unilateral wing of party.

**Beveridge** William Henry, 1st Baron Beveridge of Tuggal (1879–1963): Economist and author of Beveridge Report on *Social Insurance and Allied Services* (1942), which became blueprint for Britain's welfare state policies and institutions; particularly interested in unemployment; director of labour exchanges 1909–16; director of London School of Economics, 1919–37; master of University College, Oxford, from 1937; Liberal MP, Berwick-on-Tweed, 1944–45.

**Bevin** Ernest (1881–1951): Labour MP for Central Wandsworth 1940–50, East Woolwich 1950–1; chairman TUC General Council, 1937; Minister of Labour 1940–45; Foreign Secretary 1945–51; Lord Privy Seal 1951. Rose through Dockers' Union to unite 50 unions into Transport and General Workers' Union in 1921, the largest union in the world; prominent in TUC. General Council service, 1925–40; supported creation of NATO in Apr. 1949; summoned Commonwealth Foreign Ministers' Conference, Feb. 1950.

**Blair** Anthony (1953– ): Labour leader since 1994. MP for Sedgefield since 1983. Educated at St John's College, Oxford; shadow Treasury spokesman 1984–87; Trade spokesman 1987–88; Energy spokesman 1988–92; shadow Home Secretary 1992–94. Defeated Margaret Beckett and John Prescott for the leadership of the party following John Smith's death. Advocated reform of party constitution at his first party conference in October 1994. Has since swept away Clause IV but has aroused undercurrents of hostility to his style of leadership and right-wing agenda as 'New Labour' increasingly adopts centrist policies.

**Bolingbroke** Henry St John, 1st Viscount (1678–1751): MP 1701–8; Secretary of State for Northern Department 1710; prominent in reign of Queen Anne (1702–14), when he became major political propagandist opposing Whig Party. Attempts to advance Tory cause led to dismissal by George I; fled to France 1715, where he supported Jacobites; returned to England 1725, and attempted to renew literary and political career. Leader of opposition to Walpole and author of *The Idea of a Patriot King.*

**Booth** Charles (1840–1916): Shipowner and social investigator. Privy councillor 1904; member of Royal Commission on Poor Law 1905–9; contributed greatly to knowledge of social problems and statistical methodology in 17-volume *Life and Labour of The People in London* (1891–1903); advocate of old age pensions for all.

**Booth** William (1829–1912): Founder and first general of Salvation Army, which began as Christian Mission intended to evangelize and serve London poor; originally ordained minister of Methodist New Connexion 1852; resigned 1861 to become itinerant evangelist and social worker; particularly interested in problems of alcoholics and released prisoners.

**Bright** John (1811–89): Radical MP 1840; Liberal MP 1843–89; President of Board of Trade 1868–70; Chancellor of Duchy of Lancaster 1873–74 and 1880–82. First entered politics in 1840s and became associated with Cobden (*q.v.*) in leading Anti-Corn Law League; ardent supporter of Free Trade; supported admission of Jews to House of Commons 1858, and campaign leading to 1867 Reform Act; opposed Crimean War, Irish Home Rule and Gladstone government's Egyptian venture of 1882.

**Brougham** Henry Peter, 1st Baron Brougham and Vaux (1778–1868): Politician, barrister and writer. Founder of *Edinburgh Review* 1802;

associated himself with cause of Queen Caroline in 1820; helped found London University in 1828; Lord Chancellor 1830–34; as Lord Chancellor, introduced rational reforms in legal system and supervised passage of 1832 Reform Bill through Lords; gave his name to the carriage henceforth known as 'brougham'.

**Burdett** Sir Francis (1770–1844): Radical politician. MP for Westminster 1807–37; MP for Wiltshire 1837–44; became mouthpiece of discontent with wartime taxation and repression in early nineteenth century; first chairman of Hampden Club; defence of radical orator John Gale Jones led to arrest and committal to Tower; release marked by demonstrations in London; became Tory Democrat in 1830s.

**Burgoyne** John (1723–92): Soldier, MP and playwright, Burgoyne began his army career in 1740. He took part in raids on Cherbourg 1758 and St Malo 1759, and raised and commanded a light cavalry regiment in Portugal 1762. He was sent to Boston in 1774, then to Canada as second-in-command to Carleton. He proposed a plan for a threefold attack on the rebel Americans, but due to bungling in London, the plan went awry. Advancing from Canada, Burgoyne found himself cut off and surrounded, and was forced to surrender his army to General Gates at Saratoga on 17 Oct. 1777. A storm of controversy broke out in England over responsibility for this fiasco, which did much to secure foreign aid for the rebel colonists. Burgoyne was commander-in-chief in Ireland 1782–83.

**Burke** Edmund (1729–97): Whig polemicist and conservative thinker; MP from 1766; first established reputation through opposition to duties on American trade; 1770 published attack on power of Crown under George III entitled *Thoughts on the Causes of our Present Discontents*; advocated economic reform during 1780s and attacked corruption of Indian administration of Warren Hastings; *Reflections on the Revolution in France* (1790) initiated years of debate on the subject, and estranged Burke from Foxite Whigs.

**Bute** 3rd Earl of, John Stuart (1713–92): Stuart succeeded as Earl of Bute in 1723. A favourite of George III, he was a Secretary of State 1761–62, and followed Newcastle as First Lord of the Treasury in 1762. He resigned office in 1763.

**Butler** Richard Austen 'Rab' (1902–82): Leading Conservative politician. As President of the Board of Education 1941–45 he pushed through the 1944 'Butler' Education Act, establishing free secondary education for all. On the liberal wing of the party, he was instrumental in adjusting its policies after the 1945 election defeat to meet aspirations for improved housing and social welfare. His centrist, consensus policies as Chancellor of the Exchequer 1951–55 became dubbed Butskellism for similarity to those of Labour's Hugh Gaitskell (*q.v.*). Butler filled every major office of state and as Deputy Prime Minister was seen by many as the natural successor to Macmillan in 1963. His failure to capitalize on his advantage and the choice of the more patrician Home as premier was a pivotal moment in postwar Conservative politics, followed by the narrow loss of the 1964 general election. He took a peerage in 1965, effectively retiring from active politics.

**Callaghan** (Leonard) James, Baron Callaghan (1912– ): Labour politician. MP for South Cardiff 1945–50 and for South East Cardiff 1950–87. He was Parliamentary Secretary to the Ministry of Transport 1947–50; Parliamentary Secretary and Financial Secretary to the Admiralty 1950–51; Chancellor of the Exchequer 1964–67 and Home Secretary 1967–70. In 1974 he became Foreign Secretary, relinquishing the post when he was elected leader of the Labour Party and made Prime Minister in 1976. He remained Prime Minister until Labour's general election defeat of May 1979. Although an experienced Labour politician, Callaghan faced a difficult task in trying to secure continuing trade union support for his government's counter-inflation policy. He also had to shore up his party's weak parliamentary position by the Lib–Lab Pact, two factors which severely hindered his freedom of manoeuvre as premier.

**Campbell-Bannerman** Sir Henry (1836–1908): Liberal MP for Stirling Burghs 1868–1908. He was Financial Secretary to the War Office 1871–74 and 1880–82; Financial Secretary to the Admiralty 1882–84; Chief Secretary for Ireland 1884–85. He served as Secretary for War in 1886 and 1892–95. He led the Liberal Party in the Commons between 1899 and 1908, and was Prime Minister 1905–8, when he retired through ill health. Campbell-Bannerman was the last Liberal PM to win office with a Liberal majority, and succeeded in uniting a party previously divided on imperial questions.

**Canning** George (1770–1827): MP for Newport 1794–96 and 1806–7; Wendover 1796–1802; Tralee 1802–6; Hastings 1807–12; Liverpool

1812–22; Warwick 1823–26; Newport 1826–27; Seaford 1827. He held the offices of Under-Secretary for Foreign Affairs 1796–99; president of the India Board 1799–1800; Paymaster-General 1800–1; Treasurer of the Navy 1804–6; Foreign Secretary 1807–9 and 1822–27; president of the India Board 1816–21. He became Prime Minister and Chancellor of the Exchequer in 1827, shortly before his death. Better known for his liberal views on foreign policy, Canning was also able to hold together a Tory–Whig coalition in 1827. After his death the government was unable to continue for long.

**Cardwell** Edward (1813–86): Conservative MP 1842–46; Peelite and Liberal MP 1847–74; President of Board of Trade 1852–55; Secretary for Ireland 1859–61; Secretary for Colonies 1864–66; Secretary for War 1868–74. Prepared ground for colonial military campaigns during imperialist period by expansion and modernization of army to meet challenge of Prussian unification and militarization.

**Carington** Peter, Lord Carrington (1919– ): Conservative politician and Foreign Secretary in the Thatcher administration of 1979. Previously served as First Lord of the Admiralty 1959–63; Defence Secretary 1970–74; Energy Secretary 1974. In 1979 supervised Lancaster House conference which ended the guerrilla war in Rhodesia, paving the way to free elections and black majority rule. Resigned as Foreign Secretary in 1982 following the Argentine invasion of the Falkland Islands. Secretary-General of NATO in 1984–88 and in 1991 put in charge of European Community peacekeeping attempts in former Yugoslavia, a position from which he resigned in 1992.

**Carson** Sir Edward (1854–1935): Unionist MP, Dublin University, 1892–1918; Belfast, 1918–21. Appointed Solicitor-General 1900–5. Leader of the anti-Home Rule movement. Founded the Ulster Volunteer Force in 1913. Attorney-General 1915–16; First Lord of the Admiralty 1916–17.

**Cartwright** John (1740–1824): Radical who began political career in Society for Constitutional Information; pamphlet *Take Your Choice* (1776) outlined reform programme including annual parliaments, payment of MPs, secret ballot and adult manhood suffrage for which he campaigned throughout latter decades of eighteenth century and Napoleonic Wars of early nineteenth century; founder of Hampden Clubs which sought enfranchisement of all taxpayers and abolition of income tax.

**Castle** Barbara, Baroness Castle of Blackburn (1910– ): Labour politician and only female member of Wilson Cabinet of 1964 as Minister for Overseas Development 1964–65. As Transport Minister 1965–68 introduced Breathalyzer and worked on an abortive Transport Bill to distribute goods traffic between road and rail. Appointed to newly created Department of Employment and Productivity in Apr. 1968 charged with enforcing Prices and Incomes legislation. Defeated by TUC and Cabinet pressure in attempts to back up industrial relations bill, *In Place of Strife*, with penal sanctions to enforce strike ballots and a 'cooling off' period for unofficial strikes. As Secretary of State for Social Services 1974–76 ended private beds in National Health hospitals. Removed from government following Callaghan's assumption of the leadership in April 1976. A dynamic figure on the left of the party, she relinquished her long tenure as MP for Blackburn, 1945–79, for a seat in the European Parliament 1979–89.

**Castlereagh** Viscount, Robert Stewart, 2nd Marquess of Londonderry (1769–1822): Secretary for Ireland 1798–1801; Secretary for War and Colonies 1805–6, 1807–9; Foreign Secretary 1812–22. Advocate of union of Britain and Ireland; resigned when George III vetoed Catholic Emancipation; quarrel with Canning led to duel and resignation of both men in 1809; very influential at Congress of Vienna in implementing ideas regarding European balance of power, but rapidly disillusioned with functioning of Congress System. Committed suicide 1822.

**Chamberlain** (Arthur) Neville (1868–1940): Conservative politician, Lord Mayor of Birmingham 1915–16, and Director-General of National Service 1916–17. He entered Parliament as MP for Birmingham Ladywood in 1918, a seat he held until 1929. From 1929 to 1940 he was MP for Birmingham Edgbaston. Chamberlain held office as Postmaster-General 1922–23; Paymaster-General 1923; Minister of Health 1923; Chancellor of the Exchequer 1923–24, Minister of Health 1924–29 and in 1931. From 1931 to 1937 he was again Chancellor of the Exchequer, and was Prime Minister from 1937 to 1940. In 1940 he resigned the premiership and became Lord President of the Council in Churchill's War Cabinet. That same year he retired from politics completely on health grounds. Chamberlain proved a dynamic and efficient administrator at the Ministry of Health and the Exchequer, but as PM displayed a less sure touch in foreign affairs and has been much criticized for his attempts to appease the Axis powers. His apparent complacency in the face of wartime defeats brought forth the pressure both within and without the Conservative Party that resulted in his resignation as PM.

**Chamberlain** Joseph (1836–1914): Politician. Mayor of Birmingham 1873–75; MP for Birmingham 1876–1910, first as a Liberal, later as a Unionist; President of Board of Trade 1880–85; Colonial Secretary 1895–1903; Unitarian and reformer who pioneered slum clearance in Birmingham; broke away from Gladstone to form Liberal Unionists in 1886 in opposition to Irish Home Rule; joined Salisbury's Conservative–Unionist government, and as Colonial Secretary became great exponent of tariff reform and imperial federation.

**Chamberlain** Sir (Joseph) Austen (1863–1937): Conservative politician. Unionist MP for Worcestershire East 1892–1914; Birmingham West from 1914. Chancellor of the Exchequer 1903–5, 1919–21; Secretary of State for India 1915–17; Lord Privy Seal 1921–22, when also Conservative leader; Foreign Secretary 1925–29; First Lord of Admiralty 1931. Son of Joseph Chamberlain (*q.v.*) whose parliamentary seat he took over in 1914. Won Nobel Peace Prize for prominence in discussions leading to Locarno treaties of 1925.

**Chatham** 1st Earl of, William Pitt ('the Elder') (1708–78): MP for Old Sarum 1735–47; Seaford 1747–54; Aldborough 1754–66; Okehampton 1756–57; Bath 1757–66. He became Vice-Treasurer of Ireland in 1746; Paymaster-General 1746–55; Secretary of State 1756–57, 1757–61. He was Lord Privy Seal, acting as Prime Minister, 1766–68. He was Leader of the Commons 1756–61. Pitt was created Earl of Chatham in 1766. A major opponent of Walpole (*q.v.*), Pitt earned a great reputation for his parliamentary speeches. During the 1750s Pitt came increasingly to represent the voice of the country against maladministration, but the disfavour of the King and his lack of parliamentary connections kept him from high office until 1756. His aggressive war policy helped Britain to victory in the Seven Years War, but he was forced to resign shortly after the accession of George III. Though Prime Minister again in 1766, ill-health and Cabinet divisions prompted his resignation. He supported the claims of the American colonists, but could not prevent the drift to war.

**Churchill** Lord Randolph Henry Spencer (1849–94): Conservative MP 1874–94; Secretary for India 1885–86; Leader of the House and

Chancellor of the Exchequer 1886. During the 1880s, became leader of Tory Democracy, which sought a core working-class support by maintaining Disraeli's policy of social reform; resigned from government in response to increased expenditure, thus prematurely ending his political career.

**Churchill** Sir Winston Leonard Spencer (1874–1965): Churchill entered Parliament as Conservative MP for Oldham in 1900. In 1904 he became a Liberal in protest at the Conservative policy on tariff reform, but remained member for Oldham until 1906. He was Liberal MP for Manchester North West 1906–8 and for Dundee 1908–22. He represented Epping 1924–45, originally as a Constitutionalist, but later as a Conservative. He was Conservative MP for Woodford 1945–64. Churchill held office as Under-Secretary for the Colonial Office 1906–8; President of the Board of Trade 1908–10; Home Secretary 1910–11; First Lord of the Admiralty 1911–15; Chancellor of the Duchy of Lancaster 1915; Minister of Munitions 1917–19; Secretary for War and Air 1919–21; Secretary for Air and Colonies 1921; Colonial Secretary 1921–22; Chancellor of the Exchequer 1924–29; First Lord of the Admiralty 1939–40; Minister of Defence and Prime Minister 1940–45. He was leader of the opposition 1945–51; Prime Minister 1951–55; Minister of Defence 1951–52. In 1953 Churchill was appointed Knight of the Garter. Churchill's career was long and varied. After leaving the Conservative Party he became a radical and reforming minister. In the First World War disputes at the Admiralty and the failure of the Gallipoli expedition led to a temporary fall from grace, but he returned to office and served in the postwar coalition. He returned to the Conservative Party as Chancellor of the Exchequer and presided over Britain's return to the Gold Standard. During the inter-war period suspicions that he was at heart a reactionary appeared confirmed by his militant attitude against the General Strike and his opposition to the movement for Indian independence. But India and the question of rearmament also distanced him from his leaders in the 1930s and allowed his return as an alternative to Chamberlain. His natural dynamism inspired the country during the Second World War, but he was less in tune with the electorate's desire for postwar reform, and led his party to defeat in 1945. By 1951 he had come to terms with the demands of postwar Britain and led his party back to power.

**Citrine** Walter McLennan, 1st Baron (1887–1983): General Secretary of TUC 1926–46; chairman, Central Electricity Authority, 1947–57;

Merseyside trade union leader; assistant general secretary of Electrical Trades Union 1920–23; led moderate wing of TUC after 1931, and worked with Bevin (*q.v.*) in support of moderation and against fascism; organized Second World War production policies, and presided over nationalization of electricity.

**Clive** Robert, 1st Baron (1725–74): Clive was posted to Madras in the service of the East India Company in 1743. In the 1750s his actions established British supremacy over the French in India. In 1751 he seized Arcot to distract Chanda Sahib from the siege of Trichinopoly, and followed this up with victories at Arni and Covrepauk. In 1757 he led the expedition which recaptured Calcutta and defeated Surajah Dowlah at Plessey on 23 June 1757. Clive served as governor of Bengal 1757–60 and 1765–67. He was acquitted of corruption in India before parliamentary committees in 1772–73, but committed suicide on 22 Nov. 1774.

**Cobbett** William (1763–1835): Radical journalist and politician. MP for Oldham from 1832; began publication in 1802 of weekly *Political Register* which became organ for his highly individualistic radical criticism; published *Parliamentary Debates* in 1804; imprisoned in 1810 following his attack on flogging in army; zealous parliamentary reformer; published *Rural Rides*, account of tours through England, in 1830; successfully defended case of inciting violence in reform agitation of 1831.

**Cobden** Richard (1804–65): Liberal MP 1841–65; active after 1835 as pamphleteer, chiefly concerned with issues of Free Trade and disarmament; together with Bright (*q.v.*) led Anti-Corn Law League; responsible for commercial treaty with France in 1860, reducing tariffs; helped maintain relations between Lincoln and Palmerston administrations during American Civil War.

**Cole** George Douglas Howard (1889–1958): British socialist writer who published over 50 volumes in field of economics, socialist theory and working-class history; socialist and pacifist during First World War; became prominent in Labour politics as a leading Fabian; during Second World War he made important contributions to social policy through organizing Nuffield College's Social Reconstruction Survey.

**Cook** Arthur James (1885–1931): Trade union leader prominent in

General Strike of 1926; active after 1905 in syndicalist and pacifist causes; led Miners' Federation of Great Britain after First World War, and built up alliance with road, railway and engineering workers to resist anticipated attempt to cut miners' wages.

**Cornwallis** Charles, 1st Marquess (1738–1805): Cornwallis joined the Grenadier Guards in 1756, and distinguished himself in the Seven Years War. He was sent to America as a major-general in 1776, and made second-in-command of the forces there in 1778. In 1780 he was given the task of stamping out resistance in the southern states, defeating the Americans at Camden, 1780, and Guilford Courthouse, 1781. However, at a time when Britain had temporarily lost command of the seas, he was surrounded at Yorktown and forced to surrender on 19 Oct. 1781. Cornwallis was governor-general and commander-in-chief in India 1786–93, and defeated Tippoo Sahib in the Third Mysore War. On his return to England he was master-general of the ordnance 1795–1801, and viceroy and commander-in-chief in Ireland 1798–1801. He was again appointed to command in India in 1805, but died there on 5 Oct.

**Cripps** Sir Richard Stafford (1889–1952): Labour MP for Bristol East, later South East, 1931–50; Solicitor-General 1930–31; Lord Privy Seal and Leader of House of Commons 1942; President of Board of Trade 1945–47; Chancellor of the Exchequer 1947–50. He was expelled from the Labour Party in 1939 for advocating a Popular Front; readmitted 1945; as Chancellor advocated policy of 'austerity', but strict taxation and voluntary wage freeze failed to check inflation, and the pound was devalued Sept. 1949.

**Crosland** (Charles) Anthony Raven (1918–77): Labour politician and theorist. His highly influential book *The Future of Socialism* (1956) advocated improved economic performance to advance socialist policies of welfare provision. The emphasis on economic competence was seen as setting the agenda for the Wilson governments of the 1960s in which Crosland served as Minister of State at Economic Affairs in 1964–65. As Secretary of State for Education and Science 1965–67 he played a major role in promoting comprehensive schools. Subsequently as Secretary of State for the Environment 1974–76 he called a halt to local authority spending in the face of unresolved economic difficulties. Appointed Foreign Secretary in 1976, his death in office deprived Labour of one of its intellectual heavyweights.

**Crossman** Richard Howard Stafford (1907–74): Labour MP for Coventry East 1945–Feb. 1974. Minister of Housing and Local Government 1964–66; Lord President of the Council and Leader of the House of Lords 1966–68; Secretary of State for Social Services 1968–70. Editor of the *New Statesman* 1970–72. Major intellectual force in the first Wilson government and pursued active housing policy. Broke tradition of Cabinet secrecy with the publication of his *Diaries* (1975–77) after legal-political battle, paving the way for subsequent Cabinet memoirs to appear.

**Dalton** Hugh, Baron Dalton (1887–1962): Labour politician, educated Eton and Cambridge; one of the leading intellectual figures in Labour's revival from the late 1930s. Taught at the London School of Economics between the wars and published works on public finance and planning, serving as MP 1924–31 and 1935–59. Entered the War Cabinet in 1940 as Minister of Economic Warfare; as President of Board of Trade from 1942 advocated nationalization of coal and power. Appointed Chancellor of the Exchequer in Attlee's Cabinet in 1945, he oversaw the nationalization of the Bank of England in 1946 and weathered the severe financial and fuel crisis of 1947. He was forced to resign for a premature leak of Budget information in 1947; returned as Chancellor of the Duchy of Lancaster in 1948 and Minister for Town and Country Planning in 1950–51.

**Davitt** Michael (1846–1906): Irish nationalist leader. Son of an Irish Roman Catholic peasant; joined the Fenians in 1865; founded Land League 1879; Irish Nationalist MP 1892–93, 1895–99; endured several spells of imprisonment. Supporter of democratic nationalism, land nationalization and anti-clericalism.

**Derby** 14th Earl of, Edward George Geoffrey Smith Stanley (1799–1869): Stanley was Whig MP for Stockbridge 1820–26; Preston 1826–30; Windsor 1831–32; Lancashire North 1832–44. In 1844 he was elevated to the House of Lords as Lord Stanley of Bickerstaffe. Stanley served as Under-Secretary to the Colonial Office 1827–28; Chief Secretary for Ireland 1830–33; Colonial Secretary 1833–34. In 1834 he resigned office in protest at the proposed lay appropriation of surplus Irish Church revenue. He served in Peel's government as Colonial Secretary 1841–45. In 1845 he resigned in protest at proposals to repeal the Corn Laws. He became Prime Minister of Conservative governments 1852, 1858–59 and 1866–68. The major aim of Stanley and his colleagues in repeatedly agreeing to form minority governments was to establish the Conservative Party as a credible governing force. It was probably the desire to achieve this which prompted his 1866–68 government to extend the franchise.

**Devonshire** 4th Duke of, William Cavendish (1720–64): Styled the Marquess of Hartington, Cavendish was MP for Derbyshire 1741–51. In 1751 he became Lord Cavendish of Hardwicke. He was made Master of the Horse and a privy councillor in 1751. In 1755 he became Lord Treasurer of Ireland, and later the same year Lord Lieutenant and Chief Governor of Ireland. He also succeeded as Duke of Devonshire in 1755. He became First Lord of the Treasury (Prime Minister ) in 1756, serving until 1757. In 1756 he was made Lord Lieutenant of Derbyshire and in 1757 a Knight of the Garter. His period as prime minister was the result of Pitt's refusal to serve with Newcastle and the Whigs' success in keeping Pitt out of office. Devonshire was a reluctant and unsuccessful prime minister and when Pitt and Newcastle came to terms he was soon replaced. In 1757 he became Lord Chamberlain of the Household and held that post until 1762.

**Disraeli** Benjamin, 1st Earl of Beaconsfield (1805–81): Disraeli was Conservative MP for Maidstone 1837–41; Shrewsbury 1841–47; Buckinghamshire 1847–76. He served as leader of the Commons and Chancellor of the Exchequer in 1852, 1858–59 and 1866–68. He was Prime Minister in 1868 and again from 1874 to 1880, also holding the office of Lord Privy Seal 1876–78. Disraeli was created Earl of Beaconsfield in 1876. He led the Conservative Party until shortly before his death in 1881. Disraeli was a leading Conservative opponent of repeal of the Corn Laws. In 1867 he was responsible for a large extension of the franchise and as Conservative Prime Minister sought to emphasize Tory interest in social reform and the benefits of the Empire to the working class. As a novelist he dramatized the themes of his Toryism, in particular attacking the existence of 'two Englands'.

**Douglas-Home** Sir Alec (Alexander Frederick), Lord Home of the Hirsel (1903–95): Home was styled Lord Dunglass from 1918 to 1951. He was Conservative MP for South Lanark 1931–45; Lanark 1950–51. In 1951 he succeeded as the 14th Earl of Home. He renounced his title in 1963 and between 1963 and 1974 was Conservative MP for Kinross and West Perthshire. In 1974 he was made a life peer. Home was Parliamentary Private Secretary to Neville Chamberlain 1937–40; joint Under-Secretary to the Foreign Office 1945; Minister of State at the

Scottish Office 1951–55; Secretary for Commonwealth Relations 1955–60; deputy leader of the Lords 1956–57. He was Lord President of the Council 1957, 1959–60; leader of the Lords 1957–60; Foreign Secretary 1960–63. In 1963 he was chosen as leader of the Conservative Party and was Prime Minister 1963–64. From 1970 to 1974 he was Foreign Secretary. Although an experienced politician and diplomat, Home was a somewhat surprising choice as Macmillan's successor. Effectively in the position of 'caretaker' PM until the 1964 general election, Home was successful in preventing the expected large Labour victory.

**Dowding** Hugh Caswell Tremenheere, Baron (1882–1970): Air force leader. He joined the army in 1900 but served in the Royal Flying Corps during the First World War and stayed in the RAF when that was founded. From 1930 to 1936 he was air member for research and development on the Air Council where he encouraged development of Spitfire and Hurricane planes and authorized expenditure for experiments on building up a radar chain. He was appointed head of Fighter Command in 1936. He opposed the sending of fighter squadrons from England to France in 1940. He directed the British victory in the Battle of Britain. He was retired in 1942. Nicknamed 'Stuffy'.

**Eden** Sir Robert Anthony, 1st Earl of Avon (1897–1977): Conservative politician. Eden sat as Conservative MP for Warwick and Leamington from 1925 until he retired in 1957. He acted as Parliamentary Private Secretary to Sir Austen Chamberlain (Foreign Secretary) 1926–29; was Under-Secretary at the Foreign Office 1931–33, Lord Privy Seal 1934–35; Minister without Portfolio for League of Nations Affairs 1935; Foreign Secretary 1935–38. In 1938 he resigned in protest at the government's policy of appeasement. He was Secretary for the Dominions 1939–40; Secretary for War 1940; Foreign Secretary 1940–45. Between 1942 and 1945 he was also Leader of the Commons. He returned to the Foreign Office in 1951 and remained there until 1955. In 1954 he was made a Knight of the Garter. He was Prime Minister from 1955 to 1957, resigning in 1957 because of ill health. In 1961 he was created Earl of Avon. Eden was an extremely experienced diplomat but he miscalculated domestic and world opinion when authorizing the ill-fated invasion of Suez in 1956.

**Evans** Gwynfor (1912– ): Plaid Cymru MP for Carmarthen 1966–70; Oct. 1974–79. President of Plaid Cymru 1945–81; chairman, Union of

Welsh Independents 1954. First elected Plaid Cymru MP. Publications include *Plaid Cymru and Wales* (1950) and *Wales can Win* (1973). Presided over the revival of Welsh nationalism from the mid-1960s through to the devolution referendum débâcle of 1978 when Wales failed to vote for a devolved assembly.

**Ewing** Winifred (1929– ): Scottish Nationalist politician. MP for Hamilton 1967–70; Moray and Nairn 1974–79; MEP for Highlands and Islands since 1975. Her victory at the Hamilton by-election marked the emergence of the Scottish Nationalists as a major force and made her the chief celebrity of the SNP. Subsequently built up a strong position as European Parliamentary representative, confirming her popularity at the direct elections in 1979, 1984, 1989 and 1994.

**Fisher** 1st Baron, John Arbuthnot Fisher (1841–1920): Naval leader. Fisher joined the navy in 1854 and served in the Crimean War. He had great energy and enthusiasm for new developments in naval warfare. As commander-in-chief in the Mediterranean 1899–1902, he introduced new techniques in training and tactics, and as First Sea Lord 1904–10, he pushed through the creation of a British battlefleet of big-gun ships. The first, the *Dreadnought*, with ten 12-inch guns, was launched in 1906. He retired in 1910, but returned as First Sea Lord in Oct. 1914 when Battenberg resigned. Fisher resigned in 1915 after clashes with Churchill, the First Lord of the Admiralty, over the wisdom of the Dardanelles expedition.

**Fox** Charles James (1749–1806): MP for Midhurst 1768–74; Malmesbury 1774–80; Westminster 1780–1806. Secretary of State for Foreign Affairs in Fox–North coalition 1782–83; Foreign Secretary again in 1806 during 'Ministry of All the Talents'. Joined Rockingham Whigs to oppose the government's American policy in 1774; thereafter remained in opposition except for two brief periods of office. Sympathetic to reform, religious toleration and other liberal causes, he welcomed the French Revolution and opposed the war with Revolutionary France. During the 1790s he emerged as a champion of English liberties in the face of Pitt's repressive measures, but his continued support for Revolutionary France split the Whig party, reducing his followers to a small group in the House of Commons.

**Fry** Elizabeth (1750–1845): Social reformer and Quaker. A visit to Newgate Prison prompted her to become a champion of prison reform, especially regarding the treatment of women prisoners. Her activities were largely directed towards improving prison conditions in order to 'reform' prisoners. She became a European authority on prison reform.

**Gaitskell** Hugh Todd Naylor (1906–63): Labour MP in Leeds 1945–63; Chancellor of the Exchequer 1950–51; Labour Party leader 1955–63. Considered by some the outstanding representative of the social democratic tradition within the Labour Party; clashed with Bevanites over Health Service charges, but later united with Bevan (*q.v.*) to denounce Eden's Suez policy: sought unsuccessfully after 1959 election defeat to persuade party to drop socialist commitments. Died shortly after reuniting party on Common Market issue and defeating unilateralists.

**George** David Lloyd, 1st Earl Lloyd-George of Dwyfor (1863–1945): Lloyd George was Liberal MP for Caernarvon Boroughs from 1890 to 1945. President of the Board of Trade 1905–8; Chancellor of the Exchequer 1908–15; Minister of Munitions 1915–16; Secretary for War 1916; Prime Minister 1916–22. He led the Liberal Party from 1926 to 1931. In 1945 he was created Earl Lloyd-George. As Chancellor, Lloyd George proved a radical social reformer, and as Minister of Munitions and wartime PM an efficient and dynamic administrator and leader. Seeking to thwart the ambitions of socialists and the Labour Party, he was often a keen advocate of Liberal–Conservative fusion or coalition, and it was Conservative backbench unrest at such a possibility that caused them to rebel against his government in 1922. His decision to oust Asquith from the premiership in 1916, and then to continue the wartime coalition after 1918, also did irreparable harm to the Liberal Party.

**Gladstone** William Ewart (1809–98): Gladstone was Conservative MP for Newark 1832–46, then Peelite MP for Oxford University 1847–65, and subsequently Liberal MP for a variety of seats, 1865–95. In a long ministerial career he held office as President of the Board of Trade 1843–45; Colonial Secretary 1845–46; Chancellor of the Exchequer on four different occasions (1852–55, 1859–66, 1873–74, 1880–82), and Prime Minister also on four occasions (1868–74, 1880–85, 1886, 1892–94). He resigned office in 1845 over the Maynooth Grant. In 1894 he resigned over the Estimates. He was the towering figure of Victorian Liberalism, with a passionate commitment to Irish Home Rule in his later years.

**Goderich** 1st Viscount. *See* Ripon.

**Gordon** Charles George (1833–85): Military leader. Gordon joined the Royal Engineers in 1852, and took part in the Crimean War and the capture of Peking in 1860. He then took command of the Chinese forces, the 'Ever Victorious Army', which crushed the Taiping Rebellion, earning him the nickname of 'Chinese' Gordon. He later entered the service of the Khedive of Egypt and administered the Sudan 1877–80. As a devout evangelical Christian, one of his main concerns was the suppression of the slave trade. In 1884 he accepted the commission to organize the evacuation of the Sudan in the face of the rebellion led by the Mahdi. However, he remained in Khartoum. A relief expedition was sent too late, and Gordon was killed when Khartoum fell to the Mahdi's forces on 26 Jan. 1885. In England the Prime Minister, Gladstone, the 'Grand Old Man', was renamed the 'MOG' ('Murderer of Gordon').

**Grafton** 3rd Duke of, Augustus Henry Fitzroy (1735–1811): Fitzroy was MP for Bury St Edmunds in 1756, succeeding as the Duke of Grafton in 1757. He was Secretary of State for the Northern Department 1765–66 and nominal head of the 1766 Chatham administration. When Chatham (*q.v.*) resigned in 1768 he became Prime Minister and held the office until 1770. He was Lord Privy Seal 1771–75 and again in 1782.

**Graham** Sir James Robert George (1792–1861): MP from 1818, first at Hull, then St Ives and Carlisle; First Lord of the Admiralty 1830; Home Secretary 1841–46; First Lord of the Admiralty 1852. A Canningite in the 1820s, Graham joined Grey between 1830 and 1834 when he and Stanley seceded from the Whigs on the question of Irish Church Reform; as Peelite Home Secretary he was responsible for public order during Chartist disturbances.

**Granville** 1st Earl, John Carteret (1690–1763): Secretary of State for Northern Department 1742–44; as ambassador to Sweden, contributed to negotiations ending Great Northern War in 1721; protégé of Stanhope (*q.v.*); pursued energetic foreign policy aimed at isolating French; supporter of Hanoverian succession; became violent critic of government as result of struggle with Walpole and Townshend (*qq.v.*); later incurred hostility of Pelham–Hardwicke faction; failed in attempt to form ministry in 1746.

**Grenville** George (1712–70): Grenville was MP for Buckingham 1741–70. He became Treasurer of the Navy in 1756 and held that office until 1762. In 1762 he became Secretary of State. He was First Lord of the Admiralty 1762–63; Chancellor of the Exchequer 1763–65, First Lord of the Treasury 1763–65.

**Grenville** 1st Baron, William Wyndham Grenville (1759–1834): Grenville was MP for Buckingham 1782–84, and for Buckinghamshire 1784–90. In 1790 he was created 1st Baron Grenville. He was Chief Secretary for Ireland 1782–83; Paymaster and Joint Paymaster 1783–89; vice-president of the Board of Trade 1786–89; Speaker in 1789; Home Secretary 1789–90; president of the Board of Control 1790–93; Foreign Secretary 1791–1801; and Prime Minister 1806–7.

**Grey** 2nd Earl, Charles Grey, Viscount Howick (1764–1845): Grey was MP for Northumberland 1786–1807; Appleby 1807. He was styled Viscount Howick in 1806 on his father's elevation in the peerage and succeeded as 2nd Earl Grey in 1807. He held office as First Lord of the Admiralty in 1806, and as Foreign Secretary 1806–7. He was Prime Minister 1830–34. Grey was a conservative Whig, and although he accepted the need for franchise reform, and was PM when the 1832 Reform Bill was passed, he saw the 1832 Act as a final concession to popular opinion and not as the start of a continuous process of reform.

**Grey** 1st Viscount, Sir Edward Grey (1862–1933): Liberal MP for Berwick-on-Tweed 1885–1916; Foreign Secretary 1905–16. His support of Britain's obligation to help Belgium in 1914 took Britain into the First World War; he believed in international arbitration, used successfully in Balkan Wars; later a champion of the League of Nations.

**Grimond** Joseph 'Jo', Lord Grimond (1913–93): Leader of the Liberal Party 1956–67 and principal figure of its revival after 1956. Trained as a barrister, MP for Orkney and Shetland 1950–83. Took over the leadership from Davies at the nadir of the party's fortunes and gave it fresh vision and drive. His leadership saw the party achieve its first by-election success since 1928 at Torrington in 1958, further success at Orpington in 1962, and a doubling of its MPs from six in 1956 to 12 in 1966. His aim to create an effective radical, non-socialist party of the Left had achieved only partial success by the time of his resignation in 1967 with the Liberals still a minor parliamentary force. Succeeded by Thorpe, he served as interim leader in May–June 1976 after Thorpe's resignation and remained a respected elder statesman.

**Guildford** 2nd Earl of. *See* North.

**Haig** 1st Earl, Sir Douglas Haig (1861–1928): Military leader. The son of a Scottish distiller, Haig was commissioned in the 7th Hussars in 1885, and distinguished himself in the Boer War. He was principal military adviser to the reforming war minister, Haldane, 1906–8. He led the 1st Army Corps of the British Expeditionary Force to France in 1914, and fought at Mons, on the Meuse and at Ypres. In 1915 he succeeded French as British commander-in-chief on the Western Front. Haig has been fiercely criticized for the way in which he conducted the battles of attrition of the Somme, 1916, and Ypres, 1917, but his determination and confidence in 1918 overcame the shock of defeat in Mar. and led to final victory in Nov.

**Halifax** 1st Earl of, Edward Frederick Lindley Wood, 1st Baron Irwin (1881–1959): Conservative MP for Ripon 1910–25; Viceroy of India 1926–31; Lord President of the Council 1937–38; Foreign Secretary 1938–40; ambassador to USA 1941–46. As Indian viceroy, he dealt with unrest on the North West Frontier and Gandhi's campaign of civil disobedience; reached agreement with Gandhi in Mar. 1931. As Foreign Secretary he was one of the major exponents of policy of 'appeasement'.

**Harcourt** Sir William George Granville Venables Vernon- (1827–1904): Liberal MP for Derby then West Monmouthshire 1868–1904; Home Secretary 1880–85; Chancellor of the Exchequer 1886 and 1892–95; Liberal leader in the House of Commons 1894–98. An influential parliamentarian, he introduced single graduated estate duty in 1894.

**Hardie** James Keir (1856–1915): Labour leader. Independent Labour MP for West Ham 1892–95; Chairman ILP 1893–1900, 1913–15; Labour MP for Merthyr Tydfil 1900–15; chairman, Labour Party, 1906. Coal-miner who became foremost British socialist, establishing Scottish Labour Party in 1888 and helping to establish the ILP in 1893; crucial influence in shaping political history of British Labour movement, and directing it into independence of existing major parties.

**Harris** Sir Arthur (1892–1984): A major advocate of offensive air power before 1939, Harris became head of Bomber Command in Feb. 1942, and remained there until the end of the war where he gained fame as 'Bomber Harris'. Concluding that selective bombing was impossible, he began the campaign of area bombing, which he believed would destroy Germany's war-making capacity and morale.

**Healey** Denis Winston, Baron Healey (1917– ): Labour politician, Chancellor of the Exchequer, and deputy leader, leading figure on the right of the party in the Wilson and Callaghan governments. First elected an MP in 1952 and appointed Defence Secretary under Wilson 1964–70, carrying out extensive retrenchment, including cancellation of TSR2 fighter-bomber and running down role 'East of Suez'. Opposition spokesman on foreign affairs 1970–72, then on Treasury affairs 1972–74. Chancellor of the Exchequer 1974–79; forced in 1976 to call on IMF loans and initiate major cuts in programmes because of economic crisis, but supervised gradual stabilization of the economy by 1978–79. Defeated in contest for Labour leadership by Callaghan in 1976 and by Foot in 1980 when he became deputy leader. Retained the deputy leadership by narrow margin against left-wing challenge of Benn in 1981, but stood down in 1983 following the general election defeat of that year. A consistent supporter of multilateralism, the EEC and social democracy, he was marginalized in the party's shift to the Left in 1979–83. Considered by some the best leader the Labour Party never had.

**Heath** Sir Edward Richard George (1916– ): Conservative politician. Heath was Conservative MP for Bexley 1950–74; Sidcup from 1974. He was a whip 1951–55; Chief Whip 1955–59; Minister of Labour 1959–60; Lord Privy Seal 1960–63; Secretary for Trade and Industry 1963–64. In 1965 he became the first leader of the Conservative Party to be elected by ballot. He was Prime Minister 1970–74. In 1975 he withdrew from the contest for party leadership after being beaten by Mrs Thatcher in the first ballot. As Prime Minister Heath never succeeded in coming to terms with the trade unions and could not solve the problem of inflation. The fuel crisis and the miners' strike forced him to call the Feb. 1974 election. Two electoral defeats led the party to opt for fresh leadership in 1975. He has since been a persistent and vociferous critic of Margaret Thatcher.

**Henderson** Arthur (1863–1935): Labour politician. MP for Barnard Castle 1903–18; Widnes 1919–22; Newcastle 1923; Burnley 1929–31; Clay Cross 1933–35; Labour Chief Whip 1906–14; President of Board of

Education 1915–16; Minister for Labour as Paymaster-General 1916; member of War Cabinet 1916–17; Home Secretary 1924; Foreign Secretary 1929–31. Wesleyan lay preacher and trade union official who believed in necessity of Labour Party as means of representing working-class interests; an architect of the 1918 Labour Party Constitution; helped Labour recovery from 1931 election débâcle.

**Heseltine** Michael (1933– ): Conservative politician whose challenge for the leadership in autumn 1990 brought about the fall of Thatcher. A successful millionaire publisher, he entered Parliament in 1966, becoming Minister of Aerospace and Shipping under Heath 1972–74. Highly popular figure with Conservative conferences for his rousing speeches and blond good looks, nicknamed 'Tarzan' by the media. He was appointed Minister for the Environment in the first Thatcher administration 1979–83 and given special responsibility for Merseyside following the Toxteth riots of 1981. Instrumental in setting up inner-city initiatives. Appointed Minister of Defence 1983–86, his growing opposition to the Thatcher premiership led to his resignation over the Westland Affair in 1986. A long-expected challenge to the leadership came following the resignation of Howe in 1990, when Heseltine obtained sufficient votes to force a second-round ballot of MPs, precipitating Thatcher's withdrawal and effective resignation as party leader and Prime Minister. Defeated by Major in the second-round ballot, Heseltine returned as Minister for the Environment 1989–92, overseeing the replacement of the poll tax. Appointed President of the Board of Trade 1992. Became Deputy Prime Minister when Major defeated Redwood for the leadership in 1995.

**Home of the Hirsel** Lord. *See* Douglas-Home.

**Howard** John (1726–90): Quaker philanthropist, notable for efforts to improve prison conditions, especially bad sanitation and system of paying gaolers out of fees extracted from prisoners.

**Howe** Geoffrey, Baron Howe (1926– ): Conservative politician; senior figure under Thatcher as Chancellor, Foreign Secretary and Deputy Prime Minister, whose resignation speech fatally undermined her leadership. Trained as a barrister, serving as Solicitor-General under Heath 1970–72 then as Minister of Trade and Consumer Affairs 1972–74. As Thatcher's Chancellor of the Exchequer 1979–83, presided over the application of monetarist policies to the economy, reducing inflation sharply at the price of a severe depression and the highest unemployment since the 1930s. As Foreign Secretary 1983–89, successfully negotiated the transfer of Hong Kong to Chinese control after 1997 with guarantees for maintenance of a western-style economic system. Increasingly discordant views with his Prime Minister over progress towards European unity led to his replacement as Foreign Secretary in July 1989, becoming Leader of the House and Deputy Prime Minister. Further clashes over Europe came to a head with his resignation from the government on 1 Nov. 1990, followed on the 13th with a devastating speech to the Commons directly attacking Thatcher's leadership and calling on others 'to consider their own response'. The following day Heseltine launched his long-anticipated leadership challenge which forced Thatcher's resignation as Conservative leader and Prime Minister.

**Hunt** Henry (1773–1835): MP for Preston 1830–32; radical political reformer known popularly as 'Orator Hunt'; advocate of universal suffrage and annual parliaments; presided over meeting at St Peter's Fields, Manchester, in Aug. 1819 which culminated in notorious Peterloo Massacre. Tried and convicted for radical views in 1820, Hunt wrote exposé of prison conditions. Won parliamentary seat on reform platform, but lost it in 1832 election following Reform Act.

**Huskisson** William (1770–1830): MP for Morpeth 1796–1802; Liskeard 1802–7; Hawick 1807–12; Chichester 1812–23; Liverpool 1823–30, President of Board of Trade 1823–27; Secretary for War and Colonies 1827–28. A Tory reformer and protégé of Pitt, who continued Pitt's work of fiscal reform; resigned as Secretary for War following clash with Wellington; killed by locomotive while attending opening of Liverpool & Manchester Railway.

**Hyndman** Henry Mayers (1842–1921): British Marxist; author of *England for All* (1881) and many other works of socialist propaganda; founder of Social Democratic Federation; important influence on many early socialists; failed to recognize the importance of trade unions and working-class liberals as potential supporters of working-class political party.

**Jenkins** Roy, Baron Jenkins (1920– ): Labour, Social Democrat and Liberal Democrat politician; founder and first leader of Social Democratic Party. Son of a Welsh miner, Oxford educated and entered Parliament in 1950. Home Secretary under Wilson 1965–67, overseeing liberalization of law on abortion and family planning. Took over as Chancellor on Callaghan's resignation in 1967 and through deflation in 1968–69 achieved trade and revenue surplus. His non-concessionary budget in Apr. 1970 often seen as playing a part in Labour's defeat in June. Returned as Home Secretary 1974–76, passing Anti-terrorism Act. Defeated in 1976 Labour leadership election and became President of the Commission of the European Community 1977–81. At Dimbleby Lecture in Nov. 1979 launched campaign for a new centre party in Britain. In Mar. 1981 founded SDP, becoming its leader, and formed Alliance with the Liberal Party. Achieved a close result in safe Labour seat of Warrington in 1981, starting run of Alliance by-election victories, and won Glasgow Hillhead in Mar. 1982. Named 'Prime Minister designate' in 1983 election campaign, criticism of his performance led to his resignation as leader in favour of Owen in June 1983. A close ally of Liberal leader Steel, he advocated merger of the two parties, supporting the merged Social and Liberal Democrats after 1988 and becoming leader of the Liberal Democrats in the Lords.

**Jones** Ernest (1819–69): Advocate of socialist ideas. Son of a wealthy cavalry officer who became a barrister. Joined O'Connorite chartists in 1846. Stood as Chartist candidate for Parliament. Imprisoned in 1848 for advocating 'physical force'; he wrote *Chartist Songs* (1846) and edited the *People's Paper* 1852–58.

**Keble** John (1792–1866): Anglican theologian. Professor of Poetry at Oxford 1831; became leading member of Oxford Movement following sermon in 1833 against proposed suppression of ten Irish bishoprics; contributed to *Tracts for the Times*; friend and adviser of Newman (*q.v.*) and later worked closely with Pusey (*q.v.*) to keep High Church movement attached to Church of England, Keble College, Oxford, was founded in his memory.

**Keynes** John Maynard, 1st Baron Keynes (1883–1946): British economist. Born and educated in Cambridge. Worked in the Treasury during the First World War and was chief Treasury representative at negotiations prior to the Treaty of Versailles. He achieved recognition for criticism of reparations plans in *The Economic Consequences of the Peace* (1919). In the 1920s he developed radical proposals for dealing with mass unemployment by deficit financing and state intervention which influenced Lloyd George's election campaign of 1929 and Oswald Mosley's proposals to the second Labour government in 1930. His full theoretical position was published in *The General Theory of Employment, Interest and Money* (1936) which inspired the 'Keynesian Revolution' in economic thinking during and after the Second World War. This rejected the classical belief in the self-regulating economy, arguing the benefits of government expenditure and economic management by the state to maintain maximum output and full employment. He acted as an economic adviser in the Second World War and cooperated with Beveridge over the funding of the welfare state. He was the chief British delegate at the Bretton Woods Conference in 1944 and in the discussions leading to the creation of the International Monetary Fund and the World Bank. His economic ideas proved immensely influential until the rise of monetarism in the 1970s and the apparent inability of 'Keynesianism' to cope with the simultaneous onset of stagnation and inflation.

**Kinnock** Neil (1942– ): Labour MP 1970–95 and member of the party's National Executive Committee from 1978. Elected leader of the Labour Party in 1983 following the resignation of Michael Foot. Attacks upon Militant Tendency and extremist influence in the party seen as attempt to moderate the party's image after the 1983 defeat. Promoted attempts to improve Labour Party organization, especially at Walworth Road headquarters. Led Labour Party to defeat in what was widely regarded as a highly dynamic and professional campaign in the 1987 general election. His second defeat in the 1992 general election precipitated his resignation. He became a European Commissioner in 1995. Succeeded as party leader by John Smith (*q.v.*)

**Kitchener** 1st Earl, Horatio Herbert Kitchener (1850–1916): Military leader. Kitchener joined the Royal Engineers in 1870. He served in the Sudan and Egypt 1882–85, and was governor-general of East Sudan 1886–88. As commander-in-chief ('Sirdar') of the Anglo-Egyptian army in the 1890s he undertook the reconquest of the Sudan, defeating the dervishes at Omdurman on 2 Sept. 1898. In the Boer War he acted as chief of staff to Roberts until Nov. 1900. On becoming commander-in-chief in South Africa he broke the resistance of the Boers by the use of blockhouses and concentration camps. As commander-in-chief in India 1902–9 he quarrelled over control of the Indian army with the viceroy, Lord Curzon, who resigned in 1905. Kitchener was British agent and consul-general in Egypt 1911–14, then on 5 Aug. 1914 he was appointed War Minister. He had enormous success in raising new volunteer armies for the Western Front, but the habits of military command did not fit him to work well with his political colleagues. He was drowned on a mission to Russia on 5 June 1916, when the cruiser HMS *Hampshire* struck a mine off the Orkney Islands.

**Lansbury** George (1859–1940): Labour leader. MP for Poplar, Bow and Bromley 1910–12, 1922–40; member of Labour government 1929–31 as first Commissioner of Works; Labour Party leader 1932–35; pacifist and Christian socialist; influential propagandist as editor of *Daily Herald.*

**Lansdowne** 1st Marquess. *See* Shelburne.

**Law** Andrew Bonar (1858–1923): Conservative politician. Law was MP for Glasgow Blackfriars 1900–6; Dulwich 1906–10; Bootle 1911–18; Glasgow Central 1918–23. He was parliamentary secretary to the Board of Trade 1902–5. In 1911 he became leader of the Conservative Party. He took office in the wartime coalition as Colonial Secretary 1915–16, and Chancellor of the Exchequer 1916–18. In the postwar coalition he was Lord Privy Seal and Leader of the House of Commons 1919–21. In 1921 he resigned. In 1922 he became leader of the Conservative Party again following the revolt of the Conservative back-benchers and then Prime Minister. He retired in 1923 and died the same year. The main significance of Law's premiership was that it proved the Conservatives could form a government without the Liberal Lloyd George being necessary to lead them.

**Lawson** Nigel, Baron Lawson of Blaby (1932– ): Conservative politician and Chancellor under Thatcher. Served as Financial Secretary to the Treasury 1979–81, Energy Minister 1981–85, becoming Chancellor of the Exchequer in June 1985. Lawson eased the monetarist policy of his predecessor Howe, stimulating a rapid credit boom and high growth which contributed to the Conservative election victory in 1987. His reduction of income tax to 25p in the pound and of top tax rates to 40p in Mar. 1988 was blamed for a rise in inflation and a worsening trade deficit, forcing increased interest rates and recession. Following disagreement with Thatcher and her economic adviser, Alan Walters, over membership of the European Monetary System, Lawson resigned in Oct. 1989. Has suffered a roller-coaster reputation, widely praised as author of Conservative victory in 1987 but also of the deepening recession from 1989 (and of the collapse in the housing market).

**Liverpool** 2nd Earl of, Robert Banks Jenkinson (1770–1828): Jenkinson was MP for Appleby 1790–96, and for Rye 1796–1803. In 1803 he became Baron Hawkesbury. He was Master of the Mint 1799–1801; Foreign Secretary 1801–4; Home Secretary 1804–6 and 1807–9. He succeeded as 2nd Earl of Liverpool in 1808. From 1809 to 1812 he held the office of Secretary for War and the Colonies, and became First Lord of the Treasury (and Prime Minister) in 1812, a post he held until 1827. Liverpool's ministry was perhaps more impressive than that of the more famous Pitt, and was based both on Liverpool's own political skill and on the collective talents of his ministers.

**Lloyd-George** David. *See* George.

**MacDonald** James Ramsay (1866–1937): Labour politician. MacDonald was MP (National Labour, 1931–37) for Leicester 1906–18; Aberavon 1922–29; Seaham 1929–35; Scottish Universities 1936–37. He was Secretary of the Labour Representation Committee and the Labour Party 1900–12, treasurer of the party 1912–24 and chairman 1911–14. He was chairman of the Independent Labour Party 1906–9, and of the Parliamentary Labour Party in 1922. He was leader of the Labour Party 1922–31. MacDonald was Prime Minister and Foreign Secretary in 1924, Prime Minister of the 1929–31 Labour government and of the National Government 1931–35. He was Lord President of the Council 1935–37. A servant of the Labour Party from its early days, MacDonald helped make Labour appear a plausible and competent governing force, particularly in foreign affairs. But his desire to make Labour a 'responsible' party of government led to the Cabinet split of 1931 on the reduction of unemployment benefits; and his decision to form a 'National' government and to campaign against the Labour Party in the ensuing election earned his expulsion from the party.

**Macleod** Iain Norman (1913–70): Conservative politician and leading exponent of liberal, 'one-nation' Toryism under Eden and Macmillan. Served as Minister of Health 1952–55 and Labour 1955–59; as Colonial Secretary 1959–61 implemented Macmillan's policy of accelerating independence of African colonies. Leader of the Commons 1961–63, he resigned on Home's accession to the premiership. Returned as Chancellor under Heath in 1970 but died suddenly in office.

**Macmillan** (Maurice) Harold, Earl of Stockton (1894–1987): Conservative politician. Macmillan was MP for Stockton-on-Tees

1924–29, 1931–45, and for Bromley 1945–64. He served as Parliamentary Secretary to the Ministry of Supply 1940–42; Under-Secretary to the Colonial Office 1942; Minister Resident at Allied HQ in NW Africa 1942–45; Secretary for Air 1945; Minister of Housing and Local Government 1951–54; Minister of Defence 1954–55; Foreign Secretary 1955; Chancellor of the Exchequer 1955–57; Prime Minister 1957–63. As early as the 1930s Macmillan revealed himself as an advocate of the Tory paternalist tradition in the Conservative Party, a stance which suited the mood of the 1950s and facilitated his rise to the premiership. His term in Downing Street was seen as something of a high point of postwar prosperity. But by the time of his resignation in 1963 it appeared to many people that Macmillan's style of leadership was dated and out of touch with the new decade. He retired due to ill health. In his later years Macmillan was associated with criticism of Thatcherite policies of social division and privatization, calling for a revival of 'one nation' Toryism.

**Major** John (1943– ): Conservative politician who succeeded Mrs Thatcher as leader of the Conservative Party and Prime Minister in Nov. 1990. Major left school at 16 and worked in banking, before entering local government in south London. MP for Huntingdon since 1983; served in junior posts 1985–87, joining the Cabinet in 1987 as Chief Secretary to the Treasury in charge of public spending. Foreign Secretary July–Oct. 1989, then Chancellor of the Exchequer following Lawson's resignation. Took Britain into the European Exchange Rate Mechanism in Oct. 1990. When Mrs Thatcher withdrew from the leadership contest in late Nov. 1990, he obtained the largest number of votes on the second ballot. He earned praise for his conduct of the Gulf War and oversaw the replacement of the poll tax with a more acceptable system of local government taxation. His low-key, more consensual approach, as well as his 'classless' image, were seen as important factors in his leading the Conservatives to a fourth consecutive election victory in Apr. 1992 in spite of a deep economic recession. Major's authority was quickly shattered by the currency crisis of Sept. 1992 which forced Britain out of the ERM, hitherto the centrepiece of Major's economic policy. Deep divisions over the ratification of the Maastricht Treaty in 1993 brought the government to the brink of defeat and led to widespread speculation about Major's continued leadership. He entered 1994 as the most unpopular Prime Minister since polls began, but the final passage of the Maastricht Bill and the sudden death of John Smith, the Labour leader, relieved pressure on his position. His attempts to secure a solution to the Northern Irish question in cooperation with the Irish premier, Albert Reynolds, on the basis of the Downing Street Declaration of Dec. 1993 appeared to have achieved a breakthrough with the declaration of an IRA cease-fire on 31 Aug. 1994. In a well-calculated gamble he resigned the party leadership in June 1995, forcing a leadership contest which he won comfortably against John Redwood.

**Mann** Tom (1856–1941): Trade union leader and socialist propagandist. Miner and artisan who came to London from Birmingham, and joined the trade union movement in 1881; joined Hyndman's (*q.v.*) Social Democratic Federation in 1885, and supported the movement to establish eight-hour working day; involved in dockworkers' strike 1889. A leader of the militant industrial struggles before the First World War, he became general secretary of the Amalgamated Society of Engineers 1918–21, and a leading member of the Communist Party.

**Manning** Henry Edward (1808–92): Religious leader, an evangelical who swung to Tractarian side in 1840s and became one of leaders of the Oxford Movement after Newman's (*q.v.*) secession in 1845; received into Roman Catholic Church in 1851 and reordained; Roman Catholic archbishop of Westminster from 1865 when he became a cardinal; gave support to doctrine of Papal Infallibility at Vatican Council (1869–70); prominent in social work of all kinds and in 1889 successfully mediated in London dock strike.

**Martineau** Harriet (1802–76): Philanthropist. Author of *Illustrations of Political Economy* (1832), moral tales designed to explain workings of economic laws, and of *Forest and Game Law Tales* and the novel *Deerbrook*; visited USA between 1834 and 1836 and became advocate of abolition of slavery; *Positive Philosophy* (1853) was popularization and condensation of Comte's philosophy.

**Mayhew** Henry (1812–87): Pioneer of systematic social investigation; in 1849–50 published 76 letters about London poor (*London Labour and the London Poor*) as part of *Morning Chronicle*'s nationwide survey of poverty; republished 1861–62, but then discontinued following reaction to vigour of its attack on political economy of day; joint first editor of *Punch* 1841.

**Melbourne** 2nd Viscount, William Lamb (1779–1848): Politician. Lamb was Whig MP for Leominster 1806; Portarlington 1807–12; Northampton 1816–19; Hertfordshire 1819–29. In 1829 he became Viscount Melbourne. He held office as Secretary for Ireland 1827–28 and Home Secretary 1830–40. Melbourne was Prime Minister in 1834 and 1835–41. A Whig, and disliked as such by the King, Melbourne's outdated view of the constitution helped result (in 1834) in his being the last PM to be dismissed by the monarch. Between 1835 and 1841 Melbourne proved reluctant to respond to the Chartist and Anti-Corn Law movements.

**Mill** James (1773–1836): Scottish philosopher who became early exponent of utilitarianism in government and the centre of a group of philosophic liberals including his son J. S. Mill (*q.v.*), Bentham (*q.v.*) and Ricardo; his articles on prisons in *Encyclopaedia Britannica* (1823) advocated reform through industry rather than mere punishment; supported foundation of London University 1828.

**Mill** John Stuart (1806–73): Liberal MP for Westminster 1865–68; influenced by Bentham (*q.v.*) and utilitarian philosophy of James Mill (*q.v.*), became leading philosopher of nineteenth-century liberalism; advocate of equal rights for women and respect for minorities; author of *On Liberty* (1859); humanist who saw need for state intervention to prevent abuses of *laissez-faire*; later regarded himself as a socialist.

**Montgomery** 1st Viscount, Sir Bernard Law Montgomery (1887–1976): Military leader. Son of a bishop, he joined the Royal Warwickshire Regiment from Sandhurst in 1908. Although wounded in the chest in 1914 he returned to France in 1916. He rose to the rank of lieutenant-colonel and battalion commander by the end of the war. In 1940 he was evacuated from Dunkirk with the 3rd Division which he was commanding. By December 1941 he was head of South-eastern Command and a lieutenant-general. Montgomery was chosen to command the 8th Army in North Africa in 1942. He transformed the army so that it was able to halt Rommel's advance on Cairo at Alam Halfa (31 Aug.–7 Sept.) and counter-attack at El Alamein beginning 23 Oct. The battle, well planned and methodically accomplished, was a British victory. He led the invasion of Sicily and Italy, then was appointed land commander for the invasion of Europe (Overlord). He came into conflict over personal and strategic matters with American allies. After the war he was Chief of the Imperial General Staff and Deputy Commander of NATO.

**Moore** Sir John (1761–1809): Military leader. The son of a Glasgow doctor, Moore joined the 51st Foot in 1776 and saw action in Nova Scotia during the American War of Independence. In the following years he served in many campaigns: Corsica 1794–95, West Indies 1796–97, Ireland 1797–99, Holland 1799, the Mediterranean and Egypt 1800–1, Sicily 1806 and Sweden 1808. His reputation as a military reformer was enhanced by his period at Shorncliffe Camp 1803–6, where he successfully experimented with light infantry tactics and the training of troops. He took command of the British force in the Peninsula in 1808. He advanced into Spain, but was forced to retreat to Corunna. He was fatally wounded as his army evacuated on 16 Jan. 1809.

**Morris** William (1834–96): Idealist socialist, poet, painter, designer; founder of Arts and Crafts movement; established close association between art and political beliefs; involved in creation of Socialist League 1884, and Hammersmith Socialist Society 1890; lasting artistic influence, and a major influence on later socialists.

**Mosley** Sir Oswald Ernald (1896–1980): Conservative MP for Harrow 1918–22; Independent MP 1922–24; Labour MP for Smethwick 1926–31; Chancellor of the Duchy of Lancaster 1929–30; founder of progressive socialist New Party which unsuccessfully contested 21 seats in 1931 general election; formed British Union of Fascists in 1932, which engaged in anti-Semitic and Hitlerite activities until 1936 Public Order Act banned political uniforms and street marches; interned 1940–43.

**Mountbatten** 1st Earl, Lord Louis Mountbatten (1900–79): Naval commander. At the outbreak of the Second World War Mountbatten was commanding the Fifth Destroyer Flotilla. In 1941 his ship, HMS *Kelly*, was sunk in the Mediterranean and he was nearly drowned. He was then appointed adviser on combined operations. His largest operation was the Dieppe Raid in Aug. 1942, which, though a failure, taught valuable lessons. Mountbatten was then appointed supreme commander in South-East Asia, arriving in India in Oct. 1943 to find a diversity of problems. After the war he was Viceroy of India and presided over the partition of the sub-continent and the independence of India and Pakistan. He later returned to a naval career. In 1955 he was First Sea Lord and in 1959 Chief of the Defence Staff. He was assassinated by Irish extremists in 1979. Widely admired for his overall conduct of operations in Burma in the war and his recognition of the need for a rapid transition to independence in the Indian sub-continent.

**Nelson** 1st Viscount, Horatio Nelson (1758–1805): Naval leader. The son of a Norfolk parson, Nelson entered the navy in 1770 and saw service in the Arctic, the East Indies and the West Indies. In 1793 he was sent to the Mediterranean, where he lost an eye the following year in the occupation of Corsica. In 1797 he played a leading role in the victorious battle of Cape St Vincent in Feb., but in July lost his right arm in the unsuccessful attack on Santa Cruz. In 1798 he failed to intercept the French expedition to Egypt while blockading Toulon, but destroyed the French fleet at the battle of the Nile on 1 Aug. A brilliant tactician, Nelson had the ability to inspire his subordinates to display courage and initiative. In 1801 he destroyed the Danish fleet in Copenhagen harbour, putting his telescope to his blind eye to avoid seeing his superior's order to disengage. Nelson was appointed to the Mediterranean command in 1803. The French admiral, Villeneuve, eluded his blockade of Toulon in spring 1805, but after a pursuit, Nelson defeated the Franco-Spanish fleet at Trafalgar on 21 Oct. During the battle Nelson was mortally wounded by a sniper.

**Newcastle** 1st Duke of, Thomas Pelham-Holles (1693–1768): Newcastle was Secretary of State for the Southern Department 1724–54. He held the office of First Lord of the Treasury twice, 1754–56 and 1757–62. Between July 1765 and Aug. 1766 he was Lord Privy Seal. Pelham-Holles was created Earl of Clare in 1714 and Duke of Newcastle in 1715. Newcastle was a skilled and efficient manipulator of parliamentary patronage, but as Prime Minister found that, although he had the confidence of George II, he needed the support of Pitt to secure the confidence of the Commons. When Chatham left office in 1761, Newcastle found it increasingly difficult to hold his ministry together and was replaced by George III's favourite, Bute, in May 1762.

**Newman** John Henry (1801–90): Theologian. Brought up in Church of England under evangelical influence, in 1833 he became leading spirit of the Oxford Movement; wrote 24 *Tracts for the Times* between 1833 and 1841; believed the Church of England should hold an intermediate position between Romanism and Protestantism; withdrew from Oxford following controversy over interpretation of the Thirty-nine Articles in 1841, and was received into the Roman Catholic Church in 1845; he became a cardinal and had considerable influence on the revival of Catholicism in England.

**North** Frederick, 2nd Earl of Guildford (1732–92): North was styled

Lord North from 1752 to 1790. He was MP for Banbury 1754–90. In 1790 he succeeded as Earl of Guildford. He served as Lord of the Treasury 1759–65; joint Paymaster-General 1766–67; Chancellor of the Exchequer 1767–82 and First Lord of the Treasury (Prime Minister) 1770–82. He was Secretary of State for Colonial Affairs Apr.–Dec. 1783 in the Fox–North coalition. North has been held by many historians to have been an able domestic politician, but whose handling of the American crisis and conduct of the war led to his downfall.

**O'Brien** James Bronterre (1805–86): Irish radical and advocate of land nationalization and extension to workers of credit based on it; member of Working Men's Association; Chartist who advocated violence, but after 1839 stressed need for middle-class support and thereafter advised moderation.

**O'Connell** Daniel (1775–1847): Irish nationalist; known as 'The Liberator'. Born in County Kerry, he founded the Catholic Association in 1823 as a mass movement to campaign for Catholic Emancipation. Elected for County Clare in 1828, but as a Catholic not allowed to take his seat. His efforts helped to secure the passing of the Roman Catholic Relief Act 1829. Subsequently, took seat as MP for County Clare 1830, and for Waterford 1832. Organized mass meetings in 1842 and 1843 to secure repeal of the 1800 Act of Union. His cancellation of the Clontarf meeting in Oct. 1843 discredited him with many Irish extremists. He died at Genoa.

**O'Connor** Feargus (1794–1855): Chartist leader. MP for Cork 1832–35; MP for Nottingham from 1847; leading Chartist who owned and edited Chartist periodical *Northern Star* and dominated militant northern section of movement; organized Chartist demonstration 1848.

**Orford** 1st Earl of. *See* Walpole.

**Owen** David, Baron Owen (1938– ): Labour politician and leader of the Social Democratic Party (SDP). Labour MP 1966–81, and for SDP 1981–92 for Plymouth Devonport. Foreign Secretary 1977–79 in the Callaghan government, his disillusion with the leftward drift of the party under Foot led to his co-founding of SDP with Roy Jenkins, Bill Rodgers and Shirley Williams. He became leader of the SDP during the 1983 election campaign and advocated distinct SDP views on defence and the 'social market' within the Liberal–SDP Alliance. Joint leader of the Alliance campaign (with David Steel) in the 1987 election, he opposed calls for a merger following the election and resigned the leadership of the SDP when a majority of its members showed in favour. He became leader of the 'continuing' SDP until its final demise in 1989 and was widely regarded as hindering the emergence of an effective 'third force'. He left the Commons in 1992 and was given a peerage by Major following possible discussion about a role in the Conservative Party. He was appointed EU peacekeeper in the former Yugoslavia in 1992, resigning in 1995.

**Owen** Robert (1771–1858): Utopian socialist propagandist. Scottish mill-owner who attempted at New Lanark to create model factory employing no young children, educating older children and limiting adult hours; used term 'socialist' to describe experiment; *New View of Society* (1813) expounded value of cooperative ideal; unsuccessful in attempt to establish socialistic community in USA 1825–29; helped found Grand National Consolidated Trades Union 1834.

**Oxford and Asquith** 1st Earl of. *See* Asquith.

**Paine** Thomas (1737–1809): Excise officer who emigrated to America following conflict over pay claim; published *Common Sense* in 1776 demanding complete independence for the American colonies; served with Washington, but returned to England 1787; published Parts I and II of *The Rights of Man* between 1791 and 1792 in response to Burke's (*q.v.*) criticisms of French Revolution; fled to France 1792 and was convicted of seditious libel *in absentia*; died in exile in America.

**Paisley** Revd Ian Richard Kyle (1926– ): Unionist politician. Founder and head of the fundamentalist Free Presbyterian Church. Attracted populist support for ultra-loyalist Ulster Defence Committee from 1960 and founded breakaway Democratic Unionist Party (DUP) in 1971. MP for North Antrim from 1970, he helped to organize the United Ulster Unionist Council (UUUC) which won 11 out of 12 Ulster seats in 1974. Supported the Ulster Workers' Council strike of May 1974 which brought down the power-sharing executive. Bitter opponent of the Anglo-Irish Agreement of 1985, forming an electoral pact with the Ulster Unionist Party (UUP) to oppose it and to some extent healing the rift in unionist politics present since 1971. The dominant voice of Ulster loyalism since the early 1970s.

**Palmerston** 3rd Viscount, Henry John Temple (1784–1865): Temple was Tory MP for Newport 1807–11; Cambridge University 1811–31; Whig member for Bletchingly 1831–32; Hampshire South 1832–34; Tiverton 1835–65. He succeeded as Viscount Palmerston in 1802. He was a lord of the Admiralty 1807–9. In 1809 he declined the Chancellorship of the Exchequer and became Secretary for War until 1828. He was Foreign Secretary 1830–34, 1835–41, 1846–51; Home Secretary 1852–55; Prime Minister 1855–58 and 1859–65. Palmerston captured the imagination of mid-Victorian Britain by his aggressive nationalism, and his popularity was such that he was returned as Prime Minister in 1859 despite his known hostility to the growing demand for electoral reform.

**Pankhurst** Emmeline (1858–1928): Feminist leader. Joint founder and leader after 1898 of Women's Franchise League, and with daughter Christabel of more militant Women's Social and Political Union 1903; talks with Prime Minister in 1906 led to disillusionment with Liberals and resort to more violent tactics; engaged in arson and hunger strikes while imprisoned; encouraged women to join armed forces and work in industry during First World War.

**Parnell** Charles Stewart (1846–91): Irish nationalist leader. Son of Anglican gentry family, educated at Cambridge. Nationalist MP for Co. Meath 1875–80, Cork 1880–91, leading Irish Nationalist Party in Parliament from 1878. Led agitation for Home Rule, skilfully coordinating political bargaining at Westminster with more radical movements in Ireland. Career ruined when cited in O'Shea divorce case of 1890.

**Passfield** 1st Baron. *See* Webb.

**Peel** Sir Robert, 2nd Bt (1788–1850): Conservative politician. Peel was Tory MP for Cashel 1809–17; Oxford University 1817–28; Westbury 1829; Tamworth 1830–50. He was Under-Secretary at the Colonial Office 1810–12; Chief Secretary for Ireland 1812–18; Home Secretary 1822–27 and 1828–30; Leader of the Commons 1828–30; Prime Minister and Chancellor of the Exchequer 1834–35. He again became Prime Minister in 1841, resigning in 1845, but resuming office when the Whigs could not form a government. He retained the premiership until 1846. Peel is best remembered for his financial reforms and for his endeavours to prove that Conservatism was compatible with cautious reform. His repeal of the Corn Duties in 1846 split his party and left him at the head of a band of Free Trade 'Peelites' until his death in a riding accident in 1850.

**Pelham** Henry (1695–1754): MP for Seaford 1717–22; Sussex 1722–54; Secretary at War from 1724; Paymaster of the Forces from 1730; First Lord of the Treasury and Chancellor of the Exchequer 1743–54. An able administrator, Pelham sought to re-establish the country's finances and pursue a peaceful foreign policy. His position was substantially assisted by his brother's (the Duke of Newcastle) control of parliamentary patronage.

**Perceval** Spencer (1762–1812): MP for Northampton 1796–1812. He was Attorney-General 1802–6; Chancellor of the Exchequer and the Duchy of Lancaster 1807–9. He was Prime Minister and Chancellor of the Exchequer 1809–12, when he became the only British prime minister to have been assassinated, by one John Bellingham, who had nurtured a grievance against the government.

**Pitt** William, 'the Elder'. *See* Chatham.

**Pitt** William (1759–1806): Son of William Pitt 'the Elder', he was MP for Appleby 1781–84; Cambridge University 1784–1806. He was Chancellor of the Exchequer 1782–83 and Prime Minister and Chancellor of the Exchequer 1783–1801 and 1804–6. The youngest ever prime minister, Pitt was chosen by the King as an alternative to the Fox–North (*q.v.*) coalition, but emerged as a powerful leader in the House of Commons. He carried out sweeping administrative reforms in the 1780s and was sympathetic to parliamentary reform. From 1793 he led Britain in the war against Revolutionary France, repressing radicalism at home and initiating new financial measures, such as the income tax. He resigned when George III refused to allow Catholic Emancipation in 1801, but returned to office in 1804.

**Place** Francis (1771–1854): Radical reformer. London journeyman breeches-maker prominent in London Corresponding Society and reform agitation of 1790s; later led campaign against 'Sinking Fund' and Combination Laws, repeal of the latter being secured in 1824. Helped 'Political Unions' formulate demands for parliamentary reform 1832; helped draft 'People's Charter'.

**Portland** 3rd Duke of, William Henry Cavendish-Bentinck (1738–1809):

Styled Marquess of Titchfield, Cavendish-Bentinck was MP for Weobley 1761–62. In 1762 he succeeded as Duke of Portland. He was Viceroy of Ireland in 1782, Prime Minister in 1783 and again 1807–9. He was Home Secretary 1794–1801 and Lord President of the Council 1801–5.

**Potter** George (1832–93): Trade union leader. He was a carpenter prominent in London builders' strike of 1859; ran an influential labour paper in London, *Beehive*, to encourage strikes in provinces; was an aggressive unionist who saw the vote as a necessity for members to secure legislation safeguarding union funds and protecting rights. In the summer of 1864 he organized Conference of Trades; as president of London Working Men's Association, opened Trade Union Congress in 1868.

**Powell** (John) Enoch (1912– ): Conservative and Unionist politician. Regarded as one of the most controversial politicians of the postwar era because of his outspoken views on coloured immigration. A Cambridge-educated professor of classics, he was Conservative MP for Wolverhampton South-West 1950–74, serving as Minister of Health 1960–63. His speeches against continued immigration in 1967 and 1968, one of which prophesied 'rivers of blood', and calls for repatriation of coloured immigrants, earned him considerable notoriety and led to his expulsion by Heath from the Conservative shadow cabinet. His views, however, were reflected in the tightening of the rules against Commonwealth immigration under both Conservative and Labour governments. Powell also campaigned against Britain's entry to the Common Market, isolating himself from the Conservative Party by advising voters in 1974 to support anti-European Labour candidates. From 1974 to 1987 he sat for South Down as a Unionist, opposing concessions of sovereignty over Ulster. A radical in economic affairs, he has been seen as a pre-Thatcherite, but detached from the Conservative Party after 1974. He has remained a staunch opponent of the erosion of British sovereignty within the European Community.

**Pulteney** William. *See* Bath.

**Pusey** Edward Bouverie (1800–82): Regius Professor of Hebrew and Canon of Christ Church, Oxford; leading member of Oxford Movement; became leader following Newman's withdrawal 1841; assisted in establishment of first Anglican sisterhood; sermon on absolution in 1846 led to practice of private confession in Anglican Church.

**Redmond** John Edward (1856–1918): Irish nationalist leader. Son of an Irish Catholic gentry family, he was Irish Nationalist MP for New Ross 1881–85; N. Wexford 1885–91; Waterford 1891–1918; leader of reunited Nationalist Party from 1900. Worked for Home Rule by constitutional means up to Easter Rising of 1916, but the rise of Sinn Fein made his approach seem redundant.

**Rhodes** Cecil John (1853–1902): Champion of the British imperial cause in southern Africa. Went to Africa in 1870 where he earned a fortune from diamond-mining. Founded De Beers Company in 1880 at Kimberley and acquired interests in the Transvaal gold-fields. In 1887 founded the British South Africa Company to develop the region north of the Transvaal, later known as Rhodesia, and in 1890 mounted an expedition which established a settlement in Salisbury and secured the rest of the country. Made premier of Cape Colony in 1890, but was forced to resign in 1896 because of his connection with the Jameson raid. He left most of his fortune to Oxford University.

**Ripon** 1st Earl of, Frederick John Robinson, 1st Viscount Goderich (1782–1859): Robinson was MP for Carlow Borough 1806–7; Ripon 1807–27. In 1827 he was created 1st Viscount Goderich. In 1833 he was created Earl of Ripon. Robinson was President of the Board of Trade and Treasurer of the Navy 1818–23; Chancellor of the Exchequer 1823–27; Secretary for War and Colonies Apr.–Aug. 1827 and 1830–33. He served as Prime Minister Aug. 1827–Jan. 1828; as Lord Privy Seal Apr. 1833–May 1834; as President of the Board of Trade 1841–43; and as President of the Board of Control 1843–46. Goderich was asked to serve as Prime Minister following the death of his friend, Canning. He proved unable to control his ministry and resigned following the refusal of Huskisson and Herries to serve together.

**Roberts** 1st Earl, Frederick Sleigh Roberts (1832–1914): Military leader. The son of a general, Roberts was born in India and joined the Bengal Artillery in 1851. He won the Victoria Cross during the Indian Mutiny, in Jan. 1858. As commander of the Punjab Frontier Force, he defeated the Afghans and imposed the Treaty of Gardamak in May 1879. After a British force had been defeated by the Afghans at Maiwand, Roberts became a national hero by marching his army 300 miles in 22 days to relieve Kandahar on 1 Sept. 1880. He was commander-in-chief in India 1885–93 and in Ireland 1895–99. After the initial British disasters in the Boer War, Roberts was sent to command in South Africa. He returned to England in 1901 to be commander-in-chief (until 1904). His last years were devoted to advocating conscription through the National Service League. He died on 14 Nov. 1914 after contracting pneumonia during a visit to Indian troops in France.

**Robinson** Frederick John. *See* Ripon.

**Rockingham** 2nd Marquess of, Charles Watson-Wentworth (1730–82): Watson-Wentworth succeeded as Marquess of Rockingham in 1750. He was Lord Lieutenant of the North and West Ridings of Yorkshire July 1751–Dec. 1762, and Lord of the Bedchamber 1751–62. He held the office of First Lord of the Treasury from July 1765 to July 1766, and again from Mar. 1782 until his death.

**Rodney** 1st Baron, George Brydges Rodney (1718–92): Naval leader. Rodney joined the navy in 1732. He served in the War of the Austrian Succession and the Seven Years War, and was governor of Newfoundland 1749–52. Promoted to admiral in 1778, he led a fleet to relieve Gibraltar in 1780, then sailed for the West Indies. At the battle of the Saints on 12 Apr. 1782 he defeated the French fleet under the Comte de Grasse, restoring English naval supremacy and helping to ensure a more favourable peace settlement at the end of the American War of Independence.

**Rosebery** 5th Earl of, Archibald Philip Primrose, 1st Earl of Midlothian (1847–1929): Created earl in 1868, Rosebery held first the office of Under-Secretary to the Home Office 1881–83. In 1885 he became first Commissioner of Works and later in the year Lord Privy Seal. He served as Foreign Secretary in 1886 and 1892–94. He was Prime Minister and Lord President of the Council 1894–95. In 1889 and 1890 and again in 1892 he was chairman of the London County Council. After internal party squabbles he resigned the leadership of the Liberal Party in 1896. An exceptionally gifted individual, Rosebery proved a surprisingly inept premier, and through hesitancy and indecision failed to return to office after resigning the party leadership.

**Rowntree** Seebohm (1871–1954): British manufacturer and philanthropist; son of Quaker reformer and chocolate manufacturer Joseph Rowntree, he spent a considerable time in the study and alleviation of poverty, and was involved in organizations such as the

Nuffield Trust for Special Areas, the Outward Bound Trust and the War on Want Committee. Publications include studies of urban poverty and *Poverty and the Welfare State.*

**Russell** 1st Earl, Lord John Russell (1792–1878): Liberal politician. Russell was MP for Huntingdonshire 1820–26; Bandon Bridge 1826–30; Tavistock 1831; Devon 1831–32; Devon South 1832–35; Stroud 1835–41; the City of London 1841–61. In 1861 he was created Earl Russell. He was Postmaster-General 1830–34, obtaining a seat in the Cabinet in 1831; Home Secretary 1835–39; Colonial Secretary 1839–41. He served as Prime Minister 1846–52. After resigning the premiership he held office as Foreign Secretary 1852–53; Minister without Portfolio 1853–54; Lord President of the Council 1854–55; Colonial Secretary 1855; Foreign Secretary 1859–65. In 1865 he again became Prime Minister, leaving office in 1866. Russell failed to achieve the union of Whigs and Peelites which he desired during his first premiership, and was unable to establish the control he would have wished over his Cabinet and the Commons. During his second administration he proved a bold advocate of electoral reform and alarmed some of his colleagues by his 'rapidity'.

**Salisbury** 3rd Marquess of, Robert Arthur Talbot Gascoyne-Cecil (1830–1903): Cecil was Conservative MP for Stamford 1853–66. In 1865 he became Viscount Cranbourne. He served as Secretary for India in 1866, resigning in protest at the 1867 Reform Bill. In 1868 he succeeded as Marquess of Salisbury. He returned as Secretary for India 1874–76, and as Foreign Secretary 1878–80. He was leader of the opposition in the House of Lords and joint leader of the Conservative Party 1881–85. In 1885 he became Prime Minister and sole party leader. He acted as Prime Minister and Foreign Secretary 1885–86; Prime Minister in 1886; Prime Minister and Foreign Secretary 1887–92 and 1895–1900. He was Prime Minister and Lord Privy Seal 1900–2. Salisbury was a remarkably able diplomat, while in the domestic sphere he had an incisive knowledge of the Conservative Party. As a Tory and a High Church Anglican he was able to control an unruly party, and by moderate social reform and opposition to Home Rule he succeeded in forging the Unionist alliance which dominated British politics between 1886 and 1906.

**Shaftesbury** 7th Earl, Anthony Ashley Cooper, Baron Ashley (1805–85): MP for Woodstock 1826–30; Dorchester 1830–31; Dorset 1833–46; champion of measures to improve factory conditions, including various

Factory Acts between 1833 and 1850, and Owners Act of 1842; he was a noted philanthropist and evangelist, interested in Bible Society movements at home and abroad.

**Shelburne** 2nd Earl of, William Petty, 1st Marquess of Lansdowne (1737–1805): MP for Wycombe 1760–61. In 1761 he succeeded as Earl of Shelburne. He was President of the Board of Trade Apr.–Sept. 1763; Secretary of State for the Southern Department 1766–68; Home Secretary Mar.–July 1782; First Lord of the Treasury (Prime Minister) July 1782–Apr. 1783. He was created Marquess of Lansdowne in 1784.

**Sidmouth** 1st Viscount, Henry Addington (1757–1844): MP for Devizes 1784–1805. In 1805 he was created Viscount Sidmouth. He was Speaker of the House of Commons 1789–1801; Prime Minister and Chancellor of the Exchequer 1801–4; Lord President of the Council 1805; Lord Privy Seal 1806; Lord President of the Council 1806–7 and 1812. He was Home Secretary 1812–22 and a member of the Cabinet without ministerial office 1822–24. Although an able administrator, Sidmouth proved a mediocre prime minister. He proved an efficient but repressive home secretary.

**Slim** 1st Viscount, William Joseph Slim (1891–1970): Military leader. Commissioned from the ranks in the First World War into the Royal Warwickshire Regiment, he took a regular commission in the Indian Army. In Mar. 1942 he was sent to Burma to take command of 1 Corps and from Mar. to May retreated from Rangoon to Imphal where he took up a defensive position. In Dec. 1943 he was given command of the Fourteenth Army. In Feb. 1944 he halted a Japanese attack in the Arakan. This was a turning-point in the Burmese War, a boost to morale. He repulsed the Japanese attacks at Imphal and Kohima, Mar.–July 1944, then mounted a counter-offensive, defeating the Japanese at Meiktila, Mar. 1945. By 3 May he had captured Rangoon. He was worshipped by all who knew him. There was no serious criticism of Slim during or after the war. He restored the army's offensive spirit and developed new techniques of jungle fighting.

**Smith** John (1938–94): Labour politician. MP for Lanarkshire North 1970–83; Monklands East 1983–94. Secretary of State for Trade 1978–79; shadow Chancellor 1989–92; leader of the Labour Party 1992–94. Used his authority to secure reform of trade union block vote in Labour Party and built up a commanding position as anticipated next Prime Minister in the face of John Major's leadership difficulties in 1993–94. His sudden death on 12 May 1994 was widely mourned across the political spectrum. As leader, he continued the work of Neil Kinnock in building a more moderate and modernized Labour Party.

**Smith** William Henry (1825–91): Conservative MP 1868–91; First Lord of the Admiralty 1877–80; First Lord of the Treasury and Leader of the House 1887–91; founder of W. H. Smith Booksellers; opposed Lord Randolph Churchill's (*q.v.*) budgetary proposals for economies and succeeded him as Leader of the House.

**Snowden** 1st Viscount, Philip Snowden (1864–1937): Labour MP for Blackburn 1906–18, and for Colne Valley 1922–31; Chancellor of the Exchequer 1924 and 1929–31; Lord Privy Seal 1931–32. He came into the Labour Party through the Independent Labour Party, of which he was chairman 1903–6, 1917–20. He became an expert on national finance and temperance questions and a champion of Free Trade. He opposed the First World War and championed conscientious objectors; he was a vigorous opponent of Bolshevism. In 1931, with the break-up of the Labour government, he followed MacDonald (*q.v.*) into the National Government, but resigned the following year over the adoption of Imperial Preference.

**Stanhope** 1st Earl, James Stanhope (1673–1721): First Lord of the Treasury and Chancellor of the Exchequer 1717–18; Secretary of State for the Northern Department 1716–17, 1718–21. British soldier and diplomat who aimed to build up a system of European alliances and gain Continental support for the Hanoverian succession; he negotiated the Triple Alliance 1717 and Quadruple Alliance 1718; a champion of one-party government and Whig supremacy.

**Steel** Sir David Martin Scott (1938– ): Liberal politician. Liberal MP after 1965 and leader of the Liberal Party 1976–88. Helped party to recover from the Thorpe affair and negotiated Lib–Lab Pact of 1977–78 to maintain the Labour government during the devolution referendum campaigns. Supported the formation of the Alliance with the newly founded SDP in 1981 and helped achieve almost a quarter of the popular vote in the 1983 general election. Jointly led the Alliance campaign in the 1987 general election with SDP leader David Owen, but immediately afterwards called for a merger of the two parties, precipitating a prolonged merger negotiation and a split in the SDP.

He did not put himself forward for the leadership of the newly formed Social and Liberal Democrats in 1988 but became foreign affairs spokesman. A committed internationalist, Steel was also responsible for sponsoring the legalization of abortion in 1967.

**Stephens** James (1824–1901): Irish revolutionary. Member of the Young Ireland movement. Founded the Fenians in 1858.

**Tawney** Richard Henry (1880–1962): Christian socialist, social critic, reformer and historian; the economic history of England from 1540 to 1640 became known as 'Tawney's Century'; Professor of Economic History at the London School of Economics from 1931, and Professor Emeritus 1949; adviser to numerous government bodies; critic of capitalism as corrupter of rich and poor alike. His book *Religion and the Rise of Capitalism* (1926) was an important study of the sixteenth- and seventeenth-century development of capitalism and its relationship to Protestantism.

**Thatcher** Margaret Hilda (*née* Roberts), Baroness Thatcher of Kesteven (1925– ): Mrs Thatcher was Conservative MP for Finchley 1959–92. She was Parliamentary Secretary to the Ministry of Pensions and National Insurance 1961–64, and Secretary of State for Education and Science 1970–74. In 1975 she was elected leader of the Conservative Party. Between 1975 and 1979 she led the party away from the centrist policies of Heath and adopted a tough monetarist stance on economic problems and a tough line on law and order, defence and immigration. In May 1979 she became Britain's first woman Prime Minister, following her election victory. In spite of considerable unpopularity and very high unemployment, Mrs Thatcher's conduct of the Falklands War and Labour's disarray led to a landslide victory at the polls in 1983. Mrs Thatcher's second term was marked by growing emphasis on liberalizing the economy, especially the privatization (*q.v.*) of major public concerns. In 1987 she achieved a record third term of office with a majority of over 100. Weakened by the resignation of her Chancellor, Lawson, and by the unpopularity of the poll tax, her intransigent attitude towards Europe led to the resignation of her deputy leader Howe in 1990. This led to a leadership challenge in which she failed to secure a convincing majority and withdrew from the contest, resigning as Prime Minister in Dec. She has remained an outspoken critic of European integration.

**Thistlewood** Arthur (1770–1820): Imbibed revolutionary ideas while serving in army during American and French Wars; organized Spa Fields meetings 1816; led group of London extremists arrested for conspiring to murder Castlereagh and Cabinet in 1820; convicted of high treason for Cato Street conspiracy and hanged.

**Thomas** James Henry (1874–1949): Labour MP for Derby 1910–36. Colonial Secretary 1924; Lord Privy Seal and minister responsible for unemployment issues 1929–30; Dominions Secretary 1930–35; Colonial Secretary 1935–36. Railwayman who became active in Amalgamated Society of Railway Servants; later general secretary of the National Union of Railwaymen (NUR) 1918–31; urged support for Labour Party, but later expelled from party and NUR for staying with MacDonald in National Government of 1931. His political career was ended by alleged Budget leak in 1936.

**Tillett** Benjamin (1866–1943): Trade union leader. Labour MP for N. Salford 1917–24, 1929–31; chairman TUC General Council 1928–29; helped organize unionization of dockworkers; secretary of Dock, Wharf, Riverside and General Workers' Union 1887–1922; one of leaders of 1889 London dock strike; initiative led to formation of National Transport Workers' Federation; alderman of London County Council 1892–98; a founder of the Independent Labour Party and Labour Party; member TUC General Council 1921–31.

**Townshend** 2nd Viscount, Charles Townshend (1674–1738): Secretary of State 1714–16; Lord President of the Council 1720; Secretary of State 1721; Whig statesman who directed foreign policy between 1721 and 1730. His conflict with Stanhope (*q.v.*) over pro-French policy led to Townshend's dismissal in 1716, and formation with Walpole of effective opposition movement within Whig Party; reconciled 1720; resigned 1730 because Walpole prevented aggressive policy towards Austria; his nickname 'Turnip Townshend' resulted from the crop rotation system he devised.

**Townshend** Charles (1725–67): Lord of the Admiralty 1754; Secretary for War 1761–62; President of Board of Trade 1763; Chancellor of the Exchequer and Leader of the House of Commons 1766–67. His fiscal policies, notably the Townshend duties on certain goods imported from America, contributed to revolt of American colonists in 1776.

**Walpole** Sir Robert, 1st Earl of Orford (1676–1745): MP for Castle Rising 1700–1 and for King's Lynn 1702–12, 1713–42. In 1701 he served on the Committee for Privileges and Elections and in 1705 he became a member of the council to Prince George of Denmark. He was Secretary at War 1708–11 and Paymaster of the Forces 1714–17. In 1714 he became a privy councillor and in 1715 was charged with the conduct of Bolingbroke's (*q.v.*) impeachment. He was appointed First Lord of the Treasury and Chancellor of the Exchequer by Townshend (*q.v.*) in 1715, but resigned in 1717 when Townshend was dismissed from the lord lieutenancy of Ireland. In 1720 he became Paymaster of the Forces again and in 1721 again became First Lord of the Treasury and Chancellor of the Exchequer. In 1725 he was awarded the Order of the Bath, and in 1726 was made a Knight of the Garter. He was reappointed to his offices by George II in 1727. He resigned in 1742 and was created Earl of Orford. Walpole is usually considered to be the first Prime Minister, being left with a clearly dominant position in the government when Townshend resigned in 1730. He was able to establish a disciplined control over office-holders and parliamentary groups which had not previously been achieved, and transferred the centre of power from the House of Lords to the Commons.

**Webb** Beatrice (*née* Potter) (1858–1943). *See* Webb, Sidney.

**Webb** Sidney James, 1st Baron Passfield (1859–1947): with his wife Beatrice, a pioneer of British social and economic reform; they were joint authors of numerous influential works on labour history, including *The History of Trade Unionism* (1894) and *Industrial Democracy* (1897), and were founders of the London School of Economics and of the *New Statesman*. Sidney Webb helped in reorganization of University of London and provision of public education legislation, and held various offices: MP for Seaham 1922–29; President of Board of Trade 1924; Secretary of State for Dominion Affairs 1929–30 and for Colonies 1930–31. Elevated to peerage as 1st Baron Passfield 1929.

**Wellington** 1st Duke of, Arthur Wellesley (1769–1852): Military leader and politician. Wellesley was MP for Trim 1790–95; Rye 1806; Mitchel in 1807; Newport 1807–9. In 1812 he was created Earl Wellington and then Marquess. In 1814 he was created Duke of Wellington. Between 1807 and 1809 he acted as Chief Secretary for Ireland. He was Master-General of the Ordnance 1819–27. He was Prime Minister 1828–30 and during Nov. and Dec. 1834 was Secretary of State of all departments and Prime Minister. He served as Foreign Secretary 1834–35 and Minister without Portfolio 1841–46. After rising to pre-eminence as a military leader during the Napoleonic Wars, culminating in his victory at Waterloo in 1815, Wellington found it difficult to adapt to the necessities of compromise and expediency concomitant on political life. He viewed his premiership simply as fulfilling the duty of carrying on the King's government and was on uneasy terms with many of his Cabinet. His reluctance to countenance franchise reform led to the break-up of his government in 1830.

**Wesley** John (1703–91): Central figure in the rise of Methodism. A fellow and tutor at Lincoln College, Oxford, he founded the 'Methodist' Society in 1729 for stricter religious observance and undertook missionary work in America. In 1738 he underwent a personal 'conversion' and began to devote himself to evangelistic work in England. He formed a 'United Society' for weekday meetings in 1739 and founded chapels in Bristol and London. The conference of lay preachers held in 1744 later became an annual event. Though pressures for separation built up between Methodists and Anglicans, Wesley maintained his desire to remain an Anglican. The conferring of orders in 1784 and the increasing organization of 'circuits' and classes made separation virtually certain by the time of his death.

**Whitefield** George (1714–70): Methodist evangelist; came under influence of Wesley (*q.v.*) while at Oxford and accompanied him on mission to America where he founded orphanage in Georgia; began publication of *Journal* 1739; obtained patronage of Countess of Huntingdon and opened Tabernacle in Tottenham Court Road. A rigid theologian, his oratory was influential in awakening eighteenth-century religious consciousness.

**Wilberforce** William (1759–1833): MP for Hull 1780–84; Yorkshire 1784–1812; Bramber 1812–25. A famous advocate of the abolition of the slave trade, he introduced a Bill to this end into the House of Commons in 1791; the legislation eventually passed in 1804 and became law in 1807; he later supported total abolition of slavery. A Pittite and an evangelical Christian, he was associated with the Clapham Sect (*q.v.*).

**Wilkes** John (1727–97): MP for Aylesbury 1757–64; Middlesex 1768–69 and 1774–90. The slogan of 'Wilkes and Liberty' became the battle-cry of popular radicalism in the 1760s, after Wilkes was arrested in 1763 for an alleged libel on the King in issue no. 45 of the *North Briton*. Elected for Middlesex in 1768, he was not allowed to take his seat, although re-elected three times in succession. His supporters founded the Bill of Rights Society in 1769 to support his cause and he was elected without opposition for Middlesex in 1774. He spoke in favour of reform in 1776, but thereafter concentrated on London politics.

**Wilmington** 1st Earl of, Spencer Compton (1673–1743): Tory MP for Eye 1698–1710. In 1705 he became Whig chairman of the Committee of Privileges and Elections. He lost his seat in 1710, but in 1713 was elected for East Grinstead. He was MP for Sussex from 1715 until 1728 when he was created Baron Wilmington. In 1707 he was appointed Treasurer and Receiver to George, Prince of Denmark, and Paymaster of the Queen's Pensioners. In 1709 he was on the committee which drew up the impeachment of Sacheverell. He served as Speaker in 1715 and became a privy councillor in 1716. He was Paymaster-General 1722–30. In 1730 he became Lord Privy Seal and the same year was created Earl of Wilmington. He also became Lord President of the Council. From 1741 to 1743 he was First Lord of the Treasury, but with Carteret and Newcastle in the offices of Secretaries of State was Prime Minister in a nominal sense only.

**Wilson** Sir (James) Harold, Baron Wilson of Rievaulx (1916–95): Labour politician. Wilson was director of economics and statistics at the Ministry of Fuel and Power 1943–44. He was Labour MP for Ormskirk 1945–50, and for Huyton from 1950. He served as Parliamentary Secretary to the Ministry of Works 1945–47; Secretary of Overseas Trade 1947; President of the Board of Trade 1947–51. In 1951 he resigned in protest at the government's decision to impose National Health prescription charges. In 1963 he was elected leader of the Labour Party. He was Prime Minister 1964–70 and 1974–76, when he resigned office. In 1976 he was appointed a Knight of the Garter. Perhaps Wilson's greatest achievement was in keeping an inexperienced government in power with a precarious majority from 1964 to 1966, and in steering a minority government through the months from Feb. to Oct. 1974. Wilson led the Labour Party to office in four out of five consecutive elections and became the longest-serving peacetime prime minister this century until overtaken by Margaret Thatcher (*q.v.*). He was a controversial figure whose governments were criticized on the Left for failing to carry out socialist policies, including bitter criticism over his support for the Americans in Vietnam and the retention of nuclear weapons, and, more generally, for failing to tackle fundamental problems in the economy and the trade unions. These perceived failures of the 'Wilson years' have often overshadowed their substantial social advances.

**Wolfe** James (1727–59): Military leader. Wolfe joined the Marines in 1741, but transferred to the 12th Foot in 1742. He fought at Dettingen in 1743, against the Jacobites at Falkirk and Culloden 1745–46, and was wounded at Lauffeld in 1747. In 1758 he served under Amherst in the expedition which captured Louisburg, and this led Pitt to give him command of the attempt against Quebec the following year. After the British force had scaled the Heights of Abraham, the French under Montcalm were drawn out of the Quebec defences. In the ensuing battle on 13 Sept. 1759 the French were defeated, but both Wolfe and Montcalm were killed.

**Wyvill** Christopher (1740–1822): Landowner and cleric who advocated parliamentary reform and religious toleration. Leader of Yorkshire Association, founded in 1779, which initiated petitioning campaign for reform; after collapse of movement, Wyvill supported the Foxite Whig attacks on the French Wars, and advocated Catholic Emancipation; also encouraged Hampden clubs (*see* Cartwright).

# SECTION SIX

*Glossary of terms*

**Adullamites**  A term used by John Bright on 13 Mar. 1866 to describe the independent attitude of Robert Lowe (Lord Sherbrooke), Horsman and their Liberal supporters who were opposed to the 1866 Reform Bill. The 'cave of Adullam' has biblical origins.

**Alliance**  The Alliance of the Liberal and Social Democratic Parties was formed in Sept. 1981 following the creation of the Social Democratic Party earlier in the year and the acceptance by both parties of the principle of an alliance at their conferences. The Alliance agreed to an equal share-out of seats for local and parliamentary elections and campaigned under a joint manifesto in both the 1983 and 1987 general elections. In addition, Alliance groups were formed on many local councils, following local election successes. At one point in 1981 the Alliance had an opinion poll rating of over 40 per cent, but obtained only 26 per cent and 24 per cent of the vote respectively in the two general elections of 1983 and 1987 in spite of an impressive string of by-election victories. Calls for a merger of the two parties immediately following the 1987 election and votes in favour of merger by the Liberals and the SDP led to the formation of the Liberal Democrat Party in 1988. A quite distinct Alliance Party has existed in Northern Ireland since 1970.

*Ancien régime*  (Fr. for 'old order'). Describes the structure of government prevailing in Europe prior to the French Revolution of 1789. Its use is sometimes extended in Britain to include the period up to the 1832 Reform Act to emphasize the aristocratic and hierarchical character of the unreformed system. *See also* Confessional state.

**Anglo-Catholic**  *See* High Church.

**Appeasement**  Foreign policy seeking to avert war by making concessions, typified by attempts of British and French governments between 1936 and 1939 to propitiate Germany. The Chamberlain government acquiesced in Hitler's violation of Rhineland demilitarization in 1936, the *Anschluss* of 1938 and the acquisition of Czech Sudetenland in Sept. 1938.

**Aristocracy of labour**  Collective term for members of skilled trades whose earnings and superior status gave them a distinctive political stance in Victorian Britain and later, and made them often more inclined to reformist and labourist (*q.v.*) policies.

**Artisan**  Term applied to skilled craft workers, traditionally associated with independence, higher earnings, superior status and greater political involvement than the general mass of labourers.

**Asiento**  As a consequence of the Treaty of Utrecht 1713, the Spanish government granted *Asiento*, or a contract to ship African slaves to America to the English South Sea Company, which was authorized to provide 4,800 slaves per annum for 30 years.

**Balance of power**  Doctrine of maintaining a European system in which no single power was dominant. Britain was traditionally concerned to support coalitions opposing one power gaining hegemony over Europe.

**Bevanite**  Follower of Aneurin Bevan (*q.v.*), who led left-wing group of Labour Party from 1951 to 1956–57. Particularly critical of high defence expenditure, especially on nuclear arms. Opposed proposals for dropping commitment to nationalization (revisionism) advocated by Gaitskellites (*q.v.*) and appealed for more all-embracing doctrines of socialism.

**Blackshirts**  Members of British Union of Fascists, founded by Sir Oswald Mosley in 1932, and wearing black shirts and uniforms on the Italian fascist model. The Public Order Act of 1936 banned the wearing of uniforms in public.

**Blanketeers**  Lancashire textile workers, mainly handloom weavers, who attempted to march on London in March 1817 to petition the Prince Regent and highlight distress resulting from postwar economic crises. The military arrested 200, and stopped the march.

**Blitz**  Sustained night-bombing attacks by German air force (Luftwaffe) on London and other British cities from 7 Sept. 1940 to May 1941.

**Blitzkrieg**  Literally 'lightning war'. Term originally applied to technique of attack perfected by German generals in France in 1940. The essential elements were speed and surprise of attack, resulting in shock and disorganization among enemy forces.

**Boers**  Literally 'farmers' (Afrikaans). Descendants of Dutch settlers in South Africa. Two wars fought between British and Boers in 1881 and 1899–1902 known as First and Second Boer Wars.

**Bourgeoisie** Marxist term for the middle and upper classes who own and profit from capital; the class who will destroy feudalism, but themselves be displaced by the proletariat (*q.v.*).

**Boxers** Young Chinese provoked in 1900 to engage in anti-foreign violence by the expansion of European commerce and territorial acquisitions in China by Germany, Russia and Britain. Major Boxer disturbances occurred in Peking and the provinces of Shensi and Manchuria.

**Boycott** Organized refusal to buy goods and services. Originated by Parnell during Irish land agitation of 1880, when peasants effectively ostracized an estate manager, Captain C. C. Boycott, to protest against land evictions.

**Butskellism** Term which refers to a broad consensus between the two major parties in the years after 1945 on progressive social policies and the maintenance of a mixed economy with both public and private sectors. The word is a conflation of the names of R. A. Butler, author of the 1944 Education Act and Conservative Chancellor of the Exchequer from 1951 to 1956, and Hugh Gaitskell (*q.v.*), Labour Chancellor of the Exchequer from 1950 to 1951 and later leader of the Labour Party.

**Catholic Emancipation (or Relief)** Issue of freeing Catholics from disabilities which prevented them holding offices, voting and serving in Parliament. Not finally secured until 1829.

**Chartist** One who advocated fulfilment of People's Charter of 1838, cardinal aims of which were universal male suffrage, annual parliaments, vote by ballot, payment for MPs, equal electoral districts, and abolition of property qualifications for MPs. From 1839 to 1848 the Chartists engaged in petitioning Parliament and demonstrations. The entire phase of activity is referred to as Chartism.

**Chequers** Official country residence of British prime ministers. The property was acquired by Viscount Lee of Fareham in 1909, and in 1917 he made provision for it to become a weekend retreat for the prime minister. Lloyd George was the first to occupy it in 1921.

**Chiltern Hundreds** Ancient royal sinecure office. Members of Parliament are disbarred from holding it as it is technically an 'office of profit' under the Crown. Used as a device to circumvent MPs' inability to resign from the House of Commons. An MP wishing to vacate a seat asks for Chiltern Hundreds, and once the appointment is notified, the seat automatically becomes vacant.

**Clapham Sect** Formed from leading evangelicals (*q.v.*) within the Church of England, who lived in the village of Clapham in South London. Believing in personal salvation through good works, they campaigned on behalf of the abolition of the slave trade and were involved in a number of humanitarian causes, including Sunday schools, penal reform and promoting a high standard of public morality. Leading members included William Wilberforce (1759–1833), Hannah More (1743–1833), Henry Thornton (1760–1815), James Stephen (1758–1832), and Zachery Macaulay (1768–1838).

**Clause IV** The clause in the 1918 Labour Party constitution which embodied the party's objective to 'secure for the workers by hand or by brain the full fruits of their industry and the most equitable distribution thereof that may be possible upon the basis of the common ownership of the means of production, distribution, and exchange, and the best obtainable system of popular administration and control of each industry or service'. The clause became the touchstone of Labour's socialist credentials, Labour leader Hugh Gaitskell (*q.v.*) coming into conflict with the Left by attempting to remove it, though it was effectively abandoned by Neil Kinnock (*q.v.*). His successor, Tony Blair (*q.v.*), obtained party approval in 1995 for its effective watering down as part of the 'New Labour' drive.

**Clydesiders** Militant trade union and socialist group led by shop stewards in the engineering industry around Glasgow during and after the First World War. Formed a Clyde Workers' Committee to campaign against dilution (*q.v.*) and organized series of strikes and demonstrations in 1915–19. *See also* Dilution, 'Red' Clydeside, and Shop stewards' movement.

**CND** Campaign for Nuclear Disarmament. Movement launched in Feb. 1958 by Bertrand Russell and Canon Collins to abandon nuclear weapons and reduce British defence spending. At its peak in 1960–61, it had more active supporters than any mass movement in Britain since the Anti-Corn Law League. *See also* Unilateralism.

**Collectivism**  Name applied to policies or philosophy of the pursuit of the common good and social equality, even at the expense of limiting individual liberty or traditional privilege. Usually associated with welfare legislation and government intervention of the twentieth century.

**Community charge**  Also known as the poll tax, local government taxation introduced to replace rates in Scotland on 1 Apr. 1989 and in England and Wales on 1 Apr. 1990. The charge caused widespread protests, largely because it was levied on individuals and took little account of ability to pay, and refusal to pay. In 1991 the Conservative government announced the tax's abandonment, replacing it with the council tax in 1993.

**Condition of England question**  Phrase used to describe concern for social conditions in the manufacturing districts in the 1830s and 1840s and fears of social unrest, reflected in the novels of Charles Dickens, Mrs Gaskell and Benjamin Disraeli and major parliamentary enquiries into social problems such as child and female labour.

**Confessional state**  Phrase used to describe Britain in the period prior to 1832 when support for the Anglican Church and opposition to Catholic Emancipation (*q.v.*) and full toleration for Dissenters are seen as the ideological foundations of an English *ancien régime* (*q.v.*). Largely developed in Professor J.C.D. Clark's *English Society, 1688–1832* (1985), it elevates the ideological character of pre-1832 politics over more Namierite (*q.v.*) views.

**Corn Laws**  Used to describe Corn Law of 1815, which prevented the import of foreign grain until the domestic price reached 80*s.* per quarter, and its successor of 1828 which introduced a sliding scale of tariffs.

**Country gentlemen**  *See* Independents.

**County movement**  Late eighteenth-century movement for moderate parliamentary reform led by prominent country gentlemen such as Christopher Wyvill (*q.v.*). Led to formation of Yorkshire Association in 1779 and petitioning movement for reform. *See also* Economical reform.

**Court and Treasury Party**  Group of office-holders or placemen who could generally be relied upon to support an eighteenth-century administration. Perhaps numbering as many as 100–120 MPs by 1760, their numbers were reduced by economical reform (*q.v.*) and administrative reorganization from the 1780s onwards.

**Devaluation** Reduction in the value of a country's currency relative to that of others, aiming to relieve pressure on the exchange rate and cheapen exports. Britain has devalued the pound twice since 1945, in 1949 and 1967, both under Labour governments, and again in 1992 on 'Black Wednesday' when the pound was effectively forced out of the European Monetary System or EMS (*q.v.*) and allowed to decline substantially in value.

**Devolution** Decentralization of political power to a region, usually in the case of Britain referring to Scotland and Wales, although Northern Ireland enjoyed devolved powers through Stormont (*q.v.*) between 1921 and 1972. In 1979 pressure for devolution to Scotland and Wales led to a referendum, in which only 32.85 per cent in Scotland voted for devolution and only 11.9 per cent in Wales. The issue has revived, however, and Scottish devolution remains a commitment of both the Labour Party and the Liberal Democrats. The latter retain it within a policy of devolved local government throughout Britain.

**Dilution** Use of unapprenticed labour, especially women, to do skilled work previously reserved to craftsmen. It was used to increase munitions production in the First World War and was the subject of agreements between government and unions, but continued to cause strikes and unrest in some areas, such as Clydeside. *See also* Clydesiders and Shop stewards' movement.

**Disestablishment** Process of separation of church and state, implying end of state support for the Anglican Church and of any attempt by the state to enforce religious duties or discriminate in its favour. Usually adopted in relation to the moves to disestablish the Anglican Church in Ireland, completed in 1871, and later moves to disestablish the Anglican Church in Wales, passed in 1914 and coming into effect after the First World War.

**Dreadnought** An 'all-big-gun' battleship class deriving its name from HMS *Dreadnought*, launched in Feb. 1906. It represented a revolution in naval shipbuilding, and inaugurated naval armaments race.

**'Dries'**  *See* 'Wets'.

**Durbar**  Hindustani word signifying ceremonial court of audience. Used to refer to formal assemblies such as that on the occasion of Queen Victoria's proclamation as Empress of India (1876), and the famous Delhi Durbar of Dec. 1911 when King George V announced restitution of Bengal as united province.

**Eastern Question**  Nineteenth-century term, reflecting concern about the future of the Balkan territories belonging to the declining Ottoman Empire. Britain was fearful of the expansion of Russian influence over the Balkans, Constantinople, the Dardanelles and the eastern Mediterranean and the consequent threat to the route to India. Britain often supported Turkey against Russian 'aggression' and sought arbitration of the disputes in the area.

**Economical reform**  Late eighteenth-century movement led by Edmund Burke (*q.v.*), among others, aiming to reduce the number of sinecurists and placeholders in Parliament. Economical reform legislation was passed in 1782. *See also* County movement and Christopher Wyvill.

**Eire**  Name by which Southern Ireland (now Republic of Ireland) was known from 1937 to 1948 when it was a Dominion within the British Commonwealth.

**Emancipation**  *See* Catholic Emancipation.

***Entente Cordiale***  French: 'cordial understanding'. Description of relationship between Britain and France following Anglo-French *entente* reached in 1904, and continuing in spite of foreign policy differences until 1940.

**European Monetary System (EMS)**  Attempt to stabilize European currencies developed from 1979 by which members of the European Union coordinate exchange rates through the Exchange Rate Mechanism. Rates are fixed in relation to the European Currency Unit at regular meetings of finance ministers. Between meetings members support the agreed value of each other's currencies by drawing from the European Monetary Cooperation Fund. All EU members were to have entered the EMS by 1992. Britain joined in Oct. 1990 but left 'temporarily' following 'Black Wednesday' (*q.v.*) in Sept. 1992, with apparently beneficial results for its economy.

**Eurosceptic**  Term for opponents to greater European unity via the European Union (former EEC and European Community) brought to a head in Conservative Party debates in the 1990s over the Maastricht Treaty (*q.v.*).

**Evangelicals**  Group within Church of England who in the late eighteenth century sought to combat clerical apathy, while accepting Anglican discipline. Emphasized importance of moral earnestness and proclaimed salvation by faith. They gave rise to important philanthropic movements in the nineteenth century. *See also* Clapham Sect.

**Fabian**  Follower of a largely middle-class group established in Jan. 1884 to spread socialist ideas in Britain. Early Fabians included Bernard Shaw and Sidney and Beatrice Webb. The society played an important role in founding the Labour Party, and subsequently acted as a research body attached to it. As a term, it came to be applied to a supporter of gradual social reform.

**Famine, the**  *See* Potato famine.

**Fellow-traveller**  Term used, usually in derogatory fashion, to describe one who accepts much of communism, but is not or denies being a member of the Communist Party. Sometimes used by politicians to describe left-wingers generally.

**Fenian**  Supporters of an Irish revolutionary movement which was formed in the USA in 1858 and spread to Ireland in 1865. Fenian disturbances in Chester (Feb. 1867) and bomb attacks on Clerkenwell prison and other places helped make Gladstone (*q.v.*) aware of the urgency of the Irish problem.

**'Financial Revolution'**  Development of credit instruments, notably the Bank of England (from 1694), and effectively perpetual loans, the National Debt (from 1698) during the wars of William III and Queen Anne (1693–1713), which established the basis for government borrowing in the eighteenth century and the 'fiscal-military' state. Also encompasses the development of the Land Tax and the development of excise taxes, including the Window Tax (from 1696).

**'Fiscal-military' state**   Term used in John Brewer's *The Sinews of Power* (1989) to describe eighteenth-century Britain and the very effective tax and credit-raising instruments which allowed it to maintain a succession of wars against France in the eighteenth century and to emerge as a world power after 1815. *See also* 'Financial revolution'.

**Force, physical and moral**   Phrases used in the nineteenth century to describe methods of popular agitation; moral force denoting peaceful agitation, physical the resort to arms.

**Free Trade**   *See Laissez-faire.*

**Gaitskellite**   Supporter of Hugh Gaitskell's social democratic view of Labour Party principles. As Chancellor of the Exchequer (Oct. 1950) Gaitskell and followers clashed with Bevanites (*q.v.*) on introduction of Health Service charges to finance rearmament programme. Believed in need for nuclear weapons and for reforming the Labour Party constitution, removing commitment to nationalization.

**'Gang of Four'**   Roy Jenkins, David Owen, William Rodgers and Shirley Williams, the founders of the Social Democratic Party in 1981.

**General Unions**   Phase of trade union activity in the 1830s marked by attempts to achieve a 'General Union of Trades', under the influence of the ideas of Robert Owen (*q.v.*) and the leader of the Lancashire cotton-spinners, John Doherty. Early attempts in 1810, 1818 and 1829 culminated with the formation of the Grand National Consolidated Trades' Union of Great Britain and Ireland in Feb. 1834. Achieving a maximum of 50,000 members drawn mainly from London and Lancashire, the scheme collapsed after a series of strikes in spring and summer 1834.

**'Gentlemanly capitalism'**   Phrase used to describe the predominance of financial and commercial interests over industrial in nineteenth- and twentieth-century British economic activity both at home and overseas.

**Gold Standard**   Currency system in which all money is convertible into gold on demand. The system was general in Europe and the USA before 1914 and involved keeping a gold reserve large enough to meet all likely demands to back the issue of notes. Britain went off the Standard, in effect, during the First World War but returned to it in

1925, although at a level which overvalued sterling and proved insupportable during the period of the Great Crash in 1929–31. British politicians and financiers regarded the maintenance of the Gold Standard as essential to Britain's national prestige and place as a centre of international finance, placing serious restraints upon the economic policies they could pursue in the face of the Depression. Defence of the Gold Standard led indirectly to the fall of the Labour government in Aug. 1931, but the succeeding National Government was forced finally to abandon it in Sept. 1931. Although direct convertibility with gold has been abandoned, the level of gold reserves still has a part to play in underpinning international credit arrangements and individual currencies.

**Great Depression**  Phrase applied to the period of low agricultural prices, slower industrial growth and cyclical economic depressions in the late nineteenth century, contrasting with the rapid and almost continuous expansion of the mid-Victorian period. Some historians doubt the validity of the term for a period which continued to show overall growth in the economy.

**Gunboat diplomacy**  Conduct of foreign policy by use of naval power, usually associated with Palmerston's (*q.v.*) time as Foreign Secretary.

**Hansard**  Colloquial term for official report of debates in Houses of Parliament. From 1812 Hansard family published parliamentary debates, and even after the family sold the undertaking it continued to be known as Hansard.

**Hard Left**  *See* Soft Left.

**High Church**  Section within the Church of England upholding belief in sacraments and ritual, the authority of the church hierarchy, and the close relationship between church and state. In the seventeenth and early eighteenth centuries associated with political support for the monarch as head of church and state, and later with opposition to the removal of civil disabilities on Dissenters and Roman Catholics and to disestablishment (*q.v.*). In the nineteenth century, the 'Anglo-Catholic' movement represented High Churchmen nearest to Roman Catholic doctrine and liturgy.

**High Farming**  Period of great agricultural prosperity in the interval between the repeal of the Corn Laws and the flood of cheap agricultural produce from abroad which began in the 1870s, characterized by heavy investment in new techniques, including the large-scale application of machinery.

**High Politics School** View of politics which places emphasis upon the relationships between the top politicians as the crucial determinants of policy-making and action.

**Holland House** Holland House in Kensington, London, became a fashionable *salon* during the early nineteenth century, patronized by leading Whig politicians, as well as writers, painters and actors. Hence, sometimes used as a term to describe Whig opinion generally.

**Home Rule** Policy of granting partial self-government to Ireland, including the re-creation of an Irish parliament. Home Rule Bills were introduced in 1886, 1893 and 1914.

**Hunger marches** During the depression of the inter-war years, groups of unemployed men were organized by the communist-run National Unemployed Workers' Movement to march on London and provincial centres to protest about unemployment. Major marches occurred in 1922, 1929, 1930, 1932, 1934 and 1936. However, the most famous of the hunger marches was the 'Jarrow Crusade' when the town council of the shipbuilding town of Jarrow organized a march of 200 unemployed men to London led by the local MP, Ellen Wilkinson, to seek aid for the town in 1936.

**Hungry Forties** The 1840s, so described not only because of famine in Ireland, 1845–49, but because of depression and unemployment in Britain which provoked widespread discontent, including the Chartist and Anti-Corn Law movements. Widespread concern with the 'Condition of England' question (*q.v.*) was reflected in contemporary literature.

**Hustings** Booths where voting took place at parliamentary elections, or platforms from which candidates spoke. Synonymous with election-eering and political campaigns.

**Independents** Backbench MPs not directly dependent upon the administration or opposition. Regarded as the 'floating vote' in the eighteenth- and nineteenth-century House of Commons before party discipline became more effective. Variously estimated at no more than 80 members (L. Namier) and up to 300–350 (J. Owen), the independents could usually be counted upon to support an administration unless its credibility was seriously undermined by the opposition.

**Jacobins** Radical faction of the French revolutionaries of 1789 led by Robespierre. In Britain, a derogatory term applied by loyalists to French sympathizers and reformers in general. Used by historians to denote British radicals with similar aims and ideology to their French counterparts.

**Jacobites** Supporters of hereditary succession of House of Stuart following dethronement of James II in 1689. Jacobite risings took place after the death of Queen Anne in 1715, and again in 1745–46. Sympathy was strongest in the Scottish Highlands, but many Tories supported the Jacobite cause in England. It was crushed as a political force after 1746.

**Jingoism** Chauvinistic patriotism. Derives from music-hall song of 1878 threatening Russia; a spirit prominent during the Boer and First World Wars.

**King's Friends** *See* Court and Treasury Party.

**Labourism** Phase of working-class activity after 1850 characterized by pursuit of limited objectives of wage bargaining and strengthening trade union organization. More generally, a phrase used to characterize the more cautious traditions of the Labour movement.

*Laissez-faire* Doctrine of non-interference of state in economic affairs derived from teachings of classical political economists like Adam Smith, Malthus and Ricardo, and from Benthamite tradition (*see* Utilitarians). It was a fundamental tenet of British liberalism for most of the nineteenth century.

**Leicester House** *See* Reversionary interest.

**Liberal Toryism** Reforming Toryism associated with the later years of Lord Liverpool's (*q.v.*) administration and his leading ministers, Canning, Peel and Huskisson (*qq.v.*).

**Lib–Lab**  Prior to formation of Labour Party, trade unionists and working men looked to Liberals to support their interests and a number of trade union MPs were known by this label.

**Lib–Lab Pact**  Period of cooperation between the Liberal and Labour Parties to keep James Callaghan's Labour government in office. By Jan. 1977 Labour's parliamentary majority had fallen to one. In Mar. the Conservatives threatened a 'no confidence' motion. Labour was guaranteed support in the House of Commons in return for allowing the Liberals to veto proposed legislation before it went to Cabinet. The Liberals withdrew from the pact in the autumn of 1978.

**Loyalist**  A member of the majority Protestant community who wishes Northern Ireland to remain part of the United Kingdom rather than become part of a united Ireland or become a separate independent state.

**Luddism**  Phase of widespread machine-breaking in the North and Midland counties of England between 1811 and 1817. Machine-breaking was said to be carried out on the orders of a mythical 'Ned Ludd' or 'General Ludd'. Machine-breaking began in Nottinghamshire as part of the campaign of the framework-knitters for greater regulation of their trade and higher wages for work in a period of high prices and unemployment. Disturbances spread to Yorkshire where shearing-frames were destroyed by the wool-croppers and to Lancashire where power-looms were attacked. The main disturbances were over by the end of 1812 when some 10,000 troops were deployed in the manufacturing districts.

**Maastricht Treaty**  Signed on 10 Dec. 1991 following a summit of European leaders which set out agreements reached on the Treaty of European Union. Leading a party deeply divided on Britain's relationship with Europe, Conservative Prime Minister John Major obtained opt-out clauses on a single currency and the Social Chapter (*q.v.*) on the grounds of the defence of British national interests. The treaty was ratified by Parliament, despite a vigorous campaign for a referendum on the issue led in the House of Lords by Mr Major's predecessor, Baroness Thatcher. *See also* Eurosceptics.

**Marxist history**  Interpretation of history which follows the ideas of Karl Marx (1818–83) and Friedrich Engels (1820–95) and is implied by their writings. Although many variations of Marxist theory exist, they follow broadly the view of Marx and Engels that 'all history is the history of class struggle', giving primacy to the economic forces which mould society and determine its divisions into bourgeoisie (*q.v.*) and proletariat (*q.v.*). This 'materialist conception of history' assumes inevitable progression from feudalism, through capitalism, to communism.

**Model unionism**    *See* 'New Model' unionism.

**Monetarism**    Policy of controlling the monetary supply in order to influence the operation of the economy. In contrast to Keynesian economics, money supply targets were seen as a crucial element in managing the economy. These views gained influence in economic circles in the 1970s, partly drawing upon the work of Milton Friedman, and monetary targets were set by the International Monetary Fund for the Labour government in 1976 as a condition of granting credit facilities. The adoption of monetary targets meant that the Public Sector Borrowing Requirement and money supply measures became important economic indicators and these policies were adopted by the Thatcher government from 1979 to control inflation.

**'Moral economy'**    Term coined by E.P. Thompson to describe the sense of legitimacy and the values underlying episodes of popular protest and riot in the eighteenth century. The term has been applied more widely to describe the internal rationale for popular actions and rebellions in many other contexts.

**Multilateralism**    *See* Unilateralism.

**Namierite**    Method of analysing political action and membership of political parties which stresses the role of individuals and their interests rather than beliefs and ideologies; after Sir Lewis Namier, author of *The Structure of Politics at the Accession of George III* (1929) and other studies in eighteenth- and twentieth-century politics.

**Nationalization**    Taking into state ownership of an industry, with or without payment of compensation to previous owners. The 1945–51 Labour governments nationalized the Bank of England, coal, cables and wireless, transport, electricity, iron and steel.

**New imperialism**    Term applied to the renewed phase of imperial expansion in the latter part of the nineteenth century, to distinguish it from the eighteenth-century colonial expansion.

**New industries** Capital-intensive industries – aircraft and automobile production, chemicals, electrical engineering and generation, food processing and consumer goods – developed in Britain between the wars, usually sited in the South and Midlands rather than the traditional industrial regions.

**New Liberalism** Term applied to the philosophy and phase of progressive social reform undertaken by Liberal governments after 1908 and associated with Lloyd George and Winston Churchill, distinguished from traditional Liberalism (*see* pp. 121–8) by the greater readiness to countenance state intervention and increased government spending.

**'New Model' unionism** Phase of trade union organization in the mid-Victorian period marked by the formation of the Amalgamated Society of Engineers in 1851. It set a pattern of high fees and exclusiveness, national organization and restriction to skilled craft workers. The 'New Model' unions pursued moderate, craft interests in contrast to the more ambitious aims of the General Unions (*q.v.*) and had greater permanence than the purely local trade societies.

**New unionism** A dramatic upsurge in unionization among the unskilled in 1889–92, with a socialist-led London dock strike in the summer of 1889 at its centre. In 1890 the new unions – 'new' because unlike their predecessors they levied low dues and depended for success on aggressive tactics – were 320,000 strong, but by 1896 this had fallen to 80,000.

**'Nomination' boroughs** *See* 'Pocket' boroughs.

**North–South divide** Phrase of the 1980s which came to encapsulate growing concern about the increasing disparity between the older industrial regions of the North and the expanding sectors of the South, emphasized by the deep recession of 1981–82, the persistence of heavy unemployment in traditional manufacturing sectors, and the growth of 'high-tech' and financial employment near London. Although only crudely accurate, booming house prices and lower unemployment in southern England, especially the south-east, gave some credibility to the concept. It was widely referred to in the 1987 election campaign, often in association with the allegation of the creation of 'two nations' (*q.v.*), of rich and poor, in the South and in the North.

**Old Corruption**  Term used to describe the unreformed political and ecclesiastical system before the 1832 Reform Act and the beginning of reform in the Church of England, characterized by patronage and influence.

**'Open door' policy**  Term describing principle of equal trading opportunities for great powers in parts of Africa, as adopted by the Berlin Conference, 1884–85; a policy later used by the USA towards China.

**Orange card, playing the**  Support for Ulster Protestants by British politicians in order to preserve the Act of Union (*see* Unionist) and frustrate Home Rule (*q.v.*). Normally associated with the Conservative opposition to Home Rule for Ireland in the period 1880–1914.

**Orangemen**  Members of the Orange Order, a society formed in Ulster in 1795 to preserve Protestantism in Ireland, named after William III, former Prince of Orange. The order formed the backbone of the Unionist Party which ruled Northern Ireland from 1921 to 1972 and has offshoots in the Protestant areas of Glasgow and Liverpool.

**Oxford Movement**  Group within Church of England from the 1830s seeking to restore the High Church (*q.v.*) traditions of the seventeenth century. The movement arose out of anxiety over the implications of Catholic Emancipation (*q.v.*) and the Parliamentary Reform Act of 1832. It was led by three Fellows of Oriel College, Oxford, and led to a strong Anglo-Catholic revival. Though Keble and Pusey (*qq.v.*) remained in the Church of England, Newman (*q.v.*) became a Roman Catholic.

**Parnellites**  Followers of Charles Stewart Parnell (*q.v.*), the Irish politician who launched a campaign to secure Home Rule for Ireland. Parnell lost influence in 1890s following his involvement in a divorce case.

***Pax Britannica***  Period of Britain's maritime and diplomatic supremacy (and hence 'peace') in the nineteenth century, associated particularly with Palmerston's (*q.v.*) periods as Foreign Secretary.

**Peelite** Policies associated with Sir Robert Peel (*q.v.*) of sound, efficient government dominated by concern for national rather than party interests.

**Permissive society** A loosening of the reins of cultural, political and moral authority in Britain during the 1960s marked legislatively by the Labour government's encouragement of reform in the areas of abortion, divorce, homosexuality and the ending of theatre censorship.

**Peterloo 'Massacre'** Name for the break-up of a peaceful reform demonstration in St Peter's Fields, Manchester, on 16 Aug. 1819, when the local magistrates sent in troops to arrest the radical orator, Henry Hunt (*q.v.*). Eleven people were killed and over 400 injured. 'Peterloo' was a pun on Waterloo.

**'Pocket' boroughs** Boroughs directly controlled by a patron, sometimes the government, who could dominate representation and 'nominate' its MPs. *See also* 'Rotten' boroughs.

**'Polite society'** Term associated with the shift towards greater sensibility and self-consciousness in the eighteenth century reflected in literature and manners, as in Dr P. Langford's *A Polite and Commercial People* (1989).

**Poll tax.** *See* Community charge.

**Poplarism** Support for local control over welfare payments and for fairer distribution of resources to poor areas. The term derives from the struggles of the borough of Poplar, London, led by George Lansbury (*q.v.*) to maintain higher benefits for the unemployed than were allowed by the economy measures of governments in the 1920s. Similar conflicts were exposed in the early 1930s over the operation of the 'Means Test' and in the 1970s against the imposition of higher council house rents by the Conservative government of 1970–74.

**Potato famine** In 1845 and 1846 three-quarters of the Irish potato crop, the staple diet of the four million population, was destroyed by blight. The disaster was compounded by a European corn harvest failure and British maladministration, causing a million deaths from starvation and the enforced migration of a further million people.

**Potwalloper** Franchise qualification prior to Reform Act of 1832. In

---

some boroughs, every man who had a family and boiled a pot there qualified for the franchise, if resident for six months, and not in receipt of poor rates. Such voters were considered susceptible to bribery and instructions from borough patrons.

**Powellite** Advocate of coloured repatriation and ending of Commonwealth immigration, as suggested by Enoch Powell (*q.v.*).

**Pretender, Old** James Edward Stuart (1688–1766), son of dethroned King James II. Known as 'Old Pretender' to throne of England and backed by Jacobite (*q.v.*) support in Britain. Unsuccessful in attempt to prevent succession of Elector of Hanover in 1714 and in rising of following year.

**Pretender, Young** Charles Edward Stuart, known as 'Bonny Prince Charlie'. Son of James Edward Stuart, led rising in Scotland in 1745–46; aimed to place his father on the throne. Defeat at battle of Culloden in 1746 effectively ended danger of Stuart restoration.

**Privatization** Broadly defined as the policy of limiting the role of the state and extending the operation of market forces associated with the Thatcher governments since 1979, but more narrowly associated with the sale of shares in publicly owned or partly owned corporations. The Conservative administration elected in 1979 was publicly committed to changing the boundary between public and private sectors seen as traditional since 1945. It encouraged the contracting out to private firms and the offering to competitive tender of work previously undertaken by public bodies, such as municipal cleansing and hospital cleansing, and relaxed monopoly control in such areas as buses, telecommunications and broadcasting. The government also sold all or part of its share in a number of public enterprises, including telephones, gas, steel, electricity and water.

**Profumo Affair** Political scandal involving Conservative War Minister John Profumo (b. 1915). He denied having had an affair with Christine Keeler (b. 1942), a prostitute who was also involved with the Soviet naval attaché. The revelation that he was lying forced his resignation on 4 June 1963. The Denning Report claimed that national security had not been put in jeopardy by the affair. The scandal, which coincided with a growing popularity of political satire, undermined an already unpopular government in a pre-election year.

**Proletariat** Economic and social class of industrial workers deriving income solely from sale of labour power. Identified by Marxist analysis as group which would become conscious of class difference from bourgeoisie, and would organize to promote communist revolution.

**Protestant ascendancy** Term for the political and religious dominance by the Protestant minority in Ireland from the seventeenth to the nineteenth centuries.

**Puseyite** Follower of Edward Pusey (*q.v.*), English theologian and leader of Oxford Movement (*q.v.*). In 1865 Pusey declared his belief in possibility of union of Church of England and Church of Rome.

**Radical** First used to describe the supporters of universal suffrage, annual parliaments and secret ballot. Major Cartwright contrasted 'radical' and 'moderate' parliamentary reform as early as 1776 in *Take Your Choice*, and in 1792 the London Corresponding Society promulgated a 'Plan of Radical Reform'. Proposals for 'radical' reform were taken up by MPs such as Sir Francis Burdett (*q.v.*) and popular writers and speakers such as William Cobbett and Henry Hunt (*qq.v.*). The campaign for 'radical' reform continued after 1832 in the Chartist movement. In the later nineteenth century the term became associated more broadly with sweeping social and economic reform.

**Raj** Literally 'rule' or 'sovereignty'. Refers to period of British rule in India.

**'Red' Clydeside** Period of strikes and socialist unrest in the Glasgow area from 1915 to 1919. Strikes organized by the Clyde Workers' Committee against dilution (*q.v.*) in 1915–16 led to arrests and suppression of left-wing journals by government. Attempts to form a Workers' and Soldiers' 'Soviet' in 1918 prohibited by government. Forty Hours' strike in Jan.–Feb. 1919 led to disturbances and the placing of troops and tanks in the streets. *See also* Shop stewards' movement and Clydesiders.

**Referendum** Reference of political issue to electorate for direct decision by popular vote. Unknown in Great Britain until 1973 when used in Northern Ireland, followed in 1975 by a referendum which endorsed membership of the EEC (European Economic Community), and two in 1979 which rejected devolution of government in Scotland and Wales.

**Reversionary interest**  Name given to politicians who clustered about the Prince of Wales in the eighteenth and early nineteenth centuries. In 1718 the Prince of Wales (later George II) bought Leicester House in London, hence sometimes called the Leicester House interest.

**'Robinocracy'**  Collective name for supporters of Sir Robert Walpole (*q.v.*).

**'Rotten' boroughs**  Boroughs where, prior to the 1832 Reform Act, the electorate had shrunk almost to nothing. Among the most notorious were Gatton and Old Sarum. They were a source of political influence for borough owners. *See also* 'Pocket' boroughs.

**Scot and Lot**  Franchise based on ability to pay poor rate; paying rates was deemed to be equivalent of being obliged in the Middle Ages to pay Scot and bear Lot.

**Shop stewards' movement**  Term for the growth of shop-floor trade union organization, particularly in the engineering industry, before, during and after the First World War. Committees of shop stewards were active in opposition to dilution (*q.v.*) and on the Clyde Workers' Committee. *See* 'Red' Clydeside.

**Six Acts**  Repressive legislation passed by Lord Sidmouth (*q.v.*) in 1819 in the aftermath of Peterloo (*q.v.*), prohibiting meetings of more than 50 people, preventing military drilling, increasing newspaper duties, permitting magistrates to search for arms and seditious writings, and to speed up judicial proceedings.

**Six Counties**  The counties of Northern Ireland – Antrim, Armagh, Down, Fermanagh, Londonderry and Tyrone – which remained part of the United Kingdom after the Treaty of London in 1921. They were formerly part of the nine-county province of Ulster with Cavan, Donegal and Monaghan.

**Social Chapter**  Section of the Treaty of European Union rejected by the Thatcher and Major governments. The seven Articles of the Chapter include: the improvement of living standards within the context of economic competitiveness; encouragement of health and safety at work, equality for women and consultation of workers by employers; promotion of management–worker consultation by the

European Commission; contractual relations between management and workers; European coordination of social policy; equal pay for men and women; regular reporting by the European Commission on the Chapter's progress. *See also* Maastricht Treaty.

**Soft Left**  Term used in contrast to 'Hard Left' to describe ideological and policy positions within the Labour Party since the 1970s. Hard Left referred to the uncompromising, neo-Marxist wing of the party, supporting nationalization of major companies and banks, unilateralism and withdrawal from NATO, and much closer links with the trade union movement. Soft Left was a broader grouping, sharing some policies with the Hard Left, notably unilateralism, but accepting compromise on a wide range of other issues. Mr Kinnock's leadership was widely accepted as being supported by 'Soft Left' groupings within the party.

**South Sea Bubble**  Rapid rise and slump in the value of shares in the South Sea Company in 1720. The Company was floated in 1711 to trade with South America and in 1720 Parliament accepted its offer to assume responsibility for part of the National Debt, leading to a high speculative rise in its shares. Their collapse left many bankrupt and several ministers were implicated in encouraging the speculation. Robert Walpole's (*q.v.*) management of the crisis as Paymaster-General added greatly to his reputation as a financial minister and materially assisted his rise to First Lord of the Treasury the following year, as well as disgracing several rivals, notably Stanhope (*q.v.*). A 'Bubble Act' passed in 1720 regulated the formation and activities of joint-stock companies.

**Speenhamland system**  Method of outdoor relief (i.e. given to people who remained outside the workhouse) announced by the Berkshire JPs at Speenhamland in Berkshire in May 1795 by which parochial rates were used to supplement wages on a sliding scale according to the price of bread.

**Splendid isolation**  Phrase used to describe period of British foreign policy prior to entering the system of alliances in 1902 when a treaty was concluded with Japan.

**Standard-of-living debate**  Debate over the course of living standards during the Industrial Revolution between 'optimists' who see a general real rise in living standards and the 'pessimists' who see a fall. Main protagonists include J. H. Clapham, T. S. Ashton and R. M. Hartwell ('optimists'), and J. L. and B. Hammond, E. Hobsbawm and E. P. Thompson ('pessimists').

**Storming the closet** Eighteenth-century term for seizure of major positions in government by winning the support of the monarch and forcing expulsion of existing administration.

**Stormont** The building in Belfast which housed the Northern Ireland parliament until 1972, when direct rule from London was imposed. Since then, it has been the location of the Northern Ireland Office and, in 1973–74, of the Northern Ireland Assembly.

**Suffragette** Supporter of Women's Social and Political Union, founded in 1903, and dominated by Emmeline and Christabel Pankhurst. Between 1906 and 1914 it undertook militant action to further the cause of women's enfranchisement. Women over 30 were enfranchised in 1918, and women between 21 and 30 in 1928.

**Suffragist** Supporter of National Union of Women's Suffrage Societies. Believed in constitutional methods to obtain women's suffrage, and adult suffrage in general. Mrs Millicent Fawcett was the best-known suffragist leader.

**'Sweated' trades** Refers to the domestic trades such as tailoring, hat-making and flower-making where child, female and foreign labour were often grossly underpaid for work in poor conditions. The conditions of 'sweated' workers became a major cause for concern in the late nineteenth and early twentieth centuries, leading to government legislation in 1909, and the Trade Boards Act, which set minimum wages.

**'Swing'** Term used by psephologists (investigators of voting patterns) to express percentage change in votes between major parties at elections, particularly in the years since 1945 when the operation of a virtual two-party system made its calculation much more straightforward and relevant.

**Syndicalist** Supporter of principle of ownership and running of industry by workers directly. Syndicalism was influenced by writings of Proudhon and Sorel, and obtained some following in Britain between 1910 and 1914, for which Tom Mann was a spokesman.

**Tactical voting** Voting behaviour which is determined by calculating which party has the best chance of winning in a constituency (e.g. Labour supporters voting Liberal to unseat a Conservative).

**Tariff reform** Campaign for introduction of protective tariffs associated with Joseph Chamberlain (*q.v.*) in 1903–5.

**Taxes on knowledge** Newspaper and stamp duties were attacked by radicals in the early nineteenth century as 'taxes on knowledge'. The 'unstamped' or 'pauper' press were those publications which avoided or evaded such duties. Stamp duties were abolished in 1855.

**Temperance movement** Movement to restrict or ban the consumption of alcohol. Temperance societies were started as early as the 1820s, soon achieving strong support from the Methodist and other free churches. Temperance became a major feature of the Liberal Party's programme in the latter half of the nineteenth century and resulted in Licensing Acts in 1872 and 1902.

**Thatcherite** Policies associated with the Thatcher governments from 1979 to 1990. Employed pejoratively to indicate harsh application of monetarist (*q.v.*) policies, advocacy of free market mechanism, an authoritarian line on law and order, and emphasis on strong defences. After the fall of Thatcher, the Thatcherite label has been applied to such figures as Michael Portillo and John Redwood.

**Tory** Name which became current in the Exclusion Crisis of the early 1680s for a supporter of hereditary succession, the royal prerogative, divine right and loyalty to the Church of England. After the deposition of James II many became Jacobites (*q.v.*), and the taint of Jacobitism excluded them from office for 30 years after 1715. By the end of the eighteenth century, the term was being applied to those who upheld the prerogatives of George III, resisted the removal of disabilities from Dissenters and Roman Catholics, and opposed parliamentary reform. The name 'Tory' was revived by Canning (*q.v.*) in the early nineteenth century for the natural party of government which was opposed by the Whigs (*q.v.*). In the mid-nineteenth century, the Tories also came to be called the Conservative Party.

**Tory democracy** Description of policies advocated by Disraeli (*q.v.*) and Lord Randolph Churchill (*q.v.*), combining maintenance of established institutions with cautious social reform in an attempt to win working-class support for the Conservative Party.

**Tractarians** Name applied to supporters of the Oxford Movement (*q.v.*), following J. H. Newman's *Tracts for the Times*. The revived liturgical ceremonial and the emphasis on the social obligations of the church led to the introduction of religious communities within the Church of England. Many Tractarians became Roman Catholics, including Newman who became a cardinal in 1879.

**Tribunites** Group within the Labour Party, named after the left-wing weekly, *Tribune*, founded in 1937. In the years after 1945 the group advocated a programme of further nationalization, unilateral nuclear disarmament and, later, opposition to membership of the European Economic Community. During the early 1950s the Tribune group included Aneurin Bevan (*q.v.*), Harold Wilson (*q.v.*), Ian Mikardo and Richard Crossman (*q.v.*) and was highly critical of official Labour Party policy, especially on nuclear weapons. The group remains an active force within the Labour Party.

**Triple Alliance** Agreement for mutual support between the three most powerful unions, the miners, transport workers and railwaymen. Negotiations were opened in 1914 and agreement reached in 1915, but not put into operation until after the First World War. In Apr. 1921 the Triple Alliance broke down when the other two unions failed to call sympathetic strikes in support of a miners' stoppage.

**'Troubles, the'** Period of unrest in Ireland from 1918 to 1921, characterized by virtual guerrilla war between the Irish Republican Army (IRA) and the British forces, continuing after 1921 in the civil war between the Irish government and the IRA over the terms of the truce with Britain and the exclusion of Ulster. Sometimes applied to the period of unrest in Northern Ireland after 1968.

**'Two nations'** Phrase used by Benjamin Disraeli (*q.v.*) to describe the polarization of early Victorian society into rich and poor. In his novel *Sybil*, of 1845, he wrote of 'two nations: between whom there is no intercourse and no sympathy; who are ignorant of each other's habits, thoughts and feelings, as if they were dwellers in different zones, or inhabitants of different planets...' A powerful strain in Conservative philosophy since Disraeli has emphasized its commitment to 'one

GLOSSARY OF TERMS 417

nation Toryism' by stressing the need to better the condition of the people as a whole and prevent the emergence of a divided society. As well as Disraeli, Conservative leaders such as Baldwin, Macmillan and Heath (qq.v.) were seen as operating within this tradition. The issue of 'one nation Toryism' re-emerged as implied criticism of the Thatcher administrations in the mid-1980s, led by figures such as the elderly Earl of Stockton (Harold Macmillan) and Michael Heseltine (qq.v.). See also North–South divide.

**UDI** Unilateral Declaration of Independence in Southern Rhodesia by the Rhodesian Front Government of Ian Smith on 11 Nov. 1965. The British government rejected the Declaration, which was also condemned by the United Nations, because of Smith's opposition to sharing power with the African majority and his rejection of majority rule. Britain imposed trade sanctions and an oil embargo on Rhodesia, but failed to reach an agreement with Ian Smith. The rebellion came to an end in 1980 following a protracted guerrilla war in Rhodesia which led to a settlement at Lancaster House, London, and the holding of elections which returned an African majority government led by Robert Mugabe.

**Ultra-Tories** Section of the Tory Party active from the 1820s through to the 1850s which opposed Catholic Emancipation (q.v.) and supported the Corn Laws (q.v.). Their opposition contributed to the downfall of the Tory government in 1830, precipitating the Reform Crisis of 1830–32, and they subsequently opposed Peel over the Maynooth grant in 1845 and voted against repeal of the Corn Laws in 1846.

**'Unauthorized programme'** Radical programme adopted by Joseph Chamberlain (q.v.) during the 1885 election campaign which called for free education, housing reform and a programme of smallholdings to relieve unemployment. Although Chamberlain campaigned as a Liberal the programme was not official party policy.

**Unilateralism** Policy of surrendering use and deployment of nuclear weapons without obtaining similar assurances from other governments, adopted by sections of CND (q.v.) and the Labour Party from the 1950s. Contrasted with multilateralism, insisting on mutual nuclear disarmament as only basis for peace and security.

**Unionist** Supporter of the constitutional union between Britain and

Ireland, dating from the Act of Union of 1800, and by implication an opponent of Home Rule or Irish independence. In 1886 used by Lord Randolph Churchill (*q.v.*) to describe opponents in Ireland and Britain of attempts to include Ulster in Home Rule proposals. In 1912, the Conservative Party adopted the title Conservative and Unionist Party when it formally absorbed those Liberals opposed to Home Rule. The Protestant majority in Ulster formed an Ulster Unionist Council in 1905, the forerunner of the Ulster Unionist Party which controlled the province from 1921. *See also* Liberal Unionists (p. 140).

**United Irishmen**  Society established in Belfast in 1791 by Theobald Wolfe Tone (1763–98) to seek removal of religious and political grievances. After the outbreak of war with France, many United Irishmen looked to French aid and adopted republicanism. From 1796 repression of its activities drove the movement underground, but its members conspired with the French to mount an invasion of Ireland and formed links with radicals in England. The movement was largely destroyed by the abortive 1798 rebellion, the break-up of the Despard conspiracy in 1802 and the defeat of Robert Emmet's rising in 1803.

**Utilitarians**  Upholders of Jeremy Bentham's (1748–1832) belief that government policy should be based on the need to secure the 'greatest happiness of the greatest number'. His views were very influential in the field of social policy between the 1820s and 1850s.

**'Wee Frees'**  Group of 'independent' Liberals, supporters of Herbert Asquith (*q.v.*) who resisted reunion with the Coalition Liberals led by Lloyd George (*q.v.*) after 1918. Led in the House of Commons by Sir Donald Maclean, they eventually reunited with the Lloyd George Liberals in 1923.

**Welfare State**  Term for the system of comprehensive social welfare provision proposed by the Beveridge Report and introduced after 1945 by the Attlee government. It is widely seen as being undermined by Conservative policies (over, for example, the National Health Service) under Thatcher and Major.

**'Wets'**  Term used in contrast to 'Dries' to depict positions within the Thatcher administrations since 1979. 'Dry' was the term associated with support for monetarism (*q.v.*) and associated policies of liberalization of the economy and the application of market forces, led by such figures as Sir Keith Joseph and Sir Geoffrey Howe (*q.v.*). 'Wets' supported a more traditional and centrist economic policy with higher levels of spending and greater concern for the social implications of economic policy. Leading figures associated with 'wet' views, such as Sir Ian Gilmour and James Prior, were either removed from office or given less influential positions by 1981. Criticism of the consequences of monetarist policies also surfaced in the Church of England and from Earl Stockton in the House of Lords.

**Whig** Parliamentary party which emerged in the late seventeenth century, dominated British politics in the first half of the eighteenth century and evolved into the Liberal Party in the middle of the nineteenth century. Whigs were defenders of parliamentary government, ministerial responsibility and Protestantism. The 'Glorious Revolution' of 1688–89 was regarded as a triumph of Whig principles and the Whigs monopolized power following the Hanoverian succession in 1714, but in the later eighteenth century fell from favour under George III and became associated with religious toleration, economical reform (*q.v.*) and opposition to the revival of monarchical authority. Divided by the French Revolution, they became supporters of moderate parliamentary reform in the 1820s and passed the Reform Act of 1832. The Liberal Party was formed in the mid-nineteenth century out of a fusion of Whigs, radicals and Peelites. More generally, the term has been used to refer to a paternalist, but moderately reforming, approach to politics.

**Whig history** Interpretation of history as a process of improvement from earliest times to the present, and involving viewing the past from contemporary moral assumptions. Thomas Macaulay (1800–59) and Lord Acton (1834–1902) are considered principal exponents of the Whig interpretation of history.

**Whiteboys** Association of Irish peasants, first formed in about 1761 in Co. Tipperary to redress grievances. They wore white shirts and committed agrarian outrages at night.

**'Winter of Discontent'** Period of industrial unrest in the winter of 1978–79 in opposition to the Labour government's announcement of a 5 per cent pay limit. Strikes by car workers at Ford were followed by disruptive strikes by petrol tanker and lorry drivers, water workers, hospital and municipal workers, and railwaymen. The impact of the strikes was made worse by the worst winter weather for 16 years and by the unfortunate remarks by Premier Callaghan on his return from a summit in Guadeloupe, expressing surprise at talk of a crisis. The legacy of strong anti-union feeling arising from the disruption played an important part in Mrs Thatcher's victory in 1979 and remained a theme of anti-Labour propaganda during both the 1983 and 1987 election campaigns.

**Young England** Movement led by younger Tories including Disraeli (*q.v.*) in the late 1830s and 1840s in opposition to Peel's reforming tendencies; sometimes known as 'Throne and Altar' conservatism from its professed attachment to the monarchy and the established church. Other members included George Smythe (1818–57) and John Manners (1818–1906).

# SECTION SEVEN

## *Topic bibliography*

# Topics

1. The reign of Queen Anne and the Hanoverian succession.
2. Jacobitism.
3. Walpole and the Whig supremacy.
4. The Church of England and the rise of Methodism.
5. The Agricultural Revolution.
6. Eighteenth-century society.
7. The Elder Pitt.
8. British colonial policy and the American War of Independence.
9. George III, the constitution and the parliamentary reform movement, 1760–89.
10. The impact of the French Revolution on Britain.
11. Pitt and Fox.
12. The Industrial Revolution.
13. Reform, radicalism and the Tory Party in Regency England.
14. The Great Reform Act.
15. Peel, the Tory Party and the repeal of the Corn Laws.
16. Chartism.
17. Social reform in nineteenth-century Britain.
18. Trade unionism.
19. Victorian religion.
20. British foreign policy in the nineteenth century.
21. Gladstone and Liberalism.
22. Disraeli and the late nineteenth-century Conservative Party.
23. The Irish Question.
24. British imperialism.
25. Women: feminism, the family and the franchise.
26. The rise of the Labour Party.
27. The Liberal Party in the age of Asquith and Lloyd George.
28. The causes and consequences of the First World War.
29. Britain in the 1920s.
30. Britain and the slump.
31. Appeasement and British foreign policy in the 1930s.
32. Britain and the Second World War.
33. Decolonization and foreign policy since 1945.
34. The domestic policy of the Conservative governments, 1951–64.
35. The Labour government of 1964–70.
36. The 1970s.
37. The Northern Ireland crisis.
38. The Thatcher era and after.

# List of abbreviations

| | |
|---|---|
| A | *Albion* |
| AgH | *Agricultural History* |
| AmHR | *American Historical Review* |
| BIHR | *Bulletin of the Institute of Historical Research* |
| BJPS | *British Journal of Political Science* |
| CHJ | *Cambridge Historical Journal* |
| CR | *Contemporary Record* |
| DUJ | *Durham University Journal* |
| E | *Economica* |
| EH | *Economic History* |
| EconHR | *Economic History Review* |
| EHR | *English Historical Review* |
| GO | *Government and Opposition* |
| H | *History* |
| HJ | *Historical Journal* |
| HLO | *Huntingdon Library Quarterly* |
| HT | *History Today* |
| HW | *History Workshop* |
| IHS | *Irish Historical Studies* |
| IRSH | *International Review of Social History* |
| JBS | *Journal of British Studies* |
| JCH | *Journal of Contemporary History* |
| JEcclH | *Journal of Ecclesiastical History* |
| JEconH | *Journal of Economic History* |
| JHI | *Journal of the History of Ideas* |
| JICH | *Journal of Imperial and Commonwealth History* |
| JMH | *Journal of Modern History* |
| LHSB | *Labour History Society Bulletin* |
| LJ | *The London Journal* |
| NH | *Northern History* |
| NLR | *New Left Review* |
| OH | *Oral History* |
| PA | *Public Administration* |
| PAff | *Public Affairs* |
| PBA | *Proceedings of the British Academy* |
| PH | *Parliamentary History* |
| PolR | *Politics Review* |
| PolS | *Political Studies* |
| PP | *Past and Present* |

| PQ | *Political Quarterly* |
|---|---|
| PS | *Population Studies* |
| PSQ | *Political Science Quarterly* |
| SH | *Social History* |
| SHR | *Southern History Review* |
| TCBH | *Twentieth Century British History* |
| THAS | *Transactions of the Hunter Archaeological Society* |
| TRHS | *Transactions of the Royal Historical Society* |
| WHR | *Welsh History Review* |
| WMQ | *William and Mary Quarterly* |
| VS | *Victorian Studies* |

## Introductory note

This bibliography is arranged in rough chronological order and is intended to represent a fair selection of the major topics in modern British history. The essay titles are merely intended to focus attention on some of the most commonly raised issues, but by no means exhaust the range of possibilities on each subject. The reading is deliberately greater than would be required for an average essay, but does reflect the wealth of bibliographical material now available for most of these subjects and allows a degree of specialization on particular aspects of a topic. Similarly, the article literature mentioned, while not an exhaustive list, is intended as a guide to some of the most important material from which a selection can be made according to preference. A selection of source material is also provided for each topic.

## General texts

Those seeking an introduction to the period are advised to consult the various general texts that are available. Succinct one-volume studies are R.K. Webb, *Modern England: from the Eighteenth Century to the Present* (1969); G. Alderman, *Modern Britain, 1700–1983* (1986); and J. Ramsden and G. Williams, *Ruling Britannia: A Political History of Britain, 1688–1988* (1990).

There are a number of studies of the eighteenth century, including D. Marshall, *Eighteenth Century England, 1714–1784* (2nd edn, 1975); J.B. Owen, *The Eighteenth Century, 1714–1815* (1974); and J.H. Plumb, *England in the Eighteenth Century, 1714–1815* (1950). The two volumes in the Oxford series, B. Williams, *The Whig Supremacy, 1714–60* (2nd edn, 1962) and J. Steven Watson, *The Reign of George III, 1760–1815* (1960), can now be supplemented by the more recent W.A. Speck, *Stability and Strife, England 1714–1760* (1977) and I.R. Christie, *Wars and Revolutions, Britain 1760–1815* (1982). B.W. Hill, *The Growth of Parliamentary Parties, 1689–1742* (1976) and *British Parliamentary Parties, 1742–1832* (1985) are two political narratives at parliamentary level. Other works span the eighteenth century at a more interpretative level: in J. Cannon (ed.), *The Whig Ascendancy: Colloquies on Hanoverian England* (1981), a number of distinguished historians set out their views on the period from 1680 through to 1830, attached to which are the 'colloquies' or comments by other contributors to the volume; J.C.D. Clark, *English Society, 1688–1832* (1985) is a deliberately controversial work touching upon most of the important aspects of politics and religion in the period; and

J. Black, *The Politics of Britain, 1688–1800* (1992) offers a succinct overview of the century.

For the transition through to the nineteenth century, see A. Briggs, *The Age of Improvement, 1783–1867* (1959) and E.J. Evans, *The Forging of the Modern State, 1783–1870* (1982). The nineteenth century is now served by a good range of modern texts, including N. Gash, *Aristocracy and People, 1815–65* (1980); R. Shannon, *The Crisis of Imperialism 1865–1915* (1974); D. Read, *England, 1868–1914: the Age of Urban Democracy* (1979); E.J. Feuchtwanger, *Democracy and Empire: Britain, 1865–1914* (1985); D. Beales, *From Castlereagh to Gladstone, 1815–1885* (1969); and M.J. Bentley, *Politics without Democracy* (1984). A number of texts carry the story through from the nineteenth century into the twentieth: H. Pelling, *Modern Britain, 1885–1955* (1960); M. Pugh, *The Making of Modern British Politics, 1867–1939* (1986) and his *State and Society: British Political and Social History, 1870–1992* (1994); and K. Robbins, *The Eclipse of a Great Power, Modern Britain, 1870–1975* (1983).

More exclusively concerned with the twentieth century are A. Marwick, *Britain in the Age of Total War: War, Peace and Social Change, 1900–1967* (1968); W.N. Medlicott, *Contemporary England, 1914–1964: with Epilogue, 1964–1974* (rev. edn, 1976); A. Havighurst, *Britain in Transition: The Twentieth Century* (rev. edn, 1979); T.O. Lloyd, *Empire to Welfare State, English History, 1906–1985* (rev. edn, 1986); D. Thompson, *England in the Twentieth Century, 1914–79* (rev. edn, 1979); and R. Blake, *The Decline of Power, 1915–1964* (1985). Shorter periods within the twentieth century are considered by C.L. Mowat, *Britain between the Wars, 1918–1940* (rev. edn, 1968), A.J.P. Taylor, *English History, 1914–1945* (1965); and M. Beloff, *Wars and Welfare, Britain 1914–1952* (1984). For postwar Britain see A. Sked and C. Cook, *Post-war Britain: A Political History* (4th edn, 1993); D. Childs, *Britain since 1945* (3rd edn, 1992); and K.O. Morgan, *The People's Peace: British History, 1945–1990* (1990). There are helpful contributions on post-1945 Britain in P. Hennessy and A. Seldon (eds), *Ruling Performance: British Governments from Attlee to Thatcher* (1987) and A. Gourvish and A. O'Day (eds), *Britain since 1945* (1991).

Scotland and Wales are now better served than they were. For the former see W. Ferguson, *Scotland 1689 to the Present* (1968) and the two volumes by T.C. Smout, *A History of the Scottish People, 1560–1830* (1969) and *A Century of the Scottish People, 1830–1950* (1986). Good introductions are offered too by the volumes of the Arnold New History of Scotland: R. Mitchison, *Lordship to Patronage: Scotland, 1603–1745* (1983); B. Lenman, *Integration, Enlightenment and Industrialization:*

*Scotland, 1746–1832* (1981); S. and O. Checkland, *Industry and Ethos: Scotland, 1832–1914* (1984); and C. Harvie, *No Gods and Precious Few Heroes: Scotland, 1914–1980* (1981). Wales has been well served by G.A. Williams, *When Was Wales? A History of the Welsh* (1985); K.O. Morgan, *Rebirth of a Nation: Wales, 1880–1980* (1982); G.E. Jones, *Modern Wales: A Concise History of Modern Wales, 1485–1979* (1984); and J.P. Jenkins, *A History of Modern Wales, 1536–1990* (1992). For Ireland, see R.F. Foster, *Modern Ireland, 1600–1972* (1988); J.C. Beckett, *The Making of Modern Ireland, 1603–1923* (1966); F.S.L. Lyons, *Ireland Since the Famine* (1973); and A. O'Day and J. Stevenson, *Irish Historical Documents since 1800* (1992).

Of a large output of works in economic and social history, C.H. Lee, *The British Economy since 1700: a macroeconomic perspective* (1986); P. Mathias, *The First Industrial Nation: An Economic History of Britain, 1700–1914* (1969); and B. Murphy, *A History of the British Economy, 1740–1970* (1973) are helpful one-volume studies. R. Floud and D. McCloskey (eds), *The Economic History of Britain since 1700* 2 vols (1981) represents a series of assessments of both economic and social developments. One-volume social histories dealing with all or part of this period are E. Royle, *Modern Britain: A Social History, 1750–1985* (1987) and F. Bedarida, *A Social History of England, 1851–1975* (trans. 1976). Four volumes in the Pelican Social History of Britain are concerned with this period: R. Porter, *English Society in the Eighteenth Century* (1982); J. Harris, *Private Lives, Public Spirit: A Social History of Britain, 1870–1914* (1993); J. Stevenson, *British Society, 1914–1945* (1984); and A. Marwick, *British Society since 1945* (1982). F.M.L. Thompson (ed.), *The Cambridge Social History of Britain, 1750–1950* 3 vols (1990) has a fine set of thematic essays with regional survey in Vol. 1.

# Reference

Detailed statistics on this period can be found in B.R. Mitchell and P. Deane, *Abstract of British Historical Statistics* (1962), while a wide selection of factual information is presented in diagrammatic form in C. Cook and J. Stevenson, *Longman Atlas of Modern British History: a visual guide to British society and politics, 1700–1970* (1978). For maps on economic history see also H.C. Derby (ed.), *A New Historical Geography of England after 1600* (1976).

Detailed reference works for this period are C. Cook and J. Stevenson, *British Historical Facts, 1688–1760* (1988) and *British Historical Facts, 1760–1830* (1980); C. Cook and B. Keith, *British Historical Facts,*

*1830–1900* (1975); and D. Butler and G. Butler, *British Political Facts, 1900–94* (6th edn, 1994).

# 1. The reign of Queen Anne and the Hanoverian succession

The reign of Queen Anne and the 'rage of party' has been reinterpreted in recent years. The relevance and meaning of 'party' have been subjected to examination and studies of constituency politics, particular elections and the electorate have added a new dimension to our study of politics, carrying the discussion of political attitudes beyond the confines of Westminster. The place of religious strife requires consideration and the bitter conflict over foreign policy involves some understanding of the war and the financial and political issues it involved. The 'inevitability' of the Hanoverian succession also demands critical scrutiny.

## Essay topics

- What were the causes of political conflict in England during the reign of Queen Anne?
- Was the increasing bitterness of politics in the reign of Queen Anne due primarily to a conflict between 'land' and 'money'?

## Sources and documents

G.S. Holmes and W. A. Speck (eds), *The Divided Society, 1694–1716* (1967) is a short, lively collection of documents. A. Browning (ed.), *English Historical Documents, 1660–1714* (1953) has the usual wide selection of documents for the series. Dean Swift, *The Conduct of the Allies* (1711) is a brilliant tract on foreign policy. Equally interesting is Gregory King, 'Natural and political observations . . . upon the state of England', reprinted in G.E. Barnett (ed.), *Two Tracts by Gregory King* (1936).

## Secondary works

The standard modern interpretation is G.S. Holmes, *British Politics in the Age of Anne* (1967), while *Religion and Party in Late Stuart England* (Historical Association pamphlet, 1975) is a briefer version of some of his views. J.H. Plumb, *The Growth of Political Stability in England 1675–1725* (1967) remains an important interpretation, while B.W. Hill, *The Growth of Parliamentary Parties, 1689–1742* (1976) offers a detailed account of proceedings at parliamentary level. Also helpful are chs 6 and 7 of T. Harris, *Politics under the Later Stuarts* (1993) and J.P. Kenyon, *Revolution Principles: The Politics of Party, 1689–1720* (1977). These studies implicitly refute the analysis of politics based upon family groupings in R. Walcott, *English Politics in the Early Eighteenth Century* (1956). The development of political activity in the localities is discussed in W.A. Speck, *Tory and Whig: the struggle in the constituencies, 1701–1715* (1970) and G.S. Holmes, *The Electorate and the National Will in the First Age of Party* (1976), while the capital is discussed in G.S. De Krey, *A Fractured Society: The Politics of London in the First Age of Party, 1688–1715* (1985). The broader social stability underpinning the changes of ruler in 1689 and 1714 is discussed by G.S. Holmes in ch. 1 of J. Cannon (ed.), *The Whig Ascendancy* (1981). A number of essays on the character of British politics after 1689 are also included in G.S. Holmes (ed.), *Britain after the Glorious Revolution 1689–1714* (1969). B. Kemp, *King and Commons 1660–1832* (1957) has an admirably clear view of the constitutional position, whilst for financial affairs see P.G. Dickson, *The Financial Revolution in England: a study in the development of public credit, 1688–1756* (1967), especially chs 1–3. The background of foreign policy as a source of conflict is considered in P. Langford, *Britain, 1688–1815: foreign policy in the eighteenth century* (1976) and detailed studies of important areas of foreign policy are D.B. Horn, *Great Britain and Europe in the Eighteenth Century* (1967) and J. McLachlan, *Trade and Peace with Old Spain, 1667–1739* (1940).

The growing party and religious bitterness towards the end of Anne's reign is examined in G.S. Holmes, *The Trial of Dr. Sacheverell* (1973) and Bolingbroke's role is considered in H.T. Dickinson, *Bolingbroke* (1970) and S. Biddle, *Bolingbroke and Harley* (1975). E. Gregg, *Queen Anne* (1980) rescues the Queen from the caricature role often ascribed to her, and for the manoeuvres prior to 1714, see G.S. Holmes, 'Harley, St. John and the Death of the Tory Party', in his *Britain after the Glorious Revolution, 1689–1714* (1969) and D. Szechi, *Jacobitism and Tory Politics, 1710–14* (1984); also B.W. Hill, *Robert Harley* (1988).

Finally, it is worth noting that several of G.S. Holmes's essays have been collected and published under the title *Politics, Religion and Society in England, 1679–1742* (1986).

## Articles

Two views on party affiliation are expressed in H. Horowitz, 'Parties, connections, and parliamentary politics, 1689–1714: review and revision', *JBS* (1966) and D.A. Rubini, 'Party and the Augustan Constitution: Politics and the Power of the Executive', *A* (1978). The seminal article on the growth of the electorate is J.H. Plumb, 'The growth of the electorate in England from 1600 to 1715', *PP* (1969). The controversy surrounding Sacheverell is considered in M. Ransome, 'Church and dissent in the election of 1710', *EHR* (1941), while the struggle over the succession is examined in H.N. Fieldhouse, 'Bolingbroke's share in the Jacobite intrigue of 1710–14', *EHR* (1937), M.A. Thomson, 'The safeguarding of the protestant succession', *H* (1972) and E. Cruikshanks, 'The Tories and the Succession in the 1714 Parliament', *BIHR* (1973). Two case studies of electoral behaviour at the time of the Hanoverian succession are W.A. Speck, 'The General Election of 1715', *EHR* (1975) and N. Landau, 'Independence, Deference and Voter Participation: the Behaviour of the Electorate in Early-Eighteenth-Century Kent', *HJ* (1979).

## 2. Jacobitism

Jacobitism is gradually being reclaimed from the realms of romantic fiction to reflect increasingly upon the insecurity of the Hanoverian succession and the many opportunities for division within the political nation which still existed after 1714. The role of Jacobitism as an ideology of opposition is important, especially for the way in which it shaded off into Toryism and the opposition to Walpole. The manipulation of the Jacobite issue by Walpole has also received attention.

### Essay topics

• At what point were conditions most propitious for Jacobite success?
• What does the strength of Jacobite feeling suggest about the nature of political conflict in the reigns of George I and George II?

### Secondary works

G.H. Jones, *The Mainstream of Jacobitism* (1954) is a good place to start, but the best modern treatments are now P. Monod, *Jacobitism and the English People, 1688–1788* (1989); T. Harris, *Politics under the Later Stuarts* (1993); and D. Szechi, *The Jacobites: Britain and Europe, 1688–1788* (1994). E. Cruikshanks and J. Black (eds), *The Jacobite Challenge* (1988), F. McLynn, *The Jacobites* (1986) and E. Cruikshanks and R. Hatton (eds), *Ideology and Conspiracy: Aspects of Jacobitism, 1689–1759* (1982) offer a fresh assessment of Jacobite activity; see also J.C.D. Clark, *English Society, 1688–1832* (1985), especially ch. 3. The last essay in G.S. Holmes (ed.), *Britain after the Glorious Revolution* (1969) discusses the political struggle preceding Anne's death. For the survival of Bolingbroke's influence, see I. Kramnick, *Bolingbroke and his Circle: the politics of nostalgia* (1968). A.S. Foord, *His Majesty's Opposition 1714–1830* (1964) discusses the place of the Jacobites in the other factions aiming for the overthrow of Walpole, as does C.B. Realey, *The Early Opposition to Sir Robert Walpole* (1931). For recent support for the extent of Jacobite influence on the Tory opposition to Walpole see ch. V of the introductory survey of R. Sedgewick (ed.), *The House of Commons, 1715–1754* (1970) and E. Cruikshanks, *Political Untouchables, the Tories and the '45* (1979). These views are considered critically in W. Speck, 'Whigs and Tories dim their glories', in J. Cannon (ed.), *The Whig Ascendency* (1981) and L. Colley, *In Defiance of Oligarchy, the Tory Party, 1714–1760* (1981). P.S. Fritz, *The English Ministers and Jacobitism between the Rebellions of 1715 and 1745* (1975) is an excellent study of the exploitation of the Jacobite 'threat' by Walpole, while for the risings themselves, see B. Lenman, *The Jacobite Risings in Britain, 1689–1746* (1980). R.C. Jarvis, *Collected Papers on the Jacobite Risings*, vols I and II (1971–72) are a powerful antidote to the view that Jacobitism was inevitably doomed to failure. The plot of 1722 is well analysed in G.V. Bennett, *The Tory Crisis in Church and State* (1975). Good biographical studies include H.T. Dickinson, *Bolingbroke* (1970) and D. Daiches, *Charles Edward Stuart* (1973).

### Articles

N. Rogers, 'Popular disturbances in early Hanoverian London', *PP* (1978) gives a good account of pro-Tory and crypto-Jacobite feeling in London. P.D.G. Thomas, 'Jacobitism in Wales', *WHR* (1963) is good on an often neglected area of British politics. H.N. Fieldhouse, 'Bolingbroke and the idea of non-party government', *EHR* (1937); E. Gregg, 'Was Queen Anne a Jacobite?', *H* (1972); and M.A. Thomson, 'The safe-guarding of the Protestant succession?', *H* (1954) are all relevant. See also J.C.D. Clark, 'The Politics of the Excluded: Tories, Jacobites and Whig Patriots, 1715–1760', *PH* (1983) and B. Lenman, 'The Jacobite diaspora, 1688–1746', *HT* (1980). On government measures, see P.S. Fritz, 'The Anti-Jacobite Intelligence System of the English Ministers, 1715–45', *HJ* (1973). On the '45, see N. Rogers, 'Popular Disaffection in London during the forty-five', *LJ* (1975).

## 3. Walpole and the Whig supremacy

Walpole's period of office dominated the first half of the eighteenth century. The nature of his power and its significance for the conduct of politics in this period provide a major theme. The relationship between Crown and Parliament and the position of Walpole as *de facto* prime minister shed light on the working out of the constitutional implications of the Revolution Settlement. The weakening of party feeling from the 1720s provided an opportunity for a different style of politics in which patronage and 'influence' played a more crucial part than 'party'. As a result, much of the writing on this topic concerns the 'structure' of politics. Surprisingly little attention is paid to Walpole's policies, though there has been a revival of interest in the ideological basis of the 'Whig oligarchy' and that of Walpole's opponents.

### Essay topics

- Did Walpole govern by 'corruption'?
- What did Walpole's long tenure of office reveal about the nature of politics in the first half of the eighteenth century?

### Sources and documents

E.N. Williams (ed.), *The Eighteenth Century Constitution* (1960) has a good selection of contemporary documents, as has D.B. Horn and M. Ransome, *English Historical Documents, vol. X, 1714–83* (1957). Lord Hervey, *Memoirs* (3 vols, ed. R. Sedgewick, 1931) provides a fascinating account of court politics under Walpole. There is a vast amount of material on the structure of local politics in R. Sedgewick, *The House of Commons 1715–1754* (2 vols, 1970).

### Secondary works

Good outlines exist in J.H. Plumb, *England in the Eighteenth Century, 1714–1815* (1950); W.A. Speck, *Stability and Strife: England 1714–1760* (1977); B.W. Hill, *The Growth of Parliamentary Parties, 1689–1742* (1977); and J. Owen, *The Eighteenth Century, 1714–1815* (1974). J.H. Plumb, *The Growth of Political Stability in England, 1675–1725* (1967) and B. Kemp, *King and Commons, 1660–1832* (1957) both have relevant material. J.H. Plumb, *Sir Robert Walpole* (2 vols, 1956 and 1960) is the standard life, but does not go beyond 1734, but B.W. Hill, *Sir Robert Walpole* (1989) is a brief full life. H.T. Dickinson, *Walpole and the Whig Supremacy* (1973) and B. Kemp, *Sir Robert Walpole* (1976) are both useful shorter works. A collection of essays is J. Black (ed.), *The Age of Walpole* (1984), and see also his *Robert Walpole and the Nature of Politics in Early Eighteenth Century England* (1990). See also G.S. Holmes, 'Sir Robert Walpole', in H. Van Thal (ed.), *The Prime Ministers*, Vol. 1(1974). On the pattern of politics in this period, see J. Owen, *The Eighteenth Century, 1714–1815* (1974), ch. 5; his views are also stated in J. Owen, *The Pattern of Politics in Eighteenth Century England* (Historical Association Pamphlet, 1962). Owen's views and those of other writers on the Whig oligarchy have come under scrutiny in J.C.D. Clark, *English Society, 1688–1832* (1985), see especially ch. 1. The structural interpretations of Namier and Owen are also implicitly challenged in the introduction to R. Sedgewick (ed.), *The House of Commons, 1715–1754* (1970) and the pro-party analysis of B.W. Hill, *The Growth of Parliamentary Parties, 1689–1742* (1977). Discussion of some of the issues can be found in J. Cannon, *The Whig Ascendency* (1981), chs 2 and 3. For the survival of Tory/Jacobite support, see under 'Jacobitism'. One of the most important episodes of Walpole's career is discussed in J. Carswell, *The South Sea Bubble* (1960), but see also P.G.M. Dickson, *The Financial Revolution* (1967). On other issues, see P. Langford, *The Excise Crisis* (1975) and Walpole's concern with Jacobitism in P.S. Fritz, *The English Ministers and Jacobitism between the Rebellions of 1715 and 1745* (1975). The important foreign policy background is discussed in P. Langford, *Britain, 1688–1815: foreign policy in the eighteenth century* (1976); J. Black, *British Foreign Policy in the Age of Walpole* (1986); and the more detailed D.B. Horn, *Great Britain and Europe in the Eighteenth Century* (1967) and J. McLachlan, *Trade and Peace with Old Spain, 1667–1739* (1940).

The opposition to Walpole is considered in A.S. Foord, *His Majesty's Opposition, 1714–1830* (1964); C.B. Realey, *The Early Opposition to Sir Robert Walpole* (1931); and L. Colley, *In Defiance of Oligarchy, the Tory Party, 1714–1760* (1981); see also the introduction to R. Sedgewick (ed.), *The House of Commons, 1715–1754* (1970), H.T. Dickinson, *Bolingbroke* (1970) and I. Kramnick, *Bolingbroke and his Circle: the politics of nostalgia* (1968). The important role of London is considered in L.S. Sutherland, 'The City of London in eighteenth-century politics', in *Essays Presented to Sir Lewis Namier* (eds R. Pares and A.J.P. Taylor, 1956); N. Rogers, 'Resistance to oligarchy' in J. Stevenson (ed.), *London in the Age of Reform* (1977); and other urban contexts in N. Rogers, *Whigs and Cities* (1989). Rural protest is considered in E.P. Thompson, *Whigs and Hunters* (1975), adding a new dimension to the study of the Whig oligarchy.

## Articles

See M. Ransome, 'Division lists in the House of Commons, 1715–1760', *BIHR* (1942); E.A. Reitan, 'The Civil List in eighteenth-century British politics', *HJ* (1966); B. Williams, 'The Duke of Newcastle and the general election of 1734', *EHR* (1897); T.F.J. Kendrick, 'Sir Robert Walpole, the old Whigs and the bishops, 1733–1736', *HJ* (1968); E.R. Turner, 'The excise scheme of 1733', *EHR* (1927). On the opposition to Walpole, see J.C.D. Clark, 'The Politics of the Excluded: Tories, Jacobites and Whig Patriots, 1715–1760', *PH* (1983). On foreign policy see C. Gibbs, 'Parliament and foreign policy in the age of Stanhope and Walpole', *EHR* (1962); D. McKay, 'The struggle for control of George I's northern policy', *JMH* (1973); and K. Wilson, 'Admiral Vernon and Popular Politics', *PP* (1988).

## 4. The Church of England and the rise of Methodism

The rise of Methodism inevitably reflects upon the condition of the Church of England in the eighteenth century and the problems posed by population growth and economic change, but John Wesley is a fascinating figure who would alone make this subject worth studying. Three main topics emerge: what was the condition of the eighteenth-century Church of England; why was it unable to harness Methodism as a revival movement (as with the Evangelical Revival and the Oxford Movement) and why did the two separate; and what effects did Methodism have upon an industrializing England. It is worth considering whether the Church of England was any worse than it ever had been and why it found it difficult to adjust itself to meet the new challenges. Elie Halévy's claim that Methodism prevented revolution in England deserves some attention.

### Essay topics

- Why was the eighteenth-century Church of England unable to harness Wesley's reforming zeal?
- Was the rise of Methodism a condemnation of the Church of England?
- What were the political and social effects of Methodism before 1815?

### Sources

John Wesley, *Journals*; even the smallest sample is valuable for the flavour of Methodism in its 'heroic' phase. E.N. Williams, *The Eighteenth Century Constitution* (1960) has a useful section on the church. John Wade, *The Extraordinary Black Book* (1820) is a scintillating exposé of corruption in the political and ecclesiastical establishment. Though biased, it provides a mine of information on the unreformed Anglican Church.

## Secondary works

The most accessible one-volume treatment is A. Armstrong, *The Church of England, the Methodists and Society, 1700–1850* (1973), while A.D. Gilbert, *Religion and Society in Industrial England, 1740–1914* (1976) places Methodism within the context of religious adherence in general. W.G. Ward, *Religion and Society in England 1790–1850* (1972) is also relevant. N. Sykes, *Church and State in the Eighteenth Century* (1934) is the essential work on the Church of England, but see also G.V. Bennett and J.D. Walsh (eds), *Essays in Modern Church History in Memory of Norman Sykes* (1966). A full treatment of all sides of religious life in the period is G. Rupp, *Religion in England, 1688–1791* (1987). J.C.D. Clark, *English Society, 1688–1832* (1985) argues that England was a 'confessional' state prior to 1832 and examines its defenders and assailants. Good case studies of the Church of England's response locally are A. Warne, *Church and Society in Eighteenth Century Devon* (1969) and M. Smith, *Religion in Industrial Society: Oldham and Saddleworth, 1740–1865* (1994). The older C.J. Abbey and J.H. Overton, *The English Church in the Eighteenth Century* 2 vols, (1878) is still useful, as are S.C. Carpenter, *Eighteenth-century Church and People* (1959) and *Church and People, 1789–1899* (1959).

For Methodism see R. Davies and E.G. Rupp (eds), *A History of the Methodist Church of Great Britain* (1965). On Wesley himself see F. Baker, *John Wesley and the Church of England* (1970) and V.H.H. Green, *John Wesley* (1964). For the period after Wesley's death, see M.L. Edwards, *After Wesley: a study in the social and political influence of Methodism in the Middle Period, 1791–1849* (1935). On Methodism's impact see R.F. Wearmouth, *Methodism and the Common People of the Eighteenth Century* (1945) and *Methodism and the Working-class Movements of England, 1800–1850* (1937) which contain a lot of information, but are rather uncritical. D. Hempton, *Methodism and Politics, 1750–1850* (1986) is an excellent modern study; E.R. Taylor, *Methodism and Politics, 1791–1850* (1935) is also useful. E. Halévy, *England in 1815* (1924) has an important section where he argues that Methodism prevented revolution in England. E.P. Thompson, *The Making of the English Working*

*Class* (2nd edn, 1968), ch. 11 is polemical but interesting. J.D. Walsh, 'Methodism and the mob in the eighteenth century', in G.J. Cuming and D. Barker (eds), *Popular Belief and Practice, Studies in Church History*, Vol. 8 (1972) throws light on the reception of Methodism.

On the intellectual background to eighteenth-century religious life see G.R. Cragg, *From Puritanism to the Age of Reason* (1966) and R.N. Stromberg, *Religious Liberalism in Eighteenth Century England* (1954).

The Evangelical Revival is considered in C. Smyth, *Simeon and Church Order* (1940) which has important bearings on why the evangelicals could stay within the Church of England and Methodism could not. See also E.M. Howse, *Saints in Politics* (1953) for the 'Clapham Sect'.

For Scotland in this period see A.L. Drummond and J. Bulloch, *The Scottish Church, 1688–1843* (1973) and C.G. Brown, *The Social History of Religion in Scotland since 1730* (1987).

### Articles

E. Hobsbawm, 'Methodism and the threat of revolution in Britain', *HT* (1957), also reprinted in his collection *Labouring Men* (1964), is crucial on this issue. See also J.D. Walsh, 'Elie Halévy and the birth of Methodism', *TRHS* (1975); C. Smyth, 'The evangelical movement in perspective', *CHJ* (1941–43).

## 5. The Agricultural Revolution

Like the 'Industrial Revolution', the 'Agricultural Revolution' has been placed within the context of a more gradual and complex process of economic development. Explanations for the expansion of British agricultural output no longer concentrate upon the 'discovery' of a few techniques and inventions but upon the factors which stimulated a more enterprising approach to agriculture from the middle years of the eighteenth century. The Agricultural Revolution, and the enclosure movement, in particular, was seen as a social disaster by contemporaries such as Cobbett and by later historians, such as the Hammonds, but recent work has increasingly modified this picture. The story, however, remains complex and often repays study from a regional or local perspective.

### Essay topics

- Was there a 'revolution' in agriculture during the eighteenth and nineteenth centuries?

- Have the social and economic effects of enclosure been exaggerated?

## Sources and documents

William Cobbett, *Rural Rides* (1830), immensely readable and prejudiced, is available in many modern editions. A. Young, *Tours in England and Wales* (reprinted 1932) is valuable for checking generalizations against contemporary views. A.E. Bland, P. Brown and R.H. Tawney, *English Economic History* (1914), Pt III, section II has some useful documents on enclosure, while W.E. Tate and M.E. Turner, *A Domesday of English Enclosure Acts and Awards* (1978) permits the study of enclosures county by county.

## Secondary works

Many of the standard economic histories contain sections on agriculture; see especially D.C. Coleman, *The Economy of England, 1450–1750* (1977), ch. 7; C. Wilson, *England's Apprenticeship, 1603–1763* (1965), ch. 12; P. Mathias, *The First Industrial Nation: an economic history of Britain, 1700–1914* (1969), ch. 3; P. Deane and W.A. Cole, *British Economic Growth, 1688–1959* (1969), ch. 2; R. Floud and D. McCloskey, *The Economic History of Britain since 1700*, Vol. 1 (1981); essays by Jones and Hueckel; and A. Kussmaul, *A General View of the Rural Economy of England, 1538–1840* (1990).

J.D. Chambers and G.E. Mingay, *The Agricultural Revolution, 1750–1880* (1966) is the major modern work, but see also E. Kerridge, *The Agricultural Revolution* (1967). J. Clapham, *An Economic History of Modern Britain* 3 vols (1926–38), chs 4 and 11 is still useful. E.L. Jones, *The Development of English Agriculture, 1815–1873* (1968) deals with the later stages. A.H. John, 'The course of agricultural change, 1660–1760', in L.S. Pressnell (ed.), *Studies in the Industrial Revolution* (1960) is important on the timing of change; see also the essays by E.L. Jones and A.H. John in E.L. Jones and G.E. Mingay (eds), *Land, Labour and Population in the Industrial Revolution* (1967). D.B. Grigg, *The Agricultural Revolution in South Lincolnshire* (1966) is a good regional study. J.L. and B. Hammond, *The Village Labourer* (1911) remains the classic 'pessimistic' view of the effects of agricultural change, but is now rather dated. More balanced is P. Horn, *The Rural World, 1780–1850* (1980). An important recent addition is K.D.M. Snell, *Annals of the Labouring Poor. Social Change and Agrarian England, 1660–1900* (1985). E. Hobsbawm and G. Rudé, *Captain Swing* (1969) deals with agricultural protests of 1830–32 and sheds considerable light on early nineteenth-century conditions, as does B. Reay, *The Last Rising of the Agricultural Labourers* (1990). R.A.C. Parker, *Coke of Norfolk* (1975) discusses one of the pioneers of agricultural improvement. See also G.E. Mingay, *Enclosure and the Small Farmer in the Age of the Industrial Revolution* (1968) and *The Gentry: the rise and fall of a ruling class* (1976). Scottish developments are considered in E. Richards, *The Highland Clearances* (1982), and for Wales see D.J.V. Jones, *Before Rebecca* (1973).

### Articles

G.E. Mingay's views are summarized in 'The Agricultural Revolution – a reconsideration', *AgH* (1963); see also his 'The size of farms in the eighteenth century', *EconHR* (1962). E.L. Jones, 'Agriculture and economic growth in England, 1600–1750', *JEconH* (1965) is important, while J.D. Chambers, 'The Vale of Trent, 1670–1800: a regional study of economic change', *EconHR* Supplement No. 3 (1957) is a useful case study. G.E. Mingay, 'The agricultural depression, 1730–1750', *EconHR* (1956); R.A.C. Parker, 'Coke of Norfolk and the agrarian revolution', *EconHR* (1955); T.H. Marshall, 'Jethro Tull and the new husbandry of the eighteenth century', *EconHR* (1929–30); J.D. Chambers, 'Enclosure and the small landowner', *EconHR* (1940) and 'Enclosure and labour supply in the Industrial Revolution', *EconHR* (1953) are also highly relevant. E.L. Jones, 'The agricultural labour market in England, 1793–1872', *EconHR* (1964–65) and F.M.L. Thompson, 'The second Agricultural Revolution, 1815–1880', *EconHR* (1968) deal with the later period.

## 6. Eighteenth-century society

The eighteenth century saw the beginnings of population growth, significant urbanization and major developments in agriculture and industry. One of the main problems is how far Britain differed from other European societies and the extent to which social mobility increased with the rise of commerce and industry. Is the picture of a rigidly hierarchical society accurate, and how relevant is the concept of class to a society such as this? Considerable work in recent years has been done on the areas of riot, protest and crime.

### Essay topics

• What were the principal characteristics of eighteenth-century society?

- How relevant is the concept of 'class' to a discussion of eighteenth-century society?

## Sources and documents

A portrait of village life can be found in J. Woodforde, *The Diary of a Country Parson* (ed. J. Beresford, in various editions). D. Defoe, *The Complete English Tradesman* (1735, and later editions) and James Boswell, *London Journal, 1762–1763* (ed. J. Pottle, 1950 and 1966) deal with urban life. See also T. Turner, *The Diary of a Georgian Shopkeeper* (1980), dealing with Sussex life in the 1750s. E.N. Williams, *The Eighteenth Century Constitution* (1960) has a section on social life.

## Secondary works

J.D. Chambers, *Population, Economy and Society in Pre-Industrial England* (1972) and D. Marshall, *English People in the Eighteenth Century* (1956) are good starting-points. The landed classes are considered in G.E. Mingay, *English Landed Society in the Eighteenth Century* (1956) and *The Gentry: the rise and fall of a ruling class* (1976), especially chs 3–5. See also H.J. Habakkuk, 'England', in A. Goodwin (ed.), *The European Nobility in the Eighteenth Century* (1967). H.J. Perkin, *The Origins of Modern English Society, 1780–1880* (1969), ch. 2, and L.B. Namier's chapter 'The social foundations' in *England in the Age of the American Revolution* (2nd edn, 1961) are important sections of longer works. P. Langford's two works, *A Polite and Commercial People: England 1727–1783* (1989) and *Public Life and the Propertied Englishman, 1689–1789* (1991) are two major modern contributions.

D. Marshall, *The English Poor in the Eighteenth Century* (1926) and M.D. George, *London Life in the Eighteenth Century* (1925) are mines of information on the lower classes, but see also R.W. Malcolmson, *Life and Labour in England, 1700–1780* (1979). On London, see also G. Rudé, *Hanoverian London* (1971). P. Laslett, *The World We Have Lost* (1965) re-examines the nature of 'pre-industrial' society in the light of demographic and other evidence. J.L. and B. Hammond, *The Skilled Labourer, 1760–1832* (1919, 2nd edn republished 1978), C.R. Dobson, *Masters and Journeymen* (1980) and J.R. Rule, *The Experience of Labour in Eighteenth Century England* (1981) deal with industrial relations. E.P. Thompson, *Whigs and Hunters* (1975) presents a challenging view of the social conflicts over property rights, while the essays in D. Hay, P. Linebaugh, J. Rule, E.P. Thompson and C. Winslow, *Albion's Fatal Tree* (1975) throw light upon popular attitudes. On riots see J. Stevenson,

*Popular Disturbances in England, 1700–1870* (1979), on the law J. Brewer and J. Styles, *An Ungovernable People: the English and their law in the seventeenth and eighteenth centuries* (1980), and on crime J.M. Beattie, *Crime and the Courts in England, 1680–1800* (1986). Popular recreations are discussed in R.W. Malcolmson, *Popular Recreations in English Society, 1700–1850* (1973), and the press in G.A. Cranfield, *The Press and Society: from Caxton to Northcliffe* (1978). Family life and sexual mores are discussed in L. Stone, *The Family, Sex and Marriage in England 1500–1800* (1977); see also P. Laslett (ed.), *Household and Family in Past Time* (1972).

The development of the professional classes is considered in G.S. Holmes, *Augustan England: Professions, State and Society, 1680–1730* (1982), while the wider 'commercialization' of society is examined in N. McKendrick, J. Brewer and J.H. Plumb, *The Birth of a Consumer Society. The Commercialisation of Eighteenth-Century England* (1983). Two important recent contributions are P. Earle, *The Making of the English Middle Class: Business, Society and Family Life in London, 1660–1730* (1989) and P.J. Corfield, *Power and the Professions in Britain, 1700–1850* (1995). For the contribution of religious minorities see E. Bebb, *Nonconformity and Social and Economic Life, 1660–1880* (1935); I. Grub, *Quakerism and Industry before 1800* (1930); C. Roth, *A History of the Jews in England* (1941). C.W. Chalkin, *The Provincial Towns of Georgian England* (1974) and C.W. Chalkin and M.A. Havinden (eds), *Rural Change and Urban Growth, 1500–1800* (1974) examine urban development outside London. E. Hughes, *North Country Life in the Eighteenth Century: the North-East, 1700–1752* (1950) and *Cumberland and Westmorland, 1700–1830* (1965); A. Temple Patterson, *A History of Southampton, 1700–1914*, Vol. 1, *1700–1835* (1966); J.D. Chambers, *Nottinghamshire in the Eighteenth Century* (1966); J. Money, *Experience and Identity, Birmingham, 1770–1800* (1978); G. Jackson, *Hull in the Eighteenth Century* (1972); and R. Wilson, *Gentlemen Merchants* (1971) (on Leeds), are among the most important local studies.

For cultural developments, see J.H. Plumb, 'The public, literature and the arts', in P. Fritz and D. Williams (eds), *The Triumph of Culture: eighteenth-century perspectives* (1972). Country-house life is discussed in M. Girouard, *Life in the English Country House* (1978), especially chs 6, 7 and 8; see also J. Summerson, *Georgian London* (1962).

## Articles

E.P. Thompson, 'Eighteenth-century English society: class struggle without class', *SH* (1978) raises some interesting general issues. On the

TOPIC BIBLIOGRAPHY

ownership of property, see H.J. Habakkuk, 'English landownership, 1680–1740', *EconHR* (1940); C. Clay, 'Marriage inheritance and the rise of large estates in England, 1660–1815', *EconHR* (1968); B. Holdernesse, 'The English land market in the eighteenth century', *EconHR* (1974). E. Hughes, 'The professions in the eighteenth century', *DUJ* (1951) deals with an often neglected group. D. Rapp, 'Social mobility in the eighteenth century: the Whitbreads of Bedfordshire, 1720–1815', *EconHR* (1974) is an important case study. On the 'rise of the middle classes' generally, see A. Briggs, 'Middle class consciousness in English politics, 1780–1846', *PP* (1956) and H.J. Perkin, 'The social causes of the British Industrial Revolution', *TRHS* (1968). See also L. Stone, 'Literacy and education in England, 1640–1900', *PP* (1969) and J.H. Plumb, 'The new world of children in the eighteenth century', *PP* (1975). J.M. Beattie, 'The pattern of crime in England, 1660–1800', *PP* (1974) and E.P. Thompson, 'The moral economy of the English crowd in the eighteenth century', *PP* (1971) are among the most important articles on crime and protest.

## 7. The Elder Pitt

The Elder Pitt, Earl of Chatham, has, with his son, traditionally been seen as one of the 'great men' of British history. In large part this fame rests upon his leadership in the Seven Years War and his role in the development of Britain's overseas empire. Historians have also become increasingly interested in his domestic support which in some respects pre-figured the reform movement of George III's reign. Pitt's role in the early stages of the conflict with the American colonists also should not be ignored.

### Essay topics

• Assess the significance of the career of the Elder Pitt for the development of the British Empire.
• What social and political groups supported the Elder Pitt, and why?

### Sources and documents

*The Letters of Horace Walpole* (various editions available) are valuable for the mood of the country in 1756–57 and Pitt's role generally. See also Lord Hervey, *Some Materials towards Memoirs of the Reign of George II* (3 vols, ed. R. Sedgwick, 1931). D.B. Horn and M. Ransome (eds), *English Historical Documents*, Vol. 10, *1714–1783* (1957) also has relevant material.

## Secondary works

The chapters in H. van Thal, *The Prime Ministers*, Vol. 1(1974) and in P. Brown, *The Chathamites* (1967) are essential places to start. There are several biographies of which B. Williams, *Life of Chatham* is probably the best, if old (1913) and pro-Pitt. A. von Runville, *William Pitt, Earl of Chatham* is also elderly (1907), but massive, learned and anti-Pitt: a book to be quarried rather than read. J.H. Plumb, *Chatham* (1953) and B. Tunstall, *William Pitt, Earl of Chatham* (1938) are one-volume studies. Other biographies available include those by C. Grant Robertson (1946), O.A. Sherrard (3 vols, 1952–58), P.D. Brown (1978), and S. Ayling (1976). There is a brief outline of foreign policy in P. Langford, *Great Britain, 1688–1815* (1976), but more detailed studies include D.B. Horn, *Great Britain and Europe in the Eighteenth Century* (1967); R. Pares, *War and Trade in the West Indies, 1739–1763* (1936); and K. Hotblack, *Chatham's Colonial Policy* (1917). Britain's role in the Seven Years War is covered in J. Corbett, *England in the Seven Years War* (1907) and R. Savory, *His Britannic Majesty's Army in Germany during the Seven Years War* (1966), but see the more recent R. Middleton, *The Bells of Victory: the Pitt–Newcastle Ministry and the Conduct of the Seven Years War, 1757–1762* (1985). An important contribution on the financial underpinning of British war policy is J. Brewer, *The Sinews of Power: War, Money and the English State* (1989), esp. chs 1, 4–7.

Pitt's domestic significance is reflected in Brown (1967), but also in R. Robson, *The Oxfordshire Election of 1754* (1949) which reveals some of the interplay of national and local politics in the 1750s. For the City of London's support for Pitt, see Dame Lucy Sutherland, 'The City of London in eighteenth century politics', in *Essays Presented to Sir Lewis Namier* (eds R. Pares and A.J.P. Taylor, 1956) and M. Peters, *Pitt and Popularity: the patriot minister and London opinion during the Seven Years War* (1981). For the struggle between Pitt and Henry Fox, see E. Eyck, *Pitt versus Fox* (1950). Chatham's career in the 1760s is discussed in L. Namier, *England in the Age of the American Revolution* (2nd edn, 1961) and J. Brooke, *The Chatham Administration, 1766–1768* (1956).

## Articles

P. Langford, 'William Pitt and public opinion in 1757', *EHR* (1973) is helpful. Good on the background to his war policy are C.M. Andrews, 'Anglo-French commercial rivalry, 1700–50', *AmHR* (1914–15) and R. Pares, 'American and continental warfare, 1739–63', *EHR* (1936).

## 8. British colonial policy and the American War of Independence

A complex subject embracing political conflicts on both sides of the Atlantic and the general conduct of British imperial policy in the latter half of the eighteenth century. The view of American secession as inevitable needs to be carefully scrutinized and the divisions within America given full weight. Why there was a progress from resistance to taxation to 'revolution' needs to be examined carefully and the rhetoric of the colonists put in perspective. The impact of the American crisis on attitudes to the Empire is an important aspect of the topic.

### Essay topics

- How far was American independence the result of mistakes in British policy between 1763 and 1783?
- What impact did the American War of Independence have upon the development of the British Empire?

### Sources and documents

J.R. Pole (ed.), *The Revolution in America, 1754–1788* (1970) has a very useful selection of documents; see also R.C. Birch, *1776: the American challenge* (1977). E. Burke's speeches on American taxation can be read in B.W. Hill's collection of his works, *Edmund Burke on Government, Politics and Society* (1975). M. Beloff (ed.), *The Debate on the American Revolution* (1949) is also valuable.

### Secondary works

I.R. Christie, *Crisis of Empire: Great Britain and the American Colonies, 1754–1783* (1966) is a brief introduction. B. Donoughue, *British Politics and the American Revolution: The path to war, 1773–75* (1964) is a more detailed account of the immediate crisis. J.C. Miller, *The Origins of the American Revolution* (2nd edn, 1959) is an alternative outline. P. Langford, *The Eighteenth Century, 1688–1815* (1976), chs 11 and 12 deals with foreign policy in general. His *The First Rockingham Administration, 1756–1766* (1973) is important on the Stamp Act crisis. C.R. Ritcheson, *British Politics and the American Revolution* (1954) and G.H. Guttridge, *English Whiggism and the American Revolution* (2nd edn, 1963) are both relevant. J.R. Pole, *Foundations of American Independence, 1763–1815* (1972) is important on the American background. Two useful collections are E. Wright (ed.), *Causes and Consequences of the American Revolution* (1966) and J.P. Greene (ed.), *The Reinterpretation of the American Revolution* (1968). An important historiographical essay is I.R. Christie, 'The historians' quest for the American Revolution', in A. Whiteman, J.S. Bromley and P.G.M. Dickson (eds), *Statesmen, Scholars and Merchants* (1973). P. Mackesy, *The War for America, 1775–1783* (1964) and J.R. Alden, *The American Revolution, 1775–1783* (1954) deal with military affairs, and there are important essays on the naval side in J. Black and P. Woodfire (eds), *The British Navy and the Use of Naval Power in the Eighteenth Century* (1988). The wider issues of British imperial policy are considered in V.T. Harlow, *The Founding of the Second British Empire, 1763–1793*, Vol. 1: *Discovery and Revolution* (1952); G.L. Bear, *British Colonial Policy, 1754–1765* (2nd edn, 1933); J.R. Alden, *A History of the American Revolution: Britain and the loss of the thirteen colonies* (1969). Two older studies, C.H. Van Tyne, *The Causes of the War of Independence* (1922) and H.E. Egerton, *The Causes and Character of the American Revolution* (2nd edn, 1931) are still worth consulting. See also the important essay by J.G.A. Pocock, '1776: the revolution against Parliament', in J.G.A. Pocock (ed.), *Three British Revolutions: 1641, 1688, 1776* (1980). The impact of the American crisis on the reform movement in England is discussed in J. Cannon, *Parliamentary Reform, 1640–1832* (1973) and I.R. Christie, *Wilkes, Wyvill and Reform* (1962). See also P. Langford, 'London and the American crisis', in J. Stevenson (ed.), *London in the Age of Reform* (1976). B. Bailyn, *The Ideological Origins of the American Revolution* (1967) and *The Origins of American Politics* (1969) are essential on the political ideology underlying the conflict.

### Articles

R.W. van Alstyn, 'Europe, the Rockingham Whigs and the war for American independence: some documents', *HLQ* (1961); P. Marshall, 'Radicals, Conservatives, and the American Revolution', *PP* (1962); G.H. Guttridge, 'The Whig Opposition in England during the American Revolution', *JMH* (1934); and E.S. Morgan, 'The American Revolution: revisions in need of revising', *WMQ* (1957), are all useful.

## 9. George III, the constitution and the parliamentary reform movement, 1760–89

The latter years of the eighteenth century witnessed growing concern about the working of the constitution and in particular the power of the Crown. George III's attempts to exercise his right to choose his own ministers, the Wilkes affair and the conflict with America brought fresh issues into politics and led to the first widespread demands for parliamentary reform. It is important to understand why fears grew up about Crown influence and whether they were justified. The broader factors providing support for reform need to be considered and the different meanings given to 'reform'.

## Essay topics

- 'The power of the Crown has increased, is increasing and ought to be diminished' (Dunning's motion, 1780). Discuss.
- Why did the power of the Crown become an issue in British politics in the first 20 years of the reign of George III?
- What groups supported parliamentary reform in Britain between 1760 and 1789, and why?

## Sources and documents

E. Burke, *Thoughts on our Present Discontents* (1770 and later editions) is the classic statement of grievances against George III which provided the impetus for the 'economical reform' movement. E.N. Williams, *The Eighteenth Century Constitution, 1688–1815* (1960) has documents both on the role of the monarch and parliamentary reform.

## Secondary works

The most balanced and lucid exposition of the constitutional developments after 1760 can be found in I. R. Christie, *Myth and Reality in later Eighteenth-Century British Politics, and Other Papers* (1970), especially the introduction and chs 1 and 2. See also R. Pares, *King George III and the Politicians* (1953). On the reform movement, J. Cannon, *Parliamentary Reform in England, 1640–1832* (1973), chs 3 and 4, is a good introduction. I.R. Christie, *Wilkes, Wyvill and Reform* (1962) has a full discussion of the various elements in reform; see also E. Royle and J. Walvin, *British Radicals and Reformers, 1760–1848* (1982). J. Brewer, *Party Ideology and Popular Politics at the Accession of George III* (1978) examines the political forces at work in the 1760s. A recent challenge to received orthodoxy is J.C.D. Clarke, *English Society, 1688–1832* (1985), especially chs 1 and 4. See also his *The Dynamics of Change: the crisis of the 1750s and English party systems* (1982). An old but still useful study is G.S. Veitch, *The Genesis of Parliamentary Reform* (2nd edn, 1964). G. Rudé, *Wilkes and Liberty: A Social Study of 1763–1774* (1962) is essential on the metropolitan background and Wilkes's support, but see also L.S. Sutherland, *The City of London and the Opposition, 1768–74* (The Creighton Lecture, 1958), reprinted in J. Stevenson (ed.), *London in the Age of Reform* (1976). For the ideology of the English reformers see H.T. Dickinson, *The Politics of the People in Eighteenth Century Britain* (1995) and his *Liberty and Property* (1978), ch. 6. C. Robbins, *The Eighteenth Century Commonwealthman* (1959) and C. Hill, 'The Norman yoke' in his essays *Puritanism and Revolution* (1958) trace continuities with earlier ideas. On leading personalities see J.W. Osborne, *John Cartwright* (1972); E. Foner, *Tom Paine and Revolutionary America* (1976); F. O'Gorman, *Edmund Burke* (1973).

### Articles

I.R. Christie, 'Economical reform and the "influence of the Crown" 1780', *CHJ* (1956) explains the crucial link between fears of executive 'tyranny' and the demand for reform. His 'The Yorkshire Association, 1780–4', *HJ* (1960) and H. Butterfield, 'The Yorkshire Association and the crisis of 1779–80', *TRHS* (1947) examine the 'County' movement. P.D.G. Thomas, 'The beginnings of parliamentary reporting in newspapers, 1768–74', *EHR* (1959) discusses the growing influence of the press.

## 10. The impact of the French Revolution on Britain

Traditional interest focuses upon the effects of the French Revolution on party politics, especially on the Whigs, the rise of popular radicalism and its suppression, and the longer-term effects of the French Revolution on British politics. Much attention has focused in recent years on the popular political societies, E. P. Thompson seeing this as a crucial stage in the development of 'class consciousness' among working people. Goodwin represents a reworking of the available evidence, especially strong on the provincial and dissenting origins of the early reform movement. The period after 1795 is beginning to receive more serious attention than it has hitherto.

### Essay topics

- What impact did the French Revolution have upon British politics between 1789 and 1815?
- Were there any British 'Jacobins'?

## Sources and documents

The ideological debate can be followed in the various editions of T. Paine, *The Rights of Man* (1791–92) and E. Burke, *Reflections on the Revolution in France* (1790). A. Cobban (ed.), *The Debate on the French Revolution* (1950) contains selections from contemporary writers, as does M. Butler (ed.), *Burke, Paine and the Revolution Controversy* (1984); see also G.D.H. Cole and A.W. Filson (eds), *British Working Class Movements: select documents, 1789–1875* (1951). M. Thale (ed.), *The Autobiography of Francis Place* (1972) gives an insider's account of one of the popular societies in the 1790s; see also T. Hardy, 'A memoir of Thomas Hardy', reprinted in D. Vincent (ed.), *Testaments of Radicalism* (1977). For the London Corresponding Society, see also M. Thale (ed.), *Selections from the Papers of the London Corresponding Society, 1792–1799* (1983).

## Secondary works

H.T. Dickinson, *British Radicalism and the French Revolution, 1789–1815* (1985) and his edited collection *Britain and the French Revolution, 1789–1815* (1989) offer a succinct introduction to recent debates. See also M. Philp (ed.) *The French Revolution and British Popular Politics* (1991). E.P. Thompson, *The Making of the English Working Class* (2nd edn, 1968), esp. Pt 1, chs 1–5, is a stimulating and controversial view of popular radicalism. P.A. Brown, *The French Revolution in English History* (1918) is still a useful summary, but more recent assessments exist in J. Cannon, *Parliamentary Reform in England, 1640–1832* (1973), chs 6 and 7, and in A. Goodwin, *The Friends of Liberty* (1979), the most thorough of the assessments of popular radicalism. G.A. Williams, *Artisans and Sans-Culottes: popular movements in France and Britain during the French Revolution* (2nd edn, 1989) has important comparisons with the radical movement across the Channel. Loyalism has attracted increasing attention, for which see R.R. Dozier, *For King, Constitution, and Country: the English Loyalists and the French Revolution* (1983) and L. Colley, *Britons* (1992).

C. Emsley, *British Society and the French Wars, 1793–1815* (1979) ranges widely into both the political and social repercussions of the French Wars. F. O'Gorman, *The Whig Party and the French Revolution* (1967) and L.G. Mitchell, *Charles James Fox and the Disintegration of the Whig Party, 1782–1794* (1971) examine party developments, while D.G. Barnes, *George III and William Pitt, 1783–1806* (1939) is useful on the administration. E.N.C. Black, *The Association* (1963) has a section on loyalist organizations. A.D. Harvey, *Britain in the Early Nineteenth Century* (1978) is particularly helpful on the period 1800–12, but see also R. Wells, *Insurrection: the British Experience, 1796–1803* (1984) for the survival of radicalism and the threat of revolution. I.R. Christie, *Stress and Stability in Late Eighteenth-Century England* (1984) explicitly examines the stabilizing forces in the British polity, for which see also M. Thomis and P. Holt, *Threats of Revolution in Britain 1789–1848* (1977). The development of political ideology is admirably presented in H.T. Dickinson, *Liberty and Property* (1978). For the popular disturbances of the period see J. Stevenson, *Popular Disturbances in England, 1700–1870* (1979); R. Wells, *Dearth and Distress in Yorkshire, 1793–1801* (Borthwick Paper No. 52, 1977); J. Bohstedt, *Riot and Community Politics, 1790–1810* (1985); and K.J. Logue, *Popular Disturbances in Scotland, 1789–1815* (1979).

### Articles

The fears of the government are discussed in C. Emsley, 'The London "insurrection" of December 1792: fact, fiction or fantasy', *JBS* (1978). The reaction to the French Revolution is also dealt with in R.B. Rose, 'The Priestley riots of 1791', *PP* (1960); A. Mitchell, 'The Association Movement of 1792–3', *HJ* (1961); D.E. Ginter, 'The Loyalist Association Movement of 1792–93 and British public opinion', *HJ* (1966); J.R. Western, 'The Volunteer movement as an anti-revolutionary force, 1793–1800', *EHR* (1956). For popular distress, see W.M. Stern, 'The bread crisis in Britain, 1795–96', *E* (1964) and A. Booth, 'Food riots in North-West England, 1790–1801', *PP* (1977). Local movements are discussed in F.K. Donnelly and J.L. Baxter, 'Sheffield and the English revolutionary tradition, 1791–1820', *IRSH* (1974) and W.A.L. Seaman, 'Reform politics at Sheffield, 1791–1797', *THAS* (1957). For the continuity of radical activity after 1795, see J.R. Dinwiddy, 'The "Black Lamp" in Yorkshire, 1801–1802' and J.L. Baxter and F.K. Donnelly, 'The revolutionary "underground" in the West Riding: myth or reality?', *PP* (1974), and M. Elliott, 'The "Despard conspiracy" reconsidered', *PP* (1977). For an important recent work on loyalism, see M. Philp, 'Vulgar Conservatism, 1792–3', *EHR* (1995).

## 11. Pitt and Fox

The two central characters of late eighteenth-century politics can be assessed together or separately. Pitt the Younger's career in the 1780s is now much clearer and it is important to assess the importance of the financial and administrative reforms he attempted. Discussions of his career often stop in the mid-1790s, and it is necessary to take in his conduct of the war and second administration for a full assessment. Fox remains a fascinating figure. It is equally important to see his *full* career in perspective (up to 1806) and in the context of the fortunes of his party as a whole. Some grasp of party developments and the continuing, but changing, role of the Crown is important to the careers of both men.

## Essay topics

- 'A more effective prime minister than a war leader'. Discuss this view of Pitt the Younger.
- Was the career of Charles James Fox a total failure?
- How did the careers of *either* Pitt the Younger *or* Charles James Fox reflect changes in the pattern of eighteenth-century politics?

## Sources and documents

A. Aspinall and E.A. Smith (eds), *English Historical Documents,* Vol. 11, *1783–1832* (1959) has a selection of documents on the period. A. Aspinall (ed.), *The Later Correspondence of George III, December 1783–December 1810* (1962–70) also has relevant material. R. Coupland, *The War Speeches of William Pitt* (1915) and W. Pitt, *Orations on the French War* (1906) are useful for the war years. On Fox, see A. Bullock and M. Shock (eds), *The Liberal Tradition: From Fox to Keynes* (1956).

## Secondary works

J.W. Derry, *Politics in the Age of Fox, Pitt, and Liverpool* (1990) is a useful introduction to the period and its politics. For Pitt, the basic study is J. Ehrman, *The Younger Pitt: the Years of Acclaim* (1969) and *The Reluctant Transition* (1984), but these only go up to 1795. D.G. Barnes, *George III and William Pitt, 1783–1806* (1939) carries on the story to 1806. J.W. Derry, *William Pitt* (1962) is a brief study, while the older J. Holland Rose, *William Pitt and National Revival* (1911) and *William Pitt and the Great War* (1911) are still valuable. Pitt's reaction to the French Revolution is considered in P.A. Brown, *The French Revolution in English History* (1918). P. Langford, *The Eighteenth Century, 1688–1815* (1976), chs 14 and 15, is useful on foreign affairs. See also C. Emsley, *British Society and the French Wars, 1793–1815* (1979). J. Binney, *British Public*

*Finance and Administration, 1774–92* (1958) is relevant on Pitt's administrative reforms. On the role of the Irish crisis, see G.C. Bolton, *The Passing of the Act of Union* (1966).

On Fox, L.G. Mitchell, *Charles James Fox* (1992) is the best life; also helpful is J.W. Derry, *Charles James Fox* (1973). Loren Reid, *Charles James Fox: a man for the people* (1969) is useful on Fox as an orator. An older alternative is E.C.P. Lascelles, *Charles James Fox* (1936). The early part of his career is considered in J. Cannon, *The Fox–North Coalition: crisis of the constitution* (1970). The effects of the French Revolution are considered in F. O'Gorman, *The Whig Party and the French Revolution* (1967), while L.G. Mitchell, *Charles James Fox and the Disintegration of the Whig Party, 1782–94* (1970) deals more generally with Fox's relationship with the Whig Party. The organization of the Whig Party is discussed in the introduction to D.E. Ginter, *Whig Organisation in the General Election of 1790* (1967).

Of relevance to both careers are F. O'Gorman, *The Rise of Party in England* (1975), his shorter *The Emergence of the British Two-Party System, 1760–1832* (1982) and A.D. Harvey, *Britain in the Early Nineteenth Century* (1978). See, too, R. Pares, *George III and the Politicians* (1953).

Electoral politics are now considered more fully in F. O'Gorman, *Voters, Patrons and Parties: the Unreformed Electorate of Hanoverian England, 1734–1832* (1989), esp. ch. 5; J.A. Phillips, 'Electoral Polarization in the Reign of George III', in E. Hellmuth (ed.), *The Transformation of Political Culture* (1990) and his *Electoral Behaviour in Unreformed England, 1761–1802* (1982).

### Articles

On Pitt, see R.J. White, 'The Younger Pitt', *HT* (1952); A.S. Foord, 'The Waning of the influence of the Crown, 1780–1832', *EHR* (1947). For Fox, see I.R. Christie, 'C.J. Fox', *HT* (1958); H. Butterfield, 'Charles James Fox and the Whig Opposition in 1792', *CHJ* (1947–49); A.S. Foord (above): J.R. Dinwiddy, 'Charles James Fox and the people', *H* (Oct. 1970); H. Butterfield, 'Sincerity and insincerity in C.J. Fox', *PBA* 57 (1971); M.D. George, 'Fox's Martyrs: the general election of 1784', *TRHS* (1939). More generally, see J.A. Phillips, 'Popular Politics in Unreformed England', *JMH* (1980) and F. O'Gorman, 'Party Politics in the Early Nineteenth Century', *EHR* (1987).

## 12. The Industrial Revolution

This is a huge subject which can be dealt with on several different levels. It is important to recognize that there are varying interpretations among economic historians of *how* industrialization happens. The once-fashionable 'take-off' theory is now being modified by one which stresses a much broader and complex process of economic development. Some aspects, such as population growth, have almost become separate topics, raising a host of fresh questions. Traditional concerns are reflected in the debate over the effects of industrialization on living standards and the quality of life. In general, research on the Industrial Revolution has tended to create a growing awareness of the sheer complexity of the changes taking place. A regional or one-industry approach is often the best way of tackling the question.

### Essay topics

* Why did Britain experience industrial development in the period 1750–1870?
* Have the social effects of industrialization been exaggerated?

### Sources and documents

A.E. Bland, P.A. Brown and R.H. Tawney (eds), *English Economic History: Select Documents* (1914), Pt III, sections I, III, IV, V. The collection edited by C. Harvie, A. Scharf *et al.* (eds), *Industrialisation and Culture, 1815–1880* (1970) is also useful. There is a rich literature, mainly from the 1830s and 1840s, a few examples of which are C. Bronte, *Shirley* (1849) (Luddism features prominently here), T. Carlyle, *Past and Present* (1843), Mrs Gaskell, *Mary Barton* (1848) and *North and South* (1855).

### Secondary works

R.M. Hartwell, *The Industrial Revolution in England* (Historical Association pamphlet, 1965) is a useful short guide to the sort of questions economic historians ask. P. Mathias, *The First Industrial Nation: an economic history of Britain, 1700–1914* (1969) is the standard economic history. T.S. Ashton, *The Industrial Revolution, 1760 to 1830* (1948) is an older, brief outline, but a modern treatment is P. Hudson, *The Industrial Revolution* (1992). P. Deane, *The First Industrial Revolution* (1965) and P. Deane and W.A. Cole, *British Economic Growth, 1688–1959* (1962) are also valuable, as are A.E. Musson, *The Growth of British Industry* (1978) and the series of interpretative essays in R. Floud and D. McCloskey (eds), *The Economic History of Britain since 1700* (1981): see especially D. McCloskey, 'The Industrial Revolution, 1780–1860: A Survey'. F. Crouzet, *The Victorian Economy* (1984) looks at the later stages. R.M. Hartwell (ed.), *The Causes of the Industrial Revolution* (1967) has some interesting essays; see also the wide-ranging essay on 'continuity' and 'discontinuity' in R.M. Hartwell (ed.), *The Industrial Revolution and Economic Growth* (1971). The origins of industrialization are also discussed in M.W. Flinn, *Origins of the Industrial Revolution* (1966) and C. Wilson, *England's Apprenticeship, 1603–1763* (1966). Various aspects of industrialization are dealt with in M.W. Flinn, *British Population Growth, 1700–1850* (1970); N. Tranter, *Population since the Industrial Revolution: the case of England and Wales* (1973) and *Population and Society, 1750–1940* (1985); W.E. Minchington (ed.), *The Growth of English Overseas Trade in the Seventeenth and Eighteenth Centuries* (1969); A.E. Musson (ed.), *Science, Technology and Economic Growth in the Eighteenth Century* (1972); T.C. Barker and C.F. Savage, *An Economic History of Transport* (1959).

On the social effects of industrialization, J.L. and B. Hammond, *The Town Labourer, 1760–1832: the new civilisation* (1917) is the classic 'pessimistic' case, but see also A.J. Taylor (ed.), *The Standard of Living in Britain in the Industrial Revolution* (1975), M.I. Thomis, *The Town Labourer and the Industrial Revolution* (1974) and J. Rule, *The Labouring Classes in Early Industrial England, 1750–1850* (1986). E.P. Thompson, *The Making of the English Working Class* (2nd edn, 1968) and J. Foster, *Class Struggle and the Industrial Revolution* (1974) argue the case for the rise of a working class in the course of industrialization; see also H.J. Perkin, *The Origins of Modern English Society 1780–1880* (1969); S.G. Checkland, *The Rise of Industrial Society in England, 1815–85* (1964); R.J. Morris, *Class and Class Consciousness in the Industrial Revolution* (1979); and J. Walvin, *English Urban Life, 1776–1851* (1982).

Local histories of industrial development include J.D. Chambers, *Nottinghamshire in the Eighteenth Century* (2nd edn, 1966); N.H. Chaloner, *The Social and Economic Development of Crewe, 1780–1923* (1950); H. Hamilton, *An Economic History of Scotland in the Eighteenth Century* (1963) and *The Industrial Revolution in Scotland* (1966); A.H. John, *The Industrial Development of South Wales, 1750–1850* (1959); A.H. Dodd, *The Industrial Revolution in North Wales* (3rd edn, 1971); J. Rowe, *Cornwall in the Age of the Industrial Revolution* (1953); W.H.B. Court, *The Rise of the Midland Industries 1600–1838* (1953); B. Trinder, *The Industrial Revolution in Shropshire* (1973); T.C. Barker and J.R. Harris, *A Merseyside Town in the*

454     TOPIC BIBLIOGRAPHY

*Industrial Revolution: St. Helens, 1750–1900* (1954); R.A. Church, *Economic and Social Change in a Midland Town: Victorian Nottingham, 1815–1900* (1966); J.C. Beckett and R.E. Glassock (eds), *Belfast: origin and growth of an industrial city* (1967); and I. Adams, *The Making of Urban Scotland* (1978).

For individual industries, see P. Mathias, *The Brewing Industry in England, 1700–1830* (1959); T.S. Ashton, *Iron and Steel in the Industrial Revolution* (1951); A. P. Wadsworth and J. Mann, *The Cotton Industry and the Rise of Industrial Lancashire to 1780* (1965); M.M. Edwards, *The Growth of the British Cotton Trade, 1780–1815* (1967); H. Heaton, *The Yorkshire Woollen and Worsted Industry* (1920); T.S. Ashton and J. Sykes, *The Coal Industry in the Eighteenth Century* (2nd edn, 1964); and A. and N.L. Clow, *The Chemical Revolution: a contribution to social technology* (1952).

Case studies of particular firms include J.R. Harris, *The Copper King: a biography of Thomas Williams of Llanidan* (1964); T.S. Ashton, *An Eighteenth Century Industrialist: Peter Stubs of Warrington, 1756–1806* (1939); G. Unwin, *Samuel Oldnow and the Arkwrights: the industrial revolution at Stockport and Marple* (1924); R.S. Fitton and A.P. Wadsworth, *The Strutts and the Arkwrights* (1964); A. Raistrick, *Dynasty of Ironfounders: the Darbys and Coalbrookdale* (1953); E. Roll, *An Early Experiment in Industrial Organisation, being a history of the firm of Boulton and Watt, 1775–1805* (1930); J.P. Addis, *The Crawshay Dynasty: a study in industrial organisation and development, 1765–1867* (1957); T.C. Barker, *Pilkington Brothers and the Glass Industry* (1960).

## Articles

There is a large and specialized articles literature on this topic, much of which can be followed from the secondary sources mentioned above. Some general issues are raised by M. Fores, 'The Myth of a British Industrial Revolution', *H* (1981) and A.E. Musson, 'The British Industrial Revolution', *H* (1982). Other important articles are D.C. Coleman, 'Industrial growth and industrial relations', *E* (1956–57); A.H. John, 'Aspects of economic growth in the first half of the eighteenth century', *E* (1961); E.A. Wrigley, 'Raw materials in the Industrial Revolution', *EconHR* (1962); C.H. Wilson, 'The entrepreneur in the Industrial Revolution', *H* (1957); S. Pollard, 'Factory discipline in the Industrial Revolution', *EconHR* (1963); N. McKendrick, 'An eighteenth century entrepreneur in salesmanship and marketing techniques', *EconHR* (1960); K. Berrill, 'International trade and the rate of economic growth', *EconHR* (1960); T.S. Ashton, 'Changes in the standard of comfort in 18th century England', *PBA* (1955); S.D. Chapman, 'The transition to the factory system in the Midlands cotton-spinning industry', *EconHR* (1965); J.D. Chambers, 'The Vale of Trent, 1760–1800', *EconHR* Supplement No.3 (1957). For the 'standard of living' debate, see R.M. Hartwell, 'The rising standard of living in England, 1800–50', *EconHR* (1961); E.J. Hobsbawm, 'The British standard of living, 1790–1850', *EconHR* (1958); E.J. Hobsbawm and R.M. Hartwell, 'The standard of living during the Industrial Revolution – a discussion', *EconHR* (1963); R.S. Neale, 'The standard of living, 1780–1844: a regional and class study', *EconHR* (1966).

# 13. Reform, radicalism and the Tory Party in Regency England

The later years of the Napoleonic Wars and the period up to the early 1820s have frequently been viewed as ones in which the country faced agitations of almost revolutionary proportions. A combination of wartime and postwar distress, the effects of industrial development and a revival of reform activity led to a phase of widespread agitation and government repression. The nature and implications of the popular movements of these years need examining, especially the reasons for the failure of the reformers to achieve any legislative results in spite of periods of intense activity. The government of Lord Liverpool has frequently been criticized for its reactionary character, and some assessment of its strengths and weaknesses are necessary. Liverpool's reputation has been reassessed in recent years, some seeing the years 1820–22 as marking a turning-point from which a new 'liberal Toryism' emerged.

## Essay topics

- How near did Britain come to revolution in the years between 1810 and 1822?
- Why were the Whigs so ineffective between 1810 and 1830?
- Does the government of Lord Liverpool deserve more credit than it has received for its conduct of affairs between 1812 and 1827?

## Sources and documents

G.D.H. Cole and A.W. Filson, *British Working Class Movements: select documents, 1789–1875* (1951) has documents on trade union and radical groups. S. Bamford, *Passages in the Life of a Radical* (1844, and later editions) is a famous account of radicalism in the postwar years, see especially the description of Peterloo. W. Reitzel (ed.), *The Autobiography of William Cobbett* (1967) is a compilation of Cobbett's writings on his life. See also A. Prentice, *Historical Sketches and Personal Recollections of Manchester: intended to illustrate the progress of public opinion from 1792–1832* (1851, new edn with introduction by D. Read, 1970). For ministerial politics see *The Croker Papers* (3 vols, ed. L.J. Jennings, 1884), vol. 1.

## Secondary works

The later sections of A.D. Harvey, *Britain in the Early Nineteenth Century* (1979) and C. Emsley, *British Society and the French Wars, 1793–1815* (1978) are relevant to this topic; see also, J.W. Derry, *Politics in the Age of Fox, Pitt and Liverpool* (1990), ch. 4 and F. O'Gorman, *Voters, Patrons and Parties: the Unreformed Electorate of Hanoverian England, 1734–1832* (1989), chs 5 and 6. An important appreciation of radicalism is J.R. Dinwiddy, *From Luddism to the First Reform Bill* (1986), while the older R.J. White, *Waterloo to Peterloo* (1957) concentrates on the postwar years; see also D.G. Wright, *Popular Radicalism: the working-class experience 1780–1800* (1988). On radicalism, see also E.P. Thompson, *The Making of the English Working Class* (2nd edn, 1968), Pt III. Popular disturbances of the period are discussed in F.O. Darvell, *Popular Disturbances and Public Order in Regency England* (1934); M.I. Thomis, *The Luddites* (1970); A.J. Peacock, *Bread or Blood* (1965); M.I. Thomis and P. Holt, *Threats of Revolution in Britain, 1789–1848* (1977); J. Stevenson, *Popular Disturbances in England, 1700–1832* (1992). D. Read, *Peterloo: The 'Massacre' and its background* (1958) remains the best account of the famous event and its background. G. Spater, *William Cobbett: the Poor Man's Friend* (1982) supersedes the older life by G.D.H. Cole, but see also J.W. Osborne, *William Cobbett: his thought and his times* (1966). For other reformers see J. Belchem, *'Orator' Hunt* (1985), W. Thomas, *The Philosophic Radicals* (1979) and J. Dinwiddy, *Christopher Wyvill and Reform, 1790–1820* (Borthwick Paper No. 39, 1971). For the rise of public opinion, see D. Read, *The English Provinces, c. 1760–1960* (1964) and *Press and People, 1790–1850* (1960); R.K. Webb, *The British Working Class Reader, 1790–1848* (1955).

Ministerial politics are best considered in N. Gash, *Aristocracy and People* (1979) and *Lord Liverpool* (1984). There is detailed treatment of the postwar period in J.E. Cookson, *Lord Liverpool's Administration: the crucial years, 1815–1822* (1975). W.R. Brock, *Lord Liverpool and Liberal*

*Toryism* (1941) long held sway with its view of a transition after 1821, but this has been challenged, for example in J.C.D. Clark, *English Society, 1688–1832* (1986), ch. 6, and B. Hilton, *Corn, Cash Commerce* (1977) and *The Age of Atonement* (1988), esp ch. 5. For other ministerial figures, see D. Gray, *Spencer Perceval, 1762–1812* (1963); N. Gash, *Mr. Secretary Peel: the life of Robert Peel to 1830* (1961); P. Ziegler, *Addington, a life of Henry Addington, first Viscount Sidmouth* (1965); C.J. Bartlett, *Castlereagh* (1966); C.R. Fay, *Huskisson and his Age* (1951). The Whigs are discussed in M. Roberts, *The Whig Party, 1807–1812* (1939) and A. Mitchell, *The Whigs in Opposition, 1815–1830* (1967). The principal Whig personalities are discussed in E.A. Smith, *Lord Grey, 1764–1845* (1990); C.W. New, *The Life of Henry Brougham to 1830* (1961); and Earl Fitzwilliam in E.A. Smith, *Whig Principles and Party Politics* (1975). See also J.J. Sack, *The Grenvillites* (1979) and P. Jupp, *Lord Grenville, 1759–1834* (1985).

### Articles

A.S. Foord, 'The waning of the influence of the Crown, 1780–1832', *EHR* (1947); A. Briggs, 'Middle class consciousness in English politics, 1780–1846', *PP* (1956); A. Aspinall, 'English party organisation in the early 19th C.', *EHR* (1926) are useful on the conventional aspects of politics. On Lord Liverpool see B. Hilton, 'Lord Liverpool. The Art of Politics and the Practice of Government', *TRHS* (1988). J. Dinwiddy, 'Luddism and politics in the North', *SH* (1979) is a judicious survey of the upheaval of those years. T.M. Parsinnen, 'The revolutionary party in London 1816–20', *BIHR* (1972) shows the genuine revolutionaries at work. For the North, see F.K. Donnelly and J.L. Baxter, 'Sheffield and the English revolutionary tradition, 1791–1820', *IRSH* (1974). Important radical personalities are discussed in J.R. Dinwiddy, 'Sir Francis Burdett and Burdettite Radicalism', *H* (1980) and J.C. Belchem, 'Henry Hunt and the evolution of the mass platform', *EHR* (1978); see also J.C. Belchem, 'Republicanism, popular constitutionalism and the radical platform in early 19th Century England', *SH* (1981).

## 14. The Great Reform Act

The Reform Act of 1832 occupies a central place in the history of nineteenth-century Britain, though in recent years historians have tended to stress how little rather than how much was changed by it. The passing of the Act falls into three main stages: the build-up of the reform movement in the period after 1815; the break-up of the Tory Party's dominance in the late 1820s; the reform crisis of the period 1830–32. The varying demands from radicals and reformers and how far they were met requires some attention. Considerable debate has been generated by the question of whether Britain faced a revolutionary crisis in 1831–32. The medium and longer-term effects of the Act upon the conduct and the nature of Victorian politics are also important.

### Essay topics

- How would you account for the passing of the Reform Act of 1832?
- Did Britain face a revolutionary crisis in 1832?
- What truth is there in the contemporary view that the Reform Act of 1832 gave power to the middle classes?

### Sources and documents

H.J. Hanham, *The Nineteenth Century Constitution, 1815–1914: documents and commentary* (1969) has a selection of relevant documents, as has E.C. Black, *British Politics in the Nineteenth Century* (1970). G.D.H. Cole and A.W. Filson, *British Working Class Movements: select documents, 1789–1870* (1951) and D.J. Rowe (ed.), *London Radicalism, 1830–43: a selection from the papers of Francis Place* (1970) have documents on the radical side.

### Secondary works

D.G. Wright, *Popular Radicalism*, ch. 5, has a brief outline. M. Brock, *The Great Reform Act* (1973) is the best modern study, but J.R.M. Butler, *The Passing of the Great Reform Bill* (1914) is an older narrative still of value. A broader survey can be found in J. Cannon, *Parliamentary Reform, 1640–1832* (1973); see also J.C.D. Clark, *English Society, 1688–1832* (1986) for a view of the durability of the old order. One of the issues which produced the break-up of the Tory dominance is discussed in G.I.T. Machin, *The Catholic Question in English Politics, 1820 to 1830* (1964), while J.A. Phillips, *The Great Reform Bill in the Boroughs: English Electoral Behaviour, 1818–1841* (1992) examines the Reform Act in relation to electoral developments over the period. The Whig Party is treated in A. Mitchell, *The Whigs in Opposition, 1815–1830* (1967) and the role of Grey in E.A. Smith, *Lord Grey, 1764–1845* (1990). The rise of 'public opinion' is discussed in D. Read, *Press and People, 1790–1850*

(1960) and P. Hollis, *The Pauper Press: a study in working class radicalism in the 1830s* (1970). On the reform crisis J. Hamburger, *James Mill and the Art of Revolution* (1965) pursues the important argument that the radicals 'worked up' a crisis in order to force through the Bill. This argument is considered in J. Stevenson, *Popular Disturbances in England, 1700–1870* (1979) and M. Thomis and P. Holt, *Threats of Revolution in Britain, 1789–1848* (1977), ch. 4. See also D. Fraser, 'The agitation for parliamentary reform', in J.T. Ward (ed.), *Popular Movements, c. 1830–1850* (1970). On the influence of Continental events, see N. Gash, 'The French Revolution of 1830 and the reform crisis', in *Essays presented to Sir Lewis Namier* (eds A.J.P. Taylor and R. Pares, 1956).

The effects of the Reform Bill on the structure of politics are analysed in N. Gash, *Reaction and Reconstruction in English Politics, 1832–52* (1965) and his earlier *Politics in the Age of Peel* (1953). See also G.A.M. Finlayson, *England in the Eighteen Thirties. Decade of reform* (1969) and H.J. Hanham, *The Reformed Electoral System in Great Britain, 1832–1914* (Historical Association Pamphlet, 1968). The impact of the Reform Act on Whig and Liberal politics is discussed in P. Mandler, *Aristocratic Government in the Age of Reform: Whigs and Liberals, 1830–1852* (1990); R. Brent, *Liberal Anglican Politics: Whiggery, Religion and Reform, 1830–1841* (1987); I.D.C. Newbould, *Whiggery and Reform: the Politics of Government* (1990); T.A. Jenkins, *The Liberal Ascendency, 1830–1886* (1994) and his *Parliament, Party and Politics in Victorian Britain* (1996), ch. 2.

## Articles

A. Briggs, 'Middle-class consciousness in English politics, 1780–1846', *PP* (1956); 'Thomas Attwood and the economic background of the Birmingham Political Union', *CHJ* (1947–49); 'The background of the parliamentary reform movement in three English cities, 1830–32', *CHJ* (1950–52) are important. See also H. Fergeson, 'The Birmingham Political Union and government', *VS* (1960). Also relevant are J. Milton-Smith, 'Earl Grey's cabinet and the objects of parliamentary reform', *HJ* (1972); D.C. Moore, 'The other side of reform', *VS* (1961) and 'Concession or cure: the sociological premises of the first Reform Act', *HJ* (1966); G. Rudé, 'English rural and urban disturbances, 1830–31', *PP* (1967); D.J. Rowe, 'Class and political radicalism in London, 1831-2', *HJ* (1970). For the more recent discussions of the reform, see L. Mitchell, 'Foxite politics and the Great Reform Bill', *EHR* (1993); E. Wasson, 'The great Whigs and parliamentary reform, 1809–1830', *JBS* (1985); J. Phillips, 'The many faces of reform. The electorate and the

Great Reform Act', *PH* (1982); W. Rubinstein, 'The end of "Old Corruption" in Britain, 1780–1860', *PP* (1983); and J.A. Phillips and C. Wetherell, 'The Great Reform Act of 1832 and the political modernization of England', *AHR* (1995).

## 15. Peel, the Tory Party and the repeal of the Corn Laws

For some contemporaries the end of agricultural protection raised even greater passions than parliamentary reform, and the struggle over the Corn Laws has frequently been seen as marking a decisive shift in the balance of political power in nineteenth-century Britain. Strong support for 'repeal' from middle-class interests and opposition from sections of the landed interest produced a conflict with wide economic and political repercussions. It is important to see the Corn Law issue in the context of the 'Hungry Forties' and the debate about the 'Condition of England'. In the passing of 'repeal' the role of the Anti-Corn Law League and the Manchester School has to be weighed against the personal influence of Peel over the timing of the measure. Peel's position in the Tory Party and the repercussions of the Corn Law issue for party alignments is an important aspect of the question.

### Essay topics

• Why did the struggle to repeal the Corn Laws arouse such passions in early Victorian Britain?
• Why did Peel repeal the Corn Laws?

### Sources and documents

H.J. Hanham, *The Nineteenth Century Constitution, 1815–1914: documents and commentary* (1969) has some relevant documents; see also A.E. Bland, P.A. Brown and R.H. Tawney, *English Economic History: select documents* (1914), Pt III, section VI. Peel's memoirs, *Memoirs by the Rt. Hon. Sir Robert Peel* (ed. Lord Mahon and E. Cardwell, 1856–57) reveal his own view of the situation. R.S. Surtees, *Hillingdon Hall* (1845) is a novel with some relevant social comment. See also A. Prentice, *History of the Anti-Corn Law League* (1853, reprinted 1968).

### Secondary works

A. Briggs, *The Age of Improvement, 1783–1867* (1959), ch. 6, is still a good brief introduction to the politics of the 1840s; see also the section in N. Gash, *Aristocracy and People: Britain 1815–1865* (1980). There is a useful discussion in W.H. Chaloner, 'The agitation against the Corn Laws', in J.T. Ward (ed.), *Popular Movements c. 1830–1850* (1970). More detailed studies include N. Gash, *Politics in the Age of Peel* (1953) and *Reaction and Reconstruction in English Politics, 1832–52* (1965). R. Blake, *The Conservative Party from Peel to Thatcher* (1985) has a brief outline, but see R. Stewart, *The Foundation of the Conservative Party 1830–1867* (1979) for a more detailed study. N. Gash's *Peel* (1976) or his *Sir Robert Peel* (1972) are the standard lives. See also A. Briggs, 'Sir Robert Peel', in H. van Thal (ed.), *The Prime Ministers*, Vol. 1 (1974) and the recent D. Read, *Peel and the Victorians* (1987) and E.J. Evans, *Sir Robert Peel: Statesmanship, Power and Party* (1991). N. McCord, *The Anti-Corn Law League* (1958) is essential on the famous pressure group, while W.D. Grampp, *The Manchester School of Economics* (1960) examines the economic issues. C.R. Fay, *The Corn Laws and Social England* (1932) and D.G. Barnes, *A History of the English Corn Laws* (2nd edn, 1961) analyse the long-term history of the Corn Laws. F.M.L. Thompson, *English Landed Society in the Nineteenth Century* (1963) is valuable on the position of the landed interest. G. Kitson Clark, *The Making of Victorian England* (1962), especially ch. 7, has a masterly analysis of the repercussions of the repeal of the Corn Laws. R. Stewart, *The Politics of Protection: Lord Derby and the Protectionist Party, 1841–1852* (1971) discusses one strand of Tory reaction to the Corn Law issue.

### Articles

G. Kitson Clark, 'The repeal of the Corn Laws and the politics of the forties', *EconHR* (1951); B. Kemp, 'Reflections on repeal of the Corn Laws', *VS* (1961–62) and S.S. Fairlie, 'The nineteenth-century Corn Law reconsidered', *EconHR* (1965) are of general relevance. See also G.L. Mosse, 'The Anti-Corn Law League, 1844–46', *EconHR* (1947); J.A. Thomas, 'The repeal of the Corn Laws, 1846', *E* (1929); M. Lawson-Tancred, 'The Anti-Corn Law League and the Corn Law crisis of 1846', *HJ* (1960). G. Kitson Clark, 'The country gentlemen and the repeal of the Corn Laws', *EHR* (1967) and 'The electorate and the repeal of the Corn Laws', *TRHS* (1951) are also relevant. The party political dimension is discussed in N. Gash, 'Peel and the party system', *TRHS* (1951) and A. Aydelotte, 'The House of Commons in the 1840s', *H* (1954). The reactions of the landed interest are discussed in D. Spring, 'The English landed estate in the age of coal and iron', *JEconH* (1951);

A. Aydelotte, 'The country gentry and the repeal of the Corn Laws', *EHR* (1967); W.R. Ward, 'West Riding landowners and the Corn Laws', *EHR* (1966); D. Spring, 'Earl Fitzwilliam and the repeal of the Corn Laws', *AgH* (1954).

## 16. Chartism

The diversity of Chartism almost belies its status as a single movement or 'ism'. Nonetheless, the agitations which focused around the People's Charter provide an important opportunity to examine the attitudes and motivations of the mass of unenfranchised workers in mid-nineteenth-century Britain. Chartism drew both upon strong traditions of artisan radicalism and the immediate stimulus of distress in the 'Hungry Forties'. Historians are somewhat divided between those who argue that Chartism marked the end of a period of 'insurgent' working-class activity, replaced by the 'labourism' of the mid-Victorian period, and those who see greater continuity between the Chartist and post-Chartist periods, particularly when viewed from the local level. An acceptable approach is to study Chartism in the context of a particular region, which gives both some appreciation of the interplay of the Chartists with competing interests, such as trade unionism and the Anti-Corn Law League, and some awareness of the wide range of issues which flowed into Chartism. Some examination of what happened *after* 1848 is also useful.

### Essay topics

• Account for the rise and fall of Chartism.
• How far does the local history of Chartism modify the view that it failed?

### Sources and documents

Of the memoirs of Chartists, W. Lovett, *The Life and Struggles of William Lovett* (1876 and later editions) and R.G. Gammage, *History of the Chartist Movement* (1854 and later editions) are particularly valuable. See also B. Wilson, 'The struggles of an old chartist', in D. Vincent (ed.), *Testaments of Radicalism* (1977). G.D.H. Cole and A.W. Filson (eds), *British Working Class Movements, 1789–1870* (1951); D. Thompson (ed.), *The Early Chartists* (1971); P. Hollis (ed.), *Class and Conflict in Nineteenth Century England, 1815–1850* (1973); and F.C. Mather (ed.), *Chartism and Society* (1980) also have relevant documents.

## Secondary works

F.C. Mather, *Chartism* (Historical Association pamphlet, 1965) is a useful introduction. J.T. Ward, *Chartism* (1973) and D. Jones, *Chartism and the Chartists* (1975) are two fuller studies; see also D. Thompson, *The Chartists* (1986). The older studies by M. Howell, *The Chartist Movement* (1918) and J. West, *A History of the Chartist Movement* (1920) are also still of value. A. Briggs, *Chartist Studies* (1958) is essential on the regional background and G.D.H. Cole, *Chartist Portraits* (1940) on the leaders. The social background of the 1840s is discussed in J.L. and B. Hammond, *The Age of the Chartists* (1930), J. Rule, *The Labouring Classes in Early Industrial England, 1750–1850* (1986) and M.I. Thomis, *The Town Labourer in the Industrial Revolution* (1974). D. Bythell, *The Handloom Weavers* (1969) deals with a group prominent in Chartist activity. F.C. Mather, *Public Order in the Age of the Chartists* (1959) and J. Stevenson, *Popular Disturbances in England, 1700–1870* (1979), ch. 12, discuss the public order side. The ideological background to Chartism is discussed in D. Thompson, *The Early Chartists* (1971); E.P. Thompson, *The Making of the English Working Class* (2nd edn, 1968), ch. 16; P. Hollis, *The Pauper Press: a study in working-class radicalism of the 1830s* (1970), chs 6 and 7; and G. Stedman Jones, 'Rethinking Chartism', in his *Languages of Class* (1984). See also D. Thompson and J. Epstein (eds), *The Chartist Experience* (1982). Individual biographies include D. Read and E. Glasgow, *Feargus O'Connor, Irishman and Chartist* (1961); J. Epstein, *The Lion of Freedom: Feargus O'Connor and the Chartist Movement* (1982); A. Plummer, *Bronterre: a political biography of Bronterre O'Brien* (1971); D. Williams, *John Frost: A Study in Chartism* (1939); A.R. Schoyen, *The Chartist Challenge: a portrait of George Harney* (1958). Other aspects of Chartism are discussed in A. Hadfield, *The Chartist Land Company* (1970) and H.N. Faulkner, *Chartism and the Churches* (1916). The last phase of Chartism is discussed in J. Saville, *1848: the British State and the Chartist Movement* (1987) and his *Ernest Jones: Chartist* (1952). See also M. Taylor, *The Decline of British Radicalism, 1847–1860* (1995).

For the large and growing literature of regional studies of Chartism, see the bibliography in D.J.V. Jones, *Chartism and the Chartists* (1975), but two important contributions are D.J.V. Jones, *The Last Rising: The Newport Insurrections of 1839* (1985) and D. Goodway, *London Chartism* (1982).

## Articles

Important articles include R.P. Higgins, 'The Irish influence on the

Chartist movement', *PP* (1961); D.J. Rowe, 'The failure of London Chartism', *HJ* (1968); I. Prothero, 'Chartism in London', *PP* (Aug. 1969) and 'London Chartism and the Trades', *EconHR* (May, 1971); H. Weisser, 'Chartist internationalism, 1845–8', *HJ* (1971); DJ Rowe, 'Some aspects of Chartism in the north-east', *IRSH* (1971); T.R. Tholfsen, 'The Chartist crisis in Birmingham', *IRSH* (1958); B. Harrison and P. Hollis, 'Chartism, Liberalism and Robert Lowery', *EHR* (1967).

## 17. Social reform in nineteenth-century Britain

The period from the end of the eighteenth century witnessed widespread adjustments of social policy to meet the needs of a rapidly expanding industrial society. Many aspects of government and society came under scrutiny and the result was a patchwork of measures and initiatives to deal with the consequences of population growth, industrialization and urban development. The motives and tactics of reformers require analysis, as well as the adequacy of the solutions they provided. One theme of recent work has been to criticize such reforms as a mere means of 'social control', but this demands careful scrutiny. The repercussions of social reform for the conduct and nature of government have also stimulated discussion.

### Essay topics

• Did Victorian social reform amount to anything more than a 'sop to conscience'?
• How would you characterize the nature of nineteenth-century social reform?

### Sources and documents

Many of the classic texts and reports on social reform have been reprinted in modern editions. R. Owen, *A New View of Society* (1813–14) and *Report to the County of Lanark* (1821) contain the essentials of 'Owenism'. Of central importance is *The Report of the Royal Commission on the Poor Law* (1834, new edition with an introduction by S.G. and E.O.A. Checkland, 1974). On the public health question see E. Chadwick, *Report on the Sanitary Condition of the Labouring Population of Great Britain* (1842; new edition with introduction by M.W. Flinn, 1965). E.P. Thompson and E. Yeo (eds), *The Unknown Mayhew* (1971) has selections from Mayhew's investigations into London labouring life in the 1840s and 1850s. There is an excellent selection from late Victorian social enquiries in P. Keating (ed.), *Into Unknown England, 1866–1913* (1976). See also W. Booth's passionate *In Darkest England and the Way Out* (1890, reprinted 1970). Documents on particular topics can be found in M.E. Rose, *The English Poor Law, 1780–1830* (1971); J.M. Goldstrom, *Education: elementary education, 1780–1900* (1972); J.J. Tobias, *Nineteenth Century Crime: prevention and punishment* (1972); E. Midwinter, *Nineteenth Century Education* (1970). E. Midwinter, *Victorian Social Reform* (1968) also has a selection of documents with introduction.

## Secondary works

Most of the general histories of nineteenth-century Britain include sections on social reform. E. Halévy's *History of the English People in the Nineteenth Century* (1924 and subsequent re-editions) is still an excellent starting-point. J.P. Roach, *Social Reform in England, 1780–1880* (1978) and U.R.Q. Henriques, *Before the Welfare State: social administration in early industrial Britain* (1979) are two comprehensive modern studies of the problem. H. Perkin, *The Origins of Modern English Society, 1780–1880* (1969) is relevant, especially ch. 8. Specific reform movements are discussed in J.T. Ward, *The Factory Movement, 1830–1855* (1963); S.E. Finer, *The Life and Times of Sir Edwin Chadwick* (1952); J. Burnett, *A Social History of Housing, 1815–1970* (1979); M.E. Rose, *The English Poor Law, 1870–1930* (1971) and *The Relief of Poverty, 1834–1914* (1972); G.W. Oxley, *Poor Relief in England and Wales, 1601–1834* (1974); D. Fraser (ed.), *The New Poor Law in the Nineteenth Century* (1976); F. Driver, *Power and Pauperism. The workhouse system, 1834–1884* (1993); C. Emsley, *Crime and Society in England, 1750–1900* (2nd edn, 1995); J. Hurt, *Education in Evolution* (1972); P.H.J.H. Gosden, *The Development of Educational Administration in England and Wales* (1966); A.T. Scull, *Museums of Madness: the social organisation of insanity in nineteenth century England* (1979); M. Ignatieff, *A Just Measure of Pain: the penitentiary in the Industrial Revolution* (1978).

There is an important local study in E.C. Midwinter, *Social Administration in Lancashire, 1830–1860* (1969) and of the problems which remained to be solved in G. Stedman Jones, *Outcast London: a study in the relationship between classes in Victorian society* (1971). The role of state intervention is discussed in A.J. Taylor, *Laissez-faire and State Intervention in Nineteenth Century Britain* (1972). For administrative consequences see O. MacDonagh, *Early Victorian Government* (1977) and D. Roberts, *Victorian Origins of the British Welfare State* (1960). The 'social control' theme is discussed in A.P. Donajgrodzki (ed.), *Social Control in Nineteenth*

*Century Britain* (1977); and P. McCanny (ed.), *Popular Education and Socialisation in the Nineteenth Century* (1977). See also D.N. Chester, *The English Administrative System, 1780–1870* (1981); V. Cromwell, *Revolution or Evolution: British Government in the Nineteenth Century* (1977); W.C. Lubenow, *The Politics of Government Growth: Early Victorian Attitudes towards State Intervention, 1833–48* (1971); and J. Prest, *Liberty and Locality: Parliament, Permissive Legislation and Ratepayers' Democracies in the Mid-Nineteenth Century* (1990). There is also an excellent overview by P. Thane, 'Government and Society in England and Wales, 1750–1914', in F.M.L. Thompson (ed.), *The Cambridge Social History of Britain, 1750–1950* Vol. 3 (1990).

### Articles

There is a large article literature which can be followed from the secondary works. See especially W.O. Aydelotte, 'The Conservative and Radical interpretations of early Victorian social legislation', *VS* (1967) on general issues. On poverty, see U.R.Q. Henriques, 'How cruel was the Victorian Poor Law?', *HJ* (1968); D. Roberts, 'How cruel was the new Poor Law?', *HJ* (1963); M. Blaug, 'The myth of the old Poor Law', *JEconH* (1963) and 'The Poor Law re-examined', *JEconH* (1963). More general issues are discussed in G. Kitson Clark, 'Statesmen in disguise', *HJ* (1959); J. Hart, 'Nineteenth-century social reform: a Tory interpretation of history', *PP* (1965); B. Harrison, 'Philanthropy and the Victorians', *VS* (1966) and 'Religion and recreation in nineteenth century England', *PP* (1967); O. MacDonagh, 'The nineteenth-century revolution in government: reappraisal', *HJ* (1958–59); V. Cromwell, 'Interpretations of nineteenth-century administrations: an analysis', *VS* (1966); H. Parris, 'The nineteenth century revolution in government: a reappraisal reappraised', *HJ* (1960). Two recent discussions are D. Eastwood, ' "Amplifying the Province of the Legislature": the flow of information and the English State in the early nineteenth century', *HR* (1989) and his 'Men, morals and the machinery of social legislation, 1790–1840', *PH* (1994).

## 18. Trade unionism

There has been an enormous growth of interest in labour and trade union history in recent years. Discussions of nineteenth-century trade union history almost inevitably become bound up with wider interpretations of the development of British society in general. It is important to examine the relationship between trade unionism and the working population at large at a time when trade union members made up only a minority of the labour force and reflected primarily the interests of the more skilled and more favourably placed workers. The involvement of trade unionists with radical politics and the nature of 'respectability' are two of the themes which can be pursued.

## Essay topics

- Did the experience of nineteenth-century trade unionists suggest that 'respectability' paid better dividends than violence?
- How effective were the early trade unions in protecting the interests of the working population at large?

## Sources and documents

G.D.H. Cole and A.W. Filson (eds), *British Working Class Movements: select documents, 1789–1875* (1951) has a wide selection of documents; see also A. Aspinall, *The Early English Trade Unions* (1949). On the period up to 1850, P. Hollis (ed.), *Class and Conflict in Nineteenth Century England 1815–1850* (1973) has several documents on radicalism and trade unionism. On the 1860s, see E. Frow and M. Katanka (ed.), *1868: year of the unions* (1968); S. Pollard, *The Sheffield Outrages* (1971); and on the later nineteenth century E.J. Hobsbawm (ed.), *Labour's Turning Point 1880–1900* (2nd edn, 1974).

## Secondary works

A.E. Musson, *British Trade Unions, 1800–1875* (1972) has a brief outline and helpful bibliography. H. Pelling, *A History of British Trade Unionism* (new edn, 1987), E.H. Hunt, *British Labour History, 1815–1914* (1981) and K.O. Brown, *The English Labour Movement, 1700–1951* (1982) are broader histories. A highly suggestive interpretation is A. Fox, *History and Heritage: The Social Origins of the British Industrial Relations System* (1985). The early history of trade unions is discussed in C.R. Dobson, *Masters and Journeymen: a prehistory of industrial relations, 1717–1800* (1980) and J. Rule, *The Experience of Labour in Eighteenth-century Industry* (1981); see also the introduction in A. Aspinall, *The Early English Trade Unions* (1949); E.P. Thompson, *The Making of the English Working Class* (2nd edn, 1968); J.L. and B. Hammond, *The Skilled Labourer, 1760–1832* (1919, new edn with introduction by J. Rule, 1980). G.D.H. Cole, *Attempts at General Union, 1818–1834* (1953) and J.F.C. Harrison, *The*

*Early Victorians, 1832–51* (1971), especially chs 2 and 6, are important on the 1830s and 1840s. Biographies of early trade union leaders include G. Wallas, *The Life of Francis Place, 1771–1854* (5th edn, 1951); R.G. Kirby and A.E. Musson, *The Voice of the People: John Doherty, 1798–1854* (1975); I. Prothero, *Artisans and Politics in Early Nineteenth Century London: John Gast and his times* (1979). On the Victorian years see F.E. Gillespie, *Labour and Politics in England, 1850–1867* (1927); R. Harrison, *Before the Socialists: studies in labour and politics 1861–1881* (1965); D. Kynaston, *King Labour* (1976); A. Briggs, 'Robert Applegarth and the trade unions', in *Victorian People* (1954); K. Burgess, *The Origins of British Industrial Relations: the nineteenth century experience* (1975) and *The Challenge of Labour: shaping British society, 1850–1930* (1980) and J. Hinton, *Labour and Socialism: A History of the British Labour Movement, 1867–1974* (1983).

There are a number of important collections of essays, especially E.J. Hobsbawm (ed.), *Labouring Men* (1964); A. Briggs and J. Saville (eds), *Essays in Labour History*, vol. 1 (2nd edn, 1967); J. Saville (ed.), *Democracy and the Labour Movement* (1954); and B. Pimlott and C. Cook (eds), *Trade Unions in British Politics* (1982), chs 1 and 2. For the overlap between formal trade unionism and violence, see M.I. Thomis, *The Luddites* (1970); J. Stevenson, *Popular Disturbances in England, 1700–1870* (1979), chs 11–14; and for Wales, D.J.V. Jones, *Before Rebecca: popular protests in Wales, 1793–1835* (1973), chs 3–4. For particular trades and areas see the bibliography in A.E. Musson, *British Trade Unions, 1800–1875* (1972), to which can be added H. Hikins, *Building the Union* (Merseyside) (1973); E. Ellen, N. McCord, J.F. Clarke and D.J. Rowe, *The North-East Engineers' Strikes of 1871* (1971); G. J. Barnsby, *The Working Class Movement in the Black Country, 1750–1867* (1979); B. Trinder, *The Industrial Revolution in Shropshire* (1973); W.J. Rowe, *Cornwall in the Age of the Industrial Revolution* (1953); B. Glen, *Urban Workers in the Early Industrial Revolution* (Stockport) (1984); G. Crossick, *An Artisan Elite in Victorian Society: Kentish London, 1840–80* (1978); G. Stedman Jones, *Outcast London* (1971). For agriculture see P. Horn, *Joseph Arch* (1971) and J.P.D. Dunbabin (ed.), *Rural Discontent in Nineteenth Century Britain* (1974).

For the ideology of trade unionism, see G.D.H. Cole, *Robert Owen* (1925); J.F.C. Harrison, *Robert Owen and the Owenites in Britain and America* (1969); J. Foster, *Class Struggle in the Industrial Revolution* (1974); H.J. Collins and C. Abramsky, *Karl Marx and the British Labour Movement: Years of the First International* (1965); and G. Stedman Jones (ed.), *Languages of Class* (1984). There are also useful sections in H. Perkin, *The Origins of Modern English Society, 1780–1880* (1969) and S.G.

Checkland, *The Rise of Industrial Society in England* (1964). The role of the 'aristocracy of labour' is discussed in E.J. Hobsbawm, 'The Labour Aristocracy in Nineteenth-century Britain', in his *Labouring Men* (1964) and R.Q. Gray, *The Aristocracy of Labour in Nineteenth Century Britain, 1850–1914* (1981); see also B. Harrison, 'Traditions of Respectability in British Labour History', in his *Peaceable Kingdom: Stability and Change in Modern Britain* (1982) and P. Joyce, *Work, Society and Politics: the Culture of the Factory in later Victorian England* (1980).

### Articles

M.D. George, 'The Combination Laws reconsidered', *EH* (1927) and M.D. George, 'The Combination Laws', *EconHR* (1936) are important revisions on the effects of the Combination Acts. Hobsbawm's four articles, 'The labour aristocracy', 'The machine-breakers', 'Economic fluctuations and some social movements' and 'Custom, wages and work-load', reprinted in *Labouring Men*, are all important. R.N. Price, 'The other face of respectability: violence in the Manchester brickmaking trade, 1859–1870', *PP* (1975) and S. Pollard, 'The ethics of the Sheffield outrages', *THAS* (1953–54) bear upon the place of violence in trade disputes. R.V. Clements, 'British trade unions and popular political economy, 1850–1875', *EconHR* (1961); A.E. Musson, 'The Webbs and their phasing of trade-union development between the 1830s and the 1860s', *LHSB* (1962); and S.W. Coltham, 'George Potter, the Junta and the *Beehive*', *IRSH* (1965) are also relevant.

## 19.  Victorian religion

The popular image of Victorian Britain is of a religious society in which Christian morality and principles played a greater part than in some other periods. The accuracy of this picture requires some scrutiny, particularly in regard to the working classes. The difficulties faced by churchmen in keeping pace with rapid population growth, urbanization and the threat of secularism need examining, as do the nature and impact of revivalist groups such as the Oxford Movement. The powerful influence of nonconformity and the links with social and political issues are also important.

### Essay topics

- How adequate was the response of organized religion to the needs of industrial Britain between 1815 and 1900?

- Was Victorian Britain a Christian country?
- How relevant was the Oxford Movement to the problems of Victorian Britain?

## Sources and documents

There is an excellent selection of documents in the Open University series: G. Parsons and J.R. Moore (eds), *Religion in Britain*, Vol. 1: *Traditions;* Vol. 2: *Controversies;* Vol. 3: *Sources;* Vol. 4: *Interpretations* (1988). The 1851 Religious Census occupies a central place in the textbooks; its findings are reprinted in C. Cook and B. Keith, *British Historical Facts, 1830–1900* (1975) with some other relevant tables. John Wade, *The Black Book: or corruption unmask'd* (1820) devoted its largest section to the Church of England. General Booth, *In Darkest England and the Way Out* (1890, reprinted 1970) is a remarkable comment on the social and spiritual problems of late Victorian society. Charles Booth's famous survey, *Life and Labour of the People in London* (1903) has an important section on religion in the slums. By contrast, *Kilvert's Diary* (1938–40) is a beautiful evocation of the life of a country cleric in the 1870s. Spiritual dilemmas are well conveyed in E.W. Gosse, *Father and Son* (1907) (Dar- winism) and J.H. Newman, *Apologia pro vita sua* (1864) (Catholicism). E. Royle (ed.), *Radical Politics, 1790–1900: religion and unbelief* (1971) has documents on secularism and J.H.Y. Briggs and I. Sellars (eds), *Victorian Nonconformity* (1977) on Nonconformity.

## Secondary works

There is a broad survey by J. Obelkevitch, 'Religion', in F.M.L. Thompson (ed.), *The Cambridge Social History of Britain, 1750–1950,* Vol. 3 (1990), while both A. Armstrong, *The Church of England, the Methodists and Society, 1700–1850* (1973) and W.G. Ward, *Religion and Society in England, 1790–1850* (1972) are good general accounts. A.D. Gilbert, *Religion and Society in Industrial England: church, chapel and social change, 1740–1914* (1976) provides the essential data on church-going and denominational affiliation. K.S. Inglis, *Churches and the Working Class in Victorian England* (1963) poses the major problem of urban growth, a theme taken up by H. McLeod, *Religion and Society in England, 1850–1914* (1996) and his edited collection *European Religion in the Age of Great Cities, 1830–1930* (1995), especially the introduction and Pt. 2.

The great study of the Anglican Church is O. Chadwick, *The Victorian Church* (2 vols, 1966–70), but see also D. Bebbington, *Evangelism in*

*Modern Britain* (1989); G. Kitson Clark, *Churchmen and the Condition of England, 1832–85* (1973); J.D. Haydon, S. Taylor and J.D. Walsh (eds), *The Church of England, 1688–1833* (1993); J. Wolffe (ed.), *Evangelical Faith and Public Zeal. Evangelicals and Society in Britain, 1780–1980* (1995). See also S.C. Carpenter, *Church and People, 1789–1899* (1959); W. L. Mathieson, *English Church Reform, 1815–1840* (1923); O.J. Brose, *Church and Parliament: the reshaping of the Church of England, 1828–1860* (1959). For the Oxford Movement see G. Faber, *Oxford Apostles* (1936); R.W. Church, *The Oxford Movement. Twelve years 1833–45* (2nd edn, 1932); and Y.T. Brilioth, *The Anglican Revival, Studies in the Oxford Movement* (new imp., 1934). See also D. Newsome, *The Parting of Friends* (1966). D. Hempton, *Methodism and Politics, 1750–1850* (1984) is an excellent modern study, but see also M.L. Edwards, *After Wesley: a study in the social and political influence of Methodism in the middle period, 1791–1849* (1935). R.F. Wearmouth, *Methodism and the Working-Class Movements of England, 1800–1850* (1937) and *Methodism and the Struggle of the Working Classes, 1850–1900* (1954), and E.R. Taylor, *Methodism and Politics, 1791–1851* (1935) are all relevant to the later history of Methodism, if somewhat uncritical. R. Moore, *Pit-men, Preachers and Politics* (1974) is more sophisticated in its approach, and see also the excellent case study by J. Obelkevitch, *Religion and Rural Society, South Lindsey, 1825–1875* (1976). On Nonconformity, see C. Binfield, *So Down to Prayers: studies in English Nonconformity, 1780–1920* (1977).

The Roman Catholic community can be studied through J. Bossy, *The English Catholic Community, 1570–1850* (1975) and G.A. Beck (ed.), *The English Catholics, 1850–1950* (1950). The important theme of anti-Catholicism is covered by G. Best, 'Popular protestantism in Victorian Britain', in R. Robson (ed.), *Ideas and Institutions of Victorian Britain* (1967) and E.R. Norman, *Anti-Catholicism in Victorian England* (1968).

For Scotland, see T.C. Smout, *A Century of the Scottish People, 1830–1950* (1986), ch. 8; A.L. Drummond and J. Bulloch, *The Church in Victorian Scotland, 1843–1874* (1975) and *The Church in Late Victorian Scotland 1874–1900* (1978); A.C. Cheyne, *The Transforming of the Kirk* (1983); S.J. Brown, *Thomas Chalmers and the Godly Commonwealth of Scotland* (1982); and C.G. Brown, *Religion and Society in Scotland since 1730* (1987).

### Articles

See K.S. Inglis, 'Patterns of worship in 1851', *JEcclH* (1960); D.M. Thompson, 'The 1851 Religious Census', *VS* (1967); A. Smith, 'Popular religion', *PP* (1968); W.L. Arnstein, 'The Murphey riots: a Victorian dilemma', *VS* (1975); K.T. Hoppen, 'The Oxford Movement', *HT* (1967).

## 20. British foreign policy in the nineteenth century

Britain's unique position of maritime supremacy after the Napoleonic Wars gave her a virtually free hand outside Europe, as well as a major voice in European diplomacy. The use which Britain made of this position and the role of her most famous foreign secretaries, Castlereagh, Canning and Palmerston, are traditional areas of concern. The considerations which affected the development of the Empire and colonial policy before the phase of the 'new imperialism' after 1870 have also attracted interest.

### Essay topics

- How did the foreign policies of Castlereagh and Canning differ?
- On what principles did Palmerston conduct British foreign policy?
- Did Britain have a coherent policy towards her colonies between 1815 and 1870?

### Sources and documents

K. Bourne, *The Foreign Policy of Victorian England, 1830–1902* (1970) and J.B. Joll, *Britain and Europe: Pitt to Churchill, 1793–1940* (1950) are particularly helpful collections of documents. Also available are H.M.V. Temperley and L.M. Penson (eds), *Foundations of British Foreign Policy from Pitt to Salisbury* (1938) and K.N. Bell (ed.), *Select Documents on British Colonial Policy, 1830–1860* (1969).

### Secondary works

P.M. Hayes, *The Nineteenth Century, 1814–80* (1975) has a general outline of foreign policy; see also the opening chapters of R.W. Seton-Watson, *Britain in Europe, 1789–1914* (2nd edn, 1955). The essential work on post-1848 diplomacy is A.J.P. Taylor, *The Struggle for Mastery in Europe, 1848–1918* (1954). The work of the two principal foreign secretaries of the early nineteenth century is considered in C.K. Webster, *The Foreign Policy of Castlereagh* (2 vols, 1931) and H.M.V. Temperley, *The Foreign Policy of Canning, 1822–27* (1925). See also H.A. Kissinger, *A World Restored: Metternich, Castlereagh and the problems of peace, 1812–1822* (1957). Biographical studies include C.J. Bartlett, *Castlereagh* (1966);

J.W. Derry, *Castlereagh* (1976); P.J.V. Rolo, *George Canning: three biographical studies* (1965) and W. Hinde, *George Canning* (1973). On Palmerston, H.C.F. Bell, *Lord Palmerston* (2 vols, reprinted 1966) is the basic study, but see also K. Bourne, *Palmerston: the early years, 1784–1841* (1982) and D. Southgate, *'The Most English Minister...'* The policies and politics of Palmerston (1966). C.K. Webster, *The Foreign Policy of Palmerston, 1830–41* (2 vols, 1951) deals with the early period. J. Ridley, *Lord Palmerston* (1970) offers a general biography. D.C.M. Platt, *Finance, Trade and Politics: British foreign policy, 1815–1914* (1968) is an overall interpretative study. On particular topics, see G.B. Henderson, *Crimean War Diplomacy and Other Essays* (1947); H.M.V. Temperley, *England and the Near East. The Crimea* (1936); V. Puryear, *England, Russia and the Straits Question, 1844–56* (1931); C. Sproxton, *Palmerston and the Hungarian Revolution* (1919); W.C. Costin, *Great Britain and China, 1833–60* (1937); D. Beales, *England and Italy, 1859–60* (1961).

For imperial and colonial issues, B. Porter, *The Lion's Share: a short history of British imperialism, 1850–1970* (2nd edn, 1984) and R. Hyam, *Britain's Imperial Century, 1815–1914: a study of empire and expansion* (1976) provide general outlines. B. Semmel, *The Rise of Free Trade Imperialism: classical political economy, the empire of free trade and imperialism, 1750–1850* (1970) and D.K. Fieldhouse, *Economics of Empire, 1830–1914* (1976) discuss the economic dimension. See also A.H. Imlah, *Economic Elements in the Pax Britannica* (1959) and L.H. Jenks, *The Migration of British Capital to 1875* (1927). C.A. Bodelsen, *Studies in Mid-Victorian Imperialism* (1924) is an important study, now amplified by W.P. Morrell, *British Col- onial Policy in the Age of Peel and Russell* (1930, rev. edn, 1970). A.P. Thornton, *The Imperial Idea and its Enemies* (1959) discusses policy, as does K.E. Knorr, *British Colonial Theories: 1570–1850* (1963). The later period is treated in J. Gallagher and R. Robinson, *Africa and the Victorians: the official mind of imperialism* (1961) and C.C. Eldridge, *Victorian Imperialism* (1978). J.M. Ward, *Colonial Self-Government: the British experience, 1759–1856* (1976) offers a view of colonial government.

P.M. Kennedy, *The Rise and Fall of British Naval Mastery* (1976) is particularly useful on the military aspects of the *Pax Britannica;* see also C.J. Bartlett, *Defence and Diplomacy: Britain and the Great Powers, 1815–1914* (1993).

## Articles

J. Gallagher and R. Robinson, 'The imperialism of Free Trade', *EHR* (1953) raises important issues. G.B. Henderson, 'The foreign policy of

Lord Palmerston', *H* (1938) and M. Beloff, 'Great Britain and the American Civil War', *H* (1952) are both useful. See also as case studies, M.M. Robson, 'Liberals and "vital interests": the debate on international arbitration, 1815–72', *BIHR* (1959); R.R. Florescu, 'Stratford Canning, Palmerston and the Wallachian Revolution of 1848', *JMH* (1963); F.G. Weber, 'Palmerston and Prussian Liberalism, 1848', *JMH* (1963); K.A.P. Sandiford, The British cabinet and the Schleswig-Holstein crisis, 1863–4', *H* (1973).

## 21. Gladstone and Liberalism

Victorian Liberalism is an elusive phenomenon which it is crucial to understand for the tenor of politics in the latter half of the nineteenth century, for the formation of the Liberal Party and for Gladstone's appeal to a wide range of electors. Considerable research in recent years has been devoted to the grassroots of Victorian politics, one of the most interesting aspects of the period. Gladstone himself is an enigmatic figure, at least as important for what he represented as for what he did. One line of interpretation has tended to undermine Gladstone's position as a 'heroic' crusader for good causes in favour of concentration upon the 'high politics' at Cabinet level, by which Gladstone sought to manage the coalition of interests which made up the Liberal Party.

### Essay topics

- What were the principal characteristics of mid-Victorian Liberalism and how were they represented in the formation of the Liberal Party?
- Did Gladstone's performance in office justify his reputation as the 'poor man's friend'?

### Sources and documents

Samuel Smiles, *Self-Help* (1859) represents the gospel of work and sturdy independence raised to an inspiration. J.S. Mill, *On Liberty* (1859) is the classic statement of Victorian Liberalism. M.R.D. Foot and H.C.G. Matthew (eds), *The Gladstone Diaries* (1968–95) are the authentic voice of the great man. W. Bagehot, *The English Constitution* (2nd edn, 1873) is a brilliant analysis of the mid-Victorian constitution.

## Secondary works

G. Best, *Mid-Victorian Britain, 1851–75* (1971) has a wide-ranging survey of the mid-Victorian scene. Also valuable are G. Kitson Clark, *The Making of Victorian England* (1962); W.L. Burn, *The Age of Equipoise. A study of the mid-Victorian generation* (1964); G.M. Young, *Victorian England: portrait of an age* (2nd edn, 1953); R. Robson (ed.), *Ideas and Institutions of Victorian Britain* (1967); W.E. Houghton, *The Victorian Frame of Mind* (1957). J.R. Vincent, *The Formation of the British Liberal Party, 1857–1868* (1966) is central, but see also D.G. Southgate, *The Passing of the Whigs, 1832–1886* (1962) and M. Bentley, *The Climax of Liberal Politics: British Liberalism in Theory and Practice, 1868–1918* (1987), chs 2–4. J.R. Vincent, *Pollbooks: How Victorians voted* (1967) is an important illustration of how politics worked at the local level. H.J. Hanham, *Elections and Party Management: Politics in the time of Disraeli and Gladstone* (1959) is important for the development of parties; see also the early sections of R.T. McKenzie, *British Political Parties* (1955). For Palmerston's contribution see E.D. Steele, *Palmerston and Liberalism, 1855–1865* (1991). A recent perspective on the development of Liberal politics is T.A. Jenkins, *The Liberal Ascendency, 1830–1886* (1994).

There are many biographies of Gladstone. R. Jenkins, *Gladstone* (1995) is an excellent one-volume study, replacing the older P. Magnus, *Gladstone. A biography* (1954). H.C.G. Matthew, *Gladstone, 1809–74* (1986) and *Gladstone, 1874–98* (1995) offer a definitive account from the editor of the Gladstone diaries, while E. Feuchtwanger, *Gladstone* (1975) and P. Stansky, *Gladstone* (1979) are briefer appreciations. For the early career, see also R. Shannon, *Gladstone* (1982). There is a detailed study in J.P. Parry, *Democracy and Religion: Gladstone and the Liberal Party, 1867–75* (1986). The introductions to M.R.D. Foot and H.C.G. Matthew (eds), *The Gladstone Diaries* (1968–95) are important reviews of Gladstone's career. The Second Reform Bill is discussed in F.B. Smith, *The Making of the Second Reform Bill* (1966) and M. Cowling, *1867: Disraeli, Gladstone and Revolution: The passing of the Second Reform Bill* (1967). R.T. Shannon, *Gladstone and the Bulgarian Agitation, 1876* (1963) examines the domestic repercussions of the Bulgarian crisis, and T.O. Lloyd, *The General Election of 1880* (1968) studies an important election. The later stages of Gladstone's career are discussed in D.A. Hamer, *Liberal Politics in the Age of Gladstone and Rosebery* (1972); J.R. Vincent and A. Cooke, *The Governing Passion: cabinet government and party politics in Britain, 1885–86* (1974); and M. Barker, *Gladstone and Radicalism: the reconstruction of Liberal policy in Britain, 1885–94* (1975).

The popular basis of Liberal politics is discussed in E. Biagini, *Liberty, Retrenchment and Reform: popular liberalism in the age of Gladstone* (1992); see also J.P. Parry, *The rise and fall of liberal government in Britain* (1993). On other Liberal figures, see W. Hinde, *Cobden* (1987); D. Read, *Cobden and Bright* (1967); R. Jay, *Joseph Chamberlain: a political study* (1981); D. Judd, *Radical Joe: a life of Joseph Chamberlain* (1977); P. Fraser, *Joseph Chamberlain: Radicalism and Empire, 1868–1914* (1966); A. Briggs, *Victorian People* (1954); and R. Rhodes James, *Rosebery* (1963).

Local political allegiances are discussed in H. Pelling, *The Social Geography of British Elections 1885–1910* (1967). On local politics see also D. Fraser, *Urban Politics in Victorian England* (1976) and *Power and Authority in the Victorian City* (1979); K.O. Morgan, *Wales in British Politics, 1868–1922* (1963); A. Briggs, *Victorian Cities* (1963); P. Waller, *Democracy and Sectarianism: a political and social history of Liverpool, 1868–1939* (1981); G.S. Messinger, *Manchester in the Victorian Age* (1985); I. Adams, *The Making of Urban Scotland* (1978); and S.G. Checkland, *The Upas Tree: Glasgow 1875–1975* (1976).

### Articles

Of importance are J.A. Thomas, 'The system of registration and the development of party organisation, 1832–70', *H* (1950); J.F.C. Harrison, 'The Victorian gospel of success', *VS* (1957); T.R. Tholfsen, 'The transition to democracy in Victorian England', *IRSH* (1961); F.H. Herrick, 'The Second Reform movement in Britain, 1850–65', *JHI* (1948); R. Harrison, 'The British working class and the general election of 1868', *IRSH* (1960); W.H. Mael, 'Gladstone, the Liberals and the election of 1874', *BIHR* (1963); J. Parry, 'Religion and the collapse of Gladstone's first Government, 1870–74', *HJ* (1982); C.H.D. Howard, 'Joseph Chamberlain and the Unauthorised Programme', *EHR* (1950); R. Kelly, 'Midlothian', *VS* (1960); T.R. Tholfsen, 'The origins of the Birmingham caucus', *HJ* (1959); J. Dunbabin, 'Parliamentary elections in Great Britain 1868–1900: a psephological note', *EHR* (1966); W.C. Lubenow, 'Irish Home Rule and the social basis of the great separation in the Liberal Party in 1886', *HJ* (1985).

## 22. Disraeli and the late nineteenth-century Conservative Party

Disraeli is often regarded as the founder of the modern Conservative Party and the agent of its revival in the latter part of the nineteenth century. It is important to discuss how essential and distinctive his personal contribution was, particularly in the passing of the Second Reform Bill, the fostering of imperialism and the promotion of 'Tory democracy'. Some consideration must also be given to the effects of the broader movements of electoral opinion, especially the growing disillusionment of middle-class voters with liberalism and the rise of working-class Toryism in places such as Lancashire. The character of Conservatism under Salisbury should also be considered in any discussion of late nineteenth-century conservatism.

## Essay topics

• What did Disraeli contribute to the Conservative Party?
• How would you account for the revival of the Conservative Party in the latter half of the nineteenth century?

## Sources and documents

Disraeli's novels provide some insight into his social views; see especially *Sybil* (1845) or *Coningsby* (1844). T.E. Kebbel (ed.), *The Selected Speeches of Lord Beaconsfield* (1882) is particularly useful for the Crystal Palace speech of 1872. H.J. Hanham, *The Nineteenth Century Constitution, 1815–1914. Documents and commentary* (1969) and P. Adelman, *Gladstone, Disraeli and Later Victorian Politics* (1970) also have some relevant documents. An inside view of politics can be found in J.R. Vincent (ed.), *Disraeli, Derby and the Conservative Party: the political journals of Lord Stanley, 1848–1869* (1981) and J.R. Vincent (ed.), *The Derby Diaries, 1869–78,* Camden, Fifth Series, vol. 4 (1995).

## Secondary works

R. Blake, *The Conservative Party from Peel to Thatcher* (1985) puts Disraeli in context, but Disraeli's place in the earlier history of the party can also be examined in R. Stewart, *The Foundation of the Conservative Party, 1830–1867* (1978). The standard life is R. Blake, *Disraeli* (1966), but the older W.F. Monypenny and G.E. Buckle, *The Life of Benjamin Disraeli, Earl of Beaconsfield* (2 vols, 1929) is still useful. R. Blake, 'The rise of Disraeli', in H. Trevor-Roper (ed.), *Essays in British History presented to Sir Keith Feiling* (1965) is also relevant. H.J. Hanham, *Elections and Party Management. Politics in the time of Disraeli and Gladstone* (1959) and the early part of R.T. McKenzie, *British Political Parties* (1955) discuss the political machinery of the period. The Second Reform Act is treated in

F.B. Smith, *The Making of the Second Reform Bill* (1966) and M. Cowling, *1867. Disraeli, Gladstone and Revolution. The Passing of the Second Reform Bill* (1867). See also the chapter on 1867 in R. Harrison, *Before the Socialists: studies in labour and politics, 1861–1881* (1965) for a view which stresses the popular pressure for reform as opposed to the 'high politics'. P. Smith, *Disraelian Conservatism and Social Reform* (1967) and E.J. Feuchtwanger, *Disraeli, Democracy and the Tory Party* (1968) examine some of the wider aspects of Disraelian conservatism. See also P.R. Ghosh on 'Style and substance in Disraelian Social Reform, *c.* 1860–80', in P.J. Waller (ed.), *Politics and Social Change in Modern Britain* (1987). R. McKenzie and J. Silver, *Angels in Marble* (1968) has an appraisal of the appeal of working-class Toryism, as does P. Joyce, *Work, Society and Politics* (1980), chs 8–9. For the later period, see M. Pugh, *The Tories and the People, 1880–1935* (1985) and H. Pelling, *Popular Politics and Society in Late Victorian Britain* (1968). H. Pelling, *The Social Geography of British Elections, 1885–1910* (1967) has a mass of information on local politics. The major personalities of the late Victorian Conservative Party can be examined in R. Taylor, *Salisbury* (1975), P. Marsh, *The Discipline of Popular Government: Lord Salisbury's domestic statecraft, 1881–1902* (1978) and J. Cornford, 'The parliamentary foundations of the Hotel Cecil', in R. Robson (ed.), *Ideas and Institutions of Victorian Britain* (1967). Lord Randolph Churchill's influence on the Tory Party is discussed in R. Rhodes James, *Lord Randolph Churchill* (1959) and R. Foster, *Lord Randolph Churchill* (1982). Joseph Chamberlain's gradual movement towards the Conservatives can be followed in P. Fraser, *Joseph Chamberlain, Radicalism and Empire, 1868–1914* (1966); H. Browne, *Joseph Chamberlain, Radical and Imperialist* (1974); D. Judd, *Radical Joe: a life of Joseph Chamberlain* (1977) and R. Jay, *Joseph Chamberlain* (1981).

### Articles

C.J. Lewis, 'Theory and expediency in the policy of Disraeli', *VS* (1960–61); E.J. Feuchtwanger, 'The Conservative Party under the impact of the Second Reform Act', *VS* (1959); J. Cornford, 'The transformation of conservatism in the late nineteenth century', *VS* (1963–64); J.P. Dunbabin, 'Parliamentary elections in Great Britain, 1868–1900: a psephological note', *EHR* (1966). There is a review of the debate on the Second Reform Act in G. Himmelfarb, 'The politics of democracy: the English Reform Act of 1867', *JBS* (1966). On party organization see E.J. Feuchtwanger, 'J.E. Gorst and the central organisation of the Conservative Party, 1870–1882', *BIHR* (1959). R. Greenall, 'Salford working class conservatism, 1865–86', *NH* (1974) is an important case study of Lancashire politics. The role of the Liberal Unionists and Chamberlain is discussed in P. Fraser, 'The Liberal Unionist alliance: Chamberlain, Hartington, and the Conservatives, 1886–1904', *EHR* (1962). See also P.R. Ghosh, 'Disraelian Conservatism. A financial approach', *EHR* (1984) and R. Quinault, 'Randolph Churchill and Tory democracy', *HJ* (1979).

## 23. The Irish Question

Irish affairs exerted considerable influence upon British politics at various points in the nineteenth and early twentieth centuries. As well as general concern on the nature of the 'Irish Question', interest has tended to focus on particular phases of activity, notably the Home Rule period. In this area, studies have tended to move away from the view of Gladstone 'idealistically' struggling with the intractable problems of Ireland towards the role of the Irish Question in the conduct of late Victorian politics. This 'high politics' interpretation requires placing in the context of the broader studies of the rise of Irish nationalism. The period of agitation before, during and after the First World War is also beginning to attract fresh attention.

### Essay topics

- Why did Britain not grant self-government to Ireland during the nineteenth century?
- Why did Gladstone fail to solve the 'Irish Question'?
- How far were independence and partition for Ireland inevitable by 1914?

### Sources and documents

A. O'Day and J. Stevenson, *Irish Historical Documents since 1800* (1992) and T.C. and R.B. McDowell, *Irish Historical Documents, 1172–1922* (1977) have comprehensive sets of documents. Alexis de Tocqueville, *Journeys to England and Ireland* (ed. J.P. Mayer, 1958) has a perceptive account of conditions in pre-famine Ireland. Among later writers, see J.S. Mill, *England and Ireland* (1868) and G.B. Shaw, *The Matter with Ireland* (1962) and *John Bull's Other Island* (1907). A.V. Dicey, *England's Case Against Home Rule* (reprinted, 1973) is also relevant. See also the selection of documents in G. Morton, *Home Rule and the Irish Question*

(1980). H.C.G. Matthew's introduction to the Gladstone *Diaries* and the diaries themselves, Vols 10 and 11 (1990) should also be consulted.

## Secondary works

The best modern general history of Ireland is R.F. Foster, *Modern Ireland, 1600–1972* (1988) but the older histories, J.C. Beckett, *The Making of Modern Ireland, 1603–1923* (1969) and F.S.L. Lyons, *Ireland since the Famine* (2nd edn, 1973) still offer excellent accounts. See also D.G. Boyce, *Nationalism in Ireland* (3rd edn, 1995). These largely supersede the older studies by N. Mansergh, *The Irish Question, 1840–1921* (1965) and E. Strauss, *Irish Nationalism and British Democracy* (1951). Two valuable other perspectives are J.E. Lee, *The Modernisation of Irish Society, 1848–1918* (1973) and R. Dudley Edwards, *An Atlas of Irish History* (1973) with invaluable material on political, economic and social questions.

The Repeal period can be studied through O. MacDonagh, *O'Connell: the Life of Daniel O'Connell, 1775–1847* (1991 edn); A.D. Macintyre, *The Liberator: Daniel O'Connell and the Irish Party, 1830–1847* (1965); R.B. McDowell, *The Irish Administration, 1801–1914* (1964); K.B. Nowlan, *The Politics of Repeal: a study in the relation between Great Britain and Ireland, 1841–50* (1965); G. O'Tuathaigh, *Ireland before the Famine, 1798–1848* (1972) and O. MacDonagh, 'O'Connell and Repeal, 1840–45', in M. Bentley and J. Stevenson (eds), *High and Low Politics in Modern Britain* (1983). On the land question, see R.D. Collison Black, *Economic Thought and the Irish Question, 1817–1870* (1960); J.E. Pomfret, *The Struggle for Land in Ireland, 1800–1923* (1930); B. Solow, *The Land Question and the Irish Economy, 1870–1903* (1971). R. Dudley Edwards and T. Desmond Williams (eds), *The Great Famine* (1956) is a more scholarly treatment than C.B. Woodham-Smith, *The Great Hunger* (1962). J. Mokyr, *Why Ireland Starved* (1983) is a difficult but important analysis of the pre-famine Irish economy, while popular unrest in Ireland is examined in M. Beames, *The Whiteboy Movements and Their Control in Pre-Famine Ireland* (1985). For the mid-century, see K. Theodore Hopper, *Elections, Politics and Society in Ireland, 1832–85* (1984).

For the Home Rule period J.L. Hammond, *Gladstone and the Irish Nation* (1938) represents the traditional view of Gladstone's involvement with Ireland. D.A. Hamer, *The Liberal Party in the Age of Gladstone and Rosebery* (1972) explains policy towards Ireland in terms of Liberal politics. J.R. Vincent and A. Cooke, *The Governing Passion: cabinet government and party politics in Britain, 1885–86* (1974) treat the Irish issue as an example of political manoeuvre among the top politicians. On the influence of Parnell, C.C. Cruise O'Brien, *Parnell and his party, 1880–90* (1957) is essential, but see also D.G. Boyce and A. O'Day, *Parnell in Perspective* (1991). F.S. Lyons, *Charles Stewart Parnell* (1978) is the standard biography; see also M. Hurt, *Parnell and Irish Nationalism* (1968) and A. O'Day, *The English Face of Irish Nationalism: Parnellite involvement in British politics, 1880–86* (1977). The relationship between the land question and the rise of the Home Rule issue is examined in P. Bew, *Land and the National Question in Ireland, 1858–1882* (1977). The attitude of the Conservatives is reviewed in L.P. Curtis, *Coercion and Conciliation in Ireland, 1880–1892: A study in Conservative Unionism* (1963) and P. Bew, *Conflict and Conciliation in Ireland, 1890–1910* (1986). The rise of Unionism is discussed in P. Buckland, *Irish Unionism 1885–1923: a documentary history* (1973); P. Gibbon, *The Origins of Ulster Unionism* (1975); A.T.Q. Stewart, *The Narrow Ground: aspects of Ulster, 1609–1969* (1977); P. Bew, *Ideology and the Irish Question* (1994); A. Jackson, *The Ulster Party: Irish Unionists in the House of Commons, 1884–1911* (1989); and J. Loughlin, *Gladstone, Home Rule and the Ulster Question* (1986).

The later aspects of the Irish crisis are discussed in A.T.Q. Stewart, *The Ulster Crisis* (1967); R.D. Edwards and F. Pyle, *1916: The Easter Rising* (1968); F.S.L. Lyons, *The Irish Parliamentary Party, 1890–1910* (1951); K.B. Nowlan (ed.), *The Making of 1916: studies in the history of the Rising* (1969); R.D. Edwards, *Patrick Pearse: the triumph of failure* (1979); C. Townshend, *The British Campaign in Ireland, 1919–1921* (1979); D. Fitzpatrick, *Politics and Irish Life, 1913–21* (1977); M. Laffin, *The Partition of Ireland, 1911–1925* (1983).

## Articles

The most relevant include J.H. Whyte, 'Daniel O'Connell and the repeal party', *IHS* (1958–59); M.D. Condon, 'The Irish Church and the reform ministries', *JBS* (1963–64); C.H.D. Howard, 'Joseph Chamberlain, Parnell and the Irish "central board" scheme, 1884–85', *IHS* (1952–53); R.R. James, 'C.S. Parnell', *HT* (1957); E.D. Steele, 'Gladstone and Ireland', *IHS* (1970–71); 'John Stuart Mill and the Irish Question, 1865–1975', *HJ* (1970), and his 'Ireland and the Empire in the 1860s: Imperial precedents for Gladstone's first Irish Land Act', *HJ* (1968); and A. Warren, 'Gladstone, land and social reconstruction in Ireland, 1881–7', *PH* (1983). On the politics of the Irish question, see D.A. Hamer, 'The Irish Question and Liberal politics, 1886–1894', *HJ*

(1969); M. Hurst, 'Ireland and the Ballot Act of 1872', *HJ* (1965); L.J. McCaffrey, 'Home Rule and the general election of 1874', *IHS* (1954–55). For the later period see D.C. Savage, 'The origins of the Ulster Unionist Party, 1885–6', *IHS* (1960–61); G.P. Taylor, 'Cecil Rhodes and the Second Home Rule Bill', *HJ* (1971); F.S.L. Lyons, 'John Dillon and the plan of campaign, 1886–90', *IHS* (1964–65); L.P. Curtis, 'Government policy and the Irish Party crisis, 1890–92', *IHS* (1962–63); J. Boyle, 'The Belfast Protestant Association and the Independent Orange Order 1901–10', *IHS* (1962–63); H.W. McCready, 'Home Rule and the Liberal Party, 1899–1906', *IHS* (1962–63); D.G. Boyce, 'British Conservative opinion, the Ulster Question and the partition of Ireland, 1912–21', *IHS* (1970–71).

## 24. British imperialism

This is a very large topic, but one which in terms of British history is primarily concerned with the domestic causes and effects of overseas expansion. It is widely recognized that the latter part of the nineteenth century witnessed a rapid expansion of the British Empire in the phase of so-called 'new imperialism'. Differing explanations have been given for this process, the once fashionable economic interpretation being subjected to an increasing degree of qualification. The effects of imperialism on domestic politics can usefully be focused on the issues and conflicts raised by the Boer War.

### Essay topics

- What forces promoted the expansion of the British Empire in the latter part of the nineteenth century?
- How far did the Boer War mark a turning-point in British attitudes towards the Empire?

### Sources and documents

R.W. Winks (ed.), *British Imperialism: gold, god, glory* (1966) has a useful selection of documents; see also H.M. Wright (ed.), *The New Imperialism* (1961). G. Bennet (ed.), *The Concept of Empire: Burke to Attlee, 1774–1947* (1953) also provides a range of documents. C.W. Dilke, *Greater Britain* (1868) and *Problems of Greater Britain* (1890) and J.R. Seeley, *The Expansion of England* (1883) are important contemporary analyses. See also J.A. Hobson, *Imperialism: a study* (1902).

## Secondary works

M.A. Chamberlain, *The New Imperialism* (Historical Association pamphlet, 1967) is a good survey of mid-twentieth-century thinking on the question of imperial expansion. Of the general histories, see especially B. Porter, *The Lion's Share: a short history of British imperialism, 1850–1970* (2nd edn, 1984); R. Hyam, *Britain's Imperial Century, 1815–1914: a study of empire and expansion* (1976); and P.J. Cain and A.G. Hopkins, *British Imperialism: innovation and expansion, 1688–1914* (1993). C.A. Bodelsen, *Studies in mid-Victorian Imperialism* (1924) covers the period c. 1837–87. J. Gallagher and R. Robinson, *Africa and the Victorians: The official mind of imperialism* (1961) is an important series of case studies of how expansion occurred. On the 1860s and 1870s see also C.C. Eldridge, *Victorian Imperialism* (1978). D.K. Fieldhouse, *The Colonial Empires* (1966) and *Economics and Empire, 1830–1914* (1976) reconsiders the economic arguments for imperialism. D.C. Platt, *Finance, Trade and Politics in British Foreign Policy, 1815–1914* (1968) is an important study which places imperialism in the context of British foreign policy. More recent are P.J. Cain, *Economic Foundations of British Overseas Expansion* (1980); L. David and R. Huttenback, *Mammon and the Pursuit of Empire: the political economy of British Imperialism* (1986); and A. Porter and R.F. Holland, *Money, Finance and Empire, 1790–1960* (1985). On investment see A.K. Cairncross, *Home and Foreign Investment, 1870–1913* (1953); A.R. Hall (ed.), *The Export of Capital from Britain, 1870–1914* (1968); H. Feis, *Europe, the World's Banker, 1870–1914* (1930); S.B. Saul, *Studies in British Overseas Trade 1870–1914* (1960); and P.L. Cottrell, *British Overseas Investment in the Nineteenth Century* (1975). On the diplomatic repercussions of imperialism see P. Kennedy, *The Rise of the Anglo-German Antagonism, 1860–1914* (1980) and W. Langer, *The Diplomacy of Imperialism, 1890–1902* (1935), which also has an interesting chapter on the public psychology of imperialism. This theme is followed up in R. Price, *An Imperial War and the British Working Class: working-class attitudes and reactions to the Boer War, 1899–1902* (1972). Attitudes to empire are also the theme of R. Price, 'Society, status and jingoism: the social roots of lower middle class patriotism, 1870–1900', in G. Crossick (ed.), *The Lower Middle Class in Britain* (1977) and H. Pelling, 'British labour and British imperialism' in his *Popular Politics and Society in Late Victorian Britain* (1968). A.P. Thornton, *The Imperial Idea and its Enemies* (1959) and *Doctrines of Imperialism* (1965) discuss ideologies of empire; see also J. Kemp, *Theories of Imperialism* (1967) and W. Mommsen, *Theories of Imperialism* (1980).

The collection of essays by C.J. Bartlett (ed.), *Britain Pre-eminent* (1969) has several useful studies, see especially D. Southgate, 'Imperial Britain'. Other collections of relevance are R. Hyam, *Reappraisals in British Imperial History* (1975); D.A. Low, *Lion Rampant: essays in the study of British imperialism* (1974); P. Kennedy, *The Realities Behind Diplomacy: Background Influences on British External Policy, 1865–1980* (1981) and C.C. Eldridge (ed.), *British Imperialism in the Nineteenth Century* (1984).

On the political repercussions of empire see D. Judd, *Balfour and the British Empire* (1968); H.G. Matthew, *The Liberal Imperialists: the ideas and politics of a post-Gladstonian élite* (1973); B.H. Brown, *The Tariff Reform Movement in Great Britain, 1881–1895* (1943). Chamberlain's role is discussed in R.V. Kublicek, *The Administration of Imperialism: Joseph Chamberlain at the Colonial Office* (1969).

On the Boer War see T. Pakenham, *The Boer War* (1979); J.S. Marais, *The Fall of Kruger's Republic* (1961); E. Pakenham, *Jameson's Raid* (1960); S. Koss (ed.), *The Pro-Boers* (1973); and A.N. Porter, *The Origins of the South African War: Joseph Chamberlain and the diplomacy of Imperialism* (1980).

### Articles

See particularly H. Cunningham, 'Jingoism in 1877–78', *VS* (1971); J. Gallagher and R. Robinson, 'The imperialism of Free Trade', *EconHR* (1953); S.B. Saul, 'The economic significance of "constructive imperialism" ', *JEconH* (1957); D.C. Platt, 'Economic factors in British policy during the "New Imperialism" ', *PP* (1968); and P. O'Brien, 'The Costs and Benefits of British Imperialism 1846–1914', *PP* (1988). Among a number of more detailed articles, see W.D. McIntyre, 'British policy in West Africa: the Ashanti Expedition of 1873–4', *HJ* (1962); R.L. Tignor, 'Lord Cromer: practitioner and philosopher of imperialism', *JBS* (1962–63); E. Stokes, 'Milnerism', *HJ* (1962); W. Strauss, 'Joseph Chamberlain and the theory of imperialism', *PA* (1942). For South African affairs see E. Drus, 'The question of imperial complicity in the Jameson Raid', *EHR* (1953); G. Blainey, 'Lost causes of the Jameson Raid', *EconHR* (1965).

## 25. Women: feminism, the family, and the franchise

Interest in women's history has broadened and developed enormously in recent years. From almost exclusive concern with the narrow issue of the franchise there has been not only growing interest in the origins of feminism and women's movements before the Edwardian era but also a much broader interest in women's place in society at large. The study of women in the family, at work, and in society as a whole has formed part of the burgeoning interest in social history.

## Essay topics

* To what extent did industrialization alter the place and role of women within British society?
* 'Paradise for men, hell for women'. How accurate is this as a description of family life before the twentieth century?
* Why did women's suffrage take so long to achieve?
* How far did the acquisition of formal political rights lead to the emancipation of women in the twentieth century?

## Sources and documents

Two useful anthologies for the eighteenth century are V. Jones (ed.), *Women in the Eighteenth Century* (1990); B. Hill, *Eighteenth Century Women: an anthology* (1984). Mary Wollstonecraft, *A Vindication of the Rights of Woman* is available in a number of editions, as is J.S. Mill, *On the Subjection of Women* (1869). Two collections of memoir material of relevance to the later period are M. Llewelyn Davies (ed.), *Life As We Have Known It* (1931, reprint edn, 1977) and *Maternity: Letters from Working Women* (1915, reprint edn, 1978).

## Secondary works

General works which examine the position of women in society include S. Rowbotham, *Hidden from History* (1977); J. O'Faolain and L. Martines (eds), *Not in God's Image: Women in History* (1973); J.M. Mitchell and A. Oakley (eds), *The Rights and Wrongs of Women* (1976); and M. Hartmann and L. Banner (eds), *Clio's Consciousness Raised* (1974).

The early history of feminist ideas is discussed comparatively in J. Rendall, *The Origins of Modern Feminism: Women in Britain, France and the United States, 1780–1860* (1985) and in A. Browne, *The Eighteenth-Century Feminist Mind* (1987). Mary Wollstonecraft occupies a pioneering position in the history of women's rights and there are several biographies and studies, including C. Tomalin, *The Life and Death of Mary Wollstonecraft* (1974), M. Tims, *Mary Wollstonecraft: a social pioneer* (1976) and R.M. Wardle, *The Collected Letters of Mary Wollstonecraft* (1979).

The kind of work which is being done to construct an effective women's history for the early period can be found in M. Prior (ed.), *Women in English Society, 1500–1800* (1985). R. O'Day, *Education and Society 1500–1800* (1982) also has an excellent chapter on the neglected topic of women's education. Much of the work on women inevitably turns on the nature of the family, for an introduction to which see M. Anderson, *Approaches to the History of the Western Family 1500–1914* (1980). The earlier works by E. Shorter, *The Making of the Modern Family* (1976) and L. Stone, *The Family, Sex and Marriage in England, 1500–1800* (1977) have been influential for their view of the growth of a new type of family relationship, but heavily criticized: see R. Houlbrooke, *The English Family, 1450–1700* (1984), especially chs 5 and 10. P. Laslett, *The World We Have Lost* (1968) and *Family Life and Illicit Love in Earlier Generations* (1977) are important examples of the use of demographic material to study assumptions about family size, age of marriage, and household structure in pre-industrial society. Similar concerns are pursued into the industrial period by M.S. Anderson, *Family Structure in Nineteenth-Century Lancashire* (1971). Two studies of marriage which have attracted attention are A. Macfarlane, *Marriage and Love in England: Modes of Reproduction, 1300–1840* (1986) and J.R. Gillis, *For Better For Worse: British Marriages 1600 to the present* (1986).

An early attempt to examine the impact of industrialization on family structure was N.J. Smelser, *Social Change in the Industrial Revolution* (1959), but the wider effects of industrialization are discussed in I. Pinchbeck, *Women Workers and the Industrial Revolution, 1750–1850* (1969), and there are relevant chapters in the more recent studies by J. Walvin, *The English Urban Worker, 1776–1851* (1984) and J. Rule, *The Labouring Classes in Early Industrial England, 1750–1850* (1986). A case study of one group of working women is A.V. John, *By the Sweat of their Brow. Women Workers at Victorian Coal Mines* (1980) and another is J.R. Walkowitz, *Prostitution and Victorian Society. Women, Class and the State* (1980). The role of middle-class women in entrepreneurial families is explored in L. Davidoff and C. Hall, *Family Fortunes: Men and Women of the English Middle Class, 1780–1850* (1986). M. Vicinus (ed.), *Suffer and Be Still: Women in the Victorian Age* (1980) and *A Widening Sphere: Changing roles of Victorian women* (1980) are two collections of essays on the position of Victorian women. N. Boyd, *Josephine Butler, Octavia Hill, Florence Nightingale: three Victorian women who changed their world* (1982) examines women who achieved a national reputation in the Victorian era, while F. Prochaska, *Women and Philanthropy in Nineteenth-Century England* (1980) looks at the important role of women in that sphere. B. Caine, *Destined to be Wives: the sisters of Beatrice Webb* (1986) is a fine portrait of the lives of the other Webb daughters. P. Jalland, *Women, Marriage and Politics, 1860–1914* (1986) is a study of women in the later Victorian era, but see also P. Hollis, *Women in Public: The Women's Movement, 1850–1900* (1979). A spate of more recent studies includes C. Bolt, *The Women's Movement in the United States and Britain from the 1790s to the 1920s* (1993); L. Bland, *Banishing the Beast. English Feminism and Sexual Morality, 1885–1914* (1995); J. Purvis (ed.), *Women's History: Britain, 1850–1945* (1995). The experiences of women in Wales and Scotland are examined in A.V. John (ed.), *Our Mothers' Land: Chapters in Welsh Women's History, 1830–1939* (1991) and E. Breitenbach and E. Gordon (eds), *Out of Bounds: Women in Scottish Society, 1800–1945* (1992).

Women's role in the radical and labour movements is attracting more attention. D. Thompson, *The Chartists* (1984) has a section on women, and on the unions see S. Lewenhak, *Women and Trade Unions* (1977), N.C. Soldon, *Women in British Trade Unions, 1874–1976* (1978) and S. Boston, *Women Workers and the Trade Union Movement* (1980). Women's generally shabby treatment in employment by both employers and male colleagues is examined in a number of studies, such as A. John (ed.), *Unequal Opportunities: Women's Employment in England, 1800–1918* (1986), L. Davidoff and B. Westover (eds), *Our Work, Our Lives, Our Words* (1986) on women in work from 1880 to 1939, and E. Roberts, *Women's Work, 1840–1940* (1987). See also S.S. Holton, *Feminism and Democracy: Women's Suffrage and Reform Politics in Britain, 1900–1918* (1986).

Much of the broader work on the position of women leads into the twentieth century: see J. Lewis, *Women in England: Sexual Divisions and Social Change* (1984), J. Lewis (ed.), *Labour and Love: Women's Experience of Home and Family, 1850–1940* (1986), and E. Roberts, *A Woman's Place: an oral history of working-class women, 1890–1940* (1984). The crucial question of family size and welfare is discussed in J. Lewis, *The Politics of Motherhood: Child and Maternal Welfare in England, 1900–39* (1980), D. Gittins, *Fair Sex: Family Size and Structure, 1900–1939* (1982) and J. Macnicol, *The Movement for Family Allowances, 1918–45* (1980).

The development of attitudes towards sexuality is the subject of J. Weeks, *Sex, Politics and Society since 1800* (1981) and the collection by S. Cartledge and J. Ryan (eds), *Sex and Love* (1983) has a number of useful studies including L. Bland, 'Purity, Motherhood, Pleasures or Threats? Definitions of female sexuality, 1900–1970'. The development of family planning and its place in early feminist causes is discussed in

J.A. and O. Banks, *Feminism and Family Planning in Victorian England* (1964) and A. McLaren, *Birth Control in Nineteenth-Century England* (1978). The letters edited by R. Hall, *Dear Dr Stopes* (1978) are moving evidence of the sexual problems faced by many people in the earlier part of the century. See also R. Hall's biography *Marie Stopes* (1977). The interrelationship between family, work, and women's role between the wars is discussed in J. Stevenson, *British Society, 1914–45* (1984), ch. 5, and there is an assessment of the postwar position of women in E. Wilson, *Only Halfway to Paradise: Women in Postwar Britain, 1945–1968* (1980).

The development of the women's suffrage movement is traced in M.D. Pugh, *Women's Suffrage in Britain, 1867–1928* (Historical Association pamphlet, 1980), but see also A. Rosen, *Rise up Women! The Militant Campaign of the Women's Social and Political Union, 1903–14* (1974) and J. Liddington and J. Norris, *One Hand Tied Behind Us: the rise of the women's suffrage movement* (1978). C. Rover, *Women's Suffrage and Party Politics in Britain, 1866–1914* (1967) complements the thorough, detailed overview dealing with electoral reform before and after 1914 in M.D. Pugh, *Electoral Reform in War and Peace, 1906–1918* (1978). D. Morgan, *Suffragists and Liberals* (1975) examines the relationship of the women's movement with its most likely supporters in Parliament, but much the most considered treatment of the women's suffrage question at Westminster is B. Harrison, 'Women's Suffrage at Westminster', in M. Bentley and J. Stevenson (eds), *High and Low Politics in Modern Britain: Ten Studies* (1983) and his *Separate Spheres: The Opposition to Women's Suffrage in Britain* (1978). See also J. Rendall (ed.), *Equal or Different? Women's Politics, 1800–1914* (1987) and J. Lewis (ed.), *Before the Vote was Won: Arguments for and against Women's Suffrage, 1864–1896* (1987). The effects of the world wars are considered in G. Braybon and P. Summerfield, *Out of the Cage: Women's Experiences in two World Wars* (1987).

### Articles

On the general question of the range and nature of women's history, see the articles in 'What is Women's History?' in *HT* (1985). On the family see M.S. Anderson, 'Sociological history and the working-class family: Smelser revisited', *SH* (1976) and on women's work see E. Richards, 'Women in the British economy since about 1700: an interpretation', *H* (1974) and K.D.M. Snell, 'Agricultural seasonal unemployment, the standard of living and women's work in the south and east: 1690–1860', *EconHR* (1981). For the link between work and family limitation see A. McLaren, 'Women's work and regulation of family size', *HW* (1977), D. Gittins, 'Women's work and family size between the wars', *OH* (1977) and her 'Married life and birth control between the wars', *OH* (1975). Two broad perspectives on women's history in a European context are L. Tilly and J. Scott, 'Women's work and the family in nineteenth-century Europe', *Comparative Studies in Society and History* (1975) and L. Tilly, J. Scott and M. Cohen, 'Women's work and European fertility patterns', *Journal of Interdisciplinary History* (1976). See also J. Bourke, 'Housewifery in working class England, 1860–1914', *PP* (1994) and J. Vellacott, 'Feminist consciousness and the First World War', *HW* (1987).

## 26. The rise of the Labour Party

The formation and emergence of the Labour Party was one of the most important aspects of the period prior to 1914. Overhanging this topic and the next one is the question of why the Labour Party proved, eventually, to be able to rise at the expense of the Liberals. Although the development of mass trade unionism and the spread of socialist ideas provide the background, the question of why a separate, trade-union-backed political party emerged at all needs consideration, as it was not a pattern followed by all industrial countries. Proponents of a 'new Liberalism' have argued that Labour was in a relatively weak position prior to 1914 and not necessarily bound to succeed the Liberals; the evidence for the period 1906–14 needs particular attention.

### Essay topic

• Why did the Labour Party come into existence and what had it achieved by 1914?

### Sources and documents

E. Hobsbawm (ed.), *Labour's Turning Point 1880–1900* (2nd edn, 1974) has a wide range of documents on trade union and radical politics at the end of the nineteenth century. See also H. Pelling (ed.), *The Challenge of Socialism* (1954). B. Webb, *My Apprenticeship* (1926) and *Our Partnership* (1948) are eyewitness accounts by an early member of the Fabians, of social movements before 1914. R. Tressell, *The Ragged Trousered Philanthropists* (1955) is a remarkable novel of Edwardian working-class life.

## Secondary works

H. Pelling, *The Origins of the Labour Party, 1880–1900* (2nd edn, 1965) is the standard account. See also his *Short History of the Labour Party* (8th edn, 1985) and F. Bealey and H. Pelling, *Labour and Politics, 1900–1906: A History of the Labour Representation Committee* (1958). Carl F. Brand, *The British Labour Party: a short history* (1965), J.H. Stewart Reid, *The Origins of the British Labour Party* (1962), E.H. Hunt, *British Labour History, 1815–1914* (1981), K.D. Brown, *The English Labour Movement, 1700–1851* (1982) and J. Hinton, *Labour and Socialism: A History of the British Labour Movement, 1867–1974* (1983) are alternative general treatments. Trade union attitudes are discussed in H. Pelling, *A History of British Trade Unionism* (4th edn, 1986); J. Lovell and B.C. Roberts, *A Short History of the T.U.C.* (1968); R. Gregory, *The Miners and British Politics, 1906–1914* (1968); and H. Clegg, A. Fox and A.F. Thompson, *A History of British Trade Unions since 1889* (Vol. 1, 1964, Vol. 2, 1985). E. Hobsbawm, *Labouring Men* (1964) has a number of important essays; see especially 'General labour unions in Britain, 1889–1914' and 'Trends in the British Labour Movement since 1850'. The early political fortunes of Labour are discussed in P. Thompson, *Socialists, Liberals and Labour: The struggle for London, 1885–1914* (1967) and H. Pelling, *The Social Geography of British Elections, 1885–1910* (1967). The intellectual influences on the early Labour and socialist movements are discussed in E.P. Thompson, *William Morris: romantic to revolutionary* (1955); C. Tsuzuki, *H. M. Hyndman and British Socialism* (1961); H. Pelling, *America and the British Left* (1956); M. Cole, *The Story of Fabian Socialism* (1961); A.M. McBriar, *Fabian Socialism and English Politics, 1884–1918* (1966); E.R. Pease, *The History of the Fabian Society* (2nd edn, 1963); N. and J. MacKenzie, *The First Fabians* (1977); S. Pierson, *Marxism and the Origins of British Socialism* (1973); and W. Wolfe, *From Radicalism to Socialism* (1975).

R. McKibbin, *The Evolution of the Labour Party, 1910–1924* (1974) discusses the growth of labour organization, while the argument that Labour's position was weakening prior to 1914 is made by R. Douglas, 'The strange death of Labour England, 1910–14', in K. Brown (ed.), *Essays in Anti-Labour History* (1974); see also K. Brown, *The First Labour Party, 1906–14* (1986), D. Tanner, *Political Change and the Labour Party, 1900–18* (1990) and K. Laybourn and J. Reynolds, *Liberalism and the Rise of Labour, 1890–1918* (1984). See also J. Turner, *British Politics and the Great War: Coalition and Conflict, 1915–1918* (1992), esp. chs 10–12. The rise of a more militant socialist movement is discussed in W. Kendall, *The Revolutionary Movement in Britain, 1900–21* (1969); R. Holton, *British*

*Syndicalism, 1900–1914: myths and realities* (1976); and B. Pribicevic, *The Shop Stewards Movement and Workers' Control, 1910–1922* (1959). For the industrial disputes of the pre-1914 period, see E. Phelps Brown, *The Growth of British Industrial Relations: a study from the standpoint of 1906–1914* (1959).

The character of the Labour Party representatives in Parliament is discussed in D.E. Martin, ' "The instruments of the people"?: The Parliamentary Labour Party in 1906', in D.E. Martin and D. Rubinstein (eds), *Ideology and the Labour Movement: essays presented to John Saville* (1979). On prominent Labour personalities see I. McLean, *Keir Hardie* (1975); K.O. Morgan, *Keir Hardie: radical and socialist* (1975); F. Reid, *Keir Hardie: the making of a socialist* (1978); A. Bullock, *The Life and Times of Ernest Bevin*, vol. 1 (1960); D. Marquand, *Ramsay MacDonald* (1977); and the multi-volume J. Bellamy and J. Saville (eds), *Dictionary of Labour Biography* (1972– ).

### Articles

See P. Thompson, 'Liberals, Radicals and Labour in London, 1880–1900', *PP* (1964); R.I. McKibbin, 'James Ramsay MacDonald and the problem of the independence of the Labour Party, 1910–1914', *JMH* (1970); K.O. Morgan, 'The New Liberalism and the challenge of Labour', *WHR* (1973); G.A. Phillips, 'The Triple Industrial Alliance in 1914', *EconHR* (1971); P.F. Clarke, 'The electoral position of the Liberal and Labour parties, 1910–14', *EHR* (1975); H.C.G. Matthew, R.I. McKibbin and J. Kay, 'The franchise factor in the rise of the Labour Party', *EHR* (1976); and D. Tanner, 'The parliamentary electoral system, the "fourth" reform act and the rise of Labour in England and Wales', *BIHR* (1983).

## 27. The Liberal Party in the age of Asquith and Lloyd George

The history of the Liberal Party in the early twentieth century is dominated by the question of its eventual decline and replacement by Labour as the other major party in British politics. Historians have debated whether the Liberals were already doomed by 1914 or whether a 'new Liberalism' had emerged sufficient to pre-empt Labour's appeal. For some, the decisive factor was the First World War and the splits produced in the party. Lloyd George is a fascinating figure whose career attracts considerable attention in the literature.

## Essay topics

- Was Liberalism a spent force by 1914?
- Was Lloyd George an asset or a liability to the Liberal Party?

## Sources and documents

K.O. Morgan, *The Age of Lloyd George: the Liberal Party and British politics, 1890–1929* (1971) has an excellent selection of documents bearing directly on this topic; see also A. Bullock and M. Shock (eds), *The Liberal Tradition from Fox to Keynes* (1956). T. Wilson (ed.), *The Political Diaries of C.P. Scott* (1970) and M. and E. Brock (eds), *Asquith: letters to Venetia Stanley* (1982) offer an insight into politics at the highest level.

## Secondary works

There is a good survey of the debate on the decline of Liberalism in G.R. Searle, *The Liberal Party: triumph and disintegration, 1886–1929* (1992), K.O. Morgan, *The Age of Lloyd George*, chs 1– 5 and M. Bentley, *The Climax of Liberal Politics* (1987), chs 7 and 8; see also H. Pelling, 'Labour and the downfall of Liberalism', in his volume of essays, *Popular Politics and Society in Late Victorian England* (1968). G. Dangerfield, *The Strange Death of Liberal England* (1936) argues the case for the decline of 'Liberalism' by 1914. P.F. Clarke, *Lancashire and the New Liberalism* (1971) argues in favour of a 'new Liberalism' by 1914; see the informative review by K.O. Morgan in *History* (1972) and W. Arnstein, 'Edwardian Politics: turbulent spring or Indian summer?', in A. O'Day (ed.), *The Edwardian Age: conflict and stability, 1900–1914* (1984). R. McKibbin, *The Evolution of the Labour Party, 1910–24* (1974) in essence contradicts this view, as does K. Laybourn and J. Reynolds, *Liberalism and the Rise of Labour, 1890–1918* (1984); see also T. Wilson, *The Downfall of the Liberal Party, 1914–35* (1966) which locates the crucial period of decline after 1914. H. Pelling, *The Social Geography of British Elections, 1885–1910* (1967) is a mine of information on the complex electoral forces at work prior to 1914. See also K.D. Brown (ed.), *Essays in Anti-Labour History* (1974) and C. Cook, *A Short History of the Liberal Party, 1900–1992* (1993). S. Koss, *Nonconformity in Modern British Politics* (1975); H.W. Emy, *Liberals, Radicals and Social Politics, 1892–1914* (1973); H.G. Matthew, *The Liberal Imperialists: the ideas and politics of a post-Gladstonian élite* (1973); C. Wrigley, *David Lloyd George and the British Labour Movement* (1976); and B.K. Murray, *The People's Budget 1909/10: Lloyd George and Liberal Politics* (1980) deal with important themes. The

ideology of Liberalism has attracted increasing attention; see especially
M. Freeden, *The New Liberalism: an ideology of social reform* (1978); P.F.
Clarke, *Liberals and Social Democrats* (1978); M. Bentley, *The Liberal Mind,
1914–1929* (1977). See also M. Freeden, *Liberalism Divided. A Study in
British Political Thought, 1914–39* (1986); D. Marquand, *The Progressive
Dilemma* (1991); A. Booth and M. Pack, *Employment, Capital and Economic
Policy* (1985), ch. 2 on the 'Liberal Yellow Book'.
   There are several biographies of Lloyd George; see especially K.O.
Morgan, *Lloyd George* (1974); P. Rowland, *Lloyd George* (1975); J. Grigg,
*Lloyd George* (3 vols, 1973– ). Also available are M. Thomson, *Lloyd
George* (1951); F. Owen, *Tempestuous Journey* (1954); W. Watkin Davies,
*Lloyd George, 1863–1914* (1939); A.J.P. Taylor, *Lloyd George: rise and fall*
(1961); C.L. Mowat, *Lloyd George* (1964). His later career is ably
discussed in J. Campbell, *Lloyd George: the goat in the wilderness,
1922–1931* (1977). There are also a number of useful essays in A.J.P.
Taylor (ed.), *Lloyd George: twelve essays* (1971). For Asquith, see R.
Jenkins, *Asquith* (rev. edn, 1978) and S. Koss, *Asquith* (1976). Churchill's
early career is covered in R.S. Churchill, *Winston S. Churchill*, Vols 1 and
2 (1966 and 1967). On other figures, see K. Robbins, *Sir Edward Grey*
(1971); D.A. Hamer, *John Morley* (1968); and A. Briggs, *Seebohm Rowntree*
(1961).
   The effects of the First World War have received detailed attention
in D. Tanner, *Political Change and the Labour Party, 1900–1918* (1990),
chs 11, 13 and conclusion; also in J. Turner, *British Politics and the Great
War: Coalition and Conflict, 1915–1918* (1992), chs 10–12.

### Articles

Major topics are dealt with in J.F. Harris and C. Hazlehurst,
'Campbell-Bannerman as prime minister', *H* (1970); F. Bealey,
'Negotiations between the Liberal Party and the L.R.C. before the
general election of 1906', *BIHR* (1956) and 'The electoral arrangement
between the L.R.C. and the Liberal Party', *JMH* (1956); M. Peter, 'The
progressive alliance', *H* (1973); P.F. Clarke, 'The progressive movement
in England', *TRHS* (1974); P. Thompson, 'Liberals, Radicals and
Labour in London, 1880–1900', *PP* (1964); J. Howarth, 'The Liberal
revival in Northamptonshire, 1880–95', *HJ* (1969); J.G. Kellas, 'The
Liberal Party in Scotland, 1876–1895', *SHR* (1965); C. Hazlehurst,
'Asquith as prime minister, 1908–16', *EHR* (1970); K.O. Morgan, 'Lloyd
George's premiership', *HJ* (1970). For the influence of franchise
arrangements on party support, see H.C.G. Matthew, R.I. McKibbin and

J.A. Kay, 'The franchise factor in the rise of the Labour Party', *EHR*
(1976); P.F. Clarke, 'Liberals, Labour and the franchise', *EHR* (1977)
and D. Tanner, 'The parliamentary electoral system, the "fourth"
reform act and the rise of Labour in England and Wales', *BIHR* (1983).

## 28. The causes and consequences of the First World War

The origins of the First World War remain a major concern of
historians. Although responsibility for the outbreak of the war has been
variously allocated, the crucial question arises of how Britain became
involved in a general European war in 1914. The rise of the alliance
system and Britain's role within it is important, while the Anglo-German
naval rivalry added a special dimension to Britain's relations with
Germany. Particular attention needs to be given to the considerations
affecting British policy in the summer of 1914. On the domestic front,
historians have increasingly recognized the importance of the war as a
significant agent of social, economic and political change. The effects
of the First World War on Britain can be studied either as a whole or
through the examination of a major aspect, such as the impact of the
war upon party politics, the labour movement, the role of women or
social policy.

### Essay topics

- How much responsibility did Britain bear for the outbreak of war
  with Germany in 1914?
- Were the social effects of the First World War of greater significance
  than the political ones?

### Sources and documents

J.B. Joll (ed.), *Britain and Europe: Pitt to Churchill, 1793–1940* (1950); J.H.
Wiener (ed.), *Great Britain: foreign policy and the span of empire* (4 vols,
1972); C.J. Lowe and M.L. Dockrill, *The Mirage of Power: British foreign
policy, 1902–22* (3 vols, 1972) all have useful documents. Lord Grey,
*Twenty-Five Years, 1892–1916* (2 vols, 1925) is a first-hand account by
Britain's Foreign Secretary during the crucial period. See also W.S.
Churchill, *The World Crisis, 1911–14* (1923). Both enjoyable and relevant
is E. Childers, *The Riddle of the Sands* (1903), a spy story about German
invasion plans. K.O. Morgan (ed.), *The Age of Lloyd George: the Liberal
Party and British politics, 1890–1929* (1971) has useful documents on

political developments. Lord Beaverbrook's volumes, *Politicians and the War, 1914–16* (2nd edn, 1960) and *Men and Power, 1917–18* (1956) give a personal account of the political infighting. R. Roberts, *The Classic Slum: Salford life in the first quarter of the century* (1971) discusses the impact of the war on a working-class area while J. Munson (ed.), *Andrew Clarke: Echoes of the Great War* (1986) is a wonderful account of rural life. There is a wealth of war memoir material; see especially R. Graves, *Goodbye to All That* (1929) and Vera Brittain, *Testament of Youth* (1933, and later edns).

### Secondary works

B. Schmitt, *The Outbreak of War in 1914* (Historical Association pamphlet, 1964) is a good overview of the traditional interpretation that the alliance system was to blame for the outbreak of war, a view increasingly under attack; see, for example, H.W. Koch (ed.), *The Origins of the First World War: great power rivalry and German war aims* (1972) and the more recent overview by J. Joll, *The Origins of the First World War* (1985). A.J.P. Taylor, *The Struggle for Mastery in Europe, 1848–1918* (1954) is a major diplomatic study; see also R.W. Seton Watson, *Britain in Europe, 1789–1914, a survey of foreign policy* (1937). Z.S. Steiner, *Britain and the Origins of the First World War* (1977) is the most detailed analysis of British involvement. The classic study of Anglo-German naval rivalry is E.L. Woodward, *Great Britain and the German Navy* (1935), now updated on the naval side by A.J. Marder, *From the Dreadnought to Scapa Flow. Vol. 1: The road to war, 1904–14* (1961) and on the political by P. Kennedy, *The Rise of the Anglo-German Antagonism, 1860–1914* (1980). Military preparations are discussed in M. Howard, *The Continental Commitment: the dilemma of British defence policy in the era of two world wars* (1972), ch. 2, and S.R. Williamson, *The Politics of Grand Strategy: Britain and France prepare for war, 1904–1914* (1969). On the Foreign Office, see Z.S. Steiner, *The Foreign Office and Foreign Policy, 1898–1914* (1969). A. Marwick, *The Deluge* (1965) surveys economic and social life during the First World War; see also the overall study by T. Wilson, *The Myriad Faces of War: Britain and the Great War* (1987). The political repercussions of the war are discussed in T. Wilson, *The Downfall of the Liberal Party, 1914–35* (1966); A.J.P. Taylor, *Politics in Wartime* (1964); C. Hazlehurst, *Politicians at War, July 1914 to May 1915* (1971); and M. Bentley, *The Climax of Liberal Politics* (1987), chs 7 and 8. The early role of Lloyd George is considered in R.J.Q. Adams, *Arms and the Wizard: Lloyd George and the Ministry of Munitions, 1915–1916* (1978);

but for the wartime developments, see also S. Koss, *Asquith* (1976); R.
Jenkins, *Asquith* (1978); P. Rowland, *Lloyd George* (1975); M. Gilbert,
*Winston S. Churchill,* Vols 2 and 3 (1971 and 1975). J. Ramsden, *The Age
of Balfour and Baldwin, 1902–40* (1978) covers the Conservative Party;
see also the section in R. Blake, *The Conservative Party from Peel to
Thatcher* (1985) and J. Stubbs, 'The impact of the Great War on the
Conservatives', in G. Peele and C. Cook (eds), *The Politics of Reappraisal,
1918–1939* (1975). For the Labour Party the crucial study is R.
McKibbin, *The Evolution of the Labour Party, 1910–1924* (1974); see also
H. Pelling, *A Short History of the Labour Party* (8th edn, 1985); D. Tanner,
*Political Change and the Labour Party, 1900–18* (1990); and J. Turner,
*British Politics and the Great War* (1992). Trade union developments can
be followed in H. Pelling, *A History of British Trade Unionism* (4th edn,
1987); A Bullock, *The Life and Times of Ernest Bevin,* Vol. 1 (1960); K.
Burgess, *The Challenge of Labour* (1980); C. Wrigley, 'Trade Unions and
Politics in the First World War', in B. Pimlott and C. Cook (eds), *Trade
Unions in British Politics* (1982); and H.A. Clegg, *A History of British Trade
Unions since 1889,* Vol. 2, *1911–33* (1985). For the left-wing movements
see W. Kendall, *The Revolutionary Movement in Britain, 1900–21* (1969);
R.K. Middlemas, *The Clydesiders* (1965); J. Hinton, 'The Clyde Workers'
Committee and the dilution struggle', in A. Briggs and J. Saville (eds),
*Essays in Labour History, 1886–1923* (1971); I. McLean, 'Red Clydeside,
1915–1919', in R. Quinault and J. Stevenson (eds), *Popular Protest and
Public Order: six studies in British history, 1790–1920* (1974) and his *The
Myth of Red Clydeside* (1983); and B. Pribicevic, *The Shop Stewards
Movement and Workers' Control, 1910–1922* (1959).

On the suffrage question, see M.D. Pugh, *Electoral Reform in War and
Peace, 1906–1918* (1978). There is a brief introduction to the women's
suffrage question in M.D. Pugh, *Women's Suffrage in Britain, 1867–1928*
(Historical Association pamphlet, 1980). C. Rover, *Women's Suffrage and
Party Politics in Britain, 1866–1914* (1967), D. Morgan, *Suffragists and
Liberals* (1975) and R. Fulford, *Votes for Women* (1957) provide detailed
accounts. See also J. Liddington and J. Norris, *One Hand Tied Behind Us:
the rise of the women's suffrage movement* (1978) and A. Rosen, *Rise up
Women! The Militant Campaign of the Women's Social and Political Union,
1903–14* (1974). The politics of the women's suffrage issue is discussed
in B. Harrison, 'Women's suffrage at Westminster', in M. Bentley and J.
Stevenson (eds), *High and Low Politics in Modern Britain* (1983). A.
Marwick, *Women at War, 1914–1918* (1977) has an excellent set of
photographs with commentary. On other social issues, see B.B. Gilbert,
*British Social Policy, 1914–1939* (1970), ch. 1; J. Harris, *William Beveridge:*

*A Biography* (1977), chs 9 and 10; J. Burnett, *A Social History of Housing, 1815–1970* (1978), ch. 8; M. Swenarton, *Homes Fit for Heroes: the politics and architecture of early state housing in Britain* (1981). J.M. Winter, *The Great War and the British People* (1986) examines the demographic impact of the war, and there are essays on Britain in J. Winter and R. Wall (eds), *The Upheaval of War: Family, Work and Welfare in Europe, 1914–1918* (1986).

### Articles

The major themes are discussed in K.O. Morgan, 'Lloyd George's premiership', *HJ* (1970); T. Wilson, 'The coupon and the British general election of 1918', *JMH* (1964); P. Abrams, 'The failure of social reform: 1918–20', *PP* (1963); S. Koss, 'The destruction of Britain's last Liberal Government', *JMH* (1968); J.M. Winter, 'Arthur Henderson, the Russian Revolution and the reconstruction of the Labour Party', *HJ* (1972); N. Blewett, 'The franchise in the United Kingdom, 1885–1918', *PP* (1965); C. Hazlehurst, 'Asquith as prime minister, 1908–16', *EHR* (1970). On the suffrage question, see M.D. Pugh, 'Politicians and the women's vote 1914–18', *H* (1974); D. Close, 'The collapse of resistance to democracy: Conservatives, adult suffrage and second chamber reform 1911–28', *HJ* (1977). On the social effects of the war see J.M. Winter, 'Britain's "Lost Generation" of the First World War', *PS* (1977); 'The impact of the First World War on civilian health in Britain', *EconHR* (1977); 'Some aspects of the demographic consequences of the First World War in Britain', *PS* (1976); J. Vellacott, 'Feminist consciousness and the First World War', *HW* (1987); N. Whiteside, 'Welfare legislation and the unions during the First World War', *HJ* (1970).

## 29. Britain in the 1920s

The fall of Lloyd George, the formation of the first Labour government, the emergence of Baldwin and the General Strike dominate the story of the 1920s. It was also a period when hopes of postwar reconstruction were quickly dashed by depression. It is worth asking how effective the political leaders of this period were and what, if anything, was achieved. The General Strike marked a major confrontation between organized labour and the Conservative government. Views differ as to whether it was the inevitable outcome of the growth of union power, a 'showdown' engineered by Baldwin, or an anachronistic conflict brought about by an unfortunate breakdown in negotiations. Above all, the General Strike needs placing in the context of Labour and trade union growth.

## Essay topics

* Was anything substantial achieved in British politics in the decade following the First World War?
* What was the significance of the General Strike?

## Sources and documents

Lord Beaverbrook, *The Decline and Fall of Lloyd George* (1963) is informative, if biased. K. Middlemas (ed.), *Thomas Jones: Whitehall Diary*, Vol. 1, *1916–25* and Vol. 2, *1926–30* give an inside account of politics. On the 1920s see W.S. Churchill, *The World Crisis* (1923–31) and C.F.G. Masterman, *England after the War: a study* (1922). K.O. Morgan, *The Age of Lloyd George: the Liberal Party and British politics, 1890–1929* (1971) has documents on one strand of politics. R. Page Arnot, *The General Strike* (1926) has a comprehensive set of documents on the strike.

## Secondary works

A.J.P. Taylor, *English History, 1914–45* (1965) and C.L. Mowat, *Britain between the wars, 1918–1940* (1955) are both important general studies; see also A. Marwick, *Britain in the Age of Total War: war, peace and social change, 1900–1967* (1968). K.O. Morgan, *Consensus and Disunity: the Lloyd George Coalition government, 1918–22* (1979) is the essential study of the Lloyd George Coalition. On his fall, see M. Kinnear, *The Fall of Lloyd George: the political crisis of 1922* (1973). R. McKibbin, *The Evolution of the Labour Party, 1910–24* (1974) and M. Cowling, *The Impact of Labour, 1920–24* (1971) take rather different approaches to the question of Labour's rise. R.W. Lyman, *The First Labour Government, 1924* (1957) and D. Marquand, *Ramsay MacDonald* (1977) consider Labour in office. The Liberals are discussed in T. Wilson, *The Downfall of the Liberal Party, 1914–35* (1966); C. Cook, *A Short History of the Liberal Party, 1900–1992* (1993) and in the essays by J. Campbell and C. Cook in G. Peele and C. Cook (eds), *The Politics of Reappraisal, 1918–39* (1975). S. Koss, *Asquith* (1976) and J. and K.O. Morgan, *Portrait of a Progressive: the political career of Christopher Addison* (1980) discuss personalities on the Liberal side. See also J. Campbell, *The Goat in the Wilderness: Lloyd George, 1922–1931* (1977) and S. Koss, 'Asquith versus Lloyd George: the last phase and beyond', in A. Sked and C. Cook (eds), *Crisis and Controversy:*

*essays in honour of A.J.P. Taylor* (1976). For the Conservatives see J. Ramsden, *The Age of Balfour and Baldwin, 1902–40* (1978); M.D. Pugh, *The Tories and the People, 1880–1935* (1986); J. Barnes and K. Middlemas, *Baldwin* (1969); H. Montgomery Hyde, *Baldwin* (1973); H. Pelling, *Winston Churchill* (1977); M. Gilbert, *Winston Churchill,* Vol. 5: *1922–1939* (1976) and D.D. Dilks, *Neville Chamberlain* (1985). The last phase of the period has received fresh insight from P. Williamson, *National Crisis and National Government, British politics, the economy and Empire, 1926–32* (1992) and S. Ball, *Baldwin and the Conservative Party: the Crisis of 1929–31* (1988). C. Cook, *The Age of Alignment: electoral politics in Britain 1922–1929* (1976) provides an analysis of the electoral shifts of the period.

The controversy about the conduct of economic policy and the return to the Gold Standard is covered in D.E. Moggeridge, *The Return to Gold, 1925: the formulation of economic policy and its critics* (1969) and R.S. Sayers, 'The return to gold, 1925', in L.S. Pressnell (ed.), *Studies in the Industrial Revolution* (1960); see also D.H. Aldcroft, *The Inter-War Economy: Britain, 1919–1939* (1970), ch. 9; S. Pollard, *The Development of the British Economy, 1914–1950* (1962), ch. 4; S. Glynn and J. Oxborrow, *Interwar Britain: a social and economic history* (1976), ch. 4.

On the General Strike see K. Laybourn, *The General Strike* (1993); P. Renshaw, *The General Strike* (1975); G.A. Phillips, *The General Strike: the politics of industrial conflict* (1976); M. Morris, *The General Strike* (1976); W.H. Crook, *The General Strike* (1931). The strike from the trade union side is discussed in A. Bullock, *The Life and Times of Ernest Bevin,* Vol. 1 (1960) and P. Davies, *A. J. Cook* (1987); see also H. Pelling, *A History of British Trade Unionism* (4th edn, 1987). See also the essay by G. McDonald, 'The defeat of the General Strike', in G. Peele and C. Cook (eds), *The Politics of Reappraisal, 1918–1939* (1976). The trade union background is discussed in H. Pelling, *A History of British Trade Unionism* (4th edn, 1987), H. Clegg, *A History of British Trade Unions since 1889,* Vol. 2, *1911–33* (1985) and P. Renshaw, 'The depression years, 1918–1931', in B. Pimlott and C. Cook (eds), *Trade Unions in British Politics* (1982). A mining area of particular importance is discussed in H. Francis and D. Smith, *The Fed: The South Wales Miners' Federation* (1982).

Social policy is outlined in S. Glynn and J. Oxborrow, *Interwar Britain,* as well as the general works by Taylor, Mowat and Marwick (see above). See also M. Bruce, *The Coming of the Welfare State* (1961) and D. Fraser, *The Evolution of the British Welfare State* (1973). See also the essays by Crowther, Ryan and Brown in P. Thane (ed.), *The Origins of British Social Policy* (1978).

*Articles*

See K.O. Morgan, 'Lloyd George's premiership', *HJ* (1970); P. Abrams, 'The failure of social reform: 1918–20', *PP* (1963); S. Macintyre, 'British Labour, Marxism and working class apathy in the nineteen twenties', *HJ* (1977); and D. Williamson, ' "Safety first": Baldwin and the General Election of 1929', *HJ* (1983).

## 30. Britain and the slump

The 1930s appear dominated by the theme of economic depression and mass unemployment. The years of the slump have been portrayed as a particularly turbulent period in which both fascism and communism seemed to challenge the established political parties. The reasons for the break-up of the Labour government in 1931 require close analysis, as does the reaction to the depression. Recent work has stressed the more prosperous side of the decade (at least for some) and the need to explain the relative weakness of radical discontent in the decade overall. Some consideration of the evolution of more interventionist strategies in the economy and social policy is useful, as well as the extent to which Labour was poised for electoral victory prior to the Second World War.

*Essay topics*

- How would you account for the failure of political extremism in Britain after 1929?
- What was the significance of the collapse of the Labour government of 1931?
- Do the domestic policies of the National Government deserve more credit than they have received?

*Sources and documents*

G. Orwell, *The Road to Wigan Pier* (1937) is a brilliant survey of social conditions and political attitudes. W. Hannington, *Unemployed Struggles, 1919–1936* (1936) is particularly useful on unemployed movements. J. Stevenson (ed.), *Social Conditions in Britain between the Wars* (1977) has documents on social conditions. H. Macmillan, *The Middle Way* (1938) represents an influential plea for a fresh approach to economic and social management. O. Mosley, *My Life* (1968) and *The Greater Britain* (1932) are important on British fascism. On the higher levels of politics see H. Macmillan, *Winds of Change, 1914–1939* (1966) and T. Jones, *A Diary with Letters, 1931–50* (1954).

## Secondary works

There are a number of good surveys of economic affairs; see especially S. Pollard, *The Development of the British Economy, 1914–1980* (1983); D.H. Aldcroft, *The Inter-War Economy: Britain 1919–1939* (1970); S. Glynn and J. Oxborrow, *Interwar Britain: a social and economic history* (1976). A. Booth and M. Pack, *Employment, Capital and Economic Policy: Great Britain, 1918–39* (1985) specifically examines the various alternative economic policies put forward.

The major study of the fall of the Labour government is R. Skidelsky, *Politicians and the Slump: the Labour government of 1929–1931* (1967), though the older R. Bassett, *Nineteen Thirty-One: political crisis* (1958) remains useful. A major modern work is P. Williamson, *National Crisis and National Government, British politics, the economy and Empire, 1926–32* (1992), while A. Thorpe, *The British General Election of 1931* (1991) offers the best account of the conversion from emergency Cabinet into a National Government. D. Marquand, *Ramsay MacDonald* (1977) remains definitive on the Labour leader. J. Stevenson and C. Cook, *Britain in the Depression: society and politics, 1929–39* (2nd edn, 1994) offers a general interpretation and there is a helpful overview of debates in A. Thorpe, *Britain in the 1930s* (1992). S. Constantine, *Unemployment in Britain Between the Wars* (1980) focuses on the effects of unemployment. For the Communists see N. Branson, *History of the Communist Party of Great Britain, 1927–41* (1985); H. Pelling, *The British Communist Party* (1958); and R. Martin, *Communism and the British Trade Unions, 1924–33* (1969). For the British Union of Fascists see R. Benewick, *The Fascist Movement in Britain* (1972); R. Thurlow, *Fascism in Britain, 1918–1985* (1986); and D.S. Lewis, *Illusions of Grandeur: Fascism and British Society, 1931–81* (1987). R. Skidelsky, *Oswald Mosley* (1975) examines the central figure in British fascism. See also K. Lunn and R.C. Thurlow (eds), *British Fascism: essays on the radical right in inter-war Britain* (1980). A useful guide to the Labour Party's subsequent history in the 1930s can be found in H. Pelling, *A Short History of the Labour Party* (8th edn, 1985); see also B. Pimlott, *Labour and the Left in the 1930s* (1977). For the Conservatives see R. Blake, *The Conservative Party from Peel to Thatcher* (1985), J. Ramsden, *The Age of Balfour and Baldwin, 1902–1940* (1978) and M. Pugh, *The Tories and the People, 1880–1935* (1986). Trade union reactions can be followed in A. Bullock, *The Life and Times of Ernest*

*Bevin*, Vol. 1 (1960) and S. Pollard, 'Trade union reactions to the economic crisis', in his collection of essays *The Gold Standard and Employment Policies between the Wars* (1970). Social conditions are discussed in J. Stevenson, *British Society, 1914–1945* (1984) and S. Constantine, *Social Conditions in Britain, 1918–1939* (1983). An excellent case study is K. Nicholas, *The Social Effects of Unemployment in Teeside, 1919–1939* (1987); see also H. Francis and D. Smith, *The Fed: A History of the South Wales Miners in the Twentieth Century* (1982). S. McIntyre, *Little Moscows – Communism and Working Class Militancy in Inter-war Britain* (1980) is a study of areas of militancy. An important organization of the unemployed is discussed in R. Croucher, *We Refuse to Starve in Silence: A History of the National Unemployed Workers' Movement, 1920–46* (1987).

### Articles

R. McKibbin, 'The economics of the second labour government, 1929–31', *PP* (1975); F.M. Miller, 'The unemployment policy of the National government, 1931–1936', *HJ* (1976); A. Marwick, 'Middle opinion in the thirties', *EHR* (1964) are all useful. Two important articles on economic affairs are D.H. Aldcroft, 'Economic growth in Britain in the inter-war years: a re-assessment', *EconHR* (1967) and H.W. Richardson, 'The basis of recovery in the nineteen thirties: a review and a new interpretation', *EconHR* (1962). An important left-wing organization is discussed in R. Hayburn, 'The National Unemployed Workers' Movement, 1921–36: a Reappraisal', *IRSH* (1983).

## 31. Appeasement and British foreign policy in the 1930s

The conduct of British foreign policy in the 1930s has attracted controversy, primarily over the question of appeasement. Inevitably, judgements of appeasement as a policy demand some assessment of whether the dictators, especially Hitler, were appeasable. Even if appeasement might have worked, some appreciation is required of whether the policy was conducted effectively and what forces politicians were influenced by in adopting it. The Munich Crisis of 1938 occupies a central place in the literature, but some consideration of the evolution of foreign policy during the 1930s as a whole is necessary, as well as the role of Italy and Japan in shaping Britain's attitudes. Cowling's close study of the positions taken up in response to Hitler introduce a more complex dimension to the debate on foreign policy at the higher levels of politics. 'Economic' appeasement and the economic and military context of foreign policy has attracted much recent attention.

## Essay topics

• What forces shaped British foreign policy in the 1930s?
• Had appeasement anything to be said for it as a policy?

## Sources and documents

Lord Avon, *Facing the Dictators* (1962) and *The Reckoning* (1965) are important memoirs by a foreign secretary of the 1930s; see also W.S. Churchill, *The Second World War*, Vol. 1, *The Gathering Storm* (1949). G. Orwell, *Collected Essays, Journalism and Letters*, Vol. 1, *An Age Like This* (ed. S. Orwell and I. Angus, 1970) expresses many of the political and intellectual conflicts of the decade.

## Secondary works

There is a useful introduction to the topic in the historiographical essay by D.C. Watt in A. Sked and C. Cook (eds), *Crisis and Controversy: essays in honour of A.J.P. Taylor* (1976); see also P.M. Bell, *The Origins of the Second World War in Europe* (1986) and G. Martel (ed.), *The Origins of the Second World War Reconsidered: the A.J.P. Taylor Debate after Twenty-five Years* (1986) for reviews of the historiography. D.C. Watt, *How War Came: the Immediate Origins of the Second World War* (1989) and R.A.C. Parker, *Chamberlain and Appeasement: British Policy and the Coming of the Second World War* (1993) are modern treatments. See also G. Schmidt, *The Politics and Economics of Appeasement* (1986). A.J.P. Taylor, *The Origins of the Second World War* (1961) and M. Gilbert, *The Roots of Appeasement* (1966) are classics. D.C. Watt, *Personalities and Policies: Studies in the formulation of British foreign policy in the twentieth century* (1965) has a number of important essays on the formulation of foreign policy; see also W.N. Medlicott, 'Britain and Germany: the search for agreement, 1930–7', in D. Dilks, *Retreat from Power*, Vol. 1, *1906–1939* (1981). M. Cowling, *The Impact of Hitler: British politics and British policy, 1933–1940* (1975) re-evaluates the responses of politicians to foreign affairs. The role of public opinion is considered in M. Ceadel, 'Fulham revisited', in C. Cook and J. Ramsden (eds), *By-Elections in British Politics* (1973); F.R. Gannon, *The British Press and Germany, 1936–1939* (1971); R.B. McCallum, *Public Opinion and the Lost Peace* (1944). Also valuable are K. Robbins, *Munich* (1968); K. Middlemas, *Diplomacy of Illusion: the British government and Germany, 1927–1939* (1972); S. Aster, *1939: The coming of the Second World War* (1974). See also M. Ceadel, *Pacifism in Britain, 1914–1945* (1980).

Particular episodes are discussed in K.G. Watkins, *Britain Divided: the effect of the Spanish Civil War on British political opinion* (1963); J. Edwards, *The British Government and the Spanish Civil War, 1936–39* (1979); D. Waley, *British Public Opinion and the Abyssinian War, 1935–6* (1975); and T.R. Emmerson, *The Reoccupation of the Rhineland* (1976).

The attitude of Labour and the Left towards appeasement is discussed in T.D. Burridge, *British Labour and Hitler's War* (1976); A. Bullock, *The Life and Times of Ernest Bevin*, Vol. 1 (1960); H. Pelling, *A Short History of the Labour Party* (1961). See also S. Aster, 'Ivan Maisky and Parliamentary Anti-appeasement 1938–1939', in A.J.P. Taylor (ed.), *Lloyd George: twelve essays* (1971).

Military and economic considerations are the themes of M. Howard, *The Continental Commitment: the dilemma of British foreign policy in the era of two world wars* (1972); B. Bond, *British Military Policy between the two world wars* (1980); R. Shay, *British Rearmament in the Thirties* (1977); and G.C. Peden, *British Rearmament and the Treasury, 1932–1939* (1979).

Biographical studies of the major protagonists include M. Gilbert and R. Gott, *The Appeasers* (1963); J. Barnes and R.K. Middlemas, *Baldwin* (1969); K. Fielding, *The Life of Neville Chamberlain* (1946); M. Gilbert, *Winston S. Churchill*, Vol. 5, *1922–1939* (1976); H. Pelling, *Winston Churchill* (1977); D. Carlton, *Eden* (1981); and R. Rhodes James, *Anthony Eden* (1986).

## Articles

See D.C. Watt, 'Appeasement: the rise of a revisionist school?', *PQ* (1963); F. Coglan, 'Armaments, economic policy and appeasement', *H* (1972); C.A. MacDonald, 'Economic appeasement and the German "Moderates"', *PP* (1972); T. Mason, 'Some origins of the Second World War', *PP* (1964); D.H. Lammers, 'Fascism, Communism and the Foreign Office, 1937–1939', *JCH* (1971); R. Helder, 'East Fulham revisited', *JCH* (1971); R. Eatwell, 'Munich, public opinion and Popular Front', *JCH* (1971); R.A.C. Parker, 'Great Britain, France and the Ethiopian Crisis, 1935–1936', *EHR* (1974). Also relevant on British public opinion is A. Marwick, 'Middle opinion in the thirties', *EHR* (1964). On the crisis of 1939, see G.C. Peden, 'A matter of timing: the economic background to British foreign policy, 1938–1939', *H* (1984).

## 32. Britain and the Second World War

The impact of 'total war' was perhaps even more significant in the case of the Second World War than the First. Domestic politics were dominated by the leadership given by Churchill to the coalition government and the remarkable mood of social optimism which gave rise to the Beveridge Report and the Butler Education Act. The reasons for Labour's victory in the 1945 general election require explanation, as well as some assessment of what it accomplished.

### Essay topics

• Why did the Labour Party win the general election of 1945?
• Assess the impact of the Second World War on British politics and society.

### Sources and documents

G. Orwell, *Collected Essays, Journalism and Letters,* Vol. 2. *My Country Right or Left* (ed. S. Orwell and I. Angus, 1970) provides an interesting commentary on contemporary attitudes. T. Harrison, *Living Through the Blitz* (1976) contains the Mass Observation reports on the impact of bombing on civilian morale and attitudes. See also H. Macmillan, *The Blast of War, 1939–1945* (1967) and W.S. Churchill, *The Second World War* (6 vols, 1949–54). See also the collection of photographs with commentary in A. Marwick, *The Home Front: the British and the Second World War* (1976). A good diary of wartime life is R. Broad and S. Fleming (eds), *Nella Last's War* (1981).

### Secondary works

Of the general studies, A. Marwick, *Britain in the Century of Total War: War, Peace and Social Change, 1900–1967* (1968) and A.J.P. Taylor, *English History, 1914–45* (1965) have relevant sections. P. Addison, *The Road to 1945: British Politics and the Second World War* (1975) has a brilliant analysis of wartime politics. See also H. Pelling, *Britain and the Second World War* (1970) and the essays by P. Addison and A. Marwick in A. Sked and C. Cook, *Crisis and Controversy: Essays in Honour of A.J.P. Taylor* (1976). For Churchill see R. Rhodes James, *Churchill: A Study in Failure* (1973); H. Pelling, *Winston Churchill* (1977); R. Blake, *The Conservative Party from Peel to Thatcher* (1985). For the Labour Party see H. Pelling, *A Short History of the Labour Party* (8th edn, 1985); C.F. Brand, *The British Labour Party: A Short History* (1965). Major personalities of the period are covered in J. Harris, *William Beveridge: A Biography* (1977); A. Bullock, *The Life and Times of Ernest Bevin*, Vol. 2 (1967); B. Donoughue and G.W. Jones, *Herbert Morrison* (1973). A. Calder, *The People's War* (1969) discusses the war from the point of view of the civilian population. The effects of the war on social policy and politics are surveyed in H.L. Smith (ed.), *War and Social Change* (1987); D. Fraser, *The Evolution of the British Welfare State* (1973); J. MacNicol, 'Family allowances and less eligibility', in P. Thane (ed.), *Origins of British Social Policy* (1978); J. Harris, 'Social planning in wartime: some aspects of the Beveridge Report', in J.M. Winter (ed.), *War and Economic Development* (1975). C. Barnett, *The Audit of War* (1986) is a major critique of the war effort and its long-term effects, but see also A.S. Milward, *The Economic Effects of the Two World Wars on Britain* (1970).

The 1945 general election is discussed in R.B. McCallum and A. Readman, *The British General Election of 1945* (1947). The Attlee governments have received excellent treatment in K.O. Morgan, *Labour in Power, 1945–1951* (1983); H. Pelling, *The Labour Governments, 1945–51* (1984); M. Sissons and P. French (eds), *The Age of Austerity* (1963); N. Tiratsoo (ed.), *The Attlee Years* (1992).

Biographies of the major Labour politicians can be consulted in K. Harris, *Attlee* (1982); B. Pimlott, *Hugh Dalton* (1984); A. Bullock, *Ernest Bevin: Foreign Secretary* (1982); M. Foot, *Aneurin Bevan, 1945–60* (1975); J. Campbell, *Nye Bevan* (1987). The performance of the Labour governments has been reviewed recently in the essays by Addison and Hennessy in P. Hennessy and A. Seldon (eds), *Ruling Performance: British Governments from Attlee to Thatcher* (1987). A crucial aspect of the postwar period, economic survival, has been the subject of debate, see Barnett (above), but has received fuller treatment in A.K. Cairncross, *Years of Recovery: British Economic Policy, 1945–51* (1985). Foreign policy is discussed in V. Rothwell, *Britain and the Cold War, 1941–47* (1983); R. Ovendale, *The Foreign Policy of the British Labour Governments, 1945–51* (1984), and Bullock's life of Bevin (above).

Of the large literature on postwar decolonization, most relevant here are J. Darwin, *Britain and Decolonization: The Retreat from Empire in the Post-war World* (1987); M.E. Chamberlain, *Decolonisation: The Fall of the European Empires* (1985); D. Judd and P. Slinn, *The Evolution of the Modern Commonwealth, 1902–80* (1982). On India see B.R. Tomlinson, *The Political Economy of the Raj, 1914–47* (1979) and R.J. Moore, *Escape from Empire: The Attlee Government and the Indian Problem* (1987). The decision to pursue a nuclear future is discussed in M. Gowing and L. Arnold, *Independence and Deterrence: Britain and Atomic Energy, 1945–51* (1974).

For the Conservative response to the postwar situation see R. Blake, *The Conservative Party from Peel to Thatcher* (1985); B. Schwartz, 'The tide of history, the reconstruction of conservatism, 1945–51', in N. Tiratsoo (ed.), *The Attlee Years* (1992); J.D. Hoffmann, *The Conservative Party in Opposition, 1945–51* (1964); J. Ramsden, *The Conservative Party: the Age of Churchill and Eden, 1940–1957* (1995) and *The Making of Conservative Party Policy: The Conservative Research Department since 1929* (1980).

## Articles

The general acceptance of 'consensus' and its ramifications are examined in R. Lowe, 'The Second World War, consensus, and the foundation of the Welfare State', *TCBH* (1990); J.C. Hess, 'The social policy of the Attlee government', in W.J. Mommsen (ed.), *The Emergence of the Welfare State in Britain and Germany* (1981); B. Pimlott, 'Is postwar consensus a myth?, *CR* (1989). On politics see H. Pelling, 'The 1945 election reconsidered', *HJ* (1980) and J. Ramsden, ' "A party for owners or a party for earners?" The Conservative Party after 1945', *TRHS* (1987). On social policy see A. Marwick, 'The Labour Party and the Welfare State in Britain, 1900–48', *AmHR* (1967). On foreign policy, see R. Ovendale, 'Britain, the USA and the European Cold War, 1945–48', *H* (1982).

# 33. Decolonization and foreign policy since 1945

While the theme of imperial expansion has attracted considerable attention, no less important was the dismantling of Britain's overseas Empire and the decline of influence in many different parts of the world. The Suez crisis provides one focal point for the discussion of Britain's changing role in the world. Britain's withdrawal from her remaining colonies and the entry into the European Common Market bring the topic up to the 1970s.

## Essay topics

- Why did Britain grant independence to so many of her colonies after 1945?
- What was the significance of the Suez crisis for the conduct of British foreign policy in the postwar period?

## Sources and documents

The later sections of G. Bennet (ed.), *The Concept of Empire: Burke to*

*Attlee, 1774–1947* (1953) are relevant. See also N. Mansergh (ed.), *Documents and Speeches on Commonwealth Affairs, 1952–1962* (1963); Lord Avon, *Full Circle* (1960) and *The Reckoning* (1965); and W. Strang, *Britain in World Affairs* (1961).

## Secondary works

General studies of foreign affairs include D. Reynolds, *Britannia Overruled: British Policy and World Power in the Twentieth Century* (1991); C.M. Woodhouse, *British Foreign Policy since the Second World War* (1961); F.S. Northedge, *British Foreign Policy, The Process of Readjustment, 1945–1961* (1962) and *Descent from Power: British Foreign Policy, 1945–73* (1974); and W.N. Medlicott, *British Foreign Policy since Versailles, 1919–63* (1968).

For the Empire, see the survey by B. Porter, *The Lion's Share: Short History of British Imperialism, 1850–1970* (2nd edn, 1984). C. Cross, *The Fall of the British Empire 1918–1968* (1968) is an outline of decolonization; see also J. Darwin, *Britain and Decolonization: The Retreat from Empire in the Post-war World* (1987) and P.J. Cain and A.G. Hopkins, *British Imperialism: Crisis and Deconstruction, 1914–1990* (1993). M.E. Chamberlain, *Decolonisation: The Fall of the European Empires* (1985) and D. Judd and P. Slinn, *The Evolution of the Modern Commonwealth* (1982) are good studies. Other features of British policy are considered in P.S. Gupta, *Imperialism and the British Labour Movement, 1914–64* (1975); P. Darby, *British Defence Policy East of Suez 1947–1968* (1973); P.M. Kennedy, *The Rise and Fall of British Naval Mastery* (1976); C.J. Bartlett, *The Long Retreat: A Short History of British Defence Policy, 1945–70* (1972); M. Gowing and L. Arnold, *Independence and Deterrence: Britain and Atomic Energy, 1945–1951* (1974).

The immediate postwar period is discussed in M.A. Fitzsimmons, *The Foreign Policy of the British Labour Government, 1945–51* (1953); A. Bullock, *Ernest Bevin: Foreign Secretary* (1982); M. Edwards, *The Last Years of British India* (1963); M. Zinkin and T. Zinkin, *Britain and India: Requiem for Empire* (1964); B.R. Tomlinson, *The Political Economy of the Raj, 1914–47* (1979); and R. J. Moore, *Escape from Empire* (1987).

The background to the Suez affair can be found in E. Monroe, *Britain's Moment in the Middle East, 1914–56* (1963). On the crisis itself, see K. Kyle, *Suez* (1991); H. Thomas, *The Suez Affair* (1966); S. Lloyd, *Suez 1956: A Personal Account* (1978); A. Nutting, *No End of a Lesson* (1967). Eden's role is discussed in D. Carlton, *Eden* (1981) and R. Rhodes James, *Anthony Eden* (1986). Also see D. Carlton, *Britain and the Suez Crisis*

(1989) and R. Louis and R. Owen (eds), *Suez 1956: The Crisis and its Consequences* (1992).

On attitudes to Europe, see E. Barker, *Britain and a Divided Europe, 1945–70* (1971); R.B. Manderson-Jones, *The Special Relationship: Anglo-American Relations and Western European Unity, 1947–56* (1972); M. Camps, *European Unification in the Sixties* (1967); U. Kitzinger, *The Second Try: Labour and the EEC* and *Diplomacy and Persuasion: How Britain Joined the Common Market* (1973); J.W. Young, *Britain, France and the Unity of Europe, 1945–51* (1984); J. Young, 'The parting of the ways: The 1955 Messina Conference', in M. Dockrill and J. Young, *British Foreign Policy, 1945–56* (1989).

### Articles

J. Darwin, 'The fear of falling; British politics and imperial decline since 1900', *TRHS* (1986) and 'British decolonization after 1945: a pattern or a puzzle', *JICH* (1992); R. Butt, 'The Common Market and the Conservative Party, 1960–61', *GO* (1967); S. George, 'Britain in the EEC', *CR* (1992).

## 34. The domestic policy of the Conservative governments, 1951–64

Although many of the official documents and papers relating to Britain's recent history are still not available, the main features of these years are beginning to receive serious historical analysis. Economic difficulties are one dominant theme of the period, which in recent years has begun to be debated in terms of the 'decline' of Britain. The nature of postwar politics and the adequacy of existing institutions to meet the demands of a more sophisticated electorate provides another approach to the period. Some analysis of the most significant social changes of the period is beginning to be possible.

### Essay topics

- Were the 'thirteen wasted years' really wasted?
- Why did the Conservatives rather than Labour enjoy the support of the electorate between 1951 and 1964?

### Sources and documents

Of the political memoirs of the period, see Lord Avon, *Full Circle* (1960); R.A. Butler, *The Art of the Possible* (1971); the later volumes of

Harold Macmillan's *Memoirs* (6 vols, 1966–73). A.H. Halsey (ed.), *Trends in British Society since 1900* (1972) has a wealth of statistics on social developments, while A. Sampson, *Anatomy of Britain Today* (1965) is an interesting survey of Britain in the 1960s.

## Secondary works

On the Conservative administrations see R. Blake, *The Conservative Party from Peel to Thatcher* (1985); V. Bogdanor and R. Skidelsky (eds), *The Age of Affluence* (1970), chs 2–4; J. Ramsden, *The Conservative Party: the Age of Churchill and Eden, 1940–1957* (1995); and P. Addison, *Churchill on the Home Front 1900–1955* (1992), ch. 12. On a crucial election see D.E. Butler and R. Rose, *The British General Election of 1959* (1960), chs 2–5; on 1951–55 see A. Seldon, *Churchill's Indian Summer: The Conservative Government 1951–5* (1981). For the Eden and Macmillan premierships, see D. Carlton, *Eden* (1981); R. Rhodes-James, *Anthony Eden* (1986); A. Horne, *Macmillan*, Vol. 2 (1991); A. Howard, *RAB: The Life of R.A. Butler* (1987), chs 11–16. More generally see K. Middlemas, *Power, Competition and the State*, Vol. 1 (1986), chs 7–11; P. Hennessy and A. Seldon, *Ruling Performance: British Governments from Attlee to Thatcher* (1987); S. Ball and A. Seldon (eds), *The Conservative Century, 1900–1994* (1994).

On the Labour Party in this period, see the sections in H. Pelling, *A Short History of the Labour Party* (8th edn, 1985) and C. Cook and I. Taylor (eds), *The Labour Party* (1980). Discussion of Labour figures can be found in P. Williams, *Hugh Gaitskell* (1979); M. Foot, *Aneurin Bevan, 1945–60* (1973) and J. Campbell, *Nye Bevan* (1987); shorter profiles are in K.O. Morgan, *Labour People* (1986). S. Haseler, *The Gaitskellites* (1969) examines an important group. J. Cronin, *Labour and Society in Britain, 1918–1979* (1980), chs 8–10 examine the unions' role. Some of the dissident forces are examined by D. Howell, *British Social Democracy* (1976), chs 6–8; E. Shaw, *Discipline and Discord in the Labour Party* (1992), chs 2–5; and F. Parkin, *Middle Class Radicalism* (1968), ch. 6.

## Articles

See B. Pimlott, 'Is the "post-war consensus" a myth?', *CR* (1989); D. Dutton, 'Anthony Eden and the judgment of history', *CR* (1991).

## 35.  The Labour government of 1964–70

The Labour governments of the 1960s have attracted much criticism; there are those who see the promises of economic advance cruelly betrayed in the problems of balance of payments, devaluaton, and meeting Labour's historic commitments to expanded social welfare provision. The Wilson governments have also earned portmanteau criticism for their concessions to 'permissiveness' and sixties 'liberalism'. In practice, kinder views suggest that many problems were inherited or endemic, and that the social changes promoted by the Labour governments were generally progressive.

## Essay topic

- Did the social achievements of the Labour government of 1964–70 outweigh its economic failures?

## Sources and documents

See especially R.H.S. Crossman, *The Diaries of a Cabinet Minister* (1975–77, abridged edn, ed. A. Howard, 1979), the outstanding set of memoirs for the period. The 'official' version is available in H. Wilson, *The Labour Government, 1964–1970: a personal record* (1971). B. Castle, *The Castle Diaries, 1964–1976* (1980–84), available in one volume, *The Castle Diaries* (1990) are also valuable.

## Secondary works

For the general course of events see A. Sked and C. Cook, *Post-War Britain: A Political History* (4th edn, 1993), chs 8 and 9; K.O. Morgan, *The People's Peace: British History, 1945–1990* (1990); P. Hennessy and A. Seldon (eds), *Ruling Performance: British Governments from Attlee to Thatcher* (1987). For analysis of the decade see D. McKie and C. Cook (eds), *The Decade of Disillusion: British Politics in the 1960s* (1972); N. Tiratsoo (ed.), *The Wilson Years* (1993); B. Pimlott, *Harold Wilson* (1992); B. Donoughue, *Prime Minister: The Conduct of Policy under Harold Wilson and James Callaghan* (1987). C. Ponting, *Breach of Promise: Labour in Power, 1964–70* (1989) is a useful account. On the central issue of the management of the economy see S. Pollard, *The Development of the British Economy, 1914–1980* (3rd edn, 1983); D.W.E. Alford, *British Economic Performance since 1945* (1986). The broader context of decline is considered in A. Sked, *Britain's Decline: Problems and Perspectives* (1987) and A. Gamble, *Britain in Decline: Economic Policy, Political Strategy and the British State* (1985).

For the major social developments of the period see A. Marwick, *British Society since 1945* (1982); J. Weeks, *Sex, Politics and Society* (1991);

P. Foot, *Immigration and Race in British Politics* (1965); A.H. Halsey, *Change in British Society* (1978); J. Burnet, *A Social History of Housing* (1992); and H. Jones, *Health and Society since 1900* (1993).

## Articles

P. Anderson, 'Origins of the present crisis', *NLR* (1964); A.H. Albu, J. Bray and R. Prentice, 'Lessons of the Labour government', *PQ* (1970); W.B. Gwyn, 'The Labour party and the threat of bureaucracy', *PolS* (1971).

## 36. The 1970s

The 1970s saw the Heath, Wilson and Callaghan governments attempting to cope with a variety of problems in which the issues of economic decline, regional and national disparities, and the 'ungovernability' of Britain became significant issues. The rise of Scottish and Welsh nationalism became significant, as did the more persistent challenge from the revived Liberal Party. The decade ended with a Labour government grappling with both devolution and union power, with the historiography somewhat predictably focusing on the Conservative victory in 1979.

### Essay topics

* To what extent was Britain 'ungovernable' in the 1970s?
* Did either Heath or Callaghan have any answer to Britain's industrial decline?
* Why did devolution become an issue in British politics during the 1970s?

### Sources and documents

B. Castle, *The Castle Diaries, 1964–1976* (1980–84), available in one volume, *The Castle Diaries* (1990) and T. Benn, *The Benn Diaries* (1988–90) are available as day-to-day records of politics. See also D. Healey, *The Time of my Life* (1989), J. Callaghan, *Time and Chance* (1987) and R. Jenkins, *A Life at the Centre* (1991).

### Secondary works

For the Heath government see P. Hennessy and A. Seldon (eds), *Ruling Performance: British Government from Attlee to Thatcher* (1989) and R. Blake, *The Conservative Party from Peel to Thatcher* (1985). On Heath himself see

J. Campbell, *Edward Heath* (1993). For the ill-fated Industrial Relations Act see M. Moran, *The Politics of the Industrial Relations Act of 1971* (1977). For union reactions see C. Wrigley, 'Trade unions, the government and the economy', in T. Gourvish and A. O'Day (eds), *Britain in 1945* (1991); G. Dorfman, *Government versus Trade Unionism in British Politics since 1968* (1979); and R. Taylor, *The Trade Union Question in British Politics: Government and Unions since 1945* (1993). See also B. Pimlott and C. Cook (eds), *Trade Unions in British Politics* (2nd edn, 1991).

For the Wilson and Callaghan administrations see K. Laybourn, *The Rise of Labour: The British Labour Party, 1890–1979* (1988); P. Hennessy and A. Seldon (eds), *Ruling Performance* (1989); D. Kavanagh and P. Morris, *Consensus Politics from Attlee to Thatcher* (1989). For the 'Social Contract' see G. Dorfman, *Government versus Trade Unionism in British Politics since 1968* (1979) and W.J. Fishbein, *Wage Restraint by Consensus* (1984). The Liberals are discussed in C.A. Cook, *Short History of the Liberal Party, 1900–92* (1993) and J. Stevenson, *Third Party Politics in Britain since 1945* (1992).

On the rise of the Left, see J. Callaghan, *The Far Left in British Politics* (1987); P. Seyd, *The Rise and Fall of the Labour Left* (1987); H. Wainwright, *Labour: A Tale of Two Parties* (1987); and A. MacIntyre, 'The strange death of social-democratic England', in D. Widgery (ed.), *The Left in Britain, 1956–1968* (1976). The rise of fascist, racist politics are discussed in M. Walker, *The National Front* (1977); R. Thurlow, *Fascism in Britain* (1987), chs 10–12; and Z. Layton-Henry, *The Politics of Race and Race Relations since 1945* (1992).

On nationalism see R. Coupland, *Welsh and Scottish Nationalism: A study* (1954); A. Butt Philip, *The Welsh Question: Nationalism in Welsh Politics, 1945–1970* (1975); H.J. Hanham, *Scottish Nationalism* (1969); C. Harvie, *Scotland and Nationalism: Scottish Society and Politics, 1707–1977* (1977). T. Nairn, *The Break-up of Britain* (1977) was an influential analysis of the pressures on the British state in the 1970s, while V. Bogdanor, *Devolution* (1979) examines the devolution issue. J. Brand, *The National Movement in Scotland* (1992), G. Webb, *The Growth of Nationalism in Scotland* (1992) and R. Levy, *Scottish Nationalism at the Crossroads* (1992) examine further the issue of Scottish nationalism. Wales is examined into the post-referendum period in K.O. Morgan, *Rebirth of a Nation: Wales, 1880–1980* (1982), chs 3, 9, 13. T. Gallagher (ed.), *Nationalism in the Nineties* (1992) examines the fortunes of nationalism at the end of the century; see also A. Marr, *The Battle for Scotland* (1992) and A. Midwinter, M. Keating and J. Mitchell, *Politics and Public Policy in Scotland* (1991).

## Articles

On the Left, see R. Samuel, 'The lost world of British communism', *NLR* (1985–86); N. Wood, 'The empirical proletarians: a note on British communism', *PSQ* (1959).

## 37. The Northern Ireland crisis

The revival of the 'Irish Question' to produce the longest-running security problem in the British Isles this century and to present politicians of all parties with one of their most intractable difficulties raised all kinds of issues about social justice, regional government and civil liberties, many of them barely resolved by the late 1990s.

### Essay topic

* What was the 'Irish Question' after 1960 and why did successive British governments fail to solve it?

### Sources and documents

See the collection by A. O'Day and J. Stevenson, *Irish Historical Documents since 1800* (1992), Pt. 8. B. Devlin, *The Price of my Soul* (1970) has the authentic voice of the early nationalist movement.

### Secondary works

There are useful general accounts in D.G. Boyce, *The Irish Question and British Politics, 1968–1988* (1988); P. Arthur and K. Jeffrey, *Northern Ireland since 1968* (1988); and J.J. Lee, *Ireland, 1912–1985* (1989). On British policy towards Ireland, see M.J. Cunningham, *British Government Policy in Northern Ireland 1969–89: Its Nature and Execution* (1991); A. Kenny, *The Road to Hillsborough: The Shaping of the Anglo-Irish Agreement* (1986). A useful collection on the background to the crisis is J. Darby (ed.), *Northern Ireland: The Background to the Conflict* (1983). Another perspective is given by R. Rose, *Governing without Consensus: An Irish Perspective* (1971). Key personalities in the evolution of the conflict are examined in J. Campbell, *Edward Heath* (1993), chs 22, 29.

On the security issue, see C. Townshend, *Political Violence in Ireland: Government and Resistance since 1848* (1983); P. Bew and H. Patterson, *The British State and the Ulster Crisis from Wilson to Thatcher* (1985); C. Townshend, *Britain's Civil Wars: Counter-insurgency in the Twentieth*

*Century* (1986), ch. 2; P. Bishop and E. Mallie, *The Provisional IRA* (1987); and R. Thurlow, *The Secret State* (1994).

### Article

A. Liphart, 'The Northern Ireland problem', *BJPS* (1975).

## 38. The Thatcher era and after

The coming to power of the Thatcher administration in 1979 has been widely interpreted as marking the start of a less consensual era in British politics. Arguments about what Thatcherism was and when it began, even whether it existed, are commonplace. Whether the Conservative administrations of Mrs Thatcher and then John Major signalled as drastic a change in the structure of politics as was once thought remains a major question. The impact of defeat on the Labour Party and the attempt of the SDP to 'break the mould' of British politics are important sub-themes. Also significant is the growth of 'Europe' as an issue, particularly within the Conservative Party.

### Essay topics

* Was Mrs Thatcher a Conservative?
* To what extent did the Thatcher premiership mark a decisive shift in the conduct of British politics?
* Why did the SDP fail to 'break the mould' of British politics in the 1980s?

### Sources and documents

Documents and memoirs relating to different parts of the political spectrum can be found in M. Thatcher, *The Downing Street Years* (1993); N. Lawson, *The View From No. 11: Memoirs of a Tory Radical* (1992); R. Jenkins, *A Life at the Centre* (1991); D. Steel, *Against Goliath* (1992); and D. Owen, *Time to Declare* (1991).

### Secondary works

The Thatcher era is put into longer-term perspective in R. Blake, *The Conservative Party from Peel to Thatcher* (1985) and S. Ball and A. Seldon (eds), *The Conservative Century 1900–94* (1994). P. Riddell, *The Thatcher Government* (1989) and the section in P. Hennessy and A. Seldon (eds),

*Ruling Performance* (1987) offer an analysis of her premiership, though not of the last phase. For an analysis of 'Thatcherism' see D. Kavanagh, *Thatcherism and British Politics* (1987); R. Skidelsky (ed.), *Thatcherism* (1988); and S.R. Letwin, *The Anatomy of Thatcherism* (1992). On specific aspects of policy see N.M. Healy (ed.), *Britain's Economic Miracle: Myth or Reality* (1993); P. Byrd (ed.), *British Foreign Policy under Thatcher* (1988); H. Butcher, I. Law, R. Leach and M. Mullard, *Local Government and Thatcherism* (1990); and the essays in D. Marsh and R. Rhodes (eds), *Thatcherism: Audit of an Era (1992).*

Opposition to Thatcher's government from within is considered in I. Gilmour, *Inside Right* (1987) and for her final period in N. Lawson, *The View from No. 11* (1992). The Labour Opposition is examined in P. Seyd, *The Rise and Fall of the Labour Left* (1987). For Labour's leaders in the period see K.O. Morgan, *Labour People* (1987). G. Elliott, *Labourism and the English Genius: The Strange Death of Labour England?* (1993) and P. Seyd, 'Labour: the great transformation', in A. King (ed.), *Britain at the Polls, 1992* (1992) examine the later developments. For the growth of the Alliance and Liberal support see C. Cook, *A Short History of the Liberal Party* (4th edn, 1993); J. Stevenson, *Third Party Politics since 1945* (1992). The definitive account of the SDP is now I. Crewe and A. King, *The Birth, Life and Death of the Social Democrat Party* (1995).

Accounts of the European dimension include S. George, *An Awkward Partner: Britain and the European Community* (1990), his shorter *Britain and European Integration since 1945* (1991) and the collection S. George (ed.), *Britain and the European Community: The Politics of Semi-detachment* (1992). See also S. Bulmer, S. George and A. Scott, *United Kingdom and EC Membership Evaluated* (1992); N. Nugent in P. Dunleavy, A. Gamble, I. Holliday and G. Peele (eds), *Developments in British Politics 4* (1994).

Margaret Thatcher's foreign policy impact can be examined in D. Kavanagh and A. Seldon (eds), *The Thatcher Effect* (1989) and P. Byrd (ed.), *British Foreign Policy under Thatcher* (1988). The Falklands conflict is examined in L. Freedman, *Britain and the Falklands War* (1988) and her Irish policy in A. Kenny, *The Road to Hillsborough* (1985).

For the Major period see A. King (ed.), *Britain at the Polls, 1992* (1992); E. Pearce, *The Quiet Rise of John Major* (1992); B. Anderson, *John Major* (1992); P. Dunleavy, A. Gamble, I. Holliday and G. Peele (eds), *Developments in British Politics 4* (1994); I. Budge and D. McKay, *The Developing British Political System: The 1990s* (3rd edn, 1994).

## *Articles*

M. Wickham-Jones and D. Shell, 'What went wrong? The fall of Mrs Thatcher', *CR* (1991); I. Crewe, 'Why Mrs Thatcher was returned with a landslide', *SSR* (1987); 'Why did Labour lose (yet again)?', *PolR* (1992); R. Taylor, 'Thatcher's impact on the TUC', *CR* (1992).

# Index

'Tamworth Manifesto', 22, 114
Tantia, Topi, 289
Tariff Reform, 116, 343, 415
Tawney, Richard H., 384
taxation, 268–9
taxes on knowledge, 415
Tea Act (1773), 11
Tebbit, Norman, 58, 59, 64, 120, 121
Teheran Conference (1943), 42
Teignmouth, Lord, 232
Television Act (1954), 184
temperance movement, 415
Temple, Sir Gerald, 293
Temple, Viscount see Palmerston
Temple, William, 236
Templewood, Viscount see Hoare
Ten Hours Act (1847), 225
Tenby, Viscount see Lloyd-George, G.
tenure, housing, 175
Territorial Reserve Forces Act
    (1907), 297
Test and Corporation Acts, 20, 229,
    232
textile industry, 265
    disturbances, 19, 192–3, 207–11, 405
Thailand, 310
Thatcher, Margaret H., 54, 56–64,
    74, 107, 108, 119, 120, 127, 311,
    319, 323, 324, 362, 384, 410,
    515–17
Thatcherite, 415
Theft Act (1969), 190
Theodore, King of Abyssinia, 289
Thibaw, King of Burma, 287
Thistlewood, Arthur, 193, 385
Thomas, J.H. (Jimmy), 38, 39,
    217–18, 385
Thompson, E.P., 406, 414
Thompson, George, 52
Thorne, G., 124
Thorne, Will, 214
Thorneycroft, Peter, 46, 76, 118–19
Thornton, Henry, 232, 396
Thorpe, Jeremy, 50, 54, 126, 360
Thring, Edward, 157
Tibet, expedition to (1903–4), 291
Tientsin, Treaty of (1856), 287, 331
Tillett, Benjamin, 29, 216, 385
Tindal, Matthew, 229

Tippoo Sahib, 286, 353
Tithe Act (1838), 314
Toleration Act (1721), 229
Tolpuddle Martyrs (1834), 212
Tone, Theobald Wolfe, 16, 312, 313,
    418
Topping, R., 118
Torrens' Act (1868), 172
Torrey Canyon, 177
Tory, 415
Tory democracy, 415–16
Toryism, 355, 369, 460–2
    see also Conservative Party, elections
Town and Country Planning Act
    (1947), 43, 173, 176
Townshend, Charles, 2nd Viscount,
    3–5, 75, 77, 80, 359, 385
Townshend, Thomas, 13, 80
Toxteth riots, 57, 363
Tractarians, 416
trade, 247–55
    disputes, 226–8
    legislation, 10, 39, 64, 182, 207
Trade Boards Acts (1901, 1909,
    1918), 165, 414
Trade Disputes Acts,
    (1906), 33
    (1965), 219
Trade Disputes and Trade Union Act
    (1927), 38, 219
Trade Union Acts,
    (1871), 26, 213
    (1913), 216
Trade Union and Labour Relations
    Act (1974), 220–1
Trade Union and Labour Relations
    (Consolidation) Acts (1992), 223
trade unionism, 207–23, 462, 466–9
    'New Model', 407
    unionists, 341, 344, 352–3, 362–3,
    370, 377, 385
transport, 271–6
    legislation, 48
transportation of criminals, 191
treaties, 301–11
'Trent incident' (1861), 25
Trevelyan, C.P., 123
Trevelyan, George, 28
Tribunites, 416